HISTORY AND DESTINY OF THE JEWS

Also by Josef Kastein

THE MESSIAH OF ISMIR

HISTORY AND DESTINY OF THE JEWS

BY JOSEF KASTEIN

TRANSLATED FROM THE GERMAN BY HUNTLEY PATERSON

THE VIKING PRESS · NEW YORK

1935

PUBLISHED, APRIL, 1933
SECOND PRINTING, FEBRUARY, 1934
THIRD PRINTING, MAY, 1935

EINE GESCHICHTE DER JUDEN

PRINTED IN THE UNITED STATES OF AMERICA

DISTRIBUTED IN CANADA BY THE MACMILLAN COMPANY OF CANADA, LTD.

PRINTED BY THE CORNWALL PRESS, INC.

DEDICATED

WITH PROFOUND RESPECT

TO

ALBERT EINSTEIN

CONTENTS

PART I

FROM
THE RISE OF THE THEOCRACY
TO
THE DOMINION OF THE LAW

THE THEME OF THE BOOK

AMONG the civilized races of the world, the Jewish people are at once the best and the least known. It is one of the tragic peculiarities of their fate that they could never be ignored, and have thus been constantly obliged to face the criticism of the rest of the world—their non-Jewish environment—and stand or fall by it. Various attempts have been made, from time to time, to correct the inaccuracies which have crept into the Gentile portraits of the Jew—inaccuracies which were inevitable since they were the outcome of judgments inspired by particular motives, by human passions, animosity, and incompatibility. But they served no useful purpose. For a people as intensely vital as the Jews stand in no need of an apologia. On the contrary, they require above all to be constantly reminded of their true nature, so that they may never be in danger of forgetting the stupendous responsibilities which have been imposed upon them on this earth.

The main object of this book is to reveal the nature of these responsibilities, that is to say, the *raison d'être* of the Jewish people. Its further object is to give a just and accurate account of the part they have played in history, and this will necessitate passing the panorama of their life and fate in swift and sweeping review. For they are now standing on the threshold of a new historical period, a fresh beginning. To make this plain it will be necessary to recapitulate two previous periods of exceptional activity and importance.

The first was inaugurated by the destruction of the Jewish state at the hands of Rome and the final dispersion of the Jewish people. From that day they were obliged not only to live their own history but also that of the people about them. And, while they were caught up in the wheel of external events, they lived an eventful inner life of their own. Alien forces, more particularly Christianity, hurled them again and again into the limelight, and in combating them they concentrated all their energy on endeavouring once more to mould their own destiny, continue their national existence in all its manifestations, and again make themselves an individual force in history. And they carried out this undertaking in a manner wholly different from that of other nations; for they lacked nearly all the means of expression which have enabled other peoples to make their mark. They could not wage war or make conquests; colonies, the position of rulers, and revolutions were not for them! In the Diaspora Jewish history knew war only as a state of self-defence against murder and murderous attacks; conquest only as victory in the struggle for bare sustenance and living room; colonization only as the settlement of a community in a strange land; the position of rulers only in the form of scholars, artists, and rabbis, and revolutions only in the realm of the spirit. Everything was there, but it was all fatally concentrated on one plane.

This state of affairs ended when the governments of Europe granted the Jews equal rights of citizenship. Whereupon for a brief century the ideal of again making themselves an individual force in history sank into comparative insignificance and gave place to a desire to become adapted to environment. This was comprehensible enough not only owing to the barbaric suppression the Jews had suffered for centuries, but also in view of a tendency which seems to have become almost a law of their being in their dispersion. For their intellectual achievements were irrevocably bound up with the problem of securing the bare means of existence. That is to say, the greater the straits they happened to be in, the more narrowly and exclusively did their intellectual activities tend to become concentrated upon their inner being, and particularly upon the religious foundations of their race. As soon as they secured more breathing-space, their intellectual range automatically widened, and whenever mere survival ceased to be a specially Jewish problem, or merely appeared to have done so, they showed themselves capable of cultural achievements quite mundane in character and divorced from all religion and faith.

This is also what took place after the emancipation, when the Jews resolutely refused to admit that mere survival still constituted a problem for their race and, moreover, overrated the readiness of their environment to allow even the intellectual consequences of the spirit of emancipation to be realized. For, truth to tell, though nominally emancipated, they were never really granted freedom and equality by the states that professed to have liberated them, and whenever the recognition of equal rights threatened to become more than mere theory, it inevitably gave rise to renewed tension and friction. Owing to these strained relations, the spirit of Jewish history began to be falsified, not merely because the Jews had abandoned the desire to make themselves an individual force in history, but also because they tried to relieve the tension by means of innumerable concessions to those about them, endeavouring to win and deserve equal rights alike in the civil, intellectual, social, artistic, and even human sense, and to frame both their thought and action with an eye to the opinion and point of view of others. Thus they hoped to create a Judaism that was inconspicuous, that is to say, to make it survive as an innocuous concept and to exterminate it as a living force with perfect and unique legitimate rights of its own.

It stands to the credit of the Zionist ideology that it arrested this retrograde movement, and paved the way for an intellectual attitude which freed the independent achievements of the Jewish people and their mission in the world from all the attacks and criticisms of the Gentile world. Thanks to it, the foundation has been laid for fresh productivity on the part of Judaism, as the possessor of a world mission, and Jewish history may now be resumed. This is the point at which the Jewish world now stands.

Wherein this productivity lies, it will be the object of this book to show by a study of the course of Jewish history. When nations cease to live in isolation and really learn to consort together, the mere fact of being different, of being differently constituted, may lead to productivity. And it is for this reason that we propose to lay stress on the peculiarity of the Jews, that is to say, their difference from other people, believing, as we do, that it is not differentiation or distinction, but only separation dictated by prejudice that is really pernicious. For mere differentiation or distinction—at least such is the pious hope of all devout souls—must one day be blotted out, and rendered superfluous by a moral development of mankind which will refuse any longer to tolerate distinctions. Separation, on the other hand, immortalizes the spirit of enmity, and makes even the sublimest faith assume the aspect of a hostile attitude.

But this point of view apart, it must forthwith be acknowledged that in this book we have no intention of adopting a neutral standpoint. No man who feels impelled by a deep passion to write history, more especially the history of his own people, can remain neutral; if he did he could not breathe his own soul into the narrative. The man who does not feel history as he feels his own fate, affecting and embracing him, remains no more than a compiler. But since the soul's vigilance and uprightness are behind every experience, he is filled with so deep a responsibility towards himself, towards his own people, and towards the outside world, that his readers may rest assured that although it has been worked out as a subjective experience, the finished work contains the objective truth and the fundamental meaning of the events narrated.

CRYSTALLIZATION

THE growth of a people is always a mysterious process. From out mere groups, hordes, tribes, or individual families, whose one thought is themselves, there suddenly arise confederations and communities sharing the same manners and destiny; birth and death, happiness and nemesis suddenly acquire a new meaning, while new feelings and modes of thought arise to put a new face on the world. It serves no purpose to tell us that certain demonstrable causes lie at the root of all this—climate, food, economic conditions. This may be so, but as an explanation it is inadequate. Like man himself, human communities grow organically as a part of nature. The decisive factor is the part played by the soul, the spirit, the idea. This is the undemonstrable and mysterious factor in every case of historical development. It is impossible to demonstrate the existence of an idea. All it does is to manifest itself. Whether a man can accept it or not is a matter of faith.

Such manifestations may be discerned in the very earliest known period of Jewish history, and they appear as a process of crystallization pregnant with meaning.

About 3000 B.C. certain groups of the Semitic race began to spread over the Near East. Their original home may perhaps have been the Arabian peninsula, whence they penetrated northward, towards the region between the Euphrates and the Tigris, known as Mesopotamia. The Akkadian group spread over southern Babylonia, the Amurru or Amorites settled in the west, on the borders of Canaan, sending out offshoots in the direction of Palestine and various nomadic tribes as far south as the confines of Egypt. They were half nomad, half peasant. Though restlessness was in their very bones, they all felt the longing to settle down somewhere and consequently wandered much farther afield than is usually the case with nomads in search of fresh pastures. A vast restless horde, ever pressing onwards, they ranged the country between the two centres of civilization—Egypt and Babylon. Again and again they traversed the land lying between the two opposite poles—Palestine, the natural bridge between Asia and Africa. Group after group remained behind and settled down. Numberless little sovereign communities came into being and appropriated the available free space in the country. At the same time the two great powers north and south stretched forth their hands to seize this country as a line of communication and a trade route. As early as 2500 B.C. Babylon had already occupied the whole country, with the result that the nomadic hordes were dammed up artificially, as though by dikes, and were ultimately forced to overflow into the forbidden land. Then Egypt in her turn pressed forward and took possession of the country, thus creating similar conditions to those brought into being by the Babylonians—she dammed up the wandering tribes. Consequently, about 1400 B.C. Semitic groups once again invaded Palestine in force. But on this occasion the people concerned were a special clan of that race—the Hebrews.

How and when they cut themselves adrift from the larger body cannot be definitely ascertained, but within the narrow circle of their family clans, they were all inclined to do so. Their very name and the historical kernel of legends connected with their patriarchs may lead us to infer the following facts. They first made their appearance on the lower reaches of the Euphrates, then travelled northward into Mesopotamia, and followed the route used by all groups of people at that time and in that part of the world—the road via Syria to Canaan and the wilderness beyond; when hunger drove, they even penetrated into Egypt. The nations they encountered called them the people "from the other side" of the river. The Hebrew for "the other side" is *'eber*. Those who hailed from the other side were *'Ibrim,* or in English, "Hebrews." These migrations occurred about the beginning of 2000 B.C.

A portion of this Hebrew group of the Semite race settled on the confines of Canaan. But a stationary and a nomadic existence are not only opposed as concepts, they also lead to different ideologies and different habits of life, and the Hebrew group was obliged to split up as the greater Semitic race had done. Owing partly to this process of cleavage, the tribe of the Bne Yisrael, the Children of Israel, eventually made their appearance in history as the outcome of a twofold process of selection, first from the Semites and then from the Hebrews.

But the process of differentiation did not end here, and in Canaan and the districts adjacent to it the Children of Israel became split up into twelve family groups, known as the twelve tribes. Though intimately connected, both by descent, language, and customs, they soon separated and followed wholly different paths. Some remained within the confines of Canaan, others settled down along the great military highway of the East and in the neighbouring deserts and wildernesses, where they led a nomadic existence, while a smaller section, driven by hunger, finally succeeded in reaching Egypt, where the Pharaohs took them under their protection.

Everything was calculated to make these bands of emigrants to Egypt become disintegrated in that country, or be swallowed up in other branches of the Semitic race who had also emigrated thither.

The land of Goshen, formed by the delta lying between the eastern arm of the Nile and the desert, where they penetrated, was much coveted as a place of settlement by the various nomadic Semitic tribes in the neighbourhood, who either by means of slow infiltration or violent invasion had long been in possession of its extensive pasture-land. Yet no disintegration or intermingling took place. On the contrary, it was the emigration of these Hebrews into Egypt which first led to the development of a really promising and definite national character on their part.

When Egypt wished to extend her sway as far as Babylon, it was imperative that stable conditions should first be established in the land of Goshen, the restless district on her frontier. The inhabitants of this area were therefore made Egyptian subjects. But, according to the social order of the Egyptians, subjects were not free men but slaves. Thus the Children of Israel were not treated in any way differently from the rest of the Egyptians; but they reacted differently. They had entered the land of Goshen as members of a free tribe, and their love of freedom, including freedom to move about as they pleased, was still as strong as ever. A state of affairs which the native Egyptians took as a matter of course seemed to these immigrants, whose separation from their main body had proved them to be individualists, absolutely intolerable. This led to an insurrection and a demand to be liberated from the position of thralls and to be allowed to migrate to another country.

Even at this stage in Jewish history, three factors may already be plainly discerned, which had a lasting and decisive influence, and which we must now make clear in the light of subsequent events. The Jewish people came into being only through a process of progressive isolation lasting over centuries. This striving after isolation has in fact continued throughout the ages to the present day, and constitutes a spiritual characteristic of the race, a metaphysical factor. Fate furthermore imposed the law of selection on the Jews. At every turning-point in their history their numbers were reduced, the external husks being stripped away, as it were, from the kernel. If this compulsory selection led to the survival of the most viable elements in the race, it is not surprising that these people acquired a vital character which made them rise superior to any environment in which they happened to be placed. Finally, as soon as any signs of hostility appeared in their neighbourhood, they immediately discovered a means of resistance, either active or passive, according to the age and the place in which it arose. Such efforts were always fruitful, inasmuch as they invariably led again and again to further feats of self-determination and self-control, and constantly added strength to their will to live.

Isolation, selection, and concentration are in themselves but the names of processes. They do not answer the question why things happened in this way, and yet at this point in Jewish history—the end of the Egyptian period—the question must perforce be answered. These people vegetated within the confines of a religious idea. No historical development can be understood in its inception apart from the predominating influence of the religious forces guiding it, and every historical event loses its importance from the standpoint of purely human affairs in proportion to the loss in strength of the religious factor in it. The early history of the Jews was much more deeply and obviously rooted in religion than the later period has been, and unless this is borne in mind it is impossible to understand the forces that directed them. Those to whom the concepts God, Faith, and Religion are meaningless must inevitably fail to grasp the decisive factors which built up this nation.

MŌSHEH

ACCORDING to the Bible account, the central figure of all these events is Mōsheh, or *anglice,* Moses. There can be no doubt that he is a historical figure. But what was the man and what was his aim? He was not the founder of a religion, for just as there is no such thing as the creator of a revolution, so there is no such thing as the founder of a religion. All we find in history is the man who breaks the sealed vessel in which the new forces are fermenting to bursting-point. Nor was Mōsheh a deliverer of his people. For no nation bursts its bonds and gains freedom unless for ages it has been prepared in every possible way for the experience of liberty. He was the highest and most sensitive embodiment of the forces of his people. What these forces were may be gathered from the historical truth that lies at the root of the traditions that have been handed down to us about him.

The historical sources lay stress on only one of his personal qualities—gentleness. Gentleness is kindness. Kindness is the chief characteristic of the man who is free and just. Injustice and lack of freedom are next of kin. Mōsheh, the man with the Egyptian name, who knew the court of Memphis as well as he knew the people of his own tribe, recognized that these two allied manifestations of malevolence were in their peculiar character the outcome of a religious form and almost the necessary attributes of ideas regarding faith which were neither his own nor those of his people. This early recognition of the different ways of regarding freedom, justice, and faith, must have marked the very beginning of his mission. Thus in him, for the first time within the memory of man, there came into being a piece of knowledge which was the outcome of a conscious act of comparison and gave birth to a sense of obligation which, in its turn, led to the perception of a definite purpose.

There can be no doubt that at this period the Egyptian conception of the world and the deity was already highly developed and complex, whereas the Children of Israel were imbued with very little more than a presentiment that beyond and outside themselves there existed a divine force, a sovereign power, upon which, for better for worse, their fate depended. But infinite possibilities lay concealed in this indefinite conception, and Mōsheh revealed to his people those possibilities which his own religious endowment led him to regard as ultimate and conclusive. He named their God for them and thus made Him knowable. The Scriptures tell us that God called unto Moses. But was it not rather Moses who called unto God? An inner voice told him that man was not meant to be a mere animal, that a free being should not be a bondsman, and that those whose eyes were raised to the stars should not crawl on their bellies. By reducing these states of independence to a sacred dependence on God, there arose within him, for the first time, the idea of order and subordination associated with freedom, with voluntary action. And thus he outlined the fundamental concept of the Jewish theocracy. He is the only man whose idea has been an actuality for four thousand years.

He did nothing and thought of nothing that was not in conformity with the spirit of his people. Otherwise they would never have followed him. But whether they immediately grasped in its full magnitude the significance of his thoughts and actions, or understood the idea upon which they were called upon to base their lives, is another matter. They must certainly have done so only hesitatingly, step by step, but their manner of setting to work proves that they had chosen the right path in their organic development, while the fact that they did so at all shows that Mōsheh was a leader of consummate ability.

Leadership constitutes the keynote of his personality. The Scriptures call him a prophet. This also is true, for his thoughts and actions are full of prophetic vision. The moment when a wandering people becomes sedentary determines its fate as a civilized nation, and the Children of Israel had reached a stage of development when it was high time for the innate longing to settle down and become a civilized people to be gratified. But Mōsheh perceived that the attempt they had made in the land of Goshen, with all the local and spiritual conditions that accompanied it, must inevitably lead to disaster. It was for this reason that he interrupted the process of settling down and wrenched his people from the soil which they had as yet hardly made their own. He inspired them with the desire to leave it by giving them an object for so doing—he promised them the land of Canaan as a prize. The idea was apparently simple enough, for countless other Semitic and Hebrew tribes had settled there. But this constant influx of settlers had filled the country to overflowing. Thus any fresh attempt to enter must necessarily involve violence and warlike invasion, and a conflict with tribes more or less closely related to themselves. And it was this conflict that he set before them as a duty. He even provided them with a good reason for it, telling them that the country was theirs by the ancient right of inheritance. What matter that actual conditions in Canaan had long effaced this right and rendered it illusory? In the teeth of the facts he threw out an idea to them—the idea of living and developing a life of their own, independent and isolated, under the ægis of their own God, who was distinct from all other gods!

It was impossible for the people to grasp the idea at once. But that at heart they were qualified to do so is shown by the fact that they followed their leader, and marched with him into the neighbouring wilderness of Sinai. In one of those mountain gorges, which from time immemorial must have served as the sanctuaries of local cults, he endowed their object with the sanctity of a mission by the revelation of a grandiose religious symbol—the conclusion of a covenant with God.

Who was their God? How did they conceive of Him? The answer must be—they did not conceive of Him at all. The Jews did not spontaneously create a God out of their own inner consciousness; they produced Him laboriously out of their lives on many a sunlit height and in many a gloomy dale, through the mere fact that they constantly inclined to the human-all-too-human, and from the scene of their various vicissitudes and experiences arrived at the conclusion that mere existence, even when it supplies every possible need and provides an adequate well-being, cannot constitute an end in itself. The seeds of this conviction already lay dormant within them on Sinai. And the communication made to them there, giving them a standard of conduct, was, therefore, first and foremost ethical in character; it amounted to a body of instructions which provided a spiritual basis for the activities of their everyday life and furthermore placed them under a moral obligation. True, the Ten Commandments (the Decalogue), and the "Tables of the Covenant," to which they then pledged themselves, were not new and original in every detail. They bear various points of resemblance to, and have much in common with, the Code of Hammurabi, King of Babylon, while now and again the wording is reminiscent of the Egyptian *Book of the Dead* dating from the sixteenth century B.C. But in their aim, general character, and the use to which they were put, these laws and regulations are fundamentally Jewish. Whereas, in the Egyptian *Book of the Dead,* the soul of the deceased pleads before the god Osiris saying: "I have done no murder," the Decalogue makes moral conduct a duty: "Thou shalt do no murder! Thou shalt not commit adultery! Thou shalt not steal! Honour thy father and thy mother! Thou shalt not covet thy neighbour's house!" And above all there is a law of supreme importance: "Thou shalt keep holy the Sabbath Day!" which introduced a break in the daily life of toil, and systematically overcame the curse of labour by the right to a day of festivity and meditation, the basis of an immortal idea.

All these are beginnings. But they were given a decisive impetus towards further development by the promulgation of an idea which was far ahead of the age. It was enunciated at the time of the symbolic acts on Sinai and has altered the face of the world—the proclamation of a God, one and invisible, of Whom no image could be made. In a world of many gods and divinities, Judaism from the depths of its soul gave birth to monotheism as an idea, and also as the aim of its development. And thus the Children of Israel were irrevocably separated from those about them and the process of isolation made a further momentous advance.

We cannot prevail upon ourselves to presuppose the control of a definite personal deity. All we can do is to extract some sort of meaning from the course of events—a meaning which amounts to an internal reason. It was not God Who willed these people and their meaning. It was this people who willed this God and this meaning. Those who inquire into the source of human qualities and capacities, human efforts and aims, are bound in the end either to confess they do not know, or else to reach the concept of a God. And thus the circle is closed.

THE TAKING OF TERRITORY

IT was only when the Israelites were in the wilderness that Mōsheh embarked upon activities which cannot be rightly understood unless they are regarded as deliberately educative. The oasis of Kadesh—the very name (*kadesh,* holy) suggests the sanctuary of a cult—became the focus of forty years of a special kind of development. The people grew in numbers. Tribal groups, closely related to the Children of Israel, were admitted into their ranks, and a new ethnic entity came into being. During the forty years of wandering between Kadesh and the Gulf of Elath, all those who could remember having eaten of the bread of bondage in Egypt gradually died out. A new nomadic race came into being, who could not, however, at a moment's notice set off on their wanderings in the wilderness again, but were dominated by the creative will of their leader Mōsheh, who gave a direction to their desire for a land of their own—Canaan. By means of an idea—Canaan, the Promised Land—he sublimated their natural inclination to stay where they were. He made them no promise; on the contrary, he set them a task—the invasion of a certain country with the sanction of their God.

Thus this people reached maturity with a peculiar relation to a country which none of them had seen, but which they spoke of and craved for as their home. This conception of home took shape not through having lived for generations in the land which was the cradle of their race, but through an idea, through the belief that the divine mission allotted to them could be fulfilled only in this particular country. Thus the country and their religious consciousness were inextricably bound together, an association which has survived intact to the present day. A people usually grow and develop in their own land, and are to a great extent influenced by the conditions prevailing in it. But here we have a people growing and developing their fundamental spiritual characteristics in anticipation of a land of their own, and thus skipping the first natural step in their evolution. First, they were given the idea of the country, and then the country itself. And this accounts for the fact that country and climate later play such a subordinate part in the history of the Jews and explains why they have been able to settle down anywhere and everywhere without any fundamental characteristic of their nature being either surrendered or lost.

The land of their dreams might be termed an "intermediate state of the soul." With its mountain ranges and the River Jordan running almost due north and south, with its coastline, fertile plains, and the wilderness beyond, lying east and west of these main natural features, Canaan, in an area of barely 9000 square miles, possessed at once all the variety of rounded mountain peaks of eternal snow, valleys enjoying subtropical warmth, verdant plains, and sandy deserts. But while it was not exposed to the dangers of wild nature on a grand scale, it could not lay claim to extravagantly sublime beauty. Its inhabitants were not doomed either to decay or to perish but could choose their own line of life.

Mōsheh endeavoured to reach this land with the least possible expenditure of effort and strength. As alien tribes barred his way by the direct route northward, he described a wide circuit round the southern extremity of the country and with the majority of his people inevitably reached the plain beyond Jordan. But the tribe of Judah remained behind and succeeded in invading Canaan from the south, and settling down in a district close to the eventual site of Jerusalem which was in possession of the Jebusites. They were accompanied by the tribe of Simeon. But the other tribes in Transjordania had no alternative but to fight all who stood in their way, otherwise they would have been squeezed out into the Syro-Arabian desert.

They fought with such determination that in a very short time they had seized the whole of Transjordania. The way now lay open for the conquest of Canaan. But at this point the process of cleavage went still further. The tribes of Gad, Reuben, and half the tribe of Manasseh declared that they wished to remain in Transjordania, and the most that Mōsheh could obtain from them was a promise to send contingents to help in the operations on the other side of the river. They refused to do more and settled down to work out their own destiny and evolution.

Mōsheh did not live to see the crossing of the Jordan, and the command was taken over by Jehoshua (Joshua), the son of Nun, the leader of the host. He crossed the Jordan, broke up the coalition of Amorite and north Canaanitish princes, and made a determined but not altogether successful raid on the country. Three districts were occupied. Judah in the extreme south was completely separated from the rest of the tribes of Israel by native peoples. A definite area was occupied in Transjordania, but it was entirely cut off and isolated by the Jordan. In the centre of the country, as far as the northern province, afterwards known as Galilee, the rest of the tribes settled down, in some places living side by side with the Canaanites who were already there, in others living actually in dependence on them. The coastal regions to the north were occupied by the Phœnicians, a Semitic race, and remained in their hands, while the seaboard to the south later came into the hands of the Philistines, immigrants from the Aegean Islands.

But the forward march of invasion was definitely stopped not so much owing to the resistance of the peoples already in occupation of the land, as through the premature splitting up of the tribal confederations themselves. With unspeakable greed, they rushed forward and seized all the land they could possibly hold, obsessed, as it were, by the idea that they were at last going to find rest. Tribe deserted tribe as soon as it had succeeded in securing a district. All concerted action was at an end. So anxious were they to settle down on their farms, that they did not even take the trouble to make the districts they had appropriated secure, but as soon as they had recovered from the first shock of the invasion, made every possible concession to the original occupants of the land rather than take up arms again. This situation had revealed a strongly individualistic tendency, but it was counterbalanced by the possession of the opposite quality—a pronounced feeling of collective sympathy. Deep down in their hearts, despite their individualistic disintegration, they never lost sight of the idea that inspired them and was common to them all. This is proved by innumerable definite events, which people have tried in vain to interpret along sociological lines.

One of the tribes—the tribe of Levi—acquired no territory at all. But it should be remembered that it had not advanced under the protection of one of the other tribes, as had been the case with Simeon and Judah. Nor, as a matter of fact, had it laid claim to any land. On the contrary, all the other tribes were agreed that it ought to have no definite district allotted to it, but that its members should be allowed to take up their abode with any tribe they chose. The Levites had been chosen to be the priestly tribe, and, as they were forbidden to acquire land, and were thus deprived of the means of earning a livelihood, the other tribes undertook the obvious duty of raising contributions for their maintenance, thus showing that they were fully aware that the functions of the priesthood were the concern of the community as a whole, and could not be shelved by allowing the Levites to acquire territory of their own or separating them from the rest of the community. Moreover, in all subsequent wars, whether waged by one tribe alone or by several together, either with the object of extending their domain or keeping what they already held, the Israelites always regarded the war not as fought by this or that tribe, but as "Yahweh's war." In all times of crisis they were bound by the communal obligation of the idea, the main object of which was the realization of the theocratic state.

THE THEOCRACY

EVERY successful war that ends in the conquerors settling down in the land they have won has as its sequel a conflict of cultures. And we know that very often the conquerors prove in the end to be the conquered. This, indeed, promised to be the case after the invasion of Canaan by the Israelites, but, strange to say, after a preliminary period of uncertainty, no such thing as a compromise between the invaders and the original inhabitants took place. On the contrary, the development of the conquerors as a nation progressed apace, and in spirit they became more than ever a race apart. Their whole environment obviously favoured a process of assimilation or even complete intermingling. The Israelites constituted a minority, and were surrounded by an unbroken circle of Phœnicians, Philistines, Aramæans, Idumæans, Moabites, Amalekites, Ammonites, Arabs, and half-Arabs, who were to some extent also permanently interspersed among them. These were engaged in agriculture, trade, and commerce, and had reached a high degree of civilization. They also possessed a well-developed religious organization, which, in spite of local differences of custom and cult, was in most respects similar to the ancient traditions of the Babylonian religion.

The Canaanitish cults were closely connected with the soil and expressive of the forces of nature, particularly the force of fertilization. This force, or deity, which was called Baal—or Dagon among the Philistines and Milcom among the Ammonites, for the attributes of the three are identical—was, therefore, the god of agriculture and closely connected with a certain locality. Consequently he also protected any place where a shrine was set up to him. As the logical outcome of the nature concept, to which he owed his worship, he was supposed to have as complement the female principle—the goddess Baalath or Astarte. Furthermore, the extension of the divine protection to particular properties or estates led to the creation of innumerable domestic deities. The subjection of the people to their god was acknowledged chiefly in the form of sacrifices of every description, from offerings in kind to the sacrifice of virginity and even human sacrifice.

With the exception of the Philistines, who, if only from their barbaric treatment of prisoners of war, betrayed their kinship with the Greeks, the Canaanites derived their laws and customs from the common source of ancient oriental law, whence the two great codes, the Babylonian and the Hebrew, emanated. Thus, if the Israelites wished to hold their own against an organization so powerful, both from the numerical and the cultural standpoint, it was imperative for them to exert considerable energy. And this they did not fail to do, fortified as they were by beliefs which they had inherited, and by the impetus derived from the new idea which fired their breasts. The various civilized rules and regulations which generations of wandering had taught them had in the very early days been sufficiently ordered and arranged to be recorded in the "Tables of the Covenant." It remained to be seen whether the laws thus formulated would hold good in a totally different environment.

Their religion also had to prove its worth. At first it was limited simply to the recognition of a divine power and expressed by the concept El or Elohim, while their nomadic mode of existence prevented this concept from being materialized into a god related to the soil. The Israelites, therefore, entirely skipped the evolutionary stage of polytheism. It is possible that each tribe conceived its god according to its own peculiar characteristics, but in all the conceptions—and this is the important point—there lay the same fundamental elements of monotheism, that is to say, the idea of a god who could not be represented by plastic images, and was not bound to any particular locality. Every tribe had its god, but he was a monotheistic deity. The Israelites were monotheists.

A generation before the conquest of Canaan they experienced the momentous disruption which separated them forever from the general scheme—they came to know their God, the God common to them all. They came to know Him as the final revelation of a primeval heritage, and learnt that the general vague idea of an almighty power could in the last event be condensed into a single definite concept.

"And God spake unto Moses, and said unto him, I am the Lord; and I appeared unto Abraham, unto Isaac, and unto Jacob, by the name of the Almighty, but by my name of YAHWEH was I not known to them."

This was the name He now revealed to them. And the revelation had a peculiar form and a peculiar purport, both of which are important, since they have both survived. The form He chose was to give a bond between the people and their God, a bond which was sealed voluntarily. They were in no way forced to seal it, and did so only for the sake of religious exclusiveness. The purport took its root in the exclusiveness of monotheism, and in the establishment of moral obligations. From that time forward, they did not live from hand to mouth, as it were, every man doing what was right in his own eyes, or as time and circumstances prompted him. But the most insignificant actions of everyday life became important, endowed with moral weight, and imbued with a loftier meaning. The Israelites were given the opportunity of having God as their ally, and they resolved to avail themselves of it. They did so with full knowledge of the profusion of obligations they would incur and of the many reasons making it impossible for them to turn back when once they had agreed. For the God they had conceived and taken to their bosom, and in whose likeness they wished to grow, would have nothing to do with shirkers and waverers. But the promise He made them was indeed magnificent:

"Now, therefore, if ye will obey my voice indeed, and keep my covenant, then ye shall be a peculiar treasure unto me above all people; for all the earth is mine: and ye shall be unto me a kingdom of priests, and an holy nation."

But the discharge of their obligations had to take place under the eyes of a zealous God, Who could not be bargained with, but was constantly reminding them of the fact that He alone was God, and of the demands He made upon them—Him or no one, everything or nothing. It is high time that we should give up the concept of a "God of Vengeance," which was due to a mistranslation and a mistaken point of view. The "God of Vengeance" never existed. We know of a "zealous God," and one who demanded nothing for Himself, for he was not a human being to be offended by deeds either of commission or omission. He did not even require sacrifices. All He demanded was a rigid standard of morality between *man* and *man,* and therefore between man and Himself, so that *man* might develop into a clean and spiritual being. It matters not that the aim of this covenant has never been realized. Suffice it that the aspiration, the striving after the goal, remained alive and potent.

Thus the preliminary steps which preceded the invasion of Canaan merely amounted to the establishment of the theocracy. True, each tribe had its own leader, but there was no supreme religious, political, and military head either for the tribe or the people as a whole. Their supreme head was their God as they understood and conceived Him. And He became their destiny. From the time of Mōsheh, they constantly adapted themselves to circumstances with an ever-increasing consciousness of their new spiritual standards, though they were not perhaps always consistent. And it was this that lent the conflict with their new environment its peculiar character.

Their craving for land could be satiated only by an immediate close connexion with the soil. And this drove them inevitably to agriculture and consequently to daily intercourse in various ways with the original inhabitants of the country. For sowing, reaping, and harvesting and for all exchange and barter they were dependent on the native rites and usages. And the more scattered they were, the more did they suffer from the results of the imperfect nature of their conquest and were driven to live on terms of peace and amity with the natives. Thus not only did they share some of their customs and cults, but, particularly along the border districts, they also began to intermarry with them. They adopted the local Baal worship, they founded their own festivals on those already existing among the peasants and agriculturists of their district, and copied the civilization they found established in the towns to which they took their surplus crops. In short, just after their seizure of the land, it seemed as though they would become assimilated and swallowed up by the Canaanites who constituted a formidable majority.

The fact that this never occurred, but that, in spite of all the dangers that threatened, the inner core continued to grow, was due to their extraordinary, one might almost say, "double religious life." For their attraction towards the local Baal worship did not prevent their submitting to their own national God everything which they undertook as a corporate body. Whenever any question arose involving their existence as a nation, they knew only one God, and recognized but one idea—the theocracy. Baal might bless their crops and safeguard their commercial transactions. But in the wars they fought to defend themselves against annihilation they were led by Yahweh. Thus even while they served Baal, Yahweh continued to develop in their hearts, and they kept to the path leading to the goal that had been set before them. Whatever their backslidings, they never really deserted Him, and all the vicissitudes they underwent constituted stages in the development of their idea of God. Moreover, in the priesthood in Shiloh, where the Ark of the Covenant was displayed, they had a constant living representation of their idea. For although Shiloh may not have been a suitable political or commercial centre, its importance from the point of view of the spirit cannot be overestimated. It was the outward and visible expression of their theocratic system.

Thus the force which ever since the flight from Egypt had been working towards their physical and spiritual unification had remained alive in them. It could only have been a spiritual law of extraordinary power that was capable of saving them from the threat of assimilation, and it made its influence felt not only in the spiritual but also in the material dangers of their situation. Danger lurked on every side. As soon as the original inhabitants had recovered from the first shock of the invasion, they gradually assumed an aggressive attitude towards the Israelites, or tried to drive them out. And where, owing to the numerical strength of the Israelitish settlers, this did not occur, the conquered peoples and borderland tribes, who were constantly invading the adjoining country, endeavoured by means of raids, surprise attacks, and well-planned campaigns to annihilate the newcomers who had just settled down in peace. In vain did the Israelites join in the worship of Baal and adopt the economic, political, and social customs of the country; they were still regarded as an alien confederation and harassed accordingly. Thus they were perforce driven to defend themselves as one people, a fact which could not fail to contribute to the development of an élite among them, the enhancement of the feeling of corporate unity, and the strengthening of their religious idea. The concrete result of this development was the appearance of the *Shophetim,* or Judges.

THE SHOPHETIM

WITH but trifling exceptions, external events during the epoch of the Judges are all similar in character—one or more of the Israelitish tribes were attacked by the common enemy, defeated, and reduced to a state of subjection amounting almost to slavery. Then, suddenly, a leader would appear, who, after mustering all the strength of his people against their oppressors, would restore them to a state of freedom even greater than they had enjoyed before. There is nothing unusual in this sequence of events, which has occurred time and again in the history of mankind and constitutes a natural stage in the evolution of nations, except that in this case religion was the really important factor. We are told of various peoples who from time to time oppressed the Israelites—the Idumæans, the Moabites, the Philistines, the Midianites, and the Ammonites. The saviours, of whom tradition has handed down the names, are Othniel, Shamgar, Balak, Gideon, Jephthah, and Samson. However different in other respects, these men had this much in common, that not one of them belonged to a family of repute; none of them, either by birth or the evidence of exceptional prowess in early life, was predestined for the office he assumed. They sprang out of obscurity from the people. Jephthah was a robber chief of Gilead, whose fellow-tribesmen drove him out. Samson, on whom legend has fastened with particular affection, was a sort of mountain sprite. Of Deborah, a figure to whom the Scriptures refer with great tenderness, we are merely informed that she was the wife of a man called Lapidoth. They were all, including Deborah, called *Shophetim,* Judges, a fact which proves fairly conclusively that the literal translation of the word does not adequately render its meaning. They were not judges in the sense that they administered the law. They appeared only at times of emergency, and sank back into oblivion when the danger was over. The feat they accomplished was to liberate their people for the time being, and, as the case of Deborah shows, it was not even necessary, for this purpose, to perform some heroic deed of arms. All that was required was to discover a formula that reached the people's hearts and quickened their spiritual powers. This constitutes the whole of Deborah's method and achievement. She never fought. She gave the people the idea of the battle and its slogan. When the Canaanite king of Hazor defeated the northern tribes, she fought his chariots of iron with the war-cry: Let us fight against Hazor for the Lord! But not all the tribes of Israel grasped the idea. Judah took no part whatsoever in the contest, and other tribes, thinking only of their own peace, also stood aloof. But the remainder who followed her won a victory, the magnitude and importance of which find an echo in the exceptionally mature and dramatically conceived Song of Deborah:

"In the days of Shamgar the son of Anath, in the days of Jael, the highways were unoccupied, and the travellers walked through by-ways. The inhabitants of the villages ceased, they ceased in Israel, until that I Deborah arose, and I arose a mother in Israel."

The conclusion of this song gives a brief outline of the spiritual situation and the significance of this martial effort:

"So let all thine enemies perish, O Lord; but let them that love him be as the sun when he goeth forth in his might."

Every conflict had the same significance, sometimes actually contained in the slogan. Gideon's battle-cry, for instance, was "The sword of the Lord and of Gideon!" The readiness to appreciate these battle-cries was awakened and kept alive in the hearts of the people by the Levites, who pointed out and elucidated the spiritual connexion between the inner and the outer dangers and between the loss by the Israelites of their national characteristics through assimilation to their environment, and total ruin through war, by explaining that all calamities came of neglecting the duties to God imposed by the Covenant. The Levites were nowhere chained to the soil. They had no personal property of their own to defend. Thus they were not exposed to the temptation of becoming assimilated to their surroundings, and their freedom from this menace led them to regard themselves as holders of office and representatives of ideas. Unlike other sacerdotal castes, they had no position of personal power; their one object was to fulfil their mission, which was to secure the spiritual development of their people and the complete establishment of the theocracy. It was they who created the spiritual atmosphere, which alone made the idea of "Judges" comprehensible, and enabled the people again and again to understand and accept it for what it was—the occasional appearance of deliverers entrusted with a mission from God.

Thus the Shophetim were not judges in the ordinary sense, nor were they tribal leaders, or mere martial heroes. Deborah never fought at all. Eli was high priest in Shiloh. Samuel, coming to the Levite community in Shiloh, was not a general, nor did he hold office of any kind. Nevertheless, these people were all Shophetim, judges. In spite of the obvious editing of the Book of Judges from a monarchical point of view, the real significance of these judges remains perfectly plain—they were the instruments of the Divine Will, who appeared from time to time whenever the exigencies of the moment made the people raise their eyes in supplication to Heaven. These men, who led them either by exhortations or deeds, were regarded by them as the authorized representatives of their real Commander-in-Chief, who was God. Thus, in their eyes, the judge was simply a man charged with a single definite mission, an official of the theocracy, who, in obedience to a command from on high, passed sentence on the enemy and sat in judgment upon him. He redressed the wrongs of his own people by *passing judgment upon the rest of mankind.* It was in the persons of the judges that the people realized their life under the theocracy. And this is proved by the Judges themselves—Deborah, Eli, and Samuel—who never regarded it as their mission to secure emancipation in the political sense. Freedom from bondage was valued only because it gave the people ever fresh opportunities of winning spiritual freedom. And thus the justification for the existence of the judges ended with the fulfilment of their mission. They were unique as phenomena and had no successors. In the intervals between their appearances, the people were once more left to their own devices, and forced to settle their own affairs with God, their Supreme Head.

But at this early stage in their development the people found it extremely onerous to be left to their own devices and to be forced always to rely on their own judgment and they would gladly have rid themselves of the responsibility. A leader of some sort relieved them of the difficulty of judging for themselves, and they only had to render him temporary obedience. Thus the demand arose for more permanent institutions. Signs of this are apparent as early as Gideon, whose name was connected with the slogan he proclaimed. Apparently he was even offered the title of King by the tribes he succoured, and in any case he remained the leader of his own tribe of Manasseh until the day of his death. But this gave rise to troubles which are usually associated with monarchy. In order to seize the power, Abimelech, one of Gideon's sons, had all his brothers except one murdered. He was supported by the tribe of Ephraim. But as soon as he tried to exercise the power he had secured, the people rebelled against him, and he was killed in the struggle that ensued.

But in spite of this discouraging example, the idea of permanent leadership once conceived continued to develop, and a terrible defeat inflicted on the Israelites by the Philistines gave it fresh impetus. In the valley of Sharon, the confederated tribes of Israel had been engaged in a conflict with the Philistines without being able to reach a decisive issue. To raise their courage and have a visible symbol of their God in their own ranks, they sent for the Ark of the Covenant from Shiloh, and had it set up in their camp. But in vain! They were repulsed, the Ark of the Covenant was captured by the Philistines, the enemy penetrated far into their country, pillaging and burning, and Shiloh, together with its sacred treasures, was destroyed.

The destruction of this religious centre dispersed the Levites who had been settled there and scattered them far and wide among the tribes all over the country. They now became more than ever zealous in their efforts to develop the idea of the theocracy, but, while the people granted them every possible authority, their desire for a permanent form of leadership remained as stubborn as ever. Whereas the Levites wished them to be united by the idea of God, they themselves were anxious to have the bond of union by which all their neighbours were bound together—they wanted a king. True, they had the wherewithal to be united under one God, a God of their own. But they felt they needed someone who would always be there to guide and encourage them. They were a young nation, afraid to be left to their own devices, and in their heart of hearts they longed for a man to exercise power over them. But they were convinced, and quite rightly, that in the position in which they found themselves, the fulfilment of their desire did not depend on themselves, and that it was not a mere matter of gathering together and electing a king. To them a king meant little more than a permanent hereditary judge, instead of a temporary regent of God's will. They were therefore obliged to appeal to those whom they acknowledged to be the servants and representatives of their Supreme Head, and to select from their ranks a man whose power and personality placed him in the front rank among them. The man they chose was Samuel, who had been sent to Shiloh to be brought up under Eli.

THE BIRTH OF THE MONARCHY

SAMUEL, the son of Elkanah of Ramah, who had been trained in the tabernacle at Shiloh, had been deprived of a stable sphere of influence when the place was destroyed. But he had secured a wider and more fruitful field for his activities by constantly touring the country from his birthplace, and exerting his influence in accordance with what he conceived to be the mission given to his people Israel, which he regarded as being the establishment of the theocracy and the keeping of the time-honoured covenant they had made with the God of their choice. He insisted on strict obedience to all the laws made at the time of the covenant and to all the rules and regulations laid down by Moses, and constantly reminded the people of them. He owed his power to the single-minded determination with which he exhorted them to turn their backs on the strange cults surrounding them and to subject themselves to the Lord. By this he meant something more profound than the adoption of peculiar religious rites and ceremonies, for the development of which among the Jews there had as yet been but little time or opportunity. Even Shiloh, before it had been destroyed, had not exercised a very much greater power of attraction than the other local shrines of Yahweh. And now that it no longer existed, worship alone could not be regarded as the main essential, which henceforward had to consist of something capable of surviving without a definite local anchorage. And it was not so much the observance of the laws of morality and justice that fulfilled this function as the idea that life without the God conceived by the people was but a dreary and meaningless existence. The attitude of Samuel and men of his stamp with regard to this is well described in the following verses from the prayer ascribed to his mother Hannah (though they date from a later age):

"The Lord killeth, and maketh alive: he bringeth down to the grave, and bringeth up. The Lord maketh poor, and maketh rich: he bringeth low, and lifteth up. He raiseth up the poor out of the dust, and lifteth up the beggar from the dunghill, to set them among princes, and to make them inherit the throne of glory . . . the Lord shall judge the ends of the earth; and he shall give strength unto his king, and exalt the horn of his anointed."

Such thoughts, which owe their origin not to active deeds or performances, but only to an act of religious surrender, necessarily produce visionaries, if they succeed in securing a following. Samuel himself was not a visionary. He was gifted with wise and penetrating understanding. He was a seer. But the circle of Levites who gathered about him already revealed the characteristics of a body in which ecstatic religious experience constituted the burning principle. Bands of them roamed the country, inciting the people, inspiring them with a restless eagerness to believe, exhorting them to wage a holy war against the conquerors, and preaching the idea of union among the tribes, who were still inclined to go each its own way. Though it may not have been the direct result of their activities, it was certainly about the time when their influence was at work that the tribe of Judah, isolated in the south and hard pressed by the enemy, sought the alliance of the rest of the Israelitish community. In its isolation, this tribe had progressed along lines of its own. True, its development was very similar to that of the tribes in the centre and north of the country, but it was less civilized, simpler and more bucolically pious. The attitude it now assumed materially promoted the idea of unity.

But regarding the means of securing this unity, which was inextricably associated with the idea of an access of power, and the final destruction of the enemy about them, the people and the Levites were far from being agreed. The Levites, with Samuel at their head, conceived of unity as being capable of realization only by the establishment of a complete theocracy, a political state of which the invisible God, of whom no image was to be made, was the Supreme Head, while the judges were His officers. The people, on the other hand, desired to be united under a permanent earthly representative of God—the king.

It was about this question alone that all the controversies in their own ranks arose at this time. When the matter first began to be discussed, the Israelites were again being attacked by the Philistines. Samuel was so successful in rousing the people that in the battle near Ebenezer they scored a victory. Samuel now assumed the position of judge, but his real sphere of influence was confined to the centre of the country. He had no authority in the north or in Transjordania. Within the limits of his jurisdiction he travelled up and down the land and every year convened an assembly of the elders of each tribe, either at Bethel, Gilgal, or Mizpah, for the purpose of administering justice, discussing matters of common interest, and working for the establishment of unity as he conceived of it. But when the Philistines and Ammonites renewed their attacks, the longing and desire of the age for a king became a stubborn and clamorous demand among the people, who came before him and asked for a king. It never entered into their heads to offer him the dignity, although he had actually saved them and been their leader; for they were only too well aware of the fundamental difference between a judge and a king. But it was from him, as the representative of their God, that they demanded an earthly monarch.

However much we may discount the narrative contained in the Book of Samuel, it is at least clear that Samuel was the anti-monarchist *par excellence*. With all the force at his command he opposed the people's demand, the gratification of which meant the end of the theocracy. The speech in which he tells them what the consequences of the fulfilment of their desire would be is the earliest extant condemnation of monarchy. It runs as follows:

"And he said, This will be the manner of the king that shall reign over you: He will take your sons, and appoint them for himself, for his chariots, and to be his horsemen; and some shall run before his chariots.

"And he will appoint him captains over thousands, and captains over fifties; and will set them to ear his ground, and to reap his harvest, and to make his instruments of war, and instruments of his chariots.

"And he will take your daughters to be confectionaries, and to be cooks, and to be bakers.

"And he will take your fields, and your vineyards, and your oliveyards, even the best of them, and give them to his servants.

"And he will take the tenth of your seed, and of your vineyards, and give them to his officers, and to his servants.

"And he will take your menservants, and your maidservants, and your goodliest young men, and your asses, and put them to his work.

"He will take the tenth of your sheep: and ye shall be his servants.

"And ye shall cry out in that day because of your king which ye shall have chosen you; and the Lord will not hear you in that day."

But in spite of this, the people insisted. They felt they could not continue any longer without a leader, and, recognizing their incapacity, Samuel yielded, considering it was wiser to give way. But though he tried to meet their wishes, he did all in his power to save what he could of the Idea. That the Israelites should have a king, such as the other peoples about them possessed, was to him inconceivable, and indeed absolute power, whether wielded by an upstart or by a hereditary sovereign, still remained incomprehensible to the Jewish mind, which could regard a king as a permanent leader only on condition that he had a divine mission. Thus, instead of being temporarily appointed for a particular task, he was now given a mission which would last for his life. This constituted the main difference between a judge and a king, and it was for Samuel to make this position and this dependence clear to the chosen monarch from the very beginning. He therefore proceeded to choose a king. All the people had to do was to accept him. By the symbolic ceremony of anointing, Samuel invested him with his mission and ratified his appointment. All the people had to do was to acknowledge this appointment. Moreover, for the rest of his life, Samuel was to remain the severe and fanatical overseer; holding himself sternly aloof, he ruthlessly insisted upon the elected king rendering unquestioning obedience to God and acknowledging his immediate dependence upon Him.

When, in after years, this control and supervision dictated by a sense of duty and spiritual concern ceased to exist, the path lay open for kingship by divine right, and for a system of irresponsible government.

KING SAUL

IN the town of Gibeah, in the land of the tribe of Benjamin, lived a man named Saul, the son of Kish. He was a brawny, energetic peasant, with the heart of a child, whose interests did not extend beyond the confines of his native village. Accustomed to a peaceful rural existence, he was entirely unsophisticated, and his religious beliefs were of the simplest. Like many others he had come into contact with the wandering Levites, and was deeply stirred. Possibly his heart had never been moved before, and the idea of a "holy war," that blend of religious service and bloody deeds, made a strong appeal to him.

Beyond the Jordan, Nahash, king of the Ammonites, was laying siege to the town of Jabesh. The hard-pressed inhabitants offered to capitulate, but Nahash would accept their surrender only on the outrageous condition that they should all have their right eyes put out. When Saul heard of this, "the spirit of God came upon him and his anger was kindled greatly. And he took a yoke of oxen and hewed them in pieces and sent them throughout the coasts of Israel, saying: 'Whosoever cometh not forth after me to Jabesh, so shall it be done unto his oxen!' " This was a primitive, virile message which the people were capable of understanding. And they relieved Jabesh and cut the army of Nahash to pieces. Whereupon Saul returned to his fields and his plough.

It was this man, half Hercules and half visionary, this passionate peasant from the smallest of the tribes of Israel, that Samuel chose to be king over the people. And thus the era of the judges drew to a close. Samuel carried out the task in a manner both haughty and portentous, not unmingled with pride and mortification. The institution of judges came to an end with an unsullied record. What would the monarchy bring forth?

"And Samuel said unto all Israel, Behold, I have hearkened unto your voice in all that ye said unto me, and have made a king over you.

"And now, behold, the king walketh before you: and I am old and grayheaded; and, behold, my sons are with you: and I have walked before you from my childhood unto this day.

"Behold, here I am: witness against me before the Lord, and before his anointed: whose ox have I taken? or whose ass have I taken? or whom have I defrauded? whom have I oppressed? or of whose hand have I received any bribe to blind mine eyes therewith? and I will restore it you."

The people were obliged to confess that the judgeship had been pure and free from all taint of self-seeking. Nevertheless, they turned to face their king, the man who towered head and shoulders above them. And Samuel went home, no longer a judge, but a seer, a spectator, a prophet, who with eyes sharpened by fervour, proceeded to keep a severe and suspicious watch over the first king of Israel.

Saul at first sustained the character which had brought him to the favourable notice of the people—that of a martial hero. He attacked the Philistines and conquered. The country was freed once more. Standing high both in his own esteem and that of the people, only now did he develop from a military leader into a real king, and began to rule, extending his sway, which at first was limited to Ephraim and Benjamin, over the neighbouring tribes. He created a standing army, and the village of Gibeah became his headquarters. From a simple peasant farmer he became a monarch with a court, retainers, guards, and officials, and all too rapidly learnt to taste of the sweets of despotic power.

Meanwhile, Samuel, who had returned to Ramah, never for a single moment forgot that the monarchy was not intended to be an end in itself, but a means, and the signs of growing despotism to be discerned in Gibeah were little to his liking. He was afraid that this display of power might lead to a dereliction of duty. He therefore told Saul that God wished him to wage war against the Amalekites, that is to say, to wage a war for which there was no apparent political or economic necessity. It could only have been a holy war against a people who, at the very beginning of Jewish history, immediately after the flight into the wilderness, had attacked the Israelites. Samuel knew that the Levites still exercised authority, and Saul undertook to do God's bidding without demur. But, in this instance, various peculiar conditions were attached to his mission—every living thing in Amalek, the hereditary foe, was to be utterly destroyed. It was not merely a cruel command, it was also extremely difficult to carry out, for it must be remembered that those who fought expected to be rewarded, by booty in the shape of prisoners and cattle, for their long absence from home. And it does not seem unlikely that Samuel deliberately imposed conditions which would force the king either to obey implicitly or else fail in his mission.

The campaign ended in victory, and Saul, highly elated, set up a trophy to himself at Carmel. But the rejoicings were short-lived. For a violent dispute took place between Saul and Samuel, and the two were never again reconciled. Was this due to the fact that Samuel disapproved of Saul's high-handed celebration of the victory as his own instead of God's? Or was it because he had not executed God's command to the letter but had allowed his men to keep cattle as booty?

Possibly it was for both reasons. Be this as it may, Saul's spiritual decline dated from this moment. The belief in the king's subjection to God was still strong enough to make a breach with the representative of pure Yahwism seem extremely dangerous. And, indeed, it was Samuel who, in the consistent pursuit of his idea, planted the seeds of tragedy in the life of the first Jewish monarch. To the people, Saul was just the man they wanted—a martial hero. Their grief at his death proves how thoroughly satisfied they were with him. But the prophet was not satisfied with him. The difference between the views of the people and those of their spiritual leaders was still apparent. It is typical of the history of the Jewish people that a custodian of their ideology is always to be found standing above their everyday life and making exorbitant demands upon them.

The king having been chosen and his appointment ratified by the most solemn rites, it was impossible for Samuel to undo what had been done. But he could prevent the king from founding a dynasty, and even during his lifetime could arrange for another and worthier representative to carry on the sacred mission later on. This he actually did, and secretly appointed David, the son of Jesse of Bethlehem in Judah, to be Saul's successor.

To be repudiated by the very man from whose hands he had received his throne was a terrible blow for Saul, and he did his best to propitiate Samuel, endeavouring to clear himself of the charge of disloyalty to his God by engaging in a number of minor campaigns against the neighbouring peoples and those Canaanites who were still to be found among the Israelitish settlers. He put them all to the sword and destroyed their shrines, thus hoping to prove the genuineness of his faith. He became a religious fanatic out of sheer uneasiness of mind. Feeling that his throne was tottering, and that a further symbol was required to strengthen his position, he set a crown on his head. Thus from a simple warrior Saul became a terrified creature scenting danger at every step; the honest martial hero had turned into a suspicious monarch, whose one thought was to claim recognition. And as though to lend dramatic intensity to his tragedy, fate brought to his doors the very man who had already been judged worthier than he and chosen to be his successor.

Saul at first befriended him, hoping that if he kept him in his presence he might forget the menace he constituted. But his action had the contrary result and only served to increase the danger, for whether he treated David well or badly, the latter's power and reputation grew visibly day by day. Twice did Saul try to break through the deadly circle that was closing about him; twice did he attempt to murder David; but both attempts failed. David took flight. Whereupon with morbid determination Saul hounded him down, fondly hoping that he might circumvent his destiny, if only he could destroy the man who was to compass his doom. But he failed.

Obsessed by anxiety regarding his own fate, Saul had lost all resolution and confidence when he was once again called upon to fight the Philistines. His relationship to the living fount of all faith, which had sustained him in the early days, had been destroyed, and in accordance with ancient custom he consulted the oracle regarding the issue of the battle. But the oracle made no reply. Whereupon he probed yet further into the world of mystery and waited for dreams to enlighten him. But no dreams came. And in his last desperate effort to obtain a reply from the prophet who had first called him, Saul, who in his religious zeal had put an end to the activities of the witches, turned to the witch of En-dor, and begged her to use her arts to call up Samuel from the grave. And now, at the eleventh hour, when it was too late, he had a vision, a spiritual experience, and at last clearly grasped that to which events had long been pointing. It is described as follows in the pithy narrative of the Book of Samuel:

"And Samuel said to Saul, Why hast thou disquieted me, to bring me up? And Saul answered, I am sore distressed; for the Philistines make war against me, and God is departed from me, and answereth me no more, neither by prophets, nor by dreams; therefore I have called thee, that thou mayest make known unto me what I shall do.

"Then said Samuel, Wherefore then dost thou ask of me, seeing that the Lord is departed from thee, and is become thine enemy?

"And the Lord hath done to him, as he spake by me; for the Lord hath rent the kingdom out of thine hand, and given it to thy neighbour, even to David . . . and tomorrow shalt thou and thy sons be with me."

On the following day Saul was defeated by the Philistines and with his own hand put a premature end to his kingship and killed himself.

His memory was kept alive in the hearts of his people not by any creative act, or contribution he made to their political or spiritual development, but only by their respect for his manly courage and martial prowess.

KING DAVID

LIBERAL historians are fond of describing King David's reign as the Augustan age of Jewish history. But this is a mistake. It was only superficially productive and important, and, as far as the real fate of the people was concerned, was not noteworthy. All it did was to raise the nation to the rank of a great power. But there is nothing in history to show that victories are ever responsible for the spiritual progress of a people; indeed the reverse is generally the case.

We find in David's reign the occurrence of crises precisely similar to those which had characterized the rule of Saul, though they were now aggravated by palace intrigues and disputes over the succession—two inevitable accompaniments of monarchy. As regards further organic development, all David did was to plant seeds both of good and of evil.

At the time of Saul's death we find David the leader of a band of free-booters, living in Ziklag, where the king of the Philistines had allowed them to take refuge. On hearing that the throne was vacant, David immediately hastened to Hebron in Judah. Nobody had summoned him, but he put forward his claim to the kingship, declaring that Samuel had secretly appointed him. The men of Judah, who nearly always found themselves isolated from the rest of Israel, were probably more concerned about securing a ruler of their own than about examining David's credentials, and resolved to proclaim him king.

The rest of Israel ignored him. They were determined to have a separate kingdom of their own, and proclaimed Ishbosheth, Saul's last surviving son, king. This shows that the idea of a dynasty had already taken firm root in their minds to the detriment of the monarchy dependent on God. It was at this time that the division of Israel into two separate kingdoms really took place. Subsequent events may have hidden the rift, but it was never really bridged.

The hostility between the two kingdoms was vented in civil wars, which were ended, not by one side definitely gaining the upper hand, but owing to the fact that Ishbosheth was killed as a result of private intrigues and feuds. Thus the north was deprived of its king, and David no longer had any opposition to fear, for Israel had no alternative but to transfer their allegiance to him. In sending a deputation to Hebron to acknowledge him as king, they were moved purely by motives of expediency and not by affection or any idea of accepting him because he had been appointed by the prophet.

After a reign of seven years in Judah David found himself sole ruler over all the land, and, at all events, proceeded to act accordingly. He accepted the idea of unity and pursued it with steady determination. He invaded the country of the Jebusites, which separated the north from the south, and conquered it, thus securing the geographical unity of the territory under his rule. Whereupon he made Urusalim, the old Jebusite capital, the capital of the new kingdom. In this city now called Jerusalem he established the headquarters of the new kingdom and built palaces, raised walls, and erected a temporary temple to house the Ark of the Covenant. True, Jerusalem was an unimportant place and not much of a capital to boast of; but at least it constituted a beginning; it was the germ-cell, and sheltered the king, the army, the civil service, and the religious treasures of the nation within its walls.

Just as events had conspired to make him sole king of Israel, so did the force of circumstances now drive him to extend the boundaries of his domain. For he was compelled to defend himself. At heart he was easy-going, tolerant, and pleasure-loving. But when he was driven to action, he did not limit his efforts to mere defensive tactics but made certain of putting an end to the menace once and for all. This explains his flight from Saul, and his escape to a place where it was impossible for anyone to reach him. It also accounts for the war he now waged against the Philistines, who were making repeated attacks with all the forces at their command. David was obliged to defend himself and opened a counter-attack which led to the capture of important Philistine territory. Perturbed by this dangerous access of power, his neighbours to the south-west, the Ammonites and the Moabites, formed a coalition with the Aramaic and Syrian princes. Once again, David was obliged to act on the defensive, and once again the exaggerated vigour of his resistance developed into a war of aggression, with the result that the Ammonites and Moabites became the vassals of the Jews. For a third time, the process was repeated in the north-east, where David, in defending his country against an Aramaic coalition, succeeded in extending his sway beyond Damascus. The subjection of the Edomites in the south was alone deliberately undertaken; the kingdom that had just sprung so rapidly into being required a coastline, and David now fought to obtain access to the Red Sea. After achieving this conquest the kingdom stretched from Egypt to the Euphrates, thus attaining the greatest political extension it ever possessed.

These conquests represented only a material gain. Politically, the extension of the kingdom may have been organic, but spiritually and socially it was not. The patriarchal system was just dying out, and the social organization was not yet sufficiently developed to meet the requirements of a great state. High political and popular interests were diametrically opposed. Whereas in Jerusalem all interest was concentrated upon the standing army, the question of mercenaries, the administration of the conquered provinces, and friendly treaties with Phœnicia, and while within the palace walls the problem of the succession was already being discussed, the people for the first time in their history were really only just entering into full possession of the land. And this development was not by any means determined by purely sociological conditions, but was due to the fact that the spiritual treasure in their hearts, long pent up and repressed during the period of their nomadic existence—the years when they exerted all their strength to conquer the country, and the difficult times of early settlement—had now at last found rest and the means of expression. They began spiritually to take possession of the land. And thus, for the first time, they developed the power of proselytizing, which led those native Semitic peoples who had not hitherto joined any of the Israelitish tribes but had held aloof to come over to them, and, by abandoning their own manners and customs, to provide the newcomers with an extraordinary access of numbers. The census taken by David shows that his subjects numbered about six millions. They occupied the country but they did not form a united whole. As in the past, so now, tribe competed with tribe, while all the northern tribes were united in rivalry against Judah. All David's efforts to compose these differences were met with resistance. The census, which probably served some purpose connected with the administration and the raising of the army, provoked the most violent indignation. The setting up of a high priest in Jerusalem, whereby David hoped to establish unity of worship, was ignored, and at Gideon in Benjamin another high priest was appointed who enjoyed equal authority with his colleague in Jerusalem. Moreover, the people did not hesitate to involve the kingdom in their venal conflicts, and to take advantage of the private disputes that arose in David's court in order to turn them into palace intrigues, conspiracies, and revolts.

Thus Absalom succeeded in having himself proclaimed king during his father's lifetime, and towards the end of his reign David was driven to secure his position by means of civil war as he had been obliged to do when he first came to the throne. After a period of great confusion, during which he conducted the struggle personally and was frequently worsted, shining as a man rather than as a ruler, he himself appointed and crowned his own successor, just as he himself had been appointed to the royal office during the lifetime of another king.

With generations of great tribulation and sorrow behind them, the imagination of the people surrounded David with the twofold halo of hero and poet. The sensational events of his life, and the versatility of his nature, justify this loving distortion of truth. For in reality David was a "man of contradictions." He was courageous and cowardly, strong and weak, a lover of pomp and yet simple in his tastes, cloaking all beneath a veneer of poetry, sensuality, and music. He wrote psalms which are real works of art. Though he was not responsible for nearly as many as have been ascribed to him, they constitute the only enduring legacy he bequeathed to his people. Even to this day the people have not lost all memory of them but find in them the same meaning they had for the contemporaries of their author—the record of a man's struggles to link his destiny with God. David was never able to raise the visible and concrete expression of this endeavour—a temple—which was the object of his secret longing. Fate overtook him before he could do so. During his last years he cowered in his palace, old, defeated, and bloodless, without a temple and without love. He was covered with clothes, but he could not get warm and, although he was an old man of seventy, he was given a fresh, kind-hearted young girl named Abishag to provide him at the end of his days with living bodily warmth.

He died after a reign of forty years.

KING SOLOMON

SHELOMO (Solomon), the Peaceable, the child of love and desire, the offspring of a pleasure-loving king and a yielding but eminently practical woman, made it clear from the very beginning of his reign that he intended to be an absolute monarch. He inaugurated his rule by committing three murders which cleared his path and got rid of his only brother, and he did so without the slightest qualms of conscience. In fact, he was nothing more or less than an oriental despot, the ruler of a great state. The problems which had confronted his father as a result of the religious nature of his preferment to office did not exist for Solomon. He inherited a kingdom; that was all! And his object was to make it secure, and to derive the greatest possible benefits from it both for himself and for the state, which was at once the sphere and the instrument of his power. As to the people themselves, their wishes, interests, cares, and problems, he considered them only in so far as they did not interfere with the smooth running of his proud and despotic rule.

He waged no wars. David had extended the boundaries of his realm to their utmost limit and Solomon secured his territory not by force of arms but by marriages. He married princesses of the royal houses of the Ammonites, the Moabites, the Aramæans, the Canaanites, and the Hittites; he even married an Egyptian princess, who brought him the only access of territory he ever had—the town of Gezer. He was a Habsburg by anticipation.

He also tried to secure himself from enemies at home. But the state of affairs which had embittered his father's declining years threatened to prove a menace to him also; for the various tribes were determined as far as possible to preserve their independence and were each almost jealously proud of their own peculiar attributes. Moreover, the life of each tribal body was still organized on patriarchal lines, and this in itself represented a principle diametrically opposed to absolute monarchy. After deep and mature deliberation Solomon set to work to destroy these tribal bonds and to abolish the frontiers between the various units. He divided the country into twelve administrative districts with a royal officer at the head of each, whereby he also achieved the further object of having at his command a supervisory body for raising his exorbitant taxes and collecting his tribute in kind. Above the district officers was a principal officer, a principal tribute-officer was responsible for the taxes, and a general was at the head of the army. Zadok was appointed high priest, and became the founder of a hereditary priesthood which lasted a thousand years. All these offices and appointments were directly calculated to give a new orientation to the tribal organizations which had been dissolved, substituting for them two objects upon which the attention of the people was fixed—the king and Jerusalem his capital.

If this centre was to take the place of the other small centres of tribal veneration scattered throughout the country, it was imperative that it should do so by reason of its splendour and pomp. And in achieving this aim, Solomon was eminently successful. Within the space of thirteen years, he built palaces and halls; he fortified Jerusalem, and had water conveyed to the city from a great distance by means of a canal. He also encouraged the wealthy citizens to build expensive and luxurious mansions.

Finally he erected a building which put the coping to his work of centralization, and proved of the utmost importance later on. He built a temple on Mount Moriah. Thus religion was given a permanent shrine, and the means of acquiring a traditional form. It was now also possible to establish a hierarchy in which the high priests, priests, and Levites were given their respective ranks. At the autumn festivals, the people began to make this temple the object of their pilgrimage.

The heavy burden of maintaining the royal court, the army, and the priesthood, and paying for the labour on the palaces, canals, and roads, naturally fell on the people. Not only were they crushed beneath a load of taxation and contributions in kind, but they were also forced to work. The fact that they were not bled dry by the system was due to the flow of wealth which Solomon, by anticipating the most modern commercial methods, managed to draw into the country. He cleverly exploited the importance of Palestine as a line of communication between Africa and Asia, and by making the most of his family connexions with the south and his political power in the north, he secured for his merchants the monopoly of dealing in Egyptian goods, particularly horses and chariots, and compelled the northern peoples to buy from them. Although the transport trade between the borderland states was not entirely in his hands, he stimulated it by making a number of good roads, with rest-houses, for caravan traffic, and derived considerable profit by levying dues and tolls along them. He also turned to commercial profit the treaty his father had made with the Phœnicians, sharing in their naval expeditions which went as far as Tarshish in southern Spain, while the Phœnicians also joined his expeditions when he sent ships from the harbours of Ezion-Geber and Eloth, in the Bay of Akaba, to the ports of Arabia and India, to fetch gold from Ophir, the site of which can no longer be determined. The tribute from vassal states and gifts from foreign princes helped to swell the stream of wealth that flowed into the country. The monarch enthroned in Jerusalem was a crowned merchant.

This economic development was far too rapid to allow the social evolution of the people to keep pace with it. Urban life was certainly stimulated, becoming variegated and luxurious, pleasure-loving and extravagant, as it were in a night. There was so much precious metal in the country that silver became almost of no account. Officials and merchants naturally benefited from this state of affairs. But no one else did. For the goods which were the source of commercial gain, with the exception of balsam and oil, were not produced in the country itself. Agriculture still formed the basis of the national economy, and the merchant class was foisted on to this agricultural order of society without any organic relationship. Far from knitting the country together or smoothing over differences, the new commercial interests divided the people into distinct classes, who had nothing whatsoever in common. Their property, the life they led, and their interests were entirely different. Thus the country fell into two sections—a small capital city, and a large provincial area. In the provinces the people groaned under the ever-increasing burden of taxation, regretted the abolition of the tribal associations, and with grave mistrust perceived that King Solomon, in spite of having built the Temple, obviously showed but little inclination to establish a uniform national cult.

They were driven to this conclusion by the ostentatious regularity with which he allowed all his wives and foreigners of every description not only complete freedom of conscience but also the privilege of setting up their own shrines and temples in the country. Monuments and altars were erected in high places to Astarte, Moloch, and Chemosh. Solomon was only too pleased that his fine kingdom should assume cosmopolitan airs. There was much opposition to this religious toleration, though religion formed merely a pretext for it, since the country was full of shrines not only to Yahweh but also to all the old local Canaanitish divinities. The real reason lay in the fact that the ten tribes in particular had never been able to adapt themselves to the idea of a single united Judean kingdom, or to acquiesce in the peaceful though extremely onerous rule of King Solomon.

In Shiloh, where the Ark of the Covenant had originally been housed, a Levite organization had survived which maintained the traditions of the prophets. Though it had no official position, it exercised considerable influence over the people, and as a result was particularly eager to represent the popular will.

Towards the end of Solomon's reign, the prophet Ahijah the Shilonite denounced the king's excessive toleration of alien cults and encouraged the separatist tendencies of the ten tribes, using as his instrument a certain man named Jeroboam, an Ephraimite, who had been a taskmaster, and had by his brutality so distinguished himself in his calling that Solomon had made him head overseer in Ephraim. This upstart became a willing instrument of disorder in the hands of Ahijah, but as Solomon ordered him to be put out of the way, he was obliged to take flight. This, however, merely gave the signal for the outbreak of disturbances.

The whole of the country, including the conquered provinces, was soon in a state of ferment. Solomon's rule, which at first had been energetic, logical, and practical, had begun to degenerate under the influence of his oriental court, and was marred by ostentatious display and pride of power. The king had lost all initiative; all he cared about was a life of royal ease. The Aramæans rose up in revolt but remained unpunished. The Edomites also cast off the yoke, and their rebellion was supported by Egypt, where Solomon's father-in-law had been succeeded by a king who regarded the all-powerful monarch of Israel as a serious menace.

Threats of danger both at home and abroad were foreshadowing catastrophe, when at the age of about sixty Solomon died, thus ending a reign of great magnificence, due not to any organic development, but to the reckless exploitation of a heritage which should have been gradually built up and consolidated. For, although Solomon reaped the benefit of it and was a man of exceptional endowments both of mind and body, his kingdom was too much of a mushroom growth to survive being used purely for pleasure. In after years the creative love of the people, in poetry and legend, depicted him as the ruler of an ideal world of beauty and peace, instead of a world in which both people and king, faith and monarchy, had yet to win their spurs. And posterity became enamoured of the fiction to which he aspired, and not of the reality which constituted his reign.

THE DIVISION OF THE KINGDOM

ONLY three kings ruled over the twelve tribes of Israel as a corporate whole. Their significance does not really lie in their respective personalities, for their influence on the history of their period amounted to little more than the provision of a name for the designation of a certain interval of time. But each of them was endowed by posterity with his own peculiar features and title of honour, and thus they became great historical figures and survived as historical forces. For subsequent generations drew their inspiration and carried on the battle of life by invoking the memory of Saul the Hero, David the Psalmist, and Solomon the Wise.

But their contemporaries derived but little benefit from the kingship, for it had not even the strength to secure its own survival. True, after Solomon's death, his son Rehoboam regarded his accession to the throne as a matter of course, but he soon learnt that the idea of a hereditary monarchy was by no means taken for granted by the people as a whole. The tribes of Judah and Benjamin certainly accepted him, but they were moved more by a feeling of loyalty to the house of David than by any devotion to Rehoboam's extremely mediocre personality. But the centre and north of the country temporized. A meeting of the elders was held at Shechem, and Jeroboam, who had hurried back as soon as the news of Solomon's death reached him, was present at the conference.

Rehoboam was also obliged to go to Shechem to receive the homage of the tribes. They did not actually refuse to accept him as king but demanded certain perfectly just and fair conditions as the price of their allegiance. He was called upon to reform the administration, and a dialogue, strangely typical of the times, took place:

"Thy father made our yoke grievous: now therefore make thou the grievous service of thy father, and his heavy yoke which he put upon us, lighter, and we will serve thee."

After three days' reflection, the people received their reply, dictated by the megalomania of absolutism:

"And now whereas my father did lade you with a heavy yoke, I will add to your yoke: my father hath chastised you with whips, but I will chastise you with scorpions."

Whereupon the people rose up in rebellion and Rehoboam was obliged to flee. Absolutism had lost the day! And the elders proceeded to elect their own king for the centre and north, choosing Jeroboam,

Solomon's former overseer. Thus the unity of the country was destroyed, and for two hundred years two states subsisted side by side—the kingdom of Israel in the north, also called Ephraim or Samaria, and the kingdom of Judah in the south.

Rehoboam's attempt to coerce the ten tribes by force of arms proved a failure, and served only to emphasize the difference between Judah and Israel, making the opposition between them clearer and more obvious. Suddenly there stood confronting each other two states which had no more in common, for good or for evil, than any other two countries with a common frontier. From time to time they waged war against each other or made treaties; but they were entirely separate—they had their own interests, pursued their own national policy, and determined their own fate. And their destinies could not well have been more different. For the kingdom of Samaria fell to pieces and vanished from existence without leaving a trace, whereas the kingdom of Judah was the nucleus out of which developed a people that has survived to this day.

The fate of Samaria cannot be adequately explained on the ground that she became involved in the international politics of that day and fell like all those nations who followed a similar course. The reasons lie deeper.

The peculiar religious consciousness of the Israelites had remained intact. Their various attempts at adapting themselves to the morals, the customs, the festivals, cults, and thought of those about them had failed to reach the inmost core of their being, which constantly reminded them that they were destined to develop as a race apart. On the contrary, their unconscious religious aspirations evolved with extraordinary speed and determination into a conscious spiritual attitude, and they came to understand ever more and more clearly that their religious edifice, their view of God, of creation, of the birth of man, and of his moral obligation in life, constituted something peculiar, which above all in its form and content demanded an order of existence fundamentally different from that of the people about them. These were differences which allowed of no process of assimilation to others. They demanded separation, absolute differentiation. And this tendency towards separation began to rise above the surface of the unconscious just about this time and immediately set to work as a creative force. But it was precisely at this moment that, in the kingdom of Samaria, events followed one upon another which were entirely opposed to this tendency, and ended in the deliberate and manifest separation of that kingdom from the kingdom of Judah and its further rapprochement to the neighbouring peoples. True, a reaction occurred, which aimed at the resumption of the old line of development. But it could effect nothing against those who were officially directing Israel's fate. The creative peculiarities which distinguished the northern tribes from those about them gradually disappeared. They ceased to believe they had a destiny apart from their neighbours, and consequently lost their individual consciousness. Voluntary purposeful differentiation came to an end, and with it all the impetus towards individual existence. In fact the history of the kingdom of Samaria consists merely of the processes whereby these various mental changes came about.

From the very beginning of his reign Jeroboam made separation from Judah as complete in the religious as it was in the political sense. To take the place of the temple of Jerusalem, he endowed two temples in Bethel and Dan with the dignity of official national religious shrines. In each place he set up a golden calf, perhaps the symbol of Apis, whose cult he may have learnt in Egypt. And thus the discontented elements in the population, who disliked the centralization of religious worship in distant Jerusalem and were unfit for a nobler abstract form of religion, were given the right of worshipping in high places, groves, and at home.

The encouragement thus given to the people to return to semi-pagan forms of worship arrested the development of pure Yahweh worship. As a matter of fact religious syncretism is a frequent and by no means surprising phenomenon in the early stages of religious evolution. The only force that can defeat it is the desire for definition and exclusiveness. But in this case all such desire was sapped of its strength, because the religious life was deprived of its obligations. This separation, however, had a further sequel—many of the Levites, who refused to worship at the semi-pagan shrines, as well as large bodies of laymen who were opposed to such religious demagogy and half-measures, left the country and went over to the kingdom of Judah.

The need of establishing itself as an independent state forced the kingdom of Samaria into conflict with its neighbours, and thus war and politics became interchangeable terms. Moreover, as far as the fate of the country was concerned, the king was much less important than the general commanding the forces. The latter was the real representative of power, for in his case there was no holy kingdom to which he was called upon reverently and piously to subordinate his authority. And since the king had been raised to the throne by means of popular rebellions, the general in command of the troops felt that a similar course lay open to him.

The first to carry this reasoning to its logical conclusion was Baasha, who inaugurated a period of regicide and military *coups d'état*. He killed Jeroboam's son and wiped out the whole of his house, thus exterminating a dynasty which did not last beyond one generation.

Twenty years later his own son suffered the same fate at the hands of Zimri; but the army chose Omri, the captain of the host, to lead them against Zimri, and Omri became the founder of an ill-omened dynasty (932 B.C.), which carried recent developments to their logical conclusion and forced the people to adopt the manners and customs of those about them. The Phœnicians, with whom they had long been on friendly terms, became the example they copied. Ahab, the second king of the house of Omri, married Jezebel, a Phœnician princess, and the process of assimilation developed rapidly and methodically. The worship of Baal and Astarte was officially introduced, and Phœnician forms of worship were observed in the temples. Hosts of Phœnician priests and prophets swarmed over the land, and Phœnicians began to settle in the country, and above all in the towns. Any sign of opposition to the new religious system was cruelly suppressed, and foreign forms of worship and culture settled like a heavy cloud over the land. New customs became established, new ways of life were stimulated by the growth of commerce and industry; riches, voluptuousness, and luxury turned the country into a second Phœnicia.

At that time a deep spiritual connexion existed between a people's manner of life and their religious beliefs, and for this reason there is some justification for associating the worship of idols with dissipation and loose living. At all events this was the attitude assumed by those who resisted these developments, whether actively or passively. The passive resistance is associated with the name of Jonadab, the son of Rechab, and the Rechabite movement which was named after him. The Rechabites were ethical and social reactionaries, who disapproved of the dangerous development of affairs in the kingdom of Samaria, and preached the simple life; they advocated living in tents, the renunciation of all wine-drinking, the abolition of agriculture, and a return to a patriarchal, pastoral life. They were opposed to the outward forms of the new existence rather than to the causes that led to them. The active opposition was identified with a personality of mysterious charm—the prophet Elijah. Elijah saw that, if things continued as they were, all hope of progress would be at an end. He knew that this religious syncretism possessed no vital force and that the increasing luxury of the towns was a symptom of decay. With all the passion at his command he endeavoured to abolish these evils; he rushed through the country like a whirlwind, preaching, stirring up the people, threatening and warning them, and like a whirlwind vanished into the wilderness only to burst forth again unexpectedly to continue his wild mission. His slogan was characteristic both of the man and his idea: "Serve the Lord thy God with all thy strength as the slave serveth his master." His followers formed a sect known as the Nazirites, who led the simple ascetic life of their master. Before he vanished from the scene leaving no trace behind, Elijah with a grand symbolic simplicity chose Elisha to be his successor, and Elisha and the Nazirites together constituted an illusive, secret, and powerful organization which played a leading part in the overthrow of the house of Omri.

Under Jehoram, the last of this dynasty, the seed sown by Elijah and Elisha had so far flourished that yet another military usurper, in the person of Jehu, was able to come forward as a candidate for the throne. Like his predecessors he wiped out every member of the house of Omri.

Anxious to show his gratitude to the party of the prophets, who had helped him to power, and above all to Elisha their leader, he abolished the worship of Baal and instituted a ghastly massacre of the priests of Baal, which led to the complete disappearance of Phœnicians from the kingdom of Samaria. But important though this was, it came too late to have much salutary effect; for it is impossible to expect spiritual improvement as the result of external reforms in the case of a people exhausted by endless wars and continual internal strife. The development of Israel had been completely arrested, and the only creation of which it could boast was the body known as the Nazirites, who by their way of life raised a silent and heartfelt protest against what they regarded as injurious alien influences in their midst. Although one member of the house of Jehu, Jeroboam II, succeeded in restoring the country to the position of a great power, and extended its boundaries from the Euphrates to the Dead Sea, his achievement proved barren and negligible, and served only to emphasize the fact that spiritually the kingdom of Samaria was no different from the other oriental and semi-oriental states; its forms of worship, its culture, its political and moral outlook were identical. This final spell of political prosperity was accompanied by a wild outburst of feverish and exorbitant voluptuousness and the evidences of deep-seated social injustices, till, in the end, all powers of resistance were completely paralysed. Usury was everywhere rampant, whether in money transactions or dealings in kind; debtors were sold into slavery, the judges were corrupt, and the priesthood immoral. Any clear and definite attitude towards God and man had ceased to exist. Only two voices were raised in a grand final protest against a state of affairs which was bound to lead to ruin—those of the prophets Amos and Hosea. We shall have occasion to discuss them later. All they could do at the time was to point out a means of escape to the few who did not wish to sink in the general wreck of things.

But for this, the march of events pursued its relentless way. Jeroboam II's successor fell by the hand of a regicide, and the latter, in his turn, succumbed to Menahem. Meanwhile, a certain power had appeared on the horizon, whose rise had long been watched with ever-growing anxiety by the prophets and men of vision. Assyria was a soulless embodiment of might; her claim to fame lay solely in vast numbers and conquests, and the most important legacy she left behind consists of inscriptions recording in bombastic terms the number of cities she destroyed, the treasures she heaped up, and the multitudes she killed and took prisoner. Her lust of expansion took a southerly direction, aiming at that other great power, Egypt, and at the coast of the Mediterranean. Babylonia, Mesopotamia, and the greater part of Syria were subdued. The usurper Menahem voluntarily offered to pay tribute and to swear allegiance to Tiglath-Pileser, King of Assyria, if only he would spare him and secure him on his throne. This constituted the first step in the process of disintegration.

Though Samaria was governed by one regicide after another, her rulers still imagined they could play a leading part in politics. Pekah made an alliance with Damascus, Tyre, and Sidon against the great power at Nineveh, whereupon Tiglath-Pileser retaliated. The Aramæan principalities were overrun and the whole of Galilee and Gilead, as far as Damascus, was subdued. Samaria lost half of her territory together with the people in it. The latter were led into captivity and made to settle down as strangers in a strange land, or were dispersed, scattered to the four winds, and left to perish. All that remained was an insignificant vassal state, defeated and desperate, riddled by vice and crime of every description.

One last desperate attempt at resistance was offered; a secret treaty was made with Egypt, and the payment of tribute to Assyria was refused. But the new ally proved a broken reed, and Shalmaneser V dealt the final blow. Samaria, the capital, alone remained, and held out against a siege lasting three years (721–719 B.C.), when it was captured by Sargon. Once again thousands were carried into captivity, while Assyrians, Babylonians, and Aramæans were sent to populate the deserted towns. Of the Israelites only a few husbandmen were left and placed under the rule of a governor. But twelve months later, as the result of an attempted insurrection, they too were carried into captivity. Only a few succeeded in escaping to the kingdom of Judah.

For centuries the situation in Samaria had been crying aloud for a strong ruler, and, since he had failed to appear, the spiritual justification for its existence as a separate people had come to an end. Retribution came in the form of a conqueror who carried the inhabitants back to the country from which they had originally started out. They had left it, bearing within them all the potentialities of the seed; they returned a broken, shattered fragment, mere unrecognizable dust, one of those failures which in nature the life-force abandons to death and decay. The ten northern tribes, with their separate development, had drifted so far away from their kindred in the south that the chronicle of their fall takes the form of a brief bald statement of fact unrelieved by any expression of grief. No epic poem, no dirge, no sympathy marked the hour of their downfall.

THE REMNANT OF ISRAEL

WHILE the northern kingdom was abandoning itself to a tumultuous spiritual and material development, life in the south, in the kingdom of Judah, pursued a peaceful, indolent, and more stable course. True, upheavals were not wanting here either, but they were encountered in a very different spirit from that prevailing in the north, and consequently served a constructive purpose.

Politically, the kingdom of Judah was negligible. With the loss of access to the Red Sea, it had even forfeited the maritime and inland trade which had been the two main sources of its extraordinary but short-lived prosperity. And it turned once more to agriculture for economic support. This economic decline was accompanied by a corresponding diminution of political power, for there was nobody in the country capable of outlining a sound foreign policy. Even Samaria was regarded alternately as friend and foe. Nevertheless, this political impotence had the effect of preventing Judah from engaging in wars on a grand scale, and incurring heavy losses. It escaped coming into conflict with the all-powerful Assyrians by having recourse to an expedient compatible with its weakness. King Ahaz offered to pay homage to Tiglath-Pileser, if the latter would liberate him from his enemies, the anti-Assyrian coalition of the north, and thus secured, for the time being, the political independence of his kingdom.

All this was consonant with the fact that Judah was no longer an absolute monarchy, the authority of the king being held in subjection by the nobility, the priesthood, and the prophets, three groups which were themselves the outcome of a logical, organic development. The nobility, the "princes of Judah," consisted of the old leading patriarchal families, who had now become men of property, royal officials, judges, etc.; they had developed into an ambitious body with interests of their own, and were eager to enrich themselves at all costs, acknowledging the king only in so far as he did not stand in the way of their private aims. Together with relatives of the reigning monarch, it was they who really did as they liked with the people and occasionally inspired the foreign policy of the country.

The second group, the priesthood, founded their claim to authority on their historic descent from Aaron, brother of Moses. Ever since King Solomon had made Zadok high priest, the office had been hereditary in this family. It represented a dignity which frequently set limitations on the royal authority and sometimes even settled the question of the succession. At one extremely critical period in the history of the kingdom, it was the priesthood alone who, through their influence, maintained the house of David in power. When in the kingdom of Samaria the house of Omri was exterminated by Jehu, Ahaziah, King of Judah, was also among the victims of the massacres. His mother, Athaliah, a daughter of the Phœnician princess, Jezebel, wreaked her revenge by having every member of the house of David murdered. Her grandson, Joash, alone was saved by the High Priest Jehoiada, who secretly brought him up in the Temple, and ultimately, with the help of the army, set him on the throne. This signal service rendered to the dynasty naturally placed the priesthood in a very prominent position, but, quite apart from that, they jealously guarded their inviolability and exclusiveness. Indeed, they frequently set greater store by the authority they wielded than by the purity and undisputed supremacy of the idea whose custodians they were. Thus, when King Ahaz, the self-appointed vassal of Tiglath-Pileser, wished to prove his loyalty by emulating his overlord, and suggested erecting an Assyrian altar in the Temple, he met with no opposition from the high priest. The idea of priesthood was not yet fully developed.

It is important to point out that what we now regard as the fundamental idea, the essence of Judaism and the Jewish point of view, had yet to be formulated and interpreted. Its form, in so far as it was manifested in religious worship, was officially centralized in the Temple at Jerusalem, though there were other centres as well. Shrines still existed in high places, where the rites solemnized were largely borrowed from alien cults, and the ruling caste was still able to introduce wholly foreign forms of worship into the country. Nevertheless, it is characteristic of the conditions prevailing in Judah at this time that, unlike the state of affairs in Samaria, reactionary movements were constantly set on foot, instigated sometimes by the king, sometimes by the priests, and sometimes by the prophets. The record of such tendencies, which are known in religious parlance as "backsliding" and "returning to the fold," very nearly sums up the history of this period. And therein lies a deep significance. Superficially, form of worship and outlook, custom and religious law, form and content, were still identical. And yet forces were already active which were aiming at distinguishing them, and which perceived the chasm between rites and mental attitude, between the formal worship of God and moral behaviour.

Then two processes took place—the old religious doctrine was once again inspired with life, and later doctrines and rites were given a new and solemn interpretation which adapted them to the central idea of Israel.

It was probably about the time of the High Priest Jehoiada that the Levites were instructed to roam the country in order to teach the people the rites and doctrines of their national religious tradition, of which the masses were almost entirely ignorant. Even such parts of the Scriptures as were then in existence were wholly unknown to them. Others had acted as trustees of this spiritual treasure for them and guarded it as a heritage—the Levites and the priests. And the kingdom of Judah now reaped the benefit of the influx of Levites, the custodians of the national tradition, of whose presence Samaria had been deprived from the beginning. It was the Levites together with the prophets who moulded the spiritual treasures that had accumulated meanwhile into a definite form. They introduced nothing fundamentally new. They merely took the tradition and the potential qualities of their people and moulded them to the type which has since characterized the Jewish soul and features. All the materials lay ready to hand, albeit in a state of dire confusion. The north had not been able to summon the strength to introduce order into chaos, but the south accomplished the feat. The very fact that the spiritual leaders in both countries made the attempt simultaneously shows that it was not an achievement peculiar to priests and prophets; it was merely a matter of developing existing material, of having the power to draw from existing conditions consequences of lasting importance.

True, the God they had first recognized was the God they served. Baal had vanished, though the ceremonies connected with his name still survived, and the God worshipped through their instrumentality was still a tribal deity. But in the end their religious aspirations were not satisfied by a separatist divinity of this description. If there were a power outside the earth, outside human spheres of influence, it could be only the ultimate, final, all-powerful Being, in which case it could not be *a* power, or *a* God, but *the* power, *the* God. Such reasoning was bound to lead to the conclusion that their God was not the God of a tribe or a people, but the God of the world, of the universe. And though they may occasionally have tried to represent Him, if not by means of images, at least here and there by symbols, they gradually began to perceive that the perfect embodiment of all power, the essence and impersonation of the unearthly, could certainly not be represented by the paltry devices of man or of anything on earth, but could only be the object of belief and faith, thought and sentiment.

Thus they approached the conception of God as unity, universality, and incomprehensible mystery of which no image could be made.

This was no mere abstract development of ideas; it found tangible form not only in a literary echo, but also in practical results.

The written echo is to be found in the Book of Deuteronomy, the fifth book of the Pentateuch. It was conceived during the period when Judah and Israel existed as separate kingdoms, although it was only subsequently that it was issued in its final form. The greater the danger of assimilation to environment became, the more vital and vigorous was the elaboration of the Jewish Scriptures, animated as the work was by the conscious desire to educate the people and strengthen the religious idea. The oldest portions of the Bible had already been written by the time of David and Solomon. But during the period of separation, and under the influence of the prophets, the old tribal sagas were collected, infused with new life, amplified, and reinterpreted, though no longer arbitrarily, or for the sake of heaping up material, but with the object of offering the work as a whole, as representative of the idea. But as the task was carried on in both kingdoms, it was inevitable that, in spite of the careful preservation of the main conception, different versions should result. Thus, when these two versions were subsequently combined, two different accounts of the creation came to be placed side by side—a cosmogonic account, according to which the earth, the vegetable kingdom, the animal kingdom, and man arose in an organic ascent out of chaos, and a geocentric account, according to which man was created out of dust, and the animals and plants came later. The different localities of origin, and the different tendencies, which the compiler had to observe for educative reasons, led to other divergencies in the description of events and the interpretation of regulations. The discovery of these discrepancies led critics to form the most curious conclusions, with which we need not concern ourselves here. All that matters is that, in these writings, we have the echoes of a certain historical development; they must be interpreted with due regard to the age and the circumstances which led to their production, and which preclude anything in the nature of prejudiced and polemical handling.

The practical interpretation of the Scriptures and the knowledge of them which was handed on to the masses struck deep roots into human life, with the result that the morals and customs of the people, their religious rites and observances, were not merely raised out of the rut of indolent routine but were authoritatively prescribed as the necessary expression of an attitude to life, of a moral and spiritual existence. Thus customs and morals, religious rites, songs, sagas, commemorations, and festivals were all welded together, and produced, not a mere unwieldy conglomeration, but a definite view of the world.

Hitherto the Israelites had led a more or less hand-to-mouth existence. But they now learned that everything that takes place is somehow mysteriously connected with a higher moral idea, and that events in the life of the individual, as well as in that of communities, are not fortuitous, but all give evidence of an ethical idea, call it God, cosmic law, or what you will. And they began to grasp the meaning that lay behind historical events. When the northern kingdom, unable or unwilling to undergo this spiritual transformation, disappeared from the face of the earth, and the time-honoured law of Jewish history once more applied the principle of selection to the "remnant of Israel," those who were left perceived a strange truth behind what had happened—God was not on the side of the mighty. Yet sometimes He used the mighty to keep alive the spiritual alertness of His followers.

Thus the chain of events which culminated in the final absorption of the remnants of Samaria by the kingdom of Judah was in its essence fundamentally spiritual. The concrete historical facts produced nothing lasting, nothing which is of the smallest interest to the modern world. But ideas came into being which have altered the whole face of the world. So powerful were they, that they produced the men to represent them—the prophets, the spiritual reserve of the Judean race.

PROPHECY

PROPHECY is the divination, acknowledgment, and perception of the moral obligation that man, during his sojourn on earth, should observe towards this world and the beyond, towards God and towards his fellow-creatures. This capacity to foresee is based upon the clear-sighted religious certainty of what the consequences of a denial of moral obligations can and will be. Such visionary knowledge must have a spiritual foundation. Dull ages are incapable of it. For centuries the Jewish prophets had an unfailing capacity for it. This is what makes them unique.

Prophecy is therefore a twofold phenomenon, consisting of a religious and an earthly factor. There can be no religion without earth. Nothing can exist in the sphere of the religious that does not also exist in the sphere of the non-religious. Otherwise religion would be merely fictitious and not real. When we speak of religion, we must include the whole of life. Anything else denotes an attitude of fear, an incapacity for experience, or else untruthfulness. Possibly the ultimate fulfilment of life and fate may be given only in heaven. But the earth is the place where man lives and moves and has his being. Heaven without earth is useless.

The prophets constitute at once a historical and a timeless phenomenon. If our attempt at defining the concept of prophecy be accepted, then prophecy must be possible in every age and among every people. It is not for us to explain why the Christian world was obliged to suppress creative prophecy within its own domain. A state of mind which might have provided the basis for the appearance of prophetic spirits can be shown to have existed times without number in history.

Even before the appearance of the Jewish prophets, prophecy itself existed. In all Semitic languages the word *nabi*—announcer (?)—is to be found. This type of man hails from a world standing in a much closer and more intimate relationship to Nature both in her sensual and supersensual manifestations. He is clear-sighted and capable of divination; he has the receptive power to absorb mystical experiences and is able, through the consequent violent religious emotion, to communicate them and give evidence of them to his fellow-men. But whereas among other nations prophecy gradually degenerated into the stock-in-trade of a sacerdotal guild, and in due course, therefore, petrified and disappeared, in the atmosphere of the Israelitish and Judean culture it continued to develop in accordance with the potentialities of its representatives and its own expression and inner meaning. Among these people, prophecy was not connected with any particular office. The prophets formed a group unhampered by any social or religious limitations and enjoyed no privileges either of rank or birth. Of the majority of them hardly more is known than their birthplace and their social calling—agriculture, cattle-rearing, etc. Out of obscurity they sprang and into obscurity they vanished. Their personalities were nothing, their office everything. Even those about them regarded them only in this light. When they recorded or conveyed their message, deference was paid, not to the man, but to what he said. And it is for this reason that we find, side by side in the records, pronouncements from various quarters all mixed together without hesitation; among them there is undoubtedly much that was uttered by prophets whose names and personalities are now quite unknown.

As the temporal and earthly and the supertemporal and religious are all factors in prophecy, it is obvious that the individual prophets must have differed from one another, that they must have expressed themselves differently, and exerted a different influence, according to the time and place of their appearance. Nevertheless, in view of the many characteristics they have in common, it is possible to speak of an evolution of prophecy, if only because it grew in proportion to the distress and needs of a particular age.

The prophecy of Deborah was still simple and primitive, and can be summed up in the desire to see the people united in a theocracy. Samuel's prophecy reveals a multiple vision. He was a soothsayer, an ecstatic, as well as a passionate advocate of theocracy. The two figures of Nathan and Gad, who appeared in the reign of David, are more shadowy, while that of Ahijah the Shilonite is somewhat more clear as a man of political influence under Solomon. Elijah, the miracle-worker of popular credence, who still dies and lives on in legendary lore, had a definite programme and set himself a definite goal—the establishment of a simple Nazirite ideal of life, the abolition of despotism, and the defence of the religious idea pure and unadulterated. His successor, Elisha, combined all this into a single definite political aim—the destruction of the house of Omri. A grander conception was elaborated in the eighth century B.C. by Amos and Hosea in Samaria and by Isaiah and Micah in Judah.

All the prophets based their activities on the same fundamental principle—the ideality of the relationship between this world and the beyond, between actual existence and its meaning, between existence and the significance of existence. They recognized that a life which is merely vegetative is unworthy of humanity. Furthermore, they saw that even where the attempt is made to lend weight and significance to life through the conception of a deity, there will always be the eternal conflict between bare existence and a life in which the deepest springs of human nature are unloosed. To their eternal credit be it said that the prophets roused their people to a consciousness of this difference and kept it alive.

If man, become conscious of his human dignity, strives to rise above himself, above his daily and limited round, he can grasp the unlimited, the unearthly, the non-diurnal only in the form of the most comprehensive concept—God in his universality. This is one of the fundamental concepts of prophecy. The other is that, if a universal God is the regulator of life, we must necessarily conceive of him as regulating the whole of life and living things, and that, moreover, not according to any law of expediency or utility, but by something transcending either, that is to say morality. Thus the second fundamental concept is that of ethical monotheism.

By subordinating life in all its manifestations—religious, economic, and political—to these fundamental concepts, the Jews made very definite demands upon each of these spheres. They insisted upon religion holding aloof from all pagan forms of worship. This amounted to something more than merely drawing a superficial line of demarcation between their own people and those about them. We have pointed out again and again how essentially, in the early stages of religious development, forms of worship and inner content are one and the same thing, and how essentially the former can adequately represent the meaning and general outlook of a religion. The meaning of strange forms of worship could be summed up in every variety of magic phenomena, in innumerable grades of exorcism. But the aim of the prophets was to make religion consist not of magic but of the sacrament. In magic the deity is exorcised, invoked, and implored, flattered and discreetly threatened, and the magic rite is performed subject to the understanding that fulfilment or reward will follow. The sick man who prays expects and demands a cure. The man who offers a sacrifice does so by way of purchasing, bartering, or bargaining for a favourable issue to his undertaking. But the man who regards prayer and sacrifice as sacramental in character places himself in direct relation with God; he presents himself to the deity, and waits in readiness for something to happen to him which has not yet taken place, but will occur as a result of his submission to God. Every sacrifice which had become petrified into a ritualistic form represented what, in the language of the prophets, was called "lip-service." That is why they were opposed to the rite of sacrifice in general. They propounded the principle—not sacrifice but sentiment. And this is what the prophet proclaimed to the people when he said: "Your new moons . . . my soul hateth . . . I hate and despise your feast days, and I will not smell in your solemn assemblies. Though ye offer me burnt offerings and meat offerings, I will not accept them; neither will I regard the peace offerings of your fat beasts. Take thou away from me the noise of thy songs; for I will not hear the melody of thy viols. But let judgment run down as waters, and righteousness as a mighty stream."

This makes it readily comprehensible that strained relations, due to intensity of spiritual feeling, should have existed between the prophets and the priests, and that the prophets should have contested the right of the priests to instruct the people. By his very office the priest was bound to forms of worship. He was not in a position to inquire into the nature of the spiritual attitude held by a man who wished to bring him a sacrifice. He was, in any case, obliged to offer it, even if its object was to secure some magic result. But the prophets made it their business to influence the spiritual attitude of the sacrificer, and of the religious man in general. They strove to overcome the rite by means of the idea. This tendency involved the adaptation of the old popular customs to the higher meaning, their modification in thought and interpretation, and their endowment with fresh spiritual associations. Thus the various festivals, which had hitherto been merely bucolic jollifications, became days of religious and national commemoration; the amulets and talismans became symbols of obligation, while the Sabbath became a spiritual holiday forming a break in the routine of daily work.

But all this transmutation of festivals and symbols would have availed nothing if the prophets had been incapable of making the people understand the unifying spiritual reason for it. They reminded them of the covenant which had been made between them and their God at the very beginning of the historico-religious development. But if they now represented this God as a universal deity common to all the world and all the peoples of the world, it seemed inevitable that the belief of the Jews regarding their position as the Chosen People must be dealt a mortal blow. Yet the contrary was the case. Amos reduced it to the briefest possible formula: "You only have I known of all the families of the earth: therefore I will punish you for all your iniquities." Here we find the other side of the picture, the idea that the practice of *noblesse oblige* was incumbent upon the elect, emphatically emphasized. And the prophets never ceased to demonstrate the effect of this principle on every action of the individual as well as of the community. Nothing that a man could do was a matter of indifference or of no consequence in the light of good and evil. Everything was inextricably bound up with a moral order, with God, or with justice, or whatever the concept might be called. And thus no historical event could be the work of chance or accident. History was big with meaning. It had a meaning. Above all it meant that man could determine and mould his own destiny, by his spiritual attitude, his spiritual orientation. The destinies of the world were as good or as bad as the spirits of the human beings inhabiting it. And this has remained true to this day.

By filling the minds of the people with such ideas as these, the prophets succeeded in establishing a reasoned and co-ordinated *Weltanschauung* in the place of a panic-stricken adaptation to a certain accepted order. Thus the Jews were the first people who regarded their fate not from the standpoint of national supremacy, but from that of moral harmony.

Wherever they encountered disharmony in a moral sense, they seized upon and condemned it, whether in the daily life of the individual or of the community, whether they found it in social or in political activities. The logical outcome of this was that, as believers in a universal God, they passed prophetic judgment on the fate of *foreign* nations also. And this they were entitled to do. They did not exclude other peoples from the blessings of a harmonious existence. "I will pour out my spirit upon all flesh." Armed with this maxim the prophets were able to cross the frontiers of every nationality. If two thousand five hundred years ago their profound faith led them to see "in the last days" universal peace in the world, they saw it for all the world and for all peoples. "And it shall come to pass in the last days . . . that they shall beat their swords into plowshares, and their spears into pruninghooks: nation shall not lift up sword against nation, neither shall they learn war any more." (Isaiah ii. 2–4.)

And just as they recognized the moral quality of historical events, they also possessed the capacity for political vision. And they exercised it, if not always with success, at least with stubborn persistence. What did it signify that not all they predicted was fulfilled? All that mattered was that they were the consistent expression, the true incarnation of all that was immortal in ideas and ideals among the people. They were not so much the people's oracle, as their innermost flame of endeavour. No people con produce a whole race of ecstatics unless they themselves possess the gift of ecstasy. This Jewish ecstasy does not lie in action. It is rather a capacity for enduring, for being obliged to endure. Not one among them *wished* to be a prophet. One and all had prophecy thrust upon them. "It" spoke within them. They were not allowed to be silent. They suffered unspeakable anguish from the threats they felt forced to hold out against their people and closed their eyes with horror before all that their prophetic vision obliged them to proclaim. To a far greater degree than the judges, they were officials of the theocracy. It was not left to them to exercise their influence or not, as they pleased. They were called and they obeyed. In the case of other men strength lay in action; with them it lay in yielding. Hundreds of years after their time people were still able to live on this strength. For hundreds of years this strength was regarded as a manifestation of the divine, and the sayings of the prophets were treated as revelations from God. Even to this day Christianity turns to Jewish prophecy to justify its existence. If we give to the work of the prophets the recognition it deserves, we are bound to admit that there is not a nation or an individual who cannot look back to it as a heritage.

In their own day their activities were chiefly spent in combating social injustices. This they did with a severity and frequency that would seem to indicate that the community in which they lived was the most corrupt that had ever existed or was ever likely to exist. Yet this was not the case. True, there were social injustices, as there are bound to be in any country where an aristocracy develops and lays claim to power, where a class of wealthy merchants suddenly superimposes itself on a community of industrious peasant farmers, and urban culture, allowed to develop without let or hindrance, is utterly unscrupulous in its choice of means. The social inequality inseparable from such conditions doubtless existed, but it was not, as in the case of Rome, for instance, sanctified by law. In Jewish law there was no such thing as a legal justification of inequality, and consequently no form of injustice that could be defended. No one could vindicate an act of injustice by an appeal to the law. God, man, and his own conscience would always condemn him. It was this that the prophets emphasized so strongly. The unusual feature in the circumstances was not the existence of social injustice, but the passionate and inexorable severity with which it was combated and condemned. Yet beneath all the menaces and warnings of the prophets an undercurrent of deep affection for their people may be discerned. They knew, since they foresaw the future, that the Jews were destined to bear an exceptionally heavy burden. They already understood the law of selection, and were aware that it would be unfailingly applied until the idea, of which the Jews were the servants and representatives, had taken final and definite shape. They were therefore convinced that the various exiles and dispersions, decimations and massacres, would result in the survival of a remnant that would be immortal. *Shear yashuv,* cries Isaiah—a remnant will return.

THE ORGANIZATION OF A TIMELESS EPOCH

THE downfall of Samaria and the total disappearance of the majority of the Israelites once again applied the law of selection to the Jewish community. The few who escaped death or captivity fled to Judah and joined the nucleus that still survived there, thus becoming witnesses of an extraordinary event that took place in that kingdom. They were once more confronted by the problem, why, with only a space of a few miles between them, the history of the two kingdoms should have been so different. The reply, based upon the spiritual influence of the prophets, was simple and impressive—external power and internal power are not the same. External power, which is violence, is temporal. Internal power, which is the absence of violence, is supertemporal.

The whole subsequent history of the kingdom of Judah, until it ceased to exist as a state, consisted in exemplifying this fateful contrast. Of the Children of Israel, a people that had once numbered possibly six millions, only a fragment survived in the shape of an insignificant little state in Palestine, which was a vassal of Assyria and, on account of its very minuteness, was left to its own resources. Nevertheless, it was upon this isolated remnant that all the great powers of heaven and earth were now converging. It became the anvil on which, from north and south, the mighty hammers of the nations now began to fall.

All about it colossal powers had sprung up who desired empire as an end in itself. Assyria, a vast organization built up entirely on conquest, was no longer able to hold her conquered peoples in subjection. Babylonia, the ancient motherland, began to raise her head again and established her independence as the kingdom of Chaldea. Egypt, anxious to have her share of the crumbling colossus, reopened her insensate attacks in the direction of the Euphrates. For Egypt, Palestine was merely a corridor. For Babylonia, she was the buffer against her rivals in the south. Thus the kingdom of Judah was a tiny state lying between the frontiers of two great rivals. On both sides foreign powers were constantly pressing upon her, threatening to annihilate her. The atmosphere in which the people lived was consequently oppressive and stifling, and made their blood-pressure so high that their condition was one of feverish anxiety.

Febrile states of this description give rise to the two extremes known as resignation and active resistance. But, in this Jewish atmosphere, both resignation and resistance had a very special meaning and a twofold significance. Here, on the one hand, was a group of people who, after the endless vicissitudes of a hazardous existence, menaced on all sides by overwhelming odds, ached to find rest and peace at last. They longed for the completion of their development, which was constantly imposing new and arduous duties upon them; they longed to be relieved from the necessity of making further sacrifices to secure a separate existence. And to this end they were ready to adopt any form of worship or culture. Let him who ruled over them determine their religion as he pleased. Spiritual lassitude turned them into opportunists.

On the other hand, there were those who, while they regarded this process of cultural assimilation as desirable, nevertheless wished at all costs to regain national independence. And thus from out the dull monotony there arose the concept of nationalism, hitherto unknown in the history of the Jews. They had learned from their neighbours that, given a certain spiritual attitude, even the state could come to be regarded as an end in itself.

Finally, submissiveness and resistance were both given a very different interpretation by yet another group of people, those who, though quite ready to be resigned, limited resignation to the political sphere; and those who, though anxious to offer resistance, wished to resist in a manner transcending earthly power, in the realm of the spirit. Their aim was spiritual self-preservation, at the cost, if need be, of sacrificing political independence.

The result of such extremes in internal politics is the formation of parties. Thus this period was apparently occupied by constant politico-religious feuds, though, as a matter of fact, the real question at issue was the point of view, the *Weltanschauung*, in the literal meaning of the word. At the beginning of the period, King Hezekiah resolutely stamped out all alien cults; his successor restored them, and King Josiah in his turn made the worship of Yahweh the one religion of the land. But all these changes had nothing to do with domestic or foreign policy. It was merely a matter of determining the attitude to be adopted, on the basis of a *Weltanschauung*, between two extreme points of view, which came into being at this time and about which a decision had to be reached, just as, while the kingdom of Samaria was in existence, the only problem to be solved was that of survival, which could be grasped only on the spiritual side. Thus once again the most rigid formulation of this *Weltanschauung*, or view of the world, which was awaiting establishment, was spiritual—it belonged to the realm of the prophets. For, after all, it was the prophets who decreed what the future of this people was to be.

The spiritual conflicts of the age found their focus in the unique figure of the prophet Jeremiah. This man, who entered upon his calling at an unusually tender age, accomplished his task with extraordinary single-mindedness and clarity of vision. He, too, was a prophet *malgré lui*, overpowered by an irresistible force and obliged to obey, little though he might relish it. The extraordinary duration of his influence is only commensurate with the wellnigh superhuman vividness of his vision. In the following references to him, our remarks relate less to him personally than to his whole figure as representative of the school of prophets of the period.

With Jeremiah the question, What now? receives its final and decisive answer. He drew the inevitable conclusions from the spectacle of a world in the throes of a great struggle. He saw people after people, state after state, growing up, spreading themselves, puffing themselves up, extending their boundaries by means of force and violence, and in the end collapsing at the feet of some other power, in the face of some other form of violence. Their existence began and ended in the exercise of might. They endured only so long as another power did not overthrow them. This was a process which might well be repeated *ad infinitum* with gruesome monotony. As might can always be surpassed by might, whether in the form of man-power or engines of war, any crystallization of might can at any moment be annihilated by another greater crystallization. Consequently it is impossible for the might of any individual community to endure. When it will go under is merely a matter of time; that it will go under is absolutely certain.

The prophet regarded all these transpositions of might merely as living demonstrations of this idea. All he saw and all he suffered was inevitably imbued with a deeper meaning. He could not rest satisfied with merely watching the course of events; for a man who starts out from the idea of a universal God cannot think that chance rules the universe. Everything must have a meaning. That the deity should exercise might for its own sake has always been inconceivable to the Jewish mind. Might could be only a means to an end. On the other hand, might, as incapable of survival in itself, could be overcome only by its opposite—"absence of might," or "anarchy" in the sense of lack of all force. But as even in the absence of might or violence, and in anarchy, there must be rules of conduct for men to obey, those rules can only be the embodiment of what is known as morality or ethics, the maintenance of a corporate whole through the definition of good and evil and the limits to be set to the individual's and the community's self-seeking impulses.

These reflections led to the formulation of certain practical precepts. In the first place, Judah was to renounce all political ambition. She was not to attempt to measure her strength with the giants about her, or try to found her existence on what was obviously bringing her neighbours to ruin, namely violence. She was to submit to the ruling power of the day, and to interpret her national ambition rightly and not wrongly. "In returning and rest shall ye be saved; in quietness and in confidence shall be your strength."

The second precept was: "Judah shall offer resistance only in the realm of the spirit." (Spirit in this context was not meant to denote anything abstract; it was not the pretext for the repetition of the old but none the less erroneous idea that the Jews were an "abstract people." They are not an abstract people, but a people that can abstract.) Spirit here means taking up a stand on spiritual grounds. Its meaning is well illustrated by an event which constitutes the central point of this period of history.

In the year 621 B.C., during the restoration of the Temple by King Josiah, who tried to establish the sole worship of Yahweh, a manuscript hoary with the dust of ages was discovered among the archives. It contained a curious version of the laws which had been codified, up to that time, a sort of repetition and variation of them, giving a host of instructions regarding man's duty to God and to his neighbour. It was couched in the form of speeches supposed to have been delivered by Moses just before his death on the farther side of Jordan. Who the author was it is impossible to say, though the task was certainly carried out in a manner strictly in keeping with the spirit of the prophets. The following are its fundamental principles. The old covenant between God and His people was still valid. God had made the Israelites His chosen people, and they in their turn had pledged themselves to God, and their fate depended on whether they kept or rejected this pledge. They might still deny the pledge. But in that case they would no longer be a peculiar people, a race apart. They might acknowledge the pledge, but in that case they were not to do so with the lips alone, they were to stake their whole existence upon the affirmation. And then it would be eternal, it would be mightier than all the material power in the world. But staking their whole existence meant, in this connexion, basing their whole relationship both to heaven and earth avowedly and unequivocally upon the dominion of the soul and the spirit, in the belief that life is not an accident to be regarded with fear, but something born of the highest living energy, from God, something which is an eternal mystery, which requires no explanation, but has only to be expressed. This expression of life, *in so far as it concerns the transcendental,* consists in the recognition of one God, who has created the universe, and who insists on being acknowledged in his own sacramental, intangible shape, not in the borrowed forms of magic, which make only a portion of Him, His creative power, comprehensible and objective in symbols. This expression of life, *in so far as it concerns earthly things,* consists in *justice,* as the formative norm of human society.

Injustice is the ultimate and inevitable expression of all violence. Violence creates inequalities. It is the function of justice to remove them. This is the basic principle underlying the social rules of the book in question; they deal in general terms with innumerable conditions of life, from the daily wage of workers, which must not be withheld until after sundown, to the rights of the newly wed; from the obligation to undergo a year's military service and the punishment for refusal to pay taxes, to the curse hanging over him who does not honour his father and his mother. Whenever the various developments of social life have led to inequality, a fresh partition or equalization of property is enjoined, not as an act of benevolence to be performed or not according to choice, but as a claim on the part of the poor, whether in the form of a right to gleanings, to the cancellation of debts, the return of land sold, or what not. Special emphasis is laid upon the duty of rendering the utmost justice to widows, orphans, and strangers. No other nation has ever shown so much concern for the welfare of the stranger in their midst, as the Jews discovered to their cost when in after years they themselves dwelt as strangers in a strange land.

None of the laws in this book are in any way utopian.

"For this commandment which I command thee this day, it is not hidden from thee, neither is it far off. It is not in heaven, that thou shouldst say, Who shall go up for us to heaven, and bring it unto us, that we may hear it and do it? Neither is it beyond the sea, that thou shouldst say, Who shall go over the sea for us, and bring it unto us, that we may hear it and do it? But the word is very nigh unto thee, in thy mouth, and in thy heart, that thou mayest do it."

This is the foundation of the moral imperative. This is the basis of a life depending not on interest but on definite sentiments. In this book the world is built up afresh and crowned with the dome of heaven. It does not set up a heaven inadequately supported by earth. In it religion is the growth of experienced reality, and a passionate affirmation of life springs from the very depths of religious resignation. The Kingdom of God is of *this* world, and the kingdom of man, who has created God for himself, is also of this world. The acceptance of this principle accounts for the resistance subsequently offered to a later Jewish conception of life on earth as being merely a temporary state of preparation. The fact that at this early stage the Jews denied that life was merely provisional afterwards enabled them to escape the necessity of living in a state of constant conflict with dogma. "For the grave cannot praise thee, death cannot celebrate thee; they that go down into the pit cannot hope for the truth. The living, the living, he shall praise thee, as I do this day." (Isaiah xxxviii. 18–19.)

Now, if on the one hand there were obligations, on the other there was a promise. And here we come to a question which has been a constant cause of controversy and attack, the question of the Chosen People. Let us at once dismiss from our minds a distortion of this concept, consisting in the idea that the Jews had a mission. Judaism has no mission and has never sent out missionaries. But it is the living paradigm of all the ultimate principles which the gregarious life of humanity requires—the recognition of a moral order in the universe, of the eternal nature of spirit and the ephemeral character of violence, of the necessity of right and justice, and of the belief in a state of peace between man and man. This at once shows what the idea of "chosen" signifies; it means the survival of a people as an example. It is the idea of being chosen for duty, not for laying claim to possessions. It is not, we may; but, we must.

"The secret things belong unto the Lord our God; but those things which are revealed belong unto us and to our children for ever, that we may do all the words of this law."

The burden of these spiritual obligations first formulated and enjoined by the prophets has, in spite of backslidings and temporary failures, been borne by the Jews in their hearts to the present day. Have they still a vocation? Possibly. For they are a people destined to endure. They still have to prove their worth. They can still serve as a paradigm. Perhaps the day will come when they will be allowed to perish. But their energies are still alive, and must therefore have some significance. They have no right to stifle them.

This book of the law, known as the Book of Deuteronomy (or *Mishneh Torah*), thus appeared at a fateful moment in the history of the Jewish people. The king himself read it aloud to the congregation in the Temple, an act which constituted a grand and formal promulgation of the law. But it was also an appeal to the people to make a decisive stand, an attack on all the vague feelings and sentiments which filled their breasts in the state of feverish excitement in which they were living. This new experience was vouchsafed them when their condition was one almost akin to sickness, in which rare sensitiveness and heightened sensory appreciation had been developed. The constant threat of danger to their country, and therefore to every individual in it, had resulted in the creation, for the first time in their history, of a clinging attachment to that which was menaced, to the outward and visible sign of their communal existence —the state. The tribal pride which was all that had existed theretofore developed into the passion of nationalism, and this in its turn, connected as it now was with a definite country, gave birth to patriotism.

Their patriotism was of a peculiar kind and led them to endow this country, which their ancestors had also regarded as home, long before they had trodden its soil or set eyes on it, with a peculiar soul, a peculiar sanctity. Samaria had perished, but the south with Jerusalem and the Temple had survived. This must have a deep significance. Sennacherib, King of Assyria, who had besieged Jerusalem (701 B.C.), had suddenly been forced to retire just when the defenders were at their last gasp. This, too, must have had a deep significance, and must have been due to some special quality of holiness attaching to the country itself, the city and the Temple. When the Scythians swept like a swarm of locusts over the land, devouring everything in their path and leaving it all bare, they merely skirted the marches of Judah. The city and the Temple had been spared. This must surely mean that they were invulnerable. Thus they began to regard their native land as endowed with a soul, as sacred. God was watching over it. Jeremiah, addressing the people, declared that God was displeased with their manner of life. "Ye defile my land!" he makes Yahweh exclaim. It was then that the "Holy Land" really came into being. With these experiences behind them, we can understand how the reading aloud of Deuteronomy stirred them to the depths, and how, overwhelmed by the idea that their country was a living entity, they were driven to insurrection.

This new spiritual orientation of the people through the prophets turned a state of anarchy into a definite conflict between two opposing camps. There could be no half-measures; one alternative or the other had to be accepted. At one moment idolatry of all kinds was tolerated only to be followed by a drastic purification of religious worship. Now pacifist councils prevailed, now secret diplomacy gained the upper hand. Babylonian bacchanalia were celebrated to the accompaniment of the most cruel and bloodthirsty persecution of the prophets. The question was always—is it to be isolation or assimilation? a separate fate or the renunciation thereof? a life of creation or a life of pleasure? salvation or damnation?

The attitude of the age is accurately reflected in Deuteronomy.

"See I have set before thee this day life and good, and death and evil. . . . I call heaven and earth to record this day against you, that I have set before you life and death, blessing and cursing; therefore choose life, that both thou and thy seed may live."

Thus the choice lay with the people themselves, and the prophets were careful to make this perfectly plain. By appealing to them to come to a decision, they set a goal before them and organized and laid the foundations of the lasting power, the undying quality, of the Jewish race. And their efforts were not in vain. For the political disasters that followed were from the first robbed of their main power for evil in the case of a people whose souls had been thus disciplined.

When King Hezekiah came to the throne, Judah was still under the suzerainty of Assyria, which King Ahaz had accepted of his own free will. But Hezekiah, who was more of a patriot than a politician, was anxious to free his country from the yoke. National feeling ran high, and urged the authorities to join the other small subject states in rebellion. This merely resulted in Sennacherib carrying thousands into captivity and laying siege to Jerusalem. But owing to attacks by Egypt and disturbances in his own country, he failed of achieving his object. Thus Judah had a narrow escape, and from a safe distance was able to watch the downfall of the Assyrian colossus.

Josiah also felt called upon, both as king and patriot, to extend the boundaries of his domain. He accordingly invaded Samaria, the former sister state, and occupied portions of it, hoping that he would one day succeed in restoring his country to what it had been under King David. Even at this time the idea that the ten tribes were irrevocably lost and that their names must be finally wiped off the roll of the Israelitish clans, was becoming transmuted into the increasing hope that they would return and become reunited with their brethren. The prophets themselves actually prophesied that the north would once more be joined with the south. This prophecy was never fulfilled. It remained a wish-dream. But the people kept it alive in their hearts for two thousand years. By making the return of the ten tribes a prerequisite for a Messianic salvation, they once more set the goal of their existence in the far distant future, in an age too remote for computation.

Josiah's ambitious dreams were also shattered by reality. The Egyptians resumed their warlike activities with a view to securing their share of the spoils of their fallen foe, but Josiah refused to allow them to cross his territory. In the fighting that ensued he was mortally wounded, and the country fell beneath the suzerainty of Egypt.

This did not last for long, however, but came to an end when Egypt fell out with the new kingdom of Babylonia over the possession of Syria and Palestine, which formed connecting links between them. Babylonia emerged victorious, and Judah became her vassal. Once again two opposite policies were advocated, one party demanding war against Chaldea at all costs, the other advising internal autonomy and the peaceful development of the nation's spiritual life. This new state of dependence had lasted for three years, when the little country rebelled and refused to pay tribute. Nebuchadrezzar immediately set off at the head of a punitive expedition, and, after a short siege, Jerusalem was captured. King Jehoiachin and all his family, together with the nobles, the wealthy citizens, the priests, and the armourers, that is to say, about ten thousand souls in all, were taken captive to Babylonia. The Temple and the palaces were looted and a vassal king, Zedekiah, was set on the throne.

This first captivity, the *Galuth Jehoiachin,* gave rise to great bitterness of feeling among the people. They hated Babylonia with a deadly hatred, while a heroic but wholly futile spirit of nationalism drove the vital forces of the country in the wrong direction. From Babylonia the exiles sent forth entreaties and exhortations, which only served to add fuel to the fire. They called upon those who had been left behind to deliver them. In vain did Jeremiah urge them to meet their fate with resignation. "Build ye houses, and dwell in them; and plant gardens, and eat the fruit of them; take ye wives, and beget sons and daughters . . . that ye may be increased there, and not diminished. And seek the peace of the city whither I have caused you to be carried away captives, and pray unto the Lord for it; for in the peace thereof shall ye have peace." (Jeremiah xxix. 5–7.)

They paid no heed to him, but denounced him as a traitor to the national cause. In Jerusalem he was an object of open hostility and suspicion, and the purity of his motives was entirely misunderstood. He was helpless! The people had taken leave of their senses. With the ridiculously inadequate forces at their command, they had the temerity to defy the proudest and most powerful country of the day. After nine years' submission, Zedekiah refused to pay tribute and proclaimed the independence of the kingdom of Judah.

Once again Nebuchadrezzar marched out, and had the whole country systematically laid waste. Crowds of people sought refuge in Jerusalem. In the winter of 587 B.C. the city was invested, and famine and pestilence wrought havoc among the inhabitants and undermined their powers of resistance. On the 9th of Tammuz, 586 B.C., the Babylonians forced an entry into the city and proceeded to an indiscriminate massacre of the inhabitants. The king had his eyes put out. His sons, the high priest, and many of the leading men were put to death, and all the people, or all those who could be seized, were carried captive to Babylon. Between the 7th and the 10th of Ab, the city was destroyed, and the Temple and palaces were burnt down. Jerusalem itself and the whole country were laid waste and deserted; nothing was left but a heap of ruins. Elegies (*Qinoth, Eikha*), ascribed to Jeremiah, express the horror and grief that was felt at the death of a hope. To this very day, two thousand five hundred years after the event, these elegies are chanted on the 9th of Ab, the *Tishah b'Ab,* in all the synagogues of the world.

A short epilogue followed the tragedy. Nebuchadrezzar, anxious to avoid the entire desolation of the province of Judah, left a few insignificant vine-dressers and husbandmen in the country and made Gedaliah governor. But rebels did not take long to creep out of hiding; they created unrest and assassinated Gedaliah. The rest were terrified of reprisals on the part of Babylonia, and many of them fled to Egypt. Nebuchadrezzar gathered together all who remained and transported them to Babylon.

Among the fugitives who escaped to Egypt and at whose disposal the city of Taphnis was hospitably placed, was Jeremiah. He lived to see the founding of a Jewish colony in which the perennial problem, Assimilation or Isolation? again provided the bone of contention. But he did not live to see its solution.

Thus this period, too, ended in grave signs and omens. Some of the people, disinherited and penniless fugitives, returned to the very land from which, full of joy in their new-found freedom and with a creative attitude towards life, they had once escaped. The rest were groaning in captivity in the region in which their remotest ancestors had led the life of nomads. Their state had been destroyed, their capital and the Temple lay in ruins. Their country was depopulated and laid waste. The inhabitants had been taken captive, dispersed, and decimated. Nothing remained! Nay–everything remained! The power of the spirit still survived!

TRANSPLANTATION

FOR the Judean people, the Babylonian captivity proved the great trial and test, the period during which all that had been laid down in Judah was confirmed and proved—the foundation of their life on the spirit. It stood for an intensification of the upward spiritual tendency; it was not the beginning of a new epoch. The external facts relating to this period may be summed up as follows. As a result of Nebuchadrezzar's first expedition, 13,000 Judeans were carried captive to Babylonia; as a result of the second, about 16,000, and a further batch of a thousand followed. But for the colony in Egypt, the remnant that remained scattered through Judah, and those who had been taken as slaves to various parts of the civilized world, these figures represent the total strength of the Jewish people at this time.

Those who had been carried into captivity enjoyed complete freedom to settle where they liked in the land of exile, to worship as they chose, to select their own calling, and to administer their own social order. They took the fullest advantage of these privileges, though subject to the very important condition that they settled down as close to each other as possible, and preserved the local and family distinctions which had existed in their native land. As far as the outside world was concerned, they constituted self-contained communities, which preserved all their native customs and usages. Thus the freedom they enjoyed, and the way in which they settled down, left their social characteristics and organization almost intact. They built houses, engaged in horticulture, agriculture, industries of all kinds, and commerce. In fact they lived much as they had done in Judah, and with the inevitable social inequalities. On the whole they enjoyed a fairly high standard of comfort and, as far as material circumstances were concerned, had no cause for complaint.

Nevertheless, from the very beginning, the majority adopted an attitude of expectation. Even those who had been carried captive to Babylon with King Jehoiachin in 597 B.C. regarded their exile merely as a misfortune which could not last indefinitely and felt certain that political developments would occur which would afford them the opportunity of returning home. This prevented them from becoming rooted to the soil. The fresh stream of exiles fared no better and no worse. Whereas the Judean colony steadily increased in numbers, and began to constitute an economic factor of some importance, while some of its members were given positions at the Babylonian court, they regarded all this merely as means to an end—their restoration to liberty. Their Babylonian masters, however, had no wish to lose so valuable an element in their state, and the Judeans were consequently forced to look for other means of salvation. With a sure instinct they discovered this in the new power which was rising on the horizon in the direction of Iran, and casting its shadow across the country. Cyrus, King of Persia, was the last of the great conquerors. His power was spreading beyond Media and Persia, as far as the Aegean Sea and the confines of Greece. And his progress was everywhere heralded by a reputation for benevolence and mercy. It was upon him that the Judeans now fixed all their hopes. Even before he set out upon the conquest of Babylonia, the prophets foretold that it was through him their liberation would be achieved.

And they were right, as subsequent events proved.

The conquest of Babylonia was achieved without difficulty; the city fell without a fight. The Judeans welcomed Cyrus with open arms, and he saw that through them he could gain a twofold object. He could repopulate the devastated province of Judah, and secure the southern frontier of his empire against his great enemy, Egypt, by having a trustworthy people settled there and bound to him by ties of gratitude. Thus, as soon as he had conquered Babylonia, in 538 B.C., he allowed them to return to their own country.

But not all the Judeans availed themselves of this opportunity. Large numbers, belonging chiefly to the possessing classes, though they gave money and equipment to help those who were returning, preferred to remain in the land of their exile. This decision cannot be adequately explained by the mere word "assimilation"; it was rather a by-product, one might almost say a waste-product, of a very consistent and far-reaching process of spiritual transposition which constituted the whole meaning of the Babylonian captivity.

Interpreted in the light of previous events, the spiritual condition of the Judeans in Babylonia may be summed up as follows. Captivity had befallen them at a moment when most of their life-problems had already been revealed and made known through the turbulent nature of their environment and the passion of their inner conflicts. Even if they had come to no decision upon them, they had at least already experienced everything that was capable of guaranteeing or destroying their material and spiritual existence. Everything had already reached consciousness in them, and was just as much a part of their lives as the tangible reality about them. And it now came home to them that they had been struck down by fate in precisely the way and for the very reasons that the prophets had foretold. Thus they were in a position to profit by the experience they had undergone.

They had taken into the land of exile the treasured possession in which the haunting question of their lives had found its loftiest record—the Holy Scriptures and the words of the prophets, in so far as they had been put into writing. If they belonged to the second or third batch of exiles, they had been met on their arrival by the nobles of their various tribes who had always looked forward to a speedy return to their own country and lived as though their exile were merely temporary. The new-comers had immediately followed the example of these older exiles, while, moreover, the manner of their settlement in definite areas and groups had prevented them from coming into undue contact with the people about them and had thus diminished the temptation to become adapted and intermingle with them. It was only among that class of the community which did not enjoy the advantages of this strict isolation, the merchant class, whose occupation inevitably brought them into contact with those about them, that a process of assimilation took place. But it did not go to the length of miscegenation. It meant at first merely the adoption of the customs, habits, pleasures, and morals of the native population. Nevertheless, even in its early stages, it implied the renunciation of their connexion with a community which represented their ancestral habits, beliefs, manners, language, and country. It is at this moment in their history that the problem of assimilation may be said to have made its first appearance in Jewish history, and in the form in which it survives to the present day.

Assimilation and riches are really identical, since an inner law makes them coextensive. (The word riches, in this connexion, is used only as a convenient paraphrase for that state of property ownership in which a man can use his money or his capital to earn him an income.) Riches in this sense alters the meaning and the spirit of every community. Money provides the means of separating one's life from the soil. Money not only makes everything purchasable, but it is also the measure whereby every value is assessed, and in the terms of which every value may be expressed. Money provides a means of existence, which is really itself independent and makes men independent of every community and particularly of every kind of communal living. Money is the means by which a man can most quickly and easily forget that life is possible only in a *particular* country, among a *particular* people, in accordance with *particular* forms, and in harmony with a *particular* spirit. It leads men to discover that life is also possible under other conditions, according to other forms, and in harmony with another spirit. Experience is therefore summed up in the formula: this other way is also possible.

This formula came into being during the Babylonian captivity. It was the plain renunciation of a principle of vital importance to the constitution of the Jewish people—the principle of a home historically bound up with, and founded on, religion. "This other way is also possible," meant in this case, "we shall remain what we are, even if we do not return to Judah."

This point of view is radically inadmissible because it is meaningless. A Judean who regarded himself as such could only be pictured as living in the country to which Providence had adapted him, with the Temple, which his God had ordained should be established there and there only, and with the sacrifices which could be offered there alone. If a man believed and professed that he was a Judean apart from these essential factors, it amounted to destroying or completely transforming them. As a matter of fact, this had actually occurred.

The Judeans found themselves confronted by an altogether new experience—the experience of being foreigners. To be a foreigner meant to lack those ties by which in his own home a man consciously or unconsciously directs his life. But when, in addition to this, his presence in a strange land happens to be compulsory, he learns through this very compulsion to know how he has directed his life hitherto. Whereas he had previously been quite unconscious of revolving about a particular centre, as soon as he is deprived of it, he knows what that centre was. He learns to understand the significance of the daily routine when he is compelled to follow it in another part of the world and in different circumstances. Exile, moreover, generates that feeling which is a blend of pride, defiance, and the will to self-preservation, which a man like Dante experienced and formulated. Exile, inasmuch as it separates a man from his native soil, provides the very conditions for making an individual of him. He loses his sure support, though he has never yet put it to the test. He is thrown amid conditions of life for which he is not responsible, and is forced to regard himself both as the subject and the object of all that happens. In any case he is bound to feel everything with peculiar intensity; for the energies which a short while previously he was spending amid the particular conditions of his native land—the struggle of political parties, economic crises, military activities, and questions of foreign politics—are now all idle. Deprived of their old sphere of action, the energies which had hitherto been fully occupied are bound to find an outlet in other directions.

This detailed explanation of the conditions prevailing in exile was necessary if we are to understand how a brief captivity of forty-nine years led to so complete and radical a transposition of spiritual interests in the Jewish race. For what we are concerned with here is not so much an effect of the so-called instinct of national self-preservation, as with an elaborate attempt to reduce all the conditions of life known theretofore to a plane which would secure their survival under completely different circumstances. The spiritual stock of Judaism thus experienced a process of transposition, which, while it gave a violent impetus to its development, nevertheless left to those Jews who did not wish to return home their quality as Jews.

The development which led to this state of affairs was wholly logical. It was carried out in two stages—the first stage being the transmutation of all living relationships, and the second the imparting of a new meaning to their destiny as a nation.

They had been deprived of the Temple. But, as communion with God was a necessity to them, they replaced it by any kind of shelter they could find, and which they consecrated by the very fact of assembling in it for the common performance of their devotional exercises. They could not offer sacrifice in such a place, because sacrifices were allowed only on the altar of the Temple at Jerusalem. So they expressed their devotion, their sacrificial attitude, in prayer. This necessarily led to the following important conclusion. If it was possible to come face to face with God elsewhere than in His Temple, then it must be possible to come face to face with Him anywhere and everywhere. Thus His habitation could not be any building made of stone and wood, but any place where someone believed in Him and called upon Him. So the seat of God was not the Temple but the heart of every man who grasped the idea of His existence. Hence it followed that He could be served not only by means of a certain form of worship in the Temple, not only by a particular set ritual, which the priest performed in the name of the whole people, but by the behaviour of the suppliant, the earnestness and sincerity of the individual worshipper. And thus individuation progressed a further step. The principle of collective worship lost its exclusive meaning. *The individual became the possible repository of all religious experience and happenings.* And this being so, the responsibility for irreligious and immoral conduct must also be transferred. It was not the whole body of believers, the people as a religious unit, but each separate person who was responsible for his own sins of commission and omission. He was no longer to be blamed for what his fathers had done, but for what he himself had done.

"The soul that sinneth, it shall die. The son shall not bear the iniquity of the father, neither shall the father bear the iniquity of the son." (Ezekiel.)

This led to the further conclusion that if the whole people, the whole community sinned, it must atone for its transgression. If the individual, who was personally responsible for his own actions, sinned, though obviously he could not undo what he had done, yet by confessing it and mending his ways, he could wipe out his sin. This was known as repentance.

"Have I any pleasure at all that the wicked should die? saith the Lord God: and not that he should return from his ways, and live? . . . Cast away from you all your transgressions . . . and make you a new heart and a new spirit," says Ezekiel.

In this way, the ineluctable fate of a community was replaced by the free and responsible attitude towards the life of the individual.

Although, strictly speaking, all these modifications of position were fictitious, they served to consolidate the actual situation. And for this reason other customs and usages belonging to their existence as an independent people were subjected to the same process. The authority of the priest, the former leader of the community, was replaced by that of the head of the family or clan for the time being. Instead of the constitution of the defunct state, communal autonomy was established, and, instead of the power of the state, there came into being another power, more reliable and more enduring—the stern and inexorable discipline enforced by the obligation to render unquestioning obedience to the regulations of the ritual. It was at this point that the equalization of ritual and law began to take place. There was no government to enforce obedience to these laws; the fact that they were nevertheless observed was due to the people's having agreed to observe them. Moreover, exile from their native land led to their festivals, which had been of a local and bucolic nature, developing into religio-national celebrations, since there was no point in preserving their original character in a foreign land and under totally different conditions. At the same time, memorials were erected in the spirit to commemorate events connected with the lost land—the four days which marked the beginning of the siege of Jerusalem, the fall of the city, the destruction of the Temple, and the murder of Gedaliah became days of national mourning and fasting.

These changes of position signified, as we have pointed out, a means of making life possible, not an act of renunciation. The homeland still remained the homeland. And that was why the Jews when praying always turned their faces towards Jerusalem. That was why in their various communities they kept the strictest genealogical records, giving the origin and antecedents of every member. Incidentally these records constituted a sort of census of their numbers at various times.

The process of transposition was most marked where the old concrete relations to the lost homeland had to be replaced by spiritual adaptations—in the elaboration and amplification of Holy Writ. The larger part of the literature we now call Scripture, together with the various oral traditions, had been conveyed as a spiritual possession to Babylonia, and all classes of the people now began to take an interest in them. In the assemblies for religious worship, portions of the Scriptures were regularly read aloud, as they are to this day; while the oral traditions were written down and became the national books.

The most important work of all was that of an anonymous compiler, who, on the basis of the Scriptures and traditions, produced a pragmatic historical work, covering the entire period from the conquest of Canaan to the Babylonian captivity. It was not a mere chronological narrative of events; a unifying idea underlay it all and gave point and meaning to the destiny of the Jewish people whose relationship to their God, based upon a covenant and a reciprocal acknowledgment of rights and duties, is represented as being the acceptance of a mission which they undertook to carry out and fulfil. But this mission, which was to make their system of government a theocracy, had not been fulfilled either by the people or by those who succeeded the judges and who should have fulfilled it—the kings. Both the people and the kings had failed in their divine mission, and it was necessary to make a fresh start. This amounted to demanding a return to pure theocracy.

On this point the anonymous compiler is in complete agreement with those who came forward as the most typical representatives of the age—the prophets. How many of them exerted their influence at this period it is impossible to say. We know the name of only one—Jehesqel (Ezekiel)—and we have the writings of another, who for the sake of convenience is called Deutero-Isaiah, or the Babylonian Isaiah.

Ezekiel was essentially a prophet of his own day. So long as only one batch of captives had arrived in Babylon, his utterances were in diametrical opposition to their premature hopes of a return and their tendency to mould their fate purely from the standpoint of national ambition. But when the great catastrophe occurred and the rest of Judah joined the first captives, he greatly widened his range, and became the comforter of his people. It was he who formulated the changes of position and sentiment which we have discussed above. He also gave expression to the people's longing to return to their own country. This return he regarded as a certainty, though its object was to be not the restoration of a national state, but the establishment of a theocracy, not a national monarchy, but a theocratic republic.

But the man who really gave an aim to this generation of Babylonian captives was Ezekiel's successor, the Babylonian Isaiah. He it was who answered the questions of those who, as far as they knew, had not sinned themselves and had yet been called upon to endure not only exile, but the destruction of their country and their Temple, and wished to know the meaning of the fate that had befallen them. He summed up the situation as follows: for the man who owes allegiance to nothing and nobody, and whose life is not bound up with some other life or organization, suffering is merely a rude and meaningless experience. But for the man who does owe allegiance to something, who knows that he is connected with the ultimate reality, namely God, suffering is a sign, a summons to call his attention to the fact that either in his own heart or in the world about him something is happening to which he ought to pay heed, if only he will listen to the summons. In his case suffering means the capacity constantly to recognize, in the kaleidoscopic sequence of events, the one unalterable fact, that a life divorced from all moral obligations inevitably leaves all those who lead it derelict by the wayside, be they individuals or communities, either today or in a thousand years, and in one form or another. Suffering is a summons to attend. It is therefore a promoter of knowledge.

The Babylonian captivity was meant to make this fundamental precept of Judaism perfectly clear. By submitting to it, by proving true to it, the Judeans would do more than work their own redemption; they would become a shining example to all ages and all peoples. With this principle, a twofold idea came into being—that of the apostolic mission of the Jewish race, and that of their perception of truth both for themselves and others through suffering. This was the basis of the subsequent Christological doctrine of the suffering Messiah-Saviour.

Even the Babylonian Isaiah regarded all spiritual concepts as applicable to this world and to reality, though their foundations might be laid in heaven, in the loftiest realms of God's Kingdom. He too expected the political renaissance of his people. This involved striving after that reality through which alone anything could be achieved. It meant, moreover, that the conditions must first be secured in which the people themselves could *experience* this idea to the full and not merely *think* it to the full. This amounted to making national ends a means to supernational ends.

But for this idea to be realized, it was necessary for God to send a messenger who would make the return of the people possible. Long before the conquest of Babylonia had even begun, the prophet prophesied that God would use Cyrus the Great, King of Persia, as his instrument for the liberation of the diminutive subject race. But if the greatest king of the age was to be an instrument in the hands of the Jewish God, it meant that this God was one who determined the fate not only of one people but of all peoples, that He determined the fate of nations, the fate of the whole world. The God of the Judeans was *the God*. There was only one God. To prove this was the mission of the theophoristic people, the Jews, and constituted the quintessence of the work carried out by the prophets at this time.

Possessed of these ideas, and confronted by this stupendous task, the Jews found the road cleared for their return to their historic home.

THE LAW AND EVERYDAY LIFE

THE exiles who set forth on their return journey home in the spring of the year 537 B.C. found themselves faced with a state of the most utter desolation. Jerusalem was a heap of ruins, the country was devastated. Only a few husbandmen eked out a wretched existence, and most of the territory had been invaded and occupied by the surrounding peoples. There was no economic organization into which the exiles could fit themselves. They were obliged to set to work from the beginning again and build up everything afresh.

The fact that they had not thought of all this beforehand, and that their first concern on returning home was to set up an altar in the place of the old one, amid the ruins of the Temple, shows what their homecoming meant. Their longing to live in their own country was greater than any anxiety regarding what they were to live on. Thus a year after their return, they were already engaged in laying the foundations of the new Temple, while they themselves were for the most part still obliged to live in tents in and around Jerusalem.

The ceremony of laying the foundation stone of the new Temple was fraught with such significance, that even the neighbouring tribes began to prick up their ears, and concluded that the core of a new community had been created. With the exception of Jerusalem, the whole country was either occupied or declared to be within the jurisdiction of the surrounding peoples, who were unanimously hostile to the new community, although it was the creation of men whose claim to the land had been uncontested for a thousand years. But as the new arrivals were under the protection of the King of Persia, and any display of violence would be dangerous, they clung to the hope of being able to assimilate the little handful of immigrants. The small sprinkling of Judeans who had remained in the country had presented no obstacle to this policy of assimilation, and miscegenation had already done much towards merging them with their neighbours.

The Samaritans adopted a peculiar attitude in the matter. They were a mixed race, a blend between the remnants of the former population of the kingdom of Samaria, and the Assyrian colonists whom Sargon had sent out to restore the devastated towns. Even their religion was a mixture—a blend of their pagan ideas and the old Samaritan forms of Yahweh worship—as was also their language. And this people, a unified body formed from such diverse elements, considered themselves the legitimate successors of the northern tribes, and were consequently inclined to regard the southern Jews as kinsmen and brothers. Their leader Sanballat accordingly sent a message to Judah saying that he and his people were anxious to share in the building of the Temple and wished to be admitted into the Judean community.

He was met with a blank refusal on the part of the elders of the people. Whereupon the Samaritans, angry and indignant, proceeded to resort to every artifice to hinder the building of the Temple. Guided by a sure instinct, they felt that this was the best means of sapping the life-blood of the idea that inspired the new community. By bringing influence to bear on certain of the Persian officials, they succeeded in having the building of the Temple arrested. The work was interrupted for fifteen years.

As soon as the work stopped, the energy with which it had inspired the people died down, and they began to be conscious of the dangers and difficulties of their position and to feel helpless in the face of the problems with which they were every day confronted. Every man did his best to satisfy his personal needs, but in the majority of cases this meant an enormous amount of labour with hardly any return. During the fifty years of exile the ground had been neglected and had run to waste. Out of the frugal returns it made, contributions in kind had to be handed over for the support of numbers of priests and Levites, tribute had to be paid to the Persian governor, and any surplus had to be devoted to the building of houses. It was only the very few who succeeded in meeting all these charges.

At such moments of extreme economic depression, those persons always come to the fore who, by means of their wealth, are in a position to exploit poverty and to commercialize distress. A rich man without principles is always a source of far greater danger to the social fabric than a poor man without principles. It was for this reason that the consequences of the state of economic decay were, in the present instance, particularly hard. There sprang up overnight, as it were, side by side with the respected families with old traditions, a new capitalist class who were in a position to lend the needy money for house building, the purchase of seed, and the payment of taxes, and accepted the arable land, the vineyards, and even the debtors themselves and their children as security for the debt. And if the loan was not repaid, they seized the property together with the owner and his family and made them slaves. Thus this young community which had set out to rebuild the Temple merely succeeded in creating a plutocracy. Deprived of the symbol of the idea that was their inspiration, economically oppressed, and divided into a plutocracy and a band of paupers, even the question of administration could not be settled. In theory it was an ideal system consisting of a temporal ruler of the house of David, a spiritual ruler of the house of Zadok, both possessing equal rights and ruling side by side as representatives of the theocracy, serving the people and answerable to God. But it never became a practical reality. For it was never they who actually ruled. They were merely the tools of the rich and noble families who dictated their actions. The theocracy remained an ideal aspiration, an unrealized ambition; for vested interests had usurped the place of the idea.

But the only principle with lasting and creative power is the idea, the idea founded on some form of belief in a higher meaning to life, and higher human obligations. No matter what task a people may set themselves, or what aspirations they may nurse, they will never succeed unless they are supported by some faith or religion.

An attempt to put this idea into practice was made by the prophets Haggai and Zechariah. They declared that no state of material distress justified postponing the building of the Temple. It only required the appearance of these advocates of the idea immediately to inspire the people with fresh hope and enthusiasm. In 520 B.C. the building of the Temple was resumed, and in four years' time it was finished and solemnly consecrated.

This spiritual revival, after which the influence of the prophets waned, was followed by a period of stagnation which was doubly dangerous since it was deeply imbued with resignation. Hardly any of the expectations of the returned exiles had been realized. Judah was an insignificant little Persian province, unable to support herself, surrounded by hostile neighbours, without help in the present or hope for the future. In these circumstances, the people grew ever more inclined to adopt a conciliatory policy towards the rest of the world. True, experience had taught them that the practice of alien cults was incapable of providing a fresh incentive or goal for their existence, but they greatly relieved the stress and strain of their material position by admitting into their ranks all who wished to become members of the Judean community, while, by tolerating miscegenation with the neighbouring tribes, they established peaceful relations based on family ties. In so doing, they were no more guilty of infringing the Mosaic law as it was understood at the time than King Solomon had been in choosing wives from every nation under the sun. They were pursuing a policy, not of assimilation, but of concession.

The consequences of such an attitude might have been incalculably serious if from the safe distance of Babylon a fiat had not gone forth which once and for all cut short and made an end of this development. True, compared with their brethren who had returned home, the Babylonian Jews now merely constituted a colony. But they once again had recourse to a measure which had already played an important part in the evolution of the Israelitish conception of God as one God. Unlike the people about them, the Children of Israel of that day did not regard their God as being connected with a particular stretch of country. And thus the members of their race who had remained in Babylon conceived of a Judaism that was not bound down to Palestine, Jerusalem, and the Temple. In their efforts to realize the fictions which were the subject of the last chapter, and inasmuch as they professed to be a community, although they possessed no country of their own, no capital, no king, no high priest, no Temple and none of its binding rites, they were obliged to set up a general instrument of power to replace all these attributes of a community. This they discovered in the law and the observance of the law, that is to say, in a voluntary submission to all the precepts, regulations, rules of faith, and standards of right and wrong, which had been incorporated in their written records. They took whole books and pledged themselves to believe their contents and to apply what they believed to life. In practice this meant that in Babylon the Torah, which was a compendium of the law, a collection of all the rules regulating everyday life, acquired greater importance than the writings of the prophets. The Jewish law was a *record* of life itself, and the Babylonian Jews began to make it the meaning of their existence. And now by transferring their manner of life and their *Weltanschauung* to Judea, they introduced a constructive principle into Judaism. They made the development regressive. Nevertheless, by so doing, they rendered signal service; for it meant that when the Jews subsequently lost their country for almost two thousand years, the essence of Judaism remained intact. They prepared a spiritual homeland for the people to inhabit instead of the actual homeland that had been lost.

The news of conditions in Judea created considerable commotion in Babylon. Those who had remained behind perceived that the homeland was in danger and felt they must help it. The priest Ezra, son of Seraiah, placed himself at the head of the movement. He was a man of profound knowledge, convinced of the importance of his people and their idea. He worked with indefatigable zeal among the Jews in Babylon and Persia, with the object of persuading them to recognize the Torah as the law of life which they were in duty bound to obey. After which he made preparations to transfer his activities to Judah. In this he received the official support of Artaxerxes I Longimanus. Over 1500 people flocked to join him; but he allowed only those to return to Judah who could point to their birth registration as providing irrefutable proof that they were either of Judean extraction or members of the family of Aaron or the tribe of Levi. This fresh batch of returned exiles reached Jerusalem in the autumn of 458 B.C.

The state of affairs that confronted Ezra on his arrival filled him with horror and dismay. He was particularly appalled by the prevalence of mixed marriages, which he regarded as extremely dangerous and bound to lead to disintegration. They were also, in his opinion, forbidden by the law, and therefore sinful. So sincere and convincing was his grief, and so great were his reputation and influence, that when he publicly proclaimed the sins of the people in the Temple, they themselves came forward with the suggestion that the mixed marriages that had taken place should be dissolved.

Ezra eagerly acquiesced in the proposal. He called the people together in the square outside the Temple, and placed two resolutions before the assembled throng—first, that all the mixed marriages that had been solemnized should be dissolved, and secondly that foreigners and everything foreign should be rigorously excluded by the people. The latter assented, and the resolutions were carried. Whereupon a commission of the elders of the people was appointed and entrusted with the task of dissolving the mixed marriages.

Ezra's measure was undoubtedly reactionary. It raised to the dignity of a law an enactment which at that time was not included in the Torah and could be justified only in the circumstances then in existence. The preservation of the race and of their religion alike indicated its necessity, while it also proved that those responsible for it recognized that the Jews might be possessed of particular qualities. But there was no intention of making the breeding of a race an end in itself; all that was aimed at was to preserve a type as a definite means to an end. The Jews were engaged in an attempt to realize an extremely lofty ideology in their life as a community, an attempt which was on the verge of ending in failure. If failure were possible even in the case of a community which was the outcome of selection, how much greater must not the danger have been where foreign elements, alien both in race and culture, had been admitted. Thus Ezra was fully justified in deliberately and methodically applying the principle of isolation as an educative means.

The practical result of Ezra's reform was to confirm the people in a new way of life. But events frequently interfered with its observance. His rigorous methods provoked the utmost hostility and opposition on the part of the neighbouring tribes who felt that they had been spurned as inferior to the Jews. They attacked Jerusalem, destroyed its walls, burned down its gates, and did as they pleased in the city. Once again it was the noble families among the Jews who first resumed friendly relations and intermarried with those about them. The majority of the populace, however, preferred to desert the defenceless city. The Temple taxes ceased to be paid, many of the Levites and Aaronites were accordingly also obliged to take their departure, and the community was on the verge of a fresh collapse.

But once again help came from the Jewish colony in Persian Babylonia. Nehemiah, son of Hachaliah, was a high official in the service of Artaxerxes. An extremely wealthy and influential man, he adopted a sterner and more uncompromising attitude towards the law than Ezra had done. He now took the situation in hand and was appointed temporary governor of Judea by Artaxerxes. He was a born administrator, and the appointment gave him the opportunity for the exercise of his greatest gift.

He went to Jerusalem in 445 B.C. His first act was to call upon the elders of the people to repair the fortifications of the city as a means of restoring popular confidence. His proposal met with the approval of all classes of the community, who offered him their services free. Sanballat of Samaria, however, tried to stop the work by force. But Nehemiah organized a service of armed watchmen to circumvent him, and in a few months Jerusalem was once again a walled and fortified city; but it was almost depopulated.

Nehemiah, therefore, decided that one in ten of the population outside the city should be chosen by lot to come to live inside the gates. Those thus selected, as also those who volunteered to return, were obliged to submit to a strict investigation of their ancestry by reference to the register of births, and any who failed to establish the undisputed purity of their stock were not allowed to enter. He then took steps to prevent the further development of the community from being hampered by the injustices which had recently come into being. He called a meeting of the wealthy citizens, and by virtue of his office, and reminding them of their duty to the community as a whole, ordered them to set free those whom they had enslaved for debt, to restore the lands they had confiscated, and to cancel all debts. He himself set the example by cancelling all debts owed to him by new settlers to whom he had lent the wherewithal to start afresh. His authority and his example had the effect of making the creditors acquiesce in his demands and swear to do as they were bidden. The binding power of the law triumphed over self-interest.

After carrying out these preliminary measures, he made a further determined advance towards giving the community a constitution based on the Torah as the law and standard of life. But to do this he required the help of Ezra. A meeting of the people was called in Jerusalem on New Year's Day, 444 B.C., but nothing happened beyond the reading aloud by Ezra of passages from the Pentateuch—a ceremony recalling King Josiah's public reading of Deuteronomy. But it made an extraordinarily deep impression upon the people. So eager were they to take their national traditions to their hearts that, on the following day, they asked for a continuation of the public readings. This was granted and was repeated until Nehemiah had achieved his object, which was to give the people some idea of the spiritual treasure that lay buried in their past.

This done, he put the coping-stone to his work, and the Torah was at last put into its final form by Ezra and publicly proclaimed as the law of the Jewish people. The representatives of the various clans and families solemnly endorsed and sealed a document, in which they pledged themselves and all who belonged to them, to keep the laws of the Torah, among which special emphasis was laid on that forbidding marriage with aliens.

After twelve years of vigilant activity, Nehemiah felt that conditions were sufficiently settled and secure for him to return to Persia. But an opposition movement was again set on foot headed by the priests. They had suffered most from Nehemiah's reforms, for, although by the terms of the constitution he had secured them a regular income, they had been deprived of their influential position as ministers by the fact that henceforward through the Torah every man was able to control, shape, and answer for his own life, without their intervention.

Nehemiah was therefore obliged to return to support the tottering edifice. He ruthlessly purged the community of all those who refused to give unquestioning and unhesitating allegiance to the established order and the law. With a view to applying rigorously the selective principle, he again carefully studied the register of births and ejected from the community even Aaronite families whose ancestry could not bear the strictest scrutiny. He forcibly dissolved all mixed marriages that had been contracted in his absence, and made any infringement of the law against them punishable by the severest penalties. He also enforced stricter regulations for the keeping holy of the Sabbath day, and made the whole people renew their oath to abide by the laws. He made a last careful examination of everything and, convinced of its necessity, completed the task of isolation, with the result that when he once again returned to Persia he left behind him a community which, agreed as it now was on all fundamental questions, was able to fend for itself. He had organized their everyday life for them and built up their spiritual foundations.

THE HEDGING ROUND

HISTORY tells us but little about what now took place in the little province of Judah. We hear of no outstanding event or personality. Yet the period is one of unique importance as far as spiritual developments were concerned. For fate gave the little Jewish community a whole century in which to draw their conclusions from the sum of experiences they had undergone both as a nation and as individuals. The result was that by becoming spiritually as well as materially exclusive, and by identifying a life based on faith with the personal fate of every individual, they returned to their original constitution—a theocracy.

When, in the early days of their existence as a nation, they had aimed at establishing a theocracy, they had received at the hands of those who from time to time acted as its functionaries the laws whereby to govern their lives and conduct. But these laws had taken the shape of such general principles as had developed at the time and had always applied to particular cases. Now, however, eight hundred years had elapsed since they first entered Canaan; they had suffered much and the idea of their life had grown with them. They could look back on a host of concrete events and spiritual experiences which had been recorded in their writings, in their oral traditions, in the consciousness of the masses, and in the idealistic demands on the part of certain individuals. And now that they had graduated in the severe school of Ezra and Nehemiah, they turned to this spiritual heritage to set it in order. They had been pledged to observe this body of religious doctrine as the law of their land, and it was therefore high time to determine the compass and content of their constitution. It was at this period that the final and conclusive editing of the Torah, or Pentateuch, took place. Once again anonymous editors examined all that the people had accepted and refused, aimed at and failed to achieve, believed and denied. By accepting the spiritual and material state they had attained at this period as the highest development of which they were capable, and the final plane from which they were thenceforward to direct their lives and realize all that time demanded of them, they lent their past history, their traditions, laws, and customs, a meaning entirely in keeping with a theocracy and applicable only to that system of government. Everything they were then doing seemed to them, after their editorial task had been completed, as though it had been willed and foreseen thus from time immemorial; and, if it had been so willed for the whole of the past, it must be so willed for the whole of the future. Consequently the form which the Torah then received was the final and conclusive form which was not to be altered by one iota; no single thought, word, or letter of it was to be changed. From that moment the Torah was firmly established, immune to all the vicissitudes of fate, unshakable and immovable, a centre which could never be taken away.

In addition to this body of law which instructed them how to behave, they also had their historical records, which were ever present with them to explain *why* they had to act in this particular way. These historical records, which had been kept during the period of the monarchy and elaborated in the prophetic schools of the Babylonian exile, were now subjected to further revision. Regarded from the standpoint of their present position, everything suddenly became perfectly plain and clear to the people; their fate had followed a continuous and unbroken line, and everything depended on whether they set to work to fulfil their divine mission or not. For better for worse, their destiny depended on the choice they made. The editors who put the Books of Joshua, Judges, Samuel, and Kings into their final form endeavoured to make this clear.

Between the law and history, between the spiritual and the material life, there had stood from time immemorial those creative interpreters, the prophets, whose life mission it was to show the connexion between religious faith and fate. Ofttimes they had been as "the voice of one crying in the wilderness." But now every fragment of their teaching was gathered together and placed on record as a precious possession. It was impossible always definitely to assign particular words to particular persons, for they had so frequently worked anonymously; and, as the editors were more concerned with the subject matter than with philological exactitude, they were content with stringing the sayings of the prophets together as best they could. Thus the works of the prophets under the names of Isaiah, Jeremiah, and Ezekiel became canonical books forming one group, while twelve "minor" prophets were appended to them.

These Scriptures formed the official constitution of the Jews, according to which they guided their lives and by which they were ruled. They no longer had a king; to communicate with the outside world the high priest served as their official representative. This was the logical and formal consequence of their theocratic form of government. But from the spiritual point of view the high priest was merely an official, whose authority, strictly speaking, rested on the Temple ritual. His power was supplemented by that of a sort of senate, a council of elders, a body whose exact composition it is now impossible to specify, but which constituted the highest administrative body, and the highest court of justice. But the power of the priesthood was even more drastically circumscribed by the existence of a group of men who, though they had no recognized social or corporate standing, were typical of the age; I refer to the *Sopherim*.

The literal meaning of *Sopher* is "writer" or one skilled in writing. But in this case it was applied to men with very special talents and activities. They were the silent successors of Ezra and Nehemiah, men whose profession it was to convey to the people the content of their Scriptures. They were teachers, though nobody appointed them or gave them a mandate to teach. Their own inner force drove them to disclose to the nation its spiritual heritage, and thus make it doubly receptive for the life demanded of it. They were the most powerful visible exponents of a standpoint which set the highest store by living according to the "law." And in so doing they rightly took into account the fact that many of the laws were merely skeleton regulations, and that life in its various manifestations was constantly changing, whereas the word, no alteration of which was to be allowed, was firmly established for all time. They therefore found themselves faced with the twofold task of outlining by means of continued research what the law enjoined and what it forbade. Whenever the law could not be unequivocably applied to the relations of life, they endeavoured to discover its interpretation. (Interpretation—*Midrash.*) It is impossible now to determine in what way they participated in the administration of the country, but tradition fully bears out the view that they were the founders of the Jewish nomocracy. Their activities were summed up in the pregnant words: "Be calm in the administration of justice; send forth many scholars and set a hedge about the law."

With the application of this fundamental principle, the development of Judaism reached its limit for the time being, and its life, rooted in a definite religious content, brought the curve of the Jews' individualization to a temporary close. They not only set a hedge about the law, but, by cutting themselves off more definitely than ever from the outside world, and by binding themselves more exclusively to a given circle of laws, they set a hedge about themselves. At this stage the process of individualization became apparent above all in the form of the religiously living individual. For one and all were now and henceforward in possession of the fundamental principles of their own spiritual existence, which had been taken out of the hands of the priests, divorced from the Temple, and introduced into every town, village, and house of prayer. The custom of collecting together for worship in halls and rooms—an inevitable result of the Babylonian captivity—was retained and developed after the return. Sacrifices of every sort and kind were still restricted to the Temple; but the system of performing private acts of worship in the houses of prayer now became established. But for the fact that the hours for their religious services were fixed, the prayers offered and the means of serving God and feeling His presence were left to the worshippers themselves.

But hedged in though they were on all sides, it must not be supposed that the Jews were completely cut off from the outside world and from their neighbours. They still felt the same concern about all the external events affecting their lives. They were even able to acquire a new language at this period—Aramaic. They also adopted a new and simpler way of writing, the *Ktab Ashurit,* derived from the primeval Semitic alphabet, which eventually developed into the Hebrew square character. They also adopted new names for the months of the year from the Assyro-Babylonians and the Aramæans, and followed these two peoples in placing the ecclesiastical New Year in the spring instead of the autumn. Such changes, unimportant and uninteresting in themselves, are symptomatic of their future attitude; they were hedged in but they were not cut off from the outside world. They were no longer guilty of assimilation, but they adopted any ways and customs that suited them. In setting such barriers about their way of life that it was no longer possible for their neighbours to absorb them, they created the real guarantee of permanency. Whereas hitherto we have been able to speak of Judaism, the changes thus brought about might be regarded as constituting the birth-throes of *Jewry*.

In short, it must be confessed that this life, hedged in on all sides, was entirely responsible for the independence necessary for reaching out into the world around; for, though they had no wish to obliterate their self-imposed barriers, they wished to make them productive. The rigorous consistency of a life based on morality and holiness alone was seeking for an outlet, some shadowy sphere in which its excess of crystal clarity could be utilized, and its soul could find activity. The unequivocality with which their history had taught them that the good and evil that had befallen them in the past was the result of moral or immoral conduct, led them to explain the dualism implicit in the existence of evil as the work of evil spirits. The Iranian religion, with its host of good and evil spirits, gave them examples of this. The good belonged to Ormuzd and the evil to Ahriman. It is true that the Jews refused to accept this dualistic interpretation of the universe, but their creative impulse nevertheless led them to people heaven with angels and the depths with evil spirits; they made the Garden of Eden paradise, and the Valley of Hinnom hell. Both these innovations constituted a regression as compared with the original clear spiritual conception. The angels were picturesque superfluities, and the evil spirits constituted a way out of a difficulty. By accepting their existence, they made it possible to shift the problem from their own shoulders on to a universe alive with demoniacal spirits. For the essential feature of this age was that "religion" was left to the mercy of the individual. Bowed down beneath the load of religious duties and responsibilities, this final stage of individualization was responsible for the religious uncertainty that followed. In the most important poetical expressions of the age, the Psalms, we find not only the proud joy felt at belonging to this community, but also the plaints, the doubts, and the fears connected with the individual's religious experiences. And in one important connexion, in which they were more than usually painfully aware of the isolated nature of their hedged-in position, they borrowed yet another principle from the Iranian religion—the idea of a "beyond."

As early as the Book of Job, which was probably written at the time of the Babylonian captivity, we find a vain and abortive attempt to solve the problem why a man who has not sinned should be called upon to suffer, while others who have not shunned evil should end their days in joy and prosperity. As the Jews could not conceive of their God as otherwise than just, they tried to discover the point at which His justice came into play. But they could not find it in the world as it was, nor did the most exhaustive examination of earthly life and phenomena reveal it to them. Beyond this they were not allowed to look, for, although their religion drew its sustenance from the intercourse between God and man through all the changing scenes of life, the stage was limited to this world. A man might prove his worth to the Powers above but it had to be done on this earth and not in a beyond; here, not yonder. When a life closed, it was finished and done with; it was beyond hope, expiation, or redemption. In primitive Judaism the immortality of the individual soul was denied. The whole alone was immortal, the generality of mankind, the reason being that it was thought of, seen, and felt cosmically. But now that the Jews were called upon to realize such an extremely lofty, strict, and conclusive ideology, they gave way and retreated a step. This was done under the influence of the Iranian religion, and the great thought behind Judaism was proportionately reduced to meet the demands of the weaker brethren who dreaded their own insignificance in the face of eternity. Thus, while the belief in angels was to the Jews merely a picturesque accessory to their creed, they accepted the resurrection of the dead almost as a dogma. They had no idea of the life of the individual after death but, in order to silence all doubts, they supplemented the "End of Days" with the idea of *Teḥiath ha-Methim,* the resurrection of the dead, as providing the means and the time for the final adjustment of all the injustices of this life. This constituted a regression, which can be understood only in the light of the intensity with which personal religious experience had laid hold of them and mastered them. But, hedged around by their law, their general attitude was so consolidated as to enable them triumphantly to survive their great historic encounter with Greece.

PART II

FROM

THE ENCOUNTER WITH GREECE

TO

THE ENCOUNTER WITH CHRISTIANITY

❁ ❁ ❁ ❁ ❁ ❁ ❁ ❁ ❁ ❁ ❁

GREECE AND JUDEA

IT was the political insignificance of the Jewish theocratic republic that secured it two hundred years of peace in which to consolidate its spiritual life. But this was followed by an upheaval in the outside world which made even Judea totter. East and West met in conflict, and Greece forced her way into Asia.

The Jewish nation had already encountered many peoples, but in every instance they had found something in common with their antagonists—a Semitic origin, a kindred language, familiarity resulting from long association as neighbours, or likenesses based upon a similar historical fate. But between the Greeks and the Jews there was nothing whatever in common. They represented two opposite poles of the human mind, and stood for entirely different human ideals and methods. And it was precisely this profound contrast which made it impossible for the Jews to shirk the encounter or to ignore the new power. They were now confronted by the alternative of either losing their own individuality in favour of the Greek, or of asserting it by a fresh consolidation of their boundaries. Fate had also placed a fresh task before them, which was really only the logical outcome of their line of development—that of holding their own not only within their own narrow bounds, but also as members of a theocratic state in the face of the whole world.

At first the Jews regarded the rise of Greece with complete indifference and learnt with comparative calm that Judea had once again to submit to a change of suzerain. They heard that Alexander, the son of Philip of Macedon, was in the throes of realizing a dream of empire which was to include Europe, Asia, and Africa under the hegemony of the Greeks and the Greek spirit. The Persian empire crumbled to bits before this new offensive, and Alexander directed his march farther to the south, to Egypt; incidentally, as it were, including Judea, which succumbed without a struggle, in his victorious progress.

When, after Alexander's death (323 B.C.), the heritage of the great conqueror was divided between the Diadochi, Judea, together with part of Cœle-Syria, fell to the share of Ptolemy Lagus, who had occupied Egypt and made Alexandria his capital. Seleucus, another of the Diadochi, founded a dynasty whose dominion was gradually extended over a mighty kingdom reaching from Lebanon to the banks of the Indus. For the time being the only difference this made to Judea was that she was politically cut off from the Jews exiled in the north, while the Jewish colony in Egypt became extremely flourishing. We shall presently deal with the latter separately, not only because of the different fate that overtook it, but also because its reaction to the advance of Greece was very different from that of Judea. Judea paralysed the Greek attack while the Alexandrian Jews brought about the disintegration of Hellenic civilization.

For a hundred years Judea was under the dominion of the Ptolemies, and during that time she had ample opportunity for coming into contact with the Greeks. The Jews had long known of the existence of the latter. From the writings of the prophets they had already learnt of the "sons of Javan," the Greek slave-traders of the Ionian islands. But they now came into contact with ever-growing numbers of pure and half-caste Greeks. A ring of Greek colonies began to form round Judea, which became a mere wedge in an area in which the Greek language, manners, and customs spread day by day, not merely owing to the steadily increasing numbers of the colonists but also because the neighbouring non-Jewish peoples were only too eager to submit to the onslaught of a new culture. At first Judea, as an enclosed area, remained unaffected, but her position of dependence on Ptolemaic Egypt brought her into contact with the manners, customs, and spirit of the new culture, which meant that in the end a struggle with the Greek *way of life* became a practical problem even for Judea.

Those aspects of Greek life which were particularly offensive to the Judean—the worship of many gods, the light-hearted, licentious existence, the symposia, homosexuality, and other forms of erotic laxity, the luxurious living, the concern with worldly things and sciences, and finally the games and gymnastics in which naked men and youths participated—naturally meant but little apart from the fundamental spiritual attitude from which they sprang. The Judeans were already a much too highly differentiated people not to be able to discern the spirit underlying all these external manifestations. And they recognized behind the Greek artist, the Greek philosopher, the Greek man of the world, the Greek erotic debauchee, the light-hearted drinker, the pessimistic and scornful scoffer at the gods, the common factor which consisted of the Greek spirit itself.

And here it is incumbent to make an important parenthetical remark. A peculiar historical perspective results from the necessity of avoiding the examination of historical periods from an artistic, æsthetic, and literary standpoint, and making the standard by which they are judged one, which for measuring the value and development of humanity, has remained of equal importance for hundreds of years —the moral standard. In the light of such a point of view, the fantastic edifices of well-meaning and tendentious history-makers collapse like castles of cards. But any other way of judging has never been possible to the Jews. And they have applied it to every people. This makes them unjust towards the individual manifestations of a culture, but eminently just towards its spirit and inner significance.

Who then was the Greek? What did he appear to be to the Jew? As in the case of every criticism of one nation by another, the Jew could understand him only with the help of comparisons; and this revealed nothing but contrasts, even in that sphere where the two peoples started from the same fundamental principles.

They both firmly believed that their life was rooted in *this* world, and that they lived in this world in a state of complete consciousness. But, whichever way you look at it, the structure each raised on this foundation reposed on the opposite extremes of the position. In the first place, the prime essential for the organization of life in this world, the creation of a state, led, in the case of the Greeks, to a number of chaotic attempts. The various forms of government they established were all experiments, which, owing to the fact that they were carried to their extreme logical conclusion, culminated in absurdity. Whether they tried an aristocracy, a tyranny, a democracy, or a Spartan system of military communism, in the end they always did violence to themselves; there was always some section of the people who were fettered and oppressed, and their frequently highly intellectual toying with the idea of a state was always stronger than their desire to realize the fundamental idea of their lives in any particular form of state. Nietzsche rightly calls them "the political fools of ancient history." The span of years separating the rule of a brutal aristocracy, which put its heel on the face of the besotted masses, to the period when the scandalous practice of ostracism was established, represents, not a line of development, but two opposite poles of feeling in a community which never inspired its members with a sense of duty either towards each other or towards the state.

In Judea, on the contrary, there existed a form of state which, although it may have been colourless and lacking in imagination, was, owing to the extraordinary acuteness of the communal sense, constructed on an organic principle, along clear and comprehensive lines; and, what is even more important, there was in the people responsible for it, a *desire* for a political constitution, which should be truly representative of the spirit and aspirations of the community.

The Greeks and Judeans, moreover, had this in common, that with them both the state and the "church" were to an extraordinary degree coextensive. It is true to say of the Greeks that their state was also their church, and of the Jews that they realized their church in their state. But, as the result of the functions of this state, arbitrary power of the most despotic description appeared among the Greeks, and held over the heads of the citizens the constant threat of an impeachment for godlessness, and made it possible for three of the greatest thinkers of the Periclean Age, Socrates, Protagoras, and Anaxagoras, to be put to death. Whereas in Judea the best brains of the nation were always concerned with establishing a real and living harmony between church and state, religion and communal organization.

The factor constituting the profound subterranean difference between them is the religious endowment of the two peoples, and their corresponding religious productivity. The most striking dissimilarity lies in the fact that, whereas Judaism produced monotheism, the Greeks with their creative imagination peopled the heavens with countless divinities of strictly limited powers who from the cloudy heights of Olympus slavishly copied and even exaggerated the pleasures and pains, the perfections and imperfections, the loftiness and baseness of life on earth. The respect of the Greeks for their gods was nothing more than a fear of demons, though, as was the case with the Judeans, their religion permeated their whole existence. The gods presided over and participated in every act of public and private life. But, for that very reason, they acquired the function and value of articles of everyday use, and were worn down because there was no lofty and impelling idea behind them. Yet the main factor in their overthrow was the fact that, in spite of the ubiquitous worship vouchsafed them, the Greeks, in their heart of hearts, really doubted their existence. Certain of their thinkers had already reached the point of explaining the origin of the gods; they had accounted for them rationalistically, and had thereby dealt them their death-blow. Though the Platonic school remained content with the evasive reply that it was possible that the gods existed, and that therefore it was advisable to abide by the old attitude of reverence towards them, Euhemerus explained the gods as having, in primeval times, been real men who had been canonized and deified for deeds of outstanding distinction; while the Stoics regarded them as personifications of the forces of nature.

Different as was the nature of their respective religions and divinities, the meaning of the theology of the Jews and the Greeks diverged just as widely. That of the Jews has already been sufficiently often outlined above. That of the Greeks might be found equally well in the Eleusinian mysteries, or in the Orphic or Dionysian rites. But neither the concrete promises of Eleusis—a happy life and escape from Hades—nor the restrained melancholy of Orphic wisdom as enunciated by Pythagoras in any true sense constituted a popular religion. They were merely the concern of a group of intellectuals. The ordinary Greek, the man in the street, who was the real and typical product of the religion of his people, was utterly at the mercy of his half-formulated doubts regarding the existence of the gods, and his semi-conscious despair regarding their true worth, their utility, and their possession of the divine attribute of justice. His real religious endowment consisted in his capacity for experiencing religious emotion. This attitude of the Greek was all the more comprehensible seeing that even his spiritual leaders who, after all, had the direction of opinion and knowledge in their own hands, towards the end retained only sufficient strength for denunciation, resignation, and nihilism. The line of scepticism, sophism, and resignation runs from Theognis, via Sophocles, to Euripides and Hippocrates. The piteous plaint of the chorus in the *Œdipus Tyrannus* even to this day compels sympathy with the despair it expresses. "How in such times can a man ward off from his soul the weapons of the gods? If such deeds lead to honour, why do we still dance before the gods?"

This accounts for the fact that the encounter between Greek and Jew constituted a clash between a world where religion was falling to bits and a world in which religion was being consolidated.

All these differences together produced a disparity which must have been glaringly obvious, particularly to the eye, when the two peoples met—the disparity between both their spiritual and material forms of life. We need not enter with any detail into the influence of religious beliefs on the life forms of communities. The Greek certainly felt that his world of gods exercised a definite influence on what he did and what he did not do, but he failed to receive any guidance from them; they were so threadbare, so disunited, and so much like himself in all they felt and did! The life form of the Judeans, whether in their private or communal lives, was an attempt to prove themselves true to the divine mission. But, in ultimate analysis, whom did the Greek serve? Whatever the form or the guise, it was himself alone, himself, in his *joie de vivre,* his sorrow, his good cheer, his artistic tendencies, his profound pensiveness, and his utter impotence in the face of the meaning of the world and of life. Apart from his fear of demons and spectres, the only force that regulated and restrained him was the power exerted by his fellow-men, who likewise served only themselves. No moral law, no injunction to consider the welfare of his neighbour or of the community had ever been imposed upon him. And it was for this reason that the Greek possessed neither ethics nor morality.

This nation of subtle and polished thinkers, of unprecedented scientific activity, whose highest intellects always conceived the idea of every action and the idea of every thing as above every action and every thing, possessed neither the power nor the means to grasp the idea of an ethical reality. While endowed with a consummate gift for harmony of body, language, movement in space, and form, they possessed no trace of any talent for moral harmony. That a few of their thinkers recognized the significance of a personal and even of a social ethic, does not alter the fact that amorality was a definite characteristic of the Greek mentality. They possessed nothing even remotely resembling a Decalogue to restrain and bind them, and their language had not even a word to express the morally reprehensible. Far be it from us to write a discourse on morality; all we wish to do is to emphasize the fact that the Jews, the people with the strongest gift for morality, in coming into contact with the Greeks, encountered a race which was held up by the whole of antiquity as the prototype of everything that was mendacious, cruel, slanderous, cunning, indolent, vain, corruptible, grasping, and unjust. The Greeks were the most inhumane people of the ancient world. Their haughty contempt for the "barbarian," which was based upon their own taste, knowledge, and intellect, did not prevent them from behaving with the utmost barbarity themselves in dealing with their enemies and the countries of their enemies, whether inhabited by foreigners or a kindred race. The qualities which a man like Socrates tried to inculcate upon them, and which he tried to impose upon Greek life, with its undeniable wealth of colour and brilliance, but its total lack of direction and purpose, the ideals of virtue and reason, remained ever beyond their reach.

Moreover, the meeting of the two peoples took place in peculiar circumstances, the outcome of the spiritual state of Greek civilization at the time. For while the overflow of Greek culture beyond the shores of its own country, and its spread throughout the East, was certainly a sign of superabundance, it was of a nervous, irritable, and unsettled kind, not the superabundance of strength and security. It was an explosion of unrest, not a calm dispersal of creative power. The Greek, the Hellene, a surfeited, supersensitive nihilist, bearing about him all the traces of fatigue and decadence, encountered the Judeans at a time when the latter were still struggling with the frequently difficult and dull problems of their existence, and the forms it was to adopt. The Greeks had had vast experience in this world; their imagination had been fertile and they had created much. But the world had returned them nothing, because heaven had hidden its face from them. And as their restlessness and lack of any true faith made them demolish heaven, the earth itself also perforce crumbled beneath their feet. That, in these circumstances, they should fall in with a people imbued with a calm and sometimes stolid and bucolic certainty where its spiritual possessions were concerned, barbarians with no sculpture or breeding, necessarily tinged their contempt with impotent wrath. The inevitable logical result of this attitude on the part of the Greeks was the growth of Anti-Semitism, or hatred of the Jews.

This statement of fact is not intended to involve any act of valuation or appreciation. At the moment when it encountered Judaism, Greek culture might quite well have become the culture of the whole world. But there was one culture it could not overcome or oust from its position, and that was the Jewish, which confronted it both in Palestine and in the Egyptian Diaspora. Whereupon, relying on its military and economic superiority, it proceeded with an exorbitant amount of contempt, duplicity, and cruelty to attack it. Yet it was the Greek culture that was defeated.

The clash of Greek and Jewish cultures did not mean merely an attack on the part of the former and defence on the part of the latter, with the restoration of the *status quo ante* in the end. A clash of cultures is bound to lead to something, and the Jews did not survive the conflict unaffected. The fact that the Greek way of life had crossed their path, not merely as the result of gradual expansion from abroad, but with the deliberate intention of imposing itself upon them by brute force, provoked a degree of resistance, which they thought out to its logical conclusions. To the Greek, incapable of founding a community, everything was merely a question of form for the individual, or at best for a number of individuals; but the Jews immediately inquired how it affected the community as a whole. Thus their peculiar problem of form—theocracy or a temporal state?—was again raised and became a subject of passionate discussion. Hitherto it had merely been a question of proving the worth of the theocratic system within their own borders. But owing to the resistance they were now called upon to offer to a determined attempt to Hellenize them, it became a matter of practical importance to prove the value of theocracy in a differently constituted *outside world*. Though the spirit of religion ultimately triumphed, the worldly principles introduced by the changes due to the influence of Greek culture were not lost. The Egyptian Diaspora in particular kept them alive. Thus Judaism, while retaining its peculiar characteristics, obtained from the Greeks its introduction to worldly wisdom, which enabled it to secure its survival in the world long after the decay of Hellenism.

The first onslaught of Hellenism, introduced from Egypt, did not assume a particularly virulent form in Judea; it merely amounted to the fact that Greek manners and customs were present. The reaction to them varied from passionate hostility, through kindly interest, to enthusiastic acquiescence and the desire to emulate. From the beginning the masses unconsciously held aloof, waiting for a decision to be reached, and signs were already visible of the existence of two parties destined to wage a bitter struggle against each other later on. While on the one hand there was a large increase in the membership of the sect of Nazirites, which had been founded in the days of the prophet Elijah and now called themselves Assidæans (Ḥasidism, the "strict pietists"), there was also formed under the leadership of the tax-farmer Tobias, son of Joseph, a party which regarded the Greek way of ordering and enjoying life as eminently beautiful and desirable. This naturally meant something more than the mere adoption of foreign customs, a fact which the Judeans recognized quite clearly. It was a matter of professing belief in the spirit behind these customs and perceiving that it was different from that which lay behind Judaism. The difference may be summed up as follows. Was life to involve obligations or was it not? Were interests to be sacrificed for something or for nothing? Was the spirit to be centred in the neighbour or in self?

For those who were living in the theocracy, it was a question of finding some justification of the Greek enjoyment of life. They themselves were entirely committed, down to the minutest detail of their existence, to the rule of abstinence, not because they were ascetics on principle, but owing to the Biblical conception of "cleanliness" and "holiness." When, moreover, it is remembered that even among those Judeans who, owing to their sympathies, proudly called themselves Jewish Hellenists, while the imitation of Greek customs was necessarily imperfect (for it is impossible merely to adopt a foreign way of life which is intimately bound up with the evolution and qualities of a particular race), it becomes all the more comprehensible that among the mass of the people resistance should have gathered unsuspected momentum. It was rightly recognized that the imitation of Greek customs had a twofold implication—the renunciation of that form of life which involved obligations, and consequently the loosening of one of the strongest bonds of Jewish nationality; and secondly, in the purely religious domain, a return to magic, to a stage of spiritual and religious evolution long since overcome.

THE MACCABEAN WARS

THIS exhaustive discussion of the principle involved in the clash of the two cultures seemed necessary in order to make the history of subsequent events comprehensible, and particularly that of the Maccabean wars, which it is impossible to explain in the approved manner merely as manifestations of heroism and a gallant struggle for freedom. At least in their earliest stages they present some extraordinary features—the spectacle of a theophoric people up in arms for the defence of the theocracy; a fight for the sake of peace; the use of violence to establish life without violence.

Under the rule of the Egyptian Ptolemies (320–198 B.C.) the influence of Hellenism on Judea was merely passive, being exercised by the pure Greeks and Greek half-castes by the fact of their presence alone. But this state of affairs changed when Antiochus III, surnamed the Great, one of the Seleucidæ, drove the Egyptians out of Cœle-Syria, and thus obtained possession of Judea. Judea now became, as it were, the southernmost province of Greece, and a constituent part of the Macedonian-Hellenic sphere of influence in Asia, ruled by the Seleucidæ, the most ardent advocates of the Hellenization of the East by fair means or foul. All the neighbouring peoples, the coast tribes, Galilee, Samaria, and Transjordania, with its hodge-podge of Greeks, Syrians, and Samaritans, were subjected to an ever more violent and rapid process of Hellenization. The Greek language ousted Aramaic. Greek trade spread over the East, opening up new highways and destroying the old frontiers. In short, Greek civilization was on the point of making the East an area of uniform culture.

The process of Hellenization was also intensified in Judea. The constant stress and strain of the life led by the Jews, intensified by the severity of the ritual, tempted them to break loose and taste of the excitements, pleasures, and distractions of their new masters, and to copy their dress, banquets, theatres, popular amusements, sports, and games. Nor did they stop at mere innocent imitation; for in a community like that of the Jews, in which everything was carried to its logical conclusion and made a question of principle, only a step separated material from spiritual adaptation. Imitation of a custom became assimilation to the spirit behind that custom. And those who disapprovingly held aloof could not rest content with mere repudiation; they were obliged to go further and become aggressive. Thus when, after a brief but stormy period of development, the Hellenists showed themselves ready to renounce all exclusiveness and national peculiarities, and to accept Hellenism unconditionally, their opponents, the Assidæans, or Conservatives, gradually strengthened the restrictions and the separatist ritualistic laws, and finally forbade all association or intercourse with the Greeks or anything that belonged to them. This difference of outlook and attitude led to the division of the country into two parties.

The surrounding districts, to which Judea had for some time paid but little attention, once more rose up against her, filled with dislike for the somewhat arrogant self-assurance of this exclusive and reserved people. The Greek element now made itself felt for the first time; for it was only when he met with resistance directed against himself that the Greek discovered the Jew. Naturally he saw in him only the barbarian, and since he adopted a superior and hostile attitude, a presumptuous barbarian to boot. That he should regard the rough, unpolished customs of the Jews, their modest art of life, the lack of colour and form in their existence, as contemptible was also comprehensible enough. But his wrath and indignation can be explained only on the plane of the unconscious—in the faith, the ethos, and the social system of the Jews, he found something entirely alien to himself; he did not like it, but he could not have attained to it even if he had. And this cultural product, which was the creation of potentialities diametrically opposed to those of his own nature and which might have brought him nearer to a knowledge of how man should behave towards his fellow-creatures and the powers above, he was driven by the instinct of self-preservation to endeavour to destroy. Historians of this period declare that the Jewish world was not yet ripe for the adoption of Greek civilization. But that is not how the matter stood. Judaism did not require Greek civilization, and what little it did adopt from Greece was powerless, in the face of its own store of spiritual achievements, to prescribe the laws for its development. Judaism had long since been in possession of the *spiritual meaning* of its existence. The struggle it now entered upon was a struggle about *form.*

The instrument of the Greek will to power was at this time Antiochus IV, surnamed Epiphanes. He had spent the decisive years of his development as a hostage in Rome, with the result that his intellectual attitude became a blend of Greek and Roman. He eagerly seized the opportunity of interfering in the domestic concerns of Judea, where Onias III now filled the office of high priest in Jerusalem. The latter's brother, Joshua, who called himself Jason, was a Hellenist and was plotting to take the office from him, as he very rightly held that it was only through the power attaching to it that anything lasting could be achieved in the direction of Hellenizing the people. On undertaking to pay a contribution and to establish a gymnasium in Jerusalem, he succeeded in securing his appointment as high priest in 174 B.C.

Now that this office had at length been placed in the hands of the Hellenists, they naturally proceeded to exploit it as they were accustomed to see offices exploited in their factious Hellenic environment—that is to say, as the means for the exercise of personal power. One of the leaders of Hellenism, Onias, who called himself Menelaus, promised Epiphanes an even larger contribution if he would depose Jason, and appoint him in the latter's place. To this Epiphanes consented without demur. Menelaus, however, found he could not raise the contribution, and thereupon without hesitation began to rob the Temple treasure, and when Onias III, the high priest who had been deposed, accused him of the crime, he had him murdered. As he had to appear before Epiphanes to defend himself, he left his brother Lysimachus in charge and told him to proceed with the robbery of the Temple treasure. But the people in Jerusalem rebelled and killed him. At the trial before Epiphanes the temple robbers and murderers were acquitted and their Jewish accusers were put to death. And thus Judea learnt to know something of the spirit so frequently displayed in the Greek *polis.*

While Antiochus Epiphanes was preparing to conquer Egypt, and all Judea was waiting in suspense for the result of the campaign, the news of his death was everywhere circulated. The people immediately seized the opportunity to put an end to the tyranny, which was still in its infancy. The Hellenizers assumed an attitude of defence, and civil war raged in Jerusalem. But Epiphanes was not dead. Rome had implied to him that he would do well to evacuate Egypt. He accordingly returned and vented his wrath at the rebuff and at the opposition of Judea by making a surprise attack on Jerusalem. And the herald of Greek culture proceeded to murder madly right and left in the city. Breaking into the Temple, he took away all that his underlings had left and, giving rein to his Greek imagination or his Greek duplicity, he helped spread the rumour that the Judeans were worshipping a golden ass's head in their Temple and that he had also found bound to a bed there a Greek who was being fattened for sacrifice. (In later days a similar accusation was made with regard to Christian children.) A Syrian garrison was left in Jerusalem to protect Menelaus and the Hellenizers. Nevertheless, the process of Hellenization made no progress. On the contrary, by his barbarity Epiphanes had aroused the most bitter hostility to Greek civilization. Crowds escaped from Judea and fled to Egypt to place themselves under the protection of the Ptolemies, as Epiphanes learnt to his cost when in 168 B.C. he undertook his second campaign against Egypt. Once again he was thwarted by Rome, once again he avenged himself on the Judeans, and under Apollonius, the commander of the Syrian garrison in Jerusalem, a fresh massacre took place. Hundreds of women and children were conveyed to the various slave-markets. The city walls were pulled down, and in their stead a fortress, known as the Akra, was built in the centre of the town for the use of the Greek troops. For Epiphanes had made up his mind to put an end to the Judeans and their resistance to the policy of Hellenization, and from merely persecuting the people he turned to persecuting Judaism. He deprived Judea of autonomy, abolished the constitution, the Torah, and forbade the observance of the Jewish religious customs, more especially that of circumcision, the keeping holy of the Sabbath day, and the food regulations. On the other hand he ordered the immediate adoption of the Greek state religion, and the offering of sacrifices to the Greek gods. In order to force the Greek religion upon the Judeans, he commanded the sacrifice of unclean animals, particularly pigs. Greek officials were installed in Jerusalem and in all the towns throughout the country, to supervise and enforce the carrying out of these orders. The slightest show of resistance was punished with death. Houses of prayer were razed to the ground, rolls of the Torah were destroyed or befouled, and people were massacred by hundreds. Thus the Greek attack on Judea lent a particular form and spirit to religious martyrdom.

In December 168 B.C., the Temple of Yahweh in Jerusalem was consecrated to the Olympian Zeus, whose statue was set up there, and a pig was sacrificed in his honour. As a result of this "horrible abomination" (*shiqquṣ shomem*) more of the inhabitants took their departure. In a very short while Jerusalem was half deserted, and the Greek soldiers and officials and the Jewish Hellenizers alone remained.

But in hiding-places along the shores of the Dead Sea, in the wilderness and in the mountain caves, the fugitives and exiles were arming themselves to offer a passionate resistance, heedless of the disparity of the forces involved. Compromise with the Greek religion was out of the question, for its complete dissimilarity to their own made it possible only to say yea or nay to it. The Hellenizers said yea, while the great mass of the people, spurred on by the Assidæans to an insensate but heroic resistance, said nay. Thus resistance both passive and active spread throughout the country. Fresh cases of martyrdom occurred in the case of those who refused to sacrifice to false and moribund deities. Ever and again zealots would emerge from ambush in order to pull down the strange altars, drive away the officials, and make surprise attacks upon the Greek troops. Epiphanes ordered them to be pursued right into their hiding-places, and to be exterminated wherever they were found. He was now determined to wipe them out. But the threat merely resulted in lending the opposition the necessary strength and powers of organization. The Hasmonean family headed the struggle against Epiphanes and the Greek culture he represented, and organized the fight for the recovery of religious independence.

The head of the family, the priest Mattathias, son of John, of Modin, together with his five sons, gave the signal for open rebellion and the gathering together of all the forces of resistance by killing the Greek officer and his troops and pulling down the Greek altar. Communications were established with all those who had escaped from the country, and with all due deference to the large numbers of Assidæans (the "Pious") it was resolved in the interests of the cause to fight even on the Sabbath day when necessary. Far and wide the call to a Holy War went forth. At first it took the form of a guerrilla war characterized by the lightning appearance and disappearance of the rebel troops. But so great was the determination with which it was waged, and so rapidly did the Jewish forces grow, that Epiphanes was forced to send out a regular army against them under the command of Apollonius. The Judeans, who were led by the Hasmonean Judas, surnamed Judas Maccabeus (the Hammerer), accepted battle and held their own, and at Bethhoron that same year (166 B.C.) they defeated a second and larger army sent against them under the command of Seron. A third army under Gorgias, which was expected to exterminate the Judeans root and branch, and which, fully confident of victory, allowed slave-dealers with their coffers and chains to join the camp from the beginning, was defeated in the neighbourhood of Emmaus. The forces of Judas Maccabeus had now increased to 10,000 men, and with them he was able in the following year (165 B.C.), when Epiphanes sent yet another army against him under the command of his lieutenant Lysimachus, to win a brilliant victory near Bethsura and to clear the Greeks out of the country. He was now master of Judea. The road to Jerusalem was clear and he took possession of the city, drove the Hellenizers and the remnants of the Greek garrison into the Akra, and made clear to all what his struggle had meant by solemnly reconsecrating the desecrated Temple. Ever afterwards Hanukkah, or the Feast of Consecration, has been celebrated among the Jews.

The Syrian empire had now lost four armies, one after the other, and was obliged to call a halt. Judas Maccabeus used the respite thus gained to embark upon a process of reorganization which gave promise of national integration and concentration as opposed to the disintegrating tendencies of the Hellenizers. He sent his brother Simon with a portion of the army to Galilee to rescue the Jews who had settled there and were being oppressed and maltreated by their Greek neighbours, and to bring them back to be settled in Judea; and, with a similar object in view, he himself went to Gilead in the territory east of Jordan. After this concentration of forces he saw to it that the country ceased to be molested by the neighbouring tribes who had been incited against it. Finally he took steps to gain possession of the Akra in Jerusalem, the last Greek stronghold in the heart of Judea.

Meanwhile Epiphanes had probably died mad. His successor, Antiochus V, was prepared to make the greatest sacrifices to keep this last Greek stronghold and sent out a fifth army under Lysias. Unfortunately for the Judeans this happened at the beginning of the *Shemittah* year, in which the fields were not allowed to be tilled. Thus there was a shortage of food, the troops, debilitated and incapable of facing the superior forces of Lysias, were obliged to shut themselves up in Jerusalem and were besieged. However, they were able to hold out until Lysias was compelled to withdraw owing to disturbances on the Parthian frontier. In 163 B.C. peace was signed; all the acts of Epiphanes were rescinded, and Judea was guaranteed religious freedom, on condition that she demolished all her fortifications. The Greek garrison was withdrawn from the Akra, and was accompanied by the extreme Hellenizers. Thus the Jewish theocracy had *de facto* made good its resistance to Hellenic polytheism.

But this did not put an end to the conflict of parties among the Judeans. The extreme Hellenizers were succeeded by the moderates, whose leader Alcimus once more secured the intervention of Antioch, where Demetrius now occupied the throne, and succeeded in being appointed high priest. Judas Maccabeus immediately retaliated by leaving Jerusalem and resolutely rousing the whole country to a fresh struggle. A punitive expedition was sent against Jerusalem under the command of Nicanor, but he was defeated by Judas near Capharsalama in 161 B.C. In the following year Nicanor returned with an even stronger army, but was defeated and killed (160 B.C.)

These last two battles, which in themselves constituted a military feat of considerable importance, brought the first part of the Maccabean wars to a close. With the conclusion of peace in 163 B.C. and the rescinding of the decrees restricting religious worship, the aim of the movement had already been attained. The previous state of autonomy, which the Judeans had enjoyed for nearly four hundred years, had been restored. The Ḥasidim in particular were inclined to hold that their object had been achieved, and to subject themselves to the political suzerainty of the Seleucidæ as they had done to that of their predecessors. But the force of the reaction against the Greek invasion made it exceed the original aim, and the Hasmoneans demanded political as well as religious freedom, in fact nothing short of the complete independence of the state. Since the matter of settling the form of government should have depended on the religious principle, this meant that the temporal, anti-theocratic, Greek view of life was gaining ground.

It was Judas Maccabeus himself who headed the movement by concluding a defensive alliance with Rome. But before it could come into operation, he was attacked by yet another Syrian army under Bacchides, on the plea that he had broken the peace treaty and was a rebel. As the Ḥasidim held aloof, he was deprived of the bulk of his forces, and was obliged to go into battle with 3000 men against 20,000. He was defeated and killed at Elasa in the spring of 160 B.C.

Bacchides pursued the fugitives into their remotest haunts. But the Hasmoneans were a family of extraordinary tenacity and determination, and Judas's brother Jonathan immediately took his place. He was, however, less of a martial hero than a calm and painstaking diplomat. With the remnants of his brother's followers, he vanished into the wilderness on the shores of the Dead Sea and quietly collected troops. Bacchides, imagining that his task was accomplished, withdrew. Whereupon Jonathan immediately emerged from his hiding-place, persecuted the Hellenized Jews, and thus increased his own following. Bacchides was therefore reluctantly obliged to return; and in an endless succession of small feuds, surprise attacks, ambuscades, and raids, he was worn out and his army almost completely destroyed. Not once did Jonathan meet him in open battle, but for three years he carried on this policy of attrition, after which he offered to cease hostilities. Bacchides eagerly agreed to the proposal, and a treaty was concluded, by the terms of which the Hasmoneans were to acknowledge the suzerainty of Syria, but were to be free from all interference in their domestic affairs, more particularly regarding the appointment of the high priest. But it was impossible for Jonathan to return to Jerusalem where a Syrian garrison was in occupation, protecting a government that was no government. The real government followed him to Michmash.

Here he waited, preparing himself for the next opportunity. It was bound to come, for the state of confusion within the Seleucid empire, which was an agglomeration of conquered provinces ruled by violence, could not fail to end in disaster. Indeed in a very few years (153 B.C.) a pretender, Alexander Balas, of Smyrna, arose against Demetrius. In the fighting that ensued, Demetrius required the troops that had been left in Judea, and he gave Jonathan permission to raise forces of his own for the purpose of defending the country. Jonathan accepted the offer and at once took possession of Jerusalem. But Alexander Balas also courted his favour, and appointed him high priest. This, too, Jonathan accepted, thus combining the highest office in the land with the leadership of the national party. Rightly estimating the balance of forces, he supported the false claimant, and after the latter's ascent to the throne, he was formally installed as Governor of Judea.

On the death of Alexander Balas, Jonathan's position had already grown so powerful that the new ruler, Demetrius II, did not even dare to prevent him from laying siege to the Akra. On the contrary, he required his help to suppress an insurrection that had broken out in Antioch, in return for which he promised to grant him further privileges and to evacuate the Akra. But as soon as his difficulties were over for the time being, he broke his promises. Whereupon Jonathan withdrew his allegiance, and made a treaty with the new pretender to the throne, Antiochus VI, who was supported by Trypho and confirmed all the promises made by Demetrius II. In return Jonathan undertook to give the pretender military assistance. So brilliant were the successes he gained in Judea and the adjoining districts, that Trypho became anxious; he lured him into his camp on the plea of holding a friendly conference, took him prisoner, and put him to death.

Jonathan's brother, Simon, immediately stepped into his shoes. He had himself officially elected leader by the people of Jerusalem and routed Trypho's army. Whereupon he offered to support Demetrius II, no longer as a vassal, however, but as a free and independent ally. Demetrius accepted the offer under the conditions imposed. Judea was officially released from the payment of tribute, and was recognized as an independent state (142 B.C.). The Akra, the last stronghold of the forces of oppression, was besieged and captured in 141 B.C. The people confirmed this new state of affairs by making Simon high priest; they also gave him temporal power by appointing him commander-in-chief of the army and placing him at the head of the community with the title of "Prince."

And thus, as far as Judea was concerned, the clash between Greek and Jewish civilization was ended for the time being.

ROME AND JUDEA

WITH the rise of the family of the Hasmoneans, and the victorious wars waged by an insignificant people in defence of their ideals against one of the greatest political and cultural powers of the age, the history of the Jews enters a new phase of dramatic interest. The passionate will of the people to mould their own destiny and frame the laws of their evolution according to the voice in their own breast, produced the necessary heroic instrument. But at the very moment when the goal was reached, this instrument became an independent force; that which had hitherto served merely as a means acquired a separate existence and chose its own ends. The Hasmoneans ceased to be the executors of the will of the people, and became candidates for the prizes suggested to them by the outside world. They became exponents of the will to power, imperialists and despots. But the people had elected them to office for very different ends. They needed a leader in the deepest sense of the word; they required a man who was prepared in mind and spirit to march at the head of a band of trustful and dependent followers and to give them help. When he had achieved what they wanted, they raised him to the rank of prince. But as soon as he exploited this position of power for ends of his own unconnected with themselves, they withdrew their support. Thus a rift appeared between the people and their ruler; they drifted apart and went their various ways, their interests coinciding only by accident now and again. But the misfortunes that pursued the rulers owing to their misinterpretation of their position ended in consummating not only their own downfall, but the destruction of the people and the state as well.

Truth to tell, Simon, the prince, the last of the Hasmonean brothers, merely took reasonable measures for securing the safety of the state; he fortified the frontiers of the country. But his son and successor, John Hyrcanus, inaugurated a policy of aggression, aiming at the formation of a great Jewish state. He began by subduing the small neighbouring states and peoples, and thus broke through the cordon surrounding Judea. He seized the important harbour of Jaffa, and again opened up his country to world trade. True, all this was Judean territory; but that section of the people which attached importance only to spiritual autonomy refused to countenance even this plea in justification of the policy. Moreover, John Hyrcanus was responsible for a measure which was to prove unique in their history, and which his people regarded with the utmost suspicion and misgiving—he forced the Idumæans to embrace Judaism on pain of transportation. This policy of conversion at the point of the sword, which afterwards played such an important part in the establishment of Christianity and Islam, gave rise to the justifiable objection that faith should be a matter of a willing heart and not of a head bowed in fear. There had already been voluntary recruits to Judaism, but now for the first time conversion was made compulsory. For this the Jews suffered terrible retribution later on, for Herod came to them from the Idumæans!

Nor were the people placated by the fact that the general prosperity of the country increased with its political power. They did not consider themselves mere subjects. They stood for an idea, and accordingly made certain demands of their rulers. As a result of the lack of agreement between the aims of the people and of the government, the country was split up into parties, and the rest of its history consists of the bitter and bloody conflicts that arose between them.

The Hasmoneans, like every other dynasty, naturally had their adherents, who in this case were recruited from the class conventionally called the aristocracy, and from those people whose existence is bound up with a dynasty. But they were also supported by that section of society which, owing to contact with Greek culture, could conceive of a national state only on the pattern of those about them. These various groups which, together, constituted the party of the Sadducees, who, in their spiritual outlook, may be described as the successors of the moderate Hellenizers of the days of the Seleucidæ, did not by any means repudiate religion and the binding force of their laws, though they set the state unconditionally above religion. It was for this reason that they combated that development of the religious idea which was constantly setting up fresh barriers against the outside world, and entered into every function of private as well as political and public life. The only written law they recognized was the Pentateuch, and the only oral tradition that which could be clearly and unequivocally derived from the written word. They refused to see that the constant extension of the law was merely an attempt to shape and deal with the constantly changing conditions of existence in the spirit of traditional teaching. For it was precisely such matters that they wished to regulate in accordance with what they had learnt to know of Greek thought and Greek culture.

Though the Sadducees constituted a minority, they were extremely powerful owing to their political position. The opposition consisted of the Pharisees, who can be regarded as a party only in so far as they opposed the Sadducees, for they really represented an overwhelming majority of the people. Their leaders were the best men of the day, the scholars and the scribes, the direct successors of the Sopherim and the Ḥasidim.

The tendentious description of the Pharisees given in the Gospels produces an altogether false impression of them. They were the consistent supporters of the theocratic idea. They understood the prophets, and a study of the world about them and of their own fate confirmed them in a belief which the Sadducees refused to accept, that the actions of the individual and of the mass of mankind must, in all circumstances, be measured according to a definite standard, if life was to have a meaning and not become the senseless sport of chance. This standard they discovered in the moral law which was the very basis of their existence. The idea of the act preceded the act itself and not vice versa. The obligations of morality and the form in which they were recorded, namely the law, stood above all else, and applied to politics also; and this meant, contrary to the view held by the Sadducees, that the state was not an end in itself. Nothing should occur through its agency or for its sake, which exceeded the requirements of the theocracy. There should be no policy of conquest, but merely one of internal consolidation. The aim should be to renounce the political for the sake of the spiritual glory of the nation.

It was over questions such as these that the parties first came into conflict. From the beginning it was a struggle as to which of them should gain the upper hand at home, and culminated in an attempt to make the government, as the representative body, and the Sanhedrin, as the supreme legislative body, their instruments. The religious and cultural differences were merely a consequence of the age, for the foundations of the state were already shaken, and the political controversy was becoming more and more purposeless. But of this later.

At this juncture in the history of the Jewish people, when once again it was a question of coming to a decision, yet another and particularly interesting body of people arose—the Essenes. They can hardly be called a party, for they took no interest in politics. Nor can they be called a sect, for they did not cut themselves off from the rest of the community as the outcome of religious differences. They were the first group of people to make up their minds to refuse any longer to share the crushing and burdensome fate of their race, and to retire to a position where their souls could make peace with God, as it was apparently forbidden to find peace in this world. While they did not deny either the Jewish religion or nationality, they felt they could no longer fight for them with the rest of the people. They were overcome by an irresistible desire to leave the problems of existence to others and to flee into solitude, into a sphere of tranquillity and contemplation, into the restfulness of the "kingdom that is not of this world," with that part of them, their soul, which was perpetually menaced with danger. Everything in the outside world, with its constant wars and party feuds and their attendant devastation, misery, struggles, oppression, religious coercion, hunger, persecution, bloodshed, and unrest, filled them with disappointment and made them sick and weary at heart. And they resumed the tradition which, hundreds of years previously, the Nazirites had started, avoiding the towns and everything connected with them. They made Engedi on the lonely shores of the Dead Sea their headquarters, where they led a simple and ascetic existence, reducing their raiment and their wants to the barest necessities. They owned no personal property, but gave all they possessed to the community to be administered for the general good. They were the first communists. They took their meals together and, as these were accompanied by prayer, they acquired a religious significance and foreshadowed the Holy Communion. They aspired to cleanliness in the Biblical sense, and symbolized it by means of daily baths, which foreshadowed the rite of baptism. They maintained strict discipline among themselves, admitted new members only after years of probation, and were very much in favour of the novice being celibate, because, as a married man, he would find it most difficult to fulfil the requirements of the Levitical law of cleanliness. Thus they were also the precursors of the religious and monastic orders and celibate communities.

After supplying their modest wants each day, they devoted all their energies to the attainment of their goal—perfect communion with God. They evolved their own mysteries as to how He should be approached. They had more than one name for Him, and could interpret and apply them. But they confided the secret only to a select few to the accompaniment of solemn mystic ceremonies. It was from their mystic striving after God that the Kabbalah and Christian Gnosticism were derived. Their doctrines included the practice of magic rites, and they peopled heaven and earth with spirits. They believed more particularly in evil spirits, *shedim,* who entered into men and possessed them; and, like Jesus of Nazareth later on, they consequently practised the art of exorcism, or the driving out of evil spirits, which appealed to the simple masses and was not above their understanding.

Thus this community, the aim of whose existence was the salvation of their own souls, took its root in the active life of the people, and in its mystic probing of the world; it yearned for the end of all things, "the Kingdom of Heaven," the kingdom which was not of this world.

John Hyrcanus, who was anxious to keep on good terms with all parties, had yet to learn what the masses, permeated with the Pharisaical point of view, thought of him. Convinced that his activities in connexion with foreign affairs would leave him no time for the things in which they themselves were wrapped up, they urged him to resign the important office of high priest. Highly incensed at this, he turned to the Sadducees, who were his staunch supporters, and with their help obtained control of the Sanhedrin, which had been such an important weapon in the hands of the Pharisees. Thus the government and the aristocracy were ranged against the people. The Pharisees did not forgive either the king or the Sadducees for this trespass on their sacred province. And from a mere difference of opinion between two parties, there rapidly arose the fanatical hatred of deadly enmity. Ten years after the death of Hyrcanus, under the rule of Alexander Jannæus, everything was ripe for civil war. Jannæus was the idol of the Sadducees. A man of the world, educated in the Greek manner, a tyrant and a warrior, his passion in life was fighting, for which the country was called upon to supply the men and money. He exploited his position as high priest to infuriate the people by flouting their most sacred traditions. During a solemn religious service in the Temple he would order his mercenaries to mow down the crowd who had expressed their disapproval of him. At last the patience of the people was exhausted, and they took up arms against him, determined to tolerate him no longer as their king, even if, like his predecessors, he considerably extended the boundaries of the state. For six years they fought against him, until at last he saw that it was impossible to rule against the wishes of the majority, and sued for peace. But the other side had no wish to come to terms, and in a paroxysm of fury against the soldiers and Philhellenes, the people invited Syrian troops into the country to help them to get rid of their king. Jannæus was hopelessly defeated and became a wandering and destitute fugitive. The people took pity on him and drove the Syrians out again. But Jannæus proved a worthy example of the school in which he had been brought up, for as soon as he was reinstated on the throne he had eight hundred Pharisees crucified in Jerusalem. That same night eight thousand Pharisees fled abroad. In the fighting between the two parties 50,000 men are said to have lost their lives.

The breach was beyond repair. After the death of Jannæus, his widow, Salome Alexandra, seized the reins of government. So well and wisely did she rule that peace and contentment spread through the land. Nevertheless, the Pharisees, and the fugitives who had returned, exploited the sympathetic attitude the queen at first adopted towards them and the powers she granted them, to avenge themselves on the hated Sadducees. The final catastrophe occurred immediately after her death. She had two sons, Hyrcanus and Aristobulus; the former, an insignificant nonentity, was high priest, and on his mother's death should have succeeded to the throne. But Aristobulus, who inherited all his father's qualities, disputed his claim and led an army against him in Jerusalem. Whereupon Hyrcanus agreed to share the functions of government provided he was allowed to retain the office of high priest. Aristobulus became king. The sympathies of the people were with Hyrcanus, those of the Sadducees with Aristobulus.

But fate, secretly preparing its blow, was impervious to either sympathy or antipathy. This monarchy, which had strayed from the appointed path, inevitably wandered in the direction from which it drew its spiritual sustenance—the Græco-Roman world of politics, whose fate it consequently shared. And the impression of retributive justice was intensified by the fact that its final downfall could be traced to its own wrong-doing. For Rome first came to intervene in Judea owing to the activities of a certain man of that race which John Hyrcanus had forcibly converted to Judaism—the Idumæan, Antipater.

Antipater was the son of Antipas the Governor of Idumæa. A recent and most unwilling recruit to the Jewish state and the Jewish religion, he had made his way to Jerusalem with others of his compatriots to try to make the most of the new situation. With the help of the Jewish aristocracy, who welcomed the proselyte with open arms, he obtained access to Hyrcanus, the high priest, and succeeded in coming to a disastrous understanding with him. Hyrcanus was weak, irresolute, good-natured, and stupid. Antipater was clever, cool, calculating, and utterly unscrupulous. It did not take him long to become aware of the influence he could exercise over this weakling, and the wonderful opportunities to which such power might lead. He accordingly contrived to make Hyrcanus completely dependent upon him, a mere tool in his hands. All the calamities that followed were the outcome of a plot conceived in the brain of Antipater, whose sole object in life was to exploit every situation for his own benefit. Spurred on by such considerations, he persuaded his creature secretly to take flight from Jerusalem and to bribe Aretas, King of Arabia Petræa, to support him. With the latter's army and his own supporters he was to march against

Aristobulus and recover the throne. Hyrcanus did as he was bidden, and the allied troops besieged the king in the stronghold of Jerusalem. The issue was still hanging in the balance and both sides were appealing for help, when Rome, the universal executioner, answered their appeal.

Ever since the time of Judas Maccabeus, that is to say, for about a hundred years, a treaty of alliance had existed between Rome and Judea. It was the type of treaty so dear to the heart of Rome; it committed her to nothing and might prove useful. If the occasion arose, it might even be repudiated or conveniently forgotten, and was typical of the Roman diplomacy of the day. Slowly but surely Rome had advanced and laid her hands on the crumbling empire of the Seleucidæ. She had conquered Macedonia, broken up the Achæan League, and gradually secured a footing in Asia Minor. And now, after the subjugation of Armenia, she was approaching the borders of Syria. In 65 B.C., Scaurus, Pompey's lieutenant, appeared in Damascus, and hearing that fraternal war was raging in Judea, he hastened to have a finger in the pie. Both brothers were utterly blind to the significance of his action. Rome had stretched out her hand, and was not to withdraw it until she had ruined the state, the people, and the country.

This situation points to two obvious conclusions. In the first place, we see the result to which Judean policy had led. By overreaching herself in her efforts of self-defence Judea had entered the arena of international politics. She had shown that she too aimed at being a great power; she had embarked upon conquests, and had thrust her way into a world from which it had been her mission to hold aloof. And having placed herself at the mercy of the laws of this world, she had no alternative but to share its fate. The second conclusion is of even greater spiritual significance—the function of leader in Judea had lost its meaning. This noble mission, born of the unique idea of theocracy, was not only cast aside but actually denied. The rulers of Judea had ceased to be functionaries; they had become rulers after the pattern of the Græco-Roman world. Their office had ceased to be a service; it had become an end in itself. As the result of this discrepancy between the office and the meaning of the office, between autocratic rule and a people who expected their ruler to be merely the representative of their ancestral idea, both institutions, the office of ruler and the state, were inevitably destroyed.

The encounter with Rome, unlike that with Greece, did not entail any adjustments either on the part of Judea or her adversary. The Greek citizen and the Greek *people* had been objects of burning interest; but Rome and her policy, which consisted of a constant extension of power and the establishment of a world empire based on political intrigue, an unscrupulous administration, and murderous wars, aroused but little curiosity. And it was for this reason that any sort of compromise between the Judeans and the Romans was neither possible nor necessary. And, as a matter of fact, it was never attempted. In the case of Rome, Judea met with no culture that could touch or influence her. Whereas Greece had attained the summit of intellectual brilliance, Rome was in every respect mediocre. The fact that she had provided the legal code and set the standard of right and wrong for the rest of the world could not be expected to impress a community whose laws sprang from a much deeper source. Thus from the very beginning Judea quite rightly saw in Rome merely the representative of unintellectual and stupid brute force. The principal lesson Judea learnt from her contact with Rome was that Janus figured prominently in Roman mythology—and not without good reason.

For her interference in the present instance Rome had not the smallest legal justification. But Judea, with whom she had a treaty of alliance, had suddenly sprung into prominence as part of the Syrian empire, whose legal heir Rome claimed to be. As a matter of fact Judea had been only temporarily under Syrian dominion, and her *de facto* independence should have been regarded as having been established for some considerable time. But she lay across the path of the advancing eagles, and, even more important, formed the bridge to Egypt.

In 64 B.C. Pompey moved his headquarters to Damascus, and commanded the parties to appear before him so that he might settle their differences. They obeyed. Naturally he had no intention whatever of doing anything of the sort. Indeed it would, in any case, have been beyond his power, for, as a Roman, the conflict of ideas in Judea lay entirely beyond his sphere of comprehension. All he did, therefore, was to hold out to them hopes for a future settlement of their differences. His main object was to make Syria secure by first defeating the Arab forces so that he might the more easily turn his attention to Judea. What this meant Aristobulus understood only at the last moment when it was too late. Pompey had persuaded him to support him with his army in a campaign against the Arabs. But on the march Aristobulus suddenly turned aside and took refuge in the fortress of Alexandrium. Pompey immediately interrupted his campaign and advanced with his army against Alexandrium, where, without the smallest right to do so, he demanded the surrender of the fortress. Under pressure of necessity, Aristobulus withdrew and repaired with his forces to Jerusalem. Pompey followed hot on his heels, and, as the Roman army was far superior to his own, Aristobulus was helpless and was obliged to go to Pompey's camp, as the latter would have liked him to do in Damascus. Whereupon Pompey sent an ambassador to Jerusalem to demand a war indemnity from the people. The latter adopted the only attitude possible in the circumstances. They declared that Judea had never made war on Rome, and dismissed the ambassador at the gates of the city. Pompey's reply was to arrest Aristobulus and lay siege to Jerusalem.

Even now opinion in the city was still divided. The followers of Aristobulus were in favour of resistance; those of Hyrcanus were for surrender. Aristobulus's party therefore sought refuge in the Temple and the surrounding fortifications, where they succeeded in holding out against Pompey for three months, that is to say, until in the autumn of 63 B.C. he seized the opportunity offered by the Sabbath day, their day of enforced rest, in order to take the city by storm. A massacre of some 12,000 Judeans marked the entry of Rome into Jewish history. Pompey had the leaders of the national party executed, and the fortifications demolished; the country was forced to pay tribute and became a Roman protectorate. Hyrcanus was deposed but was allowed to retain the office of high priest, and was also given the insignificant title of Ethnarch, while, by the good graces of Rome, Antipater, the Idumæan, was made Governor of Judea. While the semblance of autonomy had been preserved, the country was really ruled by Rome through the medium of her creature, Antipater. The Hasmoneans were now reduced to playing the part of rebels. Recognizing all too late what their duty really should have been, they entered upon a struggle against the mightiest power in the world for possession of the throne and the government. With the glamour of martyrdom about them, they were at this tragic moment of their fate accepted and supported by the people, who in a spirit of forgiveness looked upon them as their lawful representatives.

Meanwhile Aristobulus and his two sons, Alexander and Antigonus, had been sent captive to Rome. Alexander managed to escape on the way, but his father and brother, together with a number of other prisoners, were exhibited at a triumph, one of those Roman institutions which, from the point of view of taste and culture, were on the level of a circus show.

The succession of Roman procurators and governors who followed were one and all guilty of the most brutal abuse of power. Under pressure of a rule of almost unalloyed brute force everything that happened in Judea on the physical plane became merely a reaction against might and violence. The materialism of Rome created materialism in those who tried to protect themselves against her, and led to a politico-national struggle in self-defence.

Arbitrary rule, on the one hand, and a spirit of rebellion, on the other, became the order of the day under the Roman governor (proconsul) of Syria, Gabinius. He did all in his power to suck the country dry, with the result that Alexander, who had managed to escape to

Galilee, was welcomed with open arms by the people, whom hatred of the Roman rule had converted into patriots overnight, as it were. Alexander succeeded in capturing three fortresses, but he was forced to surrender them all to the troops of Gabinius. A year later Aristobulus, who had managed to escape from Rome, arrived upon the scene. In spite of all his shortcomings he met with ardent support on the part of the patriots, who flocked to join his standard for a fresh uprising. After some heavy fighting, he was wounded, taken prisoner again, and sent back to Rome. A year later, Alexander once more rallied the defenders of national freedom, and headed yet another rebellion. But he was again defeated by Gabinius.

The political upheavals in Rome, and the formation of the triumvirate, were responsible for sending Crassus to Syria. The outstanding act of his administration was the appropriation of a huge sum of gold from the Temple treasure. Though he gave his solemn assurance that he would not take any more, he did not keep his word, but financed his campaign against the Parthians by means of a similar expedient. The people were infuriated, and, as soon as they heard of the death of this robber and perjurer, a fresh insurrection broke out in Galilee, headed by Pitholaus, an old supporter of Aristobulus. This led to a further incursion of Roman legions. Their commander was now Cassius, who afterwards joined the conspiracy against Cæsar. The insurrection was suppressed, and 30,000 Jewish prisoners were sold as slaves and sent to all parts of the world.

So fateful was the course of events that, even when in Rome itself an attempt was made to restore freedom to Judea, the mighty secret forces of history willed otherwise. On the death of Crassus, Cæsar and Pompey, the two remaining triumvirs, fought for the mastery. Cæsar crossed the Rubicon and occupied Italy, which Pompey had abandoned. In order to have a reliable lieutenant in the East, Cæsar released Aristobulus from imprisonment, and put him at the head of two legions, to fight Pompey in Syria. But Pompey's supporters prevented this by poisoning Aristobulus shortly before his departure. Prince Alexander, though he had twice been defeated, was still anxious to carry on the struggle against Rome, and he raised troops and tried to make his way to Cæsar. But Pompey's proconsul had him seized and put to death. The only man to profit by this tragic extermination of a dynasty, which at the eleventh hour made a heroic attempt to save a heritage undermined by a foolish imitation of the foreigner, was Antipater, the Idumæan. When, in 48 B.C., the battle of Pharsalus confirmed Cæsar's victory, he immediately sided with the conqueror, to whom he rendered valuable service by supplying men and money, and influencing opinion among the Jews in Egypt. In return, Cæsar appointed him Epitropos, or procurator of Judea.

This was a position of virtual regency, and Antipater resolutely proceeded to found a dynasty of his own. He made his son, Phasael, Strategus, which was tantamount to making him the native administrator of the Jerusalem area, and he gave his son Herod a similar position in Galilee. Herod regarded himself as a Roman official and made up his mind to establish order in his province, which had always been a focus of rebellion. Against the patriots, who had rallied together under the command of Hezekiah the Galilean, and were carrying on a bitter guerrilla war against the Syrians, the Romans, and the friends of Antipater, Herod took the field on his own initiative. He succeeded in capturing Hezekiah and his followers and had them put to death. This raised a storm of indignation throughout the country. Jewish law was still the law of the land, and the Galilean patriots were under its jurisdiction. They ought to have been handed over to the Sanhedrin for trial. The mothers of the victims went to Jerusalem and implored the authorities night and day to take reprisals. They formed a Euripidean chorus of mourning matrons. Meanwhile the Roman proconsul helped Herod to escape a trial for murder by taking flight.

Like all that had preceded it, this menace also led to the strengthening of Antipater's party. Herod fled to Sextus Cæsar, who made him Governor of Cœle-Syria.

After the murder of Cæsar in 44 B.C., Cassius, who was one of the assassins, suddenly appeared in Asia, and took command of the Syrian legions. The country still had bitter recollections of him as the man responsible for the execution of Pitholaus. He now made exorbitant demands on Judea in the shape of war taxes. Antipater and Herod did all they could to help him in his unscrupulous extortions. Those cities which did not respond quickly had all their inmates sold into slavery. As a result a conspiracy was formed against Antipater, and he was poisoned. Antigonus, the last surviving Hasmonean, son of Aristobulus and brother of Prince Alexander, now attempted another *coup d'état*. But Herod succeeded in suppressing this fresh insurrection, and had the effrontery to enter Jerusalem with his troops and demand that he be hailed as victor. Hyrcanus actually crowned Herod's victory over the defenders of the people's liberty by betrothing his granddaughter Mariamne to him. She was the daughter of Prince Alexander, who had been put to death; and thus a connexion was established with the Hasmonean dynasty.

In view of this development, the Jews again made reasonable representations to the authorities and tried along legal lines to rid themselves of Antipater and his party. But the new master of the country, Antony, the triumvir, not only refused their requests but also appointed Herod and Phasael, the pliant tools of Rome, Tetrarchs, that is to say joint rulers of Judea, under Roman protection.

Thus the Jews were once more forced to have recourse to violence and to work out their own salvation. The wild and extortionate taxation of Antony, who as Cleopatra's lover was squandering the revenues of whole states in Egypt, provided further incentive for revolt. Moreover, the opportunity seemed favourable, as the whole East was seething with discontent against the brutal administration of Rome, and was on the brink of rebellion.

Once more Antigonus appeared on the scene, and was eagerly acclaimed by the people as the man who would save them from Roman tyranny. With the help of the Parthian troops he forced his way into Jerusalem, where the people immediately rallied to his cause. After heavy fighting in the city, Herod and Phasael entrenched themselves in the fortifications. Phasael committed suicide, but Herod managed to escape with his family and made his way to Arabia. After driving out the Roman garrison, Antigonus had himself appointed both king and high priest, for neither of which offices he had the smallest qualification.

From Arabia Herod fled to Rome. Once again death and danger had turned to his advantage. With the consent of Octavius, Antony appointed him King of Judea, and gave him instructions to put an end to the disturbances in that country. In other words, Herod was committed to fighting for his position against the people he was to rule, and against the legitimate dynasty with hereditary rights. It was not an easy task. But after three years of heavy fighting, during which he was frequently obliged to call in the help of Roman troops, he succeeded in accomplishing it. For three years the patriots held out against trained forces, and everything that Herod did merely aggravated their fury and roused them to fresh deeds of retaliation. The whole country was a prey to bitter and relentless slaughter. After unspeakable sacrifices on both sides, Herod was so far successful at the end of the second year that in the spring of 37 B.C. he was able, with the help of the Roman troops, to set about laying siege to Jerusalem. On the eve of the attack he celebrated his marriage with Mariamne, the Hasmonean princess. As the result of three years of war, both sides fought with exaggerated fury. When, in July 37 B.C., after the walls of the city had been almost continuously stormed for two months, the last bulwark fell, the Roman soldiers burst into the city like ravening beasts, and Herod was obliged to promise them large gratuities to prevent them from making him king over a city of the dead. Antigonus was taken prisoner, and Herod persuaded Antony to have him beheaded, a form of execution to which no king even in the history of Rome had ever before been subjected.

With this final and at the same time preliminary act of brutality, and with the bodies of 100,000 dead behind him, Herod, a bestial and tragic Jewish half-caste, ascended the throne of Judea.

In these times of stress and strain, Herod and his activities proved fatefully significant. His actions and the ideas that lay behind them gave rise to the fiercest, most heroic, and most spiritual forms of resistance to all violence. Through him the people were once again forced to the ultimate and most difficult decision regarding the meaning of their existence as individuals and as a community. He was responsible for their paroxysm of patriotic despair, their other-worldly estrangement from the things of this world, and their passionate longing to master the temporal only by means of the eternal—in fact, the moral idea. In the reaction against him lay hid the national fate of the people and the fundamental spiritual attitude out of which the supernational fate of a religion sprang. The actuality of the messianic idea, its spontaneity, its fatally rapid development, indicate that in Herod his contemporaries, in so far as they grasped the idea of good and evil at all, saw the embodiment, the living incarnation, of the principle of evil on earth.

His contemporaries were too close witnesses of his misdemeanours and crimes to be able to appreciate the overwhelming tragedy of his lot. As a man deliberately trained by his father with a view to the rulership of Judea, and educated in Rome, with no hereditary feeling for the fifteen hundred years of Jewish development, and whom the people by every gesture and expression and repeated acts of desperation taunted with being a "half-caste" and an "Idumæan slave"—what could he do but stubbornly and defiantly vindicate his rights by the only means with which nature had endowed him, malevolence and violence? Having now attained to power, he was prepared to defend his position in accordance with the methods he had learnt in Rome—executions and proscriptions. He was, above all, anxious to get rid of the Hasmoneans, for the Jewish people were ready to accept even the worst of them if they could thereby turn out a Herod. But through his wife, Mariamne, they were his connexions by marriage. The instinct of self-preservation, however, prevailed, and he began by placing Hyrcanus, the high priest, who had been deprived of his office, under his control. He then proceeded to bring a charge of high treason against him, and had him executed by order of a compliant Sanhedrin. He also had his brother-in-law, Aristobulus III, drowned at Jericho, on the occasion of a family festival, and his mother-in-law, Alexandra, who really was guilty of conspiring against him, put to death. At the end of 29 B.C. he had Mariamne, to whom he was passionately devoted, arrested and executed on a charge of adultery. Thus within the space of seven years, either by means of open or legal murder, he exterminated the remainder of the Hasmonean dynasty, the other members of the family being massacred *en bloc*. There was not a single day of his reign that was not marked by some cruel act of despotism. The least of his crimes was the extortion of the last farthing from the pockets of his subjects. He wanted the money for the maintenance of his luxurious oriental court and for the indulgence of his Cæsarean building mania. For he regarded himself as the king of a barbarian people devoid of culture, and was anxious to prove to the Roman world, to which he owed everything, and on whose recognition he depended, that he was a man of universal culture. He built a number of new cities in the Græco-Roman style and had old cities rebuilt on a similar pattern. On the coast between Ptolemais and Jaffa he built Cæsarea, the seat of the Roman administration, the tyrant citadel of Judea. He provided enormous sums of money for the building of temples and theatres in foreign countries, sometimes as far away as Athens and Sparta, for all of which the people had to pay. For he forced the money from them by means of his tax-gatherers. But he could not compel them to witness theatrical performances, juggling displays, and contests between men and wild beasts. They quietly but firmly refused. On one occasion only did ten citizens of Jerusalem attend the theatre, and then they went with daggers concealed beneath their cloaks—ten daggers for Herod. A spy betrayed them, and they were executed. The people tore the informer to bits.

Seeing that every patriot was his potential murderer, Herod surrounded himself with a complicated net of spies and informers. Proscriptions, executions, imprisonments, and confiscations increased and multiplied. Embittered and gloomy silence reigned throughout the country. Herod noted this with sullen fury. Abroad he was highly esteemed. But in his own country only those held him in esteem who lived at his expense. But he longed at least for the admiration of the rest, and therefore proceeded to apply his zeal for embellishment to his own capital also. For himself he built a huge, strongly fortified palace, and for the people a magnificent new Temple. But in the case of the latter edifice he spoilt its possible good effect on his subjects by his subservience to Rome, for over the great gate he had a Roman eagle carved, a symbol which the people held in detestation. Every day Herod grew more bitter and suspicious. He longed to secure adherents at all costs, and insisted on his subjects swearing an oath of allegiance to him. Thousands, more particularly among the Pharisees, refused to take the oath, and he proceeded to impose fines upon them. The wife of one of his court officials paid the fines of 6000 of these recusants. But Herod dared go no further. As soon as the murmurs of discontent grew too loud and threatening, he wavered. But this did not mend matters. For a great gulf separated his throne from the people and he protected himself by means of Teutonic, Gallic, and Thracian mercenaries.

At length the day came when he had to think of his succession. Of Mariamne's five sons, two, Alexander and Aristobulus, had been educated in Rome by Asinius Pollio. He sent for them to come home. The people, who saw in these two princes the sons of the ill-fated Mariamne, welcomed them with open arms, and Herod became uneasy. In order to damp any premature hopes they may have formed, he summoned his son Antipater, by a former marriage, to court. This set the whole machinery of palace intrigue in motion, with its inevitable accompaniment of spying, suspicion, slander, and denunciation. At length the atmosphere became so heavy with falsehood and fear, that in 7 B.C. Herod solved his difficulties by bringing his two sons by Mariamne before a Roman court in Beirut, and charging them with high treason. The Roman officials did their best to accommodate him, and the princes were condemned and hanged. Antipater now became the acknowledged heir to the throne. But the king was living too long for his liking, and one day Herod discovered an elaborate and carefully prepared plot to get rid of him by poison. Once again he was obliged to bring a son up for trial. But he hesitated to carry out the sentence of death that was pronounced against him.

He was old and suffering from an incurable disease. The ardent desire of the people for his death found voice in the rumour that he actually was dead, and excitement ran high. As though a load had suddenly fallen off their backs, crowds of people rushed to the Temple to denounce Herod and all his breed. They were led by Judas, son of Sepporæus, and Matthias, son of Margalus. The hated Roman eagle was torn down from the great gate of the Temple and smashed to atoms. Large bodies of Herod's mercenaries charged the crowd, and forty of the leaders were arrested. Herod examined them himself and was met with cold, bottomless hatred and contempt. When he inquired who had incited them, they replied without fear or hesitation, "The Law!"

This was the last straw! He had them put to death, some of them being burnt alive. He felt the end was near and hastily gave orders for the death sentence on Antipater to be carried out. "It were better to be that man's pig than his son!" exclaimed Octavianus Augustus when he heard the news. Five days after this last murder Herod's own life ended, and he was conveyed to his grave by his Thracian, Gallic, and Teutonic guards. The people heaved a sigh of relief and satisfaction. A contemporary sums up his reign as follows: "Herod stole to the throne like a fox, reigned like a tiger, and died like a dog."

But even from the grave he showed himself to be a man who regarded the land and its people as his personal property. In his will he divided the country between three of his sons. Judea fell to the lot of Archelaus. The people at once appealed to him, demanding a reduction of taxation and the liberation of political prisoners. Archelaus replied that until his position had been confirmed by Rome, he could make no promises.

When the official period of mourning for Herod was over, the people, with ostentatious and provocative determination, flaunted their own mourning. It was not for Herod, however, but for the patriots who had been murdered after the storming of the Temple. The deposition of the Herodian dynasty was openly called for, and further demands were also made—the punishment of Herod's responsible ministers, the dismissal of the sycophant he had made high priest, and the appointment of a worthier man in his place. Archelaus continued to excuse himself on the ground that the imperial ratification of his office had not arrived.

The Passover celebrations of 4 B.C. were approaching, and vast crowds of pilgrims were swarming to Jerusalem, where they held a fresh demonstration within the very walls of the Temple, thereby proclaiming the connexion, obvious enough to themselves, between the state and religion. This led to fighting, and Archelaus sent out the whole garrison against them. Three thousand victims were counted. He ordered the pilgrims to return home, and they left to spread sedition and indignation throughout the whole country.

While Archelaus was on his way to Rome, Quintilius Varus, Governor of Syria, sent a legion to Jerusalem, as the situation appeared to be menacing; and, to be on the safe side, Augustus also sent the procurator Sabinus to Judea during the interregnum. The feast of *Shabuoth* (Pentecost) was fast approaching, and with it countless pilgrims, whose main object was a political demonstration, were flocking to Jerusalem. Dividing themselves into three bodies they immediately opened an attack upon the Roman forces, and fierce fighting took place in the Temple. The soldiers fell to plundering, in which Sabinus, the procurator, joined and stole 400 talents of gold. Whereupon the people drove him and his men into the royal palace and locked them in. He appealed to Varus for help.

The provinces were also up in arms. In Galilee, Judas, the son of Hezekiah who had been executed, rose up against the Romans and the Herodians. In Transjordania a man named Simon placed himself at the head of the insurgents. Anarchy reigned supreme, and any suspicion of sympathy with the Romans or even of an attitude of neutrality, was met with violence on the part of the rebels. Varus required the help of two legions to keep the insurrection within bounds, while Sabinus relieved himself of all responsibility by taking flight.

Meanwhile, Archelaus, Herod Antipas, and Philip were in Rome quarrelling over their father's heritage. The people had also sent a deputation which made the most serious allegations against the Herodians, and demanded their removal. But Augustus refused to abandon his previous line of policy, and gave Judea, Samaria, and Idumæa to Archelaus as his portion, with the title of Ethnarch. Herod Antipas was made Tetrarch of Galilee and Peræa, and Philip tetrarch of a district on the northern confines of Palestine.

Archelaus carried on his father's policy for nine years, after which the Judeans, this time in conjunction with the Samaritans, sent another deputation to Rome and brought such a number of serious charges against him that Augustus was obliged to summon him to come and answer them. He was unable to justify himself, and was deprived of his office and banished to Vienne on the Rhône. His kingdom was made part of the province of Syria and placed in direct administrative connexion with Rome by means of a special procurator with headquarters at Cæsarea. This ultimately developed into direct Roman rule, and the curtain went up for the last act of the political and religious drama.

THE HEROIC AGE

The legions might destroy Jerusalem but they could not destroy Judaism.
—Mommsen.

IN designating the period from the rise of the Hasmonean family to the destruction of the Jewish state by Rome as the heroic age, we are well aware that we are glorifying incidents which at times dim and distort the pure image of the Jew, whose ideal is to avoid violence, to abide by the justice of the theocracy, and to oppose to the stupidity of brute force the invincibility of the spirit. But it cannot be helped! The least that the remote descendants of those men can do—swept hither and thither by intellectual and utilitarian considerations—is to vouchsafe to their own past the respect which they feel bound to accord today even to lesser manifestations of resolution in the matter of sacrifice for an idea. Although he may not impute to himself righteousness for being descended from ancestors whose heroism is unparalleled and unexampled in history, the retrospective glance of many a Jew, who is ready to bow before the most foolish humiliation at the hands of his environment, may at least teach him that nothing in his heritage forces him to such an attitude of renunciation and weakness. But when we speak of this age as heroic, we also expect from those who, for whatever reason, concern themselves with it, that minimum of consideration and deference which the smallest spark of human understanding imposes, and which they are only too willing to grant in excess to every other people and to every other war of liberation.

In examining the attitude assumed by the Jewish people from the time of their first encounter with Greek civilization to the point we have now reached, we shall not be surprised to find this last act of the tragedy extraordinarily full of dramatic figures and events. The individual sank into significance compared with the type; for the history which is now to be related was not that of the Jew as such, but of an idea. Nevertheless, the fate which overtook the idea involved the people also and made them more dramatic, more tragic, more unbridled, more brutal, and more confused. They were possessed by an idea, and in their souls the pendulum swung rhythmically to and fro. Extremes suddenly sprang into being. On the one hand there was the struggle against the Romans, and the parrying of blows delivered by dull, stupid, and senseless brutality, while, on the other, there was the attempt wholly to withdraw the perpetually creative nucleus of the people from the tumult of external events, and to save it by deepening and strengthening the spiritual attitude. Lastly there was also the effort utterly to deny both the world and the people, and to find security for the life of the soul in a "kingdom that is not of this world."

The parties occupied a peculiar position half-way between politics and religion. As a matter of fact, they had not changed since the time of Herod. If they are to be named, they must be called the theocrats, on the one hand, and the partisans of Rome on the other. But even the theocrats held divergent views regarding the kind of resistance to be offered. Until the very eve of the outbreak of the war of liberation, the majority were in favour of passive resistance, while only a minority urged recourse to active measures. The more oppressive the rule of Rome became, and the more apparent it grew that her aim was annihilation at the expense of every dictate of humanity, the more clearly were the two extremes defined; on the one side were the passivists culminating in the Messianists; on the other the activists, culminating in the Sicarii, who carried daggers concealed beneath their cloaks. Both sides were heroic in their own way, performing deeds of the utmost valour and enduring untold hardships in their struggle for freedom and spiritual and intellectual independence. Even the armed conspirators were religious patriots. When they declared war on Rome, their resistance took its root in religion.

They refused to accept any more sacrificial gifts from Gentiles, which was tantamount to declaring that they would not offer sacrifice in honour of the Roman emperor.

The age in which severe spiritual oppression produces the man who can only wield a dagger, also produces the man who, far removed from all the brutal technical appliances of life, expresses his desire to serve his people, the world, and God by a wonderful efflorescence of clear ethical vision. In the person of Hillel this spiritual manifestation found its most perfect exponent. He saw that the striving after exclusiveness was crippling the people beneath an ever-growing load of regulations, precepts, and laws. His object was to prevent the latter from becoming ends in themselves, and in the most unassuming way he accordingly shifted their centre of gravity. In the juxtaposition of ethic and law, he perceived the hidden relation between purpose and technique, action and the motive for action, content and form. The law involved the idea of service. It organized the gregarious life of man, which in itself amounted to an act of devotion to God. Thus, in the sequence of values and obligations, duty towards man preceded duty towards God; whereby the fact emerged that the Jews had created their God in order to impose obligations on themselves, and not, as in the case of the Greeks, in order to place themselves in a state of absolute dependence, only occasionally relaxed by scepticism and weariness. Religion was made for man, not for God. Hillel formulated these ideas, and the love of man implicit in them, quite briefly. On the objective side he said: "Do not unto others that which thou wouldst not have done unto thee. Herein lieth the first principle of the Torah; the rest is but an explanation thereof." And on the subjective side he said: "If I do nothing for myself, who will do it for me? But if do it for myself alone, what am I? And if I do not do it now, when shall I do it?"

Hillel was not an innovator but a consummator. The clear enunciation of a principle long since made known had, however, become necessary because the undue importance attached to the law and to forms and ceremonies required correction. The distorted notion of the Pharisees and their way of life given in the Gospels may perhaps have been necessary for the Gentiles, but certainly not for the Jews. For the latter had expressed their disapproval of the Pharisees' religious excrescences often enough in innumerable contemporary utterances.

The appearance of a figure like Hillel was in itself an indication of the persistent viability of the religious life. In spite of severe external shocks, the process of formation had not been checked, and every party, including that of the Sadducees, was contributing towards it. It is to this century that we owe the Psalms of Solomon, religious poems of an age of unrest. Their lamentations over the sufferings of the time lead up to pious hopes for the future and the expectation of a royal Messiah of the house of David. They bear clear indications that their author had learnt the lesson of history, for in them the Messiah is once more depicted as a functionary of the theocratic idea. "The Lord Himself is our King, now and for evermore." They look to His sending down the just executor of His will. "In His day there shall be no injustice, for all the people will be holy." The defensive struggle against Rome had not as yet so narrowed the outlook of the people as to leave no room for a highly imaginative development of the idea of salvation. To the Jews their fate was so pregnant with meaning, so deeply rooted in the order of the universe, and so far removed from all idea of accident or the envy of the gods, as in the case of Greece and Rome, that they could envisage even disintegration only as part of that universal scheme of things implicit in this world, and as the transfiguration of man in a new community and a new realm. The nature of this realm became the subject of wild conjectures, visions, and hopes, tinged at times with magic. The Essenes, far removed from this life, and no longer reckoning with it at all, turning their eyes not to the world, but away from it, peopled the road to heaven, or to the kingdom that was to come, with hosts of angels and demons. Now for the first time there appeared the doctrine of the mediator between God and man—the Son of Man, or the Son of God, different expressions for the same idea. In any case they both amounted to a confession of the fact that direct relations between God and man had been broken off through weariness, despair, and estrangement from the world, and that reconciliation through a mediator was necessary. This introduced an idea quite alien to Jewish thought, according to which even the priest had never been a mediator; for the Babylonian captivity had already shown him to be not indispensable in that capacity.

If visionary eschatological principles were already to be found in the utterances of an Ezekiel, a Zechariah, and a Daniel, they became even more clear and pronounced in a book which was the product of this period, the Book of Enoch, a work which, with its mixture of Pharisaic and Essenic elements, is also typical of the heroic age and of spiritual heroism. For, from the spiritual point of view, it was indeed heroic in times of such acute distress to emphasize belief in the unconditioned, and not only to escape becoming brutal and besotted as the result of physical slavery and spiritual oppression, but also to conceive of the ultimate liberation of the soul and to raise this belief to the plane of a dogma of their creed. In the midst of anarchy and the most unscrupulous acts of political violence, the idea of human free will was maintained. "Sin was not sent into the world; man created it out of himself." Euripides, on the contrary, says: "Man may sin if a god so wills." It is not surprising that Christianity honoured the Book of Enoch with so many elaborations and interpolations; for in it lay the seed of its own beginnings.

But it was impossible in that age for even the most unworldly ideas to resist the assaults of reality, and the time came when hostile pressure became so brutal and overpowering that one and all, even the most passive and yielding, were driven to adopt an attitude of resolute self-defence. The events which led to this crisis were of harrowing uniformity. The same situations were repeated again and again, and the Jews were ill-treated with an extraordinary refinement of cruelty and stupidity. They retaliated with every means in their power, even resorting to assassinations and acts of the most foolhardy bravery, which revealed that clarity and reason had been suspended and that the *idée fixe* of resistance had taken its place.

The Roman administration had its headquarters at Cæsarea, where the troops, on which Rome chiefly relied for administering her provinces, were concentrated. Judea still enjoyed a certain degree of autonomy at home, particularly in the sphere of religion, though even here the Roman procurators made their power felt. This they did partly in order to annoy, as, for instance, when they insisted on keeping the high priest's vestments in the Tower of Antonia and producing them only when they were wanted. But their attitude was also partly due to lack of understanding; for, as undisputed conquerors of the world, they failed to see any point in the extreme importance which this absurdly insignificant nation attached to its own peculiar religious beliefs. For example, the emperor's head could not be used on Jewish coins, for, if it had been so used, the people would have refused to handle the money; and the Roman troops were not allowed to expose to public view in Jerusalem any standards bearing the image of the emperor. True, the Jews professed their readiness to offer up sacrifices for the emperors and the Roman people in the Temple, but declared that, if a Roman or any other Gentile set foot within the inner court of the Temple, he would be punished with instant death. These were all conditions which the Romans could only interpret as due to contempt and disloyalty. And they retaliated with contempt and oppression. At all the chief festivals the procurators repaired to Jerusalem with their troops and posted them in the outer colonnades throughout the celebrations. This they did not only because they expected disturbances at such times, but also because they knew that one of the uses to which the Jews put their Temple was to stiffen the will of the people and to organize disturbances and revolts. Moreover, they regarded the native population as their legitimate prey to be exploited for their own enrichment. Even

Tacitus acknowledges that the country had already been drained dry by the time of the first procurators.

The first procurator inaugurated his period of office by taking a census and making a list of all the landed estates, a proceeding which opened the eyes of the people to the extent of their dependence, and immediately gave rise to disturbances. But, whereas in Jerusalem reason prevailed once more, in Galilee, the hotbed of revolution among the Jews, there arose by way of protest a party which was destined to play an extremely important part in the future—the Zealots, the extremists and fanatics of political liberty. They differed from the Pharisees of all shades of opinion, not by reason of any religious doctrine, but because they maintained that the country could not wait for God's help or the coming of the Messiah. It must help itself. In the Zealots, the hatred of the materialism and brutality of Rome became a mania, and they ran amuck in their defence of the national idea against the assaults of violence. This was the only attitude it was possible for them to assume towards Rome. When Greece had encountered Judea, she had at least wished to bestow something—culture, religion, thought, a way of life, and artistic ideals. But Rome had nothing to offer, except citizenship. On the strength of exaggerated notions of imperialism, all she did was to make demands, insisting on subordination and above all on contributions in money. In due course the worship of the deified emperors was also insisted upon, an idea which originated in the crazy brain of Caligula. The Judeans had not the smallest reason to admire the political gifts of the Romans and their powers of organization as desirable qualities. Since their politics consisted wholly of the exercise of power for selfish ends, and their organization merely served the purpose of deriving every possible advantage from the power they wielded, there was no point in coming to any spiritual understanding with them. Not only among the Jews, but also throughout the Gentile world, matters of far greater importance were arousing interest at this time—the problem of man's place in the universe, for instance. But such things were beyond the comprehension of Rome.

The various procurators were almost without exception men of inconceivable cupidity and violence, who proved the constant cause of disaffection and unrest. Conspicuous among them was the Pontius Pilate of the Gospels, whose tenure of office was characterized by such exaggerated brutality towards the people under his care and such high-handed despotism, that it was only the tendentious spirit of the Gospels that caused him to have been credited with having washed his hands of all responsibility for the blood of Jesus. He held the religious scruples of the Jews in peculiar detestation, and, in order to irritate them, he made his troops leave Cæsarea and enter Jerusalem by night carrying standards which bore the image of the emperor on them. When this insult was discovered the next day, a deputation at once set out for Cæsarea to demand the removal of the standards. For five days the deputation besieged Pilate's house, whereupon he enticed them into the arena, surrounded them with troops, and threatened them with death if they persisted in their demand. But they only protested the more loudly, and Pilate ordered his troops to advance. The Jews dropped silently to the ground and bared their necks in readiness for the swords of the soldiers. In the face of such resolution, Pilate, becoming afraid, gave way and ordered the standards to be removed. But he made another attempt to impose his will, and put up shields inscribed with the emperor's name in Herod's palace. But even this suggestion that the emperor was an object of veneration led to a protest on the part of the people being lodged with the emperor himself, and the shields had to be removed.

Disagreements based upon religion grew more pronounced when Caligula ascended the throne. In him the Roman consciousness of power undoubtedly developed into megalomania. Augustus had been content to have his step-father Cæsar deified by the Senate, but Caligula insisted upon being deified in his own lifetime and being worshipped as a god. To bestow divine honour upon any man, emperor or no emperor, had always been alien to Jewish thought, and they refused to grant the title to a Roman emperor who, in any case, was a man of exceptionally feeble endowments. Caligula ordered Petronius, Proconsul of Syria, to set his image up in the Temple at Jerusalem. And very rightly suspecting that resistance would be offered, he gave him two extra legions. The Judeans sent a deputation to Petronius to inform him that he would only be able to set up the image when there were no Judeans left alive to see it. Thus warned, he continued his journey to Jerusalem with considerable trepidation; but he was bound to carry out his orders. When he arrived at Tiberias, demonstrations took place and lasted for forty days, during which the people even gave up tilling the land. A deputation was also sent from Jerusalem with the object of urgently warning him, and the result was that he took the responsibility on his own shoulders and refrained from carrying out his orders.

The Romans were only capable of appreciating such threats of immediate insurrection; they could not understand the meaning of this stubborn resistance. The Judeans persisted, however, because they saw that, if they once gave way on the question of forbidding the use of images in their religious observances, it would be the beginning of the end! For a thousand years or more they had been witnesses of the fate that had overtaken both themselves and their neighbours whenever images of the gods had been used in religious worship. It had always led to disaster, to the extermination of a type, due to and expedited by the fact that the worship of idols can never lead to that clear spiritual vision out of which a life which rises above the purpose of each individual existence can be built up and established on a sure and lasting foundation.

For a short period the Jews had respite from the rule of Rome, when Claudius made Agrippa I, a grandson of Herod, King of Judea in return for important services rendered on the occasion of his accession. It soon became clear, even to this last member of the house of Herod, what the country was suffering from and what a mine of energy lay ready to explode at his feet. He did his best to calm the people and to rule them in accordance with their wishes. But he died in the fourth year of his reign, just when his nationalist policy was beginning to meet with unfavourable comment in Rome.

After this brief spell of peace, conditions became worse than ever. Under the new procurators, the most insignificant incident inevitably led to bloodshed, and the least sign of resistance was treated with the utmost severity. Thus relations between the Jews and the Romans grew more and more strained, and Messianic manifestations took place. Under the Procurator Fadus, a visionary named Theudas succeeded in making huge crowds follow him to the banks of the Jordan to witness his miracles. As the Romans could not understand such examples of religious exaltation except as part of the general political unrest among the people (and they were fundamentally right), Fadus had the miracle seekers arrested, and many were killed or executed.

In spite of the horrors perpetrated by both sides, worse was in store. The names of the three procurators, Felix, Albinus, and Florus, represent a steady crescendo in vindictive and unscrupulous brutality. Of Felix, Tacitus says: "He exercised the prerogatives of a king with the spirit of a slave, rioting in cruelty and licentiousness"; and of Albinus: "There is no crime that he did not commit." But compared with Florus, a Greek by birth, his predecessors were decent upright men. Under his rule thousands of Judeans left the country, and, to make up for this loss of objects of plunder, he allowed thieves and robbers to go unpunished provided they shared their spoils with him and his agents.

Violent persecution of the Zealots forced them to go to fatal extremes. The hotheads among them formed themselves into a body known as the Sicarii, or dagger bearers, who not only constantly wreaked their revenge on the Romans by means of secret murders but also endeavoured by similar means to force reluctant Judeans to adopt active hostile tactics against Rome. In the face of this organization, the secrecy of which made it possible only to apprehend individuals, even the procurators were powerless.

The rule of Florus eventually led to the general insurrection which had been simmering for many years, and ultimately to the outbreak of the War of Liberation. The immediate cause of the upheaval lay in events in Cæsarea, where differences of long standing between the Greeks and the Jews led to fighting and bloodshed. Florus, when called upon to intervene, refused, although he had already accepted bribes to do so; instead he demanded further huge contributions to the imperial treasury, but it was a matter of common knowledge that the money was used for gratifying his own insatiable greed. The people, mad with rage, sent hawkers with baskets through the streets of Jerusalem begging for pennies "for poor, unfortunate Florus." Florus himself arrived on the scene with troops to wreak his revenge, and in May of the year 66 of the Christian era, he held a regular court-martial and had many Jews crucified. But now the popular indignation could no longer be controlled. The people flew to arms, attacked the Roman troops, and drove them back into the palace. Florus escaped responsibility by taking flight. This marked the outbreak of the War of Liberation.

The decision to undertake this war, in which an insignificant and, from the military point of view, wholly unorganized nation made up its mind to fight the rulers of the world, forced to a head those basic party differences which, in an age of general disintegration, when passions ran high, were in any case apt to involve cruelty and bloodshed. Moreover—and in view of the religious movement then on foot, this is important—the intellectuals among the Jews, who might have headed the forces of resistance, and directed the ideas and moulded the opinions of the public, had been exterminated or forced to leave the country, or else held aloof from any participation in public affairs. In these circumstances the question, Is it to be war with Rome or not? led temporarily to civil war. The upper city, occupied by those who were against war, and the Temple together with the lower city, occupied by the Zealots, fell to fighting each other. The Zealots were supported by the Sicarii, and their first act in Jerusalem was one which so often in history has been symbolic of revolution—they burned down Agrippa's palace, the home of the last of the Herods, and destroyed the archives containing the records of debts. Whereupon in August of the year 66 they stormed the Tower of Antonia and put the whole of the Roman garrison to the sword. Cestius Gallus hurried up with his legions and Agrippa II's auxiliary forces to punish the insurgents, laying waste everything as he went. The Zealots marched out to meet him, defeated his advance guard, occupied the passes, and demoralized his troops. Pulling himself together, Cestius made a fresh start and, overcoming all obstacles, attacked the upper city. But so determined was the defence that he was obliged to retire. The Zealots pursued him. His rear guard was cut to pieces, and the main body of his army was attacked and almost completely annihilated in the gorges of Bethhoron by the Zealot leader, Simon bar Giora. All his engines of war were also captured.

After this there could be no turning back, and party differences were sunk for the time being. The first step towards organizing the War of Liberation was the formation of a provisional government, in which even the passive Pharisees, the aristocracy, and the Temple priests were represented. A mass meeting was also called at which leaders were elected to organize the defence of the various districts. The man chosen for the important revolutionary centre of Galilee was Joseph, son of Matthias, better known as Josephus, the historian.

His election was a fatal mistake, and may have been chiefly responsible for the various disasters that brought the War of Liberation to a close. A member of the Pharisee intelligentsia, he had spent some years among the Essenes and had also been to Rome. As an enthusiastic admirer of Rome's political genius, he was too dispassionate not to weigh the chances of success coolly; with the result that, from the very beginning, he was a lukewarm supporter of his country's cause. In fact, he may be regarded as the first member of the Jewish faith who was self-consciously a Roman citizen. This dualism probably accounts for the equivocal part he played in the war. Even if we have to admit that in him cool calculation was bound to gain the upper hand of patriotism, it is still impossible to regard him as anything but a passive traitor. He had under him a national militia of 100,000 men, but owing to hesitation, incapacity, and lack of enterprise he frittered it away. As a result, when in the year 67 Vespasian, the greatest general of the day, was entrusted with the conduct of the war against Judea, Galilee was unable to offer adequate resistance. Vespasian mustered his forces in Antioch, while his son, Titus, joined him with legions from Alexandria. Altogether there must have been 60,000 regulars in Ptolemais. With these Vespasian was able to overrun Galilee, and Josephus was obliged to retreat. The main body of the Jewish army sought refuge in the mountain fastness of Jotapata, where Josephus joined them. After a siege lasting six weeks, the fortress capitulated, and forty of the survivors, among them Josephus, resolved to kill each other rather than surrender to the Romans. Josephus, however, contrived that the order in which the mutual slaughter was to take place should be decided by lot, and thus succeeded in escaping with his life. But possibly it was fate that spared him, so that at least there might be somebody to write the history of the Jews during this period.

After superhuman efforts and terrible slaughter, continued on boats and rafts on the Lake of Tiberias, the Romans captured Tarichea and Gamala. When the latter place was stormed, the survivors of the Jewish garrison flung themselves into the gorges rather than surrender to the Romans.

The heavy fighting had so exhausted the Roman troops that Vespasian was obliged to take them into winter quarters. Meanwhile the final party conflicts took place in Jerusalem. Events in Galilee had convinced the Zealots that the participation of the aristocracy in the War of Liberation had merely served to hamper the whole movement and burden it with an unreliable and irresolute factor. The conflict in Jerusalem ended in the complete and relentless extermination of the aristocracy. John of Giscala became master of the capital, while in the provinces Simon bar Giora was supreme. The rivalry between these two men led to fierce fighting inside Jerusalem itself, and it was only on the very eve of the siege that they sank their differences in order to defend the city.

The situation of the Jews was desperate from the beginning. Only a few of the defenders were trained in arms, and the city was overcrowded owing to the numbers of pilgrims who had flocked thither for the Passover celebrations of that year (70). In the party conflict vast stores of foodstuffs had been burned, and the remainder had to feed over half a million people. Against them they had in the Roman army professional troops supplied with the most perfect and up-to-date equipment. The attack was opened by four legions and large bands of auxiliaries. Titus's offer to accept the voluntary surrender of the city was rejected, and both sides fought with exceptional ferocity, making full use of engines of war. The attack, as usual, began on the north. After a fortnight's fighting the wall fell. But behind it the Romans were suddenly confronted by a second wall. The fighting grew fiercer than ever, and continued without interruption night and day. The second wall was taken by storm, lost, and taken again. Whereupon the four legions attacked the upper city and the Tower of Antonia. So determined was the resistance, that Titus again endeavoured to secure a voluntary capitulation, using as his go-between Josephus, who was in the Roman camp with him. But Josephus was howled down. And although the city was in the grip of famine, the people refused to yield. Many noncombatants were driven out of the city by hunger, but the Romans sent them back with their hands cut off, hoping that this would undermine the morale of the inmates; or else they crucified them before the walls in such vast numbers that before long there was no wood for the crosses, and no space left in which to set them up.

When all the preparations had been made for the final assault, John of Giscala made a sortie through underground passages, and destroyed all the entrenchments and siege works of the enemy. Whereupon Titus came to the conclusion that he could take the city only with the help of a dangerous ally—famine. He therefore built a stone wall all around it and posted sentries to prevent anyone from leaving.

This method was successful. Inside Jerusalem the people died like flies, and the city was full of the stench of rotting corpses. Having prepared the ground in this way, Titus was in a position to attempt storming the fortress. He destroyed the walls of the Tower of Antonia. But the half-starved defenders had meanwhile built another behind it. When at last this wall also fell, the defenders retreated to the Temple and converted it into a fortress. Once more Titus tried to persuade the remainder of the garrison to capitulate. Only a few priests surrendered, and the fighting continued. The besieged then laid a trap for the Romans, and lured them into a blazing furnace they had prepared. Titus retaliated by setting fire to the colonnades of the Temple and forcing the Jews to retreat to the inner courts. On the 10th Ab (August 29th or 30th) of the year 70, while the Jews were making a sortie, firebrands were hurled into the Temple, and it was burnt to the ground. The Romans proceeded to indiscriminate slaughter, and many Jews who could not bear to witness the destruction of their sacred treasures flung themselves into the flames. A little handful of survivors under John of Giscala managed to escape to the upper city, which was defended by Simon bar Giora.

In view of the almost impossible task of carrying on the defence with half-starved men, whose morale, moreover, had been rudely shaken by the destruction of the Temple, the leaders asked to be allowed to withdraw honourably. But Titus insisted upon unconditional surrender. This was refused, and the fight continued. In September of the year 70 the legions succeeded in forcing their way into the upper city, where they killed every living thing they met. Half-starved bodies lay piled up in heaps. The city was set on fire, but the fighting continued in the underground passages. All that remained standing among the ruins were three towers of Herod's palace, and a wall, the Kotel Maarabi, which the faithful maintained was a remnant of the Temple wall.

The victors celebrated the defeat of the little country with elaborate banquets and gladiatorial shows, in which many thousands of Jewish prisoners were killed, whilst others were exhibited in the great triumph, in which Titus appeared with the vessels plundered from the Temple. Simon bar Giora was executed in front of the temple of Jupiter Capitolinus, while the war booty, consisting of the Temple vessels, was placed in the temple of the Roman "Goddess of Peace."

It took nearly three years after the fall of Jerusalem to clear the country of the last remnants of Jewish troops and insurgents, and to capture the three fortresses of Herodeion, Machærus, and Masada. In

Masada, the fanatics swore they would never surrender, and when, after prolonged fighting, the Romans at last took the place, they found only two women and five children alive inside. All the rest had committed suicide.

Vespasian declared Judea to be conquered territory and his own personal property, which he proceeded to distribute among the Romans and Greeks, his own veterans, and any survivors that remained. In commemoration of his victory, he had special coins struck, bearing the inscription: "*Judaea devicta, Judaea capta*" (Judea conquered, Judea captured). As a Roman he was justified in using these words, for he grasped only the external significance of the events that had taken place. But, as it happened, he had not succeeded in destroying the spirit which could not surrender to any spirit less sublime than that which inspired the War of Liberation.

ALIENS

THE ten tribes, the first large body of Jews to be carried into captivity, had vanished without leaving a trace. They had been people who had not reached their final stage of development and were therefore incapable of determined resistance to environment. The second captivity, the Babylonian, consisted of men who were spiritually fully equipped, and consequently their numbers did not diminish. But as though the Jews had had a presentiment that one day their centre of concentration would be finally destroyed, and fresh places of refuge would have to be found, there also sprang up outside the country, that is to say, scattered about in foreign lands, a network of settlements, and a chain of Jewish quarters, centres of communication, houses of prayer, communities, schools, and connexions of all kinds, which together made up what is generally known as the Diaspora or *Galuth*. It was chiefly the determined hostility of the surrounding peoples that created these new centres. In Babylon the Jews arrived as captives taken from a conquered country. They first entered Asia Minor and the Ionian Islands as slaves, while Pompey took them to Rome as prisoners of war. Even in their historic refuge, Egypt, they arrived in the time of the first Ptolemies either as prisoners of war or as fugitives from their own country. But, from being victims of some superior power, they always succeeded in struggling up to a state of comparative freedom. Their consciousness of self, which took its root chiefly in the conviction that spiritually they were a peculiar people, endowed them in every situation, at every moment, and in every place with a buoyancy which prevented the loss of their personality. But for this preparation of the outside world by Jews already scattered abroad, the dispersal of the national kernel in Palestine would probably have meant the death of the people and their idea. Like Babylon of yore, Egypt was now ready to fulfil her historic mission. Babylon had saved the nation, but Egypt saved the idea by creating access for it into the outside world.

The first Jewish settlement in Egypt probably dated from the time of the fugitives who escaped thither from the Assyrian invasion. Be that as it may, the Judeans who with Jeremiah left their country after the destruction of Jerusalem in 586 B.C. found many Jewish communities already settled there. They enrolled themselves as a separate military corps in the frontier defence force formed on the Island of Elephantine (Yeb) out of Egyptian, Syrian, Greek, and Jewish mercenaries for protection against the attacks of the Nubians. They constituted a close community, grouped according to their several colours or standards; they led a secluded life and built their own temple, which was ultimately destroyed by an attack led by the Egyptian priests. There were various reasons for this. The Egyptians felt that the religious exclusiveness of the Jews showed that they despised and spurned their own form of faith; they also included the Jews in their hatred of their suzerain, Persia, for the Jews naturally defended the Persians, who had helped them to restore their state. Other causes of hostility were the determination shown by the Jews not to become assimilated with the Egyptians, their secluded life, and the fact that among themselves they used a language of their own, and their deep and unchanging devotion to Jerusalem.

These were points of difference in which the whole problem of the Diaspora was already implicit, and which recur again and again, slightly modified according to time and place. The fundamental difficulty was that the Jews could not possibly become entirely assimilated with the people about them or identify themselves wholly with the country of their adoption. Their interests were always determined by the fate of their people as a whole; in the first place by the kernel of the nation, the Judean state, and, after its downfall, when the Diaspora became a world phenomenon, by every event in every country that had anything to do with the Jews. The profound spiritual necessity of keeping in touch with every branch of the nation, the call for loyalty towards every group of their own people, however fragmentary, was bound to affect the integrity of their citizenship of a particular state. The reluctance of the people among whom they lived to grasp their attitude of loyalty towards the Jews as a whole, as well as a frequently exaggerated political pride and sense of nationality and patriotism, made the Jews feel they were strangers with inferior rights, and resulted in the adoption of a haughty attitude generally associated with those who have a definite country or even territory of their own.

After the conquest of the country by Alexander the Great, the Egyptian Jews concentrated themselves where they could keep in touch with life and the world, in that capital of mushroom growth—Alexandria, where they soon appropriated a whole quarter to themselves. Here they found a new means of livelihood ready to hand; for, with the constant influx of Greeks, travellers of all descriptions, and merchants, they could engage in an occupation with which, owing to the social structure of their people, only very few of them had hitherto been connected, namely commerce. And it was not long before the Greeks and the Jews, between whom there was constant rivalry, gained control of the whole trade of the East.

But the chief attraction of Alexandria, as far as the Jews were concerned, was the fact that it brought them into contact with Greek civilization. We described the similar phenomenon in Judea as the encounter of the Jews with the Greek *as man,* but here, where conditions were very different, it might legitimately be called the encounter with Greek *culture* or Greek civilization simply. They were now confronted with all that was best and worst in the Hellenic world, and from the process of giving and taking, attraction and repulsion, spiritual absorption and deadly hostility, there arose reciprocal effects of outstanding importance both for Judaism and the world at large.

This came about owing to the fact that in this Diaspora the problem of existence for the Jews was very different from what it had been in Judea. The idea of the theocracy had in Judea constituted the central problem both for the country and for the people. But now that the homeland, the land of their ancestors, tradition, historical unity, and communal life within a state no longer existed, or were merely matters of memory and sentiment, the idea of theocracy became a problem for the personal conscience, to be treasured in the heart of the individual and solved as he thought fit. Thus in Egypt all questions, from the simplest detail of daily life to the mystery of the origin of existence, could be discussed between man and man, or between one intellectual group and another, whereas Judea had only been able to defend her heritage, rebel, and fight. Though Judea might contemn, Alexandria saw in the intellectual culture of the Greek world of that day, in Alexandrianism, a flowering though possibly somewhat overblown blossom. It was for this reason that some Jews applied themselves strenuously to the study of this new world. They knew the Academy of Plato as well as the Lyceum of Aristotle. They were as much at home in the "garden" of Epicurus as in Zeno's "Stoa." And in Stoicism more particularly they found an ethico-philosophic system akin to their own.

The most curious feature of this encounter was that both parties claimed to have conquered the other. But whereas the Jew was essentially persuasive, the Greek, after a brief interval which he required in order to be able to discover the Jew as a fact at all, quickly assumed an aggressive attitude. At first it appeared as if the Jew were destined to be the only receptive, and therefore the defeated party. He was influenced in two extremely important respects; in the first place in the matter of language. In a few generations Aramaic was so completely ousted by Greek, that the Jew could no longer understand his sacred or profane literature in the original tongue. This loss of the primitive national vernacular, however, led to a twofold gain. In the first place it became necessary for the Jews to translate their literary heritage, and above all the Bible, into Greek, the direct result of which was that the principles of Jewish monotheism spread through the whole of the Hellenistic world. Secondly, the Hebrew language by being confined to the Holy Scriptures, acquired an odour of sanctity, and developed into the "sacred tongue." Thus it was much more securely safeguarded than if it had been a common vehicle of expression, and was able subsequently to constitute one of the secret spiritual bonds which held the Jews of the Diaspora together.

Moreover, mastery of the Greek language and intimacy with Greek ways of life, together with the growing interest in commerce resulting from the emulation of the Greek merchants, to a great extent mitigated the hardships of transplantation for the Jews; this was the second respect in which Greek influence made itself felt. However far the Jews were scattered throughout the Greek world, they were in familiar surroundings at least where material matters were concerned. But in addition to this an adaptation which is generally associated only with the individual applied to them as a people. When once they began to move and had succeeded in tearing themselves away from their centre of attraction, constant change of place and scene became a familiar experience to them. And it was along the tracks of this widespread Diaspora that Pauline Christianity was able to conduct its propaganda.

The Jew showed far greater readiness to exchange his spiritual possessions than did the Greek, which is comprehensible enough in view of the psychological position of the two peoples. The Jew had a safe anchorage in his traditions, and relying on this felt he could indulge in new thoughts and sensations, which might appear too worldly and unorthodox in the eyes of strict members of his race at home. But the Greek had no such unifying anchorage. Just as his gods had sprung up in different parts of his native land and its colonies abroad, so did his individuality find footing now here, now there, clinging to various masters, schools, systems, and cults. He could bestow his allegiance as he pleased. Consequently his allegiance was a matter for himself alone, and not, as in the case of the Jew, for the community as a whole. But the Greeks at least had this much in common—they all suffered from the religious unrest which in that age of mature development shook the world like an earthquake. Dying gods are more terrible in their last agony than in the heyday of their semi-human power. And in this Alexandrian period the Olympians were beginning to grow uneasy and to writhe beneath the pressure of a strange and astonishing idea. This idea was Jewish monotheism, communicated through the Greek translators of the books of the Bible and through the new Jewish literature which had just come into being in Alexandria.

The Greeks discovered the Jews in somewhat the same manner as people discover a race of pygmies in a virgin forest. Hecatæus was one of the first to attempt to describe them in his *History of Egypt*. His statement of historical facts is incorrect, but he does his best to explain why they were so strange, so thoroughly un-Greek in their morals, outlook, mode of thought, and exclusiveness. The next authentic work, the *History of Egypt* by the Hellenistic Egyptian priest Manetho, though a mass of confusion from the historical point of view, is quite consciously tendentious. According to him the ancient Israelites were the lepers of legend, who under a Pharaoh named Amenophis were forced to work in the Egyptian quarries. He placed Moses in the age of the Hyksos, the Semitic Shepherd Kings, and describes him as having obtained the upper hand in Egypt with the help of the latter and ruled there until he was banished. He declares that Moses was the originator of laws forbidding the worship of the Egyptian gods, and allowing the slaughter of their sacred animals.

This line of argument gives the burden of the objections afterwards brought against the Jews under different circumstances—they were foreigners with their eyes constantly turned to Jerusalem (after a time this no longer applied); they had their own peculiar religion and despised other forms of faith to which their laws and regulations proved them to be hostile. In fact their detractors could find nothing good to say about them or their origin, and the aim of all their statements was to slander them in every possible way. Manetho's example was widely followed by the Greeks; in this they must have been prompted by some deep psychological instinct, for whereas all the other peoples with whom the Jews had come into contact did not go beyond overt hostility of every kind and frank dislike, the Greeks had recourse to slander. It is not sufficient to point to their lively imaginations or their innate mendacity, of which history affords so many examples, as supplying the explanation. In the circumstances, slander was rather a spiritual weapon of self-defence. And for this reason, Greek civilization in its final phase, when it was on the eve of its death agony, encountered the very culture to which the futility of its own achievements and efforts inevitably made it most hostile. The foundations of its world, its religious substructure, were collapsing. The Stoa might have developed into a system, a doctrine, but it had failed to capture men's hearts or to produce a human community. Then suddenly there appeared before their very eyes a world which, in spite of the clumsiness of its external manifestations, was possessed of a powerful spiritual force. The critical situation of the ancient world became obvious as soon as it came into contact with that monotheism which the Jewish people alone had to offer it, in the shape, that is to say, of a living idea that could be realized on earth. Let us quote Harnack: "The Bible appeared eminently 'philosophical,' for it taught a spiritual principle, that of the Universal Father. It included an account of the creation which seemed far superior to all other similar accounts, and a history of primitive man which known traditions partly confirmed and partly explained. . . . In its Ten Commandments it set forth a code of law which, in its grandeur and simplicity, revealed the personality of a most sublime lawgiver. . . . Finally, owing to the inexhaustible wealth of its material, its variety, versatility, and scope, it was like a literary cosmos, a second creation, the twin of the first. . . . Among the Greeks . . . what produced the deepest impression was that this book and the universe seemed to belong to each other, and stood or fell together. . . ."

This appreciation of the impression made by the Bible is paralleled by an appreciation of its profound influence, how it gradually shook the man of antiquity, shattered his certainty in regard to his own possessions, relegated him to the limbo of doubt, and forced him to leave his own gods and beg for one God. He now learnt to know the monotheistic world, where there was no such thing as arbitrary fate, no blind subjection to capricious and unjust gods. For the first time, the pagan learnt what it was to believe and to mould his own destiny in accordance with all that was best and deepest in himself. His previous awestruck attitude, which had obliged him to regard himself as irredeemably relegated to the lowest place in the world and in the universe, was suddenly changed, and he found himself possessed of the right to consider himself a cosmic being, and to find a place for himself in the network of the universe. Whereas hitherto he had enjoyed, suffered, and endured, he was now in a position to experience life to the full and shape it. From a slave of the gods, he had become a free agent made in God's image, capable of giving and receiving. With the death of the pagan and his polytheism, a new man was born, and the road for Christianity was opened up. This birth dates from the translation of the Bible into Greek, which was then the universal language; and ever since, the putting of the Bible into a new form and language has always heralded a new age, the opening up of a new form of knowledge, and has provided explosive material for blowing up petrified forms of thought and belief. This has been proved time and again—by the Septuagint, by the Wycliffe and the Luther translations.

The Greeks rightly appreciated the danger menacing their world and took refuge in hostility and self-defence. In their anxiety to believe anything that would lend them strength and the power to resist, they had recourse to the last weapon of those in fear and dread—slander.

In keeping with the psychological development outlined above, the result of the encounter of Jew with Greek manifested itself in the Jewish world of thought in three ways—in an untrammelled outburst of creativeness, which was not unaffected by the spirit of Greek civilization; in apologetic writings defending the Jewish view of the world against Olympus; and in the aggressively proselytizing literature of the Roman-Alexandrian period, in which there was a conscious pitting of God against the gods, and of a moral life against philosophic systems.

Two works, which though they do not owe their origin to Alexandria were yet deeply influenced by the Greek spirit, stand out conspicuous in this age. Both were worldly productions, and both for the sake of effect—and also, perhaps, as a result of the glorifying power of memory—were attributed to King Solomon. They were the *Shir ha' shirim,* the Song of Songs, also called the Canticles, and the *Koheleth* (*koheleth* means literally, calling together), also called Ecclesiastes or the Preacher.

The Song of Songs, a duet between bride and bridegroom in the charming bucolic guise of shepherd and shepherdess, the form and embellishments of which betray the influence of Theocritus, the pupil of Callimachus, is undoubtedly a vivacious and vital piece of old Hebrew poetry, perhaps all that remains of the old love songs and epithalamia, which were never put into writing, and were lost because owing to the strictness exercised in choosing the canonical books they were rejected as profane. But the mellow perfection and maturity of feeling and expression in this song proclaim it to have been the fruit of long growth, the reflection of a world of emotion that actually existed, and not a mere isolated production. Its love making is both ardent and refined, in the wooing and in the resistance thereto; it is chaste in the subtlest sense; the poem is a solemn, softly ringing and gently vibrating recitative, as primitive and close to nature as the calling of the lovers themselves; it is a piece of nature and the cosmos, and as eternal as both. "For love is strong as death. . . . Many waters cannot quench love, neither can the floods drown it."

The other work, the *Koheleth,* is far removed from that happy world so eagerly accepted by those fresh from the experience of passion. In this work a man who has passed through the Greek schools of thought gives us the sum of his experiences of life and the world. He presents us with the answers he has received to the questions he has put to life and the forces that sustain him—reason, faith, joy, and abstinence. And the answer is a great negation, an attitude of scepticism with an undertone of restrained melancholy. He has been disappointed by everything—possessions, luxurious living, scientific study, and reason. Nothing has helped him to attain to peace and knowledge. Good exists and evil exists and the sun shines on them both. Often evil prospers and goodness comes to grief. Where is the law which makes for justice here? One thing alone is certain—at the end stands death which obliterates everything, equalizes everything, and makes everything of no account. No law can prevent death from carrying off rich and poor alike, the headstrong and those who strive after righteousness. Thought fails in the face of this harsh conclusion. And so it is best for a man to get all he can out of existence by exploiting his own gifts and the chances that come his way, and to give up worrying over problems. Let him enjoy life and not make it hard for himself. Epicureanism, not Stoicism! This was the mental attitude of a man long since permeated with the Greek spirit; that spirit which had lost all harmony, that no longer had any centre to which it could gravitate, and was therefore bound to cast doubt on everything. The following words from one of the choruses of the *Hercules Furiosus* of Euripides might have been taken straight from the *Koheleth*: "But between good and evil the gods have drawn no clear line and the rolling wheel of time only serves to heap up wealth."

Jewish thinkers of a later age were shocked and disquieted by this record of a negative spirit, and for nearly three hundred years they worked hard to try to discover some means of removing the sting from its denial of the love of life. And when it was ultimately included among the canonical books of the Bible, a chapter was added which amounted to an eleventh-hour recantation, and in which the author is supposed to remember the eternal verities. Thus at the end, out of the ruins of sceptical negativism, there arises a solemn and imposing acknowledgment of the idea of the immortality of the soul. "Then shall the dust return to the earth as it was; and the spirit shall return to God who gave it."

Between these original works, which served no set purpose, and the later apologetic literature, the translation of the Bible stands as the core and starting point of a tremendously powerful influence. The first five books, the Pentateuch, had already been translated by the middle of the third century B.C., and the translation of the Prophets and of the works that had been included among the canonical books at that time, the *Kethubim* (the Writings or Scriptures) occupied almost the whole of the second century B.C. We must now say a word or two about the translation, round which many a loving legend afterwards sprang up. Important though it was, we must not overlook its defects. On the one hand, the desire to produce an absolutely faithful Greek rendering of the Hebrew original led to the production of a number of obscure passages which the philologist alone can understand. On the other hand, the translation was undertaken with a definite object in view, that of making it comprehensible to the Greek; this led to the distortion and twisting of words, changes of meaning, and the frequent substitution of general terms and ideas for those that were purely local and national. Thus the obscurities in the translation provided material for many attacks in the controversies and disputes that arose between the pagan and the Christian world; and although this seizing on obscurities was comprehensible enough, it was a fundamentally dishonest practice.

The Jewish literature connected with the translation of the Bible forms the connecting link between the latter and the apologetic literature. It consists chiefly of historical works, glorified versions of Jewish history, full to overflowing with legends meant to illustrate the ideas underlying Judaism. Jason of Cyrene, who wrote the history of the Hasmonean wars in five books, adorns his narrative with tales describing the proud resistance of the Jews to the efforts made by the Seleucidæ to convert them, scenes full of a passionate certainty regarding his own religious possessions, and of a simple and grandiose acknowledgment of a man's duty to suffer even martyrdom for the truth in which he believes. Later writings reveal a more conciliatory and at the same time more complex attitude towards the Greek world. The Jewish philosopher, Aristobulus of Alexandria, a profound student of Greek literature and philosophy (who lived about 150 B.C.) wrote a book on the *Laws of Moses,* with the object of proving that all the doctrines of the Greek philosophers had long ago been known and recorded in the Scriptures. It was he who first introduced the method of making the Bible story clear and more familiar to the pagan or Greek world by means of picturesque interpretations and allegories.

A number of Jewish writers followed in his footsteps. Among them we may mention Eupolemus, who was responsible for the assertion that Moses invented the art of writing, that the Phœnicians learnt it from him, and the Greeks from the Phœnicians. Moreover, according to him, the whole of Egyptian wisdom—and this was a thrust at Manetho—emanated from the Jews. Their master had been Musæus, the teacher of Orpheus, and Musæus was none other than Moses. An aggressive note can already be detected here. But the Jews found a much more effective way of influencing the Greek world; they ascribed their own statements and writings to well-known authorities, and issued them under pseudonyms, in order to profit by the names and reputations of the famous. This led to the production of a mass of literature—the pseudepigraphic writings—which are not so much creative works as vehicles of expression in a controversy which necessarily became ever more specific, harsh, and offensive in character. The disputants even used the name of the Sybil, the prophetess of the Græco-Roman world, in both her Erythræan and Cumæan forms in connexion with their propaganda. A Jewish Sybil named Sabbe, or Sambethe, also made her appearance and her name was used to cover a number of works, of which the first were written by Jewish authors and had the object of holding up Jewish monotheism as an example to the pagan world, while the later ones were produced by Christian authors in defence of the dogma of the divinity of Christ.

Just as in the days when Israelitish monotheism was in process of development, the cults of Yahweh and of the local oriental divinities had formed themselves into a syncretic whole, so now the mythologies of Judaism and Greece were syncretized in order to enlist the sympathy and to give the idea of a common source in antiquity. But in each case the ultimate result was always the demonstration of the Jewish spiritual world, of one God, and of morality as the principle by which all life is moulded, as against the arbitrary nature of pagan superstition, which was disdainfully distinguished from the former, and sharply and ruthlessly criticized and refuted. While this propaganda, both in its essentials and its details, from time to time made concessions, it emphasized its own value and absolute superiority with undue pride and aggressiveness. It challenged the moribund pagan world to capitulate before the idea of monotheism.

Paganism clearly understood the challenge and, like men besieged in a fortress, it had recourse to all the guile and cruelty of war in defending itself; but all to no purpose. True, the Gentiles were informed that the revelation on Mount Sinai had been intended for all peoples and all ages, and that, as soon as the whole of mankind had submitted to the law of justice, the age of peace would be inaugurated for every nation in the world. But their primary objection was that they constituted the overwhelming majority, and that it was for the insignificant Jewish people to receive the law and not to lay it down for others. Undoubtedly most of them, and particularly the best, were, in their heart of hearts, longing for a haven of refuge in which their restless and excited spirits could find rest; but their worldliness was perhaps stronger in their communities abroad than in their ancestral home. For, away from the latter, differences were too sharply emphasized, since no communion with that which underlay all life widened their vision. And, wherever they went, the Jew was the enemy *par excellence,* in his way of life, his morals, his politics, his domestic arrangements, and his religion. There was nothing in their own natures and manner of life which was not diametrically opposed to the Jew. And thus it was impossible for them not to regard every manifestation of the Jewish world, no matter on what plane, as being directed against themselves and hostile to their interests. When, therefore, Roman power and influence also began to make themselves felt, an outburst of hatred, bloodthirstiness, and cruelty occurred, equalled only by the massacres which took place during the Crusades and the Cossack holocausts of the seventeenth century.

The ground was being similarly prepared for these conflicts in almost the whole of the Jewish Diaspora, where Jews constituted a minority among the Greeks. The Greek, though really an "immigrant" and a "foreigner" himself, was deeply prejudiced by the traditions of his city-state politics and petty urban interests, and regarded the religious autonomy of the Jews as incompatible with the general position of the citizen of a city, a province, or a country. All the Greek understood was: *cujus regio, ejus religio.* Moreover, the Jew had proved far too apt a pupil in commerce, and was essentially opposed to him in religion. Consequently throughout the Diaspora, and particularly in Syria and Asia Minor, conflicts due to this strained relationship broke out, limited at first to Greek attacks on the equal rights and autonomy enjoyed by the Jews, and to the energetic resistance of the latter. This problem had to be faced wherever the Jew made his appearance, and he covered a vast distance in a surprisingly short space of time. Even Strabo, the contemporary of Herod, declared that it would not be easy to find a single place on the face of the earth where there were no Jews. Except for Mesopotamia and Babylon, countries which could hold aloof from the influence of Greece and Rome, the common life of Greek, Jew, and Roman alike, and particularly of the latter, was dominated by an idea to which Cicero gives expression in his defence of Flaccus: Where Rome has conquered and established her rule, her laws prevail, even the laws of religion; not, forsooth, merely because she is the conqueror, but because the very fact that she has conquered proves that she is in possession of a superior religion, a superior faith.

The clash between Rome and Judea gave the signal throughout

the Græco-Roman world for the outbreak of conflicts arising from these strained relations. In rebelling against Rome, Judea rebelled against the whole of the pagan world. And it was only natural that the latter should take up the challenge. Once again, Alexandria set the example. When Caligula in his megalomania ordered that his images should be set up and worshipped, the Egyptian Jews refused, just as their brethren in Judea had done. Their religious autonomy justified them in adopting this attitude. This gave the Greeks the pretext for which they were waiting. Two demagogues, the gymnasiarchs Isidor and Lampon, constituted themselves the leaders of the people and the so-called executors of the popular will, and had the images of Caligula set up in the synagogues by force. The Jews smashed them to atoms. The Roman Præfect upheld the Greeks; he declared that the Jews, who at that time already numbered almost a million, were "foreigners and immigrants," deprived them of their religious freedom, and, on the plea that they had no right to be there, turned them out of the quarters of the city which they occupied. The Greek population shared in their forcible ejection, plundering, destroying, and killing. This was the first time that Anti-Semitism was put into practice, and it at once assumed all the features it was to have in later days—illegality, the refusal of judicial rights, provocative action on the part of demagogues and agitators, the fomenting of popular passions, brutality, robbery, and murder, and, of course, the religious argument—the refusal of the Jews to bow down before the image of the emperor—was also brought against them. In later days, changed circumstances altered the charge, according to the requirements of the moment, either to one of desecrating the Holy Sacrament, the murdering of infants, the crucifixion of Jesus, or the poisoning of wells, and the like. But it should not be forgotten that beneath it all the pagans were partly animated by horror at seeing their own world finally collapsing about their ears.

It is true that Claudius temporarily restored the *status quo ante*, and ordered the ringleaders together with the two demagogues to be executed. But naturally the differences which had led to the conflict still remained, and needed only the fresh pretext provided by the Jewish War of Liberation to come to a head once more. In Cæsarea, the Greeks retaliated by massacring nearly 20,000 Jews, and the Zealots retorted by calling upon their people as a whole to exterminate the Greeks. Mutual slaughter became the order of the day. Alexandria outdid the rest of the Diaspora by massacring some 50,000 Jews, and a further pretext was afforded the pagans by the destruction of Jerusalem. The fugitive Zealots carried undying hatred of Rome in their breasts and were prepared to bear it to the ends of the earth, as long as the breath remained in their bodies. On arriving in Alexandria, they tried to incite the Jews to an insurrection against Rome. The Roman authorities made many of them prisoners, and tortured them with the view of extorting from them an oath of loyalty to Rome. They preferred to die. Many fled to Upper Egypt. Vespasian, afraid lest they might succeed in forming a new centre of rebellion there, ordered the temple in Leontopolis to be closed. The Zealots then pushed on further and reached Libya, where they made a last desperate effort to stir up rebellion against Rome. The revolt was suppressed, and the Zealot leader, Jonathan, was burnt alive in Rome.

They all retained their freedom until the very moment of death. The survivors, who were definitely committed to a life in foreign lands, became the heirs of a fate which consisted in struggling against a hostile world and by pertinacity, sacrifice, and martyrdom securing freedom of thought for their race.

JESUS OF NAZARETH

OUT of the chaos of a national existence, which, in the face of a pagan world doomed to death, was itself painfully striving towards the extinction of its own external forms in order to gain eternal life; out of the anarchy of forces which laid bare the ultimate basis of spiritual possibilities in a community, accustomed for generations to live a strenuous and full existence; out of the heroism of body, soul, and spirit, there arose a twofold historical fact which was to influence the fate of whole worlds and millenniums—the life and work of Jesus of Nazareth and the creation of a new form of faith, Christianity. These two facts bear the same relation to each other as the typical does to the unique. That is to say, Jesus, in the power he exercised, the effect he produced, and the fate he suffered, was the embodiment of all that was best in the Jew of his day, if not in knowledge and science, or in patriotism, desire for freedom, and fidelity to type, at least in those qualities which could assuage the suffering and misery of the age, in compassion for all earthly creatures, in the pitiful conquest of suffering through calmness and love, and through the capacity for shunning the everyday life of men. The rise of Christianity, on the other hand, was a unique event, implicit in the requirements of the historical situation resulting from the state of Judaism and paganism at the time.

We shall therefore discuss Jesus *as a figure of Jewish history* irrespective of all theological or religious concepts, and Christianity only in so far as it remained a Jewish concern, and in later times, that is to say, until the present day, only so long as it made the Jew its butt and the object of its hatred and hostility.

The background against which the tragedy of the man Jesus was enacted was extraordinarily animated and full of colour. It was an age of unbridled passions and little joy, an age in which the individual, the state, and the faith were called upon to endure untold suffering owing to the terrible trials conditions imposed. The Jews have never been able to tear themselves away from their age, and at this particular period every aspect of their environment seemed to spell Nemesis for them. Although five hundred years had elapsed since the Babylonian captivity, they still felt as though they had only just returned. In Babylon their prophets had taught them their mission, and they had spent five hundred years in trying to fulfil it. Two hundred years after their return, when Ezra and Nehemiah were putting the finishing touches to their work of restoration, they had been suddenly confronted by Greek civilization, and the struggle for self-preservation began. They proved victorious. With the first achievements of the Hasmonean wars, they began to dream of the fulfilment of their mission. But it was a fond delusion, shattered first by Herod, then by Rome, and lastly by the whole giant force of paganism, which with its exaggerated assurance, in itself an indication of decay, was determined to destroy their last remnants of resistance. Their whole material and spiritual existence was at stake, and their extermination was decided upon just as they felt their goal was within reach.

In this conflict between hope and reality, endeavour and result, idea and violence, the centre of Judaism, which had never yet achieved stability but was at last striving to acquire a settled form, was burst asunder. All the potentialities which lay dormant in Judaism now found their expression, and that at first in an extreme form, in individuals, communities, groups, parties, and sects. Now that everything was at stake, everything was also possible. But even in this bursting asunder, this falling to pieces, the astounding vitality of Judaism was preserved. Everything that followed was the expression of a stupendous will to live, and even at this moment of dire collapse not a trace of resignation is to be found. Even the Essenes, who had withdrawn from ordinary existence with its organization and routine, were tired only of the practical considerations of life, not of life itself. They shunned the state because they knew that in so doing they were shunning struggle and violence. In this they were moved not by cowardice, but by the conviction that there was nothing more to be gained by remaining in the state. Their one aim was to concern themselves about their souls, though this did not make them wish to be relieved of their bodies. But as misery increased, and the last vestiges of freedom and human dignity were destroyed by the swords of the Herodians and the Romans, they conceived of the end of the Jewish community as the "End of Days" for the whole world, the dawn of an age in which other forces than those which had just failed would become effective. They renounced the kingdom of this world, and prepared themselves for the "Kingdom of Heaven." But the latter, too, was to be realized on earth, not in some vague beyond, for at that time the idea of the Kingdom of Heaven had nothing whatever to do with a celestial kingdom; it was merely a name for God, for Him in whom the Kingdom of Heaven was embodied, and which the people expected Him one day to establish on earth. They were simply consistent Pharisees, who cast their eyes back to the Nazirites.

Even those among the people who might be described as passive or moderate Pharisees had only lost faith in the *technique* of resistance, in resistance with violence; their belief in life, in the future, in the permanence and immortality of the nation was much stronger than ever. But, as the prophets had intended, they wanted their resistance to be spiritual resistance. They wished to save their nation by means of religious discipline, by spiritual measures of segregation, when the struggle demanded it, even at the cost of sacrificing the existence of the state itself, if it could not be achieved in any other way. While the War of Liberation was still raging, Johanan ben Zaccai, a disciple of Hillel, founded a college at Jamnia near Jerusalem, thus proclaiming the continuation of the struggle against the pagan world in a different sphere from the one he saw about to collapse under the assaults of Vespasian. As to the positive attitude of the Zealots and Sicarii, there is little more to be said. They were optimists to the point of desperation. They surrendered only in death.

This will to live, manifested in every shape and form by all classes and parties of the Jewish people, culminated in the firm belief common to all strata of the community, that the coming of the Messiah was at hand. Messianism was an essential doctrine of Judaism. Every Jew believed it. Even the Sicarii, who were bent on killing all Romans or friends of Rome, believed that they were committing murder for the sake of the kingdom that was to come, the Kingdom of God! Whether a man resorted to political murder or to contemplation, the idea was the same differently expressed.

Messianism was the central problem of the age. It did not make its appearance for the first time at this juncture, but merely manifested itself in different forms under the stress of the times. As an idea it had already been quite clearly indicated in the Book of Daniel, where, as so often happened in Jewish history, the world was interpreted in the light of what had already taken place. After the downfall of the four great world empires, Daniel, in his visions, saw the rise of a fifth, the Empire of the Messiah. This Messiah was not a personal Messiah but the Jewish people. Messianism, however, had already become a universal conception applied to the whole of mankind. The concept gained strength and became closely connected with the idea of the Jews being the Chosen People, the immortality of the soul, life after death, and the resurrection of the body—all of which were eminently controversial doctrines, particularly those of the immortality of the soul and the resurrection of the body, which were bones of contention between the Pharisees and the Sadducees. But the intensive religious life ultimately turned the scales in favour of absolute faith in them all. For in the conditions prevailing in Israel, particularly during the five hundred years after the Babylonian captivity, religious life meant much more than the mere observance of ritual laws and religious statutes; it was much more than a theology and a dogma. For dogma did not exist. There was no compulsion to believe anything, but only to act. That which was called "hedging round," and the outcome of which was the "Jewish religion," was a body of beliefs entirely related to real life, a national *Weltanschauung*, a culture and a philosophy, a juridical system, a solution of social problems, a system of natural science, a technique, and a practical morality. If out of all this there arose a religious idea, it was not a mere abstract idea, but was necessarily based on the realities of life, from which it had sprung, and was effective only in that connexion. Moreover, even out of the people's creative life, no religious thought could arise which they were not convinced was capable of realization. And this constitutes the conclusive reason why the overwhelming majority of the Jewish people repudiated and denied the doctrine of Jesus Christ, or rather that of his later interpreters, as of no use in practical life.

Thus, even the Messianic idea, universally held by the Jews, had to be conceived as capable of realization before it could mean anything to them. Some saw in the Messiah God's ambassador, who would free them from the yoke of Rome and restore the theocracy. Others regarded this as a side issue. For them the real importance of the idea lay in the belief that God, through the Messiah, would at last establish justice on earth. He would hold a great court at which the whole world would be judged, after which the Empire of Peace and the brotherhood of mankind would be founded on earth. This Messianism was still of this earth, and was awaiting the moment when the disasters of the age would be swept away in one great act of retributive justice and national vengeance. And even of this idea there were variations. The people all felt that they could no longer deal with the situation with their own strength alone, but that God must come to their help. But while some imagined they could actively expedite the end of time, and pressed towards it, others thought it better to make the spirit capable of resistance and to await the consummation.

Nevertheless, the manifold experiences and shocks of the age gave birth to a spiritual principle which led to a very definite modification of the Messianic idea; they led to individualism.

In dealing with the Babylonian captivity we called attention to the possible developments of Judaism to which the importance attached by the prophets to an individual attitude towards religion might lead. For the religious life of the individual to become free and liberated always indicates a substantial advance in the realm of the spirit. But, after all, the most important consideration for a religion which is not a private but a communal affair is the attitude of the individual to the community, to its mode of belief, that is to say, to the official collective faith. The greater the claim made on the individual and the deeper his religious consciousness, the greater becomes the possibility of his being entirely divorced from the collective fate. The Essenes were the first to take this step to individuality. But it is characteristic that they chose for the individualistic form of life the most intimate and closely knitted form of communal existence—communism. Another section of the people which tended to become ever more individualistic was that which in ordinary times consists of husbandmen, workmen, day-labourers, craftsmen, and artisans, for whom the endless wars and persecutions, devastations, burdensome taxation and requisitions, meant economic extermination. They were utterly ruined and done for. They no longer found any support, any hope for the future, or any comfort, in the community, in the state. Their only source of help was another man, a neighbour, provided, of course that he possessed anything and was willing to help. Instead of a social order, in which they could make their way, and instead of the charitable provisions for which the community, in accordance with the obligations imposed by the law of the Torah, should have been responsible, the only refuge was the sympathetic, compassionate individual. And thus the ideal type to come to their relief was the deliverer, the saviour, free from every social tie, whom God was going to send them for this purpose. He was in duty bound to send a deliverer. Their belief in the Messiah was, in the first place, connected with their private individual problems; but it was also a direct and necessary consequence of their unshakable belief in God. They became social revolutionaries through faith.

In addition to these, there was another class of people who renounced all worldly activities not so much from material as from spiritual distress. They were the quiet, weary, and peace-loving, who asked only for rest. They were entirely self-centred, and their one thought was for their own salvation.

Wherever the belief in a collectivity, in that form of existence which might be called the communal unit, is abandoned, and the people follow the path of the individual, of the individual let loose, so to speak, there is always a lack of reserve force; pride of ancestry has ceased to provide a safe anchorage, and the idea is deprived of the momentum which would have enabled it to shape the future. And whatever is lacking in power has to be compensated for by mysticism and a confident belief in a future which it will no longer be possible for anybody to control. Thus the Messianic idea is shattered, and a conception arises whereby the fulfilment of all hopes of compensation, justice, and peace is transferred from earth to heaven, which behind a screen of mysticism and ecstasy is far removed from the control of him whom it is to benefit—the living man.

In addition to these various conditions which constituted the spiritual basis of the age, there were the political disasters already described. The whole formed the general background, and play of forces in the background, against which the drama of Jesus was enacted.

Now what are the alternatives open to a man in such circumstances —no matter of what type you may imagine him to be? In any case they can be only those which the age has to offer him. He cannot invent or discover any others. And this is what Jesus by his life and death proved. In the description which we are now about to attempt, both space and the object of this work forbid our entering into any discussion regarding which narratives and records we consider historical or not, or giving any reason for the views we hold about them.

Jesus, the son of Joseph the carpenter and Mary his wife, was born in Nazareth in the reign of the Emperor Augustus, a few years before the beginning of our era. (He was afterwards said to have been born in Bethlehem because it became important to be able to trace his descent from David. But at the time the idea that the Messiah must be of the house of David had not been established.) He had four brothers and two sisters, and the family led the simple, industrious life of the people of Galilee. Galilee, and more particularly Nazareth, were far removed from the beaten track, and from the busy and inspiring atmosphere of Jerusalem, the capital. The province could not boast of much learning, and the people were all the more simple and unsophisticated, less obsessed by ideas, and very strong and primitive in all their reactions. In depth of religious feeling, they yielded to no one in Jerusalem, for all its scholars; but they were wont to settle many a question, which in Jerusalem would have led to a discussion, possibly a heated discussion, by resorting to revolt and the virile expedient of fisticuffs and fighting. Indeed Galilee was always the centre of insurrection and rebellion, and its inhabitants reacted with extraordinary strength and sensitiveness to the slightest encroachment on their spiritual or material liberty. And they did not stop at blows. Being simple and uncultivated, even their religious emotions were far from being animated by an unimaginative fidelity to the letter, but were endowed with a meditative and naturalistic quality and a depth of feeling upon which the serene and variegated beauty of their native land had left its stamp. And this accounts for the fact that among them many thoughtful seekers after God were to be found. There were also many whose spiritual powers were not equal to a constant state of fighting and rebellion. Their daily work, their poverty, the straining of their simple faith, the repeated shattering of their hopes of a change and of an end to their trials and tribulations, placed too heavy a spiritual and intellectual toll upon them, with the result that they became nervous wrecks whose powers of resistance were shattered. As the people were too ignorant to find any other explanation, they believed such persons were possessed of devils, and their cure became the everyday concern of anyone who chose to help them. They were accustomed to look to the Essenes to do this, or anybody else upon whom their fancy fixed.

They were constantly receiving offers of help, and willingly put themselves into the hands of those who felt that they could be of use, and pinned all their hopes on anybody whom they understood and who understood them. Such a man they would regard as their saviour, or Messiah. He was the Messiah for whom their spiritual and religious life had led them to look—the King-Messiah, the man who was to bring God, that is to say, the Kingdom of Heaven, to earth, whereby their mission as men and Jews would be fulfilled. But the expectation never got beyond the realm of faith, a goal to be striven for. The Romans and Herodians were lynx-eyed masters, and were well aware that at this juncture even the most religious of Messianic expectations, which did not, as in the case of the Essenes, declare itself to be wholly indifferent to the external world, was a real, creative, and earthly movement, and therefore represented a political menace. Consequently the leaders, saviours, and Messiahs were always suppressed by those in power, as soon as they made their appearance, and it was fatal to the progress of the age that it was always the leaders, and therefore the best and most intelligent, who were removed in this way. Time and again the people were disappointed, and fanatics were constantly appearing from their ranks. It was for this reason that Galilee in particular was the land of insurgents, fighters for freedom, robber bands, mystics, and hysterics or those possessed of devils, and that here, next to the sword, the miracle was given the place of honour as the instrument of divine power and deliverance. Like a mighty stream, gathering its forces from all directions, the fate of the age and of the people swept over Galilee, and all those of its inhabitants who had eyes to see and hearts to feel were aware of the vital current coursing through their veins.

In such circumstances, and at such a time, what therefore was a man to do who felt himself caught up in the grip of what was taking place around him and was conscious of playing a part in it? What if he could not allow the misery about him to leave him untouched and unresponsive? He was necessarily driven to acknowledge that such matters were his concern as an *individual,* and that as an individual, a *personality,* he was partly responsible for the state of affairs. The next step was to endeavour to get into touch with the whole; from which it followed that he eventually reached the conclusion that the fate of the community certainly depended upon his help. Whereupon all that was left for him to do, if he felt he had been called, was to discover the nature, the extent, and the strength of the summons. If he accepted it, he was morally bound to take action.

This is precisely what Jesus did. He was so completely the child of the Jewish life of his age, that it would only be necessary to write a history of the period, the country, and the people in it, in order to marshal all the details of his personality and fate. His peculiar tragedy lay in that part of his *personality* which failed to strike the right note in those whom he wished to serve and to save. The overemphasis of his personality, and the failure of the expectations, which he himself had awakened, led and could not help leading to the hopeless and tragic disillusionment of his followers. When the Messiah ceases to be a leader, a fulfiller, and a herald, and moved by exaggerated egoism aims at being an example and a reformer, his office falls to pieces in his hands. This constituted the tragedy of Jesus, and the turning point in his career. And, if we may be allowed to anticipate, this will constitute the keynote of our description of him.

We may conclude from his subsequent activities that Jesus, in early youth, was fairly well acquainted with the literature of his people. He had as profound a knowledge of the Torah as many a Pharisee. He also knew the prophets, the psalms, the Book of Daniel, and perhaps also the Book of Enoch. His intellectual range was that of the Jew of his time, and his spiritual range was certainly no wider, as is shown by the first momentous, stirring, and determining event of his life, his meeting with John the Baptist.

John the Baptist appeared about the year 28 in south Transjordania, on the Jordan, in Galilee, and in Peræa. He was a recluse, an ascetic of Nazirite tendencies and manner of life. He borrowed many of his principles from the Essenes. In fact he was a typical figure of the age, who was fully alive to the decadence of the times and heralded the downfall in the spirit of his day. "Repent, for the Kingdom of Heaven is at hand!" In the language of the period this meant, "Be done with half-measures and compromise! For the day is coming when God will send his perfect one to rule on earth!" It was for this reason that he told the people to carry on their daily work, to be kind to their neighbours, and not to allow their obligations to the law—this was a thrust at the Pharisees—to make them neglect their duty to man.

John did not in any way regard himself as the Messiah, but he was convinced that he was the forerunner of the Messiah, whom the people were expecting in the form of a reincarnation of the prophet Elijah. And this conviction, which implied a firm belief that the Messiah would make his appearance in the near future, lent extraordinary power and persuasiveness to his religious fervour and his preaching. Multitudes flocked to hear him, and went through the symbolic ceremony of baptism at his hands. It was a ceremony in common use among the Essenes, and also one to which the Pharisees subjected all proselytes. But John differed from the unworldly Essenes in not withdrawing into mystic inactivity. On the contrary he came forward urging men to follow him, and boldly advanced into the open, into the life of those about him, and took part in the controversies and political activities of the day. This proved his undoing. His public denunciation of Herod Antipas for marrying Herodias, a union which offended his strict interpretation of Jewish law, provided the pretext for his arrest, and, as his influence appeared to constitute a political menace, he was executed.

As one of the crowd that flocked to John the Baptist, Jesus, unknown and unnoticed by the latter, also came to be baptized by him. But whereas all the others piously made themselves the passive objects of the ceremony, Jesus, as the result of the deep emotions stirred by the symbolic act, made himself the central figure and participator in it. This cannot have been the result of a sudden impulse. It can only have been the culminating point of a long process of active development, and all that happened afterwards indicates what must have led up to it. All the forces within himself as well as all the forces of the age and country had led him to feel that he had been called to an office, to a mission. Like the preachers sent out by the Essenes, or those who felt driven to preach on their own account, he also went about preaching. He was, as he himself again and again declared, a rabbi, or one who had taken upon himself the task of strengthening the spiritual foundations of the people, so that they might be ready for the coming age; he felt he was responsible for preparing them. But he had no intention whatsoever of being an innovator, or even the destroyer of an old and the founder of a new religion. He would have regarded this as being entirely beyond the bounds of possibility and he never aimed at anything that seemed impossible to his age. He was merely a propagandist, and his teaching was pure Judaism. Even his diatribes against the Pharisees were but the counterpart of their own condemnation of excessive formalism and concern about outward observances and of their own attack on the theoretical intricacies of religion, in which severe and rigid ceremonial was growing ever more remote from all contact with actual life, until at length participation in religious worship and ritual meant that the living soul, the creature, was wantonly sacrificed to the slavish observance of rules and regulations. In this calamitous age, in which law was merely the framework and man with his burden of woe was all that mattered, any other attitude constituted a crime against the human soul and was rightly condemned. And this is what Jesus did. But the Pharisees did so too, and had nothing good to say of those of their followers who degraded their doctrines. They reviled them as the "Plague of the Pharisees," the *Ṣebuʿim,* the "painted ones," who were all surface show, that is to say, whitewashed with outward forms and ceremonies.

Thus it was unconsciously rather than consciously that the efforts of Jesus were directed towards relaxing the law by which men lived and were to continue to live and making it more a matter of the heart. And in this he was entirely guided by his instincts as a Galilean Jew, whose character has been described above. In this respect he followed in the footsteps of Hillel, and his teaching was entirely in keeping with the spirit of that great master, though his method was not that of a teacher of the law, of a scholar. He was a free and independent individual, who felt that he had received a call. Regarded from the point of view of the purity and nobility of his intentions, he may be said to have been, in the best sense of the word, a functionary of the theocracy, like the judges, the prophets, and, at least as far as their office, though not always their character was concerned, like the kings. And like the best of them, he was not spared the ordeal of that moment when the nature and scope of his mission were tested.

For Jesus, the whole gravity of the conditions in the age in which he lived were implicit in his meeting with John the Baptist. There in front of his very eyes stood the forerunner of the Messiah, the first or possibly even the last step towards fulfilment! The advent of the Messiah was a matter of days or at most a few years. The great day was at hand and it was high time for those whom it might concern to examine themselves with a view to discovering whether they had done all that lay in their power, or whether still further efforts might not be expected of them. It was incumbent on every man to look into his own heart and decide whether he was a rabbi, a teacher, or a fulfiller, a Messiah. This is what Jesus did. And to carry out his tests he withdrew into the wilderness, where the Essenes, and men like Elijah and John the Baptist had found strength for the eventual accomplishment of their mission.

The man who was to be the Messiah was expected at that time to have a threefold qualification. He was to be the King-Messiah, the destroyer of the pagan world, whose representative was now Rome. The terrible fate of those who had fought the War of Liberation did not encourage Jesus to choose this path, and it would perhaps have been unreasonable to expect him to do so, seeing that, like the moderate Pharisees, he believed in spiritual and not in material resistance. The second qualification of the Messiah was that he should be a great student of the Torah, in the sense in which Isaiah had been, that is to say, emotionally rather than intellectually. If it was not modesty that made Jesus repudiate the possession of this quality, it was at all events his recognition of the fact that the age in which he lived required understanding rather than knowledge, which the course of events had brought into serious disrepute. Thirdly, the Messiah was expected to establish a rule of peace and happiness on earth and to free mankind from sorrow for evermore. Implicit in this expectation was a firm conviction that unrelieved distress was an unfavourable basis for the free development of the soul. But to the thoughtful Galilean, brought up in poor and humble circumstances, with the example of John the Baptist, a penniless and ascetic recluse, before his eyes, such an idea did not appeal in the light of a life mission. And, as a matter of fact, when later on he and his disciples had wealthy supporters, more particularly women, he refused to take material problems seriously.

These three aspects of the Messiah were emphasized in the picturesque language and symbolism of the Gospels. And Jesus was forced to repudiate them all. That is to say, he did not feel that he had it in him to fulfil all three. The result of his self-examination took the form of resignation. He was silent, and for the next few years the records are also silent about him.

At last the news spread through the country that John the Baptist had been violently removed from the scene of his activities, with the result that the mission which he had taken upon himself had fulfilled its destiny in him. Whereupon Jesus suddenly appeared again and began preaching. What had happened meanwhile? Cautious historians aver that nothing had happened. We, on the other hand, maintain that everything had happened. For, like all profound experiences, what Jesus had gone through in the wilderness had been working subterraneously within him. Temporarily he seemed to have abandoned the struggle, but, as a matter of fact, his conflict in the wilderness constituted merely the birth-throes of a call, similar to those provoked time and again by the religious force of Judaism.

Probably not one among the prophets had been spared this decisive battle in his soul. In their heart of hearts all of them were filled with awe at the thought of their great mission. Even Moses before the burning bush protested, almost with tears of despair, against his summons. Nor did a man like Amos go forth willingly into the world as a herald. Only when he had felt the call repeatedly did he ultimately yield. "The lion hath roared, who will not fear? the Lord God hath spoken, who can but prophesy?"

Thus the early attitude of renunciation gave way to one of acceptance, and Jesus returned to Galilee. He did not resume his ordinary calling, however, but went about preaching with a definite, though for the time being secret, object in view. Like John the Baptist before him, he now endeavoured to obtain a following. Two pairs of brothers joined him, Simon and Andrew, and the sons of Zebedee, James and John. He wandered through the towns and villages and preached in the synagogues, and the people listened to him, as they listened to every rabbi who had something to say to them. But already a peculiar note could be detected in his preaching which at first did not seem to conflict in any way with the beliefs of the age, with the Messianic idea, or with the authority and binding force of the Torah. Apparently the peculiarity was merely one of form and language. As regards form, he had a special fondness for parables, the graphic clothing of moral ideas in simple similes. It was a plastic form which made a much deeper appeal to the hearts of the people than the learned prosiness of the Pharisees. The peculiarity of language consisted in the fact that, time and again, the antithesis and the thesis began with the words: "But *I* say unto you . . ." and that he constantly referred to himself as "the Son of Man."

But the latter expression was not really a mere peculiarity of language. It constituted a confession, a secret confession, but yet a confession that he was the Messiah. Otherwise it is impossible to understand why he began preaching again. True, "Son of Man," Ben Adam, originally meant nothing more than man, particularly as distinguished from the beast and the angel. But it had gradually come to have a further significance, particularly after the time of the Book of Enoch, when it became a synonym for "Messiah." By using this expression, first in one sense and then in another, and making a point of frequently confusing the two terms "I" and "Messiah," he left it open to his listeners to identify the two, and thus he both concealed and revealed himself at the same time.

But it very soon became clear that he confessed himself to be the Messiah in a very special sense, that is to say, he was a Messiah who had given up all idea of gratifying the longings of his people, but came forward with claims of his own. True, in the wilderness Jesus had at first repudiated and then accepted the call. But that first act of repudiation was really a refusal, a failure, a denial. The fact that his spiritual self-examination led to a denial can never be expunged from his life. He did not acknowledge it, but it was not without its effect. The Gospels call these tests to which Jesus subjected himself in the wilderness "temptations." But according to all the laws of spiritual evolution, they were really tests, self-examinations. The tendentiousness of his followers necessarily led to their being misinterpreted in such a way as to conceal the spiritual breach in the life of their master, and to justify in the eyes of posterity what seemed a contradictory attitude. In his threefold resistance to the three temptations, or his threefold denial of a threefold task, lies the problem of his fate as a *man*. A peculiar complexion is imparted to the moulding of his destiny precisely by the fact that he was constantly drawing his private ego into his activities, into the range of his ideas, and into the fashioning of his will. But this was inevitable; for, by his threefold denial, he had ceased to be a functionary of the idea. From that moment it became impossible for him to give to mankind with the full strength of his being that which they had a right to demand of him, if he came forward as a rabbi, a teacher, and a secret Messiah. Thus in ultimate analysis, his own conception of his Messianic mission arose out of his flight from the people whose hopes, thoughts, and feelings he was no longer in a position to satisfy. He failed to reach universality, and ended in the "ego." But just as he broke down in his relation to the community, he inevitably also broke down in his relation to its vast substructure, the world. He had no alternative but ultimately to deny it. All the resistance, trials, tests, and mortifications he encountered in the world about him he connected with himself, and shrank back, retiring into isolation himself and thus isolating his doctrine also from the world. Isolated both in himself and his idea, and divorced from his origin, he was irrevocably lost to his own people. But in return those belonging to an age which the "egos" of its religious leaders had time and again brought on to the rocks, were able to appreciate him and make him the object of their pious submission. But they did not receive salvation because they were obliged to remain living *in the world*.

As we have said, he was unconscious of having failed. He still wished to serve the people and to remain in their midst. When he sent forth his disciples he gave them the following explicit instructions: "Go not into the way of the Gentiles, and into any city of the Samaritans enter ye not; but go ye rather to the lost sheep of the house of Israel." And when, in order to escape the persecutions of his enemies, he sought refuge on foreign soil, he rudely rebuffed a Canaanitish woman who brought her sick child to him to be healed, telling her that it was not meet to take the children's bread and cast it to the dogs. True, in reply to the mother's supplications he healed the child, but the incident provided a glaring example of his Jewish chauvinism. His conscious aim was to influence the Jews. Yet there was something strange about his method, for though it was persuasive and solicitous, it was also veiled. In the light of the facts, this was not in itself curious or particularly unusual in the age to which he belonged. The Essenes acted in much the same way. They too were sending out preachers, because they believed that by repentance they could hasten the end of time. In its spiritual means it also had much in common with the activities of the Pharisees and the sticklers for the law. Like them he interpreted the Scriptures, discussed the arguments they contained, and used the same quotations. Lastly, in practice, he was both Essene and Pharisee. And in the eyes of the people the Essenes and the learned Pharisees were saints, and therefore miracle-workers.

There is no need to enter into any detailed discussion of the miracles. Suffice it to refer to one important point. When, in his wanderings, he came to his native village of Nazareth, where he was a familiar figure, and where no one was inclined to pay much attention to the carpenter with whom they had all hobnobbed in everyday life, but where, on the contrary, the inhabitants, who knew all about his family, were more ready to regard him as an idiot than as a saint, a strange phenomenon occurred—he was unable to work any miracles. The people did not believe in him! In a flash the essence of the miracle is revealed! A miracle is that which the believer can conjure up before his own eyes out of the depths of his own heart. It is for this reason that all discussion of miracles is futile, and that nothing definite is to be inferred about miracles as such from those Jesus performed, except that he happened to encounter a good deal of faith.

And he *insisted* on meeting with faith. He desired at all costs to exercise influence and to win success. That was the object of his sending out apostles to support his cause and that was why he cursed the cities in which the people had no faith in him, and prophesied that disaster would overtake them. And to avoid jeopardizing his success, he told his disciples immediately to leave those places in which they did not receive a friendly welcome, and to be most cautious in all they did. He enjoined them to be "wise as serpents." At the same time, he was terrified of his successes, and did not wish people to talk about his miracles of healing. He fled like a fugitive from Capernaum, Simon's home, the first place in which he tried to exercise influence, because he wished to avoid being asked to perform any more miracles. And perturbed by the fact that his disciples' successes drew attention to himself, he retired to Bethsaida, where he stayed without any of his followers. And when the hostility to him increased, he did not face his adversaries and proclaim himself to be the Messiah, but moved about from place to place. He even went for some time to the country east of the Jordan, where the people were chiefly pagans, and acted in the same way when he went to Cæsarea-Philippi. Suddenly something decisive occurred. Deprived of his customary environment and following, and of the acclamations without which he could no longer exist, he asked his disciples: "Whom do men say that I the Son of Man am? . . . Whom do men say that I am?" He knew very well what people thought of him; they thought he was a rabbi, or a miracle-worker, or a prophet. But what he now longed to hear was the reply which he had hitherto tried by every means in his power to avoid—that he was the Messiah. It was Simon who gave it, and he was rewarded with a gift of undying glory, the name of Peter. But he still forbade his disciples to talk about it.

What did all this signify—this desire to exercise influence, this flight from success, this concealment of his calling, and this challenging of his disciples to confirm his thoughts with their own lips? It meant that the break, the flaw, that had been created by his denial and failure, was playing an ever-increasing part in his life. It was this flaw that was responsible for his secret fear of a public confession; out of it arose his exaggerated, overcompensated desire to exercise influence, his hastening of the course of events, and the desire not to be called Messiah, combined with the secret wish that, after all, someone should one day call him Messiah and not merely prophet. It was this flaw that marred the clear conception of the man as a Messiah of a people, and made room in the person, in the personality, for the individual. It introduced the tragic element into his life. It created hostility animated less by differences in point of view than by dislike of his private life. When Jesus, the man, was disappointed, Jesus, the teacher, withdrew from the synagogue. When Jesus, the rabbi, was criticized, Jesus, the man, immediately became pugnacious and frequently offensive. He must have had a heavy load of anger and hostility in his heart and allowed it to influence his actions. He even cursed a fig tree because there was no fruit on it for him to eat, and that, too, at a time of year when figs were not in season. All this was perfectly human and comprehensible, the behaviour of a man tortured by the sufferings of his ego; but it was private and belonged to the realm of purely personal matters which could not be expected to make a universal appeal, or win popularity. The great mass of the people could see nothing in a figure so essentially and emphatically personal that prompted them to follow in his footsteps, and, above all, nothing in the nature of a general example for all.

He himself was responsible for casting doubt on the exemplariness of his way of life. True, he was a faithful observer of the law; he also paid Temple-money, and in the last dark days of his life he celebrated the Passover in orthodox fashion. "I am not come to destroy the law but to fulfil," he declared; but his handling and interpretation of it, his understanding and valuation of it, all reveal the germs of repudiation. And, in those days, to repudiate the law was tantamount to denying the very foundations of his people's existence. For the laws were not a mere cold catalogue of rules and regulations. They were the crystallized expression of a view of life and of the world. In the rapidly changing conditions of existence, they constituted the guide whereby every man directed his attitude towards God and towards his neighbour. And, more particularly at this juncture, they were a means to an end—the winning of salvation, the coming of the Kingdom of God. As instructions (*Torah* means order, direction), they were, despite national peculiarities, universal in their aim, and were intended to apply to *all* mankind, to the *whole* world. The denials and disavowals of Jesus were frequently affirmations inspired by a deep understanding of the human mind, and, in such instances, he was always abundantly justified compared with those who revered the law for its own sake, and entirely in agreement with those who, like himself, put the living man above the law. When his enemies taunted him with associating with publicans and sinners, he very rightly replied: "They that be whole need not a physician, but they that are sick." And he was forced to acknowledge that this argument satisfied his opponents. But this was an almost unique occurrence, overshadowed by numberless other occasions when he was wrong, if not in substance at least in form, and above all in the nature of his reaction. Whenever his conduct was criticized, whether because of his breach of the Sabbath rest day, or of the rules of diet, or because at a time when others were answering the call to repentance he attended drinking bouts, he always assumed an aggressive attitude, and invariably met views opposed to his own with extraordinary arrogance and impatience, and fanatical contempt. He insisted on people accepting all he did unconditionally and, though he preached gentleness and love, he roundly abused his opponents, calling them hypocrites, a generation of vipers, and serpents. He denounced his disciple, Simon, as Satan, and referred to the heathen as dogs; he cursed the fig tree and whole cities. He unreservedly denied, condemned, and repudiated everybody and everything that refused to do him homage, even members of his own family; and resistance of any kind drove him back into hopeless confusion and further denials.

Thus his denials of that which his appeals had led the people to expect of him assumed a threefold form—inability to recognize the laws and the objects of veneration of the collective whole, the people; flight from the demands of reality, and retreat into a kingdom that was not of this world; and finally exaggerated personal reactions which in the end amounted to the identification of his official calling with his private life. But conduct allowable in a man may be utterly unsuitable for the Messiah. In these circumstances, it inevitably followed that the people, doubtless under the influence of his opponents, withdrew their original support from him, and turned disappointed away. Thus, at the height of his power, he suffered an inevitable and sudden collapse. He had not proved his worth. He might still have passed for a prophet among his own people; but he was not a man entitled to represent himself as the Messiah for whom the age was expectantly waiting.

Such is the deeper significance of the events that took place in Cæsarea-Philippi, and which led him to make up his mind to go to Jerusalem, and plunge desperately into the vortex of Jewish life in order to fulfil his mission, as it were, by assault, by force. It was a piece of terrible human tragedy, a decision arrived at without either hope or elation, and full of dark forebodings that here too he might be refused the success he had been unable to achieve elsewhere. Even more tragic was the fact that the people themselves ceased to play any part in this decisive struggle of their rabbi, their prophet. They had almost forgotten his existence, and took no further notice of him. But matters pursued their relentless course. The vital problems of the people were still in existence, unrelieved and unsolved. Their hopes and aspirations had become concentrated on a war of liberation against Rome in defence of the theocratic state, as though Jesus had never lived or given them any sort of aim. All the historian notices is that the leading supporters of the new faith fled from Jerusalem and refused to share the fate of their brethren, on the very eve of this decisive struggle, just a second before the curtain fell.

Thus, at the very moment when the role of Messiah was played out, though Jesus refused to believe it, the man himself really entered upon the cruel path of suffering and agony. As he had anticipated this suffering, he warned his disciples about it, and it is characteristic of his whole being that he should have used the expression current at the time, *"Ḥeble mashiaḥ yabo le'olam,"* the birth-throes of a world awaiting the Messiah, not in its only possible connexion as applying to the sufferings of the whole Messianic age, but only to himself personally. And it was also only his misery, his fear of being left alone in Jerusalem that can explain his having promised his disciples high honours in the kingdom he was to establish, if they would remain with him. This promise once again reveals his Messianic ideal with all its admixture of spiritual, material, and politico-worldly principles—that is to say, therefore, as a purely Jewish-Messianic conception. Thus he again consciously placed himself in the Jewish tradition. To the objection that, before the coming of the Messiah, his forerunner, Elijah, must appear, he replied that Elijah had already come in the person of John the Baptist. And for his journey he deliberately chose the time of the Passover, the festival which commemorated Jewish emancipation from the yoke of Egypt, rather than any pagan holiday.

He took up his abode in Bethphage, the most outlying suburb of Jerusalem. His will to power now led him to have recourse to symbolic demonstrations. According to a prophecy of Zechariah, the Jewish Messiah was to appear humbly riding on an ass, and Jesus accordingly entered Jerusalem in this way. Legend has transfigured the event. In reality he was hardly noticed. Here and there, among the crowds of pilgrims flocking to the city, were some who recognized him as the prophet from Nazareth. He was able to go to the Temple—incidentally, as a Jew, it was his duty to do so—and to leave it without incident. In the evening he returned to Bethphage outside the city walls. On the second day he appeared again in order to proclaim himself by a further symbolic act. It is possible, though by no means historically proved, that in the outer courts of the Temple there were venders of sacrificial doves and money-changers. As the Roman coins bore the image of the emperor, they were not allowed to be used inside the Temple. This practical arrangement was no more objectionable than, for instance, the trade in devotional objects at many a Christian place of worship today. But Jesus and his disciples proceeded to take violent measures and forcibly drove the sellers of doves and money-changers from their stalls. It was a symbolic act of extremely doubtful value, but it delighted the populace notwithstanding. Preachers, leaders, and potential Messiahs who acted with resolution and violence were always acknowledged and acclaimed by the people, who looked with approval on any action that gave promise of energy and determination in face of the oppressor—Rome. When Jesus again retreated to Bethphage that evening, he had succeeded in winning considerable sympathy.

It was an evasive act, because he could not have been in any doubt that such behaviour was bound to provoke hostility. This was proved on the following day, when he again repaired to the Temple. The priests demanded to know on what authority he had acted as he had done on the previous day. He evaded the question. Following the example of the Pharisees, he replied with another question, and as his opponents could not answer him, he himself refused to enlighten them or to proclaim himself. They proceeded to argue with him, obviously in the hope of making him commit himself, and in the discussion both sides, but especially Jesus, had recourse to the usual Pharisaical methods. In parables Jesus proclaimed himself to be the Messiah, but he avoided any definite assertion. He carefully circumvented all pitfalls; but he nevertheless became entangled in his own evasions. They asked him whether it was right to pay tribute to Cæsar or not. The people expected the reply of the revolutionary, an emphatic "No!" But Jesus said: "Render unto Cæsar the things which are Cæsar's and unto God the things that are God's." This was the attitude adopted both in theory and practice by the moderate Pharisees. But the people merely jumped to the conclusion that, after all, this was not the Messiah who was to save them from the yoke of Rome, and even in Jerusalem they immediately lost all interest in him. He was popular with nobody. The masses were indifferent and the priests and the extreme Pharisees hated him. The Sadducees were also opposed to him. They constituted the most powerful Jewish party in the city, and the constant revolts and disturbances filled them with perturbation and alarm, as they invariably led to sterner measures on the part of the Romans. At this moment Jesus was also confronted by a private enemy in the person of Judas Ish Keriyoth, or in its Greek form Judas Iscariot, the only disciple who had come to him in Galilee from Judea. He had been passionately convinced that Jesus was the Messiah, and was now bitterly disillusioned. The man before him showed no readiness to illuminate, no ardent desire to fulfil; he was merely aiming at power. Entangled in ambiguity and prevarication, and obviously full of conceit and presumption, he was quite unable to give an aim to the people from whom he sprang. Judas had set forth to seek a Messiah. He had found a man. But the age was full of men who were sufferers and whose lives were fraught with tragedy. He did not require Jesus for that! And he secretly broke with him.

The next day dawned, on the evening of which the feast of the Passover was to be held. Jesus celebrated it with his disciples in Jerusalem, strictly in accordance with all the usages of the law. He even observed the regulation that the night following the feast was to be spent in Jerusalem. So he could not go back to Bethphage, but retired to the Mount of Olives and spent the night there in a garden with his disciples. Close at hand lay the city, where he knew that he had no friends but many enemies. He was at its mercy, because both by word and deed he had challenged it to be either for him or against. He had been obliged to do this, for it was the object of his visit, the final object. But the fact that he had failed filled him with burning deadly fear. His belief that he had been sent to fulfil gave way to mortal terror. And in this state of panic the man's elemental instinct of self-preservation made itself felt. The Galilean in him came to the rescue. He wished his disciples to get swords and fight his enemies when they came to seize him. His was the ecstasy of one who was no longer fit for his office, and for whom, therefore, there could be no more peace. In this most wholly human hour of his life, the despairing cry of the tortured and imperfect creature rent the night: "O my Father, if it be possible, let this cup pass from me." But as he could see no trace, no sign of help about him, and as even the disciples who were keeping him company, had fallen asleep, he bowed his head to his fate for the first time with genuine humility. "Nevertheless, not as I will, but as Thou wilt."

Meanwhile the Sadducees, who were in a majority in the Sanhedrin, had been consulting with the priests. They had decided to bring the Galilean up for trial, not merely on account of his past conduct, but also because of certain utterances to which they could attach no meaning, and which they consequently imagined must have all kinds of suspicious meanings. He had boasted, for instance, that he could "destroy the Temple of God and build it up in three days." He was therefore arrested. Witnesses gave evidence against him, but did not succeed in bringing any definite charge. Jesus remained dumb. Only when the high priest, Joseph, the son of Caiaphas, asked him whether he was the Messiah, did he open his mouth to reply, declaring that he was the "Son of Man, who would sit on the right hand of power." Whereupon the high priest rent his clothes, as a sign that the words he had just heard were blasphemous. And he was in the right. Hitherto Jesus had not said, done, or accomplished anything which might have compelled the people to acknowledge him. His strongest argument had always been: "But I say unto you . . ." an argument which did not coerce or bind those to whom it was addressed. It could therefore only amount to arrogance, or in religious phraseology, blasphemy.

The Sanhedrin confined itself to this preliminary examination, which was by no means thorough. This was comprehensible enough at a time of latent revolution. It had been carried out not by the people or the Pharisees, but by the oligarchs, the Sadducees, who had just been called upon to deal with an attempted insurrection under the leadership of Barabbas. They drew their own conclusions from the political events of the age, and to avoid the responsibility of passing judgment one way or the other, they delivered up Jesus to Pontius Pilate, the Roman governor. From that moment the Jews had nothing further to do with Jesus. The fact that at this point the Christian records falsified the facts and made the Jews responsible for what followed is due to the fear felt by the Christians of facing Rome with the truth. This was comprehensible enough though not on that account excusable.

The final failure and misunderstanding took place before Pilate. The famous question was put: "Art thou the King of the Jews?" At that time the concept King-Messiah conveyed a very different meaning to the Jew from what it did to the Roman. The latter regarded the title as one which in any case laid claim to an office, and a position of authority, which was directed against the Roman imperium, and was therefore high treason. The reply: "Thou sayest," given by Jesus, amounted at once to a confession and an evasion; but in any case it was a reply which sealed his fate and delivered him up to it.

And thus fate struck him down. It was a Jewish fate, the fate of a particular period, and of a man of that period, who, to the best of his ability, had tried to serve his people. It was not his fault, but his misfortune, that the personal, subjective, individual, and private element in his nature failed in its encounter with his people, whom, from the bottom of his heart, he wished to benefit. But after his death fate dealt kindly by him, and, in the minds of those who called themselves his followers, he was endowed with immortality in other worlds and other spheres.

But the people were forced to deny him. And the law that ruled his people's fate drove him willy-nilly to end his unfinished career in agony. His countrymen, regarding him as a man who had not fulfilled his promise, deserted him and left him to Rome to punish in her own way. He was crucified. In his last despairing moments he cried aloud to God, reproaching him with having forsaken him, and giving voice to the cry in Aramaic, the native vernacular of his Galilean home. But he was not the only one to give vent to such a cry. Hundreds of thousands were uttering a similar cry at that time, and tens of thousands of the best of them on crosses. He met with a terrible fate. But others did likewise. The cry of the one, and the cry of the hundred thousand, the martyrdom of the one and the martyrdom of the hundred thousand–by what right do the cry and the agony of the one outweigh the cry and the agony of the hundred thousand? By what right, human or divine, have the followers of one man avenged themselves for his death by the murder of millions? In the eyes of God and of all creation, before the tribunal of universal justice as well as of this world pain is always pain, and agony of soul the sublime fate of all mankind. For the Jews, the tragedy of Jesus forms part of their own life and experience. *Nostra res agitur!* His life and death are *our* affair!

SAUL OF TARSUS

JESUS of Nazareth was dead. His personal followers, who could not possibly have foreseen this tragic end to his noble but incomplete existence, fled in terror and confusion to Galilee, whence they had come. Their situation was desperate. With the death of Jesus, their own spiritual life had also been put in question. The harassed longings of the age had led them to accept precisely *this* man as the Messiah of the Jewish people; they had transferred all their hopes to *him* and to no other, believing that he would set up the Kingdom of Heaven on earth. According to Jewish conceptions, the Messiah was bound to fulfil their expectations. And Jesus himself had sworn to do so. "Verily I say unto you, there be some standing here, which shall not taste of death, till they see the Son of Man coming in his kingdom." And on another occasion: "Verily I say unto you, this generation shall not pass, till all these things be fulfilled."

But, instead, what had happened? Nothing—no act of fulfilment, no change in conditions, not the smallest sign of the promised Kingdom of God! On the contrary, he had been delivered up for judgment to the temporal powers and had been condemned like a felon. He had cried aloud in his death agony on the cross that God had forsaken him! And this had been followed by the final and irrefutable fact of his biological death.

Such a crushing consummation could be faced only in one of two ways. His followers could either have confronted the facts and, admitting their mistake after the event, have transferred their Messianic hopes to a fresh candidate for office—and there were many such candidates in those days. Such a resolve would, of course, necessarily have involved the destruction of their faith. For in that case Jesus would have been a Messiah who had falsely proclaimed his mission, or who had unjustifiably laid claim to the title of Messiah. Or else if, as might well have been the case among these people in that age, their capacity for faith and their readiness to believe were abnormally developed, it was also possible for them to deny the fact of the death, or put a different interpretation upon it, and thereupon proceed to fit this new and unique occurrence into the edifice of their belief, and thus prevent it from falling to pieces. Each one of them in his heart of hearts gave utterance to the despairing cry of the disciple on the road to Emmaus: "But we trusted that it had been he which should have redeemed Israel." For this to be true, however, the idea had to be twisted round. This they succeeded in doing by making their idea conform not to any *reality* either in the far distance or close at hand, on earth or in heaven, but to the distressful state of their souls. Never before in the history of the world, except in pagan mythology, had a case of the kind occurred, and a man's death been made the starting point of his life. As their rational minds could not deny the death of the Messiah, their faith demanded his resurrection. Between the undeniable and conclusive fact of his biological death, and his continued life in another sphere, there was interposed that power for which the impossible is not impossible—faith. And this faith sprang from the religious power of the Jewish mind. It could have had no other origin, for at that time there was no other creative religious power in existence.

After some time had elapsed, there came into being the legend—and within the sphere of a man's belief, legend is identical with truth—that Jesus of Nazareth had risen from the dead and had ascended to heaven. By means of this extraordinary act of faith, not only was the survival of the Messiah guaranteed, but a basis was also created upon which the followers of Jesus could found faith in all its various manifestations. Thus they succeeded in moving a personality, which in their own lifetime had attracted only a small circle of followers, to a sphere where it could not be judged by any standard of reality, and where its influence would therefore be as unlimited as the possibilities of faith itself.

The representatives of this faith were obviously Jews. How could it possibly have been otherwise? They stood for no particular party or tendency. They merely constituted a group of individuals who believed in Jesus as the Messiah who had already appeared. In so far as a clearly defined *separate point of view* had developed at this time—and at first this was the case only to a very limited extent—the doctrine of Jesus differed from the fundamental attitude of the Jews merely in the sense that it narrowed down the conception of what the actual achievement of the Messiah would be, and emphasized the personal and individual factor, both in the believer and in the Messiah. For anything else, and more particularly for the doctrine of salvation, there was no room for the moment. If Jesus, in his lifetime, had really conceived and preached such an idea, and if it had been regarded as a fundamental precept of his doctrine, how came it that Judaism, which was sick with longing for some religious solution and satisfaction, did not eagerly seize upon it? Why, in that case, was it adopted only by individuals? Because, possibly, Judaism, as a whole, was not ripe for it? And yet it was a Jew, a pure Jew, who was said to have preached it! Or can it be supposed that the pagan, the idolater of yesterday, was better able to grasp such ideas than the heir of two thousand years of religious tradition? There is only one possible reply: the idea of salvation played no part whatever during the lifetime of Jesus. There were other differences which separated him from his people.

There was no party which could give him its unconditional support. The Pharisees were bound to take exception to the doctrine of the "kingdom that was not of this world," if to nothing else; for even if they had been able to grasp the stupendous universal powers that lay implicit in such a conception, they were not prepared to renounce the national basis of their creed and their hopes of a Messiah. The Zealots were too much the slaves of political passion to be able to envisage the problem of redemption from a spiritual angle. The Sadducees, whose worldly interests made them opportunists, were far too little interested in a living form of religiosity to adopt any but a negative attitude. Those whose doctrines had most in common with the ideology of Jesus were the Essenes, and there can be no doubt that the Christian faith borrowed a good deal from their fund of mysticism. But they too rejected the idea of deifying a man, and making him a mediator between God and man. They conceived of God as being in direct communion with man, albeit through the medium of various mysteries.

The first supporters of Jesus were therefore renegades from all the Jewish parties, isolated individuals, who, for the sake of a common hope, joined together on a basis of Judaism. They lived, as they had always done, according to the Jewish law, and regulated their existence in accordance with one of the manifestations which Jewish Messianism had produced, forming a fraternal community on communistic lines, as the Essenes had done long before. But the idea that their Messiah had already appeared was a new conception peculiar to themselves, and their belief that the Messiah who had been crucified had risen from the dead formed the pivot of their faith. Thus they possessed all the essential characteristics of a sect.

As such they represented an important element of Judaism. What has been said concerning Jesus as a personality is, of course, also true of those who believed in him; that is to say, their attitude towards everything whether material or spiritual was determined by personal considerations; the communal or collective point of view was either given secondary importance or altogether neglected. But it would be a mistake to regard this as being prompted by a mere spirit of contradiction. For it is by no means true that religious individualism was to be found exclusively among the followers of Jesus, and that the Jews, on the other hand, were pure collectivists. It was certainly not the gospel of Jesus that was responsible for the disintegration of collective religious feeling among the Jews through the growth of free, personal, religious feeling; for they had been schooled in the latter by their prophets centuries before this. And just at this juncture, with the help of the best minds in their midst, they were making a fresh attempt at its realization. As a matter of fact on both sides there was a conflict between individualism and collectivism; both sides were trying to arrive at a synthesis, and there had not yet been sufficient time for either of them to reach its goal. Jesus, who rightly from his own viewpoint emphasized the importance of the individual in religion, thereby forfeited the basis from which belief as a world concept, as a truly constructive view of the world, springs; that is to say, the common ground of everyday life, the common bond of association.

The Judeans who hoped that one day the substructure of morality underlying the sublime ordinances of the law would receive the voluntary recognition of the whole of mankind, rightly feared they might lose their clarity in a religiosity which could not make the most beautiful and sublime demands tangible and real; for it is only on a superlatively high plane of evolution that religious feeling can dispense with the actual and practical application to life of the forms which are stamped by life itself.

Such then was the spiritual connexion between Judaism and this new Jewish sect. And it was persecuted by the rest of the Jews, not because of its stupendous importance, or because of its revolutionary spirit, for of this it showed no signs, but rather because, in the fateful struggle in which the Jewish people were then engaged, any split or schism denoted a weakening and a danger which justified defensive measures of every description. But this sect also emphasized the idea of suffering, which Jesus for the first time transferred from the Jewish people as a whole and applied to himself; and thus it became possible for the sectarian to grow stronger and prosper on the suffering of persecution. But apart from this purely passive attitude of believing and suffering, there was nothing in the sect which would have enabled it to sever its connexion with Judaism and its limitations, and spread its influence beyond the confines of the latter. Judaism, on the other hand, had no surplus energy which would have enabled it to reabsorb this sect. The impulse which had given rise to the War of Liberation had not yet been spent, and it drained the whole strength of the nation.

Moreover, during the first decades after the death of Jesus, nothing of what was subsequently known as Christianity was in existence. What was taking place was rather the continuation, on a grander scale, of a process which had already been operating for some time—the gradual spread of the spiritual power of Judaism over the whole of the pagan world. How this came about in Alexandria has already been described, and it was precisely in this quarter that Philo, a Jew of great learning and an extraordinary feeling for form, now made his appearance and endeavoured to fling a bridge between Judaic monotheism and Greek paganism. Deeply rooted in Judaism though he was, he had yet allowed himself to become thoroughly permeated with Greek thought. He regarded them both as creative powers, which should no longer be allowed to work separately or in antagonism. He undertook the hopeless attempt (hopeless, because the most powerful philosophic thought is impotent in the face of even the weakest emotion) by means of writings addressed to the international intelligentsia of the age to acquaint the Jews with the philosophic burden of his doctrine, and the Greeks with the importance of Jewish monotheism.

But as he owed his philosophy to Greece, he was obliged to present it in a roundabout way through the Bible allegories, instead of deducing it directly from its own source of development. This prevented him from exercising any influence over the Jews, who were not at all inclined to abandon the real content of their sacred traditions. And as, on the other hand, he regarded the Jewish people as the "priests and prophets" of all mankind, and urged the Greeks to accept the Mosaic law as the true natural law, and to yield to Judaism as the universal religion he himself conceived it to be, he could count on the agreement only of those among them who accepted his line of thought. Thus, he remained a man of vast knowledge and noble intentions, a great but useless figure. In later days he was read only by the Church Fathers; no one else troubled about him. And the bridge he had built was used not by those for whom it was intended, but by the Christians when they came to develop their dogma; for in Philo they thought they had discovered confirmation of the idea that God could beget a Son. But they were mistaken. When he had enunciated the doctrine of the divine emanation and the Logos, he had meant something very different. Bowed down as he was beneath the load of Greek wisdom, he was constrained to come to terms with it, and he accordingly supported the Platonic doctrine of ideas against the pantheism of the Stoics. Between the world and God, whom he conceived as infinite Being without attributes, he placed the creative force which emanated and radiated from Him into the world. He did not allow God Himself to perform the task of creation, but declared that in the beginning, "on the first day," He created the world of ideas, not the things themselves, but the ideal prototypes of things. And this mundane universe of ours was built up on the pattern of these prototypes, in accordance with the "example given by God." This is the doctrine of emanation, and its creative powers. By means of numerous similes and illustrations, he endeavoured to make this power manifest, now as an instrument, with the help of which God formed and created, as demiurgus, and again as a mediator, as an "archangel," the "first-born Son of God." To those who could make use of it, therefore, he supplied the proof of the existence of a Son of God.

In those parts of the world, however, where, unlike Alexandria, a high degree of intelligence was not common, and differences of culture did not bear fruit in philosophic speculations and literature, the pagan, and more particularly the Greek population was gradually inclining towards the fundamental beliefs and doctrines of Judaism, as a result of coming into daily contact with it. This was the case in Rome, where Horace, Fuscus, Ovid, and Persius complained of the spread of Jewish ideas, and Seneca waxed eloquent against the Sabbath day, because it was responsible for the waste of one seventh of the working life of men. "The customs of this criminal nation are gaining ground so rapidly," he declared, "that they already have adherents in every country; and thus the conquered force their laws upon the conqueror." This was the case in Italy, Syria, Greece, and Asia Minor. Conversions to Judaism had become the order of the day. But as its endless rules and regulations, and particularly the one relating to circumcision, prevented an actual mass conversion, large groups of sympathizers with Judaism were everywhere formed. They called themselves the "God-Fearing," or the "God-Revering," upheld the doctrine of one God, observed the Sabbath, and followed Jewish rites and ceremonies. At the same time the religion of paganism was rapidly falling to bits; in Asia Minor particularly the structure of Greek religion was seriously undermined by orientalism. Gods of all kinds and nationalities had been included in a chaotic syncretism, and frequently their only claim to veneration lay in their orgiastic rites.

Judaism, which had opened its first decisive assaults in this field, was too crippled in strength to pursue the attack consistently and systematically. Yet it was Jewish principles alone that could in this sphere come forward as a world against a world. And it was for this reason that the Jewish sect consisting of the followers of Jesus, who had shaken themselves free from the fate of their people, found their sphere of activity precisely here. This was only logical. For if a sect, born and brought up in Judaism, was to make its way in the outside world at all, and exercise influence, it had to bear its patrimony with it, and once more for the reason that, however much religious power might accrue to mankind, it was bound to have as its foundation the two indispensable and primeval principles of Judaism—monotheism and the insistence on moral conduct in man. And this happened by means of Judaism within the confines of the Jewish colonies. "Christianity spread under the ægis of the Jewish community." (Hoenicke.)

If, however, it had been merely a matter of propagating these two fundamental ideas, the task would not have remained in the hands of Christianity. For that to happen, highly controversial mystical elements borrowed from Jewish heterodoxy and also from paganism had to be added to the two fundamental ideas. Finally, it was necessary for the universal power that lay dormant in Judaism to be released, as the result of a special effort, and for the fountain-head and nursery of this universal power, which was the sense of responsibility for the whole of mankind, that had developed among the Jews, to be denied and denounced. All this was achieved in a single generation by means of the Jew, Saul of Tarsus.

Let us here repeat our contention that there is no such thing as the founder of a religion; all that we find are men who are able to release a certain fund of energy that is ready to hand. Saul, however, is as near to being the founder of a religion as any man who has ever lived, and is the most forcible and vivid example of the potentialities that lay hid in Judaism in his day. Of all the upheavals that took place among the Jews at this time, his advent among them was the most violent. With rare power and a phenomenally sure instinct, he recognized and used those elements in Judaism and paganism which were either capable of fusion or refractory to it.

Just as in the above outline it has been impossible to describe the inner or spiritual relationship, that is to say, the relationship of Judaism to this Judæo-Christian sect, as being merely contradictory, so it is also impossible to describe the external relationship, that is to say, the relationship between Judaism and its pagan environment as being merely contradictory. Both Judaism and paganism were in a state of extreme religious disorder. Judaism was full to overflowing with religious zeal. Paganism was dying out owing to the decay and decline of religious feeling. A superlatively negative force was confronted by a superlatively positive force, both of which might, and indeed actually did, become united in a general collapse. The Jew succumbed under the crushing weight of events, in an attempt to continue sublimating reality. The pagan succumbed before his gods by overloading them with his own confused reality which was not co-ordinated by any religious aim. Between the Jew, on the one hand, trying to evade the issue by seeking refuge in another and purer reality, and the pagan, attempting to escape from a heaven that had collapsed to one that would endure, there was created the atmosphere in which it was possible to establish Christianity.

Thus paganism and Judaism faced each other in an attitude of despair, the Jew as the result of exaggerated hopes of deliverance, and the pagan as the result of an exaggerated fear of disintegration. In each case this meant flight from the realities of existence as they had hitherto been lived, in the case of the Jew flight from the ever-fresh evidences of the discrepancy between the ideal and the real; and in the case of the pagan, flight from a way of life that had never been affected, sublimated, and satisfied either in the intellectual, the spiritual, or the religious sphere. The Jew lived his life under a crushing burden of rules and regulations; the pagan under a crushing burden of divine waywardness, or, what amounted to the same thing, lawlessness. The Jew, through his faith, had built too confidently on the hope of salvation. The pagan still lacked the assurance that his spiritual difficulties would ever be overcome. In both cases, the continuance of their religious life was bound up with the idea of salvation. Jew and pagan alike were insistently demanding a Messiah. Judaism required the help of a Messiah to reach the ultimate realization of its ideology. Paganism required a Messiah to show it how to escape from the stranglehold of a moribund pantheon and attain a spiritual, that is to say, a human and moral way of life. In themselves these were clearly two fundamentally different attitudes. It was the great creative achievement of Saul that he succeeded in acting as the intermediary, and giving to paganism, not what would bring it fulfilment, but what it did not possess.

Among those who, in Jerusalem and Palestine, were trying to persecute the new sect, and prevent it from conducting its propaganda, or publicly preaching in the Temple, was a young Jew, Saul, a native of Tarsus in that part of Asia Minor known as Cilicia. He had come to Jerusalem to study under the great teacher Gamaliel. He once quite openly described himself as "a Pharisee, the son of a Pharisee." As a matter of fact, it was not the Pharisees who persecuted the new sect, but the Sadducees, whose active interference had determined the fate of Jesus. When Peter and other leaders of the sect were brought up before the Sanhedrin to be tried for their activities, it was the Pharisees who secured their release by pointing out that, after all, they were really strict Jews. The fanatical zeal with which Saul persecuted the sectarians is extraordinary. When the followers of Jesus were joined by Jews who had moved to Jerusalem from the Greek-speaking areas, and the increased propaganda led to disturbances, one of their number, a man named Stephen, was brought up before the Sanhedrin on a charge of blasphemy and was afterwards stoned by the people. His supporters fled, but continued to carry on their propaganda in the neighbouring districts occupied by Jews, and farther afield among the Jews in Samaria, Phœnicia, Antioch, Damascus, and on the island of Cyprus. Saul had been one of Stephen's persecutors, and he now volunteered to give his services to carry on the persecution of Stephen's followers, and with the object of exterminating this sect of "heretics" he set out for Damascus.

On the way thither he suddenly changed his mind. What it was that induced him thus to give up persecuting the followers of Jesus and to declare himself one of them, it is impossible to say. He may actually have had a vision, which released some pent-up force within him. Or possibly his fanatical persecution of heretics was merely due to a strong feeling of attraction towards the mysticism of the Jesus-Messiah, which owing to being repressed manifested itself in the obverse character. Any attempt to explain the process itself would be futile. One can only point out that he had been brought up in a Judæo-Hellenistic environment, in which different cultures and points of view came into contact and gave rise to all manner of mixed and intermediate forms. Moreover, an incident of this kind, occurring at a time when religious feeling ran high, is neither so uncommon nor of such outstanding importance as it is often supposed to be. For, after all, what did it amount to? Merely that a certain Pharisaic Jew had decided to join the sect consisting of the followers of Jesus. Never was it suggested by thought, word, or deed, that, on his way to Damascus, Saul the Jew had been metamorphosed into Paul the opponent of the Jews. The change that had taken place had not made him either outwardly or inwardly any more hostile to the Jews than membership of the Jesus sect implied. It was only when he reached a later stage of development that we find him entering a domain which to a man of his religious endowment must have appeared full of hope, and which he conquered by intellectually transmuting and transforming the latent opposition of two worlds into a dogma resting on God and Jesus.

A man of Saul's activity could not rest content with being one among many others within a sect. The indefatigable energy which had always urged him on drove him still further, and the man who had persecuted with passion now began to preach with passion. From the very beginning he showed himself to be possessed, as Jesus had been, of an overbearing will to power. The sectarian, convinced of having discovered the only true way to salvation, always has recourse to propaganda and does all in his power to increase his following, and, whereas an established religion makes converts by the sword, the sect, as long as it has no power, has recourse to every other expedient, both justifiable and otherwise, for propagating its beliefs. "What then?" said Paul, "notwithstanding, every way, whether in pretence, or in truth, Christ is preached; and I therein do rejoice, yea, and will rejoice." It could do him no harm and the office could suffer no spiritual loss by allowing the will to power free rein. For he was not the Messiah, but found support in a Messiah who had already appeared. Thus his position was much more secure, and there was no necessity for him, either by his life or actions, to produce anything more or to prove anything more. He was in a position to assert and to draw conclusions, and this he did with increasing vehemence, the genius of which is beyond dispute.

Antioch now became the centre from which propaganda was deliberately and systematically conducted. It was here that among this group of Jews and Gentiles who believed that Jesus had been the Jewish Messiah that the word *Mashiaḥ* (Messiah–Anointed) was translated literally into Greek–*Christos;* and the faithful who had hitherto had no appellation called themselves Christians for the first time. But they were still a Jewish sect, and it was still possible to regard them, as the Pharisees regarded Peter when they defended him before the Sanhedrin, as orthodox members of Judaism. But it was precisely this strict orthodoxy, created by a national religious life, that made it difficult for outsiders to be converted to the sect, just as it had made it difficult for the "God-Fearing" or "God-Revering" to become wholly incorporated in Judaism.

Paul made it his first aim to remove these difficulties. On his own authority he informed possible converts that there was no necessity for them to submit to all the rules and regulations of Judaism if they wished to become Christians and join the sect that believed the Messiah had already appeared. He preached this doctrine to both Gentile and Jew, and for the former he removed one of the greatest obstacles to conversion, the ceremony of circumcision, while he also gave many Jews in the Diaspora far greater freedom than they had hitherto enjoyed. The growing pressure of the times had brought in its train increased stringency in the laws. The pressure of the times fluctuated; the stringency of the laws never decreased, in fact it actually grew stronger. It could not follow the fluctuations in the pressure of external events, which was at least alleviated from time to time. Many failed to see that the stringency of the laws was dictated by far-sightedness and regarded it at most as a temporary expedient in time of danger, and they accordingly evaded the fluctuations of pressure and the ever-increasing oppression of the age, which constituted a burden too heavy for them to bear.

This form of propaganda was regarded with ever-increasing uneasiness by the Christian community in Jerusalem. For what had Jesus said? "For verily I say unto you, Till heaven and earth pass, one jot or one tittle shall in no wise pass from the law, till all be fulfilled. Whosoever therefore shall break one of these least commandments, and shall teach men so, he shall be called the least in the kingdom of heaven." Thus Paul was preaching a doctrine which was not that of their Messiah and of which he would not have approved. It was therefore necessary to curb his activities. For he taught: "Therefore we conclude that a man is justified by faith without the deeds of the law." To these weighty and compelling words James replied with words no less weighty and compelling: "What doth it profit, my brethren, though a man say he hath faith, and have not works? . . . Even so faith, if it hath not works, is dead, being alone."

Inspired by these considerations and appealing to what Jesus himself had taught, a counter-movement was inaugurated, and the community in Jerusalem sent a deputation to Antioch, under the leadership of James, the brother of Jesus. But this did not help to mend matters; it merely increased the confusion. Paul found the work he had begun being interrupted, and he was not the kind of man to allow himself to be thwarted without offering resistance. On the contrary, for every blow he received he gave back two, and in his truculence in the face of opposition he had much in common with Jesus. (As a matter of fact this is a common characteristic of Jews who have suffered from over-much opposition.) But unlike Jesus, Paul's will to power did not take refuge in repeated denials, but in repeated exorbitant conclusions. Jesus lived in a co-ordinated world in which it was necessary either to succeed or fail. Paul, on the other hand, was able to play one force against the other. If the Jewish members of the sect failed him or his purpose, he could turn to the Gentile members. Jesus lived and worked in a maturely developed and closed circle. Paul stood at the drawbridge leading out on to the infinite plains of the Gentile world. Whether he should fling it open once and for all was merely a question of consistency. And the day came when he drew the logical conclusion from his position.

Meanwhile he went to Jerusalem to lay his case before the apostles, the leaders of the community there. He could bring forward one argument to which it was impossible for them to turn a deaf ear—he had been successful and, above all, successful among the Gentiles. This success would be jeopardized if his way of teaching and of releasing converts from all obligation to Jewish law were interfered with. Quite rightly James argued: "Wherefore my sentence is, that we trouble not them, which from among the Gentiles are turned to God." It was important for the sect to secure an increase of membership. This was final, and it was agreed that Gentiles should not be under any obligation to the law. There were three regulations, however, the infringement of which appeared intolerable in the eyes of a Jew and which he felt that even Gentiles must be called upon to observe: they were forbidden to continue worshipping many gods, or idols; to practise incest; or to eat the flesh of strangled animals, or blood. (The latter was forbidden because according to the primeval Jewish view, the blood was the seat of the soul.) That in all this the only concern was one of expediency is proved by the epistle addressed by the apostles to the Gentiles in Antioch, Syria, and Cilicia. "For it seemed good to the Holy Ghost, and to us, to lay upon you no greater burden than these necessary things."

Thenceforward the one object of Saul, now already known as Paul, was to make the most of this resolution in order to win success. In his heart of hearts he was not so much concerned with *abrogating* the law as about achieving *success*. For whenever it promoted success he applied the law unscrupulously. For instance, he had Timothy, the son of a Greek father and a Jewish mother, circumcised, "because of the Jews which were in those quarters; for they knew all that his father was a Greek." And he himself confesses: "And unto the Jews I became as a Jew, that I might gain the Jews; to them that are under the law, as under the law, that I might gain them that are under the law; to them that are without law, as without law . . . that I might gain them that are without law." This shows a degree of unscrupulousness in the exercise of the will to power which, when he was afterwards brought up for trial, reached such a pitch that it is difficult to decide whether it was inspired by the sophistry of a learned Pharisee or was merely barefaced lying. Before the Sanhedrin in Jerusalem he declared: "Of the hope and resurrection of the dead I am called in question." This was not true. The truth was that he was trying to create a schism among the Jews, because he knew that the Sadducees in the council did not believe in the resurrection. And speaking in his own defence before Felix, the governor, he not only repeated this lie, but declared with the sophistry of the extreme Pharisee: "But this I confess unto thee, that after the way which they call heresy, so worship I the God of my fathers, believing all things which are written in the law and in the prophets." Finally, to avoid all discussion with the people of his own sect and the Jews, he proudly claimed that he was a Roman citizen and as such appealed to Cæsar in Rome. When it was a matter of effecting his purpose and reaching his goal, he allowed nothing to stand in his way.

On his missionary journeys, which he continued to undertake with indefatigable zeal, he did not always win success as quickly as his passionate impulse desired. And in this he revealed a further striking resemblance to Jesus as we see him. In Paul's case, too, the personal, individual, and private factor far outweighed the importance of the office he had assumed. So long as people followed him and believed him, he was mild, paternal, benevolent, and kindly. But the moment he met with resistance, he was extraordinarily quick to take offence and become aggressive. True to his principles, he continued to preach the same doctrine to both Jews and Gentiles; but, in spite of his Pharisaic scholarship, he had a very much more difficult task with the Jews. For they contradicted him. The evidence points to the fact that Paul had been expecting this, and was apparently conscious that at this stage his sect was still neither one thing nor the other, and that a clean cut was necessary; for on two occasions he suddenly retorted with truly un-Christian haughtiness and gave a reply which though spontaneous bore the stamp of having been impatiently held in readiness for some time. He said to the Jews: "It was necessary that the word of God should first have been spoken to you; but seeing ye put it from you, and judge yourselves unworthy of everlasting life, lo, we turn to the Gentiles." But as they continued to oppose him and blasphemed, he shook his clothes and said: "Your blood be upon your own heads; I am clean; from henceforth I will go unto the Gentiles."

True, it is possible to interpret this passage as meaning that he merely wished to limit his own field of activity in this way. For whereas he called Peter the apostle of the Jews, he called himself the apostle of the Gentiles. But this really meant something more than a limitation of their respective spheres of action. It indicated a further move in the direction he had already chosen and amounted to a decision to separate himself from Judaism, which was his native element. The fact that in his Epistle to the Romans he expresses his hope that the Jews may be converted, when once "the fulness of the Gentiles be come in," does not in any way confute this. It was a bill at long sight, which he was obliged to flaunt in order to make it clear to the Gentiles that a doctrine which had emanated from Judaism had been rejected by the Jews themselves. Paul had accepted an onerous legacy from Judaism—the feeling of obligation towards a thought. And thus he bound himself not only to what in himself was the outcome of a process of thought, but also to that which resistance to his effort to influence had spontaneously evoked from him. Nowhere was it written and foretold that the gospel of salvation must first be preached in vain to the Jews. This was *par excellence* a piece of blasphemy against God's people. Even in their refusal to believe, they were a holy nation, for their refusal sprang from an attempt to reach the highest conception of the idea of God. But Paul had made a statement for which he was bound to give the proof, and he gave it!

It does not enter into the scope of this work to examine this process of proof in detail. In its method it was a consummate achievement of Pharisaical intellect, a piece of unscrupulous translation and interpretation, an arbitrary allegorization, extremely clever, beautiful, and intimate. Even the psalms, which were the intimate outpourings of pious and lonely souls, liturgical chants born of the creative religious power of Judaism, he did not hesitate to twist and turn into prophecies relating to the coming of Jesus. But more important than any proof or method of demonstration, was the spiritual attitude which made such ratiocination possible at all. This attitude rapidly became more conspicuous, more especially as it was not merely opposed to the Jews, but, as it grew more arbitrary, also came into conflict with the Christians. In Syria and Asia Minor there was open hostility between the Judæo-Christian apostles and the apostles of the Gentiles; and Paul publicly opposed Peter, the "Rock of the Church." Officially the conflict continued to rage round the vexed question of the observance or non-observance of the law. But by deciding *against* the law, Paul, in meeting the well-founded attacks of his opponents, could no longer put forward the negative plea that insistence on the law endangered success. He was obliged to use a more positive argument and prove to both Jew and Gentile Christians that it was precisely the denial of the law that constituted the positive factor, that it was precisely the repudiation and rejection of the law that was the starting-point on their road to salvation.

The question is, what is the fundamental fact in the idea of "law"?

The usual translation of the word "Torah" by "law" is inaccurate. Torah means direction, instruction, precept, not law in the sense of a legal norm. Thus the law in this sense was not an independent institution; it was not obligatory of itself and through itself. It was never an end in itself; but in all circumstances a means to an end, its object being to realize the rule of God, the theocracy, and thus to bring about the perfection and salvation of mankind and the world.

A difference or a contradiction between the law and religion had therefore always been incomprehensible in Judaism. The fact that many such contradictions actually occurred in life proves nothing against the idea, but is merely a sign of human weakness; and a cursory glance at the epistles of the apostles proves that the Christians were the last who had any right to claim perfection in this respect. But Paul required this contradiction in order to account satisfactorily for the opposition he inspired in the Jews and the Jewish Christians. That is why he created it. He created and invented a thousand and one reasons for it, with an uncanny, demoniacal consistency almost amounting to genius. He ceased to insist upon the abrogation of the law for the sake of propaganda, and began to deny the law on principle. The relaxing of the law along individualistic lines, after which both Jesus and the Pharisees strove, was exaggerated to the point of destroying it altogether for the sake of the individual. And he reverted to the cardinal principle which both tacitly and explicitly formed the basis of the moral doctrine of Judaism: "Love thy neighbour as thyself." This cardinal principle, whether as thought or formula, was not invented by Paul; it was an ancient heritage of the Jewish religion. But by selecting this one principle, he did much more than refer the whole of the "law" back to one idea, one source. He seized upon the very heart of Judaism, the universal power which lay hid within it, that power which was universal for the very reason that the concept of universality is inseparable from the Jewish view of God. For, since there is only one Creator, it follows that there can be only one creation, and all men must also be one; and finally, since the concentration of the transcendental into one divine concept is applicable to the whole of mankind, it can be adopted by the whole of mankind by means of moral conduct.

But as even this selection of a universal conception was in itself a confirmation and affirmation of Judaism, it had to be immediately transformed into something different, seeing that Paul had seized upon it not merely with the idea of making it accessible to the Gentiles also, but for the sole purpose of divorcing it from its origin and handing it over to the Gentile world, with the object of ousting Judaism from its position of being the one and only repository of the knowledge of God and allowing the Gentiles to enter into possession.

And this he now proceeded to do, and made it his aim to transfer the universal power latent in Judaism to the Gentiles. And it was only logical that in so doing he should turn his back on the life of his people and the law it had produced. For if Judaism had succeeded in acquiring universal influence, it would have had to burst the bonds of nationality, though this would not necessarily have meant that Christianity and Judaism would come to grips. At most it might have led to competition with the same weapons and the same object in view, though with different degrees of religious endowment. But Paul had no wish to repeat the same phenomenon on a different plane; his aim was something entirely different, contrary and hostile, which corresponded with his own hostility, and gave it its deepest justification.

At this stage of his individual development, his creative religious gifts set to work with extraordinary power, consistency, and sureness of touch to gratify the unsatisfied yearnings of the Gentile world. The Gentiles had long been aware that the Jews were entrusted with a divine mission, but with repressed envy they had passionately fought against having to acknowledge the fact. And lo and behold! Paul now told them that the Jews had been deprived of their mission, and that it had been transferred to them. Thus they were spared the ignominy of being obliged to accept the heritage of a foreign people and to remain under a debt of gratitude to them. On the contrary, they were the heirs upon whom a special divine mission had been bestowed. Nevertheless, the matter was not quite so simple. Whether they were heirs or successors in office, the Gentiles, in any case, lacked the tradition which would have enabled them to take up and carry on their new task. Who was this one God? How could He be reached? Could He be approached like a marble statue in a pagan temple? And what was a Messiah? A man? A god? And what was this new kingdom like, which He was going to set up?

In undertaking to answer these questions, Paul, out of the chaos of Jewish and Gentile forms of belief, created Christianity as an orderly system. True, he could not transfer the concept of theocracy to the Gentile world; but, in so far as belief was a matter for the individual, he succeeded in effecting a compromise which does credit to his genius. Theoretically he made the doctrine of the equality of all men before God acceptable to the Gentiles. By adapting himself to their spiritual conditions (as opposed to Judaism which demanded adaptation on the part of others) he showed a thorough grasp of their spiritual state. The pagan pantheon was crumbling to bits, and the inevitable question on all men's lips was, what is to come next? Whereupon Paul presented them with Christianity, saying, The end is coming, the great day of reckoning is at hand! Such reasoning could emanate only from a people to whom the end of days and a final reckoning, when outraged justice would be appeased, were familiar ideas. But the idea presented in this extremely abstract form was beyond the comprehension of the Gentiles, who were incapable of receiving it. They also lacked the tradition which would have enabled them to do so. They could understand only out of fear, the fear in which they were then living, and which had to be overshadowed by a fresh fear in order to be ready to be dispersed by a message of consolation. The appalling threat of the selection that would take place in the last days had to be held over their heads! "I tell you, in that night there shall be two men in one bed; the one shall be taken, and the other shall be left. Two women shall be grinding together; the one shall be taken and the other left."

Thus they were confronted by a new fate; a fresh menace hung over their heads, but it was one that was not devoid of hope. All that was asked of them was to believe in Christ. But the change in the religious attitude which this implied was not put before them as a duty; it was an act of grace of which they could avail themselves. If they accepted it, their fate would change. "Wherefore remember, that at that time ye were without Christ, being aliens from the commonwealth of Israel, and strangers from the covenants of promise, having no hope, and without God in the world." The important point was that, deprived of all hope as they were, living in a world without God, and utterly forlorn, a haven was offered to them. "Now therefore ye are no more strangers and foreigners, but fellow-citizens with the saints, and of the household of God."

The Christ, the Messiah, who accomplished this, was of necessity very different from the Messiah created in the minds of the Jews. The very aims involved were different. For Judaism the expectation of the Messiah, far from being the end, was, as an idea, the zenith of its development. For the Gentiles, on the contrary, the coming of the Messiah was the end of an old world and the beginning of a totally different world, a fundamentally different world. And it was for this reason that Paul divorced the idea from its spiritual and national source. Out of Jesus, who had aspired to be the Messiah of the Jews, he created Christ, a heavenly being, the true Son of God, who had deigned to dwell for a time on earth, and had taken on human form to save the Gentiles. True, such an admixture of divine and human demanded a degree of credulous mysticism, of which certain men at given times and in given circumstances are capable, but of which mankind as a whole never have been and never will be capable. But the pagan world was not unfamiliar with such mystic occurrences, in their mythology. Not only did they believe that gods had sons by the daughters of men and that a man could become a god, but also that a god might die and rise again from the dead. And it was precisely in Antioch, the headquarters of Christian propaganda, that the Gentiles at a spring festival celebrated the death and resurrection of Adonis. Tarsus, Paul's native town, also celebrated this festival. The mystic cult of Adonis and Attis, into which similar ideas were woven, had spread all over Asia Minor and Syria.

Thus the Gentiles were given a figure with the idea of which they were familiar in a sublimated form, and it was precisely the concept of a true Son of God that made the rapid acceptance of Christianity possible throughout the Gentile world. And this was all the more so since not only was the figure itself acceptable to their understanding, but also the idea behind it. They understood the real significance and true meaning of the coming of the Messiah and of his death. If paganism was ever really to overcome, close the door on, and have done with a world in which it had foundered, though it had inhabited it from time immemorial, a comprehensible and tangible conclusion had to be discovered for it, a final disposal of the past, which brought consolation and did not give rise to fears of vengeance on the part of the abandoned deities. For although their pantheon had indeed been destroyed, all their gods were not yet dead, and for hours at a time the Gentiles of Ephesus were still able to shout in stubborn chorus: "Great is Diana of the Ephesians!" and to prevent Paul from speaking. Who then would save them from the sin of apostasy? For if they embraced Christianity they would certainly be renegades, who had changed their god and their faith. There was only one man who could secure salvation for them and who shared their fate, and that was Paul. Just as at first Paul had been merely a sectarian, so it was the consistency of the sectarian that had made him a renegade. By completing his breach with Judaism, and finally separating himself from it, he made all those whom he persuaded to believe in his prophecy renegades in the widest sense, whether they were Jew or Gentile. We have already pointed out elsewhere that the renegade is never anything more than a fugitive from his god; he is never finally released from him. And because he knows he is still fettered, he is constantly longing to strike out and his attitude is one of perpetual self-defence.

This explains why Paul, like Jesus, opposed the Pharisees and not the Sadducees. The renegade fights the thing to which he is closely related, the thing that fetters him. He feels no need to free himself from things that were always alien and hostile to him.

For this sin of apostasy, and for the crimes of a sinful past, in fact for everything that could be called sin, Paul presented to the pagan world the figure of Jesus as Christ the Redeemer. Jesus, he taught, had been sent into the world to save men from their sins. And sin abounded, in fact there was little besides sin in the world. "They are all gone out of the way, they are altogether become unprofitable. . . .

For all have sinned. . . . Being justified freely by his grace through the redemption that is in Christ Jesus." And as a logical conclusion of this idea, a terrible and devastating conception suddenly came into being, the doctrine of original sin. Man had sinned in the person of Adam, the first man; his sin did not merely date from yesterday, with the worship of idols. Thus sin was so irrevocably connected with the beginning of all things, that it was impossible to escape from it except by utterly renouncing a life in which there was no hope of salvation. "Therefore as by the offence of one judgment came upon all men to condemnation; even so by the righteousness of one the free gift came upon all men unto justification of life," declared Paul. And this closed the circle. There would be an end to sin, if only all men would believe that Jesus, the Son of God, had come on earth, and by his death had taken the whole burden of sin on to his own shoulders. Thus did Paul lead men to Jesus, even before he led them to God.

For it was necessary to conceive of God as without beginning and without end, as timeless and eternal. But what did "eternal" convey to the pagan? A subject of philosophic speculation for the few; it never entered into his mind to connect it with his own soul. Those who were not deified as heroes and as such had a place in an eternity which was both dubious and a matter of doubt, merely died. The pagan was familiar with chaos, but he had no knowledge of how it could be set in order or of the resulting satisfaction. He had one terrible and invincible enemy—death. And even this enemy Paul declared was now conquered, for the doctrine he preached was that not only had Jesus died to save men from sin, but he had also risen from the dead and conquered death. This doctrine of the resurrection of the dead or of eternal life was cardinal to the fear-haunted world of the Gentiles. It therefore became a cardinal point in Pauline Christianity. "And if Christ be not risen, then is our preaching vain, and your faith is also vain." And thus he did what Judaism could not prevail upon itself to do; he founded the dogma of the resurrection of the dead on the resurrection of Jesus.

In its essence the doctrine of death and resurrection was a primeval Jewish idea, that is to say as denoting a change of life it was clearly symbolized in the ceremony of anointing, which produced a transformation in the man submitting to it and endowed him with a new and higher existence, no matter who or what he had been previously. But in Pauline Christianity a new principle was introduced; for the first time, a fact, a tangible, concrete, and actual fact, to which it was alleged that witnesses could bear testimony, was made the basis of the idea pure and simple—the fact that a man had been crucified and had risen from the dead. And from this concrete fact, the idea was now once more deduced. But by this time it had been considerably modified. "The Lord's Anointed" still remained the instrument of the theocracy; but Christ was deified. The Lord's Anointed took the place of occasional manifestations of the divine. But Christ was the final and conclusive manifestation, and henceforward, almost to the exclusion of God, was to be God's representative for ever and ever. And, as God's representative, Jesus necessarily and logically became the mediator. For this idea of a mediator obviously follows from all that has been said above. Judaism did not regard even its high priests as mediators. But the pagan world had no other avenue of approach to the God which it had not even heard of the day before. "For there is one God, and one mediator between God and men, the man Christ Jesus."

But as the terror-stricken world of the pagan had developed with him, it could not suddenly be dissipated into thin air by means of a new law, or rule of faith, and, though Pauline Christianity professed to dispel it, it merely led it by means of other doctrines to a new and no less terrifying alternative—the antithesis of flesh and spirit, body and soul. It was only natural that Paul should everywhere encounter among his Gentile followers the heritage of ancient culture—unbridled sexuality; and he inevitably lived to see the ceremony of Holy Communion, or the love feast, the symbol he had introduced as a means of approach to Christ, degenerate into a sexual orgy. But whereas, with the restraint and sensitiveness of the Hebrew, he protested against it, the desire to be consistent did not lead him to the conclusion reached by Judaism, which was to recognize the divine unity of body and soul and the sanctification and sublimation of both, but to the extreme view that the flesh was altogether sinful, that marriage was merely the lesser of two evils, and that the ideal life was one of asceticism. And thus the very source of life was polluted and held suspect, and although sex perhaps no longer gave rise to the old fears and qualms of conscience, it was now connected with the new eternal horrors of original sin, hell, the devil, and purgatory. Thus before they had even mastered life on this earth, the converts were confronted with a beyond full of fresh terrors. They were held in a vice. For centuries this nightmare led to repeated outbursts of panic, until, at last, the religious impulse resigned itself and in our day has become almost extinct.

Paul continued to carry the process of assimilation to its logical conclusion, and turned every fresh step into a new dogma. When he presented the Gentiles with a belief which he maintained was the only true, the only blessed one, he was at the same time obliged to adjust his attitude to his own race and to the idea of the obligations implicit in the fact that they were the Chosen People. And he did not attempt to evade the issue. On his own authority he found a way out of the difficulty and declared that Judaism had fulfilled its mission; as it had refused to accept Jesus, the Jews had lost all claim to being the Chosen

People, and God, by a free act of grace, had rejected them and placed the Gentiles in the position they had occupied. "But ye are a chosen generation, a royal priesthood, an holy nation." But such reasoning, which was inadequate even in the realm of theology, did not satisfy him and, with the sublime technique of the Pharisee, he put the coping-stone to his work by reverting once more to an argument he had used in the early days of his conversion—the antithesis he claimed to have discovered between law and faith. "For Christ is the end of the law for righteousness to everyone that believeth." True, Judaism had endeavoured to realize God; but it had shown a lack of understanding, and had laid down laws for itself by which it hoped to realize God on earth. But the new faith required a new method. "For with the heart man believeth unto righteousness; and with the mouth confession is made unto salvation." And for his proof, as had been the case with the old religion, Paul had to turn to evidence taken from the highest Jewish authority on God, the Book of Deuteronomy: "For this commandment which I commanded thee this day . . . the word is very nigh unto thee, in thy mouth and in thy heart that thou mayest do it."

Ten years of strenuous effort enabled Paul to produce a mythology and a dogma for the new sect, and to raise it to the rank of a religion. It was an extremely difficult undertaking, for the dogmas which he gave the people were not the result of natural development, and this innate flaw was responsible for the constant outbursts of schismatic views and sects among the faithful. "Now this I say, that every one of you saith, I am of Paul; and I of Apollos; and I of Cephas; and I of Christ. Is Christ divided?" But it was not only against schism that Paul had to fight; he had also to set his face against the cult of persons and an inborn tendency to connect the faith with particular individuals. But this was inevitable; for the new congregation consisted chiefly of Greek and oriental polytheists, and Paul himself, through the deification of the man Christ, had taught the cult of persons. He himself on one occasion was actually called Mercury, while his fellow-apostle, Barnabas, was hailed as Jupiter! But these were all difficulties which arose at a time when Christianity had already completely severed itself from its Jewish source, and do not therefore belong to Jewish history and are outside the scope of the present treatise.

But there was one factor which had far-reaching results and continued to exercise a most deleterious influence over the history of Judaism; I refer to the hostility of Christianity as a religion against the Jewish people and the Jewish religion. Paul was also responsible for this, for it was through him that a difference of dogma developed into a conscious antagonism between Christianity and Judaism. A mere difference in kind became a difference in value. The whole of his propaganda is replete with valuations. He was unable to set the new doctrine on such firm foundations of its own that it would be in a position to dispense with an attitude of contempt towards the religion to which it owed its fundamental concepts. He was not content for Christianity to be different from Judaism and at the same time to show respect for it; he wished it to be better. But if valuing is allowable at all, it ought surely to be done in connexion with the nature of the demands made upon the individual, in connexion with proof of worth and those matters whereby a religion establishes its worth, that is to say, the relations of man to the world and to God, and not only to one of these. The difference between Judaism and Christianity did not arise from the difference between their dogma, but from the interpretation given to the idea of salvation. Christianity regarded salvation as the final freeing of man, once and for all, from sin through baptism. The Jew did not recognize any original sin, and when he sinned, he had no act of grace to which he could resort. Judaism recognized only the incessant and repeated striving for the realization of its mission—the perfection of the race as members of God's creation. An effort consummated in a single act of decision and confession is very different from one which is sustained throughout the whole of a man's life and beyond it through the generations that follow after. Judaism makes an appeal to mankind for an effort that should be continued for all time. The struggle follows the appeal as the effect the cause. Herein lies the living core of the creative power of the Jewish religion which is far from being dead. But why all this weighing and valuing of religions one against the other? How futile it is! How superfluous! For a similar fate awaits them all; they must prove their truth in the active life of the world.

Judaism made no systematic attempt to oppose the spread of the new faith. The subsequent controversies between Jews and Christians proved fruitless in the end, for the struggle was carried on with different arguments on different planes. And it became quite purposeless when Christianity began to spread under the protection of the state, and the fundamental difference between the methods, formulæ, dogmas, and propaganda of the two religions became unmistakable.

PART III

FROM

THE BANISHMENT FROM PALESTINE

TO

THE SETTLEMENT IN THE WEST

THE MOBILE CENTRE

JUST before the greatest nation in the world at that time was arming itself for its decisive conflict with the smallest, two groups of people left Jerusalem. The one which claimed to be acting on divine instructions consisted of the followers of Jesus of Nazareth. They left their people to their fate. The other, consisting of a few members of the "pacifist" group, teachers, scholars, and educators, repaired to Jamnia, taking the fate of their people on their shoulders so as to be responsible for it through the ages. While in Rome a triumphal arch was being erected in honour of Titus bearing the inscription: "The Senate and people of Rome return thanks to the Imperator Titus for having conquered the Jewish people and destroyed the city of Jerusalem, which all the generals, kings, and peoples of former times attacked in vain," Johanan ben Zaccai, with the help of his colleagues, was setting up in Jamnia the central body for the administration and guidance of the Jewish people.

As a rule, when a nation has been utterly routed as the Jews were on this occasion, they perish altogether. But the Jewish people did not perish. Five hundred years previously they had discovered the force which makes survival possible—the force of the spirit. But while this spirit could understand the real sense of things, it could not understand single facts. They had already learnt how to change their attitude during the Babylonian captivity. And they followed a similar course now.

True, the Christians were loud in their triumph, and saw in the fall of Jerusalem a proof that Judaism was played out. The Jewish Christians therefore immediately intensified their propaganda, fondly imagining that the common people at all events would now join them. But they did not understand what had taken place. They confounded the end of a national state with the end of a people, to whom though the form of the state was essential, the actuality was not. And just as the state could be dispensed with, so also could the Temple, the existence of which was not necessary for the religious salvation of the people. The Babylonian captivity had proved this; the prophets had proved it; and now Johanan ben Zaccai and his circle proceeded to prove it for the third time.

The first institution to be set up in Jamnia was a *Beth-din,* which formed the basis of all legislative, administrative, and judicial activities, and was merely the old Sanhedrin under a new name. In addition and closely connected with it was the *Beth-ha-Midrash,* the academy, which combined under one roof the various schools that had existed in the past. These two institutions were naturally complementary. The Jews had renounced nothing, and as they still wished to live as they had always done, according to the spirit of the Torah, they were obliged to regulate their daily life, their communal life, and their relationship to the outside world in accordance with its principles. Their state had been destroyed, but they immediately fell back upon the force which provides the idea underlying every state—the binding force of laws based on mutual agreement. When laws of this nature are held to be binding, although they are not backed by force, they acquire an extraordinary amount of power and vitality. And the vast majority of the Jewish people have for centuries obeyed one law, and do so still, not because they are *compelled* to obey it but because they *wish* to do so.

Laws not only bind, they also standardize. This is inevitable. And the Jewish people were forced to react to the death of the collective state by standardizing the behaviour of the individual, by a general attack on the individual, in whom the Christian doctrine of a beyond centred. Thus the Jews became a people in whom the idea of discipline reached its highest expression. This discipline was rigid to the point of deadliness as far as the individual was concerned, though astonishingly flexible as applied to the whole community. The law raised an insuperable barrier against the outside world. And beyond this barrier anything from sublime faith to superstition might prosper.

The new autonomous administration made it their first duty to keep the body of the nation together and protect it from danger, and, in so doing, the leaders even did all they could to keep proselytes at arm's length; for they wished to avoid the waste of strength involved in assimilating new members. Moreover, there was the danger that converts might create confusion, thanks to the vestiges of paganism which might continue to cling to them. Confusion was also to be feared from the quarter of the Jewish Christians; consequently the line of demarcation between them and the Jews was made ever more and more plain, until eventually the Jews were forbidden to buy meat, wine, or bread from them, to carry on business with them, or to perform any service for them, no matter how insignificant.

The aim was to make the life of the Jew utterly different from that of the Gentile. On the authority of Jamnia an important step was taken in this direction by dividing up the day and the year; the day was broken up by the intervals for prayer, and the year by the periodic festivals. The Temple had been destroyed, but the Temple services were replaced by forms of prayer, which were repeated three times a day at the hours at which the services had been held. The year was divided up by the various festivals, and as their nature was determined by the position of the sun or moon, and were fixed according to their phases, the Beth-din at Jamnia undertook the task of arranging that they should be celebrated simultaneously by the Jews all the world over.

Just as the body of the people themselves had been collected and bound together, so the rules and standards by which they were to regulate their lives had also to be collected and bound together. Apart from the Torah, there was no written law; but legislative enactments, orders, and instructions dealing with every department of life to which everyday occurrences, particular circumstances, and individual cases had given rise, were enshrined in the memories of the people; they formed the theoretical basis for practical conduct and were handed down from teacher to pupil. Reverence for the sacredness of the written words of the Torah had prevented anything in the nature of a written record being made of these laws, which were only derived from everyday life, and already constituted a huge unwieldy mass. Much of it was, moreover, obsolete and no longer applicable. But as the old differences of opinion regarding dogmas, which had existed between the schools of men like Hillel and Shammai, still survived in the school at Jamnia, as though disaster had not meanwhile overtaken the Jewish people, no uniformity had been established. But it was imperative to secure uniformity at all costs, if a people scattered over the face of the whole civilized world were not to fall a hopeless prey to arbitrary decisions and drift irrevocably apart. It was therefore decided to put the matter to the vote. Any law that received a majority of votes in its favour was passed. Opponents were threatened with the ban (*Niddui*), which meant being excluded from the community for a given period.

It might be imagined that as a result a rigid and unalterable code was produced which would in future render all legislation superfluous. But the contrary was the case. These laws in their entirety also represented a direction, a "Torah," and although there was some scruple about placing them immediately on record, their origin made them equally sacred and they took their place beside the written Torah and were known as the "Oral Torah." As soon as this idea had received its final form, the Oral Torah came into existence as a separate entity. And just as the Torah had been in the past, so now the Oral Torah, the *Mishnah,* became the source of fresh enactments, and gave birth to a new and peculiar spirit which left an indelible mark on the intellectual life of the Jews for over a thousand years. The Torah, as the fundamental moral norm, could be the fountain-head of new laws. The law, in order to exist, required an actual basis in fact, and if anything further was to be derived from it, that too had to have some possible, imaginary, or hypothetical basis in fact. Thus laws came into being which were ends in themselves; thus arose the solemn toying with possibility, and the advent of Talmudic methodology before the Talmud itself was produced.

When once this binding together and isolation of the people and the law had been accomplished, one last important task remained—the bestowal of a final and unalterable form to the fountain-head by once and for all determining what really constituted Holy Writ, and fixing the canon for all time. Both the national Jewish literature and more recent productions of Christian origin had to be examined and everything of a doubtful nature weeded out. The excitement prevailing at the time in religious matters had led to a vast output in both departments, but the Christian writings were particularly voluminous. In addition to much else, the Gentile had above all inherited a most precious possession from Judaism in the shape of the Bible. For the first time in his history he had at his disposal a whole body of literature dealing with matter concerning his soul, and the longing to propagate his doctrines and communicate them to the rest of the world which Paul had been the first to undertake systematically found exaggerated expression in countless epistles, treatises, revelations, and gospels written in Hebrew, Greek, and Syriac. Over forty Gospels were produced, a special one for each sect, purporting to have been written by Adam, Enoch, Moses, the Patriarchs, and Isaiah. The Psalms of David were imitated, and the most fantastic authorship assigned to these outpourings to lend them authority. Even the Torah, in its Greek version, the Septuagint, was unhesitatingly corrupted in a number of places, with the object of inserting as many proofs as possible of the appearance of Jesus and of his Messiahship. It had become imperative once and for all to purge Jewish literature of all such productions regardless of their alleged antiquity or authenticity.

The Jewish writings were subjected to an equally strict scrutiny, and any which fell under the slightest suspicion of teaching anything short of clear and unequivocal monotheism, or betrayed the faintest traces of the syncretism so characteristic of Christian literature, was unhesitatingly rejected. Not even the most profound piety and earnestness in endeavouring to trace the fundamental principles of Judaism, in examining the promises and failures which had determined the fate of the Jewish people, or in inquiring into what was to happen at the "End of Days" could save a book. Such works, called apocryphal works, appeared in large numbers. But even the best of them, "The Fourth Book of Ezra," and "The Apocalypse of Baruch," both of which are far superior to the "Revelation of St. John," were relegated to a place outside the canon. A similar fate awaited even older works, such as the "Psalms of Solomon," the "Wisdom of Ben Sira," the "First

Book of Maccabees," etc. And about the middle of the second century the canon was established in the form that is still accepted at the present day.

Thus the centre of the circle was finally fixed, and the circle itself fully described in the form of the law and the hedge that was set about the people. The Jew undertook to effect standardization through the law; but in those spheres where it did not concern his way of life, but merely his emotions, he created an outlet for himself in the shape of mystical Messianism as a form of thought, and the Haggadah as a form of expression. It was as though the soul of the people, before once more delivering itself up to a hazardous existence, wished to make a final survey to try to ascertain where its pilgrimage of pain would end, when and how salvation would come, and, if it was not to come during the lifetime of those then living, what the individual had to expect after death.

In all this the sensitive and poetical soul of the people was left entirely to its own devices. Unlike Christianity, official Judaism resolutely refused to allow ideas such as the World to Come, the Resurrection of the Dead, Retribution in a Beyond, which emanated from a Messianic age, to be rigidly fixed in a dogma. It was contrary to the conception of the theocracy; for theocracy was primarily fulfilment, through which alone salvation could come. Thus the people were allowed to speculate and to rhapsodize outside the confines of scholarly knowledge and compulsory belief, and this accounts for the vagueness of their ideas regarding the Messianic age and the beyond, and their uncertainty as to which came first. But the depression and defeatism of the age and their own sorry fate led them to seize upon anything that lay ready to hand, and the close proximity of innumerable Christian sects, all preaching and propagating their doctrines, led to Jewish thought being permeated by all sorts of ideas about hell, the last judgment, and purgatory. The Jews identified their own sufferings with the "sufferings of the last days," and a spirit of resignation spread everywhere. "For the world is growing old, and hath outlived its youthful strength." Prompted by this same spirit of resignation, they proceeded to act as Pauline Christianity had done when the prophecy made by Jesus that the day of salvation was at hand had not been fulfilled; in order not to lose faith in their faith, they postponed the day of fulfilment. Thus the idea of a Messiah of the house of Joseph, who was to precede the Messiah of the house of David, came into being. He was to fight Gog and Magog, the enemies of the Jewish people; he would be killed in the struggle, but his death would clear the path for the advent to power of the Messiah of the house of David. When all is said and done, their various devices for accounting for the postponement did actually lead them in the direction of the belief that the Messiah had already come. He was crouching among the beggars and lepers at the gates of Rome, abiding his time! Or they relegated him indefinitely to heaven, where he shared all the sufferings of his people with them, and waited for the cup to be full.

Thus in addition to the inexorableness of the world of law, the mystical element also came into its own. In addition to the law (the Halakah), opinion, emotion, faith, and the visionary, legendary, imaginative, and superstitious side of life were embodied in the Haggadah. Nevertheless, the various mystical elaborations of the Messianic idea were unable to destroy the strong political core it contained. Messianism was still largely built up on the belief that, in the near future, the rule of Rome would be replaced by the rule of Judea, the rule of might by the rule of right. To the Jews Rome constituted the quintessence of all that was odious and should be swept away from off the face of the earth. They hated Rome and her device, *arma et leges,* with an inhuman hatred. True, Rome had *leges,* laws, like the Jews. But in their very resemblance lay their difference; for the Roman laws were merely the practical application of the *arma,* the arms; they completed a formula which made a deep impression on slaves of every category. But without the arms, the *leges* were empty formulæ, and nobody dreamt of making them into repositories of justice instead of mere judicial enactments.

This resistance, this attitude of self-assertion in the face of Rome, found its final, if somewhat feeble support, in the political autonomy their stubborn perseverance enabled them to build up in a few years. Though Judea was a conquered province, the Jews still survived as a nation and were acknowledged as such. In the person of the patriarch they provided themselves with an official representative in their relations with the outside world, and particularly with Rome. The fiction of state representation was preserved, and carried to such lengths that even the laws regarding the sacredness of the land were retained, as though the country still belonged to the Jews as it had done in the old days. But so much vital energy still remained in this institution that it succeeded in creating and gathering up the strength for one more final and desperate revolt against Rome, one last attempt at recovering national freedom.

In the person of Rabbi Aqiba the nation was presented with a man who was at once its spiritual and its political co-ordinator. He was a most distinguished scholar and the first to introduce order into the oral tradition. He was also a man who had not relinquished all hope but felt that his people still had a future as a nation, and he not only succeeded in making himself the centre of a band of devoted scholars but also had a secret following among the rebels. But in those days every man was a rebel who regarded the Roman yoke as intolerable, and in this sense the whole people consisted of rebels, not only in Palestine, but throughout the Diaspora. In Palestine a perpetual cause of friction was provided by the fact that the old Temple tribute was still collected under the new designation of *fiscus judaicus* and allocated to the temple of Jupiter Capitolinus in Rome; while the Diaspora looked upon the Romans as the destroyers of the Temple, who had taken away Jerusalem from them as a place of pilgrimage. Furthermore, if we bear in mind all that has already been said regarding the general intellectual disagreement between Rome and Judea, it is easy to understand that the whole of the Jewish world should have risen up in a paroxysm of indignation when Rome stretched out her hand to that part of the Diaspora which she had hitherto left in peace.

This took place under Trajan, whose ambition it was to be a second Alexander, but who lacked both the personality and the intellect for the part. In the year 114 he inaugurated his campaign against Asia, and in the following year he occupied northern Mesopotamia, and Adiabene, which had a large Jewish population, from whom he already met with opposition. He advanced farther into Babylonia, where more particularly in the provinces of Nisibis and Nehardea he again came into contact with the Jews who had learnt to regard resistance to Rome in the light of a Holy War. They issued a general call to arms. In the rear of the Roman army Adiabene revolted, and forced Trajan to begin his work of conquest all over again. But hardly had he reconquered this territory, when the insurrection spread from Mesopotamia to Palestine, Egypt, Libya, Cyrenaica, and even to the island of Cyprus. The whole movement was carried out with such extraordinary speed and precision as to leave no doubt that it was the result of unity of command or at all events of entire unity of popular sentiment. But in the fury of this revolt, the idea of a war of liberation against Rome was suddenly lost in a tumult of hatred, revengefulness, violence, and despair against the common enemy, against paganism as such. The whole of Asiatic Judaism was soon in what appeared to be the last death agonies of a struggle against Romans, Greeks, and Hellenized Jews. Inhuman and barbaric massacres took place, and the inhabitants of whole suburbs, cities, and districts engaged in mutual slaughter. Once again the Jews defeated a Roman army under the command of Lupus and turned the city of Salamis into a heap of ruins. They are said to have killed over 100,000 Romans and Greeks in Cyrenaica and Cyprus, and to have wrought such havoc in Libya that it had to be colonized afresh.

In this insensate and hopeless insurrection it at last became clear that the incessant onslaughts of a whole world—Egypt, Assyria, Babylon, Persia, Greece, and Rome—had ended by inspiring a determined and fanatical will to self-preservation in the soul of the Jewish people.

But it also provided a further proof that the weapon of violence to which other nations had recourse was not one that the Jews could use. Trajan retorted by dispatching Roman armies to Africa and Asia. The Egyptian Diaspora received its death-blow, and ceased to exist after Martius Turbo's soldiers had done their work there. In Cyprus not a Jew was left alive. And in the year 117 Lucius Quietus suppressed the rising in Asia Minor with great slaughter.

Quietus was on the point of subduing Palestine also, when Trajan died. Whereupon a number of provinces immediately tried to make a bid for freedom. Hadrian, Trajan's successor, endeavoured to gain his ends by means of conciliation and apparent concessions. He even negotiated with the Jews, and held out to them the prospect of rebuilding Jerusalem and restoring the Temple. They then laid down their arms. But Hadrian was a Roman. He allowed the rebuilding of the city to be begun, but it soon became evident that the new Jerusalem was to be a pagan and not a Jewish city. The people were furious and exasperation increased. In 131 Hadrian himself came to Palestine and then his intentions were plainly revealed. Jerusalem was to be a centre of Roman culture in the East. True, there was to be a Temple, but it would be a temple of Jupiter. As soon as his back was turned, bands of armed men sprang up in the whole of the Jewish area. One by one they attacked each Roman garrison, separately and in very difficult country. The rebels succeeded in evading capture; they were as slippery as eels in eluding attack, and by guerrilla tactics destroyed the reinforcements sent out against them.

Rabbi Aqiba was the spiritual leader of this uprising. He was here, there, and everywhere, organizing the rebellion, and even went as far as Parthia. Every walled city, every lurking-place in the hills, was converted into a fortress, with the result that the country, which was supposed to be conquered and disarmed, suddenly bristled with arms and had all the necessary supplies and lines of communication. From all the four quarters of the Diaspora fighters poured into the country for this last struggle with Rome. In addition to the spiritual organizer, a military organizer also suddenly made his appearance. He was appointed on the authority of Rabbi Aqiba, and accepted by the people. His name was Bar Koziba, but he was popularly known as Bar Kokeba, the Son of the Stars. According to Jewish authorities, he had an army of 400,000 men; Dion Cassius puts it at 580,000.

Bar Kokeba struck his blow before Rome had fully grasped the extent of the rising. The Roman general, Tinnius Rufus, a butcher of men, was taken by surprise, and even when he had received reinforcements he failed to stem the advance of the rebels. The Proconsul of Syria was obliged to come to the rescue. But in vain! Within the space of a year Bar Kokeba had captured 50 strongholds in Samaria and Judea and 985 towns and villages, including Jerusalem.

This forced Hadrian to make up his mind to send his ablest general, Julius Severus, the conqueror of Britain, with a large army to Judea. Severus did not venture to risk an open engagement, but at the price of enormous losses he gradually wiped out the insurgents piecemeal. And this tiny little country forced him to fight for three and a half years and to engage in over fifty battles before he succeeded in shutting up Bar Kokeba, the leader, and the remains of his army in Bethar. The fortress held out for a year, but at last, owing to the treachery of some Samaritans, it capitulated in 135. The victors then indulged in an orgy of massacre which appalled even the Romans. Dion Cassius gives the number of dead as over half a million.

The Romans were silent about their own losses. When Hadrian informed the Senate that the war was over, he did not dare to use the formula usual on such occasions: "All is well with us and with our army." But in honour of this victory he was made Imperator for the second time.

Streams of fugitives now left the country, which rapidly became depopulated, and all that remained of the scattered fighting forces was gradually annihilated. But Hadrian waged war even against noncombatants, in the sense in which Antiochus Epiphanes had done so. He was quite right in thinking that the indefatigable eagerness to fight on the part of the Jews was not due to any political or imperialistic ambitions, but was the reaction of an idea to hostile attacks. He therefore made it his aim to destroy the idea. On the site of Jerusalem he built the pagan city of Ælia Capitolina, complete with a temple of Jupiter, statues of the gods, a theatre, and a circus, and settled Romans, Greeks, and Syrians within its walls. The Jews were forbidden on pain of death to practise their religion; the rite of circumcision in particular was prohibited, as well as the observance of the Sabbath and any preoccupation with Jewish law. Tinnius Rufus, an incapable general, but an efficient taskmaster, was made governor of the country. He organized a network of spies who were responsible for the martyrdom of many victims, among them Rabbi Aqiba. It was at this time that, at a secret meeting, held at Lydda, the Jewish scholars passed a resolution to the effect that if a Jew were asked under the threat of death to deny his faith, he might do so, or at least pretend to do so, but that he was bound to suffer death by martyrdom rather than consent to worship idols, or to be guilty of unchastity or murder. Later on, Christianity was again and again to make this law a ghastly reality throughout the centuries.

As soon as Hadrian's edicts were rescinded by his successor, Antoninus Pius, Jewish life once more returned to the old rhythm which had been interrupted by the fight for freedom. True, the people had been perfectly ready to sacrifice the work of spiritual settlement while there was the least chance of restoring the state as an actuality by means of insurrection. But when the attempt failed, the responsible leaders immediately came forward and took the fate of their people into their own hands.

The southern part of the country, which had formerly been Judea, had been deserted by the Jews. All who had not emigrated were concentrated in the north, in Galilee, where the fugitive or exiled teachers and scholars also found refuge. In the town of Usha, in Galilee, they formed a new Sanhedrin, and reinstated the patriarchate. So great was the authority voluntarily conceded to this institution by the people that, at the request of Usha the Babylonian Jews without demur abolished their own patriarchate, which had been created during the war carried on by Bar Kokeba. Though the Jewish community in Palestine was the smallest, it inhabited the historic home, and had always been responsible for providing the government. The people respected this government more than they had respected their former kings, whom they had forgotten all too quickly. Their sagas contain no mention of them. But with passionate resolution they kept alive their own view of what constituted history, namely the attempt to realize their own idea. It is only by bearing this in mind that we can understand how it came about that, after the failure of all their political and military activities, they not only shut themselves up in their spiritual life, but also ceased to take any notice of external events. It is extremely significant that from this moment, that is to say, from the second to the eleventh century, Jewish historical records virtually cease to exist, and even the chronology is scanty and unreliable. And this is not due to the fact, as many historians maintain, that the Jews suddenly found themselves unable to write history, or that their life was no longer influenced by the activities of the world about them, for in this respect they suffered even more than other nations. But they deliberately ceased to take an interest in external concerns, and confined their connexion with the outside world to what was absolutely necessary in the circumstances, without regarding it as worth while to make any record of it. It was a case of a people refusing to write history that was not its own, but was forced upon them and dictated from outside.

This idea can be traced in every detail of their lives and leads to the conclusion that, after the final destruction of the Jewish state, Jewish history became dependent on the particular environment of the moment; but the spiritual development of the people remained free and independent, with the result that a twofold division occurred in Jewish history—materio-historical and spirito-historical, external and internal. Sometimes the two overlapped, but as a rule they did not.

Thus the Palestine Jews continued their spiritual development in a uniform manner. External circumstances enabled them to do this in peace for two hundred years, during which they took the opportunity of examining and arranging their oral tradition once more. But it had now reached such unwieldy proportions that it was impossible to continue the tradition of committing it to memory instead of putting it into writing, and at the beginning of the third century Jehuda ha Nasi, who filled the offices of Patriarch, president of the Sanhedrin, and head of the academy, collected all the material together in one great encyclopædia, which has been handed down to us as the Mishnah. It was not a book of laws, but a compilation; not a code, but material for study. It was only at a much later date that the desire to find anchorage in an ever more distant past led to the work being accepted as canonical.

Inasmuch as the law provided a spiritual haven for the Jews, it left them free to watch and judge what was going on in the world about them. Confusion was rampant there. Three forms of religion already stood out in sharp distinction side by side—Judaism, paganism, and Christianity. But whereas Judaism set limitations about itself and grew ever more exclusive, paganism and Christianity became split up into innumerable movements, cults, and sects. In Rome the decline of imperial authority had begun as early as Commodus, and time and again the legions had invested men of their own choice in the purple. And thus the various oriental religions were enabled to find their way to Rome, where the most hybrid forms of pagan cult took root and flourished. On the virgin soil of Christianity also countless sects sprang up, while the Gnostics, who were deeply stirred by religious unrest, formed a connecting link between the leading cults. Recruited from the ranks of the three chief religions, the Gnostics endeavoured to reach an understanding of the nature of God and of his relation to the world and to life, but so closely were they allied to paganism that all they succeeded in doing was to put forward a dualistic conception of the Godhead instead of a monotheistic. At this stage in their development Christianity and paganism had, in religious syncretism, one feature in common, which favoured their subsequent convergence and amalgamation. But for the time being they were still at daggers drawn, and continued to be opposed until, by the conversion of one man, the Emperor Constantine, the new religion received a fatal and momentous gift in the shape of state power.

From the very beginning the Jews paid no attention to the Gentile Christians who were not within their jurisdiction. They were able only to exclude the Jewish Christians, the *Minim* (heretics) from their ranks; and pronounced a special curse on them; for, like all renegades, they were only too ready to give information to Hadrian's spies. But it required no effort on the part of the Jews to widen the breach between Judaism and Christianity. The synoptic Gospels (Matthew, Mark, and Luke) had followed in the footsteps of Paul, and in the Epistle to the Hebrews, which came into being in Italy at the beginning of the second century, a new note was struck, and polemics began to play a part.

Christianity, the new religion, required confirmation, and therefore turned to polemics, and, as it wished to make its way in a world of superstition, it charged even the theophoric people themselves with holding a creed that was superstitious. (This is really too much for any serious student of history to swallow!) But it was precisely the Jews who were in a position to bring a charge of blasphemy against Christianity for having made the Godhead human, and for having destroyed monotheism. Yet the polemical tactics adopted by Christianity were comprehensible enough, seeing that not only did Judaism have a strong attraction for the emotionally religious type unspoiled by false education, as was proved by the constant conversion of such men to Judaism, but that it also constituted the only storehouse from which Christianity drew the wherewithal for the development of its creed. Just as the sacraments of baptism and the holy communion were Jewish in origin, so too were the prayers and festivals, the communal institutions, and the educational methods of Christianity founded upon Jewish customs, and to some extent merely literal and slavish copies of them. And yet the Christians forbade members of their sect to have anything to do with the Jews for fear they might become like them, and the doctrine preached by the apostolic fathers was merely a diluted form of Judaism, and their morality that of the Old Testament!

The polemics gave rise to controversies. Here Christianity found itself in difficulties, and for hundreds of years, in fact nearly a thousand years, until the rule of the Christian church had supplanted the Christian religion, it safeguarded a position that was still precarious by forbidding all discussions between the Christian laity and the Jews. For the discussions turned on dogma, which was far from unassailable, more particularly as Christianity insisted at all costs on supplying proofs, whether for the Messiahship of Jesus or for the doctrine of the Holy Trinity. But such proofs could be obtained only from the Jewish Scriptures, which had to be unscrupulously falsified and distorted for the purpose. Thus any discussion with Jews was obviously difficult and unpleasant.

Moreover, the Judaism of the Halakah, or what might be termed official Judaism, would have nothing to do with such discussions, which belonged to the province of the Haggadah, or unofficial Judaism. The typical representative of the latter was the *darshan,* the itinerant preacher, whose activities kept the religious consciousness of the people alive and prevented it from becoming disordered.

Eventually the time came when, although such controversies had not ceased to be important, Christianity, having become possessed of political, legal, and military power, was in a position to decide them always in its own favour. To set up a "Kingdom which was not of this world" Christianity regarded all means as justified, and even succeeded in robbing the Jews of their historic home, and in destroying it for centuries to come as a source of creative inspiration for the whole of the Jewish world.

CHRISTIAN POLICY

UP to the fourth century Judaism and Christianity occupied entirely different positions in the framework of the Roman state. Judaism was supported by a united people, a recognized nation, whose religion was a *religio licita,* a lawful creed. The Patriarch in Judea was regarded in Rome as the supreme head of all the Jews in the Roman empire. Christianity, on the other hand, was a forbidden sect, and its form of worship one of the forbidden, secret cults. The conversion of pagans to it was, in the eyes of the law, held to be defection from the approved state religion, and was for a while actually punished as such.

The conversion of the Roman Emperor Constantine (312–337) to Christianity changed the position, inasmuch as henceforward Christianity became the state religion in accordance with the fundamental principle *cujus regio ejus religio,* the religion of the ruler is the religion of the state. When the conversion of the emperor was officially established, hundreds of thousands of Christians suddenly made their appearance. This might have been a matter of indifference to the Jews if Constantine had succeeded in realizing all his ideas and aims. But, in so far as his conversion was not purely the outcome of personal inclination, he had been led to it by political considerations and more particularly by the fact that, in conflicts with other powers, he would be able to rely on the Christian element in his army. We do not know what arrangements were come to in this respect but that some were come to is, from the psychological standpoint, a matter of course. As late as the year 313, by the Edict of Milan, he confirmed the right to freedom of conscience for all citizens of the Roman empire, but two years later he made an exception in the case of the Jews, thus abandoning his original intention of placing Judaism and Christianity on a footing of equality. In his attitude towards the Jews he wavered for a considerable time, but towards the end of his reign he became definitely hostile towards them, although they had not been lacking in any way in loyalty towards him as emperor, or in their duties as Roman citizens.

This is a clear proof that he had pledged himself to the Christians and had promised to defend their religion in return for their support in arms. And thus he made himself dependent on the representatives of Christianity, the priests. The rise of legends in connexion with his conversion was not accidental, for they frequently served the purpose of adding strength to the somewhat feeble pretexts he advanced for the step he had taken.

Jewish history is not concerned with Constantine's change of religion, but it is concerned with his change of attitude towards the Jews. So long as he remained a pagan he respected other religions, but as soon as he became a Christian he persecuted the Jews for no other reason than that they believed something different from what he believed. He did not adopt this attitude of his own accord; it was forced upon him by the Christian priesthood, who disapproved of the freedom of conscience he had intended to make the basis of his rule. The possibilities opened up by the sudden elevation of a sect to the rank of a state religion had to be exploited, and the clergy could no longer be satisfied with Christianity being placed on an equal footing with Judaism. The open and secret struggle in which, ever since its foundation, it had been engaged against Judaism must now be brought to an end, and nothing could be simpler than to use the power of the state to this end. Thus they assumed the same attitude of overbearance and intolerance as their predecessors, the pagan priests of Rome, had done in defence of the state religion and their own position of power. As soon as Christianity became the recognized religion of the state, the hostility of the clergy became too active and determined to be explained on the grounds of religious fanaticism alone; it was much more the attitude of those who regarded themselves as the successors of the state priests of pagan Rome; and the sect which but a short time previously had been the object of persecution inaugurated its career as a state religion by immediately adopting an attitude of intolerance, and persecuting in its turn. It did not feel called upon for the moment to supply the world with a practical proof of its religious spirit.

The very terms in which its edicts were couched were full of presumption and unbridled abuse. The language of the first edict of Constantine against the Jews, which was issued in 315, was redolent of Christian polemics, and revealed the spirit in which the Christian church availed itself of state support. The Jews, "that disgraceful sect," were forbidden to make Jews of their slaves by means of the ceremony of circumcision; furthermore—and this was tantamount to an infringement of their rights of autonomy—they were forbidden to punish members of their own race who abandoned the Jewish faith.

For the time being these measures were entirely religio-political in character, and are only to be understood as such. For, after all, by far the greater number of Christians had embraced the new religion as the result of a political measure which had nothing whatever to do with personal conversion. To have converted them all in such a short space of time would have been impossible, more particularly as, for the moment, there were far more urgent matters for the new religion to settle. The limitation of the legal rights of the Jews therefore reduced the sources of danger to which it was exposed not only owing to the unreliability of the new converts, but also above all owing to the splits and rifts within the new faith itself. When the Council of Nicæa in 325 endeavoured to establish order in this sphere, and introduce uniformity into the dogmas which were henceforward to govern the faith, the line of demarcation between Jews and Christians was also more sharply defined. The Easter festival, which the Asiatic communities had hitherto celebrated at the time of the Jewish Passover, which was only logical according to the Gospels, was given its own particular place in the calendar. But in this connexion the fact itself is less interesting than the reasons adduced for it: "It would be unseemly if at this sacred festival we followed the customs of the Jews, who have stained their hands with the most monstrous of all crimes, and remain spiritually blind!"

The racial barrier was supplemented at the Council of Laodicea by a ceremonial barrier between the two religions. Christians were forbidden to sit down to meals with Jews, to take any part in their festivals, to perform their rites, and above all observe their Sabbath. It was imperative for Christianity to consolidate itself, and to confine its members within certain bounds in order, as far as possible, to prevent them from feeling drawn to Judaism, an attraction which still constituted a danger. But Christianity was not content with setting bounds. The power it had acquired soon reached vast proportions, and that which only yesterday had been a religion in search of converts was now a church engaged in political activities. Under Constans a law passed in 339 punished with death or banishment any Jew who converted his slaves to Judaism and thus injured Christianity. To prevent any Christian from being under the authority of a Jew, the Jews were forbidden to keep Christian slaves. Mixed marriages between Christians and Jews were also made punishable offences. A law of 357 ran as follows: "Should anyone after the passing of this law turn from

Christianity to Judaism, or be proved to have attended its blasphemous meetings, he shall have the whole of his property confiscated for the benefit of the state treasury."

A peculiar psychological note can now be detected in Christian policy; it aimed at making its opponents and other religions appear contemptible, and at making mere difference a sufficient ground for hatred, which it used as a further means for the exercise of power. Jerusalem was established as the goal of systematic Christian pilgrimages, the members of which did not go there merely to pray but, under the leadership and influence of their spiritual guides, to perpetrate excesses against the Jews. So scanty was the respect paid to other people's religious feelings, that, although the Jews were, it is true, granted permission to pray in Jerusalem on the most momentous and fateful day in their history, the 9th of Ab, they were made to pay heavily for the privilege. In this connexion St. Jerome writes triumphantly: "Their eyes were still full of tears, their hands were still trembling, and their hair was still disarranged, when the guard demanded from them the fee for permission to shed more tears!"

Whenever bodies of people undeservedly acquire power as it were overnight, they always immediately assume the attitude of *parvenus*.

It is natural that the Christians should at first have concentrated their attacks on the Jews in Palestine, for Christianity laid claim to that country as its "Holy Land," and its aim was therefore to clear it as far as possible of all Jews and Jewish institutions. Constans, during his Persian campaign, quartered part of his army in Palestine, and the vexation and trouble caused by the behaviour of the troops once again roused the best elements among the people to rebel, with the result that thousands of Jews were killed. The power of the patriarchate was reduced again and again, and Hadrian's edicts revived. In vain did Julian, whom the church stigmatized as "the Apostate," because he respected every form of religion, promise the Jews to rebuild their Temple; in vain did Theodosius I maintain that legally Judaism was entitled to be treated as it had been in the past as a *religio licita;* the Christian clergy forced him to change his position, and to agree with them that it was pleasing in the sight of the Lord to destroy synagogues. When, after the division of the Roman empire, Palestine came under the jurisdiction of Byzantium in 395 they gained a freer hand and proceeded to dictate the legislation of the Christian emperors making their fundamental principle the idea that "the kingdom of heaven suffereth violence, and the violent take it by storm." (Matthew xi. 12.) The decree of Theodosius II that synagogues which had been destroyed, or converted into churches, were to be restored, and the sacred vessels which had been stolen returned, was met by a passionate protest. "Christians were plunged into the deepest mourning." Theodosius was obliged to rescind the decree, and the old law to the effect that damaged synagogues were to be repaired, but that synagogues that had been destroyed need not be rebuilt, was revived. Thus, if the mob, urged on by the clergy, succeeded in completely destroying a synagogue, the matter ended there!

But besides the destroying of synagogues, the clergy were particularly anxious to put an end to the Jewish administrative centre, and their various legislative enactments aimed at gradually reducing the authority of the Jewish patriarchate to a mere shadow. The law of 429 eventually made it completely impotent. True, this did not entirely strangle the mental life of the nation, but the incessant assaults of Christianity deprived it of its scientific character. However, there was still sufficient strength left to produce the supplements to the Mishnah and make a complete collective work (*Tosephta*) of it. And even the notes and comments on the Mishnah were collected to prevent them from being forgotten (*Gemara*). The Mishnah and the Gemara together make up the Talmud, or rather the Palestinian Talmud, of which, however, only the first four parts have survived.

Important as this work was for subsequent generations, it did not really represent the spiritual life of the time, which was one of terrible suffering. For the Jews of Palestine, the Middle Ages had already dawned, and their spiritual life had to be confined to the intimacy of home-life, which was not so much exposed to attack, while the centre was shifted from the academy to the synagogue, where not only were prayers said, but sermons preached and instruction given. The synagogues were now also called *Beth ha-Midrash,* or houses of preaching. In these sermons, *Midrashim,* the Scriptures were interpreted, explained by means of parables, legends, and similes, embellished, and, on occasion, elaborated to meet the spiritual demands of the people, either by practical examples, political references, polemical discourses, or comforting fictions regarding some future Messianic age. Various collections of these Midrashim have survived to this day, and there is no more convincing proof of their efficacy at the time they were delivered than the fact that the Christians in their propaganda imitated their style or simply copied them wholesale.

In the Midrashim the people found a refuge from the growing pressure of external events. But even this refuge did not remain unmolested. The Emperor Justinian in particular, a zealous Church politician, who made it his aim to extirpate all "false" religions, regarded any remnant of Jewish religious life as a menace to Christianity. He also discovered that wherever Christian sects or pagans opposed the state religion they drew their moral and spiritual sustenance from Jews and Jewish thought. There were two ways of putting a stop to this; the Jews could be made to look contemptible and thus be deprived of all claim to authority, or their religious activities could be curtailed, which would mean their spiritual annihilation. To this end a number of laws were passed. One of the first, the decree of 537, excluded Jews from all public offices, but obliged them to accept urban administrative posts, that is to say, to undertake extremely onerous unpaid duties. The motive for this was baldly stated as follows: "Let these people bear the whole burden of urban administration and groan beneath the load; but no honour must accrue to them thereby!"

For the crippling of their spiritual life, measures which had been found efficacious in the past were revived. The Jews were ordered in their public readings of the Torah to use the Septuagint version, that is to say, a version which had been tendentiously edited by Christian propagandists. Above all the Jews were forbidden to complete their religious services by means of sermons and explanations of the Scriptures. The reason is obvious.

These untiring efforts achieved their purpose. The spiritual life of the Jews in Palestine was utterly destroyed. Deprived, as they were, of all spiritual weapons, they were powerless and completely at the mercy of the Christians, who proceeded to adduce the proof they required for their followers, declaring that God had punished the Jews for their stubborn repudiation of Jesus! The Church now adopted a method which she continued to employ for centuries. All-powerful as she was in the state, she forced the Jews into a peculiarly humiliating position and then proceeded to use their resulting social inferiority as an argument against them—an extraordinarily effective method of dealing with them!

Such methods were obviously bound to create an enormous amount of bitterness and hatred, even among the oppressed Jews of Palestine. The discontent came to a head when, at the beginning of the seventh century, the Persians carried their war against Byzantium into Palestine. Armed Jews flocked to the Persian army from all sides, and were promised that Jerusalem would be given back to them. This stimulated them to special efforts, and with their help Jerusalem was successfully taken in 614. The Persians proceeded to a wholesale massacre of Christians in which the Jews participated with the fury of men bent on avenging themselves for three hundred years of oppression.

The Persians remained the masters of Palestine for fourteen years, but showed no signs of fulfilling the smallest of the promises they had made to the Jews, and the latter were therefore only too ready to negotiate with the Emperor Heraclius, when he prepared to reconquer Palestine. He promised them all kinds of privileges if they refrained from taking any part in the struggle, and above all swore that, in the event of victory, he would grant them a free pardon for all that had happened in the previous war. But as soon as he succeeded in entering

Jerusalem in 629, he was importuned by the clergy to avenge them against the Jews. Heraclius protested that he was bound by oath. The clergy replied that they would release him from his oath on condition that he did penance by abstaining from eating fish and eggs as well as meat during the first week of the great fast. (The Egyptian Copts kept this "Fast of Heraclius" until the tenth century.) After these preliminaries a wholesale massacre of Jews took place throughout Palestine, combined with efforts to force conversion to Christianity upon them.

Thus religion by means of a fast arrogated to itself the right to commit murder!

It was not until 638, when the Caliph Omar occupied Palestine, that the country was freed from Christian rule for a few centuries. But, even without this change of rule, Christianity would not have been able to succeed in its object, which was the extirpation of Judaism. For the spiritual centre which had been destroyed in Palestine another had long since been established, which carried on the tradition of national autonomy, and which, far removed from Christian influence, succeeded in inspiring a fresh spiritual renaissance. I refer to Babylonia.

THE TALMUD

FOR the second and last time in the history of Judaism, the Babylonian Jews, after the destruction of the national state by Rome, and of the centre in Palestine by the Christian church, acted as the bodily and spiritual saviours of their people. Many political and economic arguments could be advanced to explain how the vitality of the Jews remained safely stored up in the Diaspora; whatever the explanation, the fact remains that it did.

Babylonia had remained essentially unaffected by the great, decisive wars of the East. The Jewish colony was still intact, although it showed no signs of further development from the time of the return of the captives to Jerusalem to the destruction of the Jewish state. It was enough that it should have remained uninfluenced by the mixed cultures surrounding it, and that its compact organization and its indispensability to the government, from the economic standpoint, should have enabled it to survive without injury the political conflicts that raged about it. Politically it was virtually autonomous, and its exilarch, or prince of the captivity of the house of David, was the living representative of the last remnants of independence.

On two occasions—after the destruction of Jerusalem and after the insurrection of Bar Kokeba had ended in dismal failure—the fugitives who sought refuge in Babylon constituted valuable recruits both from the numerical and the intellectual point of view to the Jewish colony there. Like the various branches of the Diaspora, this colony, throughout all the political and social vicissitudes to which it had been exposed, had never ceased to regard Palestine as home, the guiding centre, and an interchange of scholars had constantly taken place. This was only natural, for in every branch of the Diaspora the Jews had established schools, or academies serving the same purpose, for the satisfaction of their intellectual needs, a state of affairs which continued to exist until Western Europe placed the Jews legally on an equal footing with other citizens.

At the beginning of the third century Babylonia already possessed important academies. The academy at Sura loyally carried on the scholastic traditions of Palestine. Abba Arika, who had been trained in Palestine, was a member of the staff; he had brought with him from Palestine the text of the Mishnah, which was the basis of the Babylonian Talmud. Nehardea was also an important scholastic centre. But the last and most famous was the Academy of Pumbedita, which eventually took the lead and was responsible for the greatest creative achievements.

Thus it came about that Babylonia rather than any other country became the centre where it was decided whether or no, seeing that the Jewish state had been destroyed, Judaism was still capable of surviving both as a nation and a religion. The problem was solved both for the Babylonian colony as such and for the Jews throughout the world—for the Babylonian colony by means of a successful struggle against Parseeism and later against Islam, and for the rest of the Jews by means of the production, or rather, the compilation of the Babylonian Talmud.

Parseeism was the state religion of Babylonia under Persian rule, and its priests were the Magi. When the rule of the Arsacides had been replaced by that of the ancient Persian family of the Sassanians, the Magi, like the priests of the Roman empire, endeavoured to improve their position by using their authority to force the various nationalities in the state to believe what hitherto they had not believed. This gave rise in the second half of the fifth century to serious discontent, followed by insurrections and bloody persecutions, from which many Jews fled to India and Arabia. But in the end the physical and spiritual energy of the Babylonian Jews proved stronger than Parseeism, and they were able to hold their own until Islam conquered the country and brought a new influence to bear on religion and politics. For reasons which will be explained later, the encounter of Judaism with

Islam actually proved beneficial to Judaism, which was never the case in the encounter between Judaism and Christianity.

The fact that in Babylon the Jews, being unhampered by mere considerations of self-preservation, were free to set their minds to the production of the Talmud, does not imply that they were peculiarly gifted intellectually. It merely meant that for a thousand years they had been in the fortunate position of being able to be the custodians of tradition. They had never abandoned their national and spiritual exclusiveness, but had only conceded just enough to the people about them to make their economic activities possible, and to avoid friction. Among these concessions, however, there was one of far-reaching importance, the fundamental rule laid down by Samuel Yarhinai in the third century, *Dina de'malkutha dina,* the law of the country (of your adoption) is (binding) law. This fundamental rule applied to everything except religion, and made it perfectly plain to the Jews all over the world what their attitude towards the government of the particular country in which they lived should be.

As has already been pointed out, the Babylonian Jews were the spiritual custodians of tradition and had remained at the stage of development forced upon them by the transposition of all their functions as the result of the Babylonian captivity. The practical result of this was that they set great store by their national unity, and organized themselves as a national unit. Although their religious energy was undiminished and permeated every detail of their lives and all their living functions, as it had always done, most of its creative power was necessarily employed in devising measures to preserve the type and in regulating everyday existence. Thus the law, which in the Jewish theocracy had originally been a means for the realization of this form of state, gradually became a means for regulating the life of the people. The laws remained essentially religious laws, but in operation they became state laws. As a result of the duality of their origin and their practical application, a curious intermediate phenomenon occurred unparalleled in the history of the civilized world—the study of the law became an end in itself, the investigation of religion was undertaken with the object of discovering theoretical laws for the everyday life of a group of people, and certain life functions were made subject to the law, not from the legal, but from the religious point of view. And as all the regulations bearing upon the complicated existence of these people with their widespread social and economic activities, could ultimately be traced either to the letter or the spirit of the Torah, trivial or profane laws were nonexistent. The simplest, most common, and ordinary everyday matters had about them the halo of obligation.

This spiritual condition necessarily led to a steady increase in power of the heads of the academies, the *Resh-Methibta.* For it was they who ultimately determined what constituted law, and who made the *Resh-Galutha,* the exilarch, bow down to it. Hence arose a conflict between the spiritual and the temporal power, which was in some respects similar to the struggle between the papacy and the empire in the Middle Ages. It ended in the exilarch becoming merely a splendid and dignified figurehead, while the president of the academy laid down the rules and regulations of daily life not only for the Babylonian Jews but for the whole of Judaism.

For with a docile acceptance of the inevitable of which only a Jewish conception of tradition and discipline is capable, the Jews throughout the world recognized the academies in Babylonia as the authoritative centre of Judaism, and regarded any laws they passed as binding. And if any regulation was not clear, or there was some doubt as to whether a particular law could be made to apply to certain new conditions of life, it was always to Babylonia that inquiries were addressed. The replies given by the academies (now called Gaonic Responses) were held in respect all over the world.

It is obvious that the activities of the Babylonian academies must have been extremely wide and varied, for they had to lay down rules of conduct for a state of existence which was by no means primitive, but, on the contrary, had reached such a degree of development that the difference between it and life today is merely one of degree and not of kind.

Economic life was already fully organized; at one end of the scale was the capitalist who let his money work for him, and at the other the beggar who roamed the town *demanding* alms. Agriculture was so highly developed that it formed the basis of commerce; manufacture existed on a large scale, and the practice of some handicraft was regarded as an honorable second calling for a scholar, who could thereby supplement the income derived from his more learned labours. But all classes of the community were equally interested in intellectual pursuits. The aristocracy owed their position not to property or birth, but to the scholarly traditions of their families. To learn, to be able to learn, was the *noblesse oblige* of all whom the struggle for existence left the smallest leisure for the purpose. It was taken for granted that children of five or six years of age should be compelled to attend school. The child was always the object of deep affection in Jewish life, perhaps chiefly because it guaranteed the continuation of the race, and therefore the fulfilment of the promise. And when owing to the destruction of the state the promise had become applicable only to the sphere of the spirit, children became the symbol of the spiritual future. There is a significant saying of the period to the effect that "every day God sends forth his angels to destroy the world. But

He has only to cast one glance at the schoolchildren, and the scholars, for his anger to be turned to pity."

Such a cult of learning and scholarship was bound to yield results beyond what was required for the mere ordering of existence. Thus it came about that there was a surplus unlinked with reality and which existed only in the minds of the thinkers; it was not even religious thought, but mere material for knowledge, for the development of which there was no pressing necessity; it was sheer casuistry. Other societies have, as a rule, allowed any surplus spiritual energy to flow into the channels of general knowledge, free research, poetical creation, natural science, or technical discoveries. But the Babylonian Jews—and at this period the Jews throughout the rest of the world also—had barred this outlet for themselves. As regards actual knowledge and culture, the period could not boast of anything except what it owed to Greek culture; and to all this the experience of centuries had led the Jews to cultivate instinctive resistance. Ever since the days of Antiochus Epiphanes, everything that had proved really hostile to them in the realm of the spirit had always presented itself in Greek form of some kind, whether as Alexandrianism or as Christianity, with its Greek translation of the Scriptures and its religious syncretism. "Greek wisdom" was a term which in the eyes of the learned Jewish world was tinged with contempt, and "profane" knowledge was banned from the schools and educational institutions.

Nevertheless, spiritual stultification was never allowed to supervene. The people themselves were endowed with the energies which led the Jewish spirit to burst the bonds of dangerous confinement and invade the boundless fields beyond. But to make these energies effective, a ring of vast proportions and colossal elasticity had at all events to be placed about them—the Talmud.

Just as in Palestine two hundred years previously the huge unwieldy mass of material had forced the scholars to examine it and determine what was to be kept, so too in Babylonia in the middle of the fourth century recent accretions faced the academies with a similar task. The explanations and interpretations of the Palestinian Mishnah had led to the production of the Gemara, which now also threatened to become unwieldy. Thus it was necessary to set it in order not merely as material but also, as after all it was nothing more than an interpretation of the Mishnah, as an organic part of the latter. The two undertakings combined led to the production of the Babylonian Talmud. This gigantic work was begun in the second half of the fourth century, and was finished about the year 500, and altogether represents over a hundred years of intellectual effort.

Even if the Jew of today were to lose all knowledge of the Talmud, a not unlikely contingency seeing that the majority know nothing whatever about it, the world about them would always be in a position to refresh their memories, because for the last thousand years this book has played an important part in the ideology of non-Jewish peoples. It became the great arsenal to which everyone resorted who wished to attack the Jews. In the eyes of those who could not tolerate the existence of the Jews with equanimity, it came to be regarded as a wicked, dangerous, strange, criminal, and blasphemous work, which to this day has been held to contain the whole secret and inviolable law of Judaism. The Inquisition put it on its trial in every conceivable way; it was sentenced to death and publicly burnt; it was foolishly picked to pieces and explained, and even now is quoted and commented on with such colossal ignorance of its meaning that it would be hopeless to attempt to combat such methods. Nevertheless, this attitude is comprehensible. The only result of opposition in the case of rare achievements which secretly increase their vital power, is that one day they are surrounded by a sublime and mysterious halo. Thus, in course of time, the Talmud became an almost sacred book for the Jews, and almost anathema to all who were not Jews.

But what in truth is the Talmud? Externally, it is a twelve- or eighteen-volume work (editions differ) in six parts subdivided into sixty-three treatises. Its contents are the record of the existence of a people scattered over the face of the earth during a period of about a thousand years, that is to say, from the end of the Pentateuch to the beginning of the sixth century. All the laws passed during this period, as well as those that could be reproduced from memory, are here set down. Criminal law, the law of debt, common law, family law, the law of inheritance—everything is included, whether obsolete or not, whether it actually passed into law or was merely a projected law, *de lege ferenda*. Moreover, mere customs or practices, or important theoretical explanations of a law, or a custom given by a school or an important scholar are also mentioned. All discussions which took place in the academies on legal matters or questions of medicine, hygiene, agriculture, natural science, morals, or customs are also reported and summarized in brief epigrammatic style. Religious rules and regulations are to be found side by side with moral exhortations, dry law is intermingled with legends from the Haggadah, the sublime concept of God is entwined with the wildest superstitions borrowed from the Magi; a pronouncement or doctrine of world-wide importance is set cheek by jowl with some utterly trivial detail. The Talmud is as great and as small as the life of a people at its best and its worst, as tranquil and as blustering, as peaceful and as aggressive. It is the encyclopædia of an age and of a type of life to which nobody can do justice who does not approach it with goodwill and judge it in the light of the circumstances of its nature, and the conditions in which it came into being.

Those who helped to make the Talmud never for one moment intended that it should be regarded as a binding or representative code of law. It was merely a collection of material, intended for use in the schools and academies. It was only much later that it became representative not only of the intellectual capacity of the post-biblical Jews, but of the spiritual life of the Jews in general. There were two reasons for this. The first was that the laws of the Talmud proved exceedingly efficacious in binding the Jewish people together in times of increasing dispersion and oppression. The second was that the accomplishment of the great work was followed by a period of exhaustion which came to an end only when the Talmud had already begun to circulate all over the world. But the real reason why Judaism clung so fiercely and passionately to the Talmud is to be found in the naturally law-abiding nature of the Jewish people in all matters relating to the spirit, a nature already fully developed at this time. In proportion as the centrifugal forces of Judaism necessarily spread out in ever wider circles under the pressure of events, its centripetal forces also grew stronger and demanded a centre to cling to. The more fiercely distress and persecution beat on the periphery of life, the more terrifying became the fear lest the day would come when there would be no centre round which the meaning or meaninglessness of their fate as individuals and as members of a corporate body could vibrate. When, on their wanderings, their actual home was bit by bit taken from them, they replaced it little by little with fragments of their fictitious home, taken from the world of the Talmud, until at last the frontiers became fluid, functions changed, and the place in which they settled became a habitation, while the Talmud, which they carried with them everywhere, became their home.

ISLAM

THE completion of the Babylonian Talmud confronted the spiritual leaders and the academies with a strange and disquieting situation—their sphere of labour was exhausted. There was still polishing to be done, passages to be elaborated, and improvements in style to be introduced. But at last the work lay completed before them. At that very moment, however, forces began to emanate from the concentrated life that lay hid within it and, like a piece of radium, diffused energy without any apparent loss of substance. The Talmud became possessed of independent life and the capacity of influencing men both for good and evil.

True, since new sources of law were regarded as inadmissible, no new laws could develop out of it. But it could achieve something far more important; it could bring about the realization of its store of actual and potential laws; it could spread them like a closely woven net over the whole Jewish community, over ordinary days and holidays, over their actions and over their prayers, over their whole lives and every step they took. And this it succeeded in doing. Even the scholars and the academies helped in the process by regulating its application to life.

A strange existence now came into being. Whether on the Volga or on the Rhine, on the Danube or along the shores of the Mediterranean, the Jews celebrated the same festivals on the same days with the same rites; they drew up their marriage contracts according to the same plan, they ate and drank in accordance with the same rules, admitted people into the covenant, and bore them to the grave in obedience to the same regulations and customs. Nothing in their external lives was any longer allowed to be the sport of arbitrary settlement or of chance. The process which had begun with the destruction of the national state was consistently carried on, and the conduct of the individual was standardized. The Talmud became the unbreakable husk round a kernel determined to survive. It encased the heart of the Jew with a spirituality which though cold as ice was strong as steel to protect.

Wherever the Jews encountered unfavourable conditions of life, they meekly withdrew behind the sheltering walls of the Talmud where they felt safe. But wherever life became easier and more peaceful, they began to question both the necessity and the justification for these rigid fetters. And this led to an attitude of mild opposition, which was, as a rule, directed—and this is typical—not against the law as such, but towards winning for the spirit the right to be creative even outside the law. This gave rise to two important movements in Judaism—the schism of the Karaites in the ninth century, and the great cultural struggle of the thirteenth and fourteenth centuries. The former was a conflict concerning the law, the latter was a struggle for spiritual freedom. The former was necessarily a vain attempt, seeing that the law was a principle of life; but the latter achieved enormous successes, as creative spiritual freedom was the integrating principle of Judaism. The former occurred in Babylonia, the latter in Spain, and constituted an attack on the rest of the Jewish world. Both came into being within the confines of a new spiritual unity—Islam.

Islam, as an integrating movement, which was at once national and religious, originated in a number of Semitic tribes, which seem to have been forgotten by history until the beginning of the seventh century. They did not lie on the great highway on which the civilizations of the world met and were forced to come to terms. On three sides they were cut off by the sea. Only the northern portion of Arabia was flanked by civilized areas, on the west by Syria and Palestine, which belonged to the Byzantine empire, and on the east by Babylonia, which was part of Persia. Whereas the centre of the great peninsula was still inhabited by nomadic Bedouin tribes, cities and kingdoms had already been formed along the coastal areas, in northern Hejaz on the Red Sea, in southern Yemen, in south Babylonian 'Iraq, and in the kingdom of the Ghassanids in southern Syria.

Through these coastal areas, the surrounding civilization was able to penetrate concentrically into the country and make the forces which lay dormant there burst forth with peculiar violence. In spite of differences of occupation, way of life, and proximity to other centres of civilization, the characteristics of these various tribes, groups, associations, cities, and kingdoms, were fundamentally similar, for they were all Semites and still led a nomadic existence.

Semitism is endowed with special qualifications for religious creativeness. They consist in the capacity for examining and carrying the experience of cosmic relations to its logical conclusion and deriving therefrom a clear and coherent idea; of concentrating this idea into the form of a monotheistic conception of God, and then of rigidly, almost fanatically subordinating everything to the obligations derived from this conception of God. This makes a nomadic civilization possessed of such spiritual potentialities extraordinarily pathetic; for it carries a contradiction in its bosom. Its members have an inordinate love of freedom and yet they can be slaves for abject obedience. They set the noble quality of truth above all else and yet respect the man of cunning for his mental alertness; they are long-suffering and yet intolerant; they rhapsodize about friendship and will yet prosecute a blood feud to the extent of exterminating a whole race; they can be moved to tears by a love song and can yet commit murder with the most callous brutality. They are children of nature in whose breasts a sense of responsibility is just beginning to awake.

At the period with which we are concerned various influences had combined to relax and disturb the uniformity of life among the Arabs. True, they were still polytheists and had made Mecca their pantheon; but in addition to all their minor deities, or above them, they already recognized in Allah one invisible God, the Father of all the rest. They worshipped him in the form of a huge stone, around which a temple was built. The Arabs of 'Iraq, however, were already joining either the Babylonian Jews, or the Persian fire-worshippers. The Ghassanids were attracted by Christianity, while from centres in Syria and Ethiopia Byzantium was carrying on more or less successful propaganda by means of missionaries and soldiers in southern Arabia. The fact that Jews, Christians, and Persians alike were successful in their propaganda, whether deliberately or unconsciously conducted, proves that the former religious beliefs of the Arabs were already beginning to decay.

In one important particular, their religion had for centuries ceased to be a native product, and that was in its historical tradition. Both the northern and the southern tribes traced their origin from Jewish sources; the north regarded Ishmael, the son of Hagar, as their ancestor, and the south Joktan, the son of Eber. This not only pointed to their kinship with the Jews, but also to a religious affinity; for in Semitic nomad civilization, tribal and religious traditions are almost always identical. This affinity had been maintained and kept alive by the Jewish settlements which from time immemorial had been scattered throughout Arabia. Except for their religion, the Arabian Jews were not very different from the people about them. They lived in tribal communities, which, like the Arabs, were constantly at loggerheads; they inhabited fortified towns, sometimes in large bodies which in the sixth century led to the formation of the Himyaritic state in southern Arabia; they carried on a caravan trade, and practised horticulture and handicrafts; they sang and wrote poetry and fought just as the Arabs did, and were in every way assimilated to the people about them. Their only superiority lay in their religion and in the fact that it was they who gave the Arabs a tradition. And for this reason conversions to Judaism were extremely frequent.

Conversions of this kind did not involve any very serious act of decision or change; it was only natural that they should occur, in the first place, owing to the common national tradition, and secondly, because the Arabs, in spite of minor differences, had after all formed the concept of one supreme God. Although their Allah was supplemented by a host of minor deities, they were all assembled in a pantheon at Mecca, whereby at least a local concentration of the divine was secured. They were polytheists on the threshold of monotheism. Moreover, when we remember that there were among them men who were gravely perturbed by the religious confusion and carelessness of the people, it becomes clear that, as a matter of principle, the conversion of an Arab from polytheism to the recognition of the one and only God was a rapid process, and, as far as his country was concerned, could be consummated without having recourse to any imposing ceremonial. Here, too, all that was required was the man who would undertake to open the way. And this man came forward in the person of Mohammed.

Mohammed was the most contradictory religious founder that history has ever known. He was inspired by a strong religious impulse, but it lost its bearings completely as soon as it ceased to find something to lean upon, and weakened when it failed to discover fresh energy in the person of its originator, Mohammed himself. Mohammed considered himself the bearer of a new gospel, which he could interpret only by founding it on the past, and regarding all the patriarchs of Jewish history and even Moses and Jesus as his forerunners. The idea of tradition assumed exaggerated proportions in his mind; but at the same time he also had an exaggerated idea of leadership, which is essentially opposed to the idea of tradition. He looked upon himself as the last genuine purveyor of a truth which claimed to conquer the world. These constitute the two main supports of the religious edifice he built up. Between them lay the attempt to raise a new world of faith on the basis of old concepts.

This was by no means an easy undertaking. The world which might have been accessible to his ideas and his age, and might have understood them, was already divided up between the various religions. There was no need of a new religion, whatever its form. Nor was any one of the existing religions capable of receiving a new form. Judaism, which had long since formulated its fundamental ideas, had just erected the encircling walls of the Talmud about itself. Christianity, both as a faith and as a church, had already proved its unsuitability for the civilized Semite. Consequently, those elements in the East which were no longer contented with idolatry, and which had, as it were, been left out of account by the development of monotheism, were forced to find a form of their own. This form was entirely the work of Mohammed. But he borrowed the principles for it from everything he found ready to hand and could understand—Judaism, Christianity, and the religious traditions of the Arabian tribes. He could neither read nor write, but he had at his fingers' ends a store of tales, stories, and legends drawn from the Old Testament, the Gospels, from Talmudic legends and Christian apocrypha. At times this material became distorted not only in his imagination but above all in the version he gave of it. Nevertheless, he managed, consistently enough, to extract from it the fundamental ideas which he lays down in the Koran—the idea of one God; the duty of serving Him only, and no other gods besides; the idea of justice and the belief in a beyond and in the resurrection of the dead. The grouping of these ideas and the reasoning based upon them were entirely determined, however, by the qualities composing his personality, by his antecedents, his intellectual capacity, his faith, his powers of imagination, his successes and failures, his loves and his hates, and lastly, as in the case of Jesus and Paul, by his individual will to power and thirst for authority. This does not mean that Islam, in its final development, is identical with Mohammed. Wherever religiously minded men are to be found, a religion can always become greater than its founder.

In 610, after a long and solitary preparation, during which he watched and prayed and led a life of strict asceticism, Mohammed had his first vision when the angel Gabriel appeared to him (the first five verses of Sura or Chapter 96 of the Koran, "Congealed Blood"). A year later he had his second vision (Sura 74, "The Covered"). His first revelation amounted to nothing more than the declaration that there was *one* God, the creator of mankind. But in the second this declaration is described as having been made to him personally, and his office is presented to him as the proclaimer of this truth, and the Prophet of Allah. Through all the changes and vicissitudes of his life he clung tenaciously to this idea; he was not the Messiah, but only the messenger, the ambassador, the herald of Allah, whom he regarded not as the national god of the Arabs, but simply as God, the God worshipped alike by Jews and Christians. Was he then to be regarded as a Jewish or a Christian prophet? As neither; but as the successor to both Moses and Jesus. But both were already the accepted representatives of existing forms of belief! What then was Mohammed's peculiar mission? He explained his mission in exactly the same way as Paul had explained the mission of Jesus when he declared that Judaism had been found unworthy and its office had been transferred to the Gentiles. Mohammed said Judaism and Christianity had been found unworthy, and their office had been transferred to Islam. "Every prophecy hath its fixed time of accomplishment" (Koran vi. 66). But Paul maintained that the law had been superseded, having been fulfilled by the Gospels. And Mohammed also declared that all previous revelations had been superseded, having been fulfilled by the Koran. "For He (Allah) had formerly sent down the law and the gospel, a direction unto men; and He had also sent down the distinction between good and evil" (Koran iii. 2). "Every age hath its book" (xiii. 38). In answer to the momentous question why this should be so, Paul explained that it was God's will. Mohammed also declared that Allah did what seemed good in His own eyes. In connexion with Paul's remonstrance about the law, the apostles in Jerusalem explained that they did not wish to lay too great a burden on the Gentiles. And Mohammed declared: "God would make this an ease unto you, and would not make it a difficulty unto you" (ii. 181). Paul traced all true belief back to Abraham. Mohammed did likewise. "Abraham was neither a Jew nor a Christian; but he was of the true religion, one resigned unto God" (iii. 60).

But in spite of these many points of resemblance, Mohammed could not avoid drawing a sharp distinction between Christianity and Islam. He regarded the doctrine of the Trinity, and even the doctrine of the Son of God, as polytheistic and destructive of the unity of Allah. He constantly combated this. "They are certainly infidels, who say, God is the third of three; for there is no God besides one God" (v. 77). "He is the maker of heaven and earth: how should He have issue, since He hath no consort?" (vi. 101).

It was on personal grounds rather than on matters of principle like these that Mohammed attacked the Jews, though he had no grievance against their religion. He was disappointed in them; above all they had made fun of him. At first he did not have much success. As had been the case with Jesus, his own family did not acknowledge him. The Koreish in Mecca saw their receipts from pilgrims threatened by his propaganda, and he was obliged to flee from them and take refuge in Abyssinia. In order to be allowed to return and gain recognition as prophet, he was prepared to admit besides Allah three other gods from the pantheon at Mecca. But he withdrew this concession, and altered the verse in the Koran in which it had been contained (liii. 19–22). His prospects began to brighten only when he succeeded in winning over part of the city of Yathrib to his side. Yathrib was a fortified Jewish city until the end of the fifth century, when it was conquered by the Arab tribes of Aus and Khazraj, who, however, did not drive out the Jews. Mohammed entered into negotiations with pilgrims belonging to these two tribes. But as the Koreish came to hear of this, he was obliged to flee from Mecca to Yathrib (June 622). This marks the official foundation of Islam, and from that day Yathrib bore the name of Medinat en-Nabi, the city of the prophet, or in abbreviated form, Medina.

His mastery of this city lent Mohammed's position a certain importance, and at the same time his tone changed. In addition to holding the office of prophet, he became a leader, a real chieftain, with all that this meant and implied in a political sense. It was in Medina that the first signs of legislative activity begin to appear in the pages of the Koran, which proves that, in order to win power and success, he was engaged not merely in religious propaganda, but was also making a deliberate bid for political power by means of negotiations. One of his main objects was to secure the adherence of the Jews of Medina, and he uses arguments about himself similar to those Paul had advanced in the case of Jesus, declaring that his advent had long since been predicted in the Scriptures, that is to say, the Torah, and that the Jews were therefore bound to acknowledge him. In addition to maintaining that he was carrying on the Jewish tradition, he was also prepared to make them concessions with regard to religious observances. For instance, he gave instructions that the *qibla,* the position in prayer, should be facing Jerusalem. Like the Jews and the Christians, he made Jerusalem his holy city, and chose the most solemn of the Jewish festivals, the great Day of Atonement, as the most important festival for Islam. He also adopted the Jewish regulations about cleanliness and the order of prayers; he forbade his followers to eat pork and copied many other Jewish observances. Nevertheless, he met with but little success, and very few Jews became converted to the new faith. To many he was merely a laughing-stock. The high esteem in which they held learning prevented them from taking this half-educated Bedouin seriously. Moreover, his private life had far too much of the unbridled, primitive, and passionate Arab about it to inspire them with belief in his high office. But for the majority of Jews the problem was settled by merely pointing out that on the one hand they were asked to believe in Jesus, and on the other they were asked to believe in Mohammed, each side maintaining that Judaism had been superseded, and that it alone was in possession of the one and only truth. The Jew, therefore, had no alternative but to reject them both.

Mohammed now began to use threats as Paul had done. He charged the Jews with having falsified the Torah, and cut out all reference to his own coming. The Christians had brought a similar charge against the Jews. He also withdrew his most important concessions–the *qibla* towards Jerusalem, and the fast of the 10th of Tishri; and before long he proclaimed in the Koran: "Thou shalt surely find the most violent of all men in enmity against the true believers to be the Jews and the idolaters" (v. 85). Thus he classed the Jews with the idolaters, just as Paul had done in his Epistles, and continued like the latter to hurl threats at their heads.

In these circumstances, it was inevitable that, owing to the demands of the age and the individual interpretations of one man, the constitution of Islam should also have owed a good deal to ancient pagan sources. Just as Christianity had been obliged to absorb and nullify the Græco-Roman pantheon, so Mohammed made Islam include in its concept of monotheism all that remained of the Semitic pantheon. Thus both religions were driven to achieving their aims through the roundabout way of syncretism. But in its final development, Islam remained essentially a national faith.

What Mohammed had failed to achieve by purely religious propaganda, he now gradually accomplished by emphasizing the idea of leadership in his office. He entered the conflict being waged at the time between Medina and Mecca, and it stands to his credit that he succeeded in endowing it with a religious significance by giving it the character of a holy war. In the settlement he reached with Mecca in 628, his position as a political representative and a religious leader are equally emphasized. In any case, it was his function as leader which was growing in importance. Unified leadership, which was unknown to the Arabs as a corporate whole, was an all the more conspicuous feature of each separate province, city, tribe, and family group, all of which could boast of a leader possessed of a certain amount of power, who exercised authority, and marched out to battle against other rulers. As long as such forces remained confined to the country itself, they necessarily exhausted themselves in feuds and deeds of warlike valour. If they could be united and a path opened up for them into the outside world, the idea of leadership would necessarily be transformed into the driving force of the conqueror.

Mohammed took the first step in this direction at this time, when the idea of leadership first began to assume an important place in his mind, and to find expression in a series of manifestoes in which he called upon the whole of the world then accessible to him—Persia, Byzantium, and Abyssinia, to be converted to Islam and to submit themselves to him, Mohammed, the prophet of Allah. He was scoffed at, but he made a beginning notwithstanding, in his immediate circle. One by one, during the years 624–628, he attacked the free Jewish tribes in their fortified cities and drove them out or massacred them. A year after the capture of Mecca (630) his following had already grown so large that he was able to raise an appeal for a holy war against the infidels. All the potentialities that lay hidden in the Arabs —their unspent nomadic strength, their warlike spirit, and their religiosity—turned towards him as the one figure that towered above the chaos of groups and conflicting interests, offering an integrating thought and an integrating aim. This aim, moreover, made a universal appeal. It involved the gathering together of all the Arab tribes and groups into one people, under one leadership and under one faith, with the object of spreading this faith, this national religion, over the whole world. The conquest of the world for Islam was the legacy Mohammed left behind him when he died in 632, and which, by recording it in the Koran, he made sacrosanct. It was only after his removal from the scene that it became possible for what is known either as Islamic Arabianism or Arabian Islamism to be realized. In any case, it was a culture whose founder was not Mohammed, but a creative power which had long been stored up and lain untouched by the progress of civilization. Islam now found itself face to face with a fate similar to that which had confronted every people that had preceded it—it was called upon once in the course of its development to measure its strength against the rest of the world.

It now entered upon this trial of strength.

THE KARAITES

THE career of conquest embarked upon by Islam after the death of Mohammed was more than merely political in character, it was something more than ordinary warfare. It was the East wreaking its revenge on the West, which through Greece and Rome had broken into Asia. East and West are not mere geographical distinctions; they represent forces whose endowments are utterly unlike. All attempts made in history to value one above the other have come to nothing. Their destiny does not lie in the overpowering of one by the other, but in the exchange of ideas and mutual fertilization, even in those spheres where their qualities seem to be diametrically opposed. This is the law governing the struggle that has constantly swayed backwards and forwards between East and West. And the only people that have remained in the area over which the conflict has ebbed and flowed and have never left it are the Jews. Consequently the incursion of Islam was for them a matter of supreme significance, more particularly, of course, in that part of the world where they had formed compact settlements and where the centre of their administration lay, that is to say in Babylonia.

The ardour and enthusiasm of Islam, in which religious fanaticism was allied with the predatory lust of the Bedouin, made short work of the conquest of Babylonia (633–638), and also very quickly subdued the rest of Persia (644–656). After which Syria, Palestine, Egypt, and the north coast of Africa were wrenched from the Byzantine empire. It took only a little over a hundred years to build up an empire of such colossal proportions that its unwieldiness necessitated its division into separate units. But it was precisely owing to this extension of Islamic rule that a very considerable portion of the Jewish Diaspora became linked together under the same authority; for wherever Islam extended its boundaries, the Jews found a dividing frontier removed. Moreover, this gathering together of the Jews within the Islamic empire was also considerably strengthened by the economic expansion of the East. Islam joined Asia and Africa to the European world. A large and important trade route was opened up, which went from Basra via Baghdad to Arabia, along the Red Sea, across Suez, and through the ports of Egypt, Byzantium, Italy, and Spain as far as the Frankish empire and beyond into eastern Europe and the Slav countries. All along the route the Jews had stations and colonies, and they travelled backwards and forwards and constituted the most important representatives of international trade.

This increased commercial activity was not wholly voluntary, but was to some extent the outcome of the conquests of Islam. As soon as Islam burst out into the world, it must have seen that the religious organizations of other nations were already too firmly established for the forcing of a new form of belief upon mankind as a whole to be possible. Thus the political factors which every conquest involves gradually thrust the religious factor ever further into the background. A world could not be converted, but it might be conquered. The example of Christianity, which always carried the cross in the wake of the sword, was of no use to Islam, since the latter possessed nothing corresponding to the international hierarchy of the clergy. Omar was therefore obliged to confine himself to converting Arabia proper into a purely Moslem country by inducing the Christians to become Mohammedans, and by getting rid of the rest of the Jews by banishing them and transplanting them to Syria. Furthermore he built up Moslem legislation on the basis of the distinction between the faithful and the infidels, between Moslems and those who professed other religions. Unlike Christianity, Islam allowed the infidel absolute economic freedom, and an autonomous administration, but by means of extortionate taxation it emphasized the difference between the true and the false faith, and the state of subjection of those who belonged to the latter category. Many of the caliphs seem to have thought the whole purpose of government to lie in drawing up strict rules and regulations for the hounding down of men of means and all on whom taxation could lay a heavy hand.

Large numbers of Jewish farmers in Babylonia found themselves unable to pay the land tax, and, together with those whose previous occupations did not bring them in sufficient money to meet the poll tax, they turned to commerce as a means of livelihood. But those who were evading the economic pressure and the general confusion of war were also following the same trade route, and making their way to Europe. Thus the spread of Islam was accompanied by the spread of Judaism. The Jewish world which, for a while, had been stationary, again began to move, and in this case the movement did not merely amount to a change of place, or geographical redistribution; it was a fresh state of restlessness, a reawakening of dynamic forces, the breaking down by the living East of the hedge which the Babylonian Jews had set about themselves and the world they ruled.

In the light of the purpose which can be traced throughout Jewish history, Babylonia had been the place of refuge in which the powers of resistance had found the chance of developing after the twofold shock of the destruction of the state and the vigorous attack made by

Christianity on the ancient home of Judaism. The production of the Talmud there had been the work of a period of powerful spiritual activity which had been followed by an uncreative phase in which all that happened was that the functions of a religious bureaucracy were exercised and the Talmud and its authority were circulated throughout the Jewish world. But Jewish spirit and intellect then reached a point at which its original purpose, the service of the theocracy, was to be transmuted into its opposite, the service of itself, the service of the law for the sake of the law itself. It now became clear that the Talmud and Judaism were not identical, that all the Talmud had accomplished was to codify one of the spiritual potentialities of Judaism, and that although it might well be a guide to *living,* it could not be a guide to a view of life.

But this had not been either its task or its intention. Its aim had been to regulate action, not belief. It recognized rules and regulations, but formulated no dogmas. It satisfied all manner of religious and ritualistic demands, but not the deeper needs of the heart. It did not touch the chasm between religion and religiosity; but the religious power of Judaism had to be tested by the emotional dislike of the law before it could be decided whether it still remained intact.

It was no easy task to assert its claims. The body which at that time represented the Jewish world in Babylonia was animated either by worldly considerations or by the desire for spiritual systematization. The exilarchs who, after the triumph of Islam, called themselves *Nasim,* princes, became increasingly powerful, and were the official representatives of the Jewish population at the court of the caliph. The nasi was the vassal of the caliph, and the greater the power and splendour of the vassal the greater the honour that redounded to the caliph whose subordinate he was. Thus the caliphs, for reasons connected with their own reputation, had an interest in increasing the power and prestige of the exilarchs. But they rendered their office entirely worldly by making it purchasable, and thus forcing those who held it to recover their expenses by taxing the Jewish communities.

Similarly the strengthening of the autonomous administration increased the prestige of the heads of the academies. The academies of Sura and Pumbedita, the heads of which were called *Gaonim,* exercised the same functions as the Sanhedrin had done in the past. The nasi was dependent on their approval, and, owing to the similarity of the religious and political laws of Judaism, their authority was constantly coming into conflict with that of the exilarch. Even if both the exilarchs and gaonim had remained conscious of their responsibility towards the people, they were, after all, only functionaries of the administration, the leading officials of a fictitious state. The one was dependent upon the political situation, the other upon the religious development. Consequently the exilarchate fell with the caliphate, while the gaonim could not survive the completion of their task.

Every law is bound one day to be asked for its credentials. This was true even of the Jewish law. But those who, weighed down beneath the luxuriant overgrowth of Talmudic regulations, now changed from an attitude of implicit obedience to one of inquiry, did not protest against the law because it was rigid and bound them down too severely; they were much more deeply concerned with the question whether the law, in the form in which they submitted to it at that time, was really, as the scholars and legislators maintained, the continuation of a tradition which could be traced back link by link to Moses as its founder. Thus it was not the coercion that disturbed them, but the question whether this coercion sprang from a sacred source. To them the Bible was the revelation of law. There could be nothing besides the Bible, unless everybody was to be allowed to derive just what he pleased from it.

This questioning of the law was due to the fact that the recognition of its necessary function was overshadowed by a stronger interest—concern regarding the object of the law, man himself. The law might be good; the question was, did it serve man? And this repeated question concerning the serviceableness to man, like the question concerning good and evil, was inspired by religion, by the fact of faith.

Strictly speaking, the world of faith lay outside the Talmud. Faith went its own way. Just when the Talmud was proving its efficacy and power in the maintenance—it might almost be said the perpetuation—of the Diaspora, the will of the people, ever anxious to make an end of the latter, manifested itself in a number of Messianic movements. To them Rome and Arabia were not merely political concepts, they were also apocalyptic. Rome was the Edom, Arabia the Ishmael of the Bible. Edom had now been supplanted by Ishmael. True, according to oft-repeated promises, Edom should have been supplanted by Judea, but this intermediate kingdom could also serve the purpose of fulfilment and the "End of Days," that is to say, the reinstatement of the theocracy in the old homeland, and its extension over the rest of the world.

A certain Abu Isa, a Jew of Ispahan, proclaimed himself to be the forerunner of the Messiah, and collected a following, with which he attempted an insurrection against the caliphate (end of the seventh century). He left behind him a sect known as the Isavites, vestiges of which survived in Damascus until the tenth century. At about the same time, at the beginning of the eighth century, Zonarias announced himself to be the Messiah in Syria, and preached the reconquest of Jerusalem. Jews hastened to join him from all quarters, even from Spain. But the movement died out in a few years.

These were open and avowed Messianic movements. But the existence of secret and simmering Messianic movements was revealed by other events which took place at this time. This applied more particularly to certain new sects, all of which had at least this much in common, that they endeavoured, by making much of some extreme or other, to get nearer to their goal, which was religious fulfilment. This was true of the Isavites, as also of a sect of one of the disciples of Abu Isa, the Judghanites, as well as of the Mushkanians, who were an offshoot of the latter. The people who are usually referred to in history as the Karaites did not originally constitute a sect at all; they were the representatives of the movement we have been discussing, which set faith above the law, because it doubted the latter's claims in the sphere of religion; it was really latent Messianism and also proved that anti-Talmudism and Messianism were essentially one in concept. The man who inaugurated this movement was Anan ben David, who, in the middle of the eighth century, unsuccessfully stood as a candidate for the vacant post of exilarch. His heretical views had already made him an object of suspicion to those who rejected his candidature, and after his failure he became an open opponent of the custodians of Talmudic thought. He was of opinion that all "oral traditions" should be rejected as spurious, and that the organization of life through law should once more be directly connected with the source from which alone it sprang—the Bible. Herein lay the seeds of a reform movement, which obtained for him a large following. The Ananites represented a popular movement, not a sect. And out of this popular movement the Messianic idea again made its appearance. The longing for Zion, which had stirred the heart of Judaism so deeply in the same country twelve hundred years previously, flared up once more, and the preliminary conditions for bringing about this period of fulfilment were held to lie in rigid asceticism, more rigorous rules of cleanliness, and a religious way of life. The opposition to the Talmud and the return to the Bible were not ends in themselves. The return to the Bible was held to be a preliminary step to the return to Jerusalem. Large numbers followed this tendency to its logical conclusion, and went back to Palestine. They were the first to exemplify an inclination on the part of the Jews of the Diaspora to emphasize the Messianic idea whenever religious fervour increased. From this time onwards, Messianism never ceased to be connected with Jewish faith.

It seems impossible that so radically sound a movement, animated by such lofty aims, should not have had the power to succeed, but should one day have been represented by an isolated party, and, after centuries of hard struggle, it is true, have finished its existence as a sect. But it was inevitable; for in the religious sphere, which is the highest in life, all undertakings that are unorganized have to pay much more heavily for this deficiency than they do in other realms. The desire to return to the source of faith was orderly and logical. But the method adopted was unorganized, and this spelt ruin. The very slogan, "Search the Scriptures carefully!" in which Anan ben David summarized his aim and object, though it contained an element of truth, was also a pitfall. His followers searched the Scriptures, and it was not long before they did so in precisely the same way as the Talmudists had done. Innumerable ritualistic changes and innovations were introduced, nearly all of which merely increased the severity of the laws already in existence. The Sabbath was overloaded with a burden of rules and restrictions, which made it resemble a day of torture rather than a festival. The prohibition against marriage between relatives was extended, the number of fast days was increased, the reading of the calendar was made more difficult by a return to obsolete methods, and the rules for ritualistic cleanliness were made more stringent. And all this was done on the authority of the Bible, and inevitably pointed to the production of a new Talmud. Even poetry, the last possible source of religious productivity, was eliminated from divine service by the Ananites. And thus they deprived themselves of all possibility of spiritual relaxation. The spirit of opposition which had animated them from the beginning gained the upper hand and ultimately had them completely at its mercy. As a matter of fact they never really returned to the Bible. Before they had gone very far, they became Talmudists. They were doomed to become a sect when they set out, not only to secure for the soul a larger share in religious life, but also to turn back what tradition had given them and fasten it to any point they thought fit. They proved that formalism is at once the criterion and the death of the sect. Thus a certain section of the people escaped the exacting claims of the Talmud by means of another Talmud. But quite as many escaped the Talmud, not because they did not respect the law, but because they had created a religious life of their own, as it were a private sphere of faith, which went to such lengths in mysticism and theosophy, in the clumsy anthropomorphization of God, in occultism, faith-healing, and belief in secret remedies and talismans, in short, in every form of profound superstition, that life in such an atmosphere was tantamount to a denial of the law, together with its foundation, the Bible.

The Ananites, who afterwards called themselves the "Bible-Loyalists" or Karaites, found followers all over the Jewish world. In the tenth century their community extended from Persia to Spain. But they never succeeded in attaining a coherent movement or a clear idea, and were held sternly at arm's length by official Judaism. Nevertheless, they did succeed in exercising a certain amount of influence. Their attacks gave rise to inquiries regarding the meaning of the law and its purpose, which were not silenced for a long time to come. These inquiries took place at a time when, close by, in the neighbouring sphere of influence, similar inquiries were being made and giving rise to hot disputes, that is to say in Islam, which now had to repeat the various stages of its development in all the districts it had conquered. Mohammed had succeeded in propagating Islam, but he had not been able to give it a form. The formative powers of the faith did not come into existence until the eighth and ninth centuries, and first revealed the capacity for culture that lay dormant in the hitherto unspent forces of Arabian Semitism. The political, intellectual, and religious disputes of the Islamic world took place in Babylonia, within earshot of the Jewish world. To draw a sharp distinction between the faithful and the infidel remained, if we except a few reactionary caliphs, the wish-dream of the Moslem priests. As a matter of fact, a relationship grew up between the Jews and Arabs which proved extremely profitable to both sides. The Jews turned the general emancipation which attended the advance of Islam in the East to such good account that their intellectual influence once again began to make itself felt in the world of culture, and before long they were in a position to convey to Islam the "Greek wisdom" of which they had fought so shy in the past. The language they used for the purpose, moreover, was actually Arabic, which was completely ousting Aramaic. Thus between the ninth and the twelfth centuries a Hebraic-Arabic literature came into being which in Spain attained to supreme heights of power and picturesqueness.

In addition to the geographic road cut by oriental Islam into the outside world, the Jews of Babylon now also made use of the intellectual route, and a Judæo-Arabic culture arose in every way similar to the former Judæo-Hellenic culture. In both cases, spheres of knowledge were entered and investigations conducted which the conservative elements in the nation, terrified of any tendency to become too thoroughly assimilated to those about them, rejected in horror. As if by way of a reaction to sterile spiritual speculation, natural science was widely studied. Jews translated not only Aristotle, Plato, and Ptolemy into Arabic, but also Greek mathematicians and naturalists. The Jews themselves also produced several distinguished mathematicians and medical men, of whom one, Isaac Israeli of Kairawan, came to be regarded as one of the founders of medieval medicine. And just as the Hellenized Jews had inclined to Christianity, the Jews of the Islamic world of thought, for lack of a definite object to which to assimilate themselves, inclined to science and free thought generally. We see here the first signs of the subsequent cultural struggles of the thirteenth and fourteenth centuries; on the one hand there were the enlightened rationalists, on the other mystics of every category, and beyond them both those who are immersed in the grossest superstition.

But when such extreme schisms arise among a people, and their religious consciousness either throws off every burden or else weighs itself down beneath every conceivable kind of spiritual yoke, it always means that the equilibrium of the creative centre has been disturbed, that something in the religious evolution of a people has been overlooked and is wanting. To be able to react to the question of faith with the impulsive spontaneity of a true child of nature Judaism had long since ceased to be young enough, and yet it was not old enough to dispose of all religious problems on the basis of schemes and standards. It needed that spiritual power which does justice both to the heart and to the head, and through both to their common object, religious faith. The Talmud was a means of survival, but it was not a means of fulfilment. And if it had set out to give a people a meaning for their existence, it had already proved abortive. A fresh attempt had therefore to be made to realize the Jewish idea, and, what is more, this required to be accomplished in accordance with what has been said above, on the plane of the spirit, with the spiritual as its basis. Even Christianity from the very first had aimed at discovering a spiritual foundation. Islam had stuck fast in the midst of its struggle to find a spiritual motivation. And now Judaism embarked upon a similar undertaking.

This endeavour found visible expression in the person of Saadya ben Joseph, of Faiyum in Upper Egypt (882–942). His was a mind of encyclopædic and universal range. At the age of twenty he had already begun to translate the Scriptures into Arabic, and the reputation he gained so early in life soon led to his being summoned to Babylonia. Here he came into conflict with the ruling exilarch, and was placed under the ban. But this period of forced retirement, during which he was able to watch the spiritual conflict, gave him leisure to mature and prepare for an important literary output. And thus he became, more especially with his treatise *Emunoth we'deoth* (Doctrines of Faith and Their Proof), a new point of orientation for the Jewish spirit. The doctrine of the Moslem rationalists, the Mutazilites (free will as the basis of religious ethics), Philo's attempt at reaching a synthesis between Judaism and Greek philosophy, and anything in the teaching of Aristotle and Plato which could be made to fit in with his monotheistic conception of the universe, he built up into a system, the object of which was to point out a *via media* to both the rationalists and the mystics, to reconcile the Talmud and the demands of religion, and to prevent the former from being wrecked by reason, and the latter from being swamped in faith. "I saw how some were drowning in the sea of doubt," he declared by way of explanation, "and some plunging into the abyss of error." He gave both of these groups of people a system to guide them and a philosophic body of doctrine, which advanced fundamental principles but provided no dogma. At the beginning of all things he postulated the creation of the world out of nothing by the will of one absolute God. The crown of creation was man, for he alone was endowed with a soul and therefore with the capacity to distinguish between good and evil, and to exercise his free will in practising virtue or being guilty of sin. The law was given to man as a revelation, to enable him to set up standards for himself, which he did not naturally possess. But he still retained the power of moral choice. He alone by his conduct was responsible for sin, which had not always existed in the world. It was for this reason that his fate was not preordained and that he was the creator of his own destiny, either sullying his soul by sin or purifying it by virtue. His good and evil deeds would be weighed in the balance only in the beyond which was reached through the gate of death; death was not the end of life, it was merely a bridge to a new and fateful path for the soul.

By establishing and systematizing such ideas, Saadya once more opened up the way to freedom of thought for the Jewish world. From his time onwards, discussions about the Talmud and religious dogma became allowable. He provided the age with the means of coming to a close. The Babylonian epoch had been unable to reach any definite conclusion. It was merely a stage, bounded and enclosed by two opposites—the law and the heart, the Halakah and the Haggadah—which already stood opposed to each other, though both came from the same source and were destined for each other. One characteristic at least they always had in common—concern about God.

THE PERIOD OF PASSIVITY

WHILE Babylonia was imparting fresh life to Judaism, in those European countries where Jews had settled a period of passivity now supervened. By this we mean that they were now compelled to play a passive part in history. A strange power, in the shape of the Christian church, not the Christian religion, thwarted them at every turn; it tried to convert them and, where it failed to do so, it did its best to exterminate them, or at all events to force them down to the lowest possible level of existence.

Events followed the same monotonous course in all the countries of Europe, and always ended in the same way. At first we find the Jews living peacefully side by side with the people of the country, enjoying normal neighbourly, business, and intellectual relations with them. But as soon as Christian missionaries appeared, the scene changed. Their efforts were directed not only towards converting the pagans to Christianity, but also towards separating them as far as possible from the Jews, and fostering hostility between them. This was not always an easy matter; for the hundred and one human and economic interests they had in common were often stronger than obedience to the new religion. But what the faith did not effect, or, to put it more accurately, what the faith had no right to effect, unless it wished to make nonsense of its claim to be the "religion of love," was accomplished by the church, that is to say by Christianity in its development as a political institution.

We have already referred to this development, and are now concerned with its effects on Jewish history. In dealing with this question we shall touch upon the darkest and most grievous chapter in the whole history of humanity. When we pass in review the countless cruelties, martyrdoms, persecutions, murders, massacres, curtailments of rights, and general molestation that Judaism has for ages been called upon to suffer at the hands of Christianity, we cannot help seriously asking ourselves whether Christianity as a religion, as a religious idea, can possibly be held responsible. If it can, and if we believe the Christians who declared at that time that they were really acting in the name of their *faith,* in the name of Jesus, we are obliged perforce to contest the value of Christianity as an ethical, social, and humane doctrine. But the Jewish respect for every faith as an expression of the highest spiritual experience, and the Jewish desire to come to an understanding on a human basis, suggest another standard of judgment, and that is that the majority of the manifestations which have claimed and still claim to be Christian have no connexion whatever with true religion, but are political acts and the outcome of political measures.

The Christian church, whether in Italy or in Gaul, in the Frankish empire or in Spain, took up the struggle against Judaism. The brutality of the conflict increased in proportion to the distance the scene of the struggle was removed from Rome. It cannot be denied that as a political fight it was justified and consistent. The idea that Christianity should be the one and only religion was accepted in the early days of the papacy. But if it were the only religion, it alone must exercise sovereignty; that is to say, Christianity should include the whole world and refuse to tolerate the existence of those who refused to submit to its rule. It was to this imperialistic conception that Christian propaganda owed its untiring energy. When the word failed to convert, the sword took its place. But everywhere was to be found a group of men who refused to capitulate either to the word or to the sword—the Jews. They were the living refutation of the right to exclusive dominion claimed by the church, and Christianity felt that this refutation must be confuted, and when this was impossible, suppressed.

The church possessed the power to do this. In an age which witnessed the downfall of the world empire of Rome, the migration of peoples, the rise of new empires, the disintegration of all the old powers, and the struggle for the formation of new ones, the only body on the scene of the struggle which had a coherent, masterful, and essentially unchanging idea was the newly formed Christian church. Backed by the Christian empires of Rome and Byzantium, it could set to work methodically and systematically to set political forces off one against the other and serve its own ends, the executive in the whole business being the clergy.

Whereas, hitherto, the Jews had been called upon to submit only to the authority of foreign kings, they now had a new authority set over them—the Christian clergy. Foreign kings, according to their views, their culture, and their mood, had treated the Jews well or badly, but the Christian clergy could not officially be anything else than hostile in their attitude. From the very first the Christian priesthood were endowed with power, originally in their own right, and afterwards more and more as the result of the idea of the apostolic succession. When the religion crossed the political frontiers of a country, the priesthood went also, but they regarded themselves as belonging to a supernational organization. The power they gradually won over mankind and over the human soul, owing to the doctrine that it was through the mediation of the priesthood alone that a man could win salvation, further strengthened this organization retrospectively, as it were, since all its members, by virtue of the power conceded to them, were deeply interested in the source of this power, that is to say, the organization. Whereas in other national units, the priesthood had hitherto been a strictly secluded caste, Christianity, after every political frontier it crossed, formed of the clergy a supernational organized community, a caste which lived on the power which it generated itself inside the caste. This explains why the clergy reacted in the same way in all countries. Financial interests alone could induce individual representatives of the church to diverge from the uniform attitude. The kings, on the other hand, as isolated powers, not united and supported by any organization, could, within the limits of their political and human capacity, do as they pleased. In certain circumstances they were able to follow the dictates of their superior human or political knowledge, and often did so in open opposition to the clergy. Such an attitude on the part of the clergy, however, would have been the death-blow to the organization and consequently to their own power. This explains why their spiritual reaction was more purposeful, more stubborn, more malicious than that of the kings, and more responsible for the centuries of human besotment and subjection that followed.

The Jews were from the beginning the predestined victims of power. They were not dangerous, for they possessed no effective weapons. Any spiritual power with which their self-government may have endowed them was taken from them in Italy and Byzantium as early as 398, by the fact that they were deprived of their rights of autonomy. And thus they were delivered up body and soul to the mercy of the state and the clergy. Nevertheless, they still constituted a danger; for new converts to Christianity did not break off relations with them with sufficient spontaneity to make secret counter-propaganda on the part of the Jews among the pagans of yesterday impossible. Just as Christianity had originally sprung from Judaism, and had in its inception and its development depended solely upon Jewish forms, so, at this period, a number of spiritual links still remained in existence which helped to make large numbers of Christians incline towards Judaism in their views, customs, and way of life. Christians attended religious services in the synagogues. They kept the Jewish fast-days and observed the Sabbath, New Year's Day, the Passover, and the Feast of Tabernacles. When at a trial an oath had to be taken, they preferred to take it in the synagogue, because it was more solemn and binding than an oath taken in church. Thus the church had to fight not only against the pagans, but also against the Judaizing members of their own flock.

There were two methods of conducting the struggle. The Jews might by guile be separated from the Christians, or they might be converted. Both ways were followed alternately, and sometimes together. Innumerable resolutions passed at the various councils dealt with regulations for separating the Jews from their Christian environment, and every kind of relationship, from mixed marriages to taking meals together, was forbidden. As early as the sixth century the Merovingian rulers of the Frankish empire decreed that at Easter no Jew was to be seen in the streets for four days.

An enactment of this kind is extremely instructive. If the segregating measures were to prove effective, it was necessary to produce ample justification for them in the eyes of the common people. Political and theological arguments were useless in this connexion. An appeal had to be made to instinct, to religious fanaticism, to the readiness of the majority to regard themselves as the elect and everybody else as the scum of the earth. And no pains were spared to make the Jews appear contemptible in the eyes of Christians by calling attention to their strange customs and observances. The church dinned these ideas into the heads of the faithful with such impressive and untiring perseverance that they at last bore fruit in such phenomena as the Crusades, the Black Death, the Shepherds' Crusades, and the Spanish Inquisition.

True, Judaism, the peculiar attributes of which naturally inclined it to exclusiveness, had, in its endless struggles against an overpowering environment, isolated itself in various ways ever more and more. But between voluntary separation of this nature, and compulsory exclusion, there is the same difference as exists between self-defence and crime. In the first case, separation was the result of spontaneous conviction, and insistence upon respect being paid to the views held; in the second case, it was the outcome of contempt and the suppression of all feelings of humanity. It was Christianity which, as the result of systematic training, first introduced a sinister note into the idea of separation.

But the attempt to solve the Jewish problem by means of conversion was independent of this. The papacy in its early days took the view that the Jews should be left in possession of their ancient rights, and should not be oppressed, provided care was taken to see that they practised no propaganda among the Christians, and above all that they owned no Christian slaves. And it was hoped that they would of their own accord soon see reason. This was the view held by Gregory I, who said: "Even if we do not win them over, we certainly win over their children." Different countries, however, had different ideas about conversion. Byzantium, the Frankish empire, and later on Spain also, showed a strong determination to convert the Jews. There were three ways of doing this—to offer special rewards and favours to converts, to impose economic disabilities on those who refused to be converted, and lastly to use force against those who continued to offer stubborn resistance.

Economic pressure was brought to bear chiefly by the application of the law concerning slaves. Economic life at that time, more particularly agriculture and horticulture, was entirely dependent on purchased human labour. The Jews were therefore forbidden, on threat of the severest penalties, to keep Christian slaves. They then had recourse to keeping pagan slaves, whereupon a law was passed by which every pagan slave who became converted to Christianity immediately obtained his freedom, that is to say, he had to be liberated. Naturally, numbers of pagan slaves availed themselves of this chance of gaining manumission, which was always obtained at the expense of the Jews.

When even this undermining of his economic existence, not to mention its destruction, failed to induce the Jew to be converted, the authorities resorted to violence, that is to say, the Jew was dragged to church and baptized. His children were taken from him, and, in order to bring them up in a Christian atmosphere, they were placed in convents or in Christian families.

Such things invariably happened wherever Christianity appeared upon the scene, and a description of what took place in Spain applies equally well to other countries where events followed the same chronological sequence.

Ever since the first century the Jews had possessed settlements in Spain, which in point of numbers, economic significance, and intellectual influence were extremely important. It was precisely their importance which led the Spanish bishops to be the first to make an attack on the Jews. As early as the year 306, before Christianity had become the state religion of the Roman empire, at a council convened to discuss the conversion of the pagans, they decided that Christians and Jews should be strictly separated and, above all, that mixed marriages should be prohibited. It was only the invasion of the Visigoths in the fifth century that interrupted their hostile manœuvres. The Visigoths were Arians, and therefore diametrically opposed to Orthodox Catholicism on matters of dogma. It is interesting to note that the Arians (that is to say, those who believed that Christ was of similar nature but not of the same substance as God the Father) were always tolerant towards those who differed from them in matters of faith. This was also true of the Ostrogoth Theodoric. It was only when they embraced Athanasianism that religious fanaticism flared up, and vented itself upon those who did not hold the same beliefs as themselves.

This also applies to the Visigoths in Spain when, under Reccared I (586–601), they renounced Arianism and became filled with a maniacal lust for power and violent religious fanaticism. The combination was possible, because in their case the church and the king for the first time worked in unison, the authority of both powers being coextensive, with the result that resolutions passed by the councils *ipso facto* became laws of the state. The legislation which resulted from this, and which Montesquieu described as "puerile, eccentric, and idiotic," aimed at bringing about the union of church and state by every possible form of violence. As not even the utmost severity of the law could prevail upon the Jews to become Christians, King Sisebut, in 613, issued an ultimatum confronting them with the alternative of baptism or emigration. Some of the Jews, who were wedded to their estates, pretended to go over to Christianity. Others emigrated to north Africa. Others, who emigrated to the empire of the Franks, fell into the hands of the Merovingian monarch, King Dagobert, who confronted them with the same alternative, baptism or exile. Apparently they chose to become converts to Christianity.

The next king, Svintilla, who was more interested in the politics than in the church of his country, allowed the pseudo-Christians to return to Judaism. This was a defeat for the church, and she wreaked a cruel revenge, not against the king, of course, but against the Jews. When they recovered a free hand under Sisemant, the bishops discussed the problem of these Jews at the Fourth Council of Toledo. The decision reached was that, although henceforward no Jew could be baptized by force, any who had already been baptized, even by force, were to remain Christians.

In order to make sure whether such baptized Jews were not guilty of observing their own faith in secret, they were delivered up body and soul to the jurisdiction of the bishops, and became little more than chattels. The bishops tormented them and extorted money from them mercilessly. The perpetrators of these inhuman extortions were threatened with excommunication, but the very council which passed the resolution contained members who were the worst offenders in this respect. The spiritual martyrdom which subsequently attained such vast proportions in the fight the Spanish Inquisition carried on against the Marranos, the Jewish pseudo-Christians, started at this early date.

But it was only the beginning. King Chintila (636–640) on his accession took an oath that he would faithfully observe all the enactments directed against the Jews. Jews who had been forcibly baptized, terrified of fresh acts of violence, submitted themselves humbly to the king and the bishops with a *placitum,* in which they swore a solemn oath that they would do their best to be good Christians and had no wish to associate with Jews any more.

But this did not set them free. For in spite of it they were involved in the attack made by King Recceswinth (649–672) on the Jews who had not yet been baptized. Before the Eighth Council he declared (653): "Whereas Almighty God has rooted out all false doctrine from our country, this blasphemous sect alone has not yet been exterminated, therefore it must either be led into the right path by force of our piety, or else struck down to the ground with the rod of vengeance."

The force of piety does not seem to have sufficed to exterminate the Jews, for the next Visigoth monarch, King Euric (680–687) was obliged to have recourse to the rod of vengeance. At his opening speech at the Twelfth Council of Toledo, he made the following appeal to the bishop: "I beg you to make one last effort to pull this Jewish pest out by the roots!" A law was passed forbidding the practice of the Jewish religion. The Jews were ordered to present themselves for baptism within the year, and, if they failed to do so, they were to be punished by being given a hundred strokes of the lash, having their hair pulled out, being driven from the country, and having their property confiscated to the crown.

In the face of this menace many of them fled to north Africa where they joined the Arabs. But the law was never carried into practice, for the governors of the provinces and the feudal lords protested against this act of economic suicide. The coping-stone of Visigoth legislation, however, was the law of the Seventeenth Council in the year 694, which made all the Jews in Spain royal property, with which the king could deal as though they were his own goods and chattels.

Political Christianity had to wait another six hundred years before it was able to realize the ideal of a wholly national Christian state. Meanwhile the power of the Visigoths waned and dwindled away in the face of the invasion of Islam, and the Jews, who had been destined to be made into slaves, became the heralds of a universal culture.

PART IV

FROM

THE SPANISH PERIOD

TO

THE BANISHMENT FROM THE WEST

CREATIVE DEVELOPMENT

THE liberated forces of the Semitic civilization of the Arabs had given rise to a movement which had spread throughout Syria, Palestine, and Egypt to north Africa. It had gathered fresh impetus from the people settled in these parts, more particularly from the Berbers and from the Jews, who had fled from the barbarian princes and priests ruling the Visigoth and Byzantine empires. The Berbers helped the Arabian movement to spread as far as Spain, while the Jews supported the enterprise with both men and money. In 711 the Berbers, under Tarik, pressed forward across the straits and occupied Andalusia. The Jews supplied pickets and garrison troops for the district, and in 712 Musa completed the conquest of southern and central Spain.

The conquered areas were regarded as part of the African province of the caliphate of Omayyad. This invasion, which was a real campaign of conquest, left its mark upon the life of the country during the following decades. Jews and Christians alike were exploited by the conquerors, who, moreover, split up into a number of small groups, waged war on each other. But the situation became clearer as soon as Abdurrahman, the Omayyad, took command. In 756 he proclaimed himself the independent Emir of Spain. And the nomadic life of the invaders, bent only on conquest, began to develop into an ordered sedentary existence. An administration was formed which certainly practised toleration towards those of other faiths, though it levied special taxes on them. But the problem raised by differences of religion was simplified by the conversion of large numbers of Christians to Islam. They were animated partly by the desire to avoid heavy taxation, partly by the wish to become eligible for public office, and partly by economic pressure. For the Arabs took a leaf out of the book of the Christians, and insisted that, if a slave belonging to a Christian became converted to Islam, he should be given his freedom. As a result, the Christians preferred to turn Mohammedan, and there came into being a whole class of Christian renegades who, to emphasize the fact that they were exceptionally true believers, always placed themselves on the side of orthodoxy in the insurrections stirred up by the clerical Mohammedan party against the government. In the economic, political, and intellectual sphere, the Christians now ceased to play any part, a fact of considerable importance from the standpoint of the development of Jewish culture.

The Jews were now, however, no longer treated as a conquered race, and were able slowly to recover from the persecution of the Christian Visigoths. When Abdurrahman III proclaimed himself caliph (929), and raised his kingdom to the rank of a great European state, the internal consolidation of the Jews was already sufficiently advanced to enable them to turn to creative production. Under the Moors in Spain they were allowed two hundred years of peace in which to do this. And they took full advantage of the respite. If any other people than the Jews had at that period shown themselves capable of similar cultural achievements, they would have been given a conspicuous place in the history of civilization.

The intellectual efforts of this Spanish period have led to its being called the Jewish Renaissance. But this is inaccurate. For its successes were not inspired by the past; it did not copy or repeat anything that had taken place before. It was rather an attempt on the part of a people to live their own life to the full, in accordance with the laws of their own being. By living their own life to the full, we mean that they exercised every function of which a corporate body of men is capable—the organization of the community, the exploiting of economic conditions, the development of art, philosophy, and religion. In all these departments feats of extraordinary vitality and power were performed, and had repercussions far and wide. The liberation of the Spanish Jews from the yoke of the Christian Visigoths had an immediate effect upon the Jews of the whole world. All the Jews inhabiting the vast empire of the Moors, which reached from Cordova to Baghdad, were now once again brought into touch with one another, and the unity of the Jewish population in all parts of the world, which, owing to the fact that it had no country of its own, was always dependent on the general political situation, was to a large extent restored. Judaism, dispersed as it was over the face of the globe, was always inclined to set up a fictitious state in the place of the one that had been lost, and always aimed, therefore, at looking to a common centre for guidance. Compulsory mobility led to the formation of a mobile centre, which the people invariably identified with the place where their spiritual leaders resided, and never with the headquarters of economic or political power. (As a matter of fact, in practice only, it turned out that economic and political freedom always provided the Jews with spiritual opportunities as well.) This centre was now held to be situated in Spain, whither the national hegemony was transferred from the East. Just as Babylonia had providentially taken the place of Palestine, so now Spain opportunely replaced Babylonia, which, as a centre for Judaism, had ceased to be capable of functioning. All that could be done there had already been accomplished; it had forged the chains with which the individual could bind himself to avoid being swallowed up by his environment—the Talmud. As the result of the Messianic agitation, the activities of the Karaites, and the philosophy of a man like Saadya, it had also pointed out how the chains could be rendered not only innocuous but actually productive. Babylonia had educated and prepared Judaism, so that it could once again make its bow to the world, though it certainly had a touch of the East, a breath of the homeland, in the shape of Arabian civilization to help it to do so. We must again beg leave to point out that Judaism was never offered such chances, such fine opportunities to flourish, from Christianity. (The only exceptions to this are afforded by the rare cases in which Christianity, casting dogmatic constraints aside, confined itself to purely human and spiritual considerations.)

This new centre necessarily acquired an utterly different complexion from any of the former centres, and the revivals of the old Babylonian institutions of the exilarchate and the gaonate, bore only a superficial resemblance to their prototypes. This period produced the learned doctor Hasdai ibn Shaprut (910–970), the political adviser and minister for foreign affairs of Abdurrahman III and Hakam II, whose influence and personal gifts led to the Jews addressing him as *Nasi,* prince. He was responsible for the foundation of the academy in Cordova to which Jewish scholars from all parts of the world flocked, and which the people would have liked to regard as a revival of the gaonate. But its position and importance as a representative institution no longer depended upon the official recognition of the government, but on the determination of the Jewish people to acknowledge it as such. Even the functions of its officials were different. True, the Talmud was still eagerly and painstakingly studied there, and there was probably no Jewish poet, philosopher, or scientist in the whole of Spain who had not passed through the school of the Talmud in his youth. Nevertheless, the spiritual atmosphere of Spain was not completely overshadowed by the Talmud as had been the case in Babylonia. The Talmud was no longer an end in itself, but merely part of a spiritual whole. The people no longer wished to give themselves up to it body and soul; all they aimed at was to apply it, and it was only with this end in view that they undertook the task of making it more wieldy, more comprehensible, and more orderly.

As a matter of fact, order and form were the two fundamental concepts underlying Jewish life in the Spanish epoch; order, with a view to making the spiritual treasures, heritage, and potentialities wieldy and available; and form, so that the general survey thus obtained might make the world brighter, more full of joy, and worthy of humanity. Herein lay both the starting-point and the goal of this spiritual life—the starting-point was the national hearth, and the goal was the world, mankind, the universe. If we add to this that the comparatively peaceful existence the Jews were now allowed to lead also gave an extraordinary impetus to their economic prosperity (if only for the simple reason that, in Spain as everywhere else, they were far ahead of those about them in economic development) it is no wonder that they attained to extraordinary heights in almost every department. Until the end of the twelfth century only two productive civilized peoples existed in that part of the world which were making history—the Arabs and the Jews.

The basis of the formative tendency consisted in that species of culture known in the history of civilization as Humanism. But among the Jews in Spain it began four hundred years earlier than it did in Italy, since it showed signs of life as early as the ninth and tenth centuries. An overpowering thirst for knowledge, enlightenment, and discovery became everywhere noticeable. They gave this knowledge a firm foundation in the past, in their medium of expression—language. Grammars were produced, and analytical dictionaries. The structure of the Hebrew tongue was analysed and examined, and its form and means of expression were endowed with fresh life and became the subject of controversy. Before long the faulty use of language, either in speech or writing, provoked the most bitter and withering scorn and ridicule. Knowledge of the Hebrew language became a science, and the application of this knowledge a high art, while, as regards form and expression, the language itself developed into an instrument of the most perfect classic beauty.

With the language as a basis, they once more ventured to return to their ultimate anchorage in the past, the Bible, and were able to throw light on all those passages which, owing either to the form in which they were written, or to faulty tradition, had become obscure. Thus, at the beginning of the twelfth century, the first real Bible commentaries were already in existence. This implied a growing interest in the Bible. But in the Jewish Diaspora any such increased preoccupation with the Bible almost always presupposed diminished interest in the Talmud, it might almost be said a tacit, though often very marked opposition to the latter book, which in Spain found its compensation in the field of the emotions. The rigid, binding, and unrelenting rites of the Talmud were opposed by the constantly changing demands of human life, of the human heart. It was the heart versus the Talmud, the intensification of the emotional side of religion, that formed the burden of the popular work *Duties of the Heart,* which Bahya ibn Pakuda wrote at the beginning of the eleventh century.

Furthermore, the supremacy of the Talmud had already been undermined as the result of the striving after order, which led to this unwieldy mass of literature being systematically dealt with and all that was unessential and confused in it being suppressed. (*The Little Talmud* by Isaac Alfasi, 1013–1103.) These philological activities, the systematization of the material, and the relegation of the Talmud to its proper place, all combined to liberate that creative religious tendency which, on ultimate analysis, was also the foundation of the Talmud itself. What under different conditions of life had to become the Haggadah, and survived as the Midrash, in the present instance was able to develop into poetry and philosophy. Incidentally, this reveals the real nature of the forces behind the Haggadah and the Midrash.

Such a systematic consolidation of the spiritual treasury of the past could not fail considerably to raise the level of general culture. Every department of contemporary knowledge was tackled and mastered—medicine, natural science, mathematics, astronomy, philology, literature, poetry, and moral and religious philosophy. Only one branch was omitted by the Spanish Jews, and that was history; they did not even write their own history. There was a deep significance in this, and the reason for it was very different from that which prevented the Jews of the Babylonian period from writing history. The fact was that they still had a secure spiritual anchorage; they felt no curiosity regarding the past. They were trying to get into touch with the spirit and soul of the world they found about them; they were examining, pondering, and rhapsodizing about the world with a view to the possibilities of the future; they stopped working only at the point where their range of knowledge ceased, and this range was exceptionally wide.

Philo in Hellenistic Alexandria, and Saadya in Talmudic Babylonia, were each, it is true, the exact expression of the age and place in which they carried on their activities; but, after all, they were solitary figures. In the Spanish epoch, on the other hand, philosophic figures were so plentiful that one is almost tempted to write a history of Jewish philosophy instead of a history of the Jewish people. As this philosophy was the outcome of extraordinary exuberance, educated people were all more or less philosophers, while every philosopher was also creative, or at least active in some other department of life. Hasdai ibn Shaprut, the foreign minister already mentioned, was a man deeply versed in philosophy, and as his office left him no time for productive work, he at least spent his ample means on the patronage of art and letters on a grand scale.

Samuel ha Nagid of Granada (982–1055) resembled him both as a statesman and a Mæcenas, but was an even greater scientist and philosopher. He was, moreover, a poet who wrote in a classical though somewhat ponderous style. He was the first Jewish poet of Europe who treated of worldly matters in his poems. This combination of philosophy and poetry made him a link between the past and those spiritual giants of whom it is difficult to decide whether they were greater as poets or as philosophers, or whether they were equally distinguished in both capacities.

The first of this series, who in the depth and range of his intellect stands out head and shoulders above everybody else in the eleventh century, was Solomon ibn Gabirol, who lived from about 1020 to 1070. His poetry reveals a complete mastery of both form and content, and he may truthfully be said to have turned the whole of his universe, the whole gamut of his existence, into poetry—from the cares and sorrows of his own private life, to his pious and intimate communion with God, and even to the metaphysical foundations of the world. "I am a child with the heart of an octogenarian," he observed of himself with patient resignation, "my body treads the earth, but my spirit hovers in the clouds!"

But all the restlessness and world-weariness of his private life settles down and grows calm when he communes with his God, or lets his God commune with his people: "Have patience yet a while longer, thou piteous soul, until I send forth my messenger to prepare my way before me; then shall I crown my king on Mount Zion!"

And at last he becomes perfectly calm and resigned when he deals with his relation to the great whole, and his interpretation of the world and the universe. He then goes right back to the "Source of Life," which is the title of the philosophic work in which he evolves a complete and unbroken harmony out of the whole gamut of creation, from the highest fundamental principle to the lowest creature in the scale of creation. The same law and the same forces underlie both macrocosm and microcosm. "The power (of the divine will) extends to the smallest tissue of the lowest creature." And just as the divine radiates energy from itself, which permeates everything, from primeval matter to the most insignificant of living things, so human life also sends heavenwards its eternal craving for God as the "Source of Life." Thus here too harmony of movement is complete.

Ibn Gabirol was the first philosopher worthy of attention in the Middle Ages. Christian scholasticism, ignorant of the fact that their author was a Jew, borrowed heavily from his works. Albertus Magnus, Thomas Aquinas, and Duns Scotus all made use of the *Fons Vitae*, written by a certain Avicebrol, who was none other than Ibn Gabirol!

At the end of the eleventh and the beginning of the twelfth century, we meet with a number of poets and philosophers who, in spite of their many differences, have this much in common, that they all set forth from a national basis in their search for the universal. And while as poets, as creators working with their hearts, they mastered the most intricate subtleties of the Hebrew language, as philosophers, as creators working with their heads, they wrote in a no less pure, classical Arabic. Even in their medium of expression, they emphasized their desire to be both separate from the rest of the world and yet one with it. Thus did this epoch set the example to the rest of the Jews for the position they should take up in the world.

The achievements of these thinkers have quite erroneously been declared to have been inspired by contemporary Arabic philosophy. But as a matter of fact all that happened was that the same problem became acute at the same time in the case of both peoples. Every philosophy bears within it a germ of autocratic feeling, which is hostile to tradition, and as such may one day prove hostile to ancestral beliefs, to religion. Between Baghdad and Spain, between the orthodox and the rationalists among the Arabs, there arose in the twelfth century a dispute as to whether faith should be set above reason, or reason above faith. Judaism had also reached a stage of development at which this problem was due to arise. Faith, in its expression as the religion of a particular nation, is, as a matter of fact, capable only of binding the people of that nation. (That is why there cannot really be any such thing as "conversion.") Thus there can be no understanding between two believers of two different nations, on the plane of religion, but only on another plane superior to both of them. If, therefore, the intellectual leaders of Judaism of that day really and truly wished to take the step from the national to the universal standpoint, they would have been forced to occupy themselves with the question whether that which was peculiar to themselves, to their religion and their tradition, could be applied to the whole, to the store of knowledge accessible to everybody. It was for this reason that it was first necessary to settle the relation in which belief and reason, religion and philosophy, stood to one another.

Extremely animated discussions began to rage round this important problem. Every thinker and poet of distinction took part in it. Among them was Moses ibn Ezra who lived from about 1070 to 1138, and whose poetical gifts were so rich and abundant that his heart was capable of breaking over an unhappy love affair. He was responsible for hundreds of hymns and prayers which constituted the melancholy religious compensation for a life whose youthful joy and vivacity were all too soon destroyed. In his philosophy he tried to reach a compromise between reason and belief, between the need of knowing with intellectual precision, and the inner necessity of regarding the traditional religion as a revelation.

There was also Abraham ibn Ezra (1092–1167), an all-round scholar, who travelled all over the world from Egypt to Rome and London and back again to Narbonne. He was poet, grammarian, Bible exegete, philosopher, and a virtuoso of the intellect, and at times fell on misfortune and was obliged to turn to some Mæcenas for help. He was pious and faithful to tradition, yet he made certain concessions to rationalism. While maintaining that man was endowed with free will and could mould his own destiny, he was nevertheless a believer in Pythagorean mysticism and in the influence of the stars on human life.

While these two philosophers, as well as many others, found themselves unable definitely to decide one way or the other in the controversy about faith and reason, the two greatest and most versatile figures of the century stand out all the more conspicuous in the unhesitating determination with which the one pronounced in favour of the superiority of faith, and the other in favour of the superiority of reason. The one was profoundly national; the other profoundly international. The former was Judah Halevi, the other Moses ben Maimon, known as Maimonides.

Judah, the son of Samuel Halevi, whose Arabic name was Abul-Hasan, was born in Cordova in 1085, and was educated under the Moorish dominion in southern Spain. He was a doctor by profession, but his spiritual mission was to be the living pulsating expression of the Jewish soul. If art consists in the creation of works so moving that they make us feel we are confronted with the secret of life itself, then Judah Halevi was certainly a great poet. Even now, eight hundred years after his death, his poems, epigrams, and elegies retain all their original brilliance and power, which was possible only because in him the national and the universal, the one and the many, the religiously ordered and the intellectually liberated, were combined to form a single harmony of marvellous rareness. In this harmony there was one principle which lent it repose, and another which endowed it with movement; the former was his deeply pious foundation in his native Judaism, the latter, his constant insatiable yearning for the salvation of his people.

In view of these elements in his being, the philosophic ideas he was called upon to express were necessarily Judæocentric, with the result that he placed faith wholly above reason. His book *Kusari* (the *Khazar*) contains his system. The very title in Arabic suggests a whole programme: "Book of proofs in defence of a humble faith." The proof is unfolded by means of a conversation between a king of the Khazars, a philosopher, a Christian, a Mohammedan, and a Jew. The argument which Halevi makes the Jew bring forward against Plato and Aristotle, against the doctrine of predestination and the dogma of the Trinity, as well as against the contention that the Koran is the final revelation of truth, is that Judaism is not the product of philosophic speculation, but the creation of religious revelation. As such it stands far above all philosophy and the origin of its laws is above reason. They are laws which, unlike those of Christianity and Islam, demand not only that the dogma should be acknowledged and believed, but also that faith should be confessed in deeds, in action, and in every manifestation of existence. The Jewish people were the first to have been selected for this knowledge and this mode of conduct, and it was for this reason that they occupied a central position in humanity. The highest purpose of all philosophy was to serve this religion, the essence of which was revelation, and the distinctive mark of which was prophecy. It was the duty of the Jewish people to strive unceasingly to secure this prophetic means of knowledge and it was a duty they would have to carry out until the advent of the Messiah.

Just as Messianism was the conclusion of his philosophy, so did it also form the burden of his hymns and elegies. In this he does not stand alone. The deeper the knowledge and the richer the poetry of this Spanish epoch became, the more luminous and fervent was the devotion to the idea of salvation. The possession of happiness, economic prosperity, high office, and intellectual freedom could not make these men forget that Spain was a foreign country and that Jerusalem was home; that, although there were many fine synagogues in the land of exile, there was no Temple; that, although there were scattered settlements, there was not one united community; and that all over the world the Jew was living in a state of indescribable misery and distress. One can almost see the tears pouring down the cheeks of Judah Halevi as he softly sings:

About them who are captive still although Thy very own,
Last remnants of Thy flock who long for Thee, and Thee alone,
Dost Thou not ask, O Zion? . . .

The yearning of the homesick exile, and grief over the failure to achieve unity, grew to alarming proportions in this loving heart.

What time in western climes I pine, my heart beats in the East.
No zest for me in meat or wine, no glamour in the feast.
But how fulfil my sacred vows, deserve my consecration,
While Zion still remains Rome's thrall, and I an Arab minion?
As trash to me all Spanish treasure, wealth or Spanish good,
When dust as purest gold I measure, where once our Temple stood!

When the death of his wife severed the last bonds connecting him with his second home, he set off at the age of fifty-five on the long and arduous journey to Jerusalem. Wonderful poems matured in his brain on the way. We know that he went to Egypt and that he trod the soil of Palestine. But after that no more is heard of him. A Saracen horseman is said to have knocked him down and killed him before the gates of Jerusalem. Hundreds of years later a certain Jew named

Heine, whose aspirations were as wayward and conflicting as Halevi's were single-minded, wrote him an ode of thanksgiving:

Pure and true and blemish free
Was his singing like his soul,
Which, when his Creator made it,
So delighted Him that He
Kissed the lovely soul, and sweet
Echoes of that kiss e'er after
Lived in all the poet's songs,
Hallowed by this grace complete.

Whereas Judah Halevi was ready to suffer the fate of his people, Moses ben Maimon aimed at moulding their destiny. The sufferer was committed to faith, the moulder was committed to knowledge. The former sang hymns, the latter stated fundamental truths. The former wished to carry on the past; the latter wished to found a future.

Maimonides (1135–1204) was the greatest synthetic spirit of his time. Just as he turned every possible science to account in his work—philology, philosophy, mathematics, astronomy, natural science, medicine, and history—so he also welded the philosophic and religious principles of Judaism into a unified whole. His object was to reconcile the eternal difference between religion and science. He lived in an atmosphere in which the spirit, no longer weighed down and muzzled by any form of Christianity, had begun to find its wings. And he wished his people to enjoy the advantages of this without suffering any loss of faith, or rather with their faith confirmed and strengthened.

For such an undertaking he naturally had to have recourse to the work in which all the manifold ideas and aspirations of Judaism had been recorded—the Talmud. He wrote a commentary of the Mishnah. Many Jewish scholars had already done this. But he hoped that his commentary would made a coherent whole out of a mass of confused detail. He tried to release the study of the Talmud from the hands of the specialist, and to make its meaning clear to all. He also endeavoured to infuse life into that which the meticulous pedantry of the commentators prevented them from seeing—the ethics and dogma of Judaism—and from the motley whole he endeavoured to disentangle the ordering and systematizing forces which would make them available for philosophic thought and speculation. He made a great mistake in regarding Aristotle as the last word in philosophy, but this does not destroy the effect of his commentary, or diminish the value of his intellectual achievement. For to this day devout Jews in their morning devotions recite the thirteen articles of faith with which Maimonides closes his work. They may be summed up as proclaiming the existence of one God, the Creator of the universe, who is absolute, one, and undivided, without substance and unchangeable, eternal and timeless; the duty of man to pray to this God alone; the truth of the Bible prophecies and of the revelation made to Moses; the genuineness and immutability of the Torah; the belief in God's omniscience, in the justice of his retribution, in the coming of the Messiah, and in the resurrection of the dead.

His second work, both as regards thought and matter, is an improvement on its predecessor. It is not a commentary on the Talmud, but instils fresh order and meaning into this chaotic production, with the result that it almost makes a new Talmud out of it. The title of the book is *Mishneh-Torah,* or *Yad ha-Ḥazaqah* (The Mighty Hand). The centuries of work on the Talmud, and all the thought and speculation of which it had been the object since the time of Saadya, certainly in this work fell into the "mighty hand" of a systematizer of genius. It is polished and perfect in form from beginning to end. The opening words are: "The foundation and pillar of all wisdom is to recognize that there is an original Being Who has called all creatures into existence." The last are: "The world will one day be as full of knowledge as the basin of the sea is full of water." Between the opening and the close, we find the precise definitions of a trained rationalist on such matters as the knowledge of God and revelation, ethics and Messianism, of what is allowed and what is forbidden. Everything that is controversial and indefinite in the Talmud he excludes from tradition, his reason being that genuine tradition is bound to be clear and uniform and to allow of only one interpretation; it cannot be the subject of dispute. But every law which admits of no dispute he makes binding, irrespective of time and place. Thus his achievement is in effect twofold; in the sphere of the Halakah he releases ordered thought and thought subject to reason, but at the same time he closes this sphere to any further development. His work was a codification. The Talmud was a compilation. The Talmud was as boundless as man's capacity for faith. His Talmud was as broad or as narrow as man's capacity for knowledge itself.

He came to the conclusion that the source of the greatest conflicts lay here, and consequently endeavoured in his last great life-work to provide for the future from a lofty plane, to reconcile philosophy and Judaism and reduce world philosophy and Jewish philosophy to the same terms. The work is entitled *Moreh Nebukim* (Guide to the Perplexed). He starts out with the assumption that, if faith is really to lead to a clear conception of God, it must conform to the demands of reason; for not only faith, but also reason is a source of revelation. The former, according to him, is embodied in the Bible; the latter in the philosophy of Aristotle. In order to reconcile the two, he created his own metaphysic, which is different from Aristotle's though it shows his influence in the conviction that the whole universe is merely a realization of God's ideas. In the beginning was God. Between Him and the world apprehended by the senses were the incorporeal spirits which issued from divine reason, and through which matter was related to the eternal. Thus all earthly things consist of both form and matter, and man consists of body and soul, the temporal and the eternal. As both reside in man, he has been endowed with the capacity of aspiring to perfection and changing himself into "acquired reason." Man's soul dies with him, because it is merely his organic vital force. But his spirit is immortal, because it is the emanation of divine reason.

The works of Maimonides had a profound and lasting influence on the spiritual development of Judaism. They were received with fanatical enthusiasm and fanatical hostility. They caused an upheaval in the intellectual world of Judaism and inaugurated a cultural conflict on a grand scale. In this conflict, the fateful burden that everywhere weighed down on Judaism became plain. Had the Jews been allowed to live like ordinary human beings, the conflict would necessarily have ended in some definite conclusion being reached regarding the philosophy of Maimonides. Everything else had succeeded in reaching finality. The language had become a science, the poetry an art, the Talmud a disciplinary system, and the philosophy a creative expression of life. It was only in the sphere of metaphysics, where it was a matter of adopting a new attitude to this world and the beyond, that Judaism was divided into two irreconcilable camps, one for and the other against, between whom no compromise was possible. For Maimonides, by means of his metaphysic, had suddenly made Judaism, from the point of view of ideas and of spiritual power, an actual problem both for itself and those about it. He it was, after all, who first opened the eyes of medieval Christian scholasticism, which eagerly made use of his works, to the possibility of reaching a settlement in the conflict between faith and metaphysic. But the rest of the Jewish world was not in a position to accept Maimonides. It was unable to do so, because it did not possess the intellectual freedom of Spain and was living in a state of deep distress. The God it needed still was one who could be addressed from the depths of a heart overflowing with grief, and whose attributes did not lie so much in absolute creative power as in absolute love and absolute grace.

How dire was its need of this love and grace will be seen if we turn for a moment to examine the rest of the Jewish world at this time.

IN HOC SIGNO . . .

THE penetration of the Jews into western Europe and the founding of settlements were temporarily suspended in the eighth century. The force of the movement from the East was now diverted to the task of development. Judaism examined its new environment and set to work to find its bearings and take stock of the forces it would have for and against it in the struggle for existence.

From the very beginning the Jews were confined within extremely narrow limits; economic prosperity was all they could hope for. Intellectually they had nothing whatever in common with those about them, from whom the most they could expect was friendly and neighbourly intercourse. While in Spain Arabic theology occupied itself with problems which also interested the Jews, in western Europe nothing that took place in the intellectual sphere made any sort of appeal to them. The medieval man with whom they came in contact was, in every respect, in the political and economic, the religious and the cultural sphere, at an elementary stage of development in which his instincts were still crude and primitive. (When we come to deal with the Crusades we shall attempt an analysis of the man of the Middle Ages.) The Jew, on the other hand, was already at that time the end result of a long line of development, all the problems of which had been settled; it only remained to apply the solutions; they no longer required to be substantiated.

But even economic prosperity, and the maintenance and continuance of bare existence, were not left to the free play of natural forces, but were made the sport of the circumstances which happened to prevail in the environment at the time and depended on political rather than economic conditions. True, the economic state of a country, whether France, Germany, or England, was extremely important from the standpoint of Jewish activities; but the Jews could not fulfil even their economic functions if political forces were against them. For from the very beginning the two ruling powers in the world of that day, the church and the state, were disagreed as to the category in which the Jew should be placed. Was he a heretic to be handed over to the authority of the church, or a foreigner, over whom the state would assume control? If the church prevailed, the Jew was certain to be oppressed and downtrodden. If the state obtained the upper hand, although the contrary would not necessarily be the case, there was at least the possibility that the ruler, in the interests of his government, would not allow any weakening of the useful economic forces he had at his disposal.

This was the point of view adopted by Charlemagne, who represented a constructive idea of the state, and consequently used the forces which served his purpose. He quite rightly valued the Jews as the mainstays of international trade. Their connexions extended from the Frankish empire as far as India and China. Their communities, scattered all over the world, acted as agencies; they possessed a wonderful gift for languages, and were admirably fitted to act as connecting links between the East and the West. Charlemagne's successor, Louis the Pious, not only insisted on having exclusive jurisdiction over the Jews, but also, by setting up a special system of guardianship over them, showed that he meant to protect them as constituting a constructive factor in the state. He took not only individual Jews but also whole communities under his personal protection, and conferred rights upon them, appointing a special *magister judaeorum* to see that these rights were respected. This attitude on his part did not of course indicate any predilection in favour of Jews as such, but even the purely political motives by which he was animated were sufficient to rouse the animosity of the church. Under Charlemagne, Pope Stephen III had already lodged a complaint with the Bishop of Narbonne (in southern France): "With deep regret and mortal anxiety we have heard from you that the Jewish people . . . on Christian soil and in enjoyment of full equality with Christians, actually hold allodial property in the towns and suburbs, which they call their own. . . . Christian men and women live under the same roof with these traitors, and defile their souls day and night by uttering words of blasphemy." In the reign of Louis, the Bishop of Lyons addressed a note to the same quarter, in which he said: "It seems passing strange to us to see the pure virgin, the bride of Christ, sitting down to eat in the company of a whore. Have matters really gone so far that many Christians, who are related to Jews, actually keep their Sabbath?"

The interesting feature of these complaints is not so much their rough, hostile tone, as the tendency they reveal. The word was passed round that the religion of a whole people was being endangered by a few thousand Jews. But in view of the fact that an attempt was being made once more to bring into force the laws relating to slaves, the economic motive animating this persecution is obvious. Not that the church had any intention of striking only at the economic position of the Jews; she was much more concerned with levelling a blow at the people as a whole. And for this reason she constantly changed her ground of attack. But by means of the slogan that the Christian religion was menaced, she always used the most dangerous of weapons

—the ignorant masses in the nation. Into minds that were still receptive to anything and everything, she constantly dinned the same argument, which sooner or later they were bound to grasp. The result was that from being mere neighbours they became the enemies of the Jews. By this means, the church secured the supreme advantage of making the desired change in the attitude of the populace take place independently of the political conditions prevailing at the time. This was proved in the period following the division of the Frankish empire (843), which involved the parcelling out of areas of power which had previously been unified. There was a consequent weakening of the constructive idea of the state, and an era of separatism and self-seeking on the part of individual rulers set in. The feudal system grew more powerful and created within the divided empire further small isolated areas of power governed by counts and bishops. These petty rulers had an interest in making their particular domains as productive as possible, and in southern France and Germany the Jews were granted full liberty to settle down and to engage in any activity they chose. In return for the favour as much was of course extorted from them as could possibly be done without actually ruining them. The state of affairs was such, that even the bishops were no longer deterred by religious scruples, and Bishop Rüdiger of Speyer was not the only prelate who did all in his power to entice Jews into his territory. With the object of establishing a new industrial centre on the Rhine, he allotted the Jews special areas in which to settle (1084), declaring, "that this would only redound to the credit of the districts."

Nevertheless, even during this period, the Jews were persecuted as the result of ecclesiastical influence. In 1007, under the Capet dynasty in France, Jews were already being murdered and forcibly baptized, on the charge of having incited Caliph Hakim to destroy churches in Palestine. In 1065, in the south of France, insurgents marched to the Spanish frontier to massacre Jews. And if we trace such incidents to their source, we almost always find that they were inspired by the machinations of monks and priests. Such isolated incidents, however, taken by themselves, are of no very great importance. Far more significant is the fact that it was characteristic of the Middle Ages as a whole that pressure should always be brought to bear on the Jews by the whole of the environment in which they lived, not by any isolated section of it. This greatly increased the difficulties of adaptation for them. The forces directed against them, whether on political, economic, or religious grounds, came at times from wholly different quarters, and it was never certain whether the same combination of forces in the environment would culminate in the same effect on the Jews. What was even worse, it made the Jews absolutely defenceless.

A complicated process of stratification now developed in medieval society. The feudal idea was carried to its logical conclusion everywhere; the system developed, and trade corporations and guilds came into being. But this stratifying process in the structure of medieval life was not accompanied by any capacity to differentiate on the part of the medieval man; consequently there was no possibility of comparisons being drawn, of increased insight, or of progress. From the standpoint of its potentialities, medieval life was quite prepared to create new forms and to leave behind it the primitive stage at which everything—economic development, politics, and religion—remained standing. But it was not given to the man of the age to realize and effect this change, or to appreciate that what he saw about him represented only a stage, a step in evolution. No matter where he turned he was always confronted with the idea that the state was under the rule of the church. But if that were so, then everything that resulted from state organization, whether in the political or the economic sphere, was influenced by religion, everything was merely a manifestation of religion, and was to be accepted as such. But religion, as it was conveyed to the medieval man by Christianity, was both as regards dogma and the idea underlying it, essentially dualistic. It was a case of the pope versus the emperor, the church versus the state, heaven versus earth, Christ versus Satan. There was no escape from this dualism. All the innate natural forces of the people, which might have been capable of producing a human and intellectual development, were artificially dammed up by the church. "The rites of the church took the place of the customs of the people, the Scriptures replaced the history of the nations, the festivals were those of the Christian year; for every expression of the soul, ecclesiastical Latin had ousted the local vernacular, and for the common blood of the tribe or nation, the church had substituted the blood of the Redeemer." There appeared to be only one way of escape from this dualism, and that was through *one* church, the Holy Catholic Church; *one* emperor, the emperor who had been crowned by the pope; *one* law, Roman law; *one* science, theology; *one* form of expression, the Gothic style.

And men were expected to live within this framework bound hand and foot, with no hope of escape. If they wished to express themselves, they could do so only within certain limits, for they had no standard of comparison. And everything that happened was the outcome of what had been fitted into the framework. It was to this that the Jews owed their terrible fate.

At first only one or two spheres of activity were open to them. Feudalism prevented them from having any connexion with the land; the guilds effectually excluded them from the practice of trades and handicrafts, while the merchant corporations restricted their activities in the sphere of commerce. All these, however, were isolated phenomena which the Jews endeavoured to make the best of. But in the face of the horrors to which they were exposed by the Crusades, they were utterly defenceless. Though to all outward seeming the Crusades were a manifestation of Christian fanaticism, they were really nothing more than the explosion of human forces that had been too severely held in check. In this connexion Christianity was merely a medium of expression, though a very highly responsible medium. It was a fateful sequence that in this case, as in many others that subsequently arose, murder, as the instinctive expression of a semi-barbarous people, should be done in the name of Christianity.

The liberation of Jerusalem from the Moslems was made the battle-cry of the crusaders. The people were told that the holy places had been desecrated, and rumours were spread to the effect that Mohammedan and Jewish fanaticism had been responsible for a holocaust of Christians. Any man who declared himself ready to take up the cross was held to be invulnerable. All his sins, both past and future, were forgiven him. The eastward direction of the movement lent it a peculiar force, and religious unrest, similar to that from which the Greeks had suffered when they had become aware of the collapse of their pantheon, found a vent. The eastern elements in the Christian faith came to life, and thirst for knowledge led to the desire to investigate them at their source. Thus piety and enthusiasm both acquired an outlet. The austere drabness of medieval life eagerly turned to this warm, variegated, and romantic form of relaxation. If, to the devout man, forgiveness of sins was the great attraction, to the peasant it was the knowledge that he would be released for a while from his drudgery; the knight was lured by hopes of fame, adventure, and plunder; the adventurer and criminal by the chance afforded of indulging his lust for murder and rapine to his heart's content with impunity; while the priest saw the opportunity of increasing his political power. In short, the Crusades provided the means for emancipation on a grand scale from the fetters of time and place, and from the dreary oppression of medieval life. Moreover, they were a means of releasing the primitive instincts, the unsublimated animal passions that still held sway over the man of the Middle Ages.

Long before the mustering of the army was completed, bands of armed men were formed under the leadership of monks, knights, and adventurers, who by a campaign of incendiarism, plunder, and murder inaugurated the local Crusade in Swabia, Lorraine, and on both banks of the Rhine. From France, where in Rouen Jews were being massacred who refused to be baptized, irregular bands of crusaders crossed Flanders and entered the Rhine provinces where, joined by the Christians of the district, they made a sudden attack on the Jews of Speyer, and a large number of Jews who refused to embrace Christianity were killed forthwith (May 3, 1096). The crusaders then turned their attention to Worms, which they attacked. Some of the Jews bribed Bishop Adalbert to allow them to take refuge in his castle. But the rest, helpless and defenceless, were left to the mercy of their assailants. Only the few who consented to be baptized were spared. The remainder were ruthlessly massacred, that is to say, all who did not prefer to escape the alternative of a cruel death, or forcible conversion, by committing suicide (May 18, 1096). A few days later the bishop informed the Jews who had taken refuge in his castle that he could no longer protect them, and advised them to be baptized. They begged for time for reflection. This was granted, and when it was over the gates were opened; but it was discovered that nearly all of them had died by each other's hand. The crusaders slaughtered the rest and dragged their bodies through the streets as trophies (May 25, 1096). On the following day, a band of crusaders under the leadership of Count Emmerich presented themselves before the gates of Mayence. Bishop Ruthard promised to give the Jews shelter in his castle and over 1300 Jews handed him their possessions and entrusted themselves to his care. When the count and his men appeared before the castle, the bishop's guard refused to fight them, the bishop took flight, and the crusaders entered the keep. Some of the Jews were massacred, but the majority, consisting of men, women, and children, killed each other. Whereupon the bishop and the count shared the Jews' fortunes between them (May 27, 1096).

On May 30th Cologne was attacked. But the people of the city and the bishop (Hermann III) hid the Jews, and the crusaders were obliged to be content with destroying their houses. When a few weeks later their hiding-places were discovered, fresh massacres occurred and compulsory baptisms, while there was also a terrible increase in the number of suicides (June 24 to July 1, 1096).

In Germany no protest was raised against these proceedings, which are not even mentioned by most of the chroniclers. Possibly they were ashamed to do so.

Wholesale massacres continued to take place wherever the irregular bands of crusaders made their way. They are recorded as having occurred at Metz, Regensburg, Prague, and other towns in Bohemia. Albert of Aix, one of the few Christian chroniclers who have recorded these events, says: "And then, laden with the spoils of the Jews, Emicho, Clarebold, Thomas, and the whole insufferable band of men and women, continued their journey to Jerusalem." It was only when they reached the frontier of Hungary that they were driven back and dispersed as robbers and marauders by King Koloman.

Altogether, between May and July 1096, about 12,000 Jews were killed in the Rhine provinces. The death of a single one would have been too many. But why consider numbers? The Jews had already faced worse massacres. It is more important to discover the effect such proceedings had upon the spiritual attitude of those who were left alive and, more particularly, what must have been the feelings of the man who preferred to commit suicide rather than allow himself even to be touched by a Christian crusader. For these mass immolations, this terrible mutual slaughter, the killing of children by their mothers, the act of jumping alive into the flames or into the water with a stone round their necks, was a spiritual phenomenon. True, the man of the Middle Ages was not responsible for all this; his worst instincts had been roused and stimulated, and every human impulse within him rudely turned to savagery. But the Jew avoided all encounter with such bestiality by resorting to suicide. The mass immolations were, so to speak, prompted by an overpowering feeling of nausea at the very thought of coming into contact with the incendiarists who bore the sign of the cross upon their garments. But this was only one of the reactions, and proceeded from the emotions and the nerves. There was another which had deeper roots. The Talmud had laid it down that, rather than be forced to commit the heinous crimes of idolatry, unchastity, and murder, the Jew should die a martyr's death. And he obeyed the Talmud. In his eyes Christianity was idolatry. The worship of images, the reverence paid to inanimate relics, he regarded as heathen superstition, and even the prayers addressed to saints as no better than the worship of pagan heroes and demigods. Moreover, he could see nothing in the outward manifestations of the Christian church which might have induced him to make an objective comparison or adopt even an attitude of respect. What was there to rouse his admiration in the fact that the pope could release men from the oath of allegiance to their superiors, or that he incited them to murder their emperor? How could he feel any impulse to respect the ignorant, greedy, and extremely dissipated clergy, or an ecclesiastical teaching which could not prevent murder and the desecration of corpses in the name of the religion of love? Could the Jew really be called upon to understand that for the death of Jesus the law of revenge was to be kept alive indefinitely, and that every street-arab was to be regarded as a constituted executor of this religious mission? Nobody is ready to die for an absurdity. And it was an absurdity for a creed to proclaim the death of Jesus as a necessary and all-important act of redemption and yet for this very act, by which the edifice of doctrine stood or fell, to continue murdering people throughout the centuries.

All that the Jew had to set against this was loyalty. He sealed his loyalty to God by dying a martyr's death. He died for the sake of the *qiddush ha-shem,* for the glory of God's name. And he did so willingly though not gladly. For this persecution had destroyed the last spark of *joie de vivre* in the Jew, and a dazed, timorous generation grew up which was always peering out suspiciously into the future for the next blow to fall. This blow was heralded by the preparations for the Second Crusade. The "kingdom of Jerusalem," that lifeless product of religious policy, was in peril. A new army was required to defend it. Pope Eugenius III published a bull declaring that all who took part in it need not pay their creditors any interest on capital borrowed if they took up the cross. Thus he achieved a twofold object which was pleasing in the sight of God; he not only secured warriors for the holy cause, but also did an injury to the Jews. But in this he was outdone by the monk, Peter Cluny, who proposed that all the property of the Jews should be confiscated to finance the Crusade. His suggestion was not carried out, though even before the Crusade started it cost the Jews the bulk of their fortunes. True, the massacres of the First Crusade were not repeated, because the kings of France, for reasons of state, and above all for the sake of the royal exchequer, prevented any repetition of these expensive disorders. In Germany also, Conrad III tried to prevent them; but he possessed no authority. All real authority over the people lay in the hands of the monks. The most influential representative of the ecclesiastical point of view was the monk Rudolph, who travelled up and down the country, preaching death to all Jews who refused to be converted. In 1146, his efforts led to further attacks being made on the Jews in the Rhineland. By paying out huge sums to bribe the feudal overlords, the Jews purchased the right to defend their lives in fortified strongholds. But all who were found on the highroads were immediately put to death. Monk Rudolph's propaganda became so violent that in the end even the church felt compelled to forbid his activities. Nevertheless, she was unable to prevent massacres and compulsory baptisms from taking place in Würzburg in February 1147. Her protest against Rudolph was of little avail against the seed which she had been sowing for centuries, and she must therefore be held responsible for the evil harvest.

This harvest began to ripen in the interval between the Second and the Third Crusade when the charge of ritual murder was first brought against the Jews. Just as the Romans had once accused the Christians of using the blood of pagans at the celebration of holy communion, so the Christians now charged the Jews with using Christian blood at the Feast of the Passover. The first instance occurred in Blois, where a Jew was accused by a farm-labourer of having flung the body of a Christian boy into the river. The judge took great pains to investigate the charge and placed the man who brought it in a boat filled with holy water, and as it did not sink a verdict of guilty was returned against the Jew. As the Jews refused to be baptized, thirty-eight of them were shut up in a wooden tower on May 26, 1171, and burned alive. This case was typical of many others that followed. They differed only in the gruesome details of their execution. The fact that such charges of ritual murder could be made can certainly only be explained on the ground of the low level of culture reached by the medieval man; it may also perhaps have its root in an erotic variation of the old pagan idea of sacrificial death. But the fact that the instinct found expression, together with the direction in which it did so, was the outcome of the religious hatred which the Christian church had created. Otherwise trials for ritual murder could not possibly have continued to take place even in the twentieth century.

This hatred pursued the Jews wherever they went; charges of ritual murder were made even in England, where the Jews migrated in large numbers after the Norman Conquest (1066). As a result of the Crusades there was a further inrush of Jews, who were attracted to the country by the economic possibilities it held out. The Norman conquerors were anxious to receive their tribute in ready cash. In a population divided into feudal lords and serfs, the financial machinery for such transactions was lacking and it was for this reason that the immigration of Jews was looked upon with favour. Henry I (1100–1135) granted them a liberal charter, but in return they were obliged to pay him a certain percentage on the profits of all businesses, whether established for mere trading or for money-lending. Moreover, from time to time he contrived to extort large sums from them, in the year 1130 no less than £80,000 in modern money. On the death of a Jew, the king became his heir. In order to meet the huge demands the government made upon them, the Jews were obliged to charge high rates of interest, and the more the kings extorted from them, the more did they plunder their debtors, until they came to be regarded by the people merely as hated money-lenders.

This pressure was not confined to the economic sphere, but also spread to the domain of religion when Normandy, Anjou, Maine, and Brittany were added to England, and the French clergy were thus able to get into close touch with their English brethren. Suddenly the charge of ritual murder was also raised against the Jews in English territory. If a man died in mysterious circumstances, it was always a Jew who was held responsible. The dead man became a martyr; his relics were preserved, and a shrine set up to his memory. The religious business thrived!

As the result of economic tension and ecclesiastical baiting, the first systematic massacres and immolations of Jews took place at the coronation of Richard I, Cœur-de-Lion, (September 3, 1189) and at the time of his departure on the Third Crusade. And with these events, England reached the level of the rest of the world.

As far as the German Jews were concerned, the Third Crusade passed off uneventfully. Frederick Barbarossa had taken the precaution of shutting up the Rhineland Jews in various fortresses until the soldiers of the cross had taken their departure. Of course the Jews had to pay heavily for this, but Barbarossa's attitude was, in any case, consistent with his determined struggle against the church for the emancipation of the state from ecclesiastical tutelage. And once again, as in the days of the Carlovingians, the question whether the Jews came under the jurisdiction of the church or the state played a part in the conflict. Barbarossa defended the claims of the state by bringing forward the argument that in the days of the Roman empire the Jews had been the wards of the emperor, and that their protection now devolved on the emperors of Germany as the legal heirs of the Roman emperors. Thus the Jews were not subjects, but wards or clients; they were not subject to law, but subject to protection; and, as Barbarossa put it, belonged to "our private exchequer." Hence the expression "exchequer Jews." This was the beginning of the process completed by Frederick II, whereby Jews were converted into chattels. The Jews had become mere objects.

But this did not perturb them in the least. The legal aspects of their existence did not interest them. All they were concerned about was to know why they had been made the victims of such murderous persecution. Many attempts have been made to show that the Jews themselves with their financial transactions were responsible for the incidents associated with the German Crusades. But facts do not bear this out. For their economic position at the time made it quite out of the question. And, after all, in spite of their comparative freedom, they were the passive victims of circumstances rather than active agents. But they took the blame on themselves in a much deeper sense. In their reaction to misfortune different people show different dispositions. Whereas one race is filled with resentment and hatred against their oppressors, others respond by turning to self-examination. The Germans belong to the former category, the Jews to the latter. Once again it was borne home to them that misfortune is the result of guilt, not guilt in regard to others, but guilt towards oneself, towards religious obligations, towards God. And as soon as they recognized this, they withdrew ever more deeply into the domain of prayer and repentance. But increased piety imposes limitations upon life. Theirs could be no joyful piety, no piety accompanied by good cheer; it was perforce a gloomy piety, encased in melancholy and involving ascetic practices; a piety of elegies and dirges, a process of self-castigation by means of laws that grew ever more severe, oppressive, and narrowing. They took refuge in the Talmud. They intoxicated themselves with rabbinical argumentations and casuistry. As their feelings could find no expression in everyday life, they turned to mysticism. And it was only when they set up in their martyrology a memorial to their dead, the real martyrs, that they broke out into words of impotent loathing, as they called to mind the inhuman butchery of their people and their desecrated bodies. Thus their poetical creations are not beautiful, but for that very reason they are all the more terribly real.

How could a people, suffering from such fundamental spiritual depression, make any contribution to culture or produce anything new or original? With no culture about them to which they were related and from which they could draw inspiration, but hopelessly oppressed by the barbarity that surrounded them, the French and German Jews endeavoured to create a cultural unit among themselves. France became the intellectual centre both for French and German Jews. Whereas southern France was able still to profit from the free life of Spain, central and northern France became the focus of intensified Talmudic studies. And just as in the past the Gemara had grown out of the Mishnah by means of commentaries, interpretations, and amplifications, so the French Talmudic schools produced the *Tosaphoth* or "additions" to the Gemara. Hence their appellation–Tosaphists. These schools, whose attitude was extremely conservative, sent numbers of rabbis out to France, Germany, and England. They became the representatives of a narrow, oppressed, but acute spirit, the kind of spirit to which a Jew, scared by the world, might cling, and in which he could find an imaginary world that could not be destroyed. True, this spirit was incapable of providing free vent for the emotions, with the result that the eternal conflict between the Halakah and the Haggadah, the head and the heart, became doubly acute. Popular writings appeared, strange compounds of religiosity and superstition, of worldly wisdom and fear of demons, of lofty morality and ghost stories. Such books constituted the favourite reading of the medieval Jews. They show how self-centred, anxious, and confused they were and where they sought consolation. But in a secret corner of their hearts they nursed a grudge against God. In the hymn *Who is like unto Thee, O God, amongst the gods?* they altered the word *ba-elim* in the phrase "amongst the gods" to *ba-ilmim,* so that the line ran "Who is like unto Thee, O God, amongst the dumb?"

MARTYRDOM AND MYSTICISM

IN the thirteenth century the Jews of France, England, Germany, and Spain were afforded the opportunity for an unusually intensive development of two qualities with which they were endowed—the capacity for passive resistance and the ability to ignore historical events. While external pressure increased from day to day, and assumed ever more barbaric forms, while they were being despoiled, ground down, tortured, burnt alive, and hounded about, they were carrying on among themselves a passionate intellectual war, a regular cultural conflict. While they were being converted into thralls, and were being trampled underfoot in all directions with morbid fury, they calmly and resolutely withdrew from a reality which to them meant insecurity, and retired into a deep world of mysticism, into another reality, where martyrdom was voluntary, and therefore not destructive, but sustaining and creative. It constituted an attempt on the spiritual plane to recover an independent position in history.

Everything that took place in the outside world had become a matter of comparative indifference to them, because, as has already been described, the result was always the same, though the methods of persecution had grown at once more brutal and more refined. While they were murdered and plundered more mercilessly than ever, they were also forced to engage in the most abstruse discussions. Proceedings were even taken against Jewish books and conducted with the utmost subtlety and learning. If distinctions are to be drawn between the various countries, it might be said that in France and England the pressure came from above, whilst in Germany and Spain it came from below. Nevertheless a certain regularity may be observed in the cruel maze of injustices. The home Crusades which the church was obliged to organize after the failure of the Crusades abroad, affected not only those Christians who longed for an opportunity of enjoying religious freedom, but also the Jews whose very existence was a refutation of the supreme authority of the church. Another regular occurrence was for the Jews to be ruthlessly driven out of the country as soon as there was nothing more to be got out of them. Lastly, they were affected by economic progress, more particularly the economic plight of their environment.

Their external status (one cannot say their status as citizens, for they were not citizens) was fundamentally the same everywhere. They were the property of the ruler they happened to be under. They were live stock. In Germany, Frederick II declared them to be *servi camerae nostrae*. They had become vested interests. Just as there were royal customs dues and royal salt monopolies, so there was a royal right of "ownership" in Jews who were placed on the same footing as customs or salt. The function of the Jews consisted in paying money to the emperor, or whoever happened to have the right of ownership over them. This explains why disputes frequently arose over the possession of Jews; particularly during the interregnum, bishops and boroughs would fight acrimoniously over them. Being classed as property, the Jews were, of course, not allowed to change their place of abode without special permission. When exploitation became particularly crushing under the rule of the Habsburgs, and the Rhineland Jews began to leave the country, Rudolph of Habsburg had their goods confiscated, on the plea that "all Jews without exception are our crown servants." It was only natural that in such circumstances the existence of the Jews should have been precarious in the extreme and that their ideas of social right and wrong should not have been very lofty. At the best the only bond between them and the people about them was one of money. When, for instance, Rabbi Meïr, who was famous among his co-religionists, tried to leave Rothenburg, he was stopped and placed under arrest. The Jews offered 20,000 marks (in the currency of the time) for his release. Rudolph demanded more. Meanwhile Rabbi Meïr died, and the authorities refused to surrender his body. Fourteen years later a rich Jew at last succeeded in obtaining possession of it. This proves that the conditions of the day were such that a dead rabbi's body could become the object of a lucrative transaction.

The rulers of France were no less skilful in exploiting the Jews. Philip Augustus (1181–1223) may well be described as the official partner in every business deal carried out by a Jew. He drew vast sums from them, and fought tooth and nail with the feudal barons and overlords for possession of Jews. But Philip the Fair (1285–1314) went to even greater lengths. He was a passionate opponent of the Inquisition, which proved an unwelcome competitor with himself in the plundering of Jews. He plied an enormous trade in Jews and kept all Jewish concerns under close supervision until at last the whole of their business fell into his hands. In July 1306, after an exhaustive secret preparation, he had the representatives of the Jewish community in almost every city and town arrested, after which he proceeded to confiscate all the account books and property of the Jews and ordered them to get out of the country within a month, leaving everything movable or immovable behind. Thus everything they possessed fell into his hands, and any debts owing to them he collected himself. The country was ruined.

In England conditions were similar, though spoliation was if possible more open. The economic gift of accumulating money evidently made a deep impression on the primitive minds of these French and English monarchs, who, for their part, had a very simple method of dealing with the superior financial capacities of the Jews; they merely had recourse to legal spoliation and extortion. Richard I ordered all Jewish money-lending businesses to be registered, and state records to be kept of all promissory notes. King John Lackland raised funds by imprisoning and torturing Jews. Henry III increased the regular levies on Jews, taxing them to the extent of one-third of their property, and, in order the better to supervise their transactions, he concentrated them in those cities in which archives were kept (for the depositing of documents relating to debts). In 1254 the Jews at last petitioned the authorities for permission to emigrate. This was refused, but their taxes were reduced to a figure they could just afford. The Jews repeated their request to be allowed to emigrate, but this merely resulted in their being handed over as security to the Italian bankers. Edward I laid hands on what little property remained to them. By means of imprisonment he extorted £12,000 out of them. At last on July 8, 1290, he ordered them all to be out of the country by November 1st, but allowed them to take their personal goods and chattels with them.

The Jews, however, did not wait for the time limit to expire. By October 1290, over 16,000 of them had already boarded vessels that took them to France, Flanders, Germany, and Spain.

In Spain, too, the Jews were the property of the king, and in this country the interest is now concentrated on the two Christian kingdoms of Castile and Aragon, where the most important historical events took place. In both kingdoms the Jews were forced to pay huge taxes, though the methods employed varied. In their struggle with Islam, the Christian states had for a long while past enlisted the help of the Jews, whom they systematically enticed into their domain when the strictly orthodox group of the Almohades of Africa invaded the south, the really Moorish region of Spain, and harassed the Jews as believers in a different creed. In the decisive conflict between the Christian north and the Mohammedan south, the Jews played an extremely active part on the side of Castile and Aragon. By their financial help they also enabled the victors to turn their victory to account and to develop both these Christian states. They were fleeced, but they obtained privileges in return. The communal treasure of the Jews gradually became converted into financial institutions for the benefit of kings and infantas, but in exchange they were granted a large measure of autonomy and were allowed to have their own administration and judicial authorities. But when the clergy established themselves in the two countries and immediately started Jew baiting, the relationship between the king and the Jews became a sort of co-operative business, the king undertaking to protect the latter in return for their financial assistance.

But royal protection, even when the king really did his best to keep his side of the bargain, frequently failed in face of the power which, in the thirteenth century, reached its zenith as a force superior and hostile to the state: the papacy. In the person of Innocent III, the idea of spiritual power reached the same extravagant proportions as did the idea of temporal power in that of his mighty lay contemporary, Frederick II. But for both pope and emperor, the Jews constituted a political problem, and one, moreover, in which the interests of each party were opposed. Both wished to exercise power over the Jews, and both in fact did so. But whereas Frederick II, as for instance in Sicily and southern Italy, was able to realize his personal ideas as to what the economic position of the Jews in his domains should be, the papacy had no alternative but to continue applying the old theory that it must be the object of Christianity to triumph over the Jews. At first, it is true, Innocent III took the view that the Christians must not oppress the Jews too heavily, "for through them the truth of our own faith is confirmed," but this comparative tolerance was bound to give way in the struggle forced on the papacy by conditions within the country. For the forces of disintegration now for the first time appeared in open and organized revolt. In the Waldenses, for instance, these forces rebelled against the constitution of the church as a whole; in the Albigenses they denied the binding and absolving powers of the priestly functions; while in the Judaizing "Wanderers" they preached a spiritual return to the Old Testament. All such movements attacked the basis on which the power of the church, in so far as it was not a purely spiritual institution, was built, and they all occurred in suspicious proximity to Jewish settlements, and often in very close intellectual relationship with Judaism itself. Innocent III rightly perceived two factors here, in the first place the extremely shaky foundation upon which the Catholic Church stood among the broad masses of the people, and in the second that the intellectual superiority of the Jews was a dangerous menace. Consequently his own policy and that of his successors was logically directed both along spiritual and material lines; spiritually, by means of war on heretics, the inculcating of church doctrines on the great mass of the people, and denunciation of the moral depravity of the clergy; and materially, by means of increased severity in the legislation against Jews, polemical attacks on all states that dared to grant them rights, and finally by attacks on the Talmud.

In the home or local Crusades (1209–1229) the clergy, let loose in Provence, ravaged the country for twenty years and killed 20,000 heretics. This gave the Jew some idea of the fate awaiting him. The proceedings opened with a campaign of slander followed by trial before the court of the Inquisition. The famous Fourth Lateran Synod (1215) was the beginning. This Synod, which was the outward and visible sign of the far-reaching power of the papacy, once more declared war on the Jews. The clergy were henceforth empowered to supervise all Jewish money-lending businesses; Jews and Mohammedans were forced to wear a special badge on their clothes, and a number of old church canons were revived and put in force. Finally, and this was the beginning of unparalleled horrors and bloodshed, it was decided to apply "salutary force" to all Jews who, having been converted to Christianity, did not remain true to their new religion. In the vast majority of cases this meant all Jews who had embraced Christianity on pain of death.

For the application of this "salutary force," two institutions were founded, the "Holy Inquisition" and the Dominican Order, the order of friar preachers. Their original function, which was to preach the Catholic faith to laymen, was subsequently taken over by the Franciscan Order, which was founded at the same time. The Franciscans, or "mendicant friars," went about among the people, while the Dominicans undertook the persecution of heretics and people of alien creeds, that is to say, principally Jews. Under Louis IX of France (St. Louis) their inquisitorial activities were displayed, and extended also to the Jews. They were called the *domini canes laterantes,* the barking dogs of the Lord, and their powers were extended by a bull of Clement IV, *Bulle turbato corde* (1267), which decreed that Christians who had been seduced to Judaism, together with their seducers, were to be brought before the tribunal. The majority of the "Christians seduced to Judaism" were Jews who had been forced to be baptized. The tribunal worked in secret and had recourse to torture for eliciting the truth. As the church abhorred bloodshed, *Ecclesia abhorret a sanguine,* the condemned victims were handed over to the secular authorities for their sentences to be carried out. And thus streams of blood began to flow.

In addition to fulfilling these savage judicial functions, the Dominicans, though perhaps with less conspicuous success, also became active in the spiritual field of disputation. These wars of words between Jews and Christians had always existed. But at the end of the twelfth century they increased, not because a larger number of conversions to Christianity were expected to result from them, but because it proved necessary again and again to justify the faith to the faithful. A thousand years of church teaching had not been able to prevent people from repeatedly feeling a spontaneous attraction to Judaism for religious reasons. Gregory IX severely condemned the fact that in

Germany Christian "slaves" inclined to Judaism, and that freemen also did so of their own accord. In order to diminish the danger, he forbade all religious discussions (1223), and in France, it became necessary to limit the Jews' rights of residence to the larger towns, to prevent them proving a menace to the faith of the simple country folk (1283).

In their zeal to spread the true faith, the Dominicans now went rather too far in their disputations, which always turned on two main themes—Christian dogma and Jesus as the Messiah. Nothing in the world is more absurd than these attempts at instruction and conversion. A dogma comes into being when a religious idea becomes petrified. This always takes place when creative religious experience is seized upon by an institution or church, and has the life strangled out of it. For a man to accept a dogma, therefore, he must not only live in accordance with the idea it conveys, he must also believe in the institution in which the idea has become petrified. But the Jews did not require the unremitting hostility of the Christian church to make it impossible to acquiesce in these two prerequisites. Quite apart from the church's attitude, Judaism had never known dogmas in the ecclesiastical sense. And in setting out to prove the Messiahship of Jesus, the church was undertaking an even more hopeless task. Messianism as an idea of salvation was probably to be found in every religiously minded community. As a form of religious thought and experience it was a Jewish product, the creation of a national religious development. When and how this development would be completed, what salvation did and did not mean, was exclusively a matter for the Jews, and could never become a subject of dispute. In affairs of the heart, every theological subtlety always becomes a blunt-edged weapon.

It was due to no merit on the part of the Jews, but was merely a natural consequence of their spiritual traditions, that they always gained the upper hand in such disputations, for which, as purely intellectual pastimes, they were more than adequately equipped. Whoever wished to defeat them, therefore, had first to deprive them of their equipment. On searching for it their adversaries discovered it in the Talmud. And a futile tragicomedy was enacted—the Talmud was brought to trial.

The Dominican, Nicholas Donin, a baptized Jew, denounced the Talmud before Gregory IX for slandering Jesus and the Christians and for its immoral doctrines, and the pope ordered the bishops of France, England, and Spain to confiscate all the copies of the Talmud they could find in the possession of the Jews and to convene a tribunal. This tribunal sat on June 12, 1240, in Paris, and was attended by the Dominicans and many dignitaries of the church. The charge consisted of thirty-five points, all drawn from the Haggadic section of the Talmud, that is to say, from that section which dealt with hundreds of years in the life of a people, with all they had to show of good and evil. The Jewish scholars who were called upon to refute the charges found themselves in an extremely difficult position, for to them everything in the Talmud was sacred, even its legends and anecdotes. This made victory for the monks easy. They deposed that the rabbis themselves admitted that certain passages were objectionable (the rabbis, of course, never admitted anything of the kind) and condemned the book to be burnt at the stake. The sentence was carried out in 1242, when twenty-four wagons piled up with copies of the Talmud were publicly burned in Paris. Two years later a similar trial was held in the provinces. In 1248 and 1250 the comedy was repeated. Moreover, it was discovered to be profitable, for the sentence of burning in the marketplace was often averted by means of bribes. Nevertheless, owing to lack of material, it resulted in the study of the Talmud being interrupted for a long while, which was the real object the monks had in view.

But in spite of this, the disputations were not abandoned. The Dominicans revived them and again sent out a baptized Jew, Paulus Christiani, surnamed Fra Pablo. He pursued his activities in Aragon, the Eldorado of the Dominican inquisition. In July 1263, in Barcelona, in the presence of the king, a debate was held which lasted four days. Fra Pablo had selected as his opponent a man whose name carried considerable weight in the Jewish world, Rabbi Moses ben Nachman (abbreviated into Ramban) of Gerona. Pablo advanced four arguments in proof of the Messiahship of Jesus, his object being once more to show that the Jewish Messiah had long since appeared. Ramban very rightly disputed this contention, and pointed out that there was nothing in the attitude of the world or of the people in it to show that the Messiah had really appeared. But he went further. He disclosed the deeper reason for the Jews' remaining hostile to any such idea; it lay in the fact that they had a different conception of the divine nature. If, argued Ramban, God and Jesus were of the same substance, Jesus must be divine; but, according to the Jewish point of view, it would be contrary both to reason and to nature to imagine that such a divine being could be born of the body of a Jewish mother, that after living an earthly existence he should be put to death, that he should rise again and once more become his divine self. Such arguments revealed the futility of the debate. The official disputation was then abandoned, but was continued in the synagogue. Pablo then declared that the doctrine of the Trinity was such a profound mystery that it was beyond the comprehension even of the angels. Whereupon Ramban retorted that in that case mere men could not be blamed for failing to understand it.

It must be admitted that this method of fighting Judaism on the part of the church showed at least a theoretical desire to reach an understanding. But this did not mean that cruder methods were neglected; among the latter there were two which were very popular—the charge of ritual murder, and the charge of desecrating the Host. The people believed that both of these crimes were being committed. The responsible clergy did not believe the charges, but they brought them forward and used them again and again in various places, *in majorem Dei gloriam*. Nothing can absolve the Christian clergy from blood guilt in this connexion.

In the thirteenth century Germany took the lead in advancing such charges, and a case of ritual murder was tried in Erfurt in 1221. In 1235 numbers of such charges were brought, among which, in view of the importance of the principles involved, the case which occurred in Fulda deserves to be described. On Christmas Eve, 1235, the house of a certain miller was burned down in Fulda. The owner and his wife were away; only the children were at home, and they were burned to death. Instead of trying to find out the cause of the disaster, the people immediately accused the Jews of having drained the children's blood and then set the house on fire. Whereupon thirty-two Jews were arrested, and tortured until the expected confession was extorted from them, after which they were killed by the irregular crusaders who happened to be on the spot. The children who had been burned to death were declared to be holy martyrs. On seeing the bodies of the Jews after execution, Frederick II, who was staying in the vicinity, said: "Bury them, they are no good for anything else." But as he was well aware of the reasons for such charges being made, he resolved to have the matter thoroughly investigated. He therefore appointed a learned commission to examine into the question of ritual murders. In the end the commission failed to reach an agreement. Whereupon Frederick took further measures. "As the commission have failed to reach a unanimous decision concerning the case, and have showed themselves incapable of coming to a satisfactory conclusion about it, as they should have done, our profound wisdom has suggested to us that the simplest way of proceeding against the Jews accused of the said crime would be through the instrumentality of persons who have themselves been Jews, but have been converted to Christianity, and who, as opponents, would not conceal anything that might be said in this connexion against the Jews or against any of the Mosaic books or the rest of the Old Testament. Although the knowledge we have ourselves obtained from these books leads us on rational grounds to regard the innocence of the said Jews as proved, nevertheless, in justice not only to the uneducated masses but also to the law, we have in our foresight and careful solicitude decided in agreement with the princes, dignitaries, nobles, abbots, and clergy connected with this case, to send special emissaries to all the kings of western Europe, asking them to send from their realms as many newly baptized Jews as possible, learned in Jewish law, to appear before us."

After a prolonged conference, the foregone conclusion was reached that nothing was to be found in the Jewish Scriptures except a severe prohibition of anything in the nature of a blood sacrifice. Whereupon Frederick II drew up an edict forbidding any such charges to be brought against the Jews in future throughout his whole empire.

But this edict was useless in the face of popular credulity, and the underhand machinations of the clergy. Even before the death of Frederick II, Innocent IV (1247) found it necessary to address to the bishops of France and Germany a bull, which incidentally sheds a good deal of light on the reasons for these charges being made. "It has come to our ears that urgent complaints have been addressed by the Jews to the effect that many ecclesiastical and secular dignitaries, as also many noblemen and official persons in your cities and dioceses, have invented malicious charges against the Jews, in order to have a pretext for despoiling them and taking possession of their property. Such persons seem to have forgotten that it is precisely the Old Testament of the Jews that bears witness to the Christian religion. Whereas the Holy Scriptures contain the law 'Thou shalt do no murder' and forbid the Jews to touch the dead during the Feast of Passover, the Jews have been falsely charged with having at this feast eaten the heart of a murdered child. If the body is found of a person who has been murdered by an unknown hand, the murder is maliciously ascribed to the Jews. All this is merely a pretext for persecuting them in the cruellest manner. Without any judicial inquiry, without any convincing proof being brought against the accused, or any admissions on his part, and in defiance of the privileges granted to the Jews by the Apostolic Chair, they are despoiled of their possessions in the most wicked and unjust manner, and are made to suffer the pangs of hunger, imprisonment in dungeons, and other tortures, and condemned to die an ignominious death. . . . As the result of such persecution, these unhappy people find themselves compelled to leave those places where from time immemorial their ancestors have resided. Fearing they may be wholly exterminated, they have now appealed to the Apostolic Chair for protection."

Such a statement, emanating from the pope as it does, spares the historian the necessity of entering into the question of the motive for these persecutions.

But even this bull, which ended with calling upon the Christians "to treat the Jews kindly and benevolently," proved ineffective in the face of the general disintegration of order into chaos, which characterized the period of the Great Interregnum. Between 1264 and 1267 massacres of Jews were frequent. After the establishment of Habsburg rule, trials for ritual murder increased (Mayence, 1283; Munich, 1286; Oberwesel, 1288). The myth about the miracle of the Host now also made its appearance, the *hostia mirifica*. Jews were accused of buying or stealing holy wafers and piercing them, thus symbolically piercing the body of Christ, whose holy healing blood was supposed to flow from the wafers. This happened in 1287 in Pritzwalk in Brandenburg. On the spot where these miracle-working wafers were found, a convent was built, to which crowds of sick folk flocked and many rich gifts were sent. After this the miracle of the holy wafer was frequently represented on the stage, and healing blood was manufactured, until even Rome was obliged to protest.

In 1298 the Jews of the little town of Röttingen in Bavaria were accused of having found a holy wafer, and of having pounded it in a mortar. A nobleman with the significant name of Rindfleisch * declared that he had received a call from heaven to avenge the dead. He gathered together a band of men and set to work to kill all the Jews in the town, after which he marched through the country, murdering and plundering; he almost wiped out the Jewish community of Würzburg, thrice raided the community of Rothenburg, and before the autumn destroyed nearly a hundred and forty Jewish settlements and communities. It was due to his influence that the tale of the miracle-working holy wafer began to be circulated in Austria also.

Such, in rough outline, was the world in which the Jew of the thirteenth century was compelled to live. It was impossible for the world in which he lived of his own free will, the religious world, to remain unaffected by such an overwhelming flood of misfortune and brutality. His religious life had at last reached a stage at which it was so deeply undermined and weakened by the adversities of his material existence that the breaking-point was visible; the living tradition which was the creative force in his life had ceased to exist, or rather had revealed itself in its true light as a make-believe and a sham. It was a great sham, the like of which has never been even remotely achieved by any other people or made the actual basis of their existence. But as the Jews were forced with their own spiritual laws and conditions to live in a constant atmosphere of strangeness and hostility, as the material conditions of their lives were entirely dependent on alien and fundamentally unfriendly powers, they lived and were able to live only in a state of temporary adaptation or defence, in which the foundation of religious life, an organized community, was more a compulsory condition of segregation than the natural product of banding themselves together. The attempt to lead the lives of Jews on this abnormal basis,

* Which means "Beef."

that is to say, to produce something in the present, to receive the power of tradition from the past, and to work hopefully towards fashioning the future, this attempt so clearly revealed the yawning gulf between faith and intellectual conceptions, between head and heart, that for centuries the problem of bringing it constituted the real problem of their existence as a people.

It was precisely in the spiritual creations which the Jews of Spain hopefully produced as the last bloom of their culture, in the works of a man like Maimonides, that this discrepancy between reality and life as it had been framed by tradition became apparent. Maimonides aimed at producing a synthesis of philosophy and faith, and the spiritual attitude produced by his work, both in his own lifetime and after his death, perceived happiness above all in free intellectual development with a *Weltanschauung* firmly rooted in national and religious feeling in the background. There was no need to repudiate anything of that which former generations had regarded as religious revelations, even if it were contrary to reason and could be substantiated only by faith in miracles. Reason and the philosophical attitude remained unassailed if legends and miracles and the anthropomorphic view of God's actions were regarded as forms of expression, imagery, symbolism. And suddenly, without their knowing it, everything which could not be understood by the light of reason alone had resolved itself into imagery and symbolism and had lost its creative religious power. They had split the unified structure of religious tradition. "In Holy Writ," declared a certain Maimonist, "there is that which is intended for the lips and that which is intended for the heart. The deeper meaning is for the wise man, the superficial meaning for the simple man." And thus Maimonides' idea of a synthesis was twisted into its opposite. If the "wise man" interpreted the meaning of the religious idea through the medium of his own personal philosophical potentialities, and did not grasp it through his emotions as fitting into the frame, as a link in the chain, as part of a single whole, then what his piety enabled him to contribute to life was a private, independent matter, and from the standpoint of a community, disintegrating. This gave rise to the most schismatic of all spiritual attitudes—the liberal attitude. Liberalism in religion is a concept of freedom which arises from the incapacity to say definitely either yea or nay.

The consequence of this liberalism was a growing neglect of the ritual laws, a gradual shaking off of fetters, and the frequent occurrence of mixed marriages. But there was no need of such developments for a steadily increasing opposition to make its appearance. The challenge to solve the problem set by Maimonides was taken up by the Jews everywhere, that is to say, in so far as the age and the place in which they happened to be allowed them to pursue spiritual interests. But the first principle from which Maimonides had set out—the necessity of reconciling religion and philosophy—was not recognized at all by a large number of Jews. It was enough for them that they believed. Nay more, belief *alone* was regarded as important. The Jews who adopted this standpoint were to be found chiefly in France and Germany, and their reason for doing so was twofold—the fate that had overtaken themselves and their anxiety regarding the destiny of their people as a whole.

To the people whose fate has been the subject of this section, of what use was reason, philosophy, and the rationalistic demonstration of their faith? Could all the reason in the world have delivered them from the paralysing feeling of impotence, with which they were left to face the manifold evils of the age and of their environment? Had they ever been allowed, like their co-religionists in Spain, to feel a breath of freedom or *joie de vivre?* Reason could never establish any connexion between their fate and the meaning of their fate. That would have been suicidal. But as their will to live was, by some miracle, still intact, they could only continue living if they surrendered themselves without question, without thought, without doubt, and unsupported by the crutches of reason, to the world of their faith. If their fate was to have any meaning at all, it must perforce lie enclosed wholly in their past, wholly in God and His laws. To make the smallest breach in this structure, to allow of the slightest relaxation even in the most insignificant of their religious laws, was to throw the world in which they lived entirely out of gear.

It was for this reason that the orthodox, the conservative tendency, necessarily grew steadily stronger among them. But it helped them to perceive the process at work in the world of Maimonides. They saw that in the hands of the rationalist every particle of tradition was transformed into a symbol. But this was anarchy and the break-up of the law. They saw that in the synagogues of Spain and Provence an enthusiastic body of youths were proclaiming their ideas of intellectual freedom. They saw that in these districts the Talmud was no more important than Plato and Aristotle. And they regarded all this as extremely dangerous, as the beginning of the disintegration of the Jewish people; and they consequently declared war on the intellectual tendency which they thought was responsible for it, that is to say, philosophy.

The Jewish world became divided into rationalists and anti-rationalists. Nevertheless, there was room for a curious intermediate party, for an attitude of mind which professed both unconditional faith and unconditional rationality; and as those adopting this attitude could not attain to a synthesis, they took refuge in dualism. This was the doctrine of "twofold truth," which was formulated by a man like Isaac Albalag as follows: "For by reason of my scientific insight I am often enough convinced that something must, in view of the requirements of nature, have been thus and thus; and yet on the authority of the prophets I believe that it must, contrary to nature, have been something quite different." The extraordinary feature of this conflict between two extremes, together with the half-way house of the "twofold truth," was that it also occurred in Christianity at the same time. Scholasticism made the same attempt that Maimonides had undertaken some time previously, that is to say, it endeavoured to reconcile the teaching of religion with the teaching of men like Aristotle. Whereas Thomas Aquinas, following this trend, came to the conclusion that philosophy was destined to be the "handmaiden of theology," others decided in favour of the dualism of the twofold truth, an attitude which was anathematized. Such coincidences, which, as we shall see when we come to consider the Kabbalah, also occurred later on, prove that, despite the difference of plane, there was, after all, a spiritual current common to both Judaism and Christianity. And herein, regardless of the countless forces arrayed against it, lies our main hope for the future of humanity.

Orthodoxy now embarked upon a struggle for which it had at its disposal various forces not only in Germany, but also in France, Spain, and Provence. But in any case the greatest enthusiasm for philosophy had not been able to prevent the influence of the Talmud, and the long established methods of studying it, from spreading even in Spain. The instinct of the Jews apparently mistrusted this first outburst of intellectual freedom, and refused to give up the help of the traditional and oft-tested methods of security. In Ramban, whom we have already mentioned, Spain possessed an authority on rabbinical lore, in Rabbi Solomon ben Adret (Rashba) of Barcelona, she had a great Tosaphist dialectician, and towards the end of the thirteenth century, Rabbi Asher ben Yehiel (Rosh), who came from Germany, represented the most bigoted German rabbinism.

The conflict was opened by the ban placed by Rabbi Solomon ben Abraham vom Berge of Montpellier in Provence and Jonah Gerondi, rabbi of Gerona, on all who occupied themselves with profane sciences and philosophy, and above all with the works of Maimonides. Other communities in Provence retaliated by placing Solomon under a ban. Saragossa and one or two other communities placed Montpellier under a ban. In the struggle the opposition became so violent that Solomon denounced the works of Maimonides before the tribunal of the Inquisition. The tribunal, needless to say, condemned both the *Book of Knowledge* and *The Guide to the Perplexed* to the stake (1232).

The wild indignation this provoked in Spain and Provence certainly made the denouncer deeply regret his action, but the position of the two camps had now been defined for the time being, and some arrangement had to be reached. At the beginning of the fourteenth century (1303) Montpellier reopened the campaign under the leadership of Don Astruc de Lunel. He was supported by Rashba of Barcelona, where in 1305, as the result of acrimonious discussions, the following edict was issued: "We hereby ordain and make it our own and our successors' duty, on pain of the ban, to insist that no member of the community under twenty-five years of age shall from now onwards and for fifty years to come engage in the study of any Greek books on natural science or theology. . . . Medicine alone is excepted from this regulation . . . for the Torah explicitly allows the practice of the medical art."

The philosopher and astronomer, Jacob ben Mahir, dean of philosophy at Montpellier, known to medieval science as Profiat or Profatius, was leader of the opposition. He placed under a ban all who dared to charge Maimonides with heresy or prevent the study of philosophy, and a host of scholars sprang up eager to defend science and the right to knowledge. But the fight could not be fought to a finish. When the struggle was at its height, the Jews were expelled from France, and once again the intervention of outside forces interrupted the organic development of Judaism, and forced the Jews to continue living with the burden of unsolved problems on their shoulders.

Nevertheless, in another quarter in which controversy did not exist, but in which secret constructive forces were constantly at work, the problem, philosophy or religion, reason or faith, once more presented itself for solution. And in this case the solution arose, not out of light or out of darkness, but out of twilight, out of that mysterious luminosity known as mysticism. Here reason played but a small part, and faith in its traditional form was inadequate. For there was something which was not accessible to reason, and which even simple faith could not grasp, and that was the mystery surrounding the nature of God, and the structure and meaning of heaven and earth. The world in which such things could be known was the world of the Kabbalah.

The Kabbalah shares with the Talmud the fate of being a word found on everybody's lips, divorced from all its technical connotations, and also of being judged in the light, not of second-hand, but of tenth-hand knowledge. The ordinary man usually emphasizes the fact that it is an excrescence, which it is safe to regard as nonsensical and obsolete. Those who take this view forget that in its origin the Kabbalah supplied a need. Regarded from the human standpoint, neither rationalism nor Talmudism could meet the need for constant religious construction and religious experience. For we must not for a moment lose sight of the fact that throughout the centuries there was in Judaism a real and constant need for such religious experience. A Jew without any religious motivation and impulses, whatever their form of expression, whether in loyalty to the Jewish law, or loyalty to the Jewish idea, is a contradiction in terms, or else a product of degeneration. In the Kabbalah, the Judaism which was beginning to develop in the thirteenth century created for itself a sphere in which religious experience could find free play apart from the control of reason and from the purely binding inexorability of the Talmudic world.

Kabbalah means: tradition for the initiated, occult doctrine for the man who perceives the hidden background behind every word and expression in the Bible. Even in the time of the patriarchs and of Moses, profound knowledge of this description was conveyed in secret ways. The Kabbalah reveals that in the beginning was God, *En Soph,* the Endless, the Limitless, the Infinite One. He had no qualities or attributes. He was the original force which sent forth emanations from Himself, creative streams of energy which in the language of the Kabbalah are called *Sephiroth. Sephirah* really means number; but both in sound and concept the word is meant to approach the Aristotelean idea of "sphere." The first sephirah, which issued from God Himself, issued the second sephirah from itself, which, in turn, issued the third and so on to the tenth. These sephiroth created the world, and keep it in order. Each of them has a different function: one controls the highest spiritual world, another the moral world, and yet another the world of the senses. These sephiroth are theosophical worlds, and mysticism which endeavours to penetrate the mystery of creation regards them as stages in the work of creation, as the categories in which the tangible world is arranged, and also as means of access for man to God; for, by prayer, man can influence the sephiroth, and thus obtain direct communion with God. The sephiroth are related to their original focus of energy, which is God; they are of like nature but not of the same substance.

And here we suddenly find ourselves face to face with the ideas of Christian Gnosticism. The opponents of the Kabbalah were quick to recognize this, and reproached its adherents with having substituted a God who was ten-in-one for the Christian God who was three-in-one, and with having made a Gnostic philosophy of history, which had nothing to do with Judaism, take the place of the clear sequence God, creation, and the existence of the world. This at once raised an extremely important problem for Jewish theology. For although the early Kabbalists quite consistently preserved the concept of God as a unity, their followers could not forestall the fate which overtakes all Gnostic ideas and which consists in those forces which are regarded as being manifestations of the deity gradually becoming more and more independent. The result is that, in the end, the mystic worlds which have developed actually hide their source, which is God, in the luxuriance of their growth. This is a provoking process! Just as the attempt to weld reason and revelation into a synthesis ended in a hopeless antithesis, so the attempt to find God by means of mystical probings ended in the necessity of seeking Him afresh. Thus the religious life of the Jews, thanks to its inner activity, was constantly confronted with a new beginning.

The scope of this survey does not permit of our going into the details of the development of the Kabbalistic world and doctrine. For the time being we must content ourselves with having described how Judaism, crushed down though it was by the difficulties of its material existence, was nevertheless able to save its spiritual existence. The mystical creed of the Kabbalah was given its first outlines and literary form in Provence and in Spain, in districts, that is to say, which were the last that can be credited with having allowed the Jews scope for creative production. We shall presently have to deal with Spain as the country in which the apocalyptic concept of hell was realized for the Jews.

BANISHMENT FROM THE WEST

THE Christian West, with the single exception of Italy, was able to find no solution of the Jewish problem confronting it, except that of banishing the representatives, the victims of the problem. At the end of the thirteenth century England ejected the Jews; at the end of the fourteenth France did likewise; at the end of the fifteenth Spain and Portugal followed suit, and throughout this period Germany was the scene of voluntary and compulsory emigrations.

The reasons for these ejections were never plain and straightforward, but always obscure and complicated. But two factors were always clearly associated—faith and economic considerations—and were indeed inextricably connected. In innumerable cases, religious scruples were overcome by means of money, while economic objections were also just as frequently hidden beneath a cloak of religion. But in every case there was one radical method of solving the problem, which one and all alike endeavoured to employ, and that was the conversion of the Jew to Christianity. From Paul to Martin Luther, this fanatical missionary zeal exploited every conceivable form of persuasion and violence. But it was not only the Jew whom this affected, but everyone, Christian or non-Christian, living under Christian rule, who did not conform to the official faith. Thus, regarded objectively, the fate of the Jews at this time once again constituted a political problem for their Christian environment. The only way of expressing power was by the use of violence. And if the pitiable results obtained by violence were not to be forfeited, a degree of cruelty had to be used which would today be regarded as sadistic, or in any case as acutely psychopathological. This is proved by the Inquisition, which, as an organization, represented the last resource of the church, and, as a system, the last word in inhumanity.

The ejection of the Jews from England has already been described. The misery and distress caused by the order for them to go repaid the proselytizing efforts of the friar preachers by securing a harvest, though a poor one, for the church. In France the results were similar, though here direct instead of indirect compulsion was used. The proposal put forward in England by the great Franciscan, John Duns Scotus, surnamed *doctor subtilis* on account of his subtle intellect, to the effect that the Jews should have their children taken away from them by force and baptized, found favour in France, where a fresh Jewish problem was looming on the horizon. The order of ejection against the Jews of the year 1306 had been allowed to lapse, for the collection of the money owing to them had proved such a difficult matter that Philip the Fair had been obliged to send for them to help him. His method of collecting these sums had been so rigorous that the people wished for the return of their Jewish creditors, particularly as they lacked the necessary funds to carry on their farms. The royal exchequer was also depleted. Consequently, at the beginning of 1315, Louis X opened negotiations with the banished Jews. They insisted upon guarantees, and a curious agreement was concluded, covering a period of twelve years subject to twelve months' notice of dismissal. The Jews obtained the free right of settlement and of engaging in trade and industry; they were to have one-ninth of the outstanding debts not yet collected by the king, and the books taken from them, with the exception of the Talmud, were to be returned. They were also to be allowed to buy back such synagogues and cemeteries as were still in existence, but were to refrain from entering into any controversies with laymen. The agreement laid it down that the Jews were being recalled owing to the *commune clameur du peuple,* the general demand of the people.

It is at once ludicrous and shocking that this could possibly have been the case and that this *clameur du peuple,* if appealed to in a certain way, could raise the call to murder. But there was nobody, not a single soul, to explain to the people the proper relations between man and man. All that existed were forces, which indicated an object upon which they could vent their ignorant feelings of unrest.

Thus once again the Jews, who laboriously set to work to build up their wretched existence afresh, were made the butt of all the savage, superstitious, and religious fanaticism of the people, and were blamed for all the latter's economic distress and exaggerated fear of material disaster. Needless to say that trials for ritual murder and for the desecration of the Host still took place, and ended in death at the stake. During this period, however, they led to a number of disasters which might have been averted, and the Christian church is severely to blame for not having prevented them.

In 1320, a rumour was spread that Philip V was preparing for another Crusade, and in a trice all the popular disturbances and upheavals connected with such an undertaking broke out. A certain young herdsman declared that the Virgin had appeared to him in a vision and called upon him to raise an army. He accordingly proceeded to muster an army consisting of herdsmen, peasants, tramps, and beggars. Two unfrocked priests placed themselves at the head of this army of "Shepherd Crusaders," and a "home" Crusade was inaugurated in the south of France and directed against the Jews. They were massacred by the hundred (unless they preferred, as had been the case in the German "home" Crusades, to immolate themselves); their children were taken from them and baptized, and a hundred and twenty communities were wiped out. Pope John XII was the first to interfere. As their career of murder and rapine was beginning to prove dangerous to the clergy and the nobles, he ordered the Crusaders to be disbanded.

Just at this time the country was suffering from certain epidemics, possibly the precursors of the Black Death. In the south of France people fell ill and died after drinking water from wells and rivers. The people could think of only one explanation—the water must have been poisoned. Who could have done it? It was suggested that it might have been the lepers, who led a wretched existence far removed from the towns. A few of them were seized and tortured until they admitted having poisoned the wells and rivers. Whereupon they were subjected to further torture until they confirmed the popular suspicion that it was the Jews who had incited them to do so. The chain of evidence was then completed by the production of forged letters purporting to prove that certain Moorish princes of Granada and Tunis had sent the Jews money and poison for the purpose of exterminating the Christian population. Jews under torture also confessed to the crime and were subjected to condign punishment. In Chinon alone 160 alleged well poisoners were burned to death. Five thousand Jews in all met their death in this way. As the fortunes of the victims fell to the state, the king ordered a searching inquiry to be held in Tours. The conclusion reached was that the charges were utterly unfounded. Whereupon a fine of 150,000 livres was imposed on the Jews. They even had to be punished for being innocent! The demand for this vast sum drove the majority of them out of the country (1322).

This was unfortunate for the government, as the exchequer had been exhausted by the war with England over the English possessions in France, and the people who had been oppressed beyond all bearing rose in insurrection (*la Jacquerie*). The Dauphin, afterwards Charles V, saw his only hope of salvation in readmitting the Jews. The agreement concluded with them reveals what their position and their conditions of life were. They were to be allowed to return for twenty years to help to restore the ruined finances of the country. In return they were given the right to trade and set up money-lending businesses, and were promised protection against injustice on the part of royal or judicial officials, for which purpose a *gardien général des juifs* was appointed. On the other hand they were to be so heavily taxed that only extremely wealthy Jews could afford the luxury of returning to France, and the crushing demands of the state made it impossible for them to live except by means of undisguised usury. Meanwhile the government was bleeding the people so unscrupulously that in Paris they ultimately rebelled, and robbed the state treasury. In connexion with these disturbances the Jewish quarter was raided. Many Jews were murdered, and numbers of Jewish children were forcibly baptized. Crowds of Jews fled from Paris. The rest were left to fall victims to an ever-increasing load of taxation and the baiting of the clergy. But as, in these circumstances, they could not produce enough to satisfy the state, they were banished from the royal provinces of France in September 1394, owing to "crimes against the Holy Faith, and abuse of their privileges." The only districts that were spared were Dauphiné, part of Provence, and papal Avignon, where some of the emigrants sought refuge; the rest went to Savoy, Italy, Germany, and Spain. But these districts served only as temporary resting-places. When Dauphiné was joined to France in 1456, the Jews voluntarily took their departure. In Provence, where Jews had been settled even under the ancient Gauls, the fresh influx led to an intensification of the economic struggle for existence, particularly in Marseilles. The clergy put the finishing touch by carrying on active missionary work among the immigrants, and stealing and forcibly baptizing their children. The handing over of the country to Louis XI and its consequent subjection to the spirit and outlook prevailing in the French crown lands immediately led to outrages on a grand scale, to which many individuals and even whole communities fell victims. The Jews then began to leave the country of their own accord and Charles VIII banished the remainder in 1496, after he had completely ruined them by repudiating all debts owing to them by Christians. And thus France was cleared of Jews for the time being.

And during this same period what happened in Germany was full of such brutality, stupidity, and barbarity in relation with both the outside world and the Jews that the student of history is almost blinded to the real cause of the trouble—the febrile condition of the man of the Middle Ages, who felt that one epoch was drawing to a close without his being prepared for the next. But no understanding of this unconscious struggle and of the morbid symptoms attending the disintegration of the ideology and social order of the Middle Ages could save the Jew from falling a victim to these birth-throes, which, although they did not concern him, were vented on him, determined his fate, and filled his life with horror. They branded his soul, and it was left to him to remove the mark as best he could. The fact that he was not altogether successful has been brought up against him by the heirs of these same medieval people.

The Jews in Germany during the fourteenth and fifteenth centuries were between the devil and the deep sea. The acquisitive instincts of those about them victimized them ever more and more, and they were constantly obliged to appeal to their "guardians," the kings, for protection against their environment. Meanwhile the rulers who had inherited this *nobile officium* from Rome made the Jews pay an ever heavier price for it. Excluded from every class of the community and from all the guilds, and yet regarded as necessary for the supply of credit in a primitive society, their calling, which was to deal in money, necessarily assumed usurious forms. And as usurers they were naturally exposed to the hatred of those who, owing to the inefficiency of their economic system, were obliged to turn to them for credit. The constant venting of this unreasoned hatred drove the Jews ever further into seclusion and isolation, which in its turn caused the superstitious fear and narrow orthodoxy of the surrounding masses to break out in displays of savage Jew baiting. It was a vicious circle from which there was no escape. The Jews had to bow their heads before everything that happened, and were quite defenceless. They could find no refuge except in their faith, and, as they wallowed and sank ever more and more deeply into it, they converted it from its original clarity into a mist, a Talmudic fog. The Talmud now performed one of its most important functions, and the fact that it did so justifies over and over again everything it contains, despite all that may be said against it. The Talmud became the spiritual refuge of the Jews against the slanderous onslaughts of the Christian church, and the brutal excesses of an environment in a continual state of ferment. If those about them repudiated them, they found their existence confirmed and affirmed afresh in the Talmud. Prevented from enjoying a free life in the open, they confined their world within four walls. And thus they hugged to their hearts a doctrine which, though it weighed down, narrowed, and restricted life, yet, with all its narrowness, was full of tragically unshakable hope and self-confidence, and with its expectation of a Messiah had about it the breath of eternity. While the life of the Christian was a gateway to the kingdom of heaven, the life of the Jew was a gateway to the kingdom of God. While both derived their origin from the same idea, what a world of difference separated them in practice!

And in the practical world about them the Jews could find nothing that was not hostile to them. In France the "Jew-Killers" were rampant; they were the crusaders of a home crusade (1336). In Alsace the innkeeper, Zimberlin, gathered round him the people of the *"Armleder,"* * to avenge the Crucified One, and in the same province whole communities were wiped out, and immolations and compulsory baptisms took place from 1337 to 1338, until at last the feudal lords themselves felt menaced by the movement, and put a stop to it. At the same time a fresh epidemic of trials for desecration of the Host broke out in Bavaria, Austria, and Bohemia, and the business side of these proceedings was no longer even disguised. An attempt made by Benedict XII to open a fresh investigation into the basis of these absurd accusations proved abortive owing to the opposition of the clergy and the civic authorities. The civic authorities derived a twofold profit from them; on the one hand they extended temporary protection to the Jews in return for heavy payments, while, on the other, they also at a price granted an amnesty to their murderers. There is an interesting document of the times consisting of the treaty made by Ludwig of Bavaria with the towns of Alsace on the subject of the murder of Jews: "In consideration of our waiving the claims which we might make against you for murdering the Jews of Mülhausen, and for the loss and damage you have brought upon them, we call upon you to place at our disposal one thousand pounds of old Basel money. And in order to enable the citizens in question to meet their respective shares of this sum, we hand over to you the whole of the goods and chattels of the Jews murdered in the city, their houses, farms, securities, and other property." Other cities also obtained absolution in this way.

In these circumstances the martyrdom of the Jews gradually reached its zenith when, in addition to the epidemic of human brutality to which they were constantly exposed, another epidemic, born of nature, suddenly swooped down upon them. The "Black Death" began to ravage Europe, the "Great Death" from plague, the pestilence which filled those living at the time with terror, crushing their spirits, making havoc of their lives, exposing their religious bankruptcy, their be-

---

* The *Armleder* consisted of a sort of badge of leather, worn on the arm. Every member of the band collected by Zimberlin wore such a badge.—*Translator.*

sottedness, and their nervous panic. It may have been bubonic plague brought in from the East. It pursued no definite course, but made its appearance sporadically, now here, now there; it died down and then broke out again; after a long period of immunity, it would burst forth afresh; individuals and even whole cities might be spared, but the uncertainty as to where it would next make its appearance was as terrifying and horrifying as the havoc it actually wrought. The deaths from it amounted to about 25,000,000. The world was seized with panic. Whence came this scourge? Guided by a sure instinct, the people suspected that a cosmic catastrophe such as this could not be the result of accident, but must form part of the rhythm of some life-force. But, in order to be able to grasp the meaning of the calamity at all, they looked for some cause, some origin in guilt. And they discovered many causes—the sinfulness of the world, the conformation of the stars, the depravity of the clergy, and the Jews. It was, however, impossible to call the stars to account, while the individual priest was protected by the claim established by Innocent III to the effect that he himself and all the clergy were by virtue of their holy office sacrosanct, even though as men they might be guilty of the worst crimes. Nevertheless, it was open to every individual to feel a consciousness of sin for which he felt he must do penance and punish himself. And thus bands of flagellants roamed the country, ravaged by religious fervour, eccentrics of faith, hysterics, beggars, criminals, and lunatics, who lashed themselves till the blood flowed, and called on all and sundry to repent. But they also clamoured for the punishment of those other sinners, who could be seized with ease and impunity—the Jews. And once more, as so often happens in the history of religion, the religious factor became associated with the erotic. The violence of these people towards themselves was self-torture; but the violence they did to the Jews now turned to bestiality.

The reason for persecuting the Jews was soon found and even more quickly proved. The Jews had poisoned all the wells, springs, and rivers in order to exterminate the Christians! (From the "Black Death" to the "wise men of Zion" is a long way.) Nobody gave a thought to the fact that the plague also raged where there were no Jews, and that, where there were Jews, they too died from it. This was understood only in the non-Christian countries which were visited by the epidemic. The first man in Christendom to furnish the proof of the Jews' guilt was Duke Amadeus of Savoy, who had the surgeon Belavigny tortured until he confessed to having poisoned the water, and even gave the ingredients of the poison he had used, which was supposed to consist of a mixture of snakes, frogs, scorpions, holy wafers, and Christians' hearts. After this explanation, thousands of Jews were burned to death. The next country to wreak vengeance on the Jews for their crime was Switzerland. In Zürich, Constance, Schaffhausen, Überlingen, and other towns on the Lake of Constance, Jews were burned to death, broken on the wheel, and hanged. The mania spread to Germany also. Only a few towns offered any resistance to these murders, while in others they actually served the purpose of settling old differences. This was the case in Alsace, where the settlement of debts arising from the murder of Jews had given rise to hot disputes. A conference of magistrates, nobles, and clergy came to the conclusion (January 1349) that the Jews were outlaws, and should be driven out of Alsace and the Rhine provinces. This was done. In Strassburg 2000 Jews were shut up in a wooden shed and burned alive, and all property belonging to Jews was distributed among the Christian citizens. In Colmar, Schlettstadt, Benfeld, Mülhausen, and Oberehnheim, Jews were burned to death, their wealth distributed, and the synagogues declared to be municipal property. The community of Speyer was almost wiped out. In Worms all the Jews were condemned to the stake, but they burned themselves to death in their own houses first. In Mayence the Jews fought to the last gasp, and then burned themselves to death, to the number of about 6000. In Cologne and Erfurt the Jewish quarters were utterly destroyed. In Frankfurt-am-Main, the Jews themselves set their quarters on fire, and flung themselves by the hundreds into the flames. And the epidemic spread through the whole of Bavaria, right into the heart of Germany, and as far as Breslau and Königsberg. By the time the plague had worked itself out, nearly 300 Jewish communities had been entirely destroyed, and their members had been either killed or burned to death. Crowds of Jews fled to Austria, Bohemia, and Poland, the forerunners of the great evacuation of the West. The headlong flight eastward had started.

Most of the fugitives remained in the East, even after the epidemic was over, and many places, which missed the taxes paid by the Jews and the facilities for credit which their wealth afforded, rescinded the decree of banishment against them. Cities, feudal lords, and bishops everywhere tried to secure the right of "possessing Jews," that is to say, serfs who would pay them in money instead of in kind. By the Golden Bull of 1356 the imperial electors were granted the right of exploiting Jews as well as of exploiting mineral mines and salt-pits. The inducements offered to the Jews to return were not particularly attractive. They were not to be allowed to acquire landed property, they were to be restricted as to occupation and place of residence, they were to pay heavy taxes, and to renounce all claim to compensation for the damage they had suffered. The reason for allowing them to return is revealed in the statute of 1400 of the magistrate of Munich. "The Jews," it reads, "must not engage in any occupation other than that of lending out money at interest." The need of possessing Jewish serfs reached such lengths that Emperor Wenceslaus, for instance, concluded an agreement with the representatives of thirty-eight Rhineland and Swabian towns, by which they were given the right to force Jews to remain where they were, and the parties to the agreement undertook to restore to each other any Jews who had managed to escape. This privilege was worth 40,000 guldens to the towns concerned, and they paid this sum to Wenceslaus in Ulm in 1385.

The fact that the Jews continued to stay in Germany in such circumstances was merely the result of accident, and at the same time a piece of blind heroism, which was really nothing but the stupor of despair. The element of accident lay in the fact that any concatenation of circumstances in their environment might affect them in a hundred different ways. The spiritual creations which marked the close of the fifteenth century in Germany, the poems and writings of men like Reuchlin, Sebastian Brant, Thomas Murner, Hans Sachs; the statues and pictures produced by Adam Krafft, Martin Schongauer, Matthias Grünewald, and Dürer, and the ideas that emanated from Thomas à Kempis and Nicolaus Cusanus, certainly pointed to the existence of a creative movement; but even those elements in the movement which were not reactionary, but progressive and prophetic, had no effect, whether formative or palliative, on the reality which was accessible to the Jews. Caught up in the everyday life of their environment, they lived in middle-class surroundings which were hostile to progress, bigoted and intolerant, and dependent upon a hopelessly corrupt priesthood. This middle-class population and their clergy were capable of any act of hostility, and indeed trials for desecration of the Host and ritual murder, as well as acts of extortion and sentences of banishment, were terribly frequent, and were carried out with such determination and passion that at the dawn of the so-called "New Era," there was only a small and sparse Jewish population in Germany.

For two hundred years this war of extermination had raged over their heads, and had forced all their activities back into the sphere of self-preservation. Not a trace of creative thought is to be found among them. They had enough to do trying to bear in mind that, in spite of everything, it was their duty to lead a national life founded on religion. They survived this period richer in one respect only—it had given them a deeper and stronger sense of their relationship to each other. There was no one in the whole world on whom they could rely as they could on members of their own race. Never in all history had a people been so forsaken and downtrodden. Even the pariah had a patch of ground on which to build his hut. But the Jew was never secure in the possession of anything even when he had it. His homeless condition was more terrible than any that had ever been created either by force of circumstances or by the attitude of human beings.

In Spain both Jewish and non-Jewish problems became clearly and definitely defined during these two hundred years. As soon as the Christian states (Aragon, Castile, Portugal, and Novarra) began to develop independent political and economic power, the measure of independence which the Jews in Spain had been able to secure under the favourable conditions of Mohammedan and early Christian rule was curtailed by the disadvantages under which they had always laboured—they were homeless foreigners with no state structure behind them to fall back on. This was plainly proved when the Spanish nobility, in conjunction with the Spanish clergy and under their leadership, began to proclaim a "Holy War" against all unbelievers in the country, meaning, of course, the Jews and the Moors. But the more cautious among the Christians recognized that, in Granada and North Africa, the Moors were still powerful, and if their fellow-countrymen in Spain were attacked, they would come over and defend them. The Moors were therefore left in peace. But the Jews could be molested with impunity. In their case, there was no fear of reprisals or even of remonstrance from any quarter. Hence the heroic courage of this holy war!

True, the Jews were intricately bound up with the economic life of Spain. Nevertheless, their economic strength was stigmatized as foreign, and depended less on economic conditions as such than on the relation of the people to these conditions. What did the Spaniards of the fourteenth and fifteenth centuries know about what was economically good or bad for their country? Nothing! All they understood was how, with the view of safeguarding their own interests, they could form themselves into classes, and that confronted by such class interests, the foreigner had to make way. The towns joined together and formed leagues, *hermandades*. In the Cortes, the nobility had both its material and social interests represented. The former were opposed to the influence of the Jews in the general economic life of the country, the latter were opposed to Jews taking any part in state administration, finance, and politics. And yet the fact that Jews were ministers of finance would have seemed to indicate that a general Jewish problem had ceased to exist in Spain. True, the Spanish kings found it necessary to have Jewish finance ministers. Even a Jew-murderer, like Henry II, was obliged to entrust the administration of his taxes to a Jew. (This did not prevent him from selling Jews as slaves in order to procure ready money!) Even Aragon, which to a man loyally obeyed all the anti-Jewish enactments of the church, depended on the Jews for keeping its domestic affairs in order. But although the position of power enjoyed by these Jewish state officials cannot be denied, they were only isolated individuals. They did not represent the leading men of a sociological community, but merely the more rapid, more successful, more powerful, and more prominent achievement of a few in the struggle for existence of a minority within a far larger group. Their position did not, therefore, constitute the pinnacle of a social hierarchy, but merely the success of isolated outsiders. The Jews, as a whole, derived no advantage from the existence of these fortune-hunters; all they gained was to be blamed for their failures, as they are even in the present day.

Thus the condition of the Spanish Jews grew more and more to resemble that of their brethren in Germany. They became the victims of an economic struggle. Their spiritual problems, and their disputes over the movement initiated by Maimonides, had long ago been settled along reactionary lines. As if in anticipation of coming events, and under the influence of the rabbis, who had come over from Germany, all speculative theology and thought withdrew into the sphere of strict law, into the Talmud, which had already ceased to be a Talmudic edifice of doctrine and had become rabbinism. All free thought was forbidden. A man like Hasdai Crescas pointed out to them the support to which even a man in the direst distress could cling, and to which thousands must cling; there could be no reconciliation and no compromise between the reasoning faculty which was a product of the human brain, and revelation which was given from above. Man's reason must accommodate itself to the rational will of God. Man's relationship to God did not consist in his intellectual knowledge of Him, but in active love. It was the morally perfect man, not the intellectually perfect man, who was the nearer to God.

Such doctrines not only prepared the people for the tribulation to come, but were the result of the recognition that the increasing economic pressure and the liberalism which emanated from the views of Maimonides led to an assimilative tendency which could be counteracted only by increased spiritual segregation. This spiritual narrowness, which, however, also made spiritual stability possible, was the only means of combating even involuntary assimilation in face of the untiring efforts of the Christian clergy to gain converts from the ranks of the Jews by means of missionary work, propaganda, and disputation. For just as the nobility and the bourgeoisie organized themselves into classes, and prepared for an onslaught on their economic and political competitors, so also did the Spanish clergy, as constituting a class of their own, begin to occupy themselves with political aims. In the kingdoms of Castile and Aragon, the clergy at first met with strong opposition on the part of the kings, who had no intention of sacrificing the prosperity of their dominions for ecclesiastical considerations. But in the fourteenth century the Catholic clergy gradually conquered Castilian society, while their power in Aragon also increased. This was not due to any religious development, but was merely a continuation of the church's policy of acquiring power, which has already been described. In Spain, however, it had been found easier than in the other countries of western Europe, to combine international with national aims, that is to say, to tend towards union with Rome and yet to pursue a national policy. The "Holy Inquisition," which in itself was merely an instrument of power in the hands of the church, became in Spain simply a weapon in the struggle of a national class, which, in so far as its position was concerned, made itself more and more independent of Rome, and even bade Rome defiance.

As the policy of the clergy was made up of a compound of economic, political, ecclesiastical, and religious factors, their activities were naturally not so simple as those of the other classes. They were carried on by the various ranks of the priestly hierarchy, by the councils as legislative authorities, by the priests at court in their capacity of confessors and advisers, by the priests who brought influence to bear on high society whether through intrigue or through the exploitation of family relationships, by the spiritual guides of the people as a whole, who worked both subterraneously and perfectly openly either by stirring up popular passion, or by the persuasive allurements of their missions, and lastly by that element in the church which never grew tired of forcing their opponents to enter into controversy in order to secure a triumph in the field of intellect.

All these various forces were bound together by the slogan of a united Christian Spain, promulgated by the clergy and adopted by the nobility. It was, so to speak, an anticipation of the Monroe Doctrine—Christian Spain for Spanish Christians. The mental attitude of Visigoth days was thus revived both as an ideal and the means for its realization. The clergy had learnt nothing from the fertile combination of three races and three religions. Any human understanding which the lapse of time might have brought about between Jews, Christians, and Mohammedans was repeatedly stifled and destroyed by the actively aggressive policy of the clergy who brought all the spiritual and temporal power at their command to bear against their adversaries. They had recourse to every imaginable form of punishment, from excommunication to death at the stake, to chastise any elements of the population which aspired to a merely human relationship with the rest. Is it possible to maintain that there was any other motive for the idea of a unified state except that of being able to exercise dominion, power, violence? Eight hundred years of Mohammedan occupation, and eight hundred years of life shared by the Mohammedans and the Jews must surely have led to certain historical developments. Or had they not? Is the national principle, when subordinated to a religious idea, entirely divorced from reality? As soon as religion denies itself and its real nature, in order to express itself as power instead of as faith, this is apparently the case.

As usual the effort to establish a unified state took the form, not of organically incorporating alien elements, but of annihilating them. Spain proclaimed a "Holy War" against all Moors and Jews within her boundaries. We have already explained why the Moors were left in peace. But against the Jews the campaign was opened with the cry of "Death or Baptism!" Its instigator was Fernando Martínez, Archdeacon of Seville, who preached a reign of terror. Rome forbade him to continue his agitation. But he merely preached on. As a punishment he was deprived of his office. Whereupon by way of consolation and reward, the ecclesiastical authorities in Spain appointed him surrogate Archbishop of Seville. In this capacity he circularized his bishops, urging them to destroy the synagogues and to bring him the sacred vessels as proof of victory. This was actually done in many towns. In Seville he himself conducted the proceedings (March 1391), but failed because the Jews and the municipal authorities resisted him. Three months later the attempt was repeated, this time with complete success. A community of about 30,000 souls was destroyed. Four thousand were killed, numbers were forcibly baptized, and numbers "taken prisoner" and sold into slavery. The small remnant that survived sought safety in flight.

After this exemplary victory, Martínez issued further orders for carrying on the conflict; all Jews who refused to embrace Christianity were to be killed. The order was obeyed, and in the fury of the fray Christianity won many new recruits. Wholesale looting took place, and many Jews committed suicide. Seventy communities in all were destroyed. The agitation spread to Aragon—Valencia, Barcelona, Gerona, Lerida, and as far as Mallorca, and everywhere met with similar results in the shape of wholesale murder, new converts to Christianity, suicide, and plunder. The number of Jews "converted" to Christianity in this holy war amounted to about 10,000.

And this was politics! But it was also religion! The facts relating to a certain age and environment do not always suffice for a historical perspective. One fine day the individual like the community is called upon to account for those failures which are the result of hostile surroundings. For the world does not listen to excuses. The Jew has always been called to account in this way, more particularly by those who refuse to be called to account themselves.

But this partial victory of Spanish policy did not mean that its ultimate aim had been achieved, and the war was therefore continued by means of compulsory baptisms, banishment, and social oppression. The Dominican, Vicente Ferrer, scoured Castile and Aragon with a band of flagellants, preaching "holy hate" against those of other faiths, and in many towns forced the Jews, by means of the most brutal terrorist methods, to embrace Christianity (1412–1413). About 20,000 were baptized. At this time pressure was also brought to bear by depriving the Jews of all civic and economic rights. Rabbi Solomon Halevi, who was baptized in 1391 and quickly promoted to the dignity of bishop and made a member of the regency council appointed to govern the country during the minority of Juan II, was the spiritual instigator of the "edict of Donna Catilina," a regulation which, by segregating the Jews and depriving them of economic liberty, reduced them to poverty and disgrace. The only remedy they had at their disposal, which was emigration, was forbidden in this order.

But neither the holy war nor the holy hate was able to obviate the consequences of this rude destruction of a living organization, which, after all, was the result of a process of evolution and was working satisfactorily. The only people who really derived any advantage from it were the plunderers. But while the impoverishment of the Jews, their emigration in large numbers, and their disappearance from commerce and industry removed their unwelcome competition, there were no substitutes at hand to fill the gap caused by their absence. Many Spanish towns, industries, and branches of commerce were ruined, and, above all, the state exchequer was empty. This made it necessary to put a stop to holy hate for a while, and Maria, viceregent of Aragon, tried by promises and every means at her disposal to keep the Jews in the country; while Castile, under Juan II, restored their ancient rights to them. But this restoration born of despair did no good to the Jews, nor did it prevent both Jews and Christians from finding themselves suddenly confronted by a situation in which the incorruptibility and impartial justice of the world force would be revealed and, in addition, a spiritual phenomenon of tragic power.

This process of political purging had considerably reduced the Jewish population in Spain, though incidentally Spanish society suffered a not inconsiderable degree of inflation by the introduction of converts, *conversos,* or new Christians. At first, both the people and high society regarded these *conversos* as a homogeneous group; the nobility and clergy in particular saw in them the fruit of victory, and in the first outburst of proud satisfaction received them into their midst. Numbers of *conversos* entered the doors held open for them and made their way into Spanish society and the Spanish priesthood; before long there was hardly a noble family which was not saturated with Jewish blood, and in the highest and most exalted positions of the clerical organization *conversos,* or men who had once been Jews, began to make their appearance. They were even to be seen at court and in high political circles. In itself, this was a natural and normal development, a result which was actually contemplated and desired by those who had promoted the holy war and the holy hate. The *conversos* had become members of Spanish society, with equal rights; but this did not mean that they had lost the qualities they had always possessed. Previously they had exercised their peculiar gifts as merchants, industrialists, financiers, and politicians. And they did so again now, but with this difference, that they were inside and not outside Spanish society. They had been forced to enter. The object had been to do away with a dangerous outsider. And he was now established in a new home. The problem had been transferred from outside to inside the social structure. What then had the ceremony of baptism accomplished after all? Was it expected to wash away the intellectual or financial genius of the Jew? Was it hoped that it would make him so excessively anxious to love his neighbour that he would cease to compete with other people? In the days of a man like Vicente Ferrer, Christianity certainly had but little power of attraction from the intellectual point of view, while, as to the value of baptism, it was not to be rated higher than a certain Jewish apologist of the day rates it in the following epigram, "There are three ways of wasting water—by baptizing a Jew, by the running of a river into the sea, and by diluting wine."

But the results were even more serious. The very *conversos* who had accepted the ceremony of baptism as final and conclusive, were most ready—and quite rightly—to turn the new situation to the best possible account for themselves. And they sought their advancement where those who had forced them to be converted also sought it, in high court circles and amongst the nobility and clergy. Their aim was not so much to gain economic power as political and social influence. To see the outlaws of yesterday the influential leaders of today was a phenomenon which filled all classes of the population with secret misgiving. "The spirits I conjured up I can no longer lay!" The simple and logical explanation was not understood, or where it was understood, particularly in the ranks of the clergy, everybody tried to shut his eyes to it; in their cruel disillusionment, they were all anxious to escape from the consequences of their own action, and by every means in their power to absolve themselves of the charge of having brought about precisely this result.

The possibility of once more sounding the alarm arose from the secret tragedy of those compulsory converts who refused to make their peace with the world and with Catholicism, and who, when faced with the ghastly peril of the terror and death, had not had the strength to sacrifice themselves but had sought safety in baptism. The suffering they endured as a result of this official lie was greater and more enduring than the suffering of the moment of suicide would have been. By consenting to be baptized, they imagined they would at least be able to enter into enjoyment of the freedom they saw everywhere about them. But, as a matter of fact, they merely entered a medieval torture chamber, in the literal traditional meaning of the word. They had become members of a church but not members of a faith. The indissoluble bonds of thousands of years of religious development forced them to bear their Judaism secretly in their hearts; still indestructible, they carried it about with them in a much deeper sense. Careful to escape the eyes of the members of their new religion, they observed all the rites and laws, all the festivals and customs of their own faith, in fear and secrecy struggled for the right to do so, and lived a double life, every man bearing a double burden.

The *conversos* who adopted this attitude of heroic suffering constituted the majority, and it was impossible for them to hide their secret indefinitely. But the discovery of it was a shattering blow for the Catholic Church, though it gave the latter something on which to fasten in order to distract attention from the fact that every victory won over a "heretic" was a defeat for the victor. A new battle cry was now raised: "The church is in danger! The Jew has forced his way into the church and into society, in order to undermine them from within!" The inevitable though absurd sequel to this was that war was declared on the "enemy within." In order to carry it on the clergy armed themselves with the machinery of the Inquisition; they appealed to the people, carried on intrigues at court, and brought all their influence to bear on high society. And the *conversos,* who had once constituted the proof of the national religious policy, became Marranos, a vulgar word with the meaning of "damned," "swinish." No distinction was now drawn between genuine and pseudo-Christian converts. They were all Marranos, and the war waged against them, like every other activity of the church in Spain, was prompted not so much by religious as by economic and social considerations, as is clearly proved by such events as those which took place in Toledo in March 1449. The government had ordered the city to make a contribution towards the war against the Moors. The city refused. Whereupon the tax-collectors, the majority of whom were Marranos, were ordered to enforce the payment of taxes. It was a duty they had frequently performed. The people rebelled. This was also only natural. The mob proceeded to storm and plunder the houses of the Marranos, many of whom were killed. At last the object of the whole affair became apparent; the municipal authorities resolved that the Marranos should no longer be allowed to hold public office. Terror and murder as a means of winning the *conversos;* terror and murder as a means of getting rid of them when they had become Marranos!

The attempts to solve the problem of the Marranos were at first quite as unco-ordinated and unsystematic as the reaction against them had been. The people were in a wild state of panic. The reappearance of the competitor of whom they hoped they were rid, the superstitious fear of this vital force that was always springing into existence again, the alarm sounded by the clergy warning them against the enemy who had found his way into society and into the church itself, made them blind and terrified and able to understand only illegal methods of self-defence. Among the nobility opinion was divided. Conservatives and liberals were disagreed, the former being in favour of excluding the Marranos, the latter wishing to absorb these new members of their order. For they found themselves faced by an extremely difficult problem, which mere violence could not solve. The church, however, studiously ignored this social problem. She was forced to do so, because she had hidden her action beneath the cloak of religion, and she could not now drop the disguise. She was mad with fury. She had not anticipated the gravity and extent of the Marrano problem. And she had no means to hand to solve it or do away with it. In her helpless impotence, she was compelled to resort to torture. As she could not conquer the spirit she must kill it. Moreover, she was obliged constantly to commit herself to a deliberate lie; for, in waging war on the Marranos as a whole, she had to pretend she was fighting for a religious principle, when obviously this was not the case, and she was concerned only with economic and social considerations. However, the methods she used in the conflict were in her opinion perfectly "legal."

The Inquisition had long been established in Spain, but for the special purpose the Spanish clergy now had in view, it was inadequate owing to its dependence on Rome. For some time past the Dominicans had been trying to create a "national" inquisition. And a political situation now arose which favoured their object. By the marriage of Ferdinand and Isabella the kingdoms of Castile and Aragon were made one. An absolute ruler of medieval cruelty and a visionary of fanatical piety had succeeded in uniting the country, and now tried to establish unity of faith within it. And, at the price of terrible slaughter and the economic ruin of their realm, they succeeded in doing so.

At the request of the Spanish government, the pope was ready to acquiesce in the creation of a national inquisition, on condition that a papal legate was attached to it. In making this proviso he was prompted not so much by a desire to ensure the strict observance of legal guarantees, as by anxiety regarding the destination of the property that would be confiscated. And Ferdinand, therefore, protested against this menace to his financial interests. Through the influence of Tomâs de Torquemada, the Queen's confessor, however, the pope, in a bull of November 1478, granted Spain the right to a national inquisition. As at first it had to meet with considerable opposition on the part of the Cortes, it came into being only in 1480, and it was legally suppressed 330 years later in 1810. In spirit, however, it was suppressed only in our own time, in 1931, when republican Spain stormed the monasteries.

The first tribunal assembled at Seville. It consisted of two Dominicans, one abbot, one royal officer of the treasury, and two other royal officials, whose business it was to take charge of the spoils consisting of the property of the condemned. No legal guarantees whatever were given for the proceedings. The basis of the charge was almost always denunciation. No examination of the charges ever took place. Accuser and accused were never confronted. Only as much of the accuser's evidence as the court deemed fit was communicated to the accused. Torture of all descriptions supplied the proof. There was no appeal. The punishment varied from imprisonment in a dungeon to burning at the stake. But part or all of the property of the accused was always confiscated; in the case of those punished by imprisonment in a dungeon, at least the greater part of it was forfeited. The accused might be alive, absent, or dead. If absent, he was burnt in effigy, if dead, his body was exhumed and burnt, and his property taken away from his heirs. And this was obviously the object of the whole proceeding, particularly as, be it remembered, by far the greater number of victims were wealthy and in a position to leave considerable property to their heirs.

The substance of the charge was "Judaizing," that is to say, secretly practising Judaism. The meaning of this was to be found in a list which gave thirty-seven distinguishing signs of Judaizing. It was sufficient for a Marrano to put on a better suit of clothes, or a clean shirt, on the Sabbath, to be suspected of Judaizing. And it was the duty of every Christian to report any cases of the kind that came to his notice. His name was kept secret, and he incurred no responsibility. Whether the accused admitted or denied the charge was of no consequence, for either a confession was forced from him by means of torture, or else his denials were interpreted as wicked obduracy.

In such circumstances eavesdropping, denunciation, house-searching, and arrest assumed vast proportions from the very beginning. By way of a start, 15,000 Marranos were arrested, and in the subterranean galleries of the monastic fortress of Seville, the torturing of them began. Even the Christians were horrified, fearing that when all the Marranos had been exterminated this instrument would be turned against themselves. A group of Marranos formed a secret conspiracy to murder the members of the tribunal. The plot was discovered. But the protests of the people and the plot itself were a warning to the tribunal, and it reduced the number of death sentences it passed. Up to November 1481, 300 persons were burnt at the stake in the district of Seville, but in the archbishopric of Cadiz the number amounted to at least 2000, chiefly wealthy people. Moreover, thousands were condemned to imprisonment for life and to other forms of punishment. The yield from confiscated property was enormous.

A special square, the Quemadero, was reserved for carrying out the death sentence. It was decorated with statues of the Jewish prophets. These "acts of faith," *autos-da-fé,* were attended by all classes of the people, from the court, the nobility, and the church, to the masses. The executioner was provided by the state, for the church did not kill. She abhorred bloodshed! The sentences were, therefore, carried out without bloodshed, *sine effusione sanguinis,* by burning the victims alive. Only those who at the last moment confessed their repentance for not having been good Christians were, as a last act of mercy, put to death by strangling, after which their bodies were burnt at the stake.

After this first session of the tribunal, there was a lull. The *sanctum officium* informed all those whom it might concern that if they came and confessed their sin before a certain date they would be granted absolution, on condition, of course, that part of their property was forfeited to the Inquisition and the king. Many presented themselves, if only because they wanted to have their inevitable trial at the hands of the Inquisition behind them. However, they discovered to their cost that the promised absolution was merely a low and brutal trick. For, after they had confessed, the tribunal called upon them to denounce any friends and relatives who secretly professed Judaism, otherwise, since they had confessed that they themselves were guilty, they would be treated as heretics. Those who really had nothing of the kind to confess, were regarded as inveterate liars who were also to be treated as heretics.

So great was the horror aroused by this fraud that even a pope like Sixtus IV, a debauchee and money-grabber, lodged an indignant protest against the methods adopted in Spain. He quite rightly saw that most of the trials "were not prompted by any religious zeal or concern about the salvation of the soul, but by covetousness," and demanded that reliable episcopal representatives should be placed on the tribunal, and that the condemned should be allowed to appeal to Rome. Ferdinand regarded this as a menace to his rich source of income and, as the Inquisition was a "national" institution, an interference with his sovereign rights. He was much more concerned about extending the activities of the Inquisition, which, owing to the opposition of the Cortes, had not yet been able to spread its tentacles over the whole country, more particularly Aragon. And Sixtus IV, in order to obtain money for his needs, granted permission for the establishment of seven new tribunals, and the creation of a "Supreme Council of the Inquisition," which was to be the chief organizing centre and bureaucratic head office of the system. Torquemada became General or Grand Inquisitor in September 1483, and with his appointment the Inquisition was in a position to exert its whole strength.

It is impossible to give details of the horrors that now began to take place, without incurring the suspicion of wishing to appeal to a morbid desire for sensationalism. No age, no people, and no church was ever again to perpetrate such outrages against humanity; the only possible exception was the slaughter of the Incas by the Spanish conquistadores. Hecatombs fell before the frenzied lust for victims. The number of Marranos seemed inexhaustible; apparently every Jew who had been converted to Christianity had remained a Jew at heart. Before the holding of each session, a period of grace was allowed for those who wished to make a voluntary confession. But once again "reconciliation with the church" was associated with the shameful stipulation that a denunciation was to be made of co-religionists sharing the same views. The punishment, moreover, was attended by some public humiliation and also, as a matter of course, with confiscation of property. But even this "mercy and leniency" is cast into the shade by the infamous rule that the tribunal was at liberty to determine whether the repentance of a Marrano were genuine or not. When it suited the tribunal, the repentance was not genuine, and the penitent sinner ended his life at the stake.

In Aragon the new activities of the Inquisition were conducted by Canon Pedro Arbúez. He allowed no "period of grace," for it led to too many fortunes slipping through his fingers. The following figures give some idea of what he did: in Toledo in 1486, 750 heretics were burnt at the stake on the 12th of February; 900 on the 2nd of April; and 750 on the 2nd of May. A panic broke out among the Marranos; a conspiracy was formed by members of the highest ranks of society and Arbúez was murdered in the church at Saragossa. The result was that the church gained a martyr, the tribunal 200 more victims for the stake, and the fortunes of hundreds of others who were condemned to imprisonment for life, while the Inquisition as a whole secured the right of increasing the severity of its methods.

This increase in severity meant that hell was let loose on the Marranos, and even those onlookers who happened to be prepossessed in favour of the institution were forced to wonder whether at this stage of its frenzied fury it was really animated by the cold political calculations of its early days, or whether its so-called administration of justice had not become so inextricably caught up and entangled in its own terminology, in its own half-truths and veiled aims, that it actually believed in the necessity and sanctity of what it did. This much at all events is certain, the greater the lengths to which the Inquisition went, the more clearly did the failure both of a policy and of a religion stand revealed; the church above all found herself in an almost tragic position. She began to see that a hundred years of compulsory baptism and the Inquisition had achieved nothing final. But the violence to which she had had recourse when she forcibly secured converts to the Christian faith was bound to lead to further displays of violence; for, unlike the rest of the world, the Jews refused to settle down quietly under an enforced religion. Thus the church found it impossible to drop the weapon she had once used, and was obliged to give the lie to herself and to deny herself in an ever more dreadful fashion, with the result that, in the end, all that was left to her was violence and dominion—sorry possessions for a religion!

The church was so wholly obsessed by her struggle against the Marranos, that for a long while the fight with the unbaptized Jew was forgotten. But—and this constitutes the perpetual irony and tragedy of the Jewish Diaspora—the country could not do without him. It required the taxpayer and the financier, because the war against Moorish Granada, which had been resumed, cost money. The Jew, Isaac Abrabanel, was therefore appointed administrator of the state finances, with instructions to raise the necessary funds. The growing success of the Spanish arms in this war, however, paved the way for a uniform solution of both the Jewish and the Marrano problems. For, as had been quite plain from the beginning and became ever more apparent, although the clergy shut their eyes to it because they did not wish to be forced to acknowledge their defeat, the problem of the Jew and the problem of the Marrano were inextricably bound up with each other. Obsessed by their belief in the universality of the Catholic faith, the opponents of the Jews failed to understand that they were in reality confronted by a spiritual phenomenon, that the obstinacy of the Jews constituted the greatest national heroism imaginable, and that their obduracy and resistance testified to the immortality of a religion rooted in the very core of life . . . and that blood can extinguish even the fire of the stake. All they knew was what their spies told them regarding externals. But that was enough! They saw that the Jews continued to maintain their connexion with the Marranos, that they instructed their children, born in the Christian faith, in the Jewish religion, that they gave the adults prayer books and told them about the festivals, and secretly performed their devotions with them in holes and corners. And all this was happening at a time when the fourth generation of new Christians was growing up!

In vain did Torquemada take the most severe and cruel measures to bring about a complete separation between Jews and Marranos. All he succeeded in doing was to create a secret atmosphere of conspiracy, in which Jews and Marranos continued to meet together in common loyalty to their ancestral heritage. His mind, therefore, inevitably turned towards discovering some plan for ridding the country of the Jews, who constituted the spiritual support of the Marranos. But, as he was fully aware, his idea was likely to arouse considerable opposition owing to the multifarious social and economic ties the Jews had formed. To work up the necessary feeling in the country, he therefore had to have recourse to the time-honoured method of bringing charges of desecrating the Host and of ritual murder. In this he was helped by external events. In 1491 Granada was occupied, and the first half of the old Visigoth ideal, "one state, one faith," was at last realized. In order to realize the second half, all that was required was to drive out the Jews.

Ferdinand entered Granada on January 2, 1492. On the 31st of March of the same year, he issued a proclamation ordering all Jews to leave Castile, Aragon, Sicily, and Sardinia within four months. They were to be allowed to take all their movable property with them, except gold, silver, coins of all descriptions, and goods the export of which was forbidden. This was tantamount to allowing them to take nothing. He gave the following reasons for his action, "In our land there is a no inconsiderable number of Judaizing and wicked Christians who have deviated from our Holy Catholic Faith; this has been brought about above all by the intercourse between Jews and Christians. . . . According to reports supplied to us by the Inquisition, there can be no doubt that this intercourse between Jews and Christians, whereby the latter have been led astray and made to believe in their damnable religion, is doing untold harm. . . . All this inevitably leads to the undermining and humiliation of our Holy Catholic Faith. . . . We have, therefore, decided to order all Jews of both sexes to leave the confines of our land for ever. . . ."

Thus about 300,000 persons, whose ancestors had lived in the country before it had been touched by Christianity, and who had been the real founders of its culture and economic life, prepared to take their departure. Troops of missionaries once more pounced upon the harassed and impoverished fugitives; but they reaped a poor harvest. From the fate of the Marranos, the Jew had learnt what awaited him if he took refuge in the bosom of the church that claimed the monopoly of the means of grace. By the end of July 1492, when the time limit expired, all the Jews had gone. The entire middle class of the country had vanished. Whole cities sank into poverty and were deserted and derelict, and a retrograde movement set in. The Marranos were able for a while to arrest this movement which was the outcome of the destruction of a social organism. But when, in the sixteenth century, they also took flight *en masse,* their influence necessarily ceased. But the stakes still survived, and were still lighted for any thinker, any heretic, and any person who yearned for freedom. All that remained was the solitude of the monk.

The catastrophe had a brief sequel in Portugal, where the scene was reminiscent of Dante's *Inferno*. Appealed to by the Jews to be allowed to pass through his country or to make a temporary sojourn in it, John II granted their request, but limited the period of their stay to eight months, at a charge of from 8 to 100 gold cruzados per head. But epidemics broke out among the 100,000 fugitives who entered Portugal in this way, and John compelled them to leave the country before their allotted time was up. The bestiality with which the fugitives were treated on the ships defies description. Those who, owing to their premature eviction, failed to get a ship, were declared to be the king's thralls and were given away or sold. The children of these slaves were dispatched to the recently discovered island of St. Thomas, which was used as a penal settlement, ostensibly with the object of being given a Christian education. The majority of them died there; that is to say, the majority of those whose mothers had not already flung themselves into the sea with them. True, John's successor, Manuel, restored the Jews to freedom, but at the request of the king and queen of Spain, whose daughter Isabella he wished to marry, he decided to expel all Jews from Portugal. The edict which was dated December 25, 1496, ordered all Jews to be out of the country within ten months. His hope was that the majority would get themselves baptized first. But he was disappointed. He thereupon gave orders for all Jewish children between the ages of fourteen and twenty to be compulsorily baptized at Easter 1497. But the stream of emigration immediately increased, and the spiritual booty was in danger of being lost. The compulsory baptisms were therefore carried out as early as March the 19th. Numbers of parents committed suicide after killing their children. The remainder were baptized amid scenes of indescribable horror.

In the harbour of Lisbon over 20,000 Jews were crowded together endeavouring to emigrate. But Manuel placed no ships at their disposal and forced them to remain until the time limit of their stay had expired. Whereupon he declared them to be his personal slaves; he took them prisoner, set missionaries to work with them, and starved them, in order to win souls for Christianity; all those who had not already committed suicide he had dragged to the baptismal font by means of ropes tied to the hair of their head. And thus he reared a new generation of Marranos. The remainder, whom in spite of all his efforts he failed to make Christians, he allowed to wander off into the unknown in 1498.

Thus these three centuries came to a close with the ejection of the

Jews from England, France, Spain, Portugal, and a large part of Germany. Hundreds of thousands had been left by the wayside, slaughtered, hanged, burned at the stake, and broken on the wheel in the name of Christ because they had been loyal to their own people. A load of debt was accumulated, for the settlement of which nothing has yet been done!

PART V

FROM

THE SETTLEMENT IN THE EAST

TO

THE RISE OF THE JEWISH CRISIS

THE FLIGHT EASTWARD

THREE hundred thousand wanderers, branded as foreigners, as strange, sinister creatures, bowed down by misfortune, living proofs that the impotent hatred of a religion and the impotent suffering of a people can always be carried one step further; three hundred thousand of such people on the highroads, on board ship, in harbours and towns along the coast of the Mediterranean, must surely have made even a callous world gasp. And it did indeed look on with horror; but only for a moment, until it understood that Providence had delivered an outlawed people and their property into its hands. Except very occasionally in Italy, wherever these wandering hordes came in contact with Christians, they were plundered, starved, flung into the sea, left forsaken on the coast of Africa, insulted, and forcibly baptized. With extremely few exceptions in the fanatical areas of north Africa, wherever they came in contact with Mohammedans they were received as a race of intelligent, industrious people, capable of being loyal citizens. For years they wandered about, decimated by disease, hunger, shipwreck, and murder; sometimes they devoured the grass in the fields like cattle, and at every place they reached they were met by monks who, with a loaf of bread in their hands, tried to lure their starving children to the baptismal font.

Nearly half a century elapsed before the last of them found a resting-place. They had settled everywhere, some in Italy, some on the Greek islands, some in north Africa, Egypt, and Palestine. But the main body met with a welcome in Turkey, in the newly formed Ottoman Empire, which from the fourteenth century onwards had gradually made an end of the reconstituted but moribund Greek empire of Byzantium. With Turkey's advance into Europe (end of the fourteenth century), the fall of Constantinople (1453), and the annexation of Palestine and Egypt (1517) a huge empire came into being, which, though it could boast of no cultural achievements, and could therefore offer no intellectual stimulus to the Jews, nevertheless guaranteed their existence. It gave them peace, allowed them to play an active part in its economic life, granted them autonomy within their own community, and, what is even more important from the standpoint of their historic continuity, afforded them breathing-space in which to draw the spiritual conclusions from their fate.

This return to the East, this backward swing of the pendulum, to a race spiritually constituted like the Jews, must have meant more than a mere geographical change. And, indeed, it had a profounder meaning, inasmuch as it was a return to the intimate circle of the oriental mind. Both the geographical and the spiritual return took a twofold path. The banishment from the West created two new colonies in the East—the colony in European and Asiatic Turkey, and the colony in Poland. It also gave the decisive impetus for the formation of a twofold extreme in the spiritual attitude of the Jews—codified rabbinism and the practical Kabbalah. Both these forms of religious thought came into being in Turkey, and were subsequently transmitted to the other eastern centre, Poland. The result was that, as soon as the world centre of Judaism had been dispersed, spiritual contact was re-established. Geographical contact soon followed also owing to the rapid spread of Jewish settlements in European Turkey, and the appearance of colonies as far west as Moldavia and Walachia. In the West the chain of Jewish settlements had been broken. In the East it was restored. The determined struggle of this homeless people to survive as an individual force in history now started afresh, and at the same time the crisis in their spiritual development also took place.

We have already several times called attention to the acute opposition which always has and always will exist between brain and heart, Halakah and Haggadah, rabbinism and mysticism. This antithesis is really nothing else than the constantly renewed endeavour to shape life, the wonderful capacity to start afresh with which Judaism has been blessed. And in this endeavour, both success and failure are included; it stands not only for progression but also for retrogression; for genuine endeavour knows of no final truth, but only searching and striving. And it was to this searching and striving that the Jews devoted themselves in Turkey as soon as they had managed to secure some small measure of freedom.

When once these people drew near to their ancestral home, and some, though but few, actually settled in Palestine, it would have been only natural for them to be stimulated by this return to an outburst of creative productivity. For the majority of them were, after all, Sephardim, Spanish Jews, the descendants of those among whom a man like Judah Halevi had been able to sing his *Songs of Zion*. Why did they not now concentrate all their energy on making Palestine their real centre once more? As a matter of fact, this was impossible, not for political reasons alone, or because monks and dervishes were firmly established in Jerusalem. Nor did it fail to come to pass because the desire no longer existed and their longing for home had vanished. The real reason lay in the fact that the idea of returning home to their native land had meanwhile undergone a profound process of sublimation, and to return home no longer meant to return to Palestine. The idea of the return, Messianism, had long since shed the last trace of its political associations. The idea now followed its original path once more, the path of pure faith in salvation. The object was, not the return home of a people, but the return home of a *perfect* people. The thousand years of exile constituted a reality embodied and rooted in this idea; it was an actuality devoid of historical significance; it was a fact which derived its importance exclusively from the domain of morality, religion, and the spirit. The Diaspora was an external phenomenon which they had not willed and for which, therefore, they were not responsible. But as they had to live in it, they lent it a meaning of their own, that is to say, they regarded it as an experience which would make them fit for salvation. That is why as a mere historical fact the Diaspora belongs to the history of the *Jews;* in its essence it belongs to the history of *Judaism.*

Thus the banished Sephardim and the Jews who had fled from the persecution of other western European countries, the Ashkenazim, were drawn together by the power of this idea, both in Palestine itself and in its neighbourhood. Their spiritual life became deeper and more intense. They were so prolific both in thought and in writing that the sum total of their activities in this respect might be regarded as having been creative. Nevertheless, they bore within them the seeds of degeneration, for once more it became plain that, as is always the case when the Jews become exceptionally rich in productivity and experience, they were living in an imaginary world and not in a real world that could be seen and felt.

In the first place, they were faced with answering the question why the centre in Spain which had been so full of hope had been broken up. They did not answer it by saying that it was because they had been living in exceptional circumstances as strangers in a strange land, where they had been confronted by brutality incarnate disguised as religion. But they answered in the words of the scholar Joseph Jabez: "It was because we forsook the holy Torah, and turned our minds to worldly science, and paid homage to profane wisdom."

Here we have the final, one-sided, and unequivocal result of the cultural struggle that had taken place in the thirteenth and fourteenth centuries, and at the same time the most extreme example of a people endowed with the capacity of feeling bound and constrained and able to endure their fate without being brought to despair by it. The function which the Jewish law had fulfilled in the early days of the Diaspora—the preservation of the Jewish type in a state that was non-existent—now became intensified on the religious side. The law became the pivot and foundation of the religious life. Man attained salvation through loyalty to the law; he served God through obedience; he must look neither to the right hand nor to the left; he must not question, brood, or doubt; not knowledge but resolution was his duty.

The written record of this point of view was supplied by Joseph ben Ephraim Karo, who, in 1564, published as part of his gigantic commentary, the code of Jewish civil and religious law, the ultimate book of the law, the final record of four hundred years of opposition to the synthesis aimed at by Maimonides. In this work there was no longer any question of philosophizing or discussing the ideas and fundamental doctrines of Judaism; it was merely an attempt to decide what was still valid in law, and should accordingly be obeyed. It was Judaism carved in stone. The title of the work was a metaphor: *Shulḥan Aruk,* the "Table Prepared."

If it had still been possible to make a work a canonical book, it would certainly have been done in this case. But even without that, it became a binding force because hundreds of thousands of Jews consented to accept this code as their pattern and rule of conduct. It was circulated throughout the Jewish world, and to say of a Jew that his life was led according to the *Shulḥan Aruk* constituted the highest meed of praise.

And yet this clinging to the law was no mere outward show devoid of feeling. It was something more than mere formalism. Even rabbinism, which in this work produced its masterpiece, was overshadowed by that other fundamental attitude of the Jewish soul, which is related to a sphere beyond rationality, and which although its aim is the same as that of loyalty to the law, leaves the latter far behind: Jewish mysticism.

As we have already pointed out, this was formulated into a system in the Kabbalah. But whereas rabbinism could be realized by a practical life led according to the law, the Kabbalah could for the time being be realized only by a speculative system, a religious metaphysic. Nevertheless, in view of the vast possibilities it held for the Jewish soul, and since its production was almost the outcome of necessity, it was inevitable that before long it should find its way into practice, and influence the conduct of everyday life. Although the Jews might not ask the reason why their existence had been so tumultuous, they might at least inquire what the end of it all would be, and how they might attain that end. That their suffering was suffering for the sake of purification was as much a certainty to the Jews, as the fact that this purification was a prerequisite of salvation. But eventually people cease to be satisfied with a theoretical reason for their suffering. They insist on its being related to some reality however fantastic, feeble, and problematical. They insist on abandoning philosophy for some practical activity.

The fact that the Kabbalah actually evolved a system of mystical practice is sufficient proof that it was imbued with the spirit of life. At all events, in its development from mere speculation to practice, it gathered up elements which, as if by way of a sharp reaction to a stimulus, first roused the spirit in order subsequently to blunt it. These elements were the Christian conception of original sin and asceticism, which were adopted not as the result of accident or arbitrary choice, but because they were, so to speak, part of the nature of things. For the more the actual communal life, the organized social existence of the Jews fell to pieces, the more fervently did they seek to save themselves on the spiritual plane. But their weakened relationship to the world and to reality, and the constant uprooting even of the fragmentary communities they were able to form, resulted in a corresponding narrowing of their spiritual conceptions, and made them just as regressive as those of Christianity became when it divorced itself from the Jewish people and the bed-rock of Judaism, in order to become a Catholic Church. This regression took the form of belief in the doctrine of the sinfulness of human nature. In so far as this was not a legacy from paganism, it was the outcome of the fear of instability felt by an uprooted people. So long as the Jews had a country, their close contact with nature and with their own people inspired them with confidence, even confidence in the goodness of man. But as homeless outcasts in a struggle against the Christian world, they fell victims to the Christian idea of original sin. They also became possessed by the Christian idea of asceticism, the belief that all earthly things were worthless and of no account, a conception entirely alien to the Jewish spirit, which held that God's creation could not be imperfect, and that life, including the life of the body, was conceived as bound up with a moral existence, to constitute an indivisible whole. But completely surrounded as they were by those who not only knew of no such view, but also made the material existence of the Jews utterly unbearable, the idea inevitably dawned on the Jewish mind that earthly things really were of no account and that, in turning towards heavenly matters, earthly possessions and joys could not be left too far behind.

The result was much more tragic than is admitted by those who see little more in Kabbalism and its mystical doctrines than an offence against sanity. The group of Kabbalists who made their headquarters in the city of Safed in Palestine started out from one reality and shaped their course towards another. Their starting-point was the conviction that the burden of suffering that had fallen upon the shoulders of the Jewish people heralded the "End of Days," and their aim was, therefore, to bring about this end by means of penance, asceticism, and religious heroism. It was only natural that people who had not found salvation either in the Bible or the Talmud should hold up the *Zohar,* which was the fundamental work of Kabbalist theory, as ultimate knowledge. It was only at this juncture that the Zohar appeared in its final form, and became, even more than the Talmud had been, the psychological record of a religious life on which exorbitant demands had been made. Its principles are clear and unequivocal—the yearning for a Messiah; the need of salvation both for the individual and the community; the sinfulness of human nature; asceticism; and demonism. All this was inextricably connected with the idea of the Sephiroth, which had long ago lost their dependence on God and their spirituality, and had become not only independent, but also realities. The dualism of Christianity and paganism found its counterpart here and allotted to everyday life the "impure Sephiroth," which were also emanations of the original force, but were encumbered with all the evil and impurity of demons. Thus the task with which a man was confronted was to purify these impure Sephiroth, that is to say, to lay aside evil, wickedness, the demonic, and everything in the world that had arisen out of sin and sensuality, and to do this not only for himself but also for the whole of mankind, for all souls both born and unborn. For when everything has become the emanation from the one original force, when there is nothing unrelated to it, then the ring joining man to God is indissolubly closed; for the soul is also in this ring, but being chained to the human body it is impure through the evil influences of sin and of demons, and stands in need of salvation. It is for this reason that it returns when one man's life has not been sufficient to cleanse it of its husk of impurity, the *Qelippah*. This was the doctrine of *Gilgul,* or the transmigration of souls. It is the terrible cycle which makes all these ideas so difficult, and so hostile to life; this uncertainty as to whose soul a particular man has within him, and how much in it still stands in need of salvation, and whether or not enough has been done to this end. But enough could be done only in a state of ecstasy, which the teachers of the Kabbalah regarded as the condition most conducive to gaining knowledge, securing salvation, and forcing an entry into heaven.

One of the leaders of this movement was Isaac Luria Ashkenasi of Jerusalem, surnamed Ari, who came to Safed in 1570. He was a man of mystery and secret premonitions, a religious ecstatic full of the knowledge of mystic lore and ceremony. After two years of preaching he suddenly died of the plague. His place was taken by his pupil, Chaim Vital Calabrese, who declared that Ari had confided to him how the "End of Days" could be expedited. He had written down what he had told him and added his own views on the subject. Further additions from various sources were also made until a dark cloud of renunciation, isolation, repentance, ecstasy, meditation, fear, and satiety of life gradually cast its shadow over the souls of the Jews. Whereupon the whole tragic contradiction came to light. Just as the Kabbalah as a whole had its aim and origin in reality, so the practical

Kabbalah was merely an attempt to connect with reality the experiences undergone in the clash with the strange world outside, irrespective of the fact that the Jews had no home. There is nothing unreal in Jewish mysticism. Life regarded as an experienced reality, heaven as a reality yet to be experienced, and between the two faith as a function of the heart alone—such was Jewish mysticism. But the practical Kabbalah failed because it was crushed beneath too heavy a burden of such concepts as demonism, original sin, and asceticism, to be related to experienced reality. Instead of mastering and shaping life, it could only teach men how to overcome life; it was, therefore, bound to lead to its own suppression, unless some event of real life came to the rescue. And this happened only once, when Sabbatai Zevi made himself the centre of a movement which will be discussed in due course.

With these two achievements, the composition of the *Shulḥan Aruk* and the development of the practical Kabbalah, the real work of the new eastern centre came to an end, as did also its importance from the standpoint of the development of Jewish history. True, it radiated other forms of energy, but they came to fruition in other lands.

The next sphere of influence was Italy, whither missionaries from Safed conveyed the doctrines of Ari. Italy, a kaleidoscopic conglomeration of states, cities, and republics, held out all manner of possibilities for the material destiny of the Jewish people. And indeed she ran through the whole scale, from the inconceivable trials and vicissitudes of the ghetto in the Papal States, to the magnificent humanity and tolerance of the d'Estes and the Ferraras. There was something kaleidoscopic also in the diversity of ways in which the Jews reacted spiritually to the events that occurred in various places. Italy in the sixteenth century appeared to be a sort of experimental laboratory for testing every tendency of the Jewish spiritual world, from profound ecstatic Kabbalism to the superior attitude adopted by the rationalists in denying the binding sanctity of the law. The first practical tests were made in this country, and subsequent developments, as it were, anticipated.

Throughout the period of the Diaspora, Messianism made constant tentative attempts to conquer reality and achieve fulfilment. These attempts represented the reflex movements of a people who were unremittingly persecuted, and knew of no other way of escape. But in some cases the attitude of search became a pose, while the quest after a way of escape led to perdition. Thus at this juncture (1502) the Kabbalist, Asher Lemlin, made his appearance in Istria and proclaimed himself to be the forerunner of the Messiah, declaring that in six months the day of salvation would dawn. But it was necessary for all to repent and do penance for their sins. Thousands in Italy, Austria, and Germany believed him and began to do penitential exercises. The six months elapsed. The repentance had not been deep and sincere enough, declared Lemlin, and sank into oblivion. But the expectation remained alive in the hearts of the people. Isaac Abrabanel, one of the most noble and distinguished of the Spanish fugitives, had calculated that Rome would be destroyed in 1531, when Israel would triumph. But Bonnet de Lattes, the Jewish doctor in the Vatican, calculated that this would happen in 1505. Between these two dates, in 1524, a man of strangely sombre appearance, the Jew David Reubeni, landed in Venice. His name indicates his origin. He belonged to the tribe of Reuben, which, over 2000 years previously had been carried into captivity by the Assyrians together with the other tribes of the kingdom of Israel. Reubeni declared that this tribe still existed, and that in the desert of Khabor (probably Khaibar in northern Arabia) it had a country of its own of which his brother Joseph was king. He himself was the commander-in-chief of the army. He declared that he had also found the descendants of the other lost tribes of Israel, who were living in Nubia. He went on to explain that he had been sent as emissary on a political mission with the object of persuading the pope and other European rulers to furnish the Jews of Khabor with arms and with their help drive the Turks out of Palestine.

Thus before presenting himself to the Jews he had first to get into touch with the Christians, and he immediately went to Rome, where he was received by Pope Clement VII. The latter welcomed the idea of a fresh crusade against Islam, both because it would create a diversion on the part of the Catholic Church against the Reformation movement inaugurated by Martin Luther, and because he hoped it would also help him to checkmate the predatory policy of Charles V. He accordingly gave Reubeni a letter of recommendation to the Emperor of Christian Abyssinia, and another to John III, King of Portugal.

Reubeni then went to Lisbon and negotiated with the king. Here, too, he was given a most sympathetic hearing, and was promised that both men and ships would be placed at his disposal. But before any active steps had been taken, it began to be suspected that his activities would favour the Jews much more than the Christians. True, Reubeni took the utmost pains to have nothing to do with the Marranos. Nevertheless, it was evident that his arrival had given rise to the utmost excitement among them. He had already confidentially informed a Jew in Rome that his aim was to conquer the Holy Land for the Jews and not for the Christians, and Marranism once more became secretly active. One of the Marranos, Diego Pires, met his doom in Reubeni. Pires, a young man of twenty-five, who was secretary to the Lisbon courts of Law, was overcome by the thought of these magic hopes, and his suppressed Judaism grew so strong that he developed into an ecstatic, believing that the Messianic age had already dawned. As a sign of the return home, he performed the operation of circumcision upon himself, gave himself the Jewish name of Salomo Molcho, and, still trembling with excitement, presented himself before Reubeni. In those surroundings the last thing the latter wanted to hear about was Marranism or Messianism. But seeing that Molcho's condition was such that he stood in eminent danger of falling into the clutches of the Inquisition, he advised him to flee to Turkey. Molcho interpreted this cautious advice as a revelation. In 1527 he reached Salonica, and shortly afterwards was in Safed, the stronghold of Kabbalism. When he heard that Charles V's troops had entered Rome, he regarded the event as the promised fall of Edom, or Rome, and immediately set out for Italy, where he landed at Ancona at the end of 1529, and went straight to Rome. Here he tried to make the old popular legend, that the Messiah would crouch among the beggars and lepers at the gates of the city and bide his time, become a reality in his own person, and sat cowering among the beggars on the Tiber bridge, quivering with religious ecstasy.

The attention of the Inquisition was directed to him and he fled to Venice, where Reubeni had also found refuge, having been expelled from Portugal owing to his dealings with the Marranos. In Venice Reubeni had renewed his activities and was trying to persuade the republic to make war on the Turks. He was playing a double game; to all intents and purposes he was the diplomatic agent of a people he had never set eyes on, and therefore a charlatan, cheat, and adventurer; but actually he was a Messiah in disguise who genuinely and sincerely wished to lead the Jews back to the Holy Land. As soon as the Signoria of Venice learnt of this, they expelled him from the republic.

Molcho regarded all this as the sufferings of the Messiah, and in spite of the risk of falling into the clutches of the Inquisition, he again went to Rome where he embarked upon a wild, but so fanatically impressive a campaign of Messianic propaganda, that even Pope Clement VII regarded him as an instrument of the divine will, and protected him against the Inquisition. When he found he could do so no longer, he helped him to escape to Germany. Here again he fell in with Reubeni, and in 1532 the two men went to Charles V at Regensburg, and informed him of their intention of calling upon the Jews of the whole world to make war upon the Turks. All that they succeeded in conveying to the mind of Charles V, however, was that they were planning to lead the Jews back to Palestine, and that their activities were, therefore, hostile to the interests of the Catholic Church. So he had them both arrested and handed over to the Italian Inquisition. Salomo

Molcho, the renegade Christian, was burnt at the stake, and Reubeni was sent to Spain, where he ended his days in some dungeon.

In this twofold tragedy Messianism gave a sign of life. And in the figure of Judah Arie (Leo) Modena, the other extreme—the first beginnings of clear critical judgment opposed to the sanctity of tradition—the decay of belief in revelation gave a sign of life.

We shall not attempt to decide whether the Renaissance and the rise of humanism in Italy really had any influence on Jewish thought and the spiritual creativeness of the Jews, or whether it was not rather the desire of Christians brought up in the new humanistic culture to become acquainted with the spiritual world of the Jews and the Arabs, through the instrumentality of learned Jews, that gave the latter the opportunity of breaking loose from their own domain of law and adopting a critical attitude. That this actually took place at this time was no new phenomenon in the case of the Jews, for we must always remember that both on the material and on the spiritual plane similar events were constantly being repeated in their history, only differing slightly according to time and place. This is explained by the fact that they came upon the scene of life with an idea, the realization of which still constitutes an exceptionally living problem even today. Job in his time had doubted; the Sadducees doubted and criticized, as did also Jesus and the Karaites, while in the philosophic system of Maimonides, doubt, either of the validity of philosophy or the binding power of revelation, is really the imaginary foundation. Doubt is either useful or superfluous according to the direction in which it works. And the reason why we refer to it here and give examples to prove that it existed, is to show that for a people whose material fate was tragic in the extreme, it also inevitably meant tragedy in the spiritual sphere and for the individual. Moreover, we shall show why it was suicidal for the Jews ever to allow themselves to doubt.

The unwillingness of the Jews of the Diaspora to engage in historical work finds its counterpart in their desire to abandon to forgetfulness everything in their earlier history which was not necessary to faith, or which might have broken the continuity they claimed for their religious traditions. Thus, for instance, the whole of the history of the Jewish Alexandrian period, which was so important, was virtually unknown, and it was left to Azaria de Rossi (1513–1578) to discover it again and to translate much of the Judæo-Greek literature into Hebrew. The importance of his work lay not in the translation, but in the discovery of historical facts and chronological connexions, as the result of which it became known that a number of historical statements in the Talmud must be untrue, that is to say, mythical, that its chronology was unreliable and therefore—and this was the severest blow to Jewish belief—the claim it made of being an unbroken chain of sacred tradition going right back to Moses was quite irreconcilable with the facts. Rossi had the courage to record these discoveries in writing and to publish them. They provoked a storm of indignation. And quite rightly; for, so long as no other form of thought had matured among them, the believing Jews could not afford to have taken from them even the most insignificant detail of that which, in the insecurity of their material position in the world at the time, bound them to a past admitting of no doubt—the belief in the continuity and sanctity of tradition.

Although Jewish orthodoxy had no Inquisition and no stakes at its disposal, the fear of being obliged to stand outside their own community was sufficient to shut the mouths of those who doubted. They did not cease to doubt, but they held their tongues. They were obliged to weigh the pros and cons of faith and scepticism in their own hearts; they could not discuss them with the outside world; and the secret conflict broke them.

In Venice, Rabbi Leo Modena, an extremely pious and cultivated man, produced scholarly works which never went beyond the bounds of what a learned rabbi of the period might legitimately be allowed to say. Yet for all his piety he was an opponent of the Kabbalah. The doctrines of the Kabbalah, however, possessed dogmatic value only for those who wished to believe in them, and it was for this reason that he was allowed to contest the sacredness of the Zohar, to pick to pieces the legends regarding its origin, to attack the doctrine of the Sephiroth, and even to bring against the practical Kabbalah the charge of being little more than a swindle. Far more daring and dangerous was his critical demonstration of the fact that Jesus had never called himself the "Son of God" in the sense represented by the subsequent ecclesiastical dogma of Christianity. Naturally on this question the censorship of the church imposed silence upon him. But when he died, two unpublished essays were found among his papers, entitled respectively *The Voice of a Fool* and *The Roar of the Lion*. In his introduction to the former he declared that he did not know the author. An unknown person had given it to him to refute. And there was indeed a good deal in it which an orthodox Jew would wish to refute, for its contention amounted to no less than that the "oral tradition" could not be traced to any revelation on Sinai, that it was the work of men, of leaders of the people who, finding themselves incapable of guiding them by means of the pure and unadulterated doctrines of the Torah, had built another edifice, the Mishnah, on the original foundation, and upon the Mishnah yet another, the Gemara, and that over both rabbinism had ultimately raised a third. This Jewish tradition was therefore not sacred and binding; it was merely a threefold burden created by man, beneath which the people were bound to collapse.

This treatise Modena entitled *The Voice of a Fool.* It merely repeated a historical truism, which was at the same time a religious blasphemy, and he gave the reply to it in *The Roar of the Lion.* The roar, however, was not so loud as the title might lead one to suppose. In fact, it was rather faint and never rose above a mild argument for the defence, which at every point was drowned by *The Voice of the Fool.* This is comprehensible enough, seeing that when two voices contend together in a single breast, one or the other must necessarily be the stronger. In other words, *both* the treatises were by Modena. His doubts, which did not dare to rise above a whisper, longed to be silenced and refuted; but even if his outward behaviour appeared immaculate and above reproach, when he was confronted by the voice of his inner conscience, he was obliged, silently and with but a feeble show of resistance, to succumb.

This, however, does not cover the whole tragedy of his life. Owing to the position he assumed in the outside world, it was inevitable that he should exercise a decisive influence on one in whom faith and tradition were likewise joined in tragic conflict: Uriel da Costa.

The da Costas were Portuguese Marranos, and all the da Costas—if, that is to say, we may conclude that all who bore the name belonged to the same family—seem to have been men of a pugnacious and rebellious turn of mind. A certain Emanuel da Costa, for instance, a Marrano of Lisbon, protested against being forced to be a Christian by nailing the following inscription to the door of the cathedral and other churches: "The Messiah has not yet come. Jesus was not the Messiah. Christianity is a lie!" He paid for this futile act by having his hands cut off, and being burned at the stake (1539). Another, later da Costa, Joseph, president of the synagogue at Amsterdam, is said to have spent his whole life engaged in violent controversies with Manasseh ben Israel (about 1651). And in Uriel da Costa a disastrous combination of similar characteristics is to be found, though on a somewhat higher plane.

He came from Oporto. His family had long been assimilated, and his father was a strict Catholic who sent his son to study law and scholastic philosophy at the Jesuit College at Coimbra. At the age of twenty-five he became canon of a church in Oporto. He had no connexion with Judaism and no knowledge of it, so that his eventual discovery that he could no longer endure to be harnessed to his mechanical ecclesiastical duties as a Jesuit and to be perpetually confessing his sins, cannot be traced to the fact that he compared his own religion with some other form of faith. It was due rather to the hereditary strain in his blood which rose up in rebellion. To be constantly confessing meant being perpetually sinful; and to be perpetually sinful meant to be hopelessly caught in the clutches of original sin. He protested against this and made up his mind to discover for himself where it was in the Holy Scriptures that man was said to be a hopelessly abandoned and sinful creature. At last his inquiry brought him to the Pentateuch, which the Jesuits always did their best to prevent from falling into the hands of their pupils; and here, to his amazement, he discovered that original sin was never even mentioned. In it man was left the free choice between good and evil; he might raise or debase himself as he pleased. This opened up to him a religious world which he recognized as his own. Whereupon he fled with his mother and two brothers to Amsterdam, where all three embraced Judaism. He changed his first name from Gabriel to Uriel, and was full of enthusiasm to start life afresh as a Jew. But the Judaism he found in Amsterdam, the rabbinism which was the inevitable historical outcome of a homeless race endeavouring to maintain its type, did not harmonize with the ideas of a man who had learnt to know Judaism at its source. This in itself proved a sore disappointment to da Costa. The fact that he was unable to understand the deviations to which history had led, made the situation even more difficult for him, since it led him to ask a question which was unjustified, and to inquire who was right, he or his environment. Both were right, and it was this that made his encounter with it so tragic. In giving to his unjustified question the reply that it was he who was right, his perspective became distorted, and he was unable to make that dispassionate investigation which would have justified his reply. The veneer of rabbinism with which Judaism was overlaid was so firmly imposed, that he could see and attack nothing else, and he made no attempt to oppose it from the standpoint of the laws of its evolution, but only from the standpoint of the fact that it actually existed. He had found his way to Judaism as the result of the free and unfettered promptings of his heart; but his environment was the result of far more than ten centuries of training. The individual stood opposed to the whole, a religious will to national necessity, heart to head, the unconstrained impulse of religious passion to the capacity for perseverance in loyalty to tradition, and in general terms, the right of the isolated person to the right of the whole community. As neither was wrong, one side was bound to suffer injustice. And in da Costa's attitude to this injustice lies the meaning of his fate—the tragedy of a point of view.

Da Costa, adopting the phraseology of the Bible, called the rabbis "Pharisees," and maintained what Rossi had already suggested, and what Modena had whispered in his own heart, that the Jewish laws were their creation and not the result of tradition. In 1616, when he was in Hamburg, he addressed to the community of Venice his *Thesis against Tradition,* in which he contested not only the justification for many of the regulations, but also their origin. Furthermore, he cast doubt on the binding force of the whole of the "oral tradition." This treatise was handed to Modena, and thus the very man whose innermost thoughts were revealed in every word uttered by this passionate sceptic, was obliged, in his capacity as rabbi of the community of Venice, to refute this thesis, and, moreover, call upon the author to recant. And as da Costa adhered to his opinion, Modena was ultimately obliged to pronounce the ban upon this secret comrade in arms. Da Costa then returned to Amsterdam, filled with eagerness for the fray. His original passionate love, finding no echo, became transformed into an attitude of truculent denial. Instead of being able to love, he was forced to go in for research, and his willingness to believe approached the unwillingness of the rationalist. In 1624, he published his *Test of the Pharisaical Tradition by Comparing it with the Written Law.* In this work he no longer attacked the laws but the dogma. He declared that Judaism knew nothing of the immortality of the soul or of retribution in a beyond. The fact that he was right did not help him. He was denounced by the pen of Samuel da Silva, and the community of Amsterdam pronounced the ban upon him even before his book appeared. He was also charged before the secular court on the ground that his doctrine was subversive of the Christian faith, and was ordered to pay a fine. His treatise was confiscated and destroyed, and he found himself alone and isolated. But he continued his religious studies for his own satisfaction, and buried himself in theistic theories. However, after ten years of a life in which he was shunned by all, he could endure his isolation no longer, and decided to crave forgiveness for his denial of the law, and was received into the community once more. But in his heart of hearts he remained unchanged. When two Christians came to him with the object of being converted to Judaism, he dissuaded them in order to spare them the pain of the conflict. For this action, and for the reasons he gave in support of it, he was once more placed under a ban. Once more he remained without the pale for six years, and then his resistance again broke down. He crept to the cross, and after being subjected to humiliating ceremonies, which the persecuted had borrowed from their persecutors of the Spanish Inquisition, he was received once more into the bosom of the church.

After having escaped from the bloody Inquisition, and being delivered up to the inquisition of his own soul, hemmed in between the ideal and the real, and punished by his own people, to whom, at the risk of his life, he had fled, his courage gave way, and in April 1640, he shot himself. In front of him, on the table, was found the autobiography he had just completed, *Exemplar Humanae Vitae,* "The Example of a Human Life."

The occurrence of such events in the life of a people indicates that a danger-point has been reached. Their importance lay not in the fact that it was possible for a Jew to doubt and deny, but that these doubts almost inevitably broke him. (All sceptics, who have rejected Judaism, or have been obliged to abandon it, bear this infirmity about with them. It is for this reason that of all renegades, the Jew is the worst.)

The contention that the danger-point had been reached seems at first sight to be contradicted by the fact that at this time the Jews had not only found a safe asylum in Turkey, but that eastern Europe, Poland, and Lithuania had also given shelter to a strong centralized Jewish settlement, with an excellent and orderly administration of its own. But this settlement was from the beginning exposed to the eternal dangers which have everywhere beset the Jews in the Diaspora, and, as we shall see from the sequel, they were not free even from spiritual dangers in this eastern centre.

The first Jewish colonies in Poland date back to the ninth century, from which time a small but constant stream of fugitives poured into the country to escape oppression either in Germany, Austria, or Bohemia. A larger influx of immigrants took place particularly when the German Jews fled from the massacres of the "home" crusades. This continued throughout the eleventh, twelfth, and thirteenth centuries. These Jewish immigrants were accompanied by ever-increasing numbers of Germans bent on escaping from the bonds of feudalism or the burdens of civil war. Both groups of immigrants gave considerable impetus to the primitive economic life of Poland and both were granted their rights as aliens in that country. But whereas the German immigrants very quickly became adapted, and began to play a leading part in browbeating the Jews who had come in with them, the Jews were immediately confronted with their hereditary foe, the Christian church, who regarded the statute granted them by the Polish government in the thirteenth century as far too generous and philanthropic. She was not interested in their economic usefulness to the country, and also regarded good neighbourly relations between Jews and Poles as dangerous. But as, for the time being, she had no influence over the government, she resolved to adopt her usual policy of framing a number of anti-Jewish regulations to be kept in reserve in case of need. Her motive for this was revealed at a conference of the Polish clergy held at Breslau in 1267. "Inasmuch as Poland represents a new field in the domain of Christianity, it is to be feared that the Christian population of this country, in which Christianity has not yet laid a firm hold on the hearts of men, may be all the more easily influenced by the erroneous beliefs and corrupt morals of the Jews living in their midst."

This point of view sedulously circulated among the people, necessarily led to a separation between the Jews and the Poles, and was bound to create the attitude of mind beautifully described at the Synod of 1542 as follows: "The church tolerates the Jews only because by their presence they remind us of the martyrdom of our Saviour"! Thus the Jews appear in the guise of a religious stimulus.

As in all the other countries into which the Jews immigrated, so in Poland, the Christian church spread a *mot d'ordre* calculated to act as a convenient cloak for all her other grounds of hostility. At the same time it once more became obvious in Poland that the enmity that arose was not spontaneous, but induced, and that a mere difference of type and habits does not of itself, as the result of natural causes, lead to hostility between peoples, but is always called into existence; though when once it has arisen in this way, it may assume various forms.

Thus, in a very short space of time, the position of the Jews in Poland did not differ in kind from that which they enjoyed in other countries, though it was distinctly worse in degree. This is true as regards the numbers of Jews concerned, the intensity of their economic activities, their autonomy, their intellectual nimbleness, and their martyrdom.

As the migrations of the Jews were not determined by any thought of finding ideal conditions, they tended to drift to areas whither they were tempted to go by the nature of the economic organization, and the presence of other Jews. All they wanted was to secure living room and neighbourly relations. Thus the growth of the colony in Poland was due more to immigration than to any increase of population resulting from the custom of early marriage, the belief that children were a blessing, abstemious living, and the reduced mortality resulting therefrom. And a Jewish population of millions came into being which was able to endure massacres of hundreds of thousands, and subsequently to furnish a large contingent to Russia notwithstanding, and even to repair the gradual exhaustion of German Jews as the result of continual depletion.

But the very existence of a mass of people is in itself a not insignificant factor in the development of their economic position. And, as a matter of fact, the activities of the Jews extended to every conceivable branch of economic life. They went in for agriculture, horticulture, handicrafts, trading in agricultural produce, buying and selling both wholesale and retail, industry, money-lending, and tax-farming. Later on they also took estates on lease, more particularly crown lands and those of the *szlachta,* or nobles. Closely connected with this was what was known as the right of "propination," or the privilege of exploiting salt mines, forests, and metal mines, and most important of all, holding licences for retailing beer, wine, and spirits. Lastly, they played a leading part as middle-man in the export trade.

The development of their economic status followed much the same course everywhere. The fresh economic territory into which they penetrated, and the chances of filling up gaps in the system, gave the Jews the chance to prosper. But in Poland they did not win prosperity quickly. The number of Jews all competing with each other was too large, and the prospects held out by Polish economic life too small. In the early days they managed to secure a position of modest competency, which they owed not merely to their industry, but also to the extreme frugality of their way of life. But the mere fact that the Jew prospered provoked the indignation of the Christian artisans and merchants. A single instance will suffice to show how primitive were Polish ideas of economic law. In the course of the economic struggles which subsequently took place, a resolution was passed to the effect that the profit on goods sold should be fixed by law; the Pole was to be allowed a profit of 8%, the foreign merchant a profit of 5%, and the Jew only 3½%. It was expected that this would lead to a considerable boom in the trade done by Christians. But of course the natural consequence was that consumers bought their goods from the Jews, for as the latter could make only a profit of 3½%, they could sell more cheaply than the Poles.

But the reaction to the activities of the Jews was not the same throughout the country. In Poland class distinctions were sharply marked. The country was divided into landed aristocracy (*szlachta*), clergy, and bourgeoisie. The vast number of peasant serfs was not regarded as constituting a class at all. When a country is divided into classes, there is generally a conflict of interests between them, and the Jews in Poland were differently affected by these different interests. To the government their international connexions and wide experience made them useful as financiers, intermediaries for loans, and tax-farmers. These were functions which Jews were called upon to undertake even when they were being cruelly oppressed in other branches of the country's economic life. The nobility were interested in the Jews because they knew how to manage their estates in such a way as to make them pay. The petty nobility, in particular, had urgent need of the Jews for the granting of credits, and the fact that they spent the money raised in this way, not for productive ends, but for keeping up their feudal rank and dignity, did not always lead to friendly feelings towards the Jews when the time came to pay back the loans. Lastly, for the national exchequer the Jews were absolutely indispensable as taxpayers, and it was one of the main duties of the Sejm at each session to settle what taxes they should pay and, in spite of the growing impoverishment of the Jewish population, to raise them if possible.

The Jews necessarily became poorer when the merchants and artisans of the bourgeois class began to suffer from their competition and, on the plea that the Jews belonged to no class, demanded special state protection for their own class interests. Again and again the government was forced to yield to these demands, and thus, in due course, the activities of the Jews were legally restricted in all manner of ways. Incidentally, it may be mentioned that it was the German immigrants who made the most determined attack on the competition of the Jews.

The first important restriction was passed by the Diet of Piotrkow in 1538. The Jews were given a "constitution," according to which it was arranged that in future the taxes could be farmed only by members of the landed aristocracy. Trading and money-lending by Jews were also placed under various restrictions. On the demand of the clergy, moreover, they were forced to wear a distinguishing badge. Thus the Jews had already fallen victims to class interests in Poland; the various sections of the community were instrumental in imposing exceptional regulations upon them, while the magnates arrogated to themselves the right to be allowed to take Jews under their personal protection, for reasons that had nothing whatever to do with humanity or philanthropy. Sigismund I (1506–1548) somewhat testily declared that those Jews who availed themselves of this privilege would forfeit the protection of the king. "Let the Jews be protected by those *who derive some advantage from them!"*

In spite of these severe restrictions, the economic superiority of the Jews was still so great that the struggle was continued without intermission, though towards the end of the sixteenth and the beginning of the seventeenth century, as the result of the Catholic Counter-Reformation, it acquired a religious complexion under the direction of the Jesuits. And thus it became possible to commit excesses against the Jews under the cloak of religion, and the popular cry of "Vengeance for the death of Jesus!" really meant "Down with the competition of the Jews!" As a result of this twofold pressure, the Jews began to leave the towns for the country. But far from producing a solution, this merely moved the problem to another sphere, and indeed led to disastrous developments. As long as the Jews restricted their activities to working as peasants on the land, their competition was negligible, though among a peasantry deeply immersed in the medieval point of view, their position soon became precarious owing to the ever-increasing agitation of the clergy. But as licensees for the sale of wine, beer, and spirits—and in course of time this came to be their main function—they were less interested in the retailing of intoxicating liquour than in the facilities the trade afforded of acting as middlemen for the sale of peasant produce locally, and for the purchase by the peasants of goods and agricultural implements. When the law eventually forbade them to engage in these activities, 60,000 families were affected. But the law was rescinded before it had been in operation for long, because the officials themselves pointed out that the Polish peasants drank spirits, not because of the Jews, but because it was their habit to do so. Spirits continued to be produced even after 60,000 families, or about 300,000 people had been reduced to want, and in addition an equal number of Polish families had been withdrawn from agriculture to occupy taverns and public-houses. In the end, there was nobody left to carry on this middle-man trade in the rural districts. But in the world's dealings with the Jews, reason has never played a prominent part. The Polish peasant did not argue that, Jews or no Jews, he always spent a good deal of his hard-earned money on spirits, but felt resentful because his money went to the Jews. He was incapable of thinking differently.

But those peasants who lived in a state of partial or complete serfdom on the large estates of the nobility and clergy were even less able to regard the state of affairs in a rational light. Taxes and forced labour had turned them into oppressed, browbeaten, poor, and miserable wretches. In some cases they never even set eyes on their masters, but the Jewish steward or bailiff was always on the spot. And it was therefore on the man who collected their taxes and forced them to work, either on behalf of the overlord, or as his lessees, that these abject people, who yearned for better conditions, concentrated all their rebellious lust of bloodshed and murder.

And thus the peculiar position of the Jews, as determined by law, their economic oppression, and the hostility they encountered at the hands of the church, was further complicated by martyrdom which now became a constant factor in their lives. The time-honoured methods of oppression—charges of having desecrated the Host and of ritual murder—were introduced from the West both by the clergy and the German immigrants, and as they were put into practice later in the East, they survived longer than they did in the West; in fact they have survived to the present day. It would almost seem as though a religious mania were bent on working itself out to the bitter end.

The first trial for desecration of the Host took place in Posen as early as 1399, and ended in one rabbi and thirteen Jews being burned at the stake. It was curious that the Jews should always be guilty of desecrating the Host at times of unusual economic depression, or when the power of the government was weakened by political disturbances, or when the church was trying to bring some religious or political manœuvre to a successful issue. The latter was the case in the present instance. The church had assisted Jagiello of Lithuania to ascend the throne of Poland, and the results of this ecclesiastical triumph were immediately visible in the systematic destruction of the good relations that had existed up to that time between Christians and Jews in Lithuania, and the frequent occurrence of trials on the charges just mentioned. As we have already hinted, the support of the church by the German element was particularly noticeable in Cracow and Posen. Even when the government, for reasons of state, ostentatiously took the part of the Jews, as happened under Casimir, a descendant of Jagiello, the church retaliated by fomenting disturbances which ended in excesses. And this subterranean propaganda was unremitting and assumed a particularly savage form in the Polish Counter-Reformation. The entry of the Jesuits into Poland is sufficient to account for the fact that there was no end to the trials for ritual murder; in fact it might have been supposed that all the Jesuits had to do in life was to produce holy martyrs. Meanwhile, the pupils of the Jesuit seminaries carried on what might be termed a sort of guerrilla war. They organized raids, sometimes attended by bloodshed, on the Jewish population, with such methodical perseverance, that the Jewish communities were forced to buy these young heroes off, at first by means of payment in kind, but subsequently by means of a regular tax.

Such was the life of the Jews in Poland until the middle of the seventeenth century and a little later. And what means had they of surviving such an existence? An iron system of autonomy, and an iron religious discipline, which inevitably resulted in the formation of an oligarchic body of administrators and the development of an extreme form of mysticism.

The very way in which Jews from every quarter of the globe always come together, in itself contains the germ of an autonomous system. Ten men meeting together for prayer constituted a community which was subject to the same religious rules and regulations. And the presence of a rabbi immediately put them in possession of an authority capable of settling all questions of civil and religious law. Those inevitable relations with the outside world, which could not be controlled automatically by the generally accepted law of the land, made it necessary to have somebody to represent the whole community; and an administration capable of dealing both with domestic and foreign matters became an obvious necessity for every Jewish community and especially for the combined communities of a particular country.

Whereas in Germany the Jews had been unable to achieve their aim, they met with complete success in Poland. They owed this in no small measure to the co-operation of the Polish government, which was interested in them chiefly in their capacity as taxpayers. In order to avoid the circumstantial method of having to account for each individual taxpayer, it made an increasing use of the Jewish system of autonomy, and handed over to the Jews themselves the task of dividing the total sum, required to be raised by taxation, among the various persons and the various communities. To facilitate matters it endowed their administrative body with ever greater authority, until, within the limits of its powers, it actually constituted an autonomous government.

The basis of Jewish autonomy was the *Kahal,* which at first included the whole community, as well as its presiding members; subsequently it consisted only of the presiding members. Every large community had a Kahal executive, which was appointed by a complicated elective process. But the heavy responsibilities entailed, which included making the individual members of the Kahal answerable for the payment of the taxes of the whole community, and for the failure to pay of any single person, naturally led to membership in this body being confined to a group of Jews capable of representing the community, and who were above all well-to-do. Similarly it was to the interest of the state to facilitate taxation by combining several Kahals together, and creating taxation areas represented by the collective Kahal of the communities concerned. Later on, even the district Kahals were further co-ordinated by the formation of a country Kahal. This system was fully developed in 1580. Thus the country *Vaads* came into existence, the *Vaad ha'araṣoth,* and later on the Vaad of the Four Countries, called the *Vaad arba araṣoth.*

Such was the constitution of the Jewish state, planted on foreign soil, hemmed in by a wall of foreign laws, with a structure partly self-chosen and partly forced upon it. It possessed its communal authority in the Kahal executive, which controlled the administration and discharged judicial functions, and was also endowed with legislative power over the dealings of man with man within the community. It possessed its country Kahals in the Vaads, and its supreme body in the combined Vaads. It had its own Jewish law, its own priesthood, its own schools, and its own social institutions. And it had its own representatives in the Polish government, who were known as *Shtadlanim.* In fact, it possessed all the elements which go to form a state. All it lacked was the most important principle of life—that freedom of action used by a state as an instrument for securing the greatest good of its citizens. Consequently the Jewish state was destroyed as soon as the outside world regarded it as superfluous.

Within the confines of this state, the Polish Jews led a spiritual existence which was at once full and cramped. Any movement in the direction of profane science was still nipped in the bud by the ingrained caution of centuries, which clung to religious science, that is to say, to the Talmud, with ever-increasing strength and tenacity. And this Talmudic science was so successful in setting standards and giving guidance that it was able to regulate the extremely complicated existence of the Jews in this age in every conceivable situation in which they might happen to find themselves. Their form of society was based upon religious convictions, and both were essentially forced upon them. All belief was in danger of becoming petrified into outward forms and ceremonies, and that which was most characteristic of the religious attitude of the Jews—the *noblesse oblige* of their difference from others—was reduced to a minimum. The *Shulḥan Aruk* had become a sacred code, but it did not even satisfy the conservatives. Moses Isserles of Cracow (*c.* 1520–1572) criticized Karo's book for not referring to the decisions of the Ashkenazian scholars, and ignoring many customs, *minhagim,* of the German-Polish communities. He therefore produced a *mappa,* or "Table-Cloth" for Karo's "Table Prepared," and the people meekly accepted this twofold complication of their difficulties, which almost made a criminal code of the table of religious rules and regulations. Polish rabbinism made this compound work almost the sole basis of its practical and theoretical activities, and the schools indulged in an extraordinary form of dialectic known as "pilpulism," the pettifogging casuistry of which bordered on the absurd. The word pilpulism is derived from a root meaning strong pepper. The method was as follows: a disputant would advance a proposition and prove it from the Talmud. He would then proceed to prove the contrary, also from the Talmud, the object being to demonstrate that although it was contrary to the original proposition, it did not contradict it. This was a species of spiritual gymnastics which is frequently practised when men's intellects, menaced with suffocation by the pressure of the outside world, find no outlet for creative expression in real life.

But we must not forget that even this sterile trifling with the powers of the intellect was connected by one last thread with the domain of profound piety. A man does not merely form his faith, he also has the capacity to endure it. The Polish Jews realized this phenomenon in a twofold way which will be discussed in the next section.

MESSIANISM

THE man of the Middle Ages did not think historically, because he regarded the world as an accepted religious phenomenon. Religion taught him that he had only himself to save. Consequently the world did not matter to him. The medieval Jew also regarded the world as a religious phenomenon, but he thought historically. His religion and his religious consciousness taught him that he had to save not only himself but all men, the whole of mankind. Consequently everything mattered to him that was important from this point of view. He was obliged to think historically, because he was bound to regard his own fate as being connected with the great whole. This attitude of mind frequently gave way under pressure of temporary distress and trouble, and was constantly threatened by the rabbinical tendency to lay too much stress on the law. But below the surface, from the deepest springs of Jewish religious thought, the consciousness of his people's mission constantly emerged, and the hope of his being, which was to return home to Jerusalem as the beginning of the fulfilment, remained unchanged. Sometimes the hope became a paroxysm of yearning. And then this secret spring of the past, which lay hid in the depths of the present, would suddenly rise to the surface, and cut out a deep bed for itself in the soil of Jewish lives which had already been loosened and broken up by every conceivable form of suffering.

No matter how different the fate of the Jews of the Diaspora may have been in different countries, their fundamental spiritual attitude remained everywhere the same. And this homogeneity can alone explain how it came about that the vast majority of them were at one time prepared to believe that the purpose of their exile had been fulfilled, that the Messiah had come, and that they were on the eve of returning home to Jerusalem. For this belief to gain ground, however, a special stimulus made up of the cumulative effect of their suffering, torture, and martyrdom was necessary, in addition to the fundamental spiritual attitude already mentioned. In order to be able to understand this effect, we must make a brief survey of the various Jewish colonies up to the decisive year 1666.

Concentrated mass suffering, it might almost be called organized suffering, still continued to exist without abatement in the Iberian peninsula. The Marrano problem, not yet disposed of in Spain, had been introduced into Portugal, where, at the request of Ferdinand the Catholic, the Inquisition was granted the right to carry on its activities. As long as it remained a non-national institution, it worked in conjunction with the Portuguese clergy, who in their turn again exploited the ignorant masses for the purposes of their own religious policy, and met with a success in no way inferior to that of the Inquisition tribunals themselves. The monks called on the people to exterminate the Jews. At Easter 1506, when certain Marranos in Lisbon were discovered making preparations for the celebration of the Passover, the monks organized the "Blood-Marriage of Lisbon," and over 2000 Jews were killed in two days. The object of the clergy was to obtain a national Inquisition similar to that with which Spain had been favoured. The pope was quite ready to grant this, on condition that the proceedings were conducted in accordance with legal guarantees. Portugal refused; legal guarantees would jeopardize the object of the Inquisition! Charles V, whose sentiments stamped him as the first genuine Habsburg, intervened, and in May 1536 the national Inquisition was able to begin operations. It inaugurated its establishment with such a barbaric and outrageous use of torture, that even Pope Paul III lodged a protest, and the Tridentine Council was obliged to examine into the horrors that had occurred in Portugal.

The mercenary side of the Inquisition became ever more and more obvious, and eventually John III concluded an agreement with the Marranos, by the terms of which the property of the condemned was not allowed to be escheated. In return the Marranos paid him a special annual tax. But even during the sixty years of the existence of the united kingdom of Spain and Portugal (1580–1640), when the Spanish kings did everything in their power to stem the decay of Catholicism and prevent the growth of the Reformation spirit, with the object of establishing an ideal Catholic state, money still played an important part. Philip III, who was in financial difficulties, obtained 200,000 ducats from the Marranos in 1601, for granting them the right to emigrate to the Hispano-Portuguese colonies. In 1604 the Marranos purchased an amnesty for themselves for one year, for which they paid the king 1,860,000 ducats, his minister Lerma 50,000 ducats, and the members of the Supreme Council of the Inquisition 100,000 ducats. These figures explain why the Inquisition worked with such enthusiasm.

The Marranos seized every possible opportunity for escape. Very few of them became resigned and abandoned the secret practice of Judaism. The majority, with incredible heroism, clung to their faith. Their achievement was superhuman. They were surrounded by spies, and at the mercy of every calumniator. But in weighing the value of life and faith they decided in favour of faith. They were more than ready for the idea of salvation.

The Marranos who succeeded in escaping, or were allowed to emigrate, sought refuge chiefly in Turkey, Holland, and America. We have already described conditions in Turkey. The immigration of Jews as well as of Marranos into Holland began immediately after the Union of Utrecht in 1579 had proclaimed freedom of conscience for the Dutch States. It was the irony of fate that at first the Marranos were regarded with great suspicion as being papists in disguise. But when in 1596 a group of them were caught by surprise celebrating service on the great Day of Atonement, they were granted the right to profess their Judaism openly. True, as time went on, relations between the Jews and the Dutch were not entirely free from friction, but no trials either for desecration of the Host or for ritual murder were held. The Jews were subjected to certain legal restrictions, but enjoyed complete autonomy as far as their own affairs were concerned. There were some towns that refused to admit them, but, generally speaking, the Dutch were obliged to acknowledge their economic usefulness both in Holland itself and in her colonies. The Jews had no reason, therefore, to complain of their material situation. And if, notwithstanding, the idea of salvation remained alive in their hearts, it was not due to the fact that they themselves had many hardships to endure for the time being, but was inspired rather by recollections of the Marranos, from whom most of them were descended, and by the conclusions drawn from the sufferings of Jews in other countries.

The history of the Jews followed much the same course in Holland as it did elsewhere, and once more proved that for the Jews to develop spiritually beyond the bounds of their religious laws, all that was required was sheer breathing-space. The spiritual achievements of the Dutch Jews were, generally speaking, not very great, but as soon as they settled down a creative tendency at least made itself felt. They were conservative, they believed in the Talmud, they were religiously intolerant, and often made an exaggerated and unjustifiable use of the word "heretic," which they had learnt in Spain. But they produced a large number of poems and dramas. Their fundamental mood was one of lyric mysticism, as though they had seen the first ray of dawn.

We shall not yield to the temptation to claim for Judaism men of outstanding intellectual gifts, merely because they happen to have been Jews. For this reason we shall omit all discussion of a figure like that of Spinoza. All that we said about the life history of Uriel da Costa also applies to the personal fate of Spinoza. The passionate intolerance of him shown by the community of Amsterdam was both futile and foolish. The Jews had not become intolerant through pride, and what has already been said regarding the fate of the Jews sufficiently explains the reasons of this attitude towards Spinoza. The Jewish world as a whole did not, of course, attempt to enter into any discussion of Spinoza's spiritual creations. His philosophy was the work of a great isolated personality, a lonely figure in the deepest sense of the word. Bonds which are subjected to too heavy a strain readily snap, and rabbinism recognizing this, strengthened them by means of the law, while the Kabbalah reinforced them still further by turning to mystical inspiration. In Spinoza's case the bonds were broken by the man himself: Spinoza, the philosopher, was a Jew only by race. His work can lay no claim to Jewish ideology, and merely proves that the intellect of the Jew is capable of covering an extremely wide range.

The freedom enjoyed by the Jews who had fled to Holland was not shared by the Marranos who escaped or emigrated to America, which had only recently been discovered at the time. It was a Marrano who first financed Columbus's expedition and made it possible; Marranos had gone with him on his voyage of discovery, and Marranos were among the first to emigrate to the New World and settle there. But even in this virgin country they were followed by the Inquisition; even this pure and unsullied part of the world was polluted by the introduction of torture and burning at the stake. Charles V officially introduced the Inquisition into Mexico, as a weapon to be used against Marranos, Lutherans, and Calvinists. Numerous *autos-da-fé* took place between 1596 and 1602. Peru also felt the lash of the Inquisition; and Brazil, which possessed a large Jewish colony as early as the sixteenth century, suffered even more. The Jews were expelled from the country when Portugal again took possession of it after it had been for a time under Dutch rule.

In the period with which we are now dealing the condition of the Jews in Germany remained unaltered, except for the fact that here, too, they showed a tendency to move eastward into Silesia, Bohemia, and Austria, that is to say, nearer to the most thickly populated Jewish colony in the world, and nearer to disaster. The Jews in other parts of the world were kept more or less constantly on the move during this period as the result of expulsion from one country or another. This happened in Mecklenburg in 1492, where during the course of a trial for desecration of the Host twenty-seven Jews were sent to the stake, and also in the Mark of Brandenburg where, on a similar charge, numbers of Jews died under torture and thirty-eight were burned to death in 1510. For thirty years after this happened, the Diet of Princes at Frankfurt was occupied in investigating the affair. The informer in the case confessed to a priest that the charges he had made were false. In the interests of justice the priest wished to make his crime public, but his superior, the Bishop of Spandau, would not allow him to break the seal of the confessional. Tortured by pangs of conscience, the priest became a convert to Protestantism, in order to be free to speak. And Melanchthon reported the whole matter to the Diet of Princes in question.

For a short time the Jews of Germany thought they saw signs of a change in the spiritual attitude of those about them, which led them to hope for a larger measure of freedom and more humane treatment. The harsh, narrow-minded, haughty and rigid attitude of mind and way of life, which, in keeping with tradition, we have termed medieval, was giving way to a more differentiated, more thoughtful, and therefore more critical, sceptical, and humanistic view of the world. Men were beginning to rebel against the constant exaggerated despotism of religion as embodied in the Catholic Church, being urged thereto both subjectively and objectively; subjectively, because they longed for freedom, and objectively because they were anxious to co-ordinate and classify the sum of human experience in a methodical and scientific manner. In the Jewish world the struggle of Reuchlin against the Dominicans was fought to a finish.

A certain Jewish renegade, named Johann Pfefferkorn, of Moravia, a butcher by trade, who had been expelled from his own parish for burglary, was incited by the Dominicans of Cologne to write pamphlets against the Talmud, more particularly the famous *Judenspiegel* (Mirror of the Jews). Through the mediation of the nun Kunigund, the sister of the Emperor Maximilian, he was given authority to examine Jewish literature to find out whether it contained any offensive allusions to Christianity (August 1509). The Jews of Frankfurt, however, refused to hand over their books to this Christian convert, and lodged a protest with the emperor, and the latter appointed a commission of experts, of whom Reuchlin was one, to examine into the matter. The majority of the commission, and above all Hochstraten, the judge of the Inquisition of Cologne, were unequivocally in favour of burning the whole of Jewish literature, and above all the Talmud. But Reuchlin, who was perhaps the only and certainly the greatest authority among them on Hebrew language and literature, was opposed to the measure. His reasons were based on insight, reason, and humanity, and also on the view that Christianity would be better employed in fighting its spiritual opponents with spiritual weapons instead of with the naked fist. Incidentally he lost no opportunity of having a sly dig at the Dominicans and their intellectual assistant Pfefferkorn. But this landed him in a hornet's nest of obscurantists, and a frenzied literary dispute ensued from which he emerged victorious. The details of the struggle do not concern us here, for it soon ceased to have any connexion with the Jews and their literature, but became concentrated on a problem which was awaiting solution within the Catholic Church itself. This problem was, should intellectual conviction be allowed free expression, or should all progress be most violently resisted by fanaticism? The episode is important for Jewish history only in so far as Reuchlin's victory might possibly have led to a more liberal and tolerant treatment of the Jewish question. The Reformation, too, at first aroused similar fond hopes.

In 1523 Luther's pamphlet, *That Jesus Christ Was Born a Jew,* was published. Luther regarded it as necessary to remind his friends of this, and to call attention to the fact that the Jews were kinsmen, cousins, and brothers of the Saviour, and that God had entrusted the

Holy Scriptures to their care and keeping. "If we wish to help them, we must act towards them according to the law of Christian and not of papal love," he declared.

Such words after twelve hundred years of political Christianity, uttered for the first time with so much fervour, caused people to think, and made them wonder whether the Reformation was not at last to bring about a return to Christianity as a religion of love. Possibly some such return was implicit in the fundamental idea of the Reformation, just as outwardly it constituted a resolute return to the Bible, where there was no mention of popes or of priests as the sole means to salvation, or of confession or of absolution. It quickly transpired, however, that these words were not a spontaneous expression of opinion; they were merely intended to serve a purpose—the mission. By the word "help" Luther understood precisely what the Catholic Church had understood for centuries—namely baptism. And just as primitive Christianity soon met its doom in the Catholic Church, so the idea of the Reformation, which was not the outcome of religious motives alone, was also soon appropriated by a church. To the Jew this meant that he was once more confronted by a religion out for power and dominion, and he was now attacked by both the Catholic and the Protestant Churches. Luther himself, when he perceived the futility of his missionary propaganda, was the first to set the example, and wrote a number of treatises against the cousins and brothers of the Saviour (*Letter against the Sabbatarians, Concerning the Jews and Their Lies, Concerning the Shem Ha-Mephorash*), in which hardly a single argument which had already been used by the Catholic Church, from the poisoning of wells to ritual murder, was omitted. Their tone is so coarse that the Swiss reformer Bullinger declared that they must have been written by a swineherd instead of by a famous shepherd of souls. At all events little of the wide measure of freedom that the Reformation eventually bestowed on the Christian world came the way of the Jews. On the contrary, Saxony and Hesse, the German states which led the movement, also played a foremost part in fighting the Jews, and it was not without reason that Charles V was obliged, in two charters of 1544 and 1546, to forbid the holding of trials for ritual murder.

The chief feature of this and the following century in the history of the Jews in Germany, Austria, Bohemia, and Moravia was the sinister instability of their condition. They were constantly migrating and being driven out, returning and again being expelled. The Thirty Years War at least secured for them the certainty of being allowed to remain in one place; for at a time when such vast sums were required for war, the Jews were indispensable, and concern about their ability to pay necessarily involved concern about their welfare. But all this was of little importance; it could not wipe out memories of the past, or give a new direction to hopes for the future. On the contrary, it was precisely the spiritual atmosphere of the German ghetto, the discipline imposed by the martyrdom of centuries, which gradually conquered the Jewish world and, in conjunction with the principles of the Kabbalah, created such an abysmal pessimism that at the slightest shock it was bound to merge into its opposite, into optimism. It never gave rise to resignation or despair, or led to surrender. The Jew does not surrender. He has the capacity to live. This constitutes the "materialism" for which he is constantly reviled.

Two very important events played a decisive part in making the spiritual outlook of the Jews more profound. The first was the invention of printing. The Jews immediately made extensive use of this innovation, and the popular work began to take the place of the precious manuscript. Written in the language of everyday life, the Judæo-German vernacular, it was printed in Hebrew characters. The Bible, the works of the prophets, the Psalms, and the narrative and poetical portions of the Talmud, which had been *studied* in the schools, were now *read* at home. Sympathetic interest in the circumstances and events of their past, which was really their present, acquired an intimacy which turned the collective into an individual experience. Through the popularization of the Book—and this constitutes the second important event—the Jewish woman, for the first time in the history of the Diaspora, was drawn into the sphere of religious experience; she was given access to the fundamental facts of history and knowledge, and was placed in a position to build up her emotional life for herself on the sagas, narratives, and poems which were presented to her. And this alone made it possible for each separate Jewish house in the ghetto to become the sounding-board of the coming Messianic movement.

The event which inaugurated this movement and caused latent Messianism to burst out and become a reality, was the disaster which overtook the Jews of Poland in 1648. We have already shown how the Jews in Poland became the victims of class interests, and the extent to which their fate was bound up in the latter. But as though this were not enough, they also became involved in the strained relations that arose between the nobility and the serfs, as well as between the Polish Catholics and the Russian Orthodox Christians. The dominion of the kingdom of Poland and of the Polish nobility had for about two hundred years extended to the Ukraine, the basins of the Dnieper and the Dniester, with Kiev as the centre, Volhynia and Podolia in the west, and Chernigov and Poltava in the east. This territory was treated like a conquered province, both the king and the nobility deriving enormous wealth from the unrestricted exploitation of the people, who were reduced to a position of serfdom. In addition to this, rancorous and fanatical religious hatred also separated master and slave. Although both were Christians, the Poles were Catholics and the Russians of the Ukraine were members of the Orthodox Greek Church. This difference which was really only a variation of the same creed, led to mortal hatred, and the revolts which eventually broke out among the oppressed Ukrainians were not only due to economic but also to religious reasons. They rose up against their Polish oppressors, the *Pans,* on the ground that they were "infidels" as well as tyrants.

But in the Jew they were also confronted by a man who bore the stigma of both infidel and tyrant. He was not only the typical infidel, he was above all the man whom the Pan was fond of choosing to be the administrator and lessee of his estates. Whereas the ground landlord hardly ever made his appearance, the Jew was always on the spot. He was the symbol of oppression, although he was as little connected with it as a stick is connected with the person who hits out with it. Thus the battle-cry of the insurrection became "Down with the Pans and the Jews!"

In these revolts the Cossacks took the lead. Half peasant, half warrior, their communities had long been in existence in the Ukraine, having been formed with the object of protecting the country against the Tatars, who, from the neighbouring steppe, were constantly pouring into the calm and cultivated lands on the western banks of the rivers. In close touch with these Cossack communities were the Zaporozhian Cossacks on the farther side of the Dnieper rapids, who had retained complete independence. They played a leading part in the Ukrainian revolts, acting as a sort of national army or as outposts of the allies.

The revolt opened as early as 1637 with an invasion of the district of Poltava. Ten years later, in 1648, it was resumed after a period of thorough preparation. The movement had secured a leader in the person of the Hetman, Bogdan Chmielnicki, who had entered into an alliance with his former foes, the Tatars. Whereas the latter were interested only in robber raids, Chmielnicki had a programme; he aimed at the propagation of the only true Greek Orthodox faith, at obtaining freedom for the Cossacks and Ukrainians, and, as a means thereto, at exterminating the Poles and the Jews.

These bands, inured to warfare, advanced with rare dash and impetus, and the Polish army of defence was driven back in two battles. The peasants of the Ukraine then rose up in rebellion, and the territory east of the Dnieper, the district of Kiev, Volhynia, and Podolia, were in a state of open insurrection. The programme of the insurgents was most conscientiously carried out, but was marred by the most bestial and unbridled barbarity. They went mad with lust for blood and rape and, abysmally ignorant in matters of religion, vented their fury on their enemies. Once more horror was heaped on horror and countless thousands were massacred, mutilated, maimed, and burned alive, in the name of religion. These maniacal hordes became intoxicated by the cry of "Baptism or Death!" It was like a magic formula. If a Jew followed them declaring that henceforward he would be a Christian, they even forgot to rob him. But if he refused to walk in the footsteps of these apostles of faith, he was subjected to tortures before which the horrors of the Spanish Inquisition paled and appeared like the work of incompetent amateurs. Chronicles of this period contain reports of scenes which even the most hardened cannot read without a shudder. Needless to say, in all but a few exceptional cases the Jews refused to be baptized. In spite of the destruction of hundreds of their communities, the massacre of their children, the rape and murder of their women, the Jews refused to become Christians, but remained true to their God and their great heritage. The *qiddush ha-shem,* the hallowing of the divine Name, meant far more to them than life itself. Thousands at a time accepted death by martyrdom; 6000 in Nemirov, 15,000 at Tulczyn, 2000 in Homel, hundreds in Polonnoya, and so on throughout the whole area of the insurrection. Those who succeeded in escaping with their lives fled, sick and ruined, half mad with fear and horror, through the country, and over the frontier into Austria, Germany, Holland, Italy, and even Turkey.

All this took place in the few months between April and September 1648. The number of Jews killed even during this short period exceeded 200,000. This does not include those who were taken prisoner; for the Tatars in particular, who, in spite of their bad reputation, were harmless and peace-loving folk compared with the Cossacks, confined themselves for the most part to taking Jews prisoner, in the hope of obtaining ransoms. The fugitives and the Jews who had been ransomed through the instrumentality of organizations specially formed for the purpose, spread all over the rest of the Jewish world, and provided witnesses of this Polish martyrdom. But the terror was not over; it had only been interrupted. The newly elected king, Jan Casimir, forced Chmielnicki to retreat and compelled him to sign a treaty of peace. After which the Jews were left undisturbed for five years. With heroic determination, they began to rebuild their administration and their communities, and to start life afresh. But in the midst of their efforts, the curtain rose on the second act of the tragedy. Chmielnicki, not satisfied with what he had achieved, made an alliance with the Tsar, Alexius Mikhailovich, and the two opened the attack in the summer of 1654. The new battle-cry was "For Russia and the Orthodox Faith!" Massacres of Jews again took place, on the ground that they were not Orthodox Christians. There were countless victims, the number of which increased when Charles X (Gustavus) of Sweden invaded Poland in 1655. He treated the Jews well, and their attitude to him was correspondingly loyal. But the Poles, who had hitherto been fighting the Jews in every conceivable way, suddenly expected them to adopt a nationalist and patriotic attitude, and because they were not ready to be killed by the Swedes as well, they were branded as traitors, and massacred by the Poles when the latter rebelled against Sweden, under the national "saviour" Stephen Czarniecki. In the struggle with the Jews the Poles altogether surpassed the Cossacks in bestiality.

Estimates of the number of Jews killed vary from 300,000 to 600,000. About 700 communities were entirely wiped out, or had only one or two members left. In eastern Ukraine not a single Jew was left alive. In Volhynia and Podolia nine-tenths had either fled or been killed or carried into captivity. The Jewish centre in Poland was annihilated. So deeply were the Jews affected by this blow that they called the catastrophe the Third Ḥurban, or the third destruction of the Temple.

The Jews met this national misfortune with the full fervour of their religious spirit and deep historical sense. They accounted for their suffering, as they had always done before; it had been sent to purify the individual and make him worthy of salvation. *Ḥeble Mashiaḥ,* the pains heralding the birth of the Messiah, constituted the essence of the idea. But in this case they connected the suffering they had undergone with the present, and the immediate future. As the result of various calculations on the part of the Kabbalists, the rumour had been spread that the Messianic epoch was to begin precisely in the year 1648, and it was readily believed. The Polish massacre of this year, terrible as it had been, was a confirmation, almost a ground for hope. The fact that the year went by without any sign of salvation, and that the Jews were once again exposed to ruthless massacres, raised their hopes to an ecstasy of expectation.

Communities in whom expectation and desire reach such a pitch of intensity are bound to produce from their midst a man who is the creation of this collective longing, and whom they accept as the redeemer and fulfiller of their hopes, as the leader. And Jewish history presents us with such a man in the person of Sabbatai Zevi of Smyrna.

Sabbatai was a member of one of those Jewish communities which, after the great immigration of the Sephardic Jews in 1492, had been formed in the East under the influence of a rabbinism which had grown ever more conservative, and of the gradual acceptance of the teaching of the practical Kabbalah. He was an apt, not to say brilliant pupil, and while he was still a mere youth was given the title of Hakam, or wise man. He was, however, a confirmed egoist, who made himself the centre of everything, and only began to understand a thing when he had brought it into some relation with himself. Such natures were rare among the Jews of that period. True, owing to the acceptance of the idea of the Chosen People, and of salvation, the Jewish world was Judæocentric, and the Jews could interpret everything that happened only from the standpoint of themselves as the centre. But this was a collective attitude; the individual Jew saw things to some extent with the eyes of the Jewish world, not with his own. And this explains why men who saw things solely and entirely with their own eyes, whose imaginations stubbornly refused to project anything except their own view of the world, made such a deep impression on the Jews, more particularly when this individual view of the world presented itself in the garb of the collective idea, common to all.

It was for this reason that Sabbatai was able in his very earliest days, and in his own native city, to collect about him a group of people who respected him as a man of extraordinary accomplishments and gifts. A further reason for his influence lay in the intensity with which he gave himself up to the study of the Kabbalah, and his ecstatic and imaginative manner of giving interpretations and making promises; for in this way he appealed precisely to the emotional side of the Jewish nature, which had always been neglected under the pressure of rabbinism. For the whole of the Kabbalah, even its theoretical side, was really nothing more than an outlet for the starved universal sympathies of the Jews.

Both the natural sense of his ego and his ecstatic imagination, however, became increasingly subordinated to his growing will to power, which, though it was uncalculating, was also unrestrained and uncontrolled. The influence his personality invariably exerted always provided fresh justification for his will to power; and he was probably unaware that his personal charm, that dazzling and eccentric quality, which in his case seemed genuine, had its necessary physical basis in the obviously homosexual nature of his being. But the balance of the effect he produced was not his work at all, but lay in the readiness of an age and a people to accept anybody who declared himself to be the Messiah.

In the circle of young men whom Sabbatai had collected about him by the time he was eighteen, he already played a part which was vaguely recognized as that of leader. But though ostensibly their teacher in science and Kabbalistic mysteries, he conveyed by various vague and secret signs that he already intended to become their leader in an even loftier and wider sense. Gradually this became more plainly defined as the wish to become their leader along the path of mystical salvation, which his profound and, in his own opinion, exclusive and intimate knowledge of Kabbalistic ideas enabled him to do. When such an idea of leadership and guidance matures, it almost inevitably develops into the materialization of the figure, which, even in the Kabbalah, is regarded as the embodiment and at the same time the releaser of all liberating forces: the Messiah.

At first Sabbatai proclaimed himself only hesitatingly by an avowal which implied nothing more than the desire to advance along the mystic path of salvation. But reports which reached him of what was taking place in the outside world first brought him into touch with reality and led him to see that no spiritual, mystical, and religious emancipation of the Jews could be conceived apart from their national emancipation. He heard of the events which had happened in Poland in the year 1648; through his father, who had become the agent of an English firm, he was told of certain currents of thought in the Christian world, which, on the authority of the Book of Revelation, was expecting the beginning of the Millennium in the year 1666; he also knew the doctrine of the *Ḥeble Mashiaḥ* and the Kabbalistic computations which fixed precisely the year 1648 as the beginning of the era of salvation. Unable by means of a single spontaneous gesture to offer himself, and yet already incapable of interpreting what was going on in the Jewish world, except with himself as the centre and pivot, he gave expression to his vague uneasiness in what might be called a preparatory manifestation. Towards the end of 1648, in the middle of a religious service, he stepped on to the *alemor* of the synagogue and pronounced the full name of God, the *Shem ha-mephorash,* in a loud voice, above the murmured prayers of the congregation. This name, as long as the Temple had been in existence, was allowed to be pronounced only by the high priest, and in the *Galuth* only by martyrs, and at the end of days—only by the Messiah.

But the Jews in the synagogue at Smyrna did not understand him, or refused to understand him, perhaps because they knew him too well as a familiar everyday figure; or possibly because they were terrified of a sudden fulfilment. The rabbis and scholars of the town followed all Sabbatai's movements with the utmost suspicion, more particularly his activities among the common people, the working men, fisherfolk, and galley-slaves. They were suspicious of him not on the ground that he was making a secret claim to the office of Messiah, but as an agitator, who was putting fantastic notions into the heads of his followers, and inciting them to acts of insubordination in which the idea of the Messiah played a vague but all the more disquieting part. They therefore decided, in order to be rid of his mischievous personality, to pronounce the ban against him.

To escape the effects of this ban, Sabbatai set out on his travels, and remained away for a number of years. He visited Constantinople and Salonica, and frequently went to Cairo, Gaza, Aleppo, and Jerusalem, always endeavouring to play a part which, with its gestures and poses, might lead people to guess its real nature. At a banquet in Salonica he confronted the rabbis with the request that they should celebrate his marriage with the Torah. This led to his being advised to resume his travels as quickly as possible. In Constantinople he wandered about the streets with a fish which he had laid in a basket like a baby in a cradle, and explained to the curious that Israel was to be saved under the zodiacal sign of Pisces. The rabbis sent a schoolmaster to him to call him to reason, and, when Sabbatai proved refractory, the man simply thrashed him. But such painful episodes did not disturb Sabbatai. His inability to attach the true value to the realities of life prevented him from seeing that such incidents were the outcome of foolish or eccentric behaviour, and he interpreted them as constituting part of the suffering which, according to the Jewish point of view, the Messiah was at first bound to endure.

But wherever he went, he always succeeded in finding one or two people who were sympathetic towards him and to whom he confided that he was really the Messiah. These various secret confessions gradually formed a series of links connecting the places he visited on his wanderings, which for a while merely constituted a loose network of friends, adherents, and believers. In the beginning Sabbatai's idea that he was the Messiah was certainly no more than a wish-thought, but this fancy, reflected in his environment and meeting with occasional response, gradually developed into a real belief in his mission. Even this belief, however, was at first weak and hesitating, and did not allow him to go beyond making symbolic suggestions and secret communications to isolated individuals here and there. But the age was so overflowing with eagerness to receive what he had to offer it, that he inevitably came in contact with people whose response to him and his alleged mission was sufficiently strong to give him every encouragement and relieve him of all hesitation in the professions he made, until at last the difference between fact and fiction was so far obliterated in his mind that the time at last arrived when he became firmly convinced that he really was the Messiah.

Among his adherents there were four men in particular who sealed his fate, each in his own way, by giving him something decisive. There was Abraham Jachini, the Kabbalist of Constantinople, who presented him with an ancient manuscript which he declared he had found in a cave and which purported to contain a prophecy that Sabbatai would come. This document was a forgery, as Sabbatai was well aware. He made no use of it himself, but allowed others to use it as a proof of his Messiahship. In Cairo, Raphael Joseph Chelebi, a tax-farmer and Master of the Mint, a well-known and immensely wealthy man, and a pious mystic, became his whole-hearted disciple and advocate, and his friendship proved an important factor in increasing Sabbatai's following. In Gaza, Sabbatai actually found his herald, his "Prophet," in one Nathan Ashkenasi, also called Nathan Gazati, who believed in him heart and soul, and was completely overwhelmed by a torrent of mystic thought and the force of his secret hopes of salvation. He sent circular letters all over the Jewish world, declaring that Sabbatai was the Messiah, and succeeded in creating a ferment of expectation. The fourth was Samuel Primo, who modestly called himself Sabbatai's secretary. But he was something more than a secretary. He was Sabbatai's mouthpiece, a master of passionate eloquence, who turned every hint let drop by Sabbatai into a manifesto. Eventually he made Sabbatai's assumption of the role of Messiah so patent, that retreat was impossible. But at the very end his efforts were all in vain!

Urged forward in this way, partly by his own desires and partly by the impetus behind him, turned from half-doubts to firm belief, and forced into reality by his unbridled ambitions, this Messiah arose, whose assumption of the role was the result of all these combined influences and not the outcome of a simple need of his heart, prompted by a profound and irresistible belief in his calling. The Jewish world at that time still believed in a personal Messiah, and as the result of its abysmal suffering and extreme readiness, it was filled with uncontrollable longing for the saviour, and accepted this man, of whom all it could understand was his stirring declarations, but not his spiritual development or the nature of his soul.

Towards the end of 1665, after an absence of almost eighteen years, Sabbatai returned to Smyrna. His appearance, as it were, put the match to a magazine of explosives long since prepared, and kept dry and compressed by means of constant news, rumours, and legends about him. Tumultuous demonstrations of joy took place; men and women fell into religious ecstasies and convulsions, and gave utterance to prophecies; and, convinced that a terrible past was about to inaugurate a glorious future, the people gave vent to pent-up emotions that could no longer be controlled. Hailed as the Messiah by the majority of the population of Smyrna, Sabbatai resolved to start on the work of salvation by dethroning the Sultan of Turkey, under whose rule the Holy Land had fallen. The last possible moment for the deed had arrived. After the year 1648 had passed by without incident, Sabbatai declared that the year 1666, which the Christians believed would inaugurate the Millennium, was to be the year of salvation, and on the 30th of December 1665, he set off on his journey to Constantinople. Before leaving, he distributed the crowns of the world among his friends.

Denounced in advance by anxious Jews in Constantinople, and destined by the Turkish government to the gallows as a rebel, he was arrested on landing and taken to the debtors' jail. But, strange to say, nothing happened to him! His fame as the Messiah, which attracted crowds of people to see him, paralysed even the resolution of the government; for Islam, too, was not unfamiliar with the idea of a saviour. With a view to cutting off Sabbatai from his followers, he was transferred to the fortress of Abydos in Gallipoli. But the result was the exact opposite of what the officials had expected. In a trice, the prison was transformed into a royal residence, to which representatives from all the Jewish settlements flocked, and before long it was furnished with the utmost luxury through gifts sent from every corner of the globe. Here Sabbatai sat enthroned, at the zenith of his power, the ruler over hundreds of thousands, who only awaited a sign from him. He only had to say the word, and they changed their day of deepest mourning, the 9th of Ab, into a day of feasting and rejoicing; they did penance and chastised themselves in order to be worthy of the salvation that was at hand; they liquidated all their businesses, and sold their goods and chattels, in order to be ready for the journey home to Palestine. And there he set enthroned, in a position no Jew had occupied for 1600 years, and allowed the time to slip through his fingers, as it must inevitably slip through the fingers of any man whose motives have not been dictated by eternal and ineluctable truth. It was a Polish Kabbalist, one Nehemiah ha-Kohen, whom he had summoned to him in the hope of obtaining from him the conclusive confirmation of his Messiahship, who sealed his doom.

He cannot be said to have exposed him, for Sabbatai lacked the resolution to be a cheat and a charlatan. But behind his passionate exterior Nehemiah discovered a man who had usurped an office for the sake of personal aggrandizement. It had not come to him as a revelation. Only in this sense did he expose the "false" Messiah. And he had no hesitation in sacrificing him for the sake of the whole people, who could not expect even spiritual or political guidance from such a usurper. He denounced him to the Turkish government as a "false Messiah."

Sabbatai was taken to Adrianople. But even now, when there was no longer any need to fear him as the Messiah, the colossal movement he had created was all the more to be dreaded, and the Turkish government was anxious to make both him and his movement innocuous without endowing the latter with a fresh impetus by creating a martyr in Sabbatai. It was a plan suggested by a renegade Jew, named Guidon, one of the Sultan's physicians, that achieved this object. He confronted Sabbatai with the alternative of either putting his Messiahship to the test by a most cruel form of martyrdom, or else of becoming converted —if he liked, it might be only pretence—to Islam. Sabbatai, who expected everything from his office without being able to give anything in return, found himself utterly powerless to vindicate it now. In deadly fear for his life, all he could do was once more to look after his own skin. The result was that in the middle of November 1666 he was converted to Islam with full pomp and ceremony, and received the name of Mehmet Effendi. He was appointed a seraglio chamberlain to the sultan and was paid a substantial monthly salary. Thus he vanished behind the walls of the seraglio.

This proved the death-blow to the Messianic movement. It survived for a little while longer because it resolutely refused to accept this appalling incident as true, and insisted upon interpreting what had happened allegorically by declaring that it was not the Messiah who had become a Mohammedan, but his phantom; it also gave itself a brief respite by advancing the recondite plea that, in order to redeem mankind and save them from their sins, the Messiah must needs become guilty of every transgression and play an active part in every religion. Sabbatai's conversion to Islam therefore constituted a step towards fulfilment. A good many of his followers not only understood this argument but also felt it their duty to imitate their Messiah and adopt the turban. As a result of this revival of the movement, Sabbatai himself was inspired with fresh hope. But he now began to play a contemptible double game, and, advancing the argument just stated, urged his followers to become converted to Islam. At the same time he led the Turkish government to believe that his aim was to win as many Jews as possible to Islam. He had become a low and despicable conspirator, who was ultimately banished to Dulcigno in Albania, where, broken and abandoned by all, he died in the autumn of 1675.

But the Sabbataian movement did not by any means come to an end with the death of its originator. On the contrary, it was only then that its decisive effects began to be felt, though they did not take the form of a great upheaval associated with his name. For the memory of this far from perfect Messiah faded comparatively fast, and it was perfectly evident that the disturbances of these years were not connected with him but with the life problems of the Jewish people. Sabbatai's personal followers split up into two groups which followed different directions. One group believed that he really was the Messiah and would return, and that his example should be followed in everything, even to conversion to Islam. This movement created a new generation of Marranos, known as Dönmehs, who in public behaved as Turks, but had their own private conventicles in which they observed Jewish customs, and carried on existence under the spell of misguided ideas of mysicism. They exist to this day.

The other group of his personal followers regarded his conversion to Islam as an isolated event which they were not called upon to imitate, and which was purely the Messiah's personal affair. But it was precisely these Sabbataians, who remained within the fold of Judaism, who exercised the greatest influence, and for a hundred years Judaism was engaged in a desperate struggle against the disturbances and dangers for which they were responsible, and which did not find expression in concrete historical events, but in something far stronger and more important—in influencing the ideology of Judaism. The historical events connected with them were merely outward and visible signs of the ideas that had been set in motion. The fact that both in the East and the West, the Jewish authorities hurled ban after ban against the Sabbataians, and that the whole of the Jewish world gradually became torn in two regarding them, had nothing to do with either approval or disapproval of Sabbatai's followers; the whole trouble was really over the consequences to which the development and elaboration of the Kabbalah gave rise, during the turbulent period of the Sabbataian age. The whole of Judaism was involved, because, in the seventeenth century, all Jewry was Kabbalistic. In this century, it had no other fundamental ideology, except that of the Kabbalah, and to wave aside the Kabbalah as the aberration of one or two eccentrics is to give an entirely false idea of the times. Only by making the Kabbalistic ideology the central point, can one understand the course of Jewish history with all its extremes, from narrow and exaggerated rabbinism, to the Christianizing Frankists, from the mystical religiosity of the Ḥasidim, to the passionate but dead world of law conceived by a man like Mendelssohn.

The doctrines of Kabbalism when fully developed attacked three of the chief elements of Judaism—the idea of God, Messianism, and morality, the latter not in its secular but in its religious, ethical sense. We have already shown that the creation of the Kabbalah was a necessity for Judaism, as a vent for its starved universal sympathies. But it is also clear that as soon as these emotions were given a theoretical basis, the latter was destined to be still further elaborated and developed. The original conception of God and His emanations was still clear and lucid, but as the result of its elaboration by the school of Safed, and also, above all, in the Lurian Kabbalah, the ten Sephiroth were multiplied into a host of emanations, forces, radiations, influences, and mystical spheres of their own. Amid all this tangled undergrowth of mysteries the wisest and most learned could no longer find God or see what He had to do with this world. Between God and this sphere of mystical mythology there was little if any connexion, and it became necessary to start afresh and build some sort of bridge between them.

Two attempts were made to achieve this object, one by the school that had emanated from the Sabbataian movement, with Abraham

Michael Cardozo as the central figure, and the other by the Ḥasidist movement.

Cardozo's doctrine, unlike Ḥasidism, did not lead to a mass movement, or enjoy the tangible material success that Ḥasidism did. It worked more subterraneously, but precisely on that account constituted a danger which immediately provoked the bitter and passionate opposition of official Judaism. The basis of his doctrine was nothing more or less than the abandonment of the idea of one absolute God. He did not regard God as the starting-point of all power, of all the Sephiroth; but went further back to a "First Cause," *Sibbah rishonah,* an original force, of which all that could be said was that it existed and was the ultimate cause of *everything,* and that it could be grasped by all by the light of pure reason alone, without the help of revelation. It was this First Cause, he declared, which was worshipped alike by pagans, Mohammedans, and Christians. But it ought not to be worshipped, since it was no more than a cause, an original force. Its first product, however, was the "God of Israel," the *Elohe Yisrael,* who was the sole creator of the universe, and alone guided the destinies of the Children of Israel. But whereas the *Sibbah rishonah* was a unity, God was androgynous. In conjunction with the *Shekinah,* which was also divine, he constituted a dynamic whole. Thus with one fell sweep he did away with the mass of mystical creations that had sprung up, and once more opened up the path for the concept of God; nevertheless he revealed Him as an elaborately concealed duality; far from being fundamentally monotheistic, He was akin to the God of Christian Gnosticism. The Kabbalistic world was saved; but God was lost!

This view of an androgynous God-Creator and his dynamic wholeness became the basis of the doctrine of salvation. According to Cardozo this true God was worshipped up to the time of the destruction of the Temple, after which dire confusion arose, and the Jewish concept of God became obscured. The Jews then began to worship not the God-Creator, but the *Sibbah rishonah,* and were no better than the pagans, inasmuch as they too worshipped a force that could be grasped by the light of reason alone without the help of revelation, and which was therefore bereft of the "mystery" of faith. The great "Secret of Faith," *raza deʿmehemanutha,* was mentioned by the wise men of old, in the book of the Zohar, which could be read with understanding in the Diaspora only by him who read with his "face uncovered." But with the advent of the Messiah the secret would be revealed to all; for the Messiah would unveil it and make it visible, not by means of any revelation vouchsafed him, but by his own perception alone, by a simple feat of rational thought. An astonishing conclusion! Thus the world of profoundest mysticism gave birth to the idea of the Messiah as "a radical rationalist."

The development of this idea of the Messiah could not remain uninfluenced by the fact that the world had witnessed Sabbatai's conversion to another faith. The interpretation put upon this by Sabbatai's faithful followers as soon as their master's apostasy became known, namely that he had been converted because, if the Messiah was to save all peoples and all forms of religion, he must become one with all peoples and all forms of religion, was intimately connected by Cardozo with the idea of a mission, which occupies such a prominent position in the Lurian Kabbalah. Just as it was the mission of every individual man to save that spark of "Original Light" that had fallen into the clutches of corrupt matter, so it was also the mission of the Messiah. But whereas the ordinary man could save only that spark which he encountered within the narrow compass of his own life, the Messiah could save every spiritual spark wherever it was to be found among any nationality under the sun. Consequently the Messiah had to go among all peoples; this was also necessary to wash away the sins of the Jewish people. For proof of this Cardozo turned to the same quarter as Christianity did for the proof of its Messiah, to the 53rd chapter of the Book of Isaiah. Incidentally, he did not regard Sabbatai as the Messiah of the house of David who was to save the world, but as his forerunner, the suffering Messiah of the house of Ephraim.

But Cardozo's doctrine had an even deeper and more vital influence on the everyday religious life of the Jews, and on their view of morality and ethics, than it had on the transformation of this concept of Judaism. The Lurian Kabbalah itself had already set out from the proposition that, in themselves, a man's actions were neither good nor bad, and that they became important only when he was confronted by his real mission, the salvation of the spark of "Original Light"; for it was only then that he returned to his original spiritual form, to Adam Qadmon. This was the sole purpose of the laws and prohibitions of the Torah, and the whole of man's life was subject to this purpose. But life was not the interval between birth and death, it was only the interval necessary for man to fulfil his mission. And Cardozo draws the logical conclusion from this idea, which is full of cosmic significance, by asking the simple question whether a man could fulfil his mission by carrying it out step by step, deed by deed, or whether he fulfilled it as a whole, straight away in its entirety. The answer to this question reveals the crisis that had supervened in the spiritual world of Judaism. Moral existence was no longer conceived as a great unity, lying implicit in the all-embracing idea of a theocracy, but as a piece of work which could be performed gradually bit by bit. When a man had accomplished a portion of his allotted task, enough had been done for the time being and for all eternity, and, if he ever returned through the process of metempsychosis, it was only to complete the still unfinished portions of his task. Thus even the greatest sin ceased to be a sin. But as this view led to dangerous freedom and laxity in the sphere of morality and religion, Cardozo introduced a safeguard against the dangerously disintegrating tendency of his doctrine, which revealed the weakness in his grand original conception, by declaring that the ordinary man did not know at which stage of existence he stood; he did not know what part of his task he had already accomplished and what there still remained for him to do. This meant that his life was no longer based on the strength of his ethical will resting on God, but that he lived in a state of uncertainty, doubt, and insecurity, with the word "perhaps" ever on his lips. But this was tantamount to doing away with the knowledge of any motive for a religious life. It meant the death of the Kabbalistic world, and it was now that the old Jewish doctrine of revelation became metamorphosed into a chimera in the hands of the consistent mystic.

We have given this somewhat lengthy description of Sabbataian doctrine, not for theological but for historical reasons. For herein, as we have already pointed out, lie the seeds of the great though short-lived religious revival of Ḥasidism, as well as of the catastrophic decline of Jewish thought in the age of Jewish emancipation.

By refusing to accept this development of the Kabbalah, Judaism was necessarily confined to the Kabbalah in the form in which it had existed before. But western Judaism could not possibly do this. For the Jews of the West were not all herded together in a great mass, like the Jews of the East. But a mass, in the sense of a real community, both as regards numbers and thought and sentiment, was the first prerequisite for the development of the idea of Messianism as a communal problem, as a collective and universal thought. Consequently, the Jews of the West inevitably lost the Kabbalah, with the result that they eventually came to lack anything in the nature of a clear-cut religious idea, and either had nothing with which to oppose so-called "enlightenment," or the process of assimilation to the egregious products of western civilization, or else merely the inadequate weapon of traditional unity, that is to say, the idea of a mission tinctured with liberalism.

Like every other spiritual movement of the Jews in the Diaspora, the one with which we are now dealing was also largely subject to the pressure of environment and of conditions at the time. This was more especially the case in Poland, which, although its Jewish population had been cruelly decimated, still constituted the mass-centre of Judaism. But most of its vital energy was absorbed in the sheer struggle for existence, for the reconstruction of the community that had been shattered by the Cossack massacres was an extremely arduous undertaking. Not only had the loss in men, money, occupation, and organizations to be made good, but the survivors had also to hold their ground against ever-increasing pressure from all sides. Poland was just recovering from the attacks of the Cossacks, Tatars, Russians, and Swedes, and the Poles regarded reconstruction as synonymous with an intensification of class distinctions and a violent clerical reaction. The old conditions were revived; the nobility despised the bourgeoisie; the bourgeoisie hated the nobility; while both alike despised the peasant and hated the Russian Orthodox Christians. The peasant, on the other hand, and the Russian Orthodox Christians both hated and despised the Pans and the Catholics; but all, without exception, were united in fraternal concord in hating and despising the Jews, unless, of course, they brought in money or became converted to the only true faith. Thus the Jews were thrown ever more on the mercy of the magistrates and were obliged to submit to them in all matters of contract. The government made ever more onerous demands on them in the form of taxes, while in the towns there were constant outbreaks of disorder, which in the official reports were modestly described as "tumults," but which were really the outcome of Jew baitings organized by the clergy. The Polish clergy, who were far more intolerant than the most fanatical Mohammedans, were not content with the existing legal restrictions imposed by the government, and, with a view to making the legal disabilities of the Jews even more crushing, they inaugurated a campaign of trials for ritual murder on a scale unparalleled in any part of the world, even Germany. The Dominicans were the prime instigators of the movement, and when the reign of terror they set up had reached such a pitch that their general, Marinis, was compelled to put a stop to their activities for a while, the work was carried on by the Jesuits. For a hundred years, from the middle of the seventeenth to the middle of the eighteenth century, charges of this nature followed on each other's heels without intermission, and, to prove them, witnesses were suborned and the victims were subjected to torture. It is a known fact that wounds were made after death in bodies found frozen or drowned, and that such corpses were used as evidence of ritual murder. An important method of proof, calculated to make a particularly profound impression on the emotional masses, was also ingeniously contrived by making the wounds on the bodies of persons killed by accident or murdered, bleed when they were brought into the vicinity of Jewish houses inhabited by those who had been marked out to be the victims of a prospective ritual murder trial. The technique of this fraud, perpetrated chiefly by means of pigeon's blood, was brought to the highest pitch of perfection. Hundreds of Jews were burnt at the stake, broken on the wheel, and drawn and quartered. The Polish clergy were well aware that Rome disapproved of such charges, but they did not care. In 1756, Pope Benedict XIV, in response to an urgent complaint from the Jews, entrusted Cardinal Ganganelli with the task of drawing up an expert report on the subject with the view of once more supplying Christianity, not for the first time in the history of the Jews, with a final and binding pronouncement on the matter. According to the long and carefully prepared expert statement, it was established that the charge of ritual murder was precisely the same sort of baseless accusation as the pagans had in ancient times brought against Christianity. This expert view, however, was not published, and thus the pope made himself an accomplice in the persecution of the Jews, which continued as though no investigation had been made. And it was only after his death that his successor, Clement XIII, in an extremely cautious manner, as though he were fearful of depriving the faithful in Poland of a time-honoured and favourite method of proving their religious zeal, had a note handed by his nuncio, Visconti, to the Polish minister, Count Brühl, in which he suggested that the proofs hitherto advanced in trials for ritual murder would not bear examination, and were, in themselves, insufficient to justify any belief in the existence of such crimes. Augustus III, acting on the information supplied by this note, restored the rights once enjoyed by the Jews, which made it necessary for such charges to be proved in fact, and not to be assumed as true. And this put an end to the epidemic of trials, which meant that, as soon as any real desire for justice was shown, the murder of Christians by Jews seemed to cease to occur.

It should be noted that in this century the clergy were opposed to the Jews for mercenary reasons also. The ecclesiastical brotherhoods had accumulated vast fortunes, which they began to use by starting money-lending businesses of their own, with the result that, eventually, they not only became formidable competitors of the Jews, but also, in spite of their peculiar position and the canonical rules against usury, lent large sums even to the Kahals. The Carmelites, the Dominicans, the Franciscans, and even the Jesuits, thus became creditors of those same autonomous Jewish bodies to which they were so hostile. When the Kahals were suppressed in 1764, they owed the clergy nearly 3,000,000 Polish zlotys. (The gold zloty is equivalent to the gold franc.)

Thus a state of affairs was continued, from which the Jews all over the world, including Poland, had for a moment hoped to be freed, and for the sufferings of which they expected the upheavals of the Messianic movement to compensate them. But as fate still denied them the opportunity of playing the leading part in history, they once more resigned themselves to a minor role. On this occasion, however, they had been concerned with an event in their own history, and as it had not brought them the promised fulfilment, they cast it from them with iron resolution, almost with brutality. As soon as Sabbatai's conversion became an established fact, the Polish rabbis and the representatives of the Kahals severed themselves from the movement. At the synod of the Vaad of the Four Countries, in 1670, the Ḥerem, or Great Ban, was pronounced on all who still professed belief in Sabbatai Zevi as the Messiah of the Jews. And, indeed, how could they indulge even in the thought of a Messianic age, when not even their morrow was secure? Instead of organizing a return to Jerusalem, they were obliged to plan defensive measures to protect themselves against the "tumults" in the towns. Instead of being able to build up their state again, they had to gather together all that remained of the autonomy they had managed to secure in foreign lands. "The only alternative left open to us," declared the Vaad of the Four Countries, "is to unite in a solid body, inspired by inviolable loyalty to the laws of God and the direction of our God-fearing masters and leaders." With these words official Polish Judaism drew the line beneath the Sabbataian movement.

But these official manifestations had no binding power over the people, who always sought religious satisfaction beyond the sphere of everyday life. Even those who submitted to the ban remained faithful to that sphere from which belief in a man like Sabbatai could be derived, the sphere of mysticism. And they followed the path which the German Jews had taken after the horrors of the "home" crusades, and sought refuge in the beyond, in a world of angels and demons, of Haggadic legend, of hell and paradise, of Kabbalistic mysticism, of magic formulæ and exorcism. Once more a wild luxuriant growth of superstition took possession of their minds, which the struggle for existence prevented from taking an interest in profane knowledge and science. And thus through the medium of the frightened heart, a popularized form of religion came into being.

On this broad basis of a popularized mysticism, which reached the point of superstition, the movement associated with the name of Sabbatai Zevi was able, in spite of bans and prohibitions, to develop yet further, with all the unfortunate consequences this involved. While Podolia was under Turkish rule (1672–1699) numbers of Jews went on pilgrimage to Salonica, in order to get into touch with the Sabbataian conventicles there. One of them, the Kabbalist, Chaim Malach, introduced secret conventicles into Poland, and taught that Sabbatai would appear again forty years after his apostasy, that is to say in 1760. The penitential movement that followed this announcement owed a great deal to the appearance of the Kabbalist Judah Ḥasid, who founded in Poland a League of Ḥasidim, or "godly men," and in conjunction with Malach, actually persuaded a group of 1500 people to migrate to Jerusalem. This "crusade" met with deep, though restrained sympathy from the Jews in the countries through which it passed, Germany, Austria, Hungary, and Italy. Many of the pilgrims died on the way, or, too tired to go any farther, remained in the various communities along the route. The remainder actually reached Jerusalem, and settled down, awaiting events that never came to pass, living on alms until at last they departed disillusioned. Some of them returned with Malach to Poland (Ḥasid had died in Jerusalem), some joined the Sabbataians, and the rest became the spoil of the German missionaries.

But the secret movement lived on in spite of this disappointment, and in spite of a fresh ban pronounced against it by the Vaad of the Four Countries in 1721, and won new adherents. The secrecy with which it everywhere worked was rudely disturbed in Germany in the middle of the eighteenth century. A rumour was officially circulated that Rabbi Eibeschütz, of the Hamburg-Altona-Wandsbeck community, had been taken to task for having supplied pregnant women with protective amulets, *kameoth,* on which the name of Sabbatai Zevi was mentioned as the Messiah. Common as was the use of such means of exorcism among the Jews at this time, they were most severe in branding as heretical everything that had any connexion with Sabbatai Zevi, particularly after the collapse of the movement. A most violent and unseemly controversy ensued, which lasted for years, in which the arguments for and against the efficacy of amulets were stoutly and tenaciously supported by the contending parties. But the influence of Kabbalistic ideology was everywhere apparent, and revealed the deeper reasons for the dispute, which could be traced to the unrest which had been introduced into the Jewish world by the development of the Sabbataian Kabbalah. A flood of essays, circulars, letters, expert judgments, accusations, and apologies came into existence, for and against, and both sides so much abused the dangerous weapon of the ban, that it soon became apparent that this disciplinary measure had lost much of its power, at least among the Jews of the West, and owing to misuse had become ineffective and no longer to be feared.

In the West the problem was discussed with hushed breath, but in the East it was given wide publicity in the movement which centred round the person of Jacob Frank, a Turkish subject, born on the frontiers of Podolia and Walachia, who often visited Salonica and Smyrna selling fancy goods and jewellery. His father before him had been a Sabbataian, and Frank believed heart and soul in the ideology connected with the movement. He was a man of poor education and mediocre gifts, but he possessed the kind of qualities calculated to make the men of his age and his circle follow him. In the first place his trade with Turkey and the support of friends enabled him to live on a lavish scale. He was extremely liberal and went about in a mock-princely style, which at any rate was sufficiently effective to make a great impression on poor people. Moreover, he came forward with a new Kabbalist-Sabbataian theory, which, though it had no profound or convincing foundation, was yet able to give something to those who welcome any means of becoming more deeply immersed in mysticism. His view of the Godhead was clearly trinitarian, although only superficially so. He distinguished the "Holy Primeval One," that is to say, God, the Holy King, whom he declared to have become incarnate in the person of Sabbatai, from the Shekinah or Matronita, whom he represented as the female hypostasis of the Godhead. But his influence was chiefly accounted for by the practical application to which he put his teaching. With a careless wave of the hand he thrust aside the whole of the Talmudic body of doctrine. To him the Zohar alone was sacred. Instead of the onerous and binding discipline of the Talmud, and instead of the asceticism enjoined by the Lurian Kabbalah, he offered an erotic mystery. The idea of the androgynous God-Creator, conceived by Cardozo with one last touch of natural sentiment, became in Frank's hands a concrete erotic symbol, which was not confined to the imagination, but was actually represented by a woman at the mystical gatherings. As an inevitable result the mysticism, instead of developing into asceticism, as was usually the case, now became its closely allied opposite, unbridled sexuality. The last followers of Sabbatai in Salonica had followed the same path. As they held that salvation could come only to a wholly good or a wholly sinful world, they resolved, as complete goodness was unattainable, to become wholly sinful, and expressed this choice in unbridled sexual promiscuity. Frank advocated similar conduct, but for other and more cogent reasons; acts which were merely a means to an end with the Sabbataians, in his case constituted a cult, almost a "divine service." Thus he released the unfortunate mystics from the burden of the law, relaxed the strict morality by which they had hitherto been bound, and gave them a joy in life which however misguided and misapplied at least supplied them with something to live for.

All this soon led to his becoming the leader of a sect. Apparently he regarded himself as an incarnation of Sabbatai. He made his followers address him as Santo Señor. He certainly believed in himself and in the correctness of his Kabbalistic doctrine, but as his influence was restricted to a sect, and was not, as in the case of Sabbatai, elevated to the plane of a great Messianic movement, his conception was bounded by the compass of that sect, which at every encounter with reality, or with resistance of any kind, was in danger of going to extremes and of being prompted to act out of pure opposition. For while every great movement endures by aiming at a utopian goal, the sect starts out with a subordinate aim, a special aim of its own, which diverges from the living concept. It is for this reason that a movement may reach a conclusion, whereas a sect can only fall into decay.

We must describe the decay of the Frankist sect, not because it had any tangible effects on Jewish history, but to show the course taken by one extreme of Jewish degeneration. By degeneration, in this connexion, we mean the loss of the capacity to understand the direction and purpose which lie implicit in the idea of the Jewish community.

In the Frankists there was from the very beginning an element of opposition, as is proved by the fact that they described themselves as anti-Talmudists or Zoharists. Thus consciously opposed as they were to their environment, which despite its Kabbalistic attitude still believed in the Talmud, their life was made so difficult for them in their centre at Lemberg, that they withdrew to the little town of Lanzcoron, where, at the beginning of 1756, they were caught by the Jews in the act of performing their orgiastic rites. Frank, as a Turkish subject, was conveyed across the frontier, and left his followers in the lurch. A rabbinical court was convened, which had every Frankist or Sabbataian it could lay hands on brought before it. Those who repented were ordered to do heavy penances, and the great ban was pronounced against those who remained obdurate. In connexion with these proceedings, the conference of rabbis at Brody dealt a heavy blow at all sectarians, placing them one and all under the ban. Whereupon—and here the reader will recall the cultural struggles of the thirteenth and fourteenth centuries—every Jew under thirty years of age was forbidden to read the Zohar, and every Jew under forty the works of Ari. In the East this ban had the effect of placing the outlaw entirely beyond the pale, and consequently deprived him of all support and legal protection. The Sabbataians and Frankists thus found themselves in a dangerous position. The logical outcome of the teaching of the Kabbalah made them Gnostics, as it were against their wills, while adherence to Sabbatai constituted them sectarians; the two together made them enemies of official Judaism, and therefore pariahs. Every means of retreat was closed to them, and the road before them led to Christianity. As an example of the general possibilities of such principles, the whole movement is extremely important, much more important than rabbinism, which, after all, now as ever, carried out a purely conservative function.

The Christian Church inevitably interfered; the development of the Kabbalistic idea of God had always led her to hope that her unremitting missionary zeal would be rewarded. And it was Bishop Dembowski who intervened in this purely domestic Jewish dispute, which had nothing to do with him, and summoned both parties to come and justify themselves before him. The sectarians eagerly agreed, and asked the bishop for a charter. He made it a condition of his consent that they should publicly announce their abandonment of the Talmud. As anti-Talmudists, this presented no difficulty to them. The bishop then forced the rabbis to hold a public debate with the sectarians, who advanced a number of propositions prepared for the occasion; among them were the following—that God consisted of three persons but was yet one and indivisible; that He could manifest Himself in human form, and that the Messiah would never come again. Against this deliberate Christianization of Judaism, the rabbis were powerless, more particularly as Dembowski appointed himself judge, and passed sentence that those who had discovered the incident in Lanzcoron were to be flogged, that the Kahal was to be heavily fined, and that the Talmud was to be burned in the diocese of Podolia. Augustus III closed the episode by granting the candidates for conversion to his faith a charter, "inasmuch as they have declared their renunciation of the blasphemous Talmud, and have risen to the height of recognizing the triune God."

As the result of these proceedings, the Frankists became a semi-Christian sect. To become entirely Christian required but one last step. Frank, who returned to Poland after a few years, and was immediately able to resume his position of leader, supplied the missing link by reviving the Sabbataian doctrine of the necessity of apostasy and introducing a variation, declaring that it was necessary for Sabbatai's followers, like their Master, to pass through the medium of another faith to reach salvation. The only possible faith in this instance was, of course, Christianity. Thus in 1759 the sect, which consisted of 15,000 members, informed the Archbishop of Lemberg that, under certain conditions, they were ready to embrace Christianity, but they were to be allowed to form separate and exclusive colonies in two places in Galicia, they were to retain the right to wear Jewish dress and to grow beards, they were not to be forced to eat pork, they were to be allowed to have a Jewish as well as a Christian name, they were to be allowed to observe the Sabbath as well as Sunday, to regard the Zohar as a holy book, and to marry only among themselves. Such were the dregs of a Judaism which had degenerated into mere rules and regulations.

True, these conditions, which were too transparent to be accepted by the Christian Church, were refused, but at a great public debate held in the cathedral of Lemberg, which lasted from July to November 1759, the sectarians, assisted by the Catholic clergy, were given an opportunity to defend a number of propositions against forty rabbis, who appeared with the utmost reluctance. These propositions were—that all the utterances of the prophets regarding the advent of the Messiah had already been fulfilled; that God Himself had taken on human form as Adonai and had suffered martyrdom to save mankind; that baptism was the only means to secure the blessings of salvation, and that the Talmud prescribed the use of the blood of Christians. The whole proceeding was, as it were, a juggling feat on the part of a man who had gone astray in mysticism and, having jumped headlong out of it again under the protection of a lofty patron, gave one last kick to the community he had forsaken and betrayed.

After this sensational debate, the sectarians became converted to Christianity in a body, and were one and all raised to the rank of Polish nobility. The best families among the Polish aristocracy undertook to be their sponsors. Frank, in keeping with his dignity, actually applied to the king himself to be invested with his title, and his request was granted. The baptisms were carried out in public with great pomp and ceremony in Warsaw.

The movement now reached the stage of conscious and unconscious fraud. Its members were Marranos, who were prepared to make no sacrifice and were devoid of all nobility; for in spite of having been baptized, they naturally wished to remain Jews, and Frank himself continued to play the part of Santo Señor so long, that the church authorities at last had him arrested and kept him a prisoner for twelve years (1760–1772) in the monastery of Chenstokhov. Here he shamelessly set to work to imitate Sabbatai Zevi, entering into conspiracies with his devoted adherents, and endeavouring to secure new ones. He even made a secret offer to the Tsar of Russia, declaring that he was ready to go over to the Greek Orthodox Church, together with 20,000 other Jews. He was half sincere and half a swindler on a grand scale, a condition which in the end left him with nothing except a morbid and hysterical desire to be the centre of mystical reverence. When he was set free from captivity as the result of the first partition of Poland, he made various vain attempts to gain a following in Austria but, meeting with no success, he went to the town of Offenbach near Frankfurt, where he purchased the castle of Prince Isenberg. He called himself Baron Offenbach, and lived in state with his daughter Eva, the "Holy Mistress," managing to maintain his reputation and position for another five years. On his death in 1791, the sect fell to pieces.

Nevertheless the last remnants of his movement still lingered on and played a certain part in the politics of the day. Like the Marranos in Spain, the neophytes, who had now become Polish aristocrats, made the utmost possible use of their freedom, and managed to secure high social positions. This horrified the old Polish nobility, who had recourse to measures of defence, "to prevent this breed of neophytes from reaching such a position as would in course of time completely overshadow the hereditary szlachta."

HEART AND HEAD

THE events we are now about to relate all took place about the middle of the eighteenth century, that is to say, at a time when the intellectual world of Europe was in the throes of a violent outburst of activity in all branches of science, research, philosophy, and art. Yet among the Jews of the Diaspora, who had hitherto been far superior to those about them from the point of view of culture, this period was one of complete sterility in all branches of thought. This condition, usually regarded as one of intellectual torpor, was, if viewed in its true historical perspective, however, merely a great pause for taking breath—a pause in which the Jews, whose position had obviously become critical, were summoning up all their forces to come to a final decision.

Let us recapitulate the course of Jewish history up to this time. The establishment of the Jewish community as a peculiar people had taken place in accordance with the concept and under the ægis of the theocracy. The state and the community both embodied an attempt to realize this aim, and this endeavour now vaguely groping its way, now guided by clear-sighted purposefulness, led before long to the extraordinarily fruitful conception that man was endowed with the capacity to give birth to ideas so great that even the combined and cumulative efforts of one generation after another were not sufficient to produce a reality worthy of them. From the beginning man had been set a holy and religious goal, but, as he was constantly being impeded by unwillingness, egoism, cruel isolation, and distress, he more often met with failure than with success, and the path to fulfilment more often than not became a path leading to disintegration. But as soon as he saw that failure, back-sliding, and imperfection inevitably lay along the path of striving, the idea of salvation was born, not as the outcome of a sense of depravity and sin, but inspired by a feeling of humility, which taught him that the creative power of a man's ideas was greater, higher, and different from all his spiritual capacities taken together. Thus Judaism produced the idea of salvation at the very moment when the state, the community, in which the striving was embodied, collapsed. This idea, in its vast all-embracing unity, was both national and universal, political and religious, earthly and heavenly.

On the return from the Babylonian captivity, a fresh attempt at realization began, which was helped by the application of the spiritual and material wealth of the Torah, the "direction." And the nomocracy arose within the theocracy. Before the result had been finally achieved, it was subjected to the rude twofold test of the Jewish encounter with Greece and Rome, the two other forms of theocracy and nomocracy. And the test was survived. Judaism showed itself to be stronger than Greece and Rome. But the encounter proved that the idea of salvation had gained in actuality, both in regard to the pagan world and also in regard to the shaping of Jewish destiny. While two figures, emanating from Jewry, Jesus of Nazareth and Saul of Tarsus, concerned themselves with salvation for the pagan world, the period of their activities coincided with the final downfall of the Jewish state, whereby, in addition to all their other general problems, the Jews were confronted with the particular problem of survival.

Just as the home of the Jewish idea was the world and not Judea, so the home of the Jewish people became the world over which they spread, and not Palestine. Under conditions against which no other people had ever held its own, their main energies were devoted to the preservation of their type, of themselves as a body. The law as a means of national discipline was embodied in the Talmud, and their spiritual productions were directly dependent upon the problem of existence. The creative power, the religious passion of Judaism, withdrew into the domain of mysticism, while the law, despite all its elasticity, became a rigid end in itself. The expression of official Judaism became rabbinism, and the domain of the subterranean and constantly active forces of Judaism became the Kabbalah. The two together produced the illusion of the continued existence of a national community, and in their form of expression constituted an attempt to control the history and destinies of the Jews, even though the latter were entirely dependent on the foreigner. Whereas in their effect they were often one, in reality they were opposed to each other. Both, however, in the course of their development, reached a crisis. While rabbinism threatened Judaism with rigid petrification and spiritual sterility, the Kabbalah led the religious life of Judaism to the verge of destruction.

Rabbinism and mysticism reached the final stage in the course they were obliged to follow in the middle of the eighteenth century. Rabbinism had drifted ever further and further from its original purpose, which was to constitute the vital link between everyday life and the storehouse of tradition, having taken upon itself rather to act as a disciplinary force for the preservation of type in the Jewish community. But, in course of time and under pressure of events, the force which made for the preservation of the type developed into an independent power of its own, superseding though still largely dependent on rabbinism. The consciousness of the obligations implicit in the idea that the Jews were the Chosen People, the pressure from outside which forced unity upon them, the retroactive animating force of martyrdom, the ever-present Messianic impulse, and finally the heroism of the Marranos—all these factors combined had created the force which made for the preservation of the type, and which no longer depended on rabbinism. It was able to support itself by its own principles, particularly those that were negative—the ability to persevere, the capacity for passive resistance, the indifference to material humiliations, which enabled the Jews to rush in even where they were not wanted. (Jewish "obtrusiveness" is nothing more than the paralysed sense of the social significance of a situation—paralysed as the result of centuries of suffering.)

With the disappearance of that function of rabbinism, which was connected with preserving the type, something else also necessarily vanished. Rabbinism had kept together and regulated the spiritual forces of the Jews. These forces were now free and could become active, and it was not surprising that the latent intellectuality of the Jewish race, which had been considerably sharpened, at least as far as the capacity for thought was concerned, by the rabbinical-Talmudic teaching, should plunge enthusiastically into the world of science, and with the greatest ease attain the superior level of culture of those about them, bridging the gulf dividing them from other nations in the shortest possible space of time. But, what was more important still, in the West the loss of the function of rabbinism had involved the loss of the impulse latent within it, which was due to the fact that its complement, the religious passion of Jewish mysticism, had also reached a crisis, or at all events, was unable any longer to impart any power to rabbinism. Thus in the West, the Jewish priesthood, no longer bound by anything, were constrained to turn their attention to mundane matters and the world of science which lay quite outside their Jewish mission and its ideology. The fact that when they were thus freed from all bonds, they were confronted by the phenomenon of equal civic rights and assimilation, proved disastrous, as we shall show in connexion with the person of Moses Mendelssohn and the intellectual circle that gathered about him.

In the East, on the other hand, where the Jews were settled in compact masses, the very power of the mass led to a different development. Here rabbinism most ably fulfilled its function as a disciplinary force and as a means of preserving the type; but here, too, its impetus had vanished and it had become wholly sterile. Here, too, it lacked the living principle of Jewish mysticism. But this mysticism, and all it meant, had not, like rabbinism, a function to perform in Jewish life, but was itself a function of this life. It was for this reason that it was always as strong or as weak, as creative or as uncreative, as the conditions prevailing at the time in the Jewish community. All that we have seen above in connexion with the development of the Kabbalah, with Sabbataianism, with the doctrines of Cardozo, and with Frankism, are nothing but variations on this theme, but, at the same time, prove that Jewish mysticism had collapsed owing to the fact that it could never be realized. All mysticism requires a reality as a starting-point and a bourne, and is distinguished from the whole sphere of rationalism, not by being either earthly or heavenly, but by suggesting means whereby earth and heaven can be united into one creative whole. Let us repeat our view of Jewish mysticism—the earth as an experienced reality, heaven as a reality to be experienced, and between the two, faith as a function of the heart alone.

The earth as an experience of reality always presupposes a living and unbroken harmony with the earth, whether it be with nature as the great proof of an act of creation, or with man himself, that is to say, with that creature who is alone endowed with creative power. For centuries the Jew had been denied both. He could not even find joy in his own community, except under conditions of such terrible oppression that it became a compulsory state rather than what a community should be—a voluntary association of people living together with one another and for one another. Thus Jewish mysticism perished as the result of a lack of reality.

This collapse of two forces filled the Jews, whose will to live could never be stifled, with a longing for some fresh activity. Western Judaism found it by gaining contact with the world, eastern Judaism by recovering contact with universal sympathies; the West by entering the field of the intellect; the East by entering the field of faith; the West, after many losses along the devious ways of assimilation, by gaining contact with the intellect of the world; the East by gaining contact with the soul of the world. When both, after a long period of separation and hostility, ultimately met once more, they were able, in our own era, to prepare the way for a new conception of the Jewish people and their destiny.

It was only in its effects, and not in its purpose or original intention, that Ḥasidism, the new movement in the East, was opposed to rabbinism. For it was a matter of a further variation of the perennially acute opposition between heart and head. The movement found its external focus in the person of Israel ben Elieser, or Baal Shem Tob Israel (abbreviated into Besht), which means "Master of the Wondrous Name of God." He was born in Podolia in 1700, and as a child showed a greater aptitude for wandering about the fields and woods than for sitting still on his form at school. As a young man, he was not attracted either by Talmudic scholarship or by the thought of earning money, but he gradually found his way into a world of solitude, contemplation and Kabbalistic studies, until, at last, he came forward as a figure common enough among the eastern Jews, as an adviser, helper, doctor, exorcizer, and maker of amulets, in fact a mixture of saint and miracle-doctor, who worked his cures as much by prayer as by the herbs he used. He was endowed, to an extraordinary degree, with those impressive and effective psychic qualities so necessary for men of his stamp. Without any effort of will, or burdening and ruining his influence by the factor of volition, he was able to give all the more forcible expression to the idea of salvation, which he did with simple open-hearted humanity. He was not the founder of a spiritual or theosophical system, and in no way the systematizer of an idea; all he did was to profess belief in an old religious truth in the simplest and at the same time deepest conception of human life. He regarded all religion as something quite apart from ritual and law, and, though he did not despise the laws, they did not, to his mind, constitute faith. To him religion meant the establishment of a living relationship with God. But God was everywhere, and those who so wished could find Him everywhere, in every deed, phenomenon, and word. The best means of communion with Him was through prayer, for which no set form was necessary. God was not served by formulæ, He could not be approached through asceticism; all that a man had to do was to listen to the dictates of his heart and gladly lay his whole life at the feet of his Maker. This meant, as the prophets had meant of old, the hallowing of everyday life; it was only thus, and not by means of expediting the "End of Days," that the salvation of the individual and of humanity could be secured. Here again, the idea of salvation does not presuppose the sinfulness of man as a necessary prerequisite. By a magnificent extension of Kabbalistic doctrine, he placed the world's need of salvation as far back as the day of creation itself. We will quote Buber's words, for the case cannot be better put: "The molten stream of creative grace poured itself, in all its fullness, over the first created primeval forms, the 'vessels,' but they were unable to resist it and broke to pieces; the stream then split asunder into an infinity of 'sparks,' around which 'crusts' were formed, and thus defects, blemishes, evil came into the world. Now imperfection lies implanted in perfect creation; a suffering world, a world in need of salvation lies at the feet of God."

Baal Shem soon had a following, and the co-ordination and development of his theories in the circle which formed about him led to the movement known as Ḥasidism, which is important in various ways in connexion with the shaping of the Jewish idea within the compass of history. It elevated the Messianic idea, which had been marred by the various attempts to realize it, to a loftier plane, suppressing the dangerous Gnostic conceptions of the Kabbalah. In the place of a number of mystical Sephiroth that had become independent, it set the concept of God as a unity and defined man's relation to Him. It also saved the domain of the heart from the excrescences of rabbinism; in fact, on the plane of religious emotion, it was responsible for a fresh attempt—and as far as we can tell it was the penultimate attempt—to make the Jews once more an individual force in history.

The Messianic idea which Baal Shem's faithful followers evolved out of his parables, similes, and didactic narratives was mainly concerned, not with the appearance of the Messiah as a political figure, but with allotting to every man his share in Messianic performance and activity. The Kabbalah also did this, but, whereas the Kabbalah choked up the free stream of life with the Christian doctrine of asceticism, Baal Shem set free the whole of life for the purpose, with all its heights and depths. This principle of joy, which Sabbatai and Frank had also endeavoured to restore to religion, gave the Ḥasidic movement a considerable access of elemental power. For its ultimate source of vitality, however, it turned to that which, as we have endeavoured to show, distinguishes Judaism from Christianity; whereas in the latter the idea of salvation is derived from a unique phenomenon, which merely requires "imitation," *imitatio;* in the former it is placed in the living present, in every second as it passes, in man's eternal striving. To the Ḥasidists such a doctrine and its adoption sanctified life and lent it a higher meaning, and the rapid growth of their movement proves that mysticism, that is to say, the religious impulse, was still far from dead. And it is for this reason that Ḥasidism, as a sphere of ideas, did not constitute a sect, and did not come to an end with Baal Shem's death.

Baal Shem's most important disciple was Rabbi Dov Bär of Mesrich, who arranged and systematized his doctrines, which though consistent enough required co-ordinating. The fact that other followers of Baal Shem eventually evolved systems of their own, and that in due course the southern section of the Jewish centre in the East, Volhynia and Podolia, produced a different form of the Ḥasidic theory from the north, where the rule of rabbinism was still much more firmly established, only testifies to the vitality of the movement.

The conditions under which it arose, both material and spiritual, though certainly extremely favourable to the development of such ideas, made their realization extremely dangerous. The idea of the purity of thought must not blind the student of history to the kind of men who appropriated it. When people, the hostility of whose environment has hardly allowed them the right to live, are called upon to rise to such lofty spiritual heights in their everyday life, they must inevitably cast about them for a mediator, to remove the unwonted burden of daily duty from their shoulders, or at least help them to bear it. The Hasidists found this mediator in the person of the *Ṣaddiq,* or "just man," who by his close proximity to God had acquired the gift of clairvoyance, or prophetic vision, who could perform miracles, and who, like the priests of the Catholic Church, undertook to act as mediators between God and man. And the people became wholeheartedly devoted to these Ṣaddiqim; their passionate longing to venerate something and the joyous certainty of having as the object of their veneration something tangible, a person who lived among them, secured for the Ṣaddiq not only a princely position, but also devotion almost amounting to worship. These people's need of love had been so much starved and neglected that similar centres of devotion and reverence sprang up spontaneously in different places at the same time. Wherever a pupil or follower of Baal Shem, or a pupil or follower in the second degree, worked, a close circle of adherents was formed about the Ṣaddiq, who with jealous love held strictly aloof from any other Ṣaddiq and his sphere of power. This breaking up of the Ḥasidic world into spheres of power resulted in regular dynasties becoming established in various places, and the dignity of Ṣaddiq being handed down from father to son without any investigation as to the latter's worthiness. Moreover, instead of a man who was really a Ṣaddiq by vocation, there arose the charlatan, the exploiter of credulous veneration, who degraded the office. Whenever the faithful cling to an individual instead of to an idea, the path to sectarianism lies open. And this happened in the present instance. The spiritual necessity which led to the Ṣaddiq being made the mediator between God and man, and to all pious activities being left to him, together with the subdivision of the parochial areas and the granting of hereditary rights to the office, led to the formation of a sect, which was equivalent to degeneration.

Various energetic attempts were made by the best of the Ṣaddiqim to arrest this development. But it proved impossible to do so, for, apart from the individual causes operating, there were too many external circumstances over which they had no control influencing the movement. A minor factor was the "enlightenment" which was gradually penetrating the East from the West, and which we shall discuss later. Its effects were inevitably slight, since there is apparently no necessary connexion between general education and the emancipation of the human heart, and consequently the one does not influence the other as a matter of course. A much stronger influence, because it was negative, came from the direction of rabbinism, which was still all-powerful in many parts of the Jewish East. The fundamental difference between Ḥasidism and rabbinism, whose relation to each other was much the same as that between religion and the church, might have enabled them to subsist peacefully side by side had it not been for the fact that rabbinism, which as a spiritual force was essentially concentrated on discipline, could not without inconsistency look on while the law, though still observed, was no longer respected as an end in itself. Moreover, the respect enjoyed by the Ṣaddiq and the influence he exercised completely overshadowed the authority of the rabbi. Thus, in addition to being guided by a different ideology, the flock was necessarily divided against itself, with the result that the unity of eastern Judaism was destroyed.

At the time of the first division of Poland, Lithuanian rabbinism, led by the last great scholastic, Rabbi Elia Wilnaer, opened the struggle in 1772. Ḥasidic writings were condemned by a rabbinical court and publicly burned, all the communities were adjured to extinguish this "blasphemous" sect, and the observance of Ḥasidic rites and ceremonies was threatened with the ban. The Ḥasidim, who constituted the majority in Volhynia, Podolia, and the district of Kiev, stoutly defended their position, and in a few years there was open and bitter warfare between them and their opponents, who called themselves *Mithnaggedim,* in which neither party shrank from deeds of violence and mutual denunciation before the government authorities. In that part of Poland which had fallen to Russia, the Russian government ultimately intervened in the dispute, which had acquired a wholly political complexion, and perpetuated the already existing schism by granting the Ḥasidim the right to have synagogues and rabbis of their own. It must be confessed that nothing creative resulted from this conflict of forces and opinions. All that happened was that the abnormal conditions already existing in the most important centre of Judaism were aggravated by a further symptom of disintegration. And once more it became clear that the sphere in which Jewish ideology was attempting to become realized was irretrievably hampered and restricted on every side.

The life of the eastern Jews was subjected to twofold oppression; not only were they still, as they had always been, the victims of economic distress and legal disabilities, but, in addition, the spiritual atmosphere in which they existed was a murky mixture of medieval ignorance and ecclesiastical stupidity. The process which usually occurred in Jewish history, after the calling of a halt to take breath and gather fresh strength—to wit, the formation of a new centre—was in this instance reversed, for the simple reason that the interval of inactivity occurred at a time when the Russian empire was expanding. For it was in this new centre that the dark and terrible tragedy of Jewish destiny reached its climax.

Even in the West, the life of the Jew was far from blissful. The fact that he lived in an environment in which intellectual progress was making rapid strides, increased rather than diminished the difficulties of his position, for it made him all the more conscious of the yawning gulf that separated him from an existence worthy of human dignity. A brief survey will enable us to form some idea of the condition of the Jews in the countries of western Europe, from the middle of the seventeenth to the middle of the eighteenth century.

Next to Poland, Austria possessed the largest Jewish colony. True, in Vienna, the capital, the authorities were in favour of reducing the Jewish population as drastically as possible, and religious sentiment combined with economic competition kept the Jews in a state of constant suspense; sometimes they were tolerated, anon they were expelled, only to be allowed to return once more. Leopold I, that pupil of the Jesuits (1657–1705), whose piety was considerably strengthened by his marriage with the Infanta Margaret Theresa, appointed a commission of experts to inquire into the Jewish problem; the gist of their report was that the Jews were engaged in an anti-Christian conspiracy. Whereupon they were expelled from Vienna and Lower Austria, and the quarter they had hitherto occupied, the Judenstadt, was renamed Leopoldstadt. However, in a few years the budget figures proved to Leopold that trade was declining, that prices were rising, that manufactures were suffering and that the treasury was empty. And his religious zeal became reconciled to the fact that the Jews might, after all, be economically useful to his country, that he required money for carrying on war, and that for raising it he needed the Jewish middleman. Facilities were therefore granted for the formation of a fresh Jewish colony, the members of which were forced, however, to accept the most crushing rules and regulations.

In the other Austrian states, Bohemia, Moravia, Silesia, and Hungary, which might be regarded as the outposts of Polish Jewry, even the fact that thickly populated colonies of Jews had been settled there for centuries did not prevent the authorities from making experiments and driving them out. Maria Theresa (1740–1780) filled with insensate and hysterical hatred of the Jews, vented her rage over the ill-success of her wars above all upon the Jews of Bohemia, whom she accused of having betrayed the country. After the withdrawal of the Prussian troops of Frederick II, she abandoned them to the excesses of the Austro-Hungarian soldiers, and in December 1744 expelled the whole lot of them at a moment's notice. For three years the Jews of Bohemia wandered about the country, not knowing where to turn. It seemed impossible that such barbarity should fail to rouse the attention of the rest of Europe. And indeed England and the Netherlands did interfere, with the result that a limit was set to the ejections, which, in consideration of an increase of taxation, were eventually stopped altogether. The fact that, with the first partition of Poland, the province of Galicia, with about 150,000 Jews, fell to the lot of

Austria, can hardly have been a source of very great satisfaction either to the empress or to the Jews themselves.

Austria's fundamental attitude to this numerically important section of her population is illustrated by two legal enactments: in the first place by "toleration," that is to say the indulgence granted to an individual Jew here and there. This form of toleration was, in some cases, hereditary, and might be continued in the family of the privileged person; in other cases it was purely personal, that is to say, all descendants of the privileged individual were obliged to emigrate. But even in the case of hereditary toleration, the privilege might be and frequently was limited to a single male descendant. This condition is somewhat similar to that created by another law which held force in Lower Austria, Bohemia, Moravia, and Silesia, and laid down that only one male descendant of a family should be allowed to remain in the country and, furthermore, that marriages among Jews should from the outset be limited to a certain number, quite irrespective of the natural increase in population, and should on no account be exceeded. The result was that thousands of Jews were condemned either to celibacy, to secret marriage, or to emigration. The openly admitted object of these laws was to reduce the number of Jews, and they constituted the legal and civilized substitute for the method used till that time, which was to get rid of them by means of massacres.

The only consideration which kept this anti-Jewish feeling in check —the expectation of getting money out of the Jews, also determined the relations between the government and the Jews in Prussia. The Mark of Brandenburg, which got rid of its Jews by means of a trial for ritual murder in 1573, received them back under the Great Elector (1640–1688) by incorporating into its domain those districts which became the basis of the state of Brandenburg-Prussia. The Elector had seen that in Holland the Jews were useful to the state. He accordingly gave them the right of sojourn and freedom to trade, and appointed a Jewish financial agent, Behrend Levi, as their "commander and representative." Against the wishes of all classes, he also concluded an agreement with fifty families, who had been expelled from Vienna, by which they were allowed to settle in the country for a fixed period. His successors, Frederick I, Frederick William I, and Frederick the Great, showed a similar mercenary interest in the Jews. All three wished to have Jews in the country, but not too many; they were, above all, to be rich, and in a position to pay rates and taxes; they were to enliven trade and to support the innovations introduced by these monarchs into the royal manufactories, by being forced to buy goods from them, particularly wedding presents and porcelain articles. Although the Jews who accepted such conditions clearly enjoyed no rights, at least they were given protection; but, as was the case in Austria, they were subject to the limitation that not more than one male descendant was to marry. As for the rest of the Jews, whom these expensive privileges did not tempt, their existence was made as difficult and as trying as possible, by means of drastic limitations of the right of settlement, marriage, and of earning a living. The obvious aim of all these regulations was to frighten them and drive them out of the country.

This system of making conditions more favourable for rich Jews and of driving the poorer to yet greater poverty, was also applied in other German states. While the economic rise of the Jews as a whole was thus hampered, a class of capitalists was also artificially created, some of whom as "court stewards" were obliged to supply loans for the various states, and many of whom, in addition, began to exercise a decisive influence on the financial world of Europe. This appearance of the Jewish financier was subsequently recorded by their non-Jewish competitors, when the latter tried to make up for the start the Jews had been given, as a heavy debit entry against Judaism. In a history of the ideology of Judaism, such developments are devoid of interest. The economic development of the Jew has really nothing whatever to do with either his nature or his ideology. When, for instance, we speak of the nature of the German, we do not mention his undoubtedly great commercial ability; and when we speak of a certain country as a nation of "shopkeepers," we are apt to do so with a touch of contempt.

To sum up, it may be said that the Jews at this time and in this environment were living in a state in which they were deprived of all rights and were the objects of ill-concealed hostility, while their persecution took the form of expulsion and limitation of population. Incidentally it must be noted that they were better treated in Catholic than in Protestant countries, though in neither were they subjected to the worst horror of martyrdom. Vital forces, which hitherto had been spent in anxious thought for the morrow, began to be set free for other activities. Moreover, the Jews began to be ever less absorbed in matters connected with their own communities, which they had before been obliged willynilly to attend to and which constituted their form of autonomy. True, communal autonomy in the West had never succeeded in developing such a strong system of organization as the Kahals in the East. The repeated subdivision of the colonized area into smaller administrative districts and the absence of a compact body of Jews were inimical to a development of this kind. But even where such strictly organized communities still existed, their authority necessarily suffered loss from the decline of rabbinism. What remained of the organization no longer regulated Jewish life or laid down strict rules for every action both within and without the community. A further change had also occurred—the governments of the various countries were beginning to interfere with the Jewish communities. So long as the European states had been organized on the basis of class privilege, they had apparently failed to see that the existence of even the most insignificant Jewish community in their midst constituted, in the ordered form it imposed on itself, the autonomous administration of a national minority. But, apart from this, the rise of absolutism led those in authority to extend their lust for dominion even to the Jewish communities, which they tried to regulate and protect. One of the least of the evils following upon this policy of interference was that the election of the presidents or elders of the community, and subsequently that of the rabbis, was not considered valid unless it had received government sanction—Prussia was the first to make this a rule—or in some places had to be conducted under state supervision. Far more serious was the state interference with the private affairs of the Jewish communities, in which Austria set the example; in addition to the legal disabilities from which they suffered, they were told what they might and might not do within their own jurisdiction, from the building of schools to the training of teachers and rabbis, from their method of bookkeeping to the clothes they should wear. Clearly such regulations were educational experiments on the part of incompetent pedagogues, who did not study the interests of those placed in their charge, but only their own. But the fact that they were educational experiments is vastly important, for it shows that the state was beginning to exercise control over the Jews for purposes other than that of getting money out of them.

This development was of the utmost importance for the future of the Jews both in the East and the West. Whereas formerly the criterion of the state had depended mainly upon the extent of the territory dominated and had had nothing to do with all the countries, peoples, languages, or cultures assembled within it, in the eighteenth century it came to mean the type of the *dominion* exercised over the territory, and dominion of the most absolute kind, which, in the case of the vast system of petty states, more particularly in Germany, liked to affect "parental airs." This led, on the one hand, to an effort to regulate the way of life and conditions of *all* the subjects, even those with minor rights, while, on the other, the homogeneity of the people, of the subjects, of the dominated group, which tended to increase as the organization based on class privilege gradually fell to pieces, was marred by the continued existence of isolated Jewish groups. A phenomenon which was the result of centuries of exclusiveness, now took the form of a differentiated section of the population, resolutely held at arm's length and despised by the rest. Just as the legal and professional restrictions to which they had constantly been subjected had not tended to strengthen ideas of right and wrong among the Jews, or to make them over-nice in their struggle for their daily bread, so the fact of being restricted to a world dependent on the rabbinical outlook, and of being excluded from the opportunities for culture enjoyed by those about them, were not calculated to make them rise to that standard of culture. Thus a condition of affairs arose in which a people belonging to an ancient civilization, through distress and the necessity for self-defence, were willynilly made to appear essentially backward and barbarous in an environment which was in the first throes of attaining culture. Consequently it was in just such a world and under just such government institutions that it was possible for the Jews to become objects of educational solicitude.

Educational experiments of this nature were not prompted by any sudden revulsion of feeling or humanitarian motives; they were far from being the outcome of any real desire to help the Jews and compensate them for generations of injustice and suffering; they were, on the contrary, attempts inspired by purely selfish considerations and regard for the interests of church and state, and of the majority of citizens, to assimilate these aliens and make them inconspicuous. They constituted an effort to dispose of the Jewish problem by disposing of the Jew. The disposing of the Jew *qua* Jew was, as a matter of fact, the ultimate and often the explicit aim of all the regulations, and even where the impossibility of such a drastic solution was recognized from the beginning, the governments by their legal enactments made a far-reaching assimilation to environment one of the first conditions of any suppression or relaxation of the restrictive measures. It was round this point of making the granting of rights dependent on cultural assimilation that the whole web of disasters was woven, which proved the undoing of the Jewish community during a century of tribulation. And, at the cost of great danger, and considerable loss of strength, the Jew forgot his sense of direction, together with the meaning and purpose of his fate and the demands his history made upon him. It is only in our own day that he has recovered any knowledge of these things.

When a people have borne an idea in their hearts throughout their history, and the idea is of such a nature as to become applicable to the whole world, they can at any moment, however low their level of culture may be by comparison with that of the people about them, immediately regain contact with the culture of the world, if only they are not forcibly prevented from doing so. And in that case *any* culture is suitable as the medium for such contact. In Jewish history the culture that has chiefly served as a medium has been that of Germany. Any other might have served equally well.

For a people to gain contact with a culture that is not their own, some attraction is an essential prerequisite. It was possible for the Jews to feel this attraction whenever the conditions of life had become sufficiently free to enable them to get into touch with those about them, and, furthermore, when the general level of culture of the latter—not the isolated achievements of specially gifted individuals—made them feel the wish to share it. This condition of affairs was reached about the middle of the eighteenth century. And it was not the prospect of making some improvement in their legal position that made the first Jews leave their isolated domain and seek contact with the culture of the outside world; their main object was to free from the old bonds their desire to exercise spiritual influence. This was no easy matter. Even where favourable conditions of life facilitated the task, and rendered access to the treasures of culture comparatively easy, it could still be attained only by rebelling against the traditional repudiation of all mundane wisdom inculcated by rabbinism. In the East it actually required heroic courage for a Jew who thirsted for knowledge to venture on the step, for it made him a heretic and placed him outside the pale of the Jewish community. In the West, the element of personal tragedy involved in falling out with the community was absent. The tragedy lay in the opposite direction, and the fact of falling out with the community was accepted with ever greater indifference as part of the bargain. For the tragedy of the Jew who had thus fallen out with his own community consisted in his not being received and adopted by the other community to whose culture and civilization he aspired.

In this connexion we use the expression "falling out with," in its broadest possible sense to include even that situation in which a Jew might insist on remaining within the fold of Judaism, though he interpreted the latter in a manner which *de facto* deprived it of the character of a community. Hitherto Judaism had not found it necessary to define either its type or its nature. It existed and that was enough; it never set up the fact of its existence as a matter for discussion; at most it called upon believers to ponder the fact that, in spite of centuries of persecution, it still existed. But now it came to be seen that Judaism no longer had an existence of its own, that it did not depend on its own strength. But where this is the case, and the mere fact of existence is not sufficient justification for a community, it is forced to bolster itself up with ideas and arguments. This is what now took place under a twofold strain which made an erroneous point of view inevitable. The people who had always refused to experience the history of other nations, now found that their capacity to understand their own history had perished; all they knew about their own race was coloured by the anxiety, by the conscious or unconscious desire, to obtain release from the legal disabilities from which they suffered.

And even this vestige of purposeful thinking was not free and unbiased. On the contrary, the very plea brought forward for this release was dictated by the arguments used by those who wished to withhold equal rights from the Jews. Educated Christians, who were interested in the matter, and qualified to express an opinion, without being moved by feelings of resentment or by obvious mercenary motives, held the view that the European states, and particularly Germany, were by nature Christian, that the state and religion formed a single corporate body, and that, while there might be room in such a structure for Jews as tolerated subjects, it was certainly out of the question for Judaism and those who professed it to be incorporated in it. Thus a difficult situation presented itself to the Jew fighting to gain contact with the culture about him, and to secure legal rights. For, not only had the whole spiritual, intellectual, and social edifice become a matter of course to the oppressed, but it had become even more so to the oppressors, the Christian environment; though the readiness to diverge from it was far greater in the Jew than in the Christian. Intolerance, pride of race, and religious hatred, were integrating factors, even in the people of the "new age." No heights of spiritual culture could make up for their inability to regard the relationship between man and man as the final determining and deciding factor in the development of humanity and of the spirit. They indulged in the sublimest emotions, but the idea of the fellowship of man in its deepest significance was utterly unknown to them. There may be considerable difference of opinion regarding the creative influence of Christianity on the culture of western Europe, but at all events the Jew, who wished to live in the countries dominated by that culture, as a citizen enjoying equal rights with the rest, was forced to defend himself against its arguments. He did this actively by appealing to the humanitarian feelings of those about him; he did it passively by attempting to interpret Judaism in such a way as to deprive it of the basic conception of nationalism that underlay it.

This expresses all that requires to be said from the standpoint of principle about a personality who may be regarded as the prototype of this attitude both in the good and in the bad sense—Moses Mendelssohn. Mendelssohn was a member of one of those small narrow Jewish bourgeois circles, in which most of the Jews of his time lived. True, he was not the first or only Jew to break loose from such an environment in order to indulge in free thought, nor did his achievements in the domain of culture, which had recently been made accessible, reveal either in form or content any particular originality or creative power. His work is interesting only in so far as it provides a proof of the productive capacity of the Jews even after an isolation lasting hundreds of years. His historical importance lies in the fact that his philosophy of enlightenment presented his own generation and those that followed with the means of divorcing from Judaism as a living whole the Jewish religion as the only criterion of what constituted Judaism, and of giving reason such an important place within that religion, that it lost both its contact with life and its transcendent power. He certainly had no wish to bring about this result. His ethical passion was sublime and seductive. He made it his aim in life to be a mediator between Judaism and its environment, and to make Christian culture acceptable to the Jews, and the Jews acceptable to the Christians as fellow-citizens. To achieve this end he had to perform a twofold task—he had to spread enlightenment among the Jews, and to vindicate the Jews to the Christians. He did both with the best and purest motives.

As a fundamental means of making the German language accessible to the Jews (the hybrid Judæo-German dialect was still in wide use at the time), and of opening the door of German culture to them, he conceived the idea of translating the Pentateuch into German. From the very beginning, however, this undertaking was doomed to failure. In a former chapter we have already emphasized the importance attaching to the translation of the Bible into a foreign tongue, inasmuch as it meant the bursting open of the gate into a domain which was not merely of interest to the Jewish people but laid claim to being of interest to all mankind. Herein we agree with Franz Rosenzweig, who said: "A people's entrance into universal history is marked by the moment at which it makes the Bible its own in a translation." Such translations, however, cannot be undertaken arbitrarily and produced whenever a man thinks fit to do so, but only at a time when the spiritual condition of a people justifies the undertaking, and when the inclusion of the Bible in a nation's language and culture make a translation a historical necessity. It is for this reason that any random translation, or any translation deliberately made with some educational or scientific object in view, always remains at best a philosophical effort. Thus Luther was *obliged* to translate the Bible, whereas Mendelssohn appeared far too late to give the Jews the Bible; all he could do was to produce a version in another idiom for educational purposes. And he himself was the living proof that no translation of the Bible was necessary in order to acquire knowledge and mastery of the German tongue.

Nevertheless, this translation, which met with the most passionate opposition on the part of the Polish rabbis in Germany and Austria, sprang from the purest motives. Mendelssohn was a whole-hearted believer in the ideas of toleration and humanity, which his friend Lessing had embodied in the figure of "Nathan the Wise" in the play of that name, and the fact that his house was the meeting-place for the circle of idealists who gathered round Lessing probably led him to believe that the class in Germany that held humanitarian views was far larger than it really was. Thus he fondly imagined that the object of his translation, which was to introduce the Jews to the German language and culture, would secure for them the same affectionate welcome into the nation as a whole as he had received from a section of it. But the first groping efforts he made in this direction roused an echo which should have made him prick up his ears. He had persuaded his friend Markus Herz to make a German translation of Manasseh ben Israel's essay, *The Salvation of the Jews,* and had written a preface to the translation, in which he pleaded for the economic and civic emancipation of the Jews. This demand met with lively opposition, and a flood of pamphlets and essays appeared, all more or less inspired by the idea already described—that Germany was a Christian state, in which Christianity was the state religion, and that in such a state it was impossible to give Jews equal rights with other citizens.

Naturally, in this controversy, Mendelssohn did not regard it as being incumbent upon him to prove that this idea of the Christian state was not based upon any Christian concept, but was due to the alliance between the power of the secular government and the dominion of the church, and that the chief, that is to say, the utilitarian value of the theory lay in its negative aspect—the institution of safeguards against the intrusion of strangers and people of different faiths. In his treatise entitled *Jerusalem, or Concerning Religious Power and Judaism,* he very rightly confined himself to a thorough examination of the question how the respective spheres of secular and religious power were to be defined in a state, and reached the sound conclusion that, while the state could force its citizens to behave in a particular way, it could not force them to hold particular opinions. But in endeavouring to apply this principle to Judaism, he outlined a type of Judaism which bore no relation whatsoever to its historical attributes. He was not in a position to be able to grasp Judaism as a historical process. He had no eye for this combination of national and religious power, for he was wholly obsessed by the idea of humanitarianism, which, noble though it may be, is dangerous inasmuch as it easily leads people to overlook the historical sequence of events by fixing their gaze upon the desired object, which is the universal brotherhood of man—a beautiful but unsatisfying obsession! The desire to humanize the world may lead to certain developments, but it cannot undo what has already been done. True, the national idea must never be allowed to become an end in itself, but must always remain a form of aspiration; but within this limit, if rightly applied, lies implicit the possibility of bringing the humanitarian ideal with all its incidental variations, to maturity.

Mendelssohn could see only the Jewish religion, and, owing to the fact that he cut it off from its sources, his understanding even of that was limited to the capacities of his own mind. To him, it was law revealed to mankind as a whole, and hallowed and transmitted through tradition. He himself was faithful to the law, and therefore tried to find a religious and devotional basis for it. Consequently he believed in revelation. But, on the other hand, being a humanitarian and an apostle of enlightenment, he required the law to be based on reason. And he emphasizes this point. "The religion of my fathers," he declares, "in its leading principles, knows nothing of mysteries which we must believe but cannot understand. Our reason can quite confidently proceed from the first, certain, and accepted basic principles of human knowledge, and rest assured that in the end it will encounter religion along that same path. There is no conflict in Judaism between faith and reason, no revolt of our natural perceptions against the oppressive power of faith."

Thus, in his hands, Judaism became a religion of reason, which was quite at home in a sphere in which, in the first great days of striving and effort, the soul of the Jew deliberately, though in fear and trembling, delivered itself up to mystery. He seemed to have lost all knowledge of the mystery of being called, which was apparently stifled by the passion of his moral earnestness. He regarded his view of Judaism as an adequate basis for his constant appeal for truth, peace, and humanity. But no truth at all is better than a half-truth. Mendelssohn was fundamentally right; the law, not religion, had been given to the Jews. But the religion was already there. It was only from the religion that the law sprang, with that necessity which makes all communities frame rules for their existence. The law helped the people to realize their religion. It was not the substance of that religion. This misunderstanding of the historical sequence, which was a product of the ghetto, led Mendelssohn to conceive of a Judaism which had never existed. So shaky and unsound was his Judaism, so much a matter of private opinion and yet so general, that a man like Lavater subsequently felt justified in attempting to win this "Socratic soul" over to Christianity.

This perversion of the Judaic idea might have had no sequel had it not been associated with that intellectual attitude traditionally known as one of "enlightenment." But this sort of enlightenment is a double-edged sword. In so far as its object is to stimulate men to use their sound common sense, to replace prejudice by knowledge, and rigid tradition by an understanding of the mutability of forms, it cannot be too highly praised. But in most cases it is associated with a dreary species of rationalism, a worship of reason and reasonableness, a foolish process of disillusionment, and an almost malicious joy in explaining the wonderful, the inexplicable. The ideal of the advocate of enlightenment is civilization and universal education. All this, if constituting an addition to life, is valuable, but, if made the substance of existence, it is inadequate.

It was along these lines that the Jewish pioneers worked who sprang from the circle about Mendelssohn. Their ambition was to educate the Jew, and to give him taste, knowledge, and æsthetic feeling. They wished to do away with the difference between the general attitude of the Jews and that of their environment. In the early stages, they aimed at accomplishing this on a twofold plane—on that of universal education and that of Jewish wisdom, by reforming the Jewish schools and by reviving Hebrew literature. The first "Jewish Free School" and the first modern Hebrew journal, *Ha-Meassef* ("The Collector"), appeared at this time (1778 and 1783). Both undoubtedly did good work in helping the Jews to make up for lost time, and expedited a process which, in any case, would have come into being in due course. But they also hampered it to a certain extent. These pioneers wished to clear the way for securing equal civic rights for the Jews, and to create a Jewish world that was in no way different, either in speech, culture, or even, if that were possible, in its way of life, from the outside world. They aimed at merging the isolated exclusive existence of the Jews into the general life of the state and of society. They regarded the reproach of the outside world to the effect that the Jew led a separate existence, as justified, and they therefore tried to remove its foundation. They loved culture with the whole-hearted intellectual passion of the Jew, and gave themselves up to it body and soul, seeing that in this sphere there were hopes of finding real humanity and toleration. Thus the feeling of having no rights became magnified into a passion for equality. They knew that, as far as love of the culture about them was concerned, they were equal to the people in their environment, and this knowledge made their legal limitations all the more galling. They felt it their duty, however, not merely to make a demand, but also to make a concession. And this concession amounted, not so much to a renunciation of their exclusiveness as Jews, as a renunciation of the ultimate reasons for this exclusiveness which lay in their being a peculiar people. As the world was not yet able to tolerate a peculiar people, the only alternative was to cease as far as possible from being a peculiar people. The only visible basis for the claim which they could see was a purely superficial one, and consisted of the petrified ideology of rabbinism and the ghetto world which no longer held out any promise of life. Consequently, instead of tackling the reasons for the development, they tackled appearances. Instead of seeking for a new basis in tradition and in their past, they burst open the door to another world, and paved the way for assimilation and adaptation.

Whereas eastern Judaism overcame the crisis by means of the heart, and was thus enabled in Ḥasidism to bequeath a new, though short-lived impulse to posterity, in the West the crisis was circumvented as the result of resentment, reason, and an intellectual humanism, in short, by means of the head. The East provided possibilities for the future, the West sought possibilities only in the present. The East deepened the Jewish problem, the West merely shifted it. The East gave a fresh justification to Jewish history, the West falsified it.

In the fact that the present Jewish world is the heir of both these tendencies lies the real problem of Judaism.

PART VI

FROM
THE STRUGGLE FOR EQUAL RIGHTS
TO
THE JEWISH RENAISSANCE

EXPERIMENTS

THE relationship of the Jews to the outside world was, until the eighteenth century, comparatively simple—they had duties but no guaranteed rights; they fulfilled economic functions, but formed no part of the social body; they were inhabitants of a country without being natives of it; they were victims of its laws but not citizens; they were human beings but condemned to be the objects on which the instincts of their environment reacted; they were the representatives of monotheism and yet were massacred in the name of monotheism.

In the eighteenth century this simple situation became more complicated both from the point of view of the Jews and from that of their environment. By neglecting the spiritual bonds of Judaism and accepting new bonds with the culture of their environment, the Jews discovered the discrepancies in their own external life, and tried to remove them by distorting their origin, their history, their evolution, and their spiritual possessions. They began the experiment with themselves. Those among whom they lived discovered that the presence of Jews in the organism of the various states was more than a mere fact, it was a problem, and in the interests of their own development they could not overlook this problem which had no real solution. Before arriving at a rough solution, which consisted in removing the inequalities imposed on the Jews, most countries tried to alter the latter's mental and cultural condition in such a way as to abolish as far as possible the difference between them and their own people. And thus experimenting with the Jews began.

In order to understand the basis on which these experiments were founded in the various countries, we must once more for a moment consider the legal position of the Jews in them. Incidentally, it is important to note that the Jewish world had been enriched by the acquisition of two new and two old countries—America and Russia had opened up fresh spheres, and in France and England two old places of domicile had just been recovered.

After the extirpation of the first Jewish settlements in America through the Inquisition, a new colonization by Jews began in 1650, and spread over the north coast of South America, the Antilles, the British West Indies, and North America. In North America, which had no ecclesiastical tradition, only faint signs of the hostility brought over from Europe were to be found. The absence of any church influence was shown during that great crisis in American history, the War of Independence (1775–1783). The Jews took part in the struggle, as a rule supporting those who were fighting for liberty. And, as might almost have been expected, it was a Jew, Chaim Salomon, who was obliged to finance the revolution. In America equality of rights for Jews did not constitute a very serious problem; it was implicitly provided for in the Declaration of Independence of 1776: "We hold these truths to be self-evident, that all men are created equal, that they are endowed by their Creator with certain unalienable Rights, that among these are Life, Liberty, and the pursuit of Happiness." Here we recognize the voice of religion and not of a church, and the terms used in the Federal Constitution were the outcome of this: "Congress shall make no law respecting an establishment of religion, or prohibiting the free exercise thereof . . ." And thus America ceased to play a part in the drama of Jewish emancipation.

In France the Jewish problem again came to the fore, owing to the immigration of Marranos into the south, and the annexation of Alsace with its old Ashkenazic Jewish elements. The French government winked its eye at the Sephardic Jews who entered the country armed with considerable wealth and extensive international commercial relations, and it pretended for the sake of principle to believe they were Portuguese even long after they had declared themselves to be Jews. In 1776 Louis XVI gave them the right of domicile in France, but the only favour he showed the Alsatian Jews was to relieve them of the poll-tax in 1784. Otherwise his treatment of them was true to tradition—without granting them any rights, he imposed extremely severe obligations upon them, and furthermore, endeavoured to reduce their numbers by the limitation of marriages. In the other provinces the Jews were only temporarily tolerated for the purpose of concluding certain business transactions.

The Jews who again landed in England shortly before the outbreak of the Grand Rebellion were also Marranos, who had escaped from the Inquisition. The situation was favourable to them. Puritanism, with its religious foundation, saw in them an opportunity for redeeming certain historical injustices, while Cromwell also saw the possibility of reaping both economic and political advantages from them. His aim was to attract Jews over to England and away from her great trade rival, Holland, and to direct the constant stream of Marrano emigrants to the shores of his country. But he never succeeded in realizing his aims by means of legislation, and for the time being the attitude of England was nothing more than one of benevolent interest. But an important part was played in this respect by the growth of economic relations between the Jews and England. Charles II, who was in exile in Flanders, promised to support the Amsterdam Jews, in return for which they undertook to give him financial assistance. This Anglo-

Dutch connexion became even closer under William III, and the economic importance of the Jews in England increased. The stock exchanges of both Amsterdam and London were controlled by Jews. Individual Jews of good repute were also allowed to take out naturalization papers. In 1753 a law was passed in Parliament allowing all Jews who had lived in England for more than three years to obtain parliamentary sanction for their naturalization, but it was repealed in the following year owing to protests on the part of those classes of the community who were interested. While their influence in trade and industry increased, and they were able to attain to a comparatively high level of culture, the Jews thus enjoyed, for at least the next hundred years, a state of freedom which only lacked a legal basis.

Holland too confined herself to granting the Jews freedom of conscience, and the right to administer their own communities autonomously. She did not grant them equal rights of citizenship, and, whereas she favoured those Jews who were substantial shareholders in the East and West Indian Companies, she oppressed the great mass of them by forbidding them to enter any calling which was represented by a guild or trade corporation.

In the Papal States, the Jewish problem was still where it had been under the old medieval ghetto conditions. The Jews were still confined to their special small quarter; they were allowed to engage only in retail trade and handicrafts; exorbitant taxes were still extorted from the poor wretches for the curia (at the beginning of the eighteenth century the tiny Roman community had accumulated debts amounting to over £50,000), and their children were still kidnapped for the purpose of being forcibly baptized.

Spain and Portugal also kept their Jewish problem alive with the help of the Inquisition. Three hundred years after the "Holy War," there were still secret Jews in Spain, consequently the Inquisition still had work to do in that country. The burning of men alive for their faith had become a form of public entertainment, like the bull fights. On the occasion of the marriage of Charles II with Louis XIV's niece, a grand *auto-da-fé* was organized in Madrid, at which 86 heretics were burned at the stake, among them 50 Judaizing Marranos. Between 1720 and 1730, 100 similar *autos-da-fé* took place, and Marranos were still fleeing the country. Obviously in Spain there could be no question whatever of granting equal rights to the Jews for the simple reason that, according to the Spanish authorities, there were no Jews in the country but only renegade Christians.

And the same applies to Portugal to an even greater degree. During the first half of the eighteenth century the Inquisition accounted for countless victims, and what Montesquieu said in 1748 in his *Esprit des Lois* about the Inquisition is very true: "If anyone in days to come should ever dare to say that the people of Europe were civilized in the century in which we are now living, you" [that is to say, the Inquisitors of Spain] "will be referred to as a proof that they were barbarians."

It is dismaying to think how slight an effort was required to put a stop to the activities of the Inquisition. In 1751 Joseph I of Portugal decreed that in future all trials held by the Inquisition should be conducted in accordance with general legal practice, and that sentences should be carried out only after they had been ratified by the government. This to all intents and purposes put an end to the Inquisition, for the compulsion to follow legal procedure prevented it from carrying on its ghastly work in private and it could no longer survive.

In Poland there was no change in the fundamental attitude towards the Jews. But how could this country be expected to adopt a rational attitude towards a foreign section of its population when even its own people could not come to an understanding under the constant disastrous partitions of the country between Prussia, Austria, and Russia? Even hatred of the Jews was not unanimous. The situation could not be more clearly outlined than it was in the declaration of the Synod of Plock in 1773: "We are well aware that people tolerate this race of infidels in other parts of the state as also abroad, but, after all, the only object of such toleration is the conversion of the remnant of Israel. . . . But our reason is that these Jews who live among us may remind us of the sufferings of Christ the Lord, and that divine justice may manifest itself in them, our slaves, by their shame and misery." But the szlachta, whose competitors they were, declared: "Prompted more by cupidity than by religious zeal, the representatives of the clergy concern themselves with discovering all kinds of pretexts for oppressing the Jews."

As we have pointed out more than once, the position of the Jews was made far worse by the partition of Poland; the lot of those who fell to the portion of Russia being particularly deplorable. Their incorporation in the Muscovite empire meant for hundreds of thousands of Jews that they were transferred to Asia and abandoned to the tender mercies of the Middle Ages, without even having to move from their homes. For, until this happened, Russia had been hermetically sealed against the Jews, and apparently it is inevitable for every people, among whom the Jews happen to appear, to go through the whole gamut of reactions inspired by their presence; it would almost seem that it is the destiny of the Jews to be the scapegoats on whom all peoples in the early stages of their development vent their savage passions. In this respect Russia had a good thousand years of headway and reaction to make up, and she left no stone unturned to prove herself equal to the task.

The Russians did not know the Jews. When the latter were dispersed and began to spread, the frontiers of Russia were already closed to them, for the profession of the Orthodox Faith in itself meant separation from the countries on her western frontier, and her isolation was further emphasized by a curious religious fanaticism. The influence of the clergy was alone responsible for making the people regard the Jews as manifestations of the Antichrist and a satanic race. The first Jews the Russian people ever set eyes upon were the prisoners of war taken from Poland in 1665–1666. Of these, some were forcibly baptized and retained, while the unbaptized were restored to Poland. In spite of this, the Jews, under the pressure of economic distress, crossed the boundary into Russia and entered Little Russia and Smolensk; but they were very soon driven out again. The Jewish population of Russia, however, was substantially increased owing to the annexation of fresh territory. In 1668 the district of Kiev, the fanatical centre of Russian orthodoxy, was joined to Russia, and in 1772 White Russia, with 100,000 Jews, was incorporated in the Russian empire. The Ukraine and Lithuania, which fell to the share of Russia by the second and third partition of Poland, together with White Russia, constituted the district known as West Russia. But the new rulers of the Jews did not allow them free access into every part of the country, but from the very beginning restricted them to the areas they had hitherto occupied. The result was the formation of the so-called pale of settlement, which at the end of the eighteenth century had already assumed the compass which in broad outline it was destined to retain—that is to say, thirteen governments, of which five were Lithuanian-White-Russian, five Ukrainian, and three New Russian.

Thus the beginnings of the Russian Diaspora were marked by the same characteristics as we have already noticed elsewhere—restrictions regarding domicile, arbitrary expulsions, and the acceptance of baptized Jews. But the full anomaly of the Jewish situation came to light only when it was found that even the inclusion of the Jews in the general legal system of the country was very far from being to their advantage. By the original treaties, which had led to the first partition of Poland, the Jews had had their existing rights safeguarded, and in White Russia might theoretically participate in the administration of the parish or municipality, by means of voting or standing for election. But in order to do so, they were obliged to submit to the class distinction which divided the urban populations into merchants and petty bourgeoisie. They were forced to enrol themselves in one of these two classes, and were consequently *compelled* to congregate in the towns. The result was that large numbers of Jews who had made their living in the country as farmers and innkeepers were not only deprived of their means of livelihood, but owing to the pressure of population in the towns were also condemned to enter upon a more severe competitive struggle than ever. Moreover, they were taxed twice as heavily as Christians.

It was upon the legal basis just described that the various authorities now began to make their experiments. In this matter of experimenting with the Jews, America, Spain, and Portugal are of course excluded, as is also England, inasmuch as in the latter country such experiments as were made were undertaken by the Jews themselves, and took the form of assimilation. In the case of the various governments who experimented with the Jews, their action was inspired by a spiritual atmosphere electrified by the consciousness of the equality of man, and upon the recognition of the fact that too marked and too glaring a contrast existed between the legal position of the Jews and their pronounced economic and increasing cultural importance.

The earliest champion of the idea of equal rights for the Jews, who was inspired by pure feelings of humanity, was probably John Toland, the philosopher of enlightenment, who was also possibly the first to set up the ideal of "free thought." In his polemic against the separatist spirit of the nations, he is akin to Lessing, who by tolerance very rightly understood not mere sufferance, but sacrifice of prestige, and the renunciation by the Christian states of the idea that godliness prevented them from treating the Jews as equal as long as they failed to embrace Christianity. Next to Lessing as the idealist comes Christian Wilhelm von Dohm, the politician and practical man, who in 1781, partly under the influence of Mendelssohn, published his treatise *Concerning the Improvement of the Civic Condition of the Jews.* This work is thoroughly typical of the age, with its humanitarian and utilitarian ideas, its goodwill, and its perplexities. It constitutes an eminently rational apology for the Jews, and ends by proposing that they should gradually be emancipated as they advanced in "civic virtue," and that they should be granted freedom to trade; but they were to be prevented, as far as possible, from engaging in commerce, and only exceptionally were they to be employed by the state. Philanthropy and justice in small doses! Utility as the basis of humanity!

The intellectual world of France adopted a somewhat similar attitude. The behaviour of Voltaire, that passionate and fanatical champion of rights, towards the Jews, can hardly be taken into account, for in the course of his numerous financial and stock exchange transactions, he was twice accused by Jews of embezzlement and forgery, and avenged himself by exploiting his powers as a publicist. Before his conflict with the Jews, however, his views were summed up as follows: "May the Christians cease from persecuting and despising those who, as human beings, are their brothers, and, as Jews, their fathers." Yet, in saying this, he was merely making his contribution to a topical subject—the concern felt by all educated people in the Jewish question. This interest was not particularly profound, it was no more than the interest of the man of culture, and even the sympathy of prominent individuals did not help to remove the utilitarian factor. Extremely characteristic was the action taken by the Royal Society of Science and Art of Metz in 1785. This body made the question the subject of a prize competition (just as prize competitions are organized for the building of a town hall) and incidentally revealed its fundamental attitude in the form in which the question was put: "Is there any means of making the Jews of France more useful and more happy?" Of the nine attempts sent in, seven suggested solving the problem by means of emancipation; some supported the suggestion extremely ably and were far less utilitarian in the solutions they offered than the framers of the question had apparently been.

The various states and governments could not, of course, be expected to show the same spontaneity and genuine warm-heartedness as a Lessing or a Mirabeau. In the case of nations, it is a long and laborious business to bring home to them that they have been guilty of injustice, and only too easily does an attitude of mind come into being, which converts a perfectly clear and simple obligation into a pathetic gesture of magnanimous and noble generosity, which forces the recipient into an attitude of grovelling gratitude bordering on the suicidal. All countries, with the exception of America, England, and Holland, steadfastly upheld the antiquated teaching of the Christian Church that Judaism should be annihilated. In the year 1800, as in the year 400, baptism still remained the gulf in which the aloofness and resistance of yesterday could be sunk. And where baptism did not come to the rescue, they aimed, as in the East, at total annihilation, and in the West, at partial annihilation by suppressing and obliterating the differentiating features. Even the *Toleranzpatent* of Joseph II of Austria was conceived in this pedagogic spirit. The Jews were expected to make themselves as indistinguishable as possible from the other representatives of Germano-Christian culture, and any who were so deeply impregnated by this culture as to be baptized were given the land they farmed by way of reward. The majority of the Austrian Jews, however, with the exception of those who belonged to the sphere of high finance or the educated upper classes of Vienna, Prague, and Budapest, met these attempts at educating them and these rewards for good conduct, with the most pronounced suspicion. For this system of meliorization reduced thousands of them, particularly in Galicia, to beggary, since they were forbidden to lease landed property or to adopt the calling of innkeepers or publicans. Nor were economic conditions any longer sufficiently fluid to enable them to build up new careers, in a night, so to speak. Moreover, they were oppressed by the most exorbitant taxation. The authorities also endeavoured, as they had done in the past, to reduce their numbers by means of restricting their marriages, while it was in Austria that Jews were first conscripted for the army. This measure meant that the manner of life traditional to Jewish youth was seriously jeopardized, while the army itself regarded the presence of Jews among them as derogatory to their caste.

Until the end of the eighteenth century the *Reglement* of Frederick the Great, conceived in the spirit of the barrackyard, and which Mirabeau stigmatized as *"une loi digne d'un cannibale,"* continued to hold sway in Prussia. Frederick William II, on his accession to the throne, made many full-throated promises "to alleviate, as far as possible, the lot of this persecuted nation." And, as a matter of fact, he did actually abolish the poll-tax. But the "improvements," which it took the Prussian government two years to draft, proved to be so inadequate, that the Jews preferred to abide by the *Reglement* of "old Fritz." And when Prussia, under the influence of the emancipation of the Jews in France, produced a fresh set of proposals, they acted in a similar way.

Poland, too, after catching a breath of the liberal tendencies of the time, made a problem of the Jewish question. The Poles, in keeping with their tradition, were almost completely unanimous on one point —that the problem could be solved only by taking drastic measures, but they disagreed as to their nature. Incapable though they were of educating themselves, they proposed to educate the Jews both politically and intellectually before they granted them the dignity of citizenship. The Sejm appointed a commission to examine the question, but it had neither the desire nor the capacity to make any definite proposals.

In the middle of all these experiments, an upheaval occurred which reverberated through the whole of Europe and led to a temporary but also precipitate and unsound solution of the emancipation question— the French Revolution. At first it was marked by strong anti-Jewish feeling, and the members of the National Assembly representing Alsace and Lorraine were armed by their constituents with instructions definitely hostile to the Jews. In the early years of the Revolution, Alsace endeavoured to influence the debates and the course of legislation by persecuting the Jews in the hope of proving that the disparity between the latter and their own people was too great to make it advisable to grant them equal rights. Thus it was plain that even the revolutionary ideas of freedom and equality, not to mention fraternity, were not, as a matter of course, intended to apply to the Jews. In spite of the general declaration that no man was to suffer any restrictions of liberty on account of his convictions, even his religious convictions, the only result of an endeavour to apply this fundamental principle was to place Catholics and non-Catholics on an equal footing as regards the right to vote and to stand for election. The Jews were obliged to send a special deputation to remind the legislature of their existence, but the authorities were content for the time being to postpone reaching a decision. The only exception that was made was in favour of the Sephardim, the Spanish Jews in the south of France, who met the legislature half-way by declaring, in opposition to the Jews of Alsace, that they renounced anything in the nature of an autonomous administration of their own community, and in other respects had nothing whatever in common with Ashkenazic Jews.

Whereupon the latter began a violent agitation for equality of rights, while behind the scenes the National Assembly started an equally violent agitation against any such concession. Jews were even excluded from the privilege granted to all foreigners of being allowed to enjoy equal rights of citizenship after five years' domicile in the country. It was only when, on the 3rd of September, the king ratified the Constitution, that the legislature, in order to avoid making nonsense of it by allowing a glaring inconsistency to remain, were compelled explicitly to acknowledge equality of political rights for the Jews. This took place on the 28th of September 1791. But the Alsatian Jews were at the same time ordered, in view of a settlement that was about to be made, to give up some of their claims against Christian debtors.

Thus, as we see, the application of the principle of the rights of man stopped short at the claims of the Jews and could not resist the temptation to resort to pedagogic methods. As a matter of fact, the authorities were not altogether pleased with those Jews who, unlike the Sephardim, were not becoming assimilated at a sufficiently high speed. Even the fact that Jews, especially in Paris, had joined the Garde Nationale and the political clubs, and were taking part in the wars of defence, giving material help to the Revolution and sacrificing themselves on the field of battle and on the guillotine, did not improve the general attitude. *Égalité,* as applied to the Jews, was not to be confounded with equality, but was at best to be interpreted as homogeneity in the sense of uniformity. Thus, under the ægis of the only revolution that had taken place in the modern world, the situation was much the same as it was in the most reactionary countries. People resolutely refused to see that the disturbing conditions were the product of history and the result of the environment in which the Jews were placed; they tried to change everything in the twinkling of an eye, and above all to force the Jew to take his place and merge himself in the more or less homogeneous mass of the people. A difficult reform of this nature, which even in more tranquil circumstances would have required time, was during this period of constant warfare and economic and financial upheavals, quite impossible. And the Jews were reproached with doing too little and showing a lack of patriotism, particularly during the wars of the Directoire, and later on under Napoleon, both as First Consul and as Emperor. Nobody stopped to inquire whether the Jews, after fifteen hundred years of barbarous oppression, did not perhaps cherish a different ideal from that of letting themselves be cut to pieces on the battlefields of the world for the sake of the ambitious designs of a single individual, however great.

Incidentally, it may be mentioned that this great man adopted the usual, conventional attitude towards the Jewish question, and it was only in his solution of it that he showed any originality. During his extraordinary campaign in the East, he had tried after capturing Gaza and Jaffa, to induce the Jews of Asia and Africa to support his efforts by promising them to restore the Holy City to them. But it was impossible for the Jews to respond to such a fantastic proposal, and Napoleon may have borne them a secret grudge on that account. In any case, he lacked both the will and the personal knowledge for an objective judgment of the question. And when the Concordat made with the pope again brought the Jewish question to his notice, he merely instructed the ministerial offices concerned to furnish him with a report on the Jews and their condition. In this report there was at least one feature calculated to infuriate him, and that was the fact that the Jews had from time immemorial constituted a nation of their own, and still did so, and that it was impossible to alter their mental status. But to Napoleon, who had seized the power over a state, the idea of the state was almost sacrosanct. He regarded the state as nothing else than a spiritually uniform order, at the apex of which he himself stood, while the base consisted of the various groups and classes of the population who looked to him as their leader. Any separate claims, either on the part of a national or an ecclesiastical group, appeared to him in the light of a damaging attack on the sovereignty of the state. Just as in his struggle with the pope and the church he was animated by the embittered reflection that subjects belonging to his state were lost to him by being ordained priests, and thus becoming part of an international corporation which he hated, so he was outraged by the idea that a group within the French nation was in the domain of the spirit leading an autonomous existence. Hence his violent attack on them at the Conseil d'État, when he said: "The Jews are to be regarded as a nation and not as a sect. They are a nation within the nation. The proper law to apply to them is not the civil but the political law, for they are not French citizens."

Napoleon soon saw that this point of view could not be reconciled with the constitution but, as he had correctly grasped the principle of the problem, he resorted to a twofold solution of it–he adopted the educative policy applied in other countries with the object of "improving" the Jews, and he also had recourse to an ingeniously disguised policy of extortion, by means of which he broke the back of French Judaism. He issued a decree staying execution of judgment in favour of Jewish creditors against the peasants of Alsace for a twelvemonth, and commanded a deputation consisting of a hundred representatives of French Jewry to come to Paris and make a declaration of loyalty.

All the communities, even the Italian ones annexed to France, hastened to elect representatives. One hundred and twelve in all assembled in Paris, Sephardim and Ashkenazim, advocates of enlightenment and conservatives, all full of expectation that momentous events were about to occur. And this was indeed the case. They were confronted with twelve questions, preceded by an introduction which contained a thinly veiled and perfectly obvious threat that, if the Jews of France returned unsatisfactory replies to them, it would not be at all to their advantage. The first three questions, of which the most important inquired whether mixed marriages were allowed between Jews and Christians, related to Jewish family law. The next three were intended to test the patriotism of the Jews–did the Jews regard the French as foreigners or as brothers? Did they regard France as their native country, which they must defend with their blood and treasure and whose laws they were bound to obey? Questions regarding the influence of the rabbis followed, and finally inquiries of an economic nature, among which there was one of particular importance in connexion with the taking of interest, and whether the Jewish law drew any distinction between Jewish and Christian debtors.

The aim of these questions is plain enough. Mixed marriages, patriotism, the functions of the rabbis, and the business attitude of Jews towards non-Jews–to all these matters the replies were expected to be in the spirit expressed by Napoleon in the introduction: *"Sa Majesté veut que vous soyez Français."* He decreed and the Jews obeyed. They regarded mixed marriages as permissible according to the "civil law"; they were quite ready to renounce autonomy in their communities; they were in every respect Frenchmen and nothing more; there was no longer any such thing as a Jewish nation. "At the present day the Jews no longer constitute a nation, since they have had the privilege of being incorporated into the great nation in which they expect to find their political salvation." In an excess of willingness to make every possible concession, they actually expressed their gratitude for the fact that the heads of the Christian Church had at all times shown them benevolence and protection. What foundation they could find in history for such a statement it is difficult to see.

The attitude of this assembly of notables has been stigmatized as servile and grovelling. This is perfectly true. But it was merely the outcome of a long and gradual process of degeneration which we must now examine more closely.

We have already called attention to the fact that the educative experiments of the various governments were inextricably connected with the question of the civic equality of the Jews, and that, on the other hand, in the efforts of the latter to secure these civil rights, there was a deep strain of utilitarianism. The combination of these two tendencies, although they started out from different principles, had the same end in view and gave rise to the idea of assimilation, which led to the Jew experimenting with himself. An extremely complex and many-sided process now came into operation which revealed down to the last detail the internal problem of the Jews.

Before the outside world had shown any signs of wishing to take the smallest positive action in favour of the Jews and was even heaping fresh burdens upon them with its vexatious educative experiments, their whole existence was already being moulded by the *possibilities* opening up before them, one of which, that of getting into touch with the culture of the rest of the world, they seized of their own accord. They were able to do this because the bonds which had hitherto bound them to their Jewish environment were breaking down and no longer held them enchained. The other possibilities, consisting of economic, legal, and political freedom, were offered to them by the outside world on certain conditions. Hitherto the Jews had enjoyed only the means of existence, and even that had only been vouchsafed them subject to endless restrictions, and now for the first time for centuries they were confronted with the chance of development. Hitherto they had, as a rule, lived in a state of bondage; now they saw the possibility of gaining freedom, though as we shall see later on they gave this concept of freedom a false interpretation. For the Jews freedom consisted in being released from bondage. In communities and states, freedom can be secured only when others are willing to respect it, and it cannot be maintained that even at the present day this condition has yet been universally realized.

The exploitation of the intellectual possibilities and the striving after others had this important result, that the isolation which had previously existed was spontaneously broken down. Wherever the Jew did not himself effect this change because he wished to abandon isolation, the aim of all the educative experiments was to make him do so. Moreover, we must remember that the changes in the economic structure of Europe had opened up new avenues to the Jew, particularly to the Jew with a large capital at his back. The less isolated he became, the more intricate were his relations with the outside world, with which points of contact were likely to lead to friction as well as to assimilation. And he now decided in the main in favour of assimilation, the scope of any discussion on the subject being predetermined by the bait of emancipation held out to him by his environment. As a matter of fact, no dispute, that is to say, no impartial, mutual examination or contest of strength, ever took place. The Jew was forced to confine himself to an attitude of apology towards the outside world, and of reform in his own. But reform was, in itself, a step towards assimilation.

Adaptation and assimilation are really natural processes which almost invariably come into operation when minorities get into touch with surrounding majorities, regardless of which party is assimilated. It is a process calculated considerably to broaden the spiritual treasures and vision of a people. The mere assimilation to a civilization is of course purely subordinate. But assimilation only becomes a vital problem for a people when, instead of regarding it as the adoption of things of spiritual and formal value from the environment, they have to regard it as the adoption of such things subject to a simultaneous renunciation of their own peculiarities. The fact the Jews assimilated themselves to French and German culture and the French and German language could redound only to their own advantage and to that of the cultures concerned. But the fact that this meant the sacrifice of Jewish culture as a whole, and above all of its fundamental principles, was, from the historical point of view, a mistake. It was clearly a possible solution, but only from the standpoint of the individual and his difficulties. As a matter of fact, many individuals adopted it. It is of interest to note that both in Mendelssohn's own family, as well as in the circle which formed about his ideas, there were many who spontaneously inclined to become assimilated. Men like Heine, Börne, Marx, and Lassalle were merely the shining lights of an intellectual set who followed the ideas that Mendelssohn had formulated with the best of intentions, and which they carried to their logical conclusion. From Mendelssohn's Judaism they separated the law, which they felt they could no longer regard as binding on themselves. What remained was a Judaism composed of resentment, not strong enough to prevent them from becoming converted to Christianity, or sufficiently binding to enable their consciousness of the homogeneity of the Jewish people, in the sense of the Jewish idea, to become creative. True, even after his conversion to Christianity, the creations of a man like Heine remained Jewish creations, the creations of the Jewish spirit; but even though they may have sprung from Judaism, it is just as impossible to place them to its credit, as the works of Paul or any other renegade who gives up his national associations. For the renunciation of the national associations is merely the external and formal aspect of the case. The important loss suffered by a community, in the present instance the Jewish, lies in the renunciation by one of its members of the will to be both a creator and an heir of the common national treasure, in order from that basis to become a benefactor to all communities. Here again, the important factor is not that a man admits his nationality, but that, when the peculiar note of a certain nationality is suppressed, the world-focus becomes distorted. Regarded from the standpoint of the whole body of nations and cultures, a nation is that which the individual is from the standpoint of the community, that is to say, a personality. And this personality possesses creative power, and is to a greater degree than the individual the representative of religion, the guarantor of human development. As long as a community understands this, it is entitled, as a personality, to defend itself against falsification and suppression, and to base its claims against every other nation upon the obligation imposed upon it by its own individuality.

But such spiritual decision presupposes a life that is real and free. The Jew of the end of the eighteenth century, however, possessed only possibilities. Confronted by the alternative of cutting the bonds that bound him as an individual, and receiving in exchange the right of citizenship, or of remaining in his state of shattered isolation, bereft of all rights, the West-European Jew decided in favour of abandoning his national form and consciousness, and accepting what was useful to him—civil rights and the nation in which he happened to be living. As in that case personality, as we have defined it, vanishes, so does also the dignified bearing which arises from the sense of personality; and, regarded from this point of view, the attitude of the Jewish notables towards Napoleon's infamous questions may indeed be stigmatized as servile and grovelling. It is not necessary to remind the historian, however, that even this renunciation of dignity was the outcome of a development that had been forced upon the Jews.

Whereas the Jewish notables were still labouring under the delusion that at a moment of historic crisis they were contributing to the salvation and emancipation of their people, they were, as a matter of fact, merely playing into Napoleon's hands and serving as the instruments of his policy. The declarations they had given him, though satisfactory in themselves, did not seem to him to be sufficiently formal and binding. He accordingly ordered an assembly of official representatives of the French Jews to be convened, who would be in a position to confirm and guarantee the declaration of the Jewish notables, and it was a stroke of genius on his part to make this gathering take the form of the old Sanhedrin, an institution whose very name was so crowded with historic memories that it might be expected to make a profound impression on the Jews not only of France but of the whole world. And in point of fact this was Napoleon's aim. In the official decree, he ordered the convocation of an assembly, "whose resolutions may be placed side by side with the Talmud, and be such as to exert the highest authority over the Jews of every country." But Champagny, Napoleon's minister of the interior, who was kept accurately informed, wrote to his master: "We must contrive to make this assembly through its resolutions provide us with a weapon not only against itself, but against the race it represents." This was Napoleon's actual intention, and he realized it, inasmuch as the Jews themselves spared him the pains of solving the Jewish problem. He achieved his object by a blend of brutal blackmailing and elaborate showmanship. Actually, he gave the Jews nothing except a magnificent display on the lines of a pageant. On the other hand he induced the representatives of western Judaism to give voice to declarations which for a long time have falsified the ideology of Judaism, and the emancipation which the notables fondly imagined they were celebrating was really nothing but one last grand act of suppression.

The "Sanhedrin" assembled in February 1807. It consisted of the traditional 71 members, of whom 46 were rabbis and 25 laymen. They met like men in a hypnotic trance; their patriotic enthusiasm surpassed all bounds; and everything the notables had declared was forthwith unhesitatingly confirmed. They went even further, and these heirs of a shattered ideal who were the representatives of western Jewry, at a moment when it was most loosely and feebly bound together, held a debate to establish what Judaism really was. They made a "declaration," in which the extinction of the Jewish nation was referred to as an accomplished fact; and this rendered it possible for them to discover a difference between religious and political laws in Judaism. Whereas they held the former to be unalterable, they declared that the latter were no longer binding *"depuis qu'ils ne forment plus un corps de nation."* And, in the event of the two clashing, even the religious laws were to be held subordinate to the laws of the state in which they lived.

This amenable attitude naturally led Napoleon to expect that they would recommend mixed marriages, abandon money-lending, and give special guarantees for the performance of military service, with the object of providing men for the army. But as they did not do so, he himself settled all these remaining questions, in so far as their practical solution could be enforced. After the resolutions of the Sanhedrin had been laid before the council, therefore, two decrees were issued. The first introduced the consistorial system for the Jews, an official institution which was really nothing more than an executive arm of the government; the other amounted to the most blatant violation of the constitution with a view to enabling Napoleon to solve the Jewish question by means of compulsion and "melioration." This was the famous *Décret Infâme* of 1808, which dealt with the economic position of the Jews. In it not only were a number of Jewish claims for debt declared null and void, but even the plying of a trade and the legality of a commercial transaction were made dependent on the acquisition of a special "patent." No further settlements were to be made in Alsace, and in the rest of France Jews were to be allowed to settle only if they took up agriculture. The right allowed to everybody else of evading military service by appointing a substitute was expressly withheld from the Jews. Such measures ran counter to the principle of emancipation, and substituted for it a system of education. Out of 68 departments, 44 were still ruled by the *Décret Infâme* up to the time of Napoleon's fall.

The granting and withdrawing of equal rights was repeated, except for Holland, in all the European states that, either from the military or political point of view, came under the influence of the French Republic or the Napoleonic empire—by the republic through enforcing the principle of the "Rights of Man," and by the empire through the compulsory establishment of the consistorial system. When, with the help of the French army of occupation, the Dutch republicans set up the Batavian Republic (1795), they proclaimed the equality of all citizens, including the Jews. And under the subsequent monarchy in Holland this state of affairs was maintained. In the other states, emancipation only lasted as long as the French remained in power over them. In Rome there were disastrous fluctuations. Because the revolution was oppressing the church in France, the pope oppressed the Jews. When in February 1789 he was deposed by General Berthier, the French gave the Jews in the "Roman Republic" the rights of Roman citizens. But when the French domination was succeeded by the Neapolitan, heavy fines were imposed on the Jews for their share in the revolution (1799). When the Papal States were annexed to France in 1809, the Jews were again granted the rights of citizenship, only to lose them on the return of the popes in 1814. Similar fluctuations occurred in Venice and in Padua. In Switzerland, which became the Republic of Helvetia in 1798, there was also a Jewish problem, although there were only 200 Jewish families in the country, and there was much anxious debating as to whether this handful of people should be granted equal rights. In the end they were refused.

The Duchy of Warsaw, created by Napoleon, was obliged at his bidding to adopt a liberal constitution, which postulated the equality of all citizens before the law. This also included the Jews. But the privilege was immediately taken from them for a period of ten years "in the hope that meanwhile they would get rid of the peculiarities which so sharply distinguished them from the rest of the people."

In Germany, between 1792 and 1794, Mayence, Worms, Speyer, and Cologne were captured, and the Jews were granted equal rights of citizenship by proclamation. The Kingdom of Westphalia, that short-lived creation of Napoleonic policy, granted the Jews equal rights of citizenship for six years; the Grand Duchy of Frankfurt-am-Main for two years (1810–1812), Hamburg for three years. It was also due to the influence of the French invasion that Frederick William III of Prussia was induced to grant concessions and to relax his absolute rule. Thus, at first, in pursuance of the new ordinance for cities, the Jews were recognized as citizens, and after the flight of the king to Königsberg, as citizens of the state of Prussia, by virtue of the "Edict concerning the Citizenship of the Jews in the Prussian State," of March 11, 1812. This edict abolished all the special laws applying to the Jews and granted them freedom to move from place to place, and liberty to choose any calling they pleased.

The other states did their best to guard against the fashion for emancipation prevalent at the time, which was comprehensible enough in itself. There were no signs of a general intellectual readiness to recognize the rights of man, and even though no state was too small and insignificant to afford the luxury of having a Jewish problem, it must be admitted that it was one that presented enormous difficulties. In forming an opinion about the Jews, they never had any standard of comparison except their own or any means of checking themselves, and were guided entirely by what an extremely intolerant church had taught them for centuries, and their own economic interests. And for this reason a liberal attitude on the part of those who could emancipate themselves from generations of constraint was all the more praiseworthy. When Bavaria in 1808 and Saxony in 1813 first abolished the poll-tax on the Jews, under pressure of the occupation of the Prusso-Russian army, they were acting consistently with their attitude and the political maturity they had reached.

But further east and further removed from French influence, the educational experiments made upon Jews became more drastic. The East was transformed into a sort of Jewish reformatory run by dragooning pedagogues. Every fresh act of repression was introduced with solemn assurances that it was all for the Jews' own good, and that it must be regarded as a preliminary step to granting them equal rights. In addition to those already described, Austria continued to devise fresh measures of oppression. Three especially were constantly re-enacted—excessive taxation, which merely reflected the old idea that the Jews must be forced to bring in money; compulsory education at the Christian schools, inspired by the idea that the Jews must be imbued with Christian culture; and a more severe application of conscription as a means of educating them in patriotism and of allowing them to make some return for the rights granted them.

We have already briefly described early conditions in Russia, and here too the nineteenth century inaugurated a more severe educational system for the Jews. Alexander I appointed a "Committee for the Proper Organization of the Jews." But bitter experience had taught the Jews what "proper organization" meant, and a meeting of the Kahal at Minsk appealed to Moscow, begging the authorities if possible to maintain the *status quo*. But it was useless. Willynilly, the Jews had to be improved. And thus, at the end of 1804, the "Statute concerning the Organization of the Jews" was passed, the main object of which was to enforce a social reshuffling of the Jewish population. Considering the callings to which the Jews had hitherto been limited, their social stratification was by no means abnormal, though it was naturally circumscribed. The Jews in the country districts were usually leaseholders, and also innkeepers, corn-dealers, and merchants. In the towns they were engaged in trade, usually retail trade, and the sale of wines and spirits; they were also to a large extent artisans. The Russian government recognized the beneficial influence exercised by the rich Jews on Russian industry, which was still in its infancy, but it regarded the activities of the village Jews as exploitation of the rural population, and it aimed at promoting industry and at the same time putting a stop to the activities of the leaseholders and making it possible for them to engage in agriculture. It therefore had recourse to drastic measures and forbade the Jews to live in the villages, with the result that about 300,000 were set on the move.

But as the Jewish quarters in the towns had not been enlarged, the people who had to leave the villages had nowhere to go to and had to be ejected by force. This was done partly by the soldiers, who drove them into the towns and left them stranded in the streets. Whereupon the Jews demanded from the government the land it had promised to give them for farming. By the end of 1806, 1500 families had already sent in applications for this. But the government was not by any means prepared to place the necessary land and the necessary means at their disposal for settling down. It managed to settle about 2000 persons in the government of Kherson in 1807, after which it could do no more. And in 1810 it was obliged to put a stop to all further colonization, although the number of applicants was enormous. It had been found necessary as early as 1808 to put a stop to driving the Jews out of the villages. Thus, except for the fact that a few thousand Jewish farmers had been created, the only result of this experiment had been to destroy innumerable lives and homes.

The Jewish response to all these experiments soon revealed a serious cleavage. At the time when the Polish centre in the East was at the height of its prosperity, western Judaism possessed no culture of its own but was spiritually entirely dependent on the East. But with the inauguration of the movement of "enlightenment" in the West, this dependence ceased and the bonds with the East were gradually loosened. This first became apparent in the attitude of the Jews towards the outside world. Whereas in the East the great majority of Jews offered bitter passive resistance to all "attempts at improvement," more especially those that affected their spiritual life, in the West we are confronted by such phenomena as the attitude adopted by the Jewish notables in Paris. At the same time, the western Jew regarded the behaviour of his brother in the East as hostile and prejudicial to his own willingness to become assimilated. He now proceeded to act towards the latter as the Sephardic Jews in France had done towards the Ashkenazic, and the difference between the Jew in the West and in the East was based precisely on the former's recent adoption of an alien culture. From this time onwards, it is possible to speak of western and eastern Jews.

A similar change, based upon the possession of a European education, also occurred among the western Jews themselves, particularly in Germany. An intellectual élite stood out from the mass of ordinary Jews, from whom they were separated, not so much by the fact that they were more educated, but by the aims and tendencies of their education, the use they made of it, and the conclusions to which it led. Here, too, when utilitarian motives did not intervene, the all too hasty cultural assimilation had been followed by national assimilation. When once they had become adapted to European culture, nothing else remained for them. It must be admitted that they embraced it whole-heartedly, and the fact that Jewish women, like Henriette Herz and Rahel Lewin, were able to make their drawing-rooms gathering places for the intellectual aristocracy of Germany, insignificant though this is in the perspective of history, at least bears witness to the warmth and enthusiasm with which the Jews interested themselves in culture in that country. It was purely as the result of this kind of surrender that cultivated Jews became converted to Christianity in ever larger numbers, and that, owing to humanitarianism or expediency, this flight to Christianity became a regular mass phenomenon. The idea behind the French Revolution, which reality so quickly suffocated, had remained rooted in the best heads and hearts of the age. But the best heads and hearts among the Jews were committed to a consistency of a peculiar kind due to their historical situation. The German who abandoned himself heart and soul to the idea behind the Revolution, though he became a cosmopolitan, yet remained a German. But the

Jew who abandoned himself heart and soul to the idea behind the Revolution, on his way to becoming a cosmopolitan became—a German. It was his Judaism that perished. Such was the result of a premature attempt on his part to pose as an internationalist.

We have already remarked that any other culture would have served the Jews quite as well as German culture for the purpose of freeing themselves from the cycle of suppression and spiritual self-constraint. Yet we may perhaps be justified in inquiring whether there was not a certain affinity between the German and the Jew which attracted the latter to German culture and made him prone to adopt it. We have no wish to add yet another to the many definitions of the German nature, but it certainly possesses three aspects which make a peculiar appeal to the Jewish spirit—in the first place its need of expression and of giving to the metaphysical a creative mundane form (which seems to us the most fertile source of the outstanding musical creativeness of the Germans); and secondly its language, not merely because the Jewish masses have irrevocably incorporated it in their Yiddish dialect, but also because in its breadth and richness it is most congenial to the Jewish spirit and seems to us to be, next to Hebrew, the most beautiful in the world. Without such an affinity, not so much between the languages as between the possibilities of the languages, Luther's translation of the Bible would have been impossible. Finally, the Jews, like the Germans, regard themselves as being the Chosen People, although their belief is based on totally different premises. At all events the old saw: "Germany will revive the world" is meant quite seriously.

That this Jewish experiment in assimilation was full of pitfalls very soon became clear, and a large section of the German people reacted in much the same way to the penetration of the Jews as Spain had done to the penetration of the Marranos. True, all the attempts at education aimed at making the Jews as like other people as possible, and, as had been the case for hundreds of years, baptism was still the passport of admission to Gentile society. Nevertheless, the mass conversions to Christianity led to a regulation being issued in Prussia making it compulsory for a candidate for baptism to present a police certificate to the priest or parson, vouching for his sincerity in wishing to be baptized. Even public opinion was roused, and Schleiermacher violently criticized the practice of securing civic advantages by means of baptism. A whole host of polemical writings for and against the Jews came into existence, which eventually became so outspoken that the censorship forbade the public discussion of the Jewish question.

Such were the material and spiritual circumstances preluding the victimization of the Jews during the violent reaction that set in throughout Europe between 1815 and 1848.

RIGHTS AND IDEOLOGIES

Interest in one's own country is important only for immature nations, for the youth of the world. It is a wretched and petty ideal to write for one nation, and to a philosophic spirit such limits are intolerable.

—SCHILLER (*writing to Körner*).

THE French Revolution, like all true ideas, was far ahead of the capacities of the period to realize it. Its mighty forward thrust was consequently followed by a conservative reaction, and the pendulum swung back against its spirit and the order created by the Napoleonic wars. In the case of the Jews, either the equal rights that had been grudgingly granted them were summarily withdrawn, as happened in the "free" Hanseatic towns, in most parts of Italy, and, of course, in the Papal States; or else the laws, though never formally repealed, were rescinded in practice by administrative means, as was the case in Prussia. In other places the tiresome Jewish question, after being more or less acrimoniously debated, was put aside and adjourned, as in Bavaria, Württemberg, Hanover, and Baden, or else the storm of reactionary fanaticism was allowed as in Russia to break with redoubled fury on the Jews. After the shock which the rulers of Europe had received from the idea of freedom, and their horror at Napoleon's destruction of all the frontiers so anxiously guarded theretofore, the various governments resolutely retired within themselves and the confines of power which recently had been so seriously menaced. As their sphere of power, the state became sacred. The nation, as the spiritual expression of the state, became exclusive and sacrosanct. The combination of both under a spiritual idea created the concept of the "Christian nation" and of the "Christian state." And over these states the rulers held sway as it were by divine right, stoutly defending "throne and altar," by a misuse of the energy with which they had been inspired by the idealism of the wars for freedom. At the Congress of Vienna (1814–1815), the "Holy Alliance" confirmed this state of affairs. Incidentally, the Jewish question happened to be just sufficiently important to give the representative of a small Hanseatic town the opportunity of proving his skill in framing judicial formulæ. The "paragraph concerning the Jews" had been shaped as follows: "The Federal Assembly will endeavour to arrive at the greatest possible unanimity regarding the means to be adopted for the improvement as citizens of those who profess the Jewish faith in Germany, and in particular for securing them the enjoyment of civic rights in return for the fulfilment of all civic duties in the federal states. Meanwhile, however, those who profess this faith will continue to enjoy the rights that have hitherto been granted to them in the various federal states." In the last half sentence, great subtlety was shown in changing the word "in" to "by." But those federal states into which the Revolution or Napoleon had introduced equal rights had not granted them to the Jews. Thus with a sigh of relief they felt they could justifiably keep the Jews in their position of inferiority. Prussia achieved this end in a most practical fashion by rescinding the edict of 1812 and by refusing to apply it to territory recently acquired by her. The result was that the Jews in the state of Prussia occupied eighteen different legal areas and enjoyed as many different legal positions, from "citizens of the state" to "protected Jews."

Every form of government, even the most reactionary, has its spiritual "claque," the members of which generally occupy professorial chairs. This was the case even in reactionary Germany, and professors of history, philosophy, and theology began to investigate the Jewish question and to define what Judaism was, and thus helped the cause by their anti-Jewish proposals. They were supported by certain sheep-like members of the literary world, with the result that a badly constructed work like the *Judenschule* was able to provoke thunders of applause from theatre audiences night after night. The picture is completed by the veritable pogrom which the patriotic students of Würzburg were able to carry out in August 1819.

But it is not these facts which made history but the way in which the Jews reacted to them. The definition of Judaism supplied by some professor of Berlin or Heidelberg is of course a matter of no importance whatsoever. The real importance lies in whether such polemics disturbed the consciousness of the Jews, and whether, as a whole, they were able to overcome these disturbances. For a false ideology is incapable of shaping or altering the destiny of a people, though it can do serious temporary damage. This is what happened in the case of the ideology which now came into being; it made its influence felt in a variety of ways, which have endured to this day. The attempt on the part of the Jews to adjust themselves and their Judaism to the world that had hitherto been closed to them was accompanied by a loss of historical perspective. Confronted for the first time for ages with the possibility of being included as subjects within the confines of an alien civilization, and in view, moreover, of the fact that being included also constituted the means of alleviating their material martyrdom, the Jews suddenly lost all consciousness of what the purpose of their previous striving had been, that is to say, to retain the initiative in spite of the fact that they were the victims of history, to *form* their Judaism and not to make it conform to the demands of the foreigner.

The leading representative of these views, who is still held in honour by many Jews as the guiding star of their lives, was Gabriel Riesser (1806–1863), a political Mendelssohn, as wholly possessed by the idea of belonging to German civilization as was Mendelssohn by the idea of belonging to the human world. Like Mendelssohn, he could on occasion give vent to the most passionate outbursts, his intentions were above suspicion, he was indefatigable in his efforts to secure equal rights for the Jews, he was a stubborn fighter for their freedom, and a great falsifier of the idea of Judaism. The fundamental conception for which he fought is revealed in the work which he published as early as 1830, *Concerning Those Who Profess the Mosaic Faith in Germany,* and it was repeated in various forms in his subsequent writings. His energies were concentrated on the question of equal rights for the Jews, on combating the detestation in which they were held, on supporting their claim for the right of domicile in Germany, and in defending Judaism against the reproach that it constituted a nation, and that, even after the Jews had been granted equal rights, it would continue to do so. He was unable to deny that Judaism had grown out of national and religious unity, but he declared that the connexion no longer held good, all that was left being a racial relationship. Communal autonomy had been due to the fact that they had no rights in the countries in which they lived, "an unsavoury feature in the life of the Jews." This shows that he was no longer conscious of the purpose of this autonomous form, or of the fact that its motive power lay in the national will, with all its aims and ambitions, including the preservation of the type and its morality; he could not see that the sorest trial to which the Jews as a nation had been exposed was to be obliged to live as strangers in a strange land, which was a home only in name. He confounded the desire for expression with the expression itself, not from malice prepense and with intent to deceive, but because assimilation to the German way of thinking and the German world of concepts compelled him to do so. He himself was a product of assimilation. He denied the existence of the Jewish nation, not because his environment demanded it, but because he could no longer see it. And he failed to see it, not because it was not there, but because he used the ideas current in his environment for the definition of a nation, in order to deny the existence of the Jewish nation. Other Jews who acted in the same way were prompted by utilitarian motives; he was animated by resentment. But even the most noble form of resentment is a bad foundation for knowledge. In his fight for equal rights, Riesser once made the following important pronouncement: "We did not immigrate here, we were born here, and, because we were born here, we lay no claim to a home anywhere else; we are either Germans, or else we are homeless." The premise is right, the conclusion is wrong and sentimentally distorted. The views current in his environment concerning the nature of a state, a citizen, a nation, had infected him. If the reasoning of the environment be accepted, then Riesser's conclusion also is right. As a matter of fact, both are wrong. But we shall enter more closely into this later on. At this point all we need do is to call attention to an important fact, which will constitute our starting-point in what remains to be told of the history of the Jews up to our own day. As to whether Judaism constitutes a nation or not, the verdict of outsiders is, of course, quite valueless. They could draw conclusions from it and affect the fate of the Jews accordingly. But for the spiritual history of the Jewish people, this was of no importance. Even the opinion of those among the Jewish masses who denied the existence of the nation was of no importance. This, too, could only provide material for party disputes, it could not wipe out the meaning of history. And they contradicted themselves daily, for their actions constituted a typical manifestation of national feeling—they were a minority fighting for their rights. All they did was voluntarily to lay aside some of the weapons which their nationality offered them. Even the Zionist ideology as such, as an ideology, has nothing to say against the existence of Judaism as a nation; but Zionism, as a movement, is merely a proof of the existence of the Jewish people. As a programme it is a party concern—no more. True, its opponents in Judaism constitute parties, but parties within the confines of the Jewish people.

Riesser, and all those who both before and after him shared his views, preached a truncated Judaism, a Judaism with but little binding force, and consequently with but little creative power, a Judaism of which everything which we said in the last chapter on the effects of denying the existence of the Jewish nation holds good. This truncated Judaism was as much responsible as was assimilation on utilitarian grounds for the severe loss in substance of the Jewish people. Heine was one of the few who, on casting a last look back on the Judaism of the type that had been abandoned, saw it once again as a complete whole, though it was too late to alter the course that had been chosen. Others had no difficulty in forsaking it, still less in forgetting it, and many actually fought it. Marx was one of the latter. (He, too, refused to be a Jew, and confounded Rothschild with Judaism; yet the reasoning on which his socialistic system is based shows that he was nothing more than an European Jew. But with his nationality he also lost the last "grain of ethic.")

In the end, for the Jew who in this spiritual sphere wished to remain in Judaism, all that was left, after the whole idea of Judaism had been truncated, was to truncate Jewish forms and ceremonies and the world of expression also, a process which was hidden under the name of reform. If reform really were what the word implies, it should mean the purging of a state or an idea of all superfluous, injurious, or degenerate elements, which had crept in during the course of time, and returning to the core. But it was precisely with the core that truncated Judaism had interfered, and all it could do was to take what remained, and instead of allowing it to develop further of its own accord, to assimilate it to the ideas generally current in Europe, and subject whatever formal attributes it possessed to a process of remoulding in keeping with European civilization and æsthetics. Thus, an undertaking which, in itself, was extremely useful, was destined, owing to the fact that it no longer had any organic coherence, to end on a note of tragicomedy. The first step was to introduce order and discipline into religious service. The old free and easy, tumultuous gatherings of yore at which the people had been accustomed to face their God, speak to Him, converse with Him intimately and unceremoniously, and altogether behave in such an everyday manner that in the synagogue even business could be discussed without committing sacrilege—these unconventional gatherings were now converted into stiff and formal Sabbath or even Sunday services, conducted in German with music, choir singing, and various officiating functionaries. The "Lord of Hosts" became the "Commander-in-Chief," and the reformed rabbi was his general. As the reformers always kept one eye on the environment, they also interfered with the subject matter of the prayers, and above all took care to eliminate any Messianic passages, in which the national appeal was too plainly evident. And in this we can already see the transition from the reformation in forms and ceremonies to the reformation in the fundamental doctrines of Judaism. And yet all the reformers who were responsible for this were undoubtedly fundamentally religious in their attitude. But as soon as they tried to account for this, either in their own case or that of Judaism as a whole, they were guided by the ideas and standards of their environment, to which they had become adapted through cultural assimilation. In addition to the fact that in the realm of religious creativeness the western European is far less gifted than the Jew, with the result that when the latter wished to find his bearings afresh he had no shining example to follow, the Christian religion at this time had become so mechanical that it could be used as a political, revolutionary, or philosophic weapon, without in any way interfering with its source.

Nothing could have been more natural, therefore, than for the Jewish reformers to seek the new reasons for their Judaism in the spirit of the age. This was the first reason for their unproductiveness. An "age" is never religious; religious ages are nonexistent.

Everybody took it for granted that Judaism was nothing more than a religion, though opinions were divided as to what it precisely represented. This led to the bitter and futile struggle between the reformers and the orthodox. Whereas a reformer like Abraham Geiger at least saw the historical factor in the religion, and rightly assumed that even the spirit and forms of the religion had undergone changes, his opponent, the orthodox S. R. Hirsch, was convinced that Judaism was an unalterable legislative creation independent of time and place. He sums up his disagreement with his adversaries as follows: "The reform which Judaism requires is an education of the age up to the Torah, not a levelling down of the Torah to this age." In opposing this view, Geiger is nearer the truth, for, as a matter of fact, changes in the fundamental doctrines had occurred more than once. But these changes had been due to natural development and reflected the religious evolution of the community; they were the outcome of experience, and had not been decreed; they were the result of growth and not of deliberate thought.

In order the better to fight the resolute opposition of the orthodox, the rabbis and laymen formed organizations; the former adopted the method of holding special assemblies, the latter developed an order known as the "Fellowship of Judaic Reform," founded in 1845, which eventually became the "Reform Association." In 1844 the first assembly of the reform rabbis met. Its spiritual attitude was very similar to that of the Paris Sanhedrin. The latter had been dominated by Napoleon, and the former was dominated by the emancipation movement. Both were equally anxious to be subservient, and the nature of their resolutions shows that they wished to subordinate what remained of the Jewish idea to the idea of obtaining equal rights of citizenship. Their first resolutions were: Jewish law must be subordinate to the law of the land; mixed marriages are permissible in those states which do not forbid the education of the children of such marriages as Jews; the *Kol-Nidre* prayer, the stirring prelude to the eve of the Great Day of Atonement, must be abolished." A year later they passed a resolution to the effect that the Hebrew language was not prescribed by Jewish law for divine service, and that its use was not desirable, and also that "the idea of the Messiah deserves every consideration in the prayers, but all requests that we may be led back to the land of our fathers and the Jewish state be restored must be dropped out of them." Thus even truncated Judaism was further purged, and Messianism, the creation born of the collective experience of the Jewish soul, was done away with by the reformed rabbis.

The whole tragedy of this garbled Judaism came to light in the appeal which preceded the foundation of the "Fellowship of Judaic Reform." In it we read: "Our spiritual religion is no longer in harmony with the external conditions of Judaism. We can no longer pray for the establishment of the kingdom of the Messiah on earth. . . . We can no longer observe laws which make no intellectual claim upon us. Filled, as we are, by the sacred spirit of our religion, we can no longer keep it in its traditional form, far less pass it on to our descendants." Written in the German language, this was the *Kaddish* on the death of Judaism as they conceived of it.

The result of these reform movements was that the ideology of the western Jew became distinguished more sharply than ever from that of the eastern Jew, to whom the word "Berliner" (man of Berlin) soon became a nickname for one who wished to save Judaism by means of enlightenment. In those parts where there were still large numbers of Jews it was possible only for occasional reforms to be introduced. But this does not by any means signify that the Jews of the East maintained a purely passive and conservative attitude. On the contrary, it was in the East that the most vital form of Judaism was developed as a counterblast to the reform movement, and, to be capable of such a feat, the powers of resistance of the eastern Jews had first to be developed to the utmost. Even in the East, the educative spirit of reaction was also opposed to Judaism, and in a much more brutal and powerful manner than in the West. But whereas the West capitulated extraordinarily quickly, the East stood firm at the cost of much bloodshed and heavy sacrifices; and whatever it accepted from the movement of enlightenment was literally enlightening, that is to say, it revealed new relations. Whereas in the West the Jews simply abandoned the Hebrew language, in the East it was modernized and developed in a genuine Renaissance spirit. And all this took place under the conditions prevailing in Russia.

By the terms of the Treaty of Vienna, the greater part of the Duchy of Warsaw, known as the "Kingdom of Poland" was handed over to Russia and with it the last large contingent of Jews. In these millions of Jews, the Russian government was confronted with a problem which it was incapable of solving; it tried everything from promising rewards for conversion to Christianity, to wholesale murder organized by the state in the form of the pogroms. As soon as Alexander I joined the Holy Alliance, severer pressure was immediately brought to bear on the Jews. In 1823 the enactments of the statute of 1804 were revived, and the Jews of White Russia were forbidden to lease land, to keep public houses, inns, hotels, or post-houses, or to reside in the country. The authorities apparently expected that this would lead to an improvement in the position of Christian agriculturists in rural districts. But the measure met with no better success than it had done before, and thousands of lives were uselessly ruined, without any advantage accruing to the Christian farmers. The Jews were even held to be chiefly responsible for the smuggling which took place on a large scale on the western frontier, and their presence was consequently forbidden in a zone of about thirty miles deep on this side of Russia. Nicholas I increased the difficulties of the Jews by introducing a special measure whereby Jews were obliged to do their military service in person instead of paying a recruiting tax as they had hitherto done. His object was not so much to oblige the Jews to perform military service as to force the Jewish youth to become assimilated by means of the knout. The period of service was twenty-five years, and boys were recruited between twelve and twenty-five years of age. But when the requisite number of recruits could not be raised, the authorities took even children of eight. It became more and more difficult, however, to find enough recruits, for as soon as the recruiting commission approached, a wild flight of Jewish youths began. And there was ample reason for this. The young recruits were transported to the remotest corners of the empire, where it was impossible for them to get into touch with Jews, and they were starved, flogged, and ill-treated in every conceivable way, with the object of inducing them, particularly if they were minors, to be baptized. Most of those who managed to survive being transported across such vast distances died under the treatment they received. Thus the performance of military service led to the "martyrdom of the children."

This method of assimilation, through the barracks, however, did not last, and the schools were then utilized. In 1844 the ukase "Concerning the Education of Jewish Children" was issued, and secret instructions were given to the minister of education to use the ordinary Jewish elementary schools for the purpose of assimilating the Jews to the Christians, and of obliterating Talmudic ideas from their minds. But the Jews were just as strenuously opposed to these schools as to the twenty-five years of slavery imposed upon their children. They were also obliged to fight for the last remnants of their autonomy, the administration of the Kahals, and to resist being placed under the general administration of the country, with the result that they clung all the more tenaciously to their rabbis and their Ṣaddiqim. They refused to yield. They were not western Jews, and even the fact that the subservient attitude of the Jews in the West had at least facilitated and expedited the granting of equal rights to them, did not lead their eastern brethren to draw any conclusions for the guidance of their own conduct.

The final step towards the emancipation of the Jews in the West was foreshadowed by the collapse of the reactionary movement controlled by Metternich. But in spite of the Revolution of 1848, there was but little sign of any desire to grant the Jews equal rights of citizenship. True, mass hatred of the Jews was not nearly so strong as it had been, and the revolution led *de jure* to the proclamation of equal rights for all, though it did not rescind the various legal restrictions already in existence. It was only after the foundation of the North German Confederation, in which Prussia took the lead, that the fundamental law of July 3, 1869, was passed: "All restrictions of civil and political rights still in existence, based on differences of religious faith, are hereby revoked, and above all the qualification to share in communal and provincial representation, and to fill official posts, shall no longer depend on religious convictions."

Prussia took the lead in putting the law into practice. Baden did not rescind its last legal restrictions until 1864. Württemberg did so in 1864. Austria, which in the constitution which was forced upon it on March 4, 1849, had proclaimed, "that the enjoyment of civil and political rights is independent of religious persuasions," revoked the constitution in 1851, and it was not until 1867 that all citizens were recognized as equal before the law. Even in other countries this change did not occur any more spontaneously. In Italy it took place only in 1870 with the establishment of Italian unity, and, when the pope became the "Prisoner of the Vatican," the prisoner of the Roman ghetto was at last set free. But his spirit was so broken that, when he eventually came into touch with the world about him, and tasted the joys of freedom, his only possible response was almost complete and all too hasty assimilation.

In England the granting of full rights of citizenship was still contingent on the fact that, in order to fill an official post, and more especially to sit in Parliament, the old practice survived of making the candidate take an oath "according to the true faith of a Christian." Consequently Jews who had been elected to the House of Commons could not take their seats. Year after year the Commons passed a bill which would allow them to do so. But year after year the Lords with conservative obduracy threw it out. This play of interests was at last brought to an end in 1858.

Free Switzerland, with its handful of Jews, continued, as in the past, to create many difficulties. And it was only when conflicts arose with France, America, and England, because Switzerland treated the Jewish citizens of these countries in the same way as it treated its own Jews, that it decided not to treat foreign Jews differently from other foreigners, and to grant its own Jews, who had been cooped up, as it were, in settlement areas in two places in the canton of Aargau, freedom to move about as they pleased (1866).

Thus, in theory, the problem of equal rights was to all intents and purposes solved in the countries of western Europe. If we reckon that the legal disabilities of the Jews in the Diaspora started from the time of Constantine, it had lasted about 1500 years. During that period this legal inequality constituted a most important factor on the liability side of Jewish history. Nor did emancipation wipe it out as a liability. We have seen with what sacrifices the Jews of the West bought their liberty. Later on we shall show how useless these sacrifices were. After the end of the actual struggle for emancipation, the result of the various changes in Jewish ideology was that the western Jews gradually became differentiated into citizens of their respective countries. The terms "German Jew" and "French Jew" were associated with a new concept, in which the emphasis was laid not on the word "Jew" but on the word "German" or "French." They not only fulfilled their obvious duty towards the states whose citizens they had become. They did much more. They so completely severed the bonds binding them to their common origin, that they felt the same strangeness and opposition towards Jews of another country as the other citizens felt towards foreigners in general. The national chauvinism of the various states of western Europe has often been ardently supported by the Jews. And here again we come across the fate of the renegade, who has denied his nationality; he suffers from the uncertainty arising from incomplete severance, which makes him go too far, because he is secretly afraid of being taunted with not having done enough for the country of his adoption.

And this severance from the original community was imperfect, for again and again international upheavals occurred which proved that, although the Jews had been divided up, forces still existed which regarded them as a unity, and which affected them in a particular way as parts of that unity. Isolated events occurred, and there were also lasting phenomena, which bore witness to this. In the year 1840, for instance, a Capuchin monk named Thomas disappeared in Damascus. Nobody could discover where he had gone. Suspicion, of course, fell upon the Jews, and the old charge of ritual murder lay ready to hand in the mental armoury of a good many people. The European world was shocked, not because it was possible for such a charge still to be brought—for in Russia it still continued to claim its victims as it had done in the past—but because the case had arisen in a sphere which was under its control and in which it was interested, that is to say in the Near East, where France, England, Prussia, and Austria all laid claim to influence. It was the French consul in Damascus, a man named Ratti-Menton, who set himself the task of investigating the charge of ritual murder; he cast a number of Jews into prison and proceeded to torture them until they either died or confessed what he expected and demanded of them. Thus the whole atmosphere of the past was suddenly revived. A similar case occurred on the Island of Rhodes, and once again the Catholic Church proclaimed her belief in ritual murder and the usefulness of such a belief for supplying her with martyrs, by the premature erection of a monument in the Capuchin church in Rome to commemorate the martyrdom of the "victim of the Jews." The European states, with the exception of France, protested, and a Jewish deputation, headed by the English Jew, Montefiore, and the French Jew, Crémieux, left London for Cairo in order to secure the release of the surviving prisoners.

In 1858 Rome staged a revival of one act of the Jewish drama. The child of a Bolognese Jew named Mortara, fell ill, and a Catholic maid who was in the house, thinking the patient was going to die and anxious to save his soul for the Christian heaven, proceeded to play the part of priest and baptized him although he was only six years old. She subsequently reported to the church what she had done. Pope Pius IX then had the child forcibly kidnapped from the house of his parents and, in spite of the protests of the whole world, kept fast hold of the soul he had purloined and made him a Catholic priest.

These deeds were performed under the eyes of the whole world, and nobody would have dared to act in such a way except against Jews. If at that time the Jews had required further proof that with all the determined atomizing of Jewry the world had not succeeded in disposing of the Jewish problem, they would have found it without difficulty as a lasting phenomenon in all the great Jewish centres of the East. When it was a question of dealing with Jews, not even diplomatic agreements guaranteed by the great powers of Europe were respected. In 1878, at the Berlin Congress, Romania was granted her independence provided she gave equal rights to all her people, including the Jews. But apparently Romania never had the slightest intention of keeping her word in this respect, for over 250,000 Jews were given the status of "foreigners" and hampered by all kinds of restrictions, and treated with a contempt which even took the form of bloody baitings.

Romania in this was following the example set by Russia, who had done everything she could to disperse and dismember her Jewish population. When the catalogue of repressive measures had been exhausted, the policy of partial alleviations was tried, with the time-honoured object of "absorbing" the Jews in the native population, and between 1856 and 1865 various reforms were carried through. In the matter of recruiting for the army, the Jews were placed on the same footing as everybody else. Big merchants who were registered in the "First

Guild," were allowed to settle down in the "Inner Radius," after which this privilege was extended to Jews who held university degrees, and subsequently to all well-educated Jews. Later on, subject to various strict conditions, artisans, and finally soldiers who had served twenty-five years, were included. After the emancipation of the peasants, the Jews acquired the right to own land. They were also given the right to vote and to stand for the provincial diets, and to become advocates. This method of procedure was extremely slow and deliberate; it was calculated to act as a constant lure, and was largely responsible for paving the way to assimilation for those who were privileged either through wealth or education. Nevertheless, it led to no amalgamation, such as had occurred in the West. The Russians wondered what could possibly be the reason why the Jews did not amalgamate with the rest of the population, and came to the conclusion that in their secret Kahals they possessed a strong reserve, and that a "World Kahal" existed of which the French "Alliance Israélite Universelle" was one of the organs. (This fact deprives similar discoveries in our own time of all originality.) Once more a commission was set to work, with the object of "loosening as far as possible the bonds which held the Jewish community together."

The methods of the Russian reaction might perhaps have succeeded if, like the countries of western Europe, the empire of the Tsars had been in a position to offer the Jews an ideology based on the general intellectual life of the nation, by which they could have taken their bearings afresh, and been divorced from their origin. But for the vast mass of the Jews this was impossible, and it was only the Jewish intelligentsia and the Jewish youth in the secondary schools and universities who were to any great extent passionately enthusiastic about the idea of Russification. But the Russian ideal outlined by these young people, in conjunction with the progressive and cultivated classes in Russia, was in form and conception essentially determined by the fact that the standardizing power of the police was hanging over the heads of countless millions, and that the fires of revolution were being stoked up to melt an iron system of suppression. Revolution as the violent outburst of the will to freedom lay at the core of the Russification of the Jewish intelligentsia. The ideology of the Jewish youth in Russia, in so far as it played any active part at all in the revolutionary movement, was Russian only in name; in its substance it was Jewish. They subordinated their oppressed lot as Jews to the general fate of the oppressed Russian people, and their aim was not so much the emancipation of the Jews, as a general freedom which would be theirs as well. Freedom is a primeval Jewish ideal, very different from the German conception of freedom. It does not mean resistance to rule, but on the contrary, absolute subordination to a rule that is voluntary. This fundamental feeling, together with its practical result, justice in everyday life, makes the Jew a predestined participator in all social and liberal revolutions. And this he has a perfect right to be. Moreover, he could not act otherwise even if he chose.

Thus it is not surprising to find a Jewess taking part in the conspiracy which led to the assassination of Alexander II in March 1881. The intensified reaction which resulted under Alexander III intimated to all concerned that the authorities had renounced all attempts to assimilate the Jews to their environment. Tsardom, which had the sword of Damocles constantly suspended over its head, required the support of loyal subjects, political partisans who were whole-heartedly devoted, and whom the throne could regard as Russian to the core. Hence the new slogan: "Russia for the Russians!" The converse was the sinister cry: "The Jew is on the move!" This meant—the Jew, the non-Russian, is a menace to Russia. And, in keeping with the traditional treatment of the Jews, everything was done to create the atmosphere in which the pogroms took place.

Thus Russia, too, followed the example of the rest of the world; first the attempt was made, by means of compulsion or compulsory education, to assimilate the Jew culturally or from the standpoint of civilization, to his environment, with a view to doing away with his peculiarities, which still seemed unfamiliar. But as soon as he had entered the appointed path and found an opportunity to develop his natural capacities, his environment spontaneously rose up in opposition against him, and every possible excuse was advanced to justify a revolt against a state of affairs which had been the creation, not of the Jew himself, but of this very environment. In the chapter on Anti-Semitism we shall have occasion to discuss this question also more narrowly. For the present, suffice it to draw from the course of events the conclusion that all the willingness on the part of the Jew to dispose of the Jewish problem in accordance with the wishes of his environment was foredoomed to failure, owing to the fact that he was constantly confronted afresh with the problem and had it forced upon him again and again by that same environment. Apparently the problem is insoluble, or is at any rate one for which all the means and methods hitherto adopted have failed to find the key.

The conviction that even the most barefaced assimilation of the western Jew could solve the problem only for the individual, and even that only in the most favourable circumstances—for often it did not solve the problem for a man himself but only for his descendants—was also subconsciously felt during this period of disintegrating ideologies. And it was this that knitted the fate of the Jews of the whole world together, and constituted the fundamental similarity of their problem. But even when such a fate is faced quite passively, when it is merely a matter of patiently submitting to it, and being unable to find a way of escape, it constitutes history. The inability either consciously or unconsciously to reach any clear understanding of the reasons for this passive endurance of fate may lead people to study history as a medium of research and enlightenment. It is for this reason that the scientific study of Jewish history almost inevitably arose in the nineteenth century, when the Jew began to do what he had hitherto always refused to do, and set to work to study the course of his development and examine into his antecedents. During the breathing-space when nothing creative was produced in the world of Judaism, but disintegration was everywhere rampant, he turned to taking his bearings, not by reference to the opinions and views of his environment, but by appealing to the objective records of what the generations preceding him had experienced and created. The vital importance of this lay in the fact that the study of history may be a source of independent experience, which may result in an intellectual position capable of separating the organic from the inorganic—that is to say, capable of making the fate of the Jewish nation comprehensible through the medium of its own determining laws, and not by the light of the disturbing accessory factors introduced into it by the compulsory nature of the Diaspora, emancipation and assimilation. Thus the act of turning to Jewish history signified for the nineteenth century the beginning of the work of reconstruction in the very midst of the perils of rapid decline. Zunz (1794–1886) may be regarded as the founder of the science of Jewish history, while its highest exponent during the nineteenth century was Graetz (1817–1891). In addition to these there were S. J. Rappoport (1790–1867), who made a special study of the Gaonic period, and N. Krochmal (1785–1840), who laid the foundations of the philosophy of Jewish history, both of whom were no less important. Mention must also be made of Geiger, the originator of the idea of the Jewish mission, and Z. Frankel, the founder of the "positive-historical" school. All these men have now become essential elements in Jewish history, but the compass of this work does not permit of any criticism of their fundamental doctrines. Nor can we attempt to value them; they are merely factors whose differences provide the historian with an opportunity for making comparisons and reaching a decision.

An organic complement of this historical research was the gradual revival of the Hebrew language, not so much for philological purposes as for use as a means of expression. Deep metaphysical meaning lies behind a proverb ascribed to King Solomon: "Life and death lie in the power of the tongue, and those who love it will enjoy the fruits thereof." Language breathes life, and offers a much more direct means than history of building up a community. And for this reason the literature that now came into being acquired an importance which is far greater from the historical than from the literary or artistic point of view. It was in Austria and Russia, where there were still large numbers of people who could echo the language, that this literature chiefly came to life. In its inception it was a literature with a purpose; it served the cause of "enlightenment"–*Haskalah*. The eastern Haskalah always strove to convey worldly knowledge and the culture of the world to the Jews, and did not try, as the West had done, to place the Jews at the mercy of both. Its aim was to achieve a genuine, not a fictitious, enrichment of Judaism. Whereas western enlightenment could act only as a link between Judaism and the outside world, the eastern Haskalah fulfilled this function between the new and the old generation within the confines of Judaism itself, between the conservatism of orthodoxy and the disintegrating will of youth. And since the national language was its means and the national-religious ideas constituted its basis, it was able in time to abandon its purpose and become really productive. Its creations gave both art and science to the community. The lyricist Micha Joseph Lebenssohn, the first modern Hebrew novelist Abraham Mapu, whose *Ahabath Zion* ("Love of Zion") became a classic studied by the youth of the Jewish ghetto, and Jehuda Leb Gordon, the champion of the liberal reform of Jewish life and customs, were the first pioneer moulders of the new age who drew their strength from the Jewish people themselves. Their influence grew deeper and more intimate when they began to write in Yiddish, in that dialect which, whatever people may care to say about it, has after all constituted the speech and means of expression of millions of men for centuries. The most lovable among these was Solomon Abramowitsch (died 1917) who, under the name of Mendele Mocher Sforim, the bookseller, dealt with every aspect of Jewish home life in the East and made it accessible to the people from a new angle. A writer not unlike Abramowitsch, in the sense that he tried to stimulate people to reform their old way of life, was Eisik Meir Dick, probably one of the most popular Yiddish writers of the East.

Thus the Jewish East seemed to be following its own course of development. And, as a matter of fact, this was the case. This eastern literature was the beginning of a development, although no trace of such a movement could yet be discovered among the mass of the people. But even in the West as well we find sporadic beginnings of a tendency to react to the knowledge of the common fate of the Jews. And here we return to the point which we made at the outset, to the effect that all attempts at atomizing the Jews were constantly opposed to outside influences which emphasized and confirmed their unity, by at least forcing upon them the knowledge of their common destiny. A certain number even of assimilated Jews perceived this, and, though the knowledge may not have been carried to its logical conclusion, at least interest in the other portions of the Jewish world was revived. It was this interest that led Munk and Crémieux, who came into contact with the Jews of the Near East through the Damascus affair, to found Jewish elementary schools in Cairo and Alexandria. It also accounted for the founding in Paris in 1860 under Crémieux's leadership of the *Alliance Israélite Universelle,* which had to objects in view—to promote the emancipation and moral progress of the Jews everywhere, and to offer energetic assistance to any Jews exposed to persecution merely because they were Jews. Such a programme was tantamount to a declaration of solidarity, for it at least assumed a common responsibility on the part of the Jews for their brethren all over the world. This solidarity, which *de facto* amounted to an international organization, was, however, bound to offend or disquiet those Jews whose newly acquired citizenship had led to a change of nationality, and who feared reproach or even worse if they had anything to do with an international Jewish organization. It therefore led to a schism. In 1871 "The Anglo-Jewish Association" was formed in London, and the "Israelitische Allianz" in Vienna. These were reflex movements resulting from assimilation, and were calculated to emphasize as politely as possible the distance which their newly adopted nationality imposed upon them.

During this same period of disintegration, however, other voices made themselves heard, which showed that the recognition of the common destiny of the Jews had led to other consequences. They were isolated manifestations, which were not consciously related in any way and did not even cumulatively constitute an intellectual movement, but nevertheless proved that there were in Judaism certain forces which always tended to expand in their own way, just as an artificially trimmed tree tends to shoot out branches in the manner natural to it and to return to its original shape. These manifestations emphasized the unity of the Jews as constituting a nation; they revealed the existence of a living national body, and endeavoured from this standpoint, that is to say, from the standpoint of the needs of the Jewish people, and not of the needs of their environment, to solve the Jewish question. One of the first of these propagandists was the politician and journalist, Mordecai Manuel Noah, who in 1825 secured Grand Island in the Niagara, and tried to get Jews to settle there as colonists forming an autonomous community preparatory to their transfer to Palestine. He was certainly not a politician of the realist school, and his plans were foredoomed to meet with failure. But he carried on a propaganda even among Christians, enlisting their help for the "rebirth of the Jews." Though such an undertaking was premature, it was not quite as absurd as it may seem, for at the conference of the Central European powers which was to decide the fate of Syria and Palestine (1840–1841) the idea of re-establishing a Jewish state in Palestine was also discussed. Colonel Churchill, the English consul in Smyrna, also seriously proposed to the Jewish "Committee of Deputies" in London, that propaganda should be started with the object of making Palestine once more the national home of the Jews, and sending large bodies of Jewish emigrants out there. A year previously an anonymous treatise entitled *New Judea,* by C.L.K., had appeared containing the suggestion that a Jewish state should be formed in North America, and at the same time another anonymous essay was printed in the Jewish weekly paper *Orient* published in Leipzig, proposing the creation of a national home in Palestine. They were all premature proposals made by individuals, each of whom had rediscovered the old truth that the Jews constituted a nation, but they were unable to rouse any enthusiastic response in the western world.

Even Graetz, the official Jewish historian of the period, did not make this response. An indefatigable worker, to whom Jewish history owes a deep debt of gratitude, he was not by any means either by instinct or desire what we understand today by a Jewish nationalist. He was in every respect an enlightened western Jew, and above all a German Jew. Yet his resolute objectivity in description led him almost unconsciously to make an admission which we find stated as follows in the fifth volume of his great *History of the Jews* (1859–1860): "Thus the history of the post-Talmudic period always bore a national stamp. It is in no wise merely the history of a religion or a church, since its subject does not consist merely of the development of a doctrine, but also of a race, which, though it possessed no land, no home, no geographical entity or state organization of its own, substituted spiritual powers for these material conditions." In the assimilated circle in which he lived, such a pronouncement could remain only a symptom. But the consistent application and recognition of this fact coincided for the first time in two figures, whose utterances may be regarded as the prelude to the history of Zionism—Moses Hess and Hirsch Kalischer, the former with his treatise *Rome and Jerusalem,* and the latter with his work *Drishath Zion* (both published in 1862). Hess was interested in the political, Kalisch in the cultural restoration of the Jewish nation. Considering the times in which he wrote and the attitude of his contemporaries, Hess's reasoning was singularly pregnant with meaning. "Judaism is primarily the expression of a nationality whose history, for thousands of years, has coincided with the history of human development. . . . As long as a Jew continues to deny his nationality, because he is not capable of the self-denial to acknowledge that he belongs to that unfortunate, persecuted, and scorned people, his false position must daily become more intolerable."

The last remark obviously aimed a blow at the assimilated Jew. It put into words for the first time the theme which forms the basis of this chapter. With it Hess drew one of the possible conclusions of his position and an extremely important one, pointing out that the assimilated Jew harboured a concept of Judaism which was constantly being repudiated by the age and by his environment, and by every action directed at the Jews. And it was precisely in those centres where the falsification of the Jewish ideology had been carried to its greatest lengths, in France, Germany, and Austria, that there now arose a new concerted movement to abrogate the decision taken by the Jews in favour of assimilation. As soon as the western Jew had discovered the ultimate formula for his relationship to the outside world, the latter also discovered its ultimate formula for its relation to the Jew. It was Anti-Semitism, to which we shall now have to turn our attention.

ANTI-SEMITISM

IF, within the compass of this history of Jewish ideas, we are devoting a special chapter to Anti-Semitism, it is because, in the course of centuries, Anti-Semitism has also become a problem for the Jews, it might almost be said, for Judaism. Nevertheless, we must not lose sight of the fact that Anti-Semitism, as such, is naturally the problem of non-Jews, and that in it they sum up their relationship, their feelings of opposition and general resistance to the Jew, his religion, his spirit, his customs and capacities, in short to his very existence. But in view of the fact that this problem of the non-Jew is to be found all over the world, though perhaps varying in form and intensity, and arising for different reasons, there must be something about the Jew and his characteristics which provokes this uniform reaction, and the very capacity to provoke such reactions forces us to regard Anti-Semitism as a passive problem, a derivative problem of Judaism.

A great deal has been written about Anti-Semitism, and many extremely subtle and intricate theories have been advanced to explain it. We do not therefore hope to contribute anything fundamentally new or original to the subject, unless the determination to examine all things in the light of history and to interpret them according to the laws of their own evolution in itself opens up new vistas. For although the word "Anti-Semitism" is of comparatively recent coinage, this should not blind us to the fact that it was only a new term for a very old phenomenon. In this new word all that is emphasized is the factor of race in the relation between the non-Jew and the Jew, the difference between the Semite and the non-Semite. In its essence, in the anti-Jewish feeling it connotes, Anti-Semitism has existed from the time that Judaism came into contact with other peoples in something more than neighbourly hostility. In order, therefore, to determine its present meaning, we must perforce examine its development, and, if in this inquiry we wish to give everything that has happened up to our own day its proper place, we must first refer to the further course of Jewish history, taking as our two outstanding dates, the Franco-German War of 1870–1871 and the World War of 1914–1918.

It is not only the existence of Anti-Semitism that makes this period one of peculiar and fateful importance in Jewish history, for, in spite of the growing dependence of the Jews on the actions and life of their environment, and the corresponding almost compulsory passivity of Jewish history, it was also a period of activity, creativeness, and consciousness. For vast masses of Jews this increased passivity was actually necessary, in order to allow them to escape into activity. In any case, it was a passivity—that is to say, the heaping of a mass of events on the heads of the Jews—which, when we take into account the difference in the stage of civilization reached, was not very different or superior to the conditions prevalent in the Middle Ages. For in its repetition of medieval methods, the age could no longer plead the excuse of intellectual immaturity, at least, not if we accept its own claims regarding the superior heights of culture to which it had risen. Yet all the old phenomena are there—charges of ritual murder, pogroms of Jews, denial of legal rights, laws devised for Jews only, social and economic boycotting, and anti-Jewish propaganda in all its forms, from the pseudo-scientific treatise to the desecration of cemeteries.

In the thirty years from 1882 to 1911, six trials for ritual murder were held, one in the East (Corfu, 1891), two in Russia (Blondes, 1900, and Beilis, 1911–1913), one in Hungary (Tisza-Eszlar, 1882), one in Bohemia (Polna, 1899), and two in Germany (Xanten, 1892, and Konitz, 1900). The Polna trial ended in sentence of death being pronounced on the Jew Hilsner; the others, of course, ended in acquittal. There is no need to give details. Suffice it to say that these trials actually took place, that it was possible for them to take place.

A more concentrated form of Jewish persecution was provided by the pogroms. People have grown accustomed to think only of Russia in connexion with the word pogrom. But this is a mistake. If we understand by pogrom, spontaneous or well-organized attacks by the masses on the Jews, we can trace the wave of pogroms westward into

Germany itself. In the summer and autumn of 1881, as a direct consequence of the campaign in favour of the "Anti-Semitic Petition," which we shall discuss later, organized raids on the Jews, attended by personal violence and plunder, took place in Brandenburg and Pomerania, and were interfered with by the government only when they threatened to become a public danger. In Galicia, Jew baiting occurred as the result of the Catholic-Polish propaganda, and troops were required to put an end to the disturbances. In Bohemia and Hungary the disturbances were merely the outcome of the trials for ritual murder already mentioned, and it is characteristic that in Bohemia the Czechs organized the pogroms, in conjunction with the Germans, because the accused Jew was condemned; while in Hungary the pogroms occurred because the accused Jews were acquitted. But the country in which the greatest and most terrible pogroms occurred was Russia. We shall confine ourselves for the moment to a plain statement of fact.

The pogroms first broke out in the south of Russia in April 1881, the first taking place in Elizavetgrad. Warning that it was going to take place was given a long time in advance. It consisted chiefly of wholesale plunder, and the military did not raise a finger to interfere. The pogroms extended over the whole district of Elizavetgrad. In Kiev it was also settled long beforehand that a pogrom was to take place on April the 26th. The reasons given were that the Jews had assassinated Alexander II, and that the Tsar had given orders that accounts were to be settled with them. This was done by the destroying and plundering of Jewish houses, the ill treatment and murder of Jews and the raping of their women. It was not until these crimes had been committed that the military interfered on the following day, the 27th of April. But the pogroms were continued in the neighbourhood in fifty villages and areas of the district of Kiev. In May, Odessa followed suit with similar outrages committed under similar conditions.

The punishments inflicted on the pogrom heroes by the Russian government were so mild and betrayed so much hesitation as to whether they should be imposed at all, that in July 1881 a further wave of pogroms began. But they were more speedily suppressed, for the government was afraid they were merely part of the general revolutionary movement. The pogrom leaders, however, continued their activities surreptitiously by means of incendiarism on a large scale. Altogether over a hundred communities and settlements in south Russia suffered by the campaign of 1881.

In the same year, pogroms were organized in the Ukraine by the revolutionary Narodniki, and also in Warsaw (December 1881) under the leadership of Russians. After 1500 Jewish homes and businesses had been destroyed, 24 Jews wounded, and damage done to the extent of many millions of roubles, the police intervened on the third day and put an end to the pogrom. In the following year, 1882, it was announced long beforehand that a pogrom would take place in Balta at Easter, and the authorities looked benevolently on! Fifteen thousand lives were wrecked, many Jews were killed and wounded, and their women were raped, and large numbers were driven mad with horror.

As the pogroms aroused too much indignation abroad, they were forbidden and replaced by legal measures on the part of the government. Nevertheless, they still occurred. There was one in Ekaterinoslav in July 1883, another in the neighbourhood of that town in the autumn of the same year, and one in Nizhni-Novgorod in 1884. These were followed by a long period of respite, during which legal methods of suppression were employed. But pogroms occurred again between February and April 1897, under the bigoted reactionary, Nicholas II. He created an atmosphere in which on the one hand everything was ripe for revolution, while on the other "the Little Father," the Tsar, was an object of exaggerated veneration. It was an atmosphere in which fresh pogroms on a grand scale became possible. In Kishinev, after the ground had been thoroughly prepared both from the spiritual and the material point of view, circulars were sent out just before Easter 1903, announcing that the Tsar had consented to a pogrom taking place on the first three days of the Easter festival (Greek Church). The signal for the opening of the pogrom was to be given by the ringing of the church bells on April the 6th. As soon as dawn broke, plundering and even murder began. Jews who tried to defend themselves were disarmed by the police. On the following day the pogrom was continued. Deeds of unprecedented bestiality occurred. At the end of the second day the troops interfered. The casualties were 45 dead, 86 seriously, and 500 slightly wounded; over 1000 houses and shops had been looted.

The Jews formed a bodyguard, which was immediately suppressed by the government. When in August 1903 the town of Homel organized its pogrom, and the Jewish bodyguard came into action, the troops fired upon them and prevented the Russians from being molested while they murdered and looted right and left. Nevertheless, both sides suffered losses in dead and wounded. In the year 1904, during which all the energies of the country were concentrated on the Russo-Japanese War, there were no pogroms, although the usual Jew baitings took place. But in 1905 all kinds of pretexts were advanced, and they started again on a larger scale than ever. The "Black Hundred," the weapon of the Tsarist government against liberals and Jews, undertook to organize them. At first small pogroms were arranged all over the country, but at Easter a pogrom on a grand scale took place at Zhitomir; it lasted three days, and fifteen Jews were killed and a hundred wounded. Between October the 18th and 25th, when the government under the pressure of a general strike had promised to establish the Duma and grant democratic suffrage, it treacherously let loose the "Black Hundred" again, and, with the help of troops and Cossacks, they proceeded to an indiscriminate slaughter of Jews in fifty towns and about six hundred villages. In Odessa alone there were 300 killed while thousands were wounded and mutilated. Even after the opening of the Duma, the pogroms were continued, and the troops still took part in them. In Bialystok, 80 were killed and 100 wounded in 1906. After the dissolution of the first Duma, the pogroms were converted into street terrorization of the Jews organized by the authorities. Those who took part in the pogroms of this year were either not punished at all, or were sentenced and immediately pardoned; whereas members of the Jewish bodyguards were punished with long terms of penal servitude.

Even the World War did not put a stop to the persecution of Jews in Russia. In fact, as far as Russia was concerned, it might have been a Judæo-Russian war. Not only were hundreds of thousands of Jews driven out of the zone of the armies, on the charge of being friendly to Germany, but they were also killed all over the country by way of punishment for the defeats suffered by the Russian arms. After the revolution of 1917 the Ukraine, that classic area for Jewish massacres, again became the scene of the wildest pogroms. In March and April 1918, when the Ukraine declared its independence, the people turned to and murdered Jews, and the subsequent fighting between the Bolsheviks and the Ukrainian separatists ultimately led to the most terrible pogroms that had taken place since the seventeenth century. Between December 1918 and April 1921, 887 large and 349 small pogroms were held, resulting in 60,000 Jews being killed and over 70,000 being wounded. General Petliura, who was chiefly responsible for these massacres, was shot in Paris on May 25, 1926, by the Jew Schalom Schwarzbart. He is the only Jew who has ever taken justice into his own hands and avenged the massacre of his people. The Ukrainians have always sung the praises of their pogromists and held them up to admiration as national heroes. But no Jew will ever sing the praises of Schalom Schwarzbart. Yet the sufferings he endured before he shot the mass-murderer of his people make *him,* and not the man he assassinated, the martyr.

Romania and Poland also produced men who were on a level with the Russian pogromists. In Romania the government has always made Jew baitings part of its programme, and these baitings developed into regular pogroms in 1907, when the peasant movement against the boyars was diverted against the Jews. But as soon as the peasants turned against the landowners also, they were repressed. After the war, the perpetration of pogrom-murders in Romania has been taken over by the nationalistic students. We have already mentioned the Warsaw pogrom of 1881. Polish chauvinism, which was the outcome of national immaturity, kept the pogrom spirit alive, and, when Poland at last recovered her independence, this spirit found a vent in massacres of Jews organized by the Polish legionaries—that is to say, by men who only yesterday had themselves been among the oppressed.

The bloodless pogroms were equal in intensity and duration to those which involved bloodshed. Their weapons were expulsion, deprivation of legal rights, economic, political, and social repression, varying according to the conditions and attitude of mind of the various countries in which they occurred. This kind of Jewish persecution had two centres—Russia, where the methods applied were practical, and Germany where they were spiritual. We shall again confine ourselves merely to the relation of facts.

In Russia the methods described in previous chapters were continued, but the earlier experiments aiming at the "improvement" and assimilation of the Jews to the native population were discarded in favour of a uniform system of suppression and extermination. The Jews were given a perfectly clear official intimation that the government intended to be rid of them, and, more particularly after the pogrom of 1881, they were definitely urged to emigrate. The authorities also considered the possibility of transporting them all, men, women, and children, to the steppes of central Asia and Siberia for purposes of "colonization." As this proved impracticable, efforts were redoubled to segregate them in the various settlement zones, and to reduce the latter artificially. The only response made by the government to the Kiev pogrom was a wholesale expulsion of Jews. By the "Provisional Regulation" of 1882 (which remained in operation for thirty-five years) they were once again forbidden to settle outside towns and villages, or to acquire or lease estates in the country. Everywhere, and particularly in St. Petersburg, regular razzias were organized to catch Jews who had possibly managed to settle down without being able to produce a satisfactory permit. The method adopted by the provincial authorities was simply to declare certain places village communities, with the result that Jews were no longer allowed to settle in them, and those who had not been settled there previously to 1882 were forthwith driven out. In Moscow, which was to be made a royal residence, the Jews were hunted out by night with the help of the police and the fire brigades, and later on even old-established artisans were driven out of the city. Altogether about 20,000 were ejected and forced to take up their abode in the Pale. But this cramming of Jews into the Pale was tantamount to expulsion in disguise, for the crushing of six million people into the towns of one or two south Russian governments inevitably gave rise to economic distress, the only possible escape from which was by death or emigration. Either alternative was equally agreeable to the Russian government, as is clear from the fact that the organization of pogroms was chiefly its work. The pogroms, as already stated, did not break out suddenly, but always occurred after a period of preparation. In every case the authorities were aware of what was happening. Almost everywhere troops were available, but either they refrained on principle from interfering, or else did so only when they thought pillage, looting, and murder had gone far enough. Sometimes they even protected the pogromists by disarming Jews who tried to defend themselves, and by shooting down the Jewish bodyguards. The government in its official declarations laid the pogroms to the charge of the Jews. Ignatiev, Alexander III's minister of the interior, maintained that they were due to the Russian people taking the law into their own hands, because they were exploited by the Jews, who were engaged in unproductive work and had obtained a hold over the whole trade and industry of the country. Two years later a commission reported to the government that ninety per cent of the Russian Jews were destitute!

As a matter of fact the government had not the slightest difficulty in putting a stop to the pogroms. When, owing to the indignation they created abroad, Ignatiev was relieved of his post, all his successor Dmitri Tolstoy had to do was to notify the local authorities that he would hold them responsible for any disturbances due to pogroms, for them to cease altogether. But they broke out again as soon as the government found it could turn them to account. This happened under Nicholas II, whose rule was responsible for all the pogroms that took place between 1903 and 1917. When the first of these occurred (Kishinev, 1903), Plehve, the minister of the interior, forbade the newspapers to publish the truth about it, but forced them to print his own version of the affair, which laid the blame for provoking it on the Jews. And yet *The Times* actually published a letter, in which, a fortnight before the pogrom began, Plehve ordered the local authorities not to allow the troops to fire in the event of disturbances. He was also responsible for forbidding the Jews to form bodies to defend themselves, and for ordering them to be fired upon if they came into action. The fact that Nicholas II made use of the "Black Hundred" and their pogroms for political ends has already been mentioned. The first Duma had the courage to question the government about the pogroms, but received the usual reply that the Jews had only themselves to blame for them. While the Duma was in session, the Bialystok pogrom took place. Moved to indignation by these massacres, Urusov, ex-Governor of Kishinev, went to the Duma, and publicly declared that he knew the government had had a hand in these mass-murders. The Duma thereupon demanded the resignation of the cabinet. The Tsar replied by dissolving the Duma because it had been guilty of "examining into the actions of the authorities appointed by the All-Highest."

It was in keeping with the general methods employed that every conceivable measure was adopted to accentuate the social misery of the Jews. After the first pogroms, and as a result of the official declaration that the Jews were exploiting the Russian people, Alexander III appointed a special commission to inquire into "the extent to which the economic activities of the Jews had an injurious effect upon the conditions of life of the native population." One of the results of the conclusion reached by these experts was that the Jews were forbidden to trade on Sundays or during important Christian festivals. Thus their working week was reduced to five days. In 1884 their technical schools were closed, "because in the towns and districts on the south-west frontier the Jews constituted the majority of the population, and their competition was unfavourable to the prosperity of the native artisans." But even the liberal professions were restricted. Between 1889 and 1895, owing to administrative machinations, Jewish advocates were prevented from practising their calling. Even educational facilities for Jews were curtailed by the introduction of what was known as the "percentage quota" for secondary schools and universities. According to this regulation Jews were allowed to have only a tenth of the number of scholars the Christians had in the settlement areas; outside these areas the number was reduced to five per cent, and in St. Petersburg and Moscow to three per cent. Under Nicholas II these percentages were reduced even further. He also introduced the government vodka monopoly, a measure directed against the Jews, and robbed 250,000 of them of their means of livelihood. Altogether, towards the end of the Tsarist regime, there were in Russia 650 laws directed against the Jews alone.

In the matter of bloodless pogroms and legally authorized reprisals, Romania ranks second to Russia. In this country the juridical monstrosity of the "native foreigner" became a concrete reality, and the position of the Romanian Jew was much more unfavourable than that of any alien. From peddling to the liberal professions, there was no activity which was not either closed to him or made onerous through legal restrictions. And it was only owing to a protest on the part of America that an attempt to exclude the Jews even from skilled trades remained unrealized. Their admission to the secondary schools and universities was exposed to all manner of restrictions, while any attempt at founding schools of their own met with vexatious measures on the part of the authorities. They were deprived of all practical or legal means of protecting themselves against arbitrary plunder, and anybody who dared to criticize was banished. The only right of which the Jews had unrestricted enjoyment was that of joining the Romanian armies in the two Balkan Wars and the World War. The government's promise to grant equal rights to the Jews who had fought in the war and who formed part of the population in the conquered districts of Bulgaria was met by frenzied opposition on the part of the Romanians. And it was only when, by the Treaty of Versailles, a large number of Jews in the Bukovina, Transylvania, and the Banat came under her rule, that Romania was forced to grant equal rights to the Jews. But she has retaliated by keeping them in a constant state of terror to this day.

The unity which the threefold partition of the country prevented Poland from realizing was at least achieved in a sense long before the signing of the Treaty of Versailles, in all those places where the Poles out-numbered the Jews, and were in a position to make their national aspirations prevail against them. In Galicia, which was part of the Austrian empire, boycotting methods were perfected in the nineties of the last century. The slogan of the Polish "National Party" was: "For Poland and Catholicism!" In 1893, the Catholic Diet of Cracow declared: "The Greek Orthodox faith and the Jews are our enemies." The boycotting movement had an official programme: "Our object is to fight the Jews by Christian means and purely economic measures. . . . A Catholic who sells a piece of land to a Jew or leases it to him undermines the welfare of our nation." Associations were formed for the purpose of carrying on the boycott, and eventually led to the complete pauperization of the Jewish masses. The Jews were also almost entirely excluded from public life. Even Russian Poland adopted the boycott system. With the cry: "There is not room for two nations on the Vistula!" the people endeavoured to shut out the Jews both economically and politically. And even after the war, when the League of Nations undertook to guarantee the rights of minorities, including the Jews, in the new Polish state, the same aim was pursued. The economic struggle was made even more severe, the exclusion of Jews from public affairs was affected by means of a tacit understanding with the government officials, and the *numerus clausus* relating to the universities may be regarded as being in practical operation although it is legally forbidden.

In those countries which have officially granted citizenship to the Jews, it is impossible for bloodless pogroms to take the form of exceptional legislation. The only alternatives are, either to oppress the Jews by deliberately misinterpreting the law, or manipulating it to their disadvantage, or by the adoption of a similar policy either by the administration or the government. Where there are no legal weapons for fighting the Jews, an ideology which serves as a pretext for doing so soon comes into being. Typical examples of such countries, up to the outbreak of the World War, were France, Germany, and Austria-Hungary; and after the war, Germany and Austria.

The unsettled attitude of official Germany towards the Jews and the Jewish question can be traced mainly to the period following the Franco-German War of 1870–1871, during which it assumed a peculiar complexion characterized by an aggressive spirit towards the Jews, which spread through every class of the community. Superficially, the reasons for this appear extremely heterogeneous, but they were not really so. The form and direction of the attacks may be gathered from the various expressions of opinion uttered at the time. Scientists, pseudo-scientists, politicians, and government servants recorded their verdict, which is not surprising, seeing that nations unfortunately have a predilection in favour of framing their ideologies and defining their problems in the atmosphere of wars, whether past or impending, lost or won. Of the scientific and popular expressions of opinion uttered at this time, the most important were those of Treitschke and Mommsen. Treitschke regarded the state as sacrosanct, and in his eyes the real heroes of history were the statesmen and generals. He published various essays in 1879 and 1880, in which he made a serious attempt to deal with the problem of the emancipation of the Jews and their unpopularity. The chief difficulty to his mind was to discover a means of amalgamating these aliens with his own people, for in the hatred of the Jews he recognized a "natural reaction of the Teutonic national sense to a foreign element which has won far too important a position in our midst." For him the only solution lay in the Jews doing all in their power to become thoroughly good Germans and abandoning all idea of possessing a nationality of their own. Equal rights of citizenship had been granted to them only in their quality of a religious community, and any other point of view must inevitably lead to encouraging them to emigrate. Even Mommsen, although opposed to any hostile attacks on the Jews, regarded the solution of the Jewish problem as lying in the conversion of the Jews to Christianity. Christianity, declared the great historian, had become identified with European culture and morals, and, as the Jews aspired to the latter, they were committed to the adoption of the former, and to the entire abandonment of their national peculiarities. One whose point of view was very similar was the philosopher Eduard von Hartmann, who in his treatise, *Judaism in the Present and the Future* (1885), insists above all on the Jews relinquishing their natural sense of race and their consciousness of solidarity among themselves, and adapting themselves whole-heartedly to the Germans and German culture.

With the "philosopher" Düring there was inaugurated that type of modern anti-Jewish literature which refuses to examine a fact objectively, but substitutes desire and emotion as the standard of valuation, making the writer's own nationality and faith the measure of all things. The inevitable result, of course, is that everything else is regarded as inferior. Thus, in his treatise, *The Jewish Question as a Problem of Race, Morals, and Culture,* he also arrived at the conclusion that the Jews were the most inferior branch of the Semitic race, that they were spiritually uncreative, and that their spiritual treasures had all been filched from other peoples. Judaism aspired to the mastery of the world, and to thwart this aspiration it was necessary to turn the Jews out of the schools and to bar them from the press and all economic activities. Above all Germany was to be on her guard against allowing her "blood to be Judaized" through the agency of mixed marriages. If in this book the contemptuous attitude towards the Jews all too blatantly serves a personal purpose, this error of taste was shortly afterwards corrected by Houston S. Chamberlain's *Foundations of the Nineteenth Century,* in which the whole history of culture is described as a struggle between the superior Aryan and the inferior Semite, and the present age as one in which the *homo Judaicus* was steadily corrupting the *homo Europaeus.* This book, the preconceived object of which places it beyond the realm of discussion, and in which a sane regard for facts is replaced by wide reading and a redundance of arguments, became the gospel of the national and racial consciousness of hundreds of thousands of people.

Wilhelm Marr in his work, *The Victory of Judaism over German Civilization,* sounds the same note of alarm as Chamberlain. He too advances proofs to show that the Jews were aiming at world mastery, describes Judaized Germany and defeated German civilization, and appeals to his contemporaries to fight the "social-political danger" and "to save their German Fatherland from complete Judaization." The fact, that to meet with success such anti-Jewish publications did not require to be either accurate in their data or tenable in their reasoning, is also proved by the *Talmud Jew* by August Rohling, a canon and professor of theology at Prague, whose treatise quotes the Talmud to demonstrate the dangerous, inferior, and criminal character of the Jews and Judaism. The German scholar, Franz Delitzsch, in the course of a trial, proved the ignorance of the author and showed that he had frequently falsified and distorted facts; but, in spite of this, the book was read with eager credulity.

The above-mentioned treatise by Marr paved the way for a transition from purely literary and cultural, to political propaganda. In 1879 Marr founded the Anti-Semitic League, and this created an atmosphere and circle which gave birth to what was known as the Petition Campaign against the Jews. Its reasoning was somewhat as follows: The Jewish element in Germany was swamping the German, whose national superiority was everywhere being undermined by the rapid ascendency of Judaism. The Jewish race had contrived "steadily to strengthen its unhealthy influence, with the result that today it afforded a serious menace not only to the economic position and welfare of the German people, but also to their culture and religion." In order to combat these dangerous conditions, four measures were demanded of the government—limitation of the influx of Jews; the removal of all Jews from responsible state offices, particularly from the judge's bench; the appointment of Christian teachers only in the elementary schools, and the admission of Jews as professors in secondary schools and universities only under exceptional circumstances; and, finally, the keeping of special Jewish statistics. And in all this, it should be noted, the petitioners were not aiming at the establishment of any utopia, but were merely placing on record a state of affairs which had long since been realized owing to the practical efforts of the administration. The real motives underlying this petition we shall discuss in due course. It was supported by about 300,000 signatories, and was handed to Bismarck in March 1881.

The political and intellectual organization of Anti-Semitism soon followed in the shape of the "International Anti-Semitic Congress" held in Dresden, but the only international feature about it was that it consisted of representatives from Germany and Austria-Hungary. The intellectual leader of the congress and of the whole movement was the Court Chaplain Stöcker, the champion of the conservative opposition to Bismarck. He submitted a number of theses to the congress, in which he emphasized the necessity of forming an international union against the ascendency of Judaism. The Jewish question was not merely a religious question, or a matter of race, it was also a cultural, economic, and moral problem. The Jews were accumulating capital in order with its help to undermine the Christian social order. As a separate nation, they could never constitute an organic part of the Christian world. Jewish emancipation was a contradiction of the very essence of the Christian state. The Jews were the pace-makers both of capitalism and of revolutionary socialism.

His policy was elaborated, and partly also combated as inadequate, by politicians of the type of Liebermann von Sonnenberg, Otto Böckel, and Rector Ahlwardt, who were very popular among the lower middle classes of Germany, to whom they promised salvation if they would fight the Jews. The legislation it was hoped to introduce through these men was inspired by the ecclesiastical canon of the Middle Ages, and the people showed their approval of it by shouting at the tops of their voices.

The attitude of Austria, and particularly of Vienna, was essentially the same as that of Germany, with this difference, that the government did not look altogether with approval on the anti-Semitic movement, whereas in Germany its activities met with the silent though obvious patronage of William I and Bismarck. The results were everywhere similar and fulfilled the demands of the Anti-Semitic Petition. True, in course of time, the level of the Anti-Semitic campaign was raised and was transferred from the gutter to the study, but the attitude was still fundamentally hostile to the Jews, both in the middle classes of Germany and in the administration, which, with the exception of the Bavarian government, did all it could to bar the military, legal, and scholastic professions to the Jews. Only for a brief space, at the beginning of the World War, when it was alleged that all party distinctions were to be abolished, were the Jews granted full equal rights in the face of death. But as early as 1916 the process of "counting the Jews" in the German army was inaugurated with the object of ascertaining whether they were making an adequate sacrifice of life in return for the benefits officially and unofficially conferred upon them by Germany.

To complete the picture of Anti-Semitism in its various forms and manifestations, we must now turn to the movement which developed in France in connexion with the war of 1870–1871. The opponents of the Jews in this case were essentially identical with the opponents of the Third Republic, which was stigmatized as Judaicized. Edouard Drumont undertook to prove this charge in his famous book, *La France Juive*. There was nothing for which the Jews could not be held responsible. Above all they constituted a danger to France. The Jews and Freemasons were in the pay of Prussia in order to keep France down. With the object of combating this danger, Drumont founded the "National Anti-Semitic League of France." And it was in this atmosphere that the Dreyfus trial occurred, a trial in which Dreyfus, the only Jew on the French general staff, was condemned by a French court martial in December 1894 to be degraded and to be sent to penal servitude for life for espionage on Germany's behalf. Two years later Colonel Picquart discovered the real culprit in the person of Major Esterhazy. A friend of the spy, Colonel Henry, a cavalry officer, did his best to prevent the exposure of this judicial murder, he himself being implicated in the affair as he had forged a certain document. Owing to the popular outcry, the ministry of war was at last compelled to put Esterhazy on his trial. But in 1898 he was acquitted because the authorities *refused* to produce the proof of his guilt. Against this verdict, Zola protested in his famous article, *J'accuse!*, for which he was sentenced to a year's imprisonment. Colonel Picquart, who continued to carry on the struggle, was also eventually sent to prison. At last

Colonel Henry confessed the truth and committed suicide in prison. Esterhazy fled abroad. This sequence of events led the clerical party and the Anti-Semites to inaugurate a frenzied campaign against the Jews. Nevertheless, it was impossible to prevent the Dreyfus trial being reopened in 1900. But in spite of the revelations that had been made meanwhile, he was again condemned and sentenced to ten years' imprisonment in a fortress, though he was immediately pardoned. To avoid further revelations an amnesty was granted to all those who had been involved in the affair. It was only in 1906, when Dreyfus, supported by the untiring efforts of men like Clemenceau and Jaurès, demanded a retrial, that he was acquitted and rehabilitated.

Other countries hardly enter into this discussion of Anti-Semitism. Perhaps Belgium might be mentioned as having for a while been infected by French Anti-Semitism, for in July 1898 a solemn procession of Belgium clergy commemorated the trial for desecration of the Host which had taken place in that country in 1370—a proof that the church had a long memory.

After this general survey of the facts we must now turn to an examination of the motives advanced by Anti-Semitism. Though they are many and various they can be divided into two categories: the first being inspired by an object to be achieved, the second by the desire to attach blame or guilt to some party. We must bear in mind that in this matter the alleged motive and the real reasons behind it did not by any means tally, and that it is typical of Anti-Semitism always to conceal its real reasons behind a purpose or a definite charge.

Among the motives inspired by a purpose to be achieved, the most important is that to which we had occasion to refer in connexion with the emancipation of the Jews in Germany—the merging of the Jewish population in the majority about them with the object of producing homogeneity in the country. It is, of course, impossible to secure such homogeneity; it does not exist even among the non-Jewish population of any country, for even Germany of the period of the emancipation, and still more after the Franco-German War, harboured all manner of racial, social, and political extremes, and, when the Anti-Semite fever was at its height, the most bitter differences existed between the various leading groups in the country. In spite of the establishment of the empire and what appeared to be an apparently powerful unity, the old military, dynastic, ecclesiastical, agrarian, and bureaucratic forces still survived. But Bismarck's aim was to treat them in the same way as he intended to treat the Jews. They were to be forced into unity by the power of the empire, just as the Jews were to be forced by the power of the German nation and German culture to abandon their peculiar type. This policy gave rise to the conflicts by which the Jews were in practice forced into an anomalous position as far as the enjoyment of rights was concerned, while special legislation was passed to place the Catholics and the Social Democrats in a similar position. But, just as Bismarck failed to unify the antagonistic sections of the German people, so did the Germans fail to unify the Germans and the Jews. Incidentally the resistance offered by the Jews to Germanization was on the whole not so strong as the resistance which the old German conservatives, for instance, offered to the "evangelical empire."

We have already noticed that a definite purpose also lay behind the attempts to deal with the Jewish question in France, Austria-Hungary, and Russia. The state of affairs in the Dual Monarchy made matters exceptionally complicated, for, in this conglomeration of peoples, each individual nation was inclined to regard itself as the sole repository of power and to assert itself against the rest, and particularly against the Jews. The Germans in Lower and Upper Austria, the Czechs in Bohemia and Moravia, the Poles in Galicia, and the Magyars in Hungary maintained an attitude of extreme hostility towards one another within their respective territories, while the Jews in each district were expected to give their whole-hearted support to the national ideals of the majority about them.

The goal of assimilation so strenuously aimed at was to a certain extent achieved, more particularly in France, though in Russia hardly any change was noticeable. In fact, it might almost be said that assimilation took place in inverse ratio to the number of Jews in a country and the density of population in their settlements. Nevertheless, complete assimilation never occurred. In every case only a financial or intellectual upper class was really affected, and the Jewish masses either stopped short when they had gone a certain distance, as was the case in Germany and Austria, or else, as in Poland and Russia, resolutely refused to become adapted in any way. But this process of complete and partial assimilation was interrupted by a movement which we have already noticed in connexion with the struggle of Spanish society against the compulsorily baptized Jews—a convulsive effort was made by the people of the various countries to defend themselves against the consequences of the assimilation that had been insisted upon, and in France, Germany, Austria, Poland, and Russia a cry of alarm was raised against these ridiculous minorities of Jews within their borders. Beware of Judaization! The actual social and cultural position of the Jews was immaterial. Even in Russia, where, of the 6,000,000 Jews, ninety per cent hardly knew how they were going to get their next day's bread, the warning cry of "The Jew is on the move!" was raised. At first there had been a real desire to put an end to the isolation of the Jews. But it had been proved impracticable, as was shown by the fact that the various peoples concerned themselves raised the alarm that they were being Judaized, which was their way of saying that some strange and deleterious process was at work to their disadvantage. The menace took a different form in every country. The state of affairs was not the same in France as it was in Germany, while the problem in Russia differed from that in either of these countries. But all without exception felt themselves exposed to danger and would have liked the former conditions, under which the Jews had been isolated, to be restored.

In this connexion it is important to note that these cries of alarm were always raised at a time of crisis in the life of the nation concerned and bore an intimate relation to local events of a momentous nature. For instance, in France Anti-Semitism came into being after the war of 1870–1871 had been lost, and in Germany after it had been won. In Austria-Hungary it arose at a time when the struggle between the various nationalities of the Dual Monarchy for cultural and political independence had become acute. In Russia it was the direct result of the reactionary regime and its struggle with the revolutionary movement among the people. Thus Anti-Semitism has always arisen in close connexion with some national problem, and the presence and influence of the Jews are always associated in some way with the national problem which happens to be uppermost at the moment. Yet there is never any question of establishing an objective connexion; the link is one forged by prejudice and an attitude of negative contempt, combined with a desire to attach blame to somebody. But the main charge advanced against the Jews is always that they are responsible for defeat in war. France blamed them for the catastrophe of 1870–1871, Russia for the loss of the Russo-Japanese War, and Germany accused them of giving her a stab in the back and bringing about her defeat in the World War. And where, as in Germany after 1871, it was a matter of a successful war, the Jews were still blamed for something or other. The same phenomenon was observed whenever disagreements arose between the Poles, Czechs, Germans, and Magyars in Austria-Hungary, and in Russia the Jews had a similar role thrust upon them in connexion with every liberal manifestation and above all revolutionary movements among the masses. Everywhere, in all circumstances, a negative attitude towards the Jews is adopted by members of the country in which they have settled down.

The nature of the accusation brought against the Jews depends upon the problem which, for the time being, happens to be perplexing a country. A simple instance is provided by Tsarist Russia. Alexander III's slogan, "Russia for the Russians!" was primitive but straightforward, and his own efforts, continued by his followers, to handicap all the liberal elements that were struggling against unlimited despotism, were brutal but obvious. Here the ulterior motive and the reasons given for the policy were identical. But, side by side with this frank and open policy of oppression, an excuse was suddenly advanced which did not fit the circumstances, and which was therefore untrue and invented to serve a particular purpose—the Jew was a danger to Russia. That is to say, he was a menace to those qualities in the Russian which constituted his particular type and value. He was a corrosive element which acted by "penetrating into Christian circles." What matter that all Christian circles were almost hermetically sealed to the Jew and that the number of those who were privileged to be summoned and therefore really "penetrated" into them was extraordinarily small? But the claim that a people consisting of many millions could be threatened with annihilation in the ancient hereditary stronghold of their culture by a handful consisting of some ten thousand Jews must necessarily either be false or else so obvious that the mere statement was sufficient and required no evidence to prove it. This was the case in the present instance owing to the prevalent belief that the Jews were an inferior race. Not all nations are as thorough as the Germans, who made a "science" of this idea. Other countries are, as a rule, satisfied with the mere statement, and we shall see later on how the motive consisting of the desire to lay the blame on someone was converted into the motive inspired by a purpose. Russia could avail herself of an even more tangible motive, and lay the whole blame for the liberal movement within her borders at the door of the Jews, excusing the pogroms against them on the score that they constituted a protest on the part of the people against the demands of the Jews, the Socialists, and the Social-Revolutionaries for a constitution. We have only to call to mind that the government itself was the instigator of these pogroms to give the lie to these statements about popular protests. Even the liberal movement, as the government itself was well aware, was, however, merely the outcome of its own system. But the obvious participation of the Jews in the movement for freedom naturally served the purpose of relieving the government of responsibility for its official policy and transferring the onus of the general discontent to the Jews. But there were other motives which were neither hidden nor dissimulated—motives connected with religion and economic conditions, which really have nothing in common, but are always associated when it is a question of browbeating the Jews. Instead of going into details we shall confine ourselves to quoting a note written by Alexander III as late as 1890 in the margin of a memorandum on the wretched condition of the Jews in Russia: "But we should not allow ourselves to forget that the Jews crucified our Saviour and shed His precious blood." On the other hand the economic success of the Jews, though there were few indeed who could boast of having achieved it, gave rise to the charge that they were obtaining the upper hand in Russian economic life, and exploiting the masses. As we have seen, this was an accusation hurled at the heads of the poorest and most miserable among the Jews who were struggling against overwhelming odds to eke out a livelihood.

The obvious motives for Anti-Semitism in Poland may readily be inferred from what we have already said about Polish history. The opposition arising from religious hostility and economic conditions was complicated, during the period when Poland was divided, by questions of nationality. In any case, as far as the nationalities in Austria-Hungary were concerned, the mere existence of the Jews and their presence was enough to stamp them as enemies and traitors to the nation and the majority. It was useless, as happened in Hungary, for the Jews to Magyarize themselves as far as possible; for, in spite of all their efforts to do so, when Hungary was made an independent state after the war, the most virulent Anti-Semitism prevailed, while Austria even today can still boast of a strong Anti-Semitic movement. But Austria at least has lost a war, whereas Hungary and Poland may almost be said to have won a war. Yet the results, as far as Anti-Semitism is concerned, are identical.

Let us now turn our attention to the motives which Germany, the classic land of Anti-Semitic ideology, advanced as an excuse for her hostility to the Jews in the eighties of last century. We are here concerned with the pronouncements of a victorious people, elated with a sense of power, to whom the establishment of imperial unity had given a peculiar idea of the nature of the state. A state is obviously something more than a mere union of individuals for a common purpose. It is a form of association for the object of securing social existence and allowing men an opportunity of developing their powers. Germany of 1870–1871, however, turned it into something else, and regarded it as a living end in itself. In spite of internal political strife, there was a revival of the most primitive medieval ideas regarding the sanctity of the state and of the alliance between spiritual and temporal power. The imperial idea, ever a matter of deep sentiment, was realized, but it was divorced from the idea of the papacy, which was replaced by the concept of the "Christian state." The state had become a personality made up of the sum of all the forces present in the people and the nation. If we add to this that the nation had just won a victory, it is no wonder that it wished to make the state exclusively its own, identified itself with the latter, and could tolerate no other gods beside it. It was this atmosphere that gave birth to the idea of the Germans being the chosen people, which, at least where practical results were concerned, far surpassed the similar Jewish idea. War was declared against everything that failed to become wholly adjusted to this triumphant nationalism, and it was only logical that the Jews should be attacked with as much ferocity as the Poles. But here we immediately encounter the phenomenon already pointed out above; as soon as ever adjustment, adaptation, and assimilation actually occurred, they provoked the most passionate protests. The utterances of official Germany already recorded show that one section of Germany was in favour and the other section wholly opposed to any mixing of the races. Nowhere was the outcry of Judaization raised more loudly than in Germany, and nowhere did it signify more emphatically that the assimilation that had once been insisted upon must be revoked. The Germans now saw not merely that it was impossible to reconcile the Jews and the German nation, but also that in the two races themselves there existed a disparity which made assimilation impossible. We cannot seriously undertake to discuss these German investigations on the subject of race, for the simple reason that they set out by taking their thesis as proved and with a resolute determination to create a Germanic ideal and prove it afterwards, and above all because, from the very beginning, their argumentation consists entirely of valuations. The further conclusion that the Semites and particularly their most inferior branch, the Jews, were engaged in an incessant struggle with the Germanic peoples, was also based on these valuations, which were assumed to be absolute.

Thus all these motives owed their origin to the mere fact that the Jews existed. But the matter did not end there. This so-to-speak passive inculpation of the Jews was supplemented by an active charge, and an argument which we have met before in our history again cropped up—the Jews were aiming at the conquest of the German people, they were set upon undermining the whole of the Christian social order, they were aiming at the economic mastery of the world. The proofs adduced were frequently far-fetched, but they dealt with every conceivable aspect of the case. Above all, the economic aims of the Jews were investigated and an endeavour made to prove that their rise was not the result of any native capacity, but was due to a "Golden International" of the Jews of the whole world. The fact that, when patriarchal conditions ceased to prevail in economic life, the economic struggle became a trial of ability, was not denied by those about them. Yet the Jews' frequent superiority was regarded as a grievance and ascribed to malice prepense. But, above all, they were accused of being the pace-makers of capitalism. Be this as it may, nobody, of course, ventured to deny that capitalism was a necessary evolution of world economics, and that consequently it would have come into being even if the Jews had not been engaged in commerce and industry at all. But in order to avoid looking foolish those who advanced these arguments were obliged to have recourse to the arsenal of valuations requiring no special proof, and it was declared that the Jews were by nature, and by the laws determining their spiritual inclinations, a race of "shopkeepers." A similar charge has been brought by the Germans against the English. In the same breath, however, the Jews were also accused of being the pace-makers for the antithesis of capitalism, the socialist working-class movement, and all organizations aiming at world revolution. But at this stage the argumentation became more than ever involved, for, in addition to the latter claim, the theory was also advanced, precisely at that period of Bismarck's cultural struggle, which concerns us here, that in the large cities the industrial masses were ground down "by capitalism and the Jews," and that it was the duty of the Prussian monarchy and of the church to come to the rescue of these unfortunate folk. It is not surprising to find that Stöcker was the champion of this theory, for, as we have seen, the essence of his reasoning was that all these contradictions culminated in the final conclusion, which required no proof, that the aim of the Jews was to destroy the Christian social order. But the members of the "Christian Social Party," which he founded, interpreted his arguments practically rather than spiritually, and employed the exceptionally clear and illuminating term—competition. But those who were ashamed to use such reasoning preferred to remain true to more spiritual slogans. The fact that the liberal press, which had many Jewish contributors, was more alive than its conservative competitors and was consequently more successful, led to the belief which prevails to this day, that "the press was in the hands of the Jews." And as the Jews were winning a name for themselves in public life, and making progress in the service of the state, an imperious demand was put forward for their exclusion, and for the purging of public life from an influence which was neither German nor Christian.

Our conclusions may be summed up as follows: the causes of Anti-Semitism lie in nationalism, and in political, religious, and racial interests. The particular form it assumes is dictated by the requirements of the place and time in which it appears. It is indifferent as to whether the arguments it uses can or cannot be proved, or whether they are mutually contradictory. It uses facts, as well as valuations and resentment, as providing a reasonable basis for its position. It comes to the fore in moments of victory as well as of defeat, and appears in times of both economic prosperity and depression. It is, therefore, clearly a problem of the non-Jewish environment, the proof being that, when the curve of a people's national, religious, or racial feeling rises, they become elated and refuse any longer to tolerate the Jews but demand their isolation on the plea that they are an inferior race and exercise a deleterious influence. But when the opposite process takes place, the Jews are again blamed, and their isolation is insisted upon as a precautionary measure and as a punishment. That clear-sighted writer, Lessing, put the whole matter in a nutshell when he said: "Do nothing, and the Jew is burned alive!"

But, from the historical point of view, this classic formula is inadequate; for it merely sums up a state of affairs and not the laws which govern it, and with which alone we are concerned. Our investigations have always taken us back to the past, and, whether we deal with facts or arguments, we find that they have all occurred before in the history of the Jewish Diaspora. The Christian religion, whether in the form of Catholicism, the Orthodox Church, or Protestantism, has been a factor perennially hostile to Judaism ever since the time of Paul. The centuries reflect each other so faithfully that even in twentieth-century Russia, owing to a sort of instinctive historical connexion, the murder of Jews took place preferably at Easter. Ever since the days of Constantine, the opposition of the Christian state to the Jews has been the primary manifestation of its being. Here, too, the modern copy is true to the original, for there is no difference between the ecclesiastical canon, raised to the dignity of a state law, which forbade a Jew to fill any official post which gave him authority over a Christian, and the practice of a modern government which does not even require the sanction of any special legal measure in order to prevent a Jew from exercising such authority. Equally hoary is the hostility shown by every country at every stage of its economic development to the Jew on account of his economic activities, and ever since the rise of Christianity every age has raised the common cry that Judaism aimed at the extermination of Christianity.

Consequently this much at least is plain—Anti-Semitism is an eternal historical problem. But there is a moment when even historical conditions become clear to the world at large and stand out above all the imponderabilia of their inception. And we have already pointed out when this happened. It occurred when Judaism encountered Hellenism, when the two extreme solutions of man's relation to God and the world were brought face to face, and Hellenism suddenly came into contact with its obverse, which was hateful to it and to which it could not aspire. Peoples like individuals feel the need of proving their superiority. And if their longing for recognition be thwarted by others who consistently deny their claim, their reaction is overcompensation in the form of hatred and the development of excessive self-consciousness. This is the real reason why nations who have been oppressed for a very long time, like the Poles and the Hungarians, are apt to show their satisfaction at any native feat of culture, however insignificant, in rapturous chauvinistic self-appreciation. The Jew in silent disdain turned his back on the Greek, showing his contempt in his intellectual and religious and national attitude; he deliberately held him at a distance as an inferior creature, and the moment it was recognized that Hellenism possessed neither the spiritual nor the temporal power to stamp its culture upon the Jew, the latter became from that moment an object of detestation. Even the Greek's most puerile argument, advanced in the time of Antiochus Epiphanes, that the Jews were fattening a Greek in the Temple, to offer him up as a sacrifice to their God, survived for 2100 years. During this period hatred of the Jews adopted a variety of forms, but underneath them all lay the fundamental feeling of a need to enjoy superiority which has met with no respect. Rome, who aimed at carrying on Greek traditions with weapons inadequate for the task, founded her hatred of the Jews on their refusal to recognize her empire and her deified rulers. Christianity, which was the religious consummation of both Greece and Rome, derived its tremendous powers of hatred and aggression from the refusal of the Jews to bow their heads to it. It is beyond dispute that, in the first stages of its development, Christianity held Judaism to be worth winning over, on account of the unique treasure of religious truth it possessed. But, from the historical point of view, this attitude lasted but a moment and changed to one of hostility against those who had scorned it—the Jews and the pagans. The pagans were worsted and the Jews were fought. This immediately gave rise to a religious tradition which became stereotyped when Christianity became petrified into a church. For, at this point, the question of power arose and, once again, an antithesis became apparent, which also for centuries led to a denial of recognition—we refer to the Christian Church's problem of power as opposed to the Jewish problem of lack of power. Power, however, can only produce the effects of power, and through all eternity can find no other basis for itself except the continuous exercise of power. That is why the Christian world is not only bound hand and foot to its tradition of hatred of the Jews, but can also find no escape from it. It could have done so if, during a period of close on 2000 years, there had been just one brief moment in which the discrepancy between life and religion had ceased to exist. But this discrepancy was always there and survives to this day. And for this reason the claim of the Christian world that the Jew should subordinate himself unconditionally to it has always been illegitimate. Subconsciously this must have been clearly felt by all ages, for it alone makes it possible to understand the eternal argument that Judaism in all its manifestations has aimed at destroying Christianity. It was the reflex action of the guilty conscience, the cry of "Stop, thief!" on the part of one to whom the ideal of annihilating Judaism had been handed down through countless generations. Thus the final product of all this, the feeling of strangeness, is not an actual fact, but a personal problem, not a problem based on concrete things, but one implicit in intellectual tendencies and spiritual potentialities. This often escapes recognition, for those who advance anti-Jewish arguments are apt to avail themselves unscrupulously of any chance fact that happens to come to hand, with the result that many Jews have even held the view that the Jew himself could do something to modify the facts lying at the root of Anti-Semitism. But they are mistaken, for there are no such concrete facts, but merely abstract conditions, and Anti-Semitism is not a Jewish, but a Gentile problem. The Jew can do nothing to alter either the substance or the nature of Anti-Semitism. Even Zionism cannot do so, inasmuch as it hopes to abolish Anti-Semitism by putting an end to the Diaspora at least as far as the nucleus of Judaism is concerned. This would be a perfectly legitimate aspiration if Anti-Semitism had been the outcome of the Diaspora. But it existed long before the Jews were scattered. All the Diaspora was responsible for was to make it permanent and endow it with eternal actuality, which for the suffering Jews was a terrible actuality. It is here that we first light on the real share of the Jews in the problem—their suffering. Even to within quite recent times men have been killing their fellows merely because they happened to be Jews, a fact of which even the most intellectual and spiritual arguments in support of Anti-Semitism will never be able to dispose. It is only the effects of Anti-Semitism that might possibly be held in check as soon as it became unsafe for the unsatisfied instincts of individuals and nations to be vented on a minority.

If a stop is ever to be put to anti-Jewish feeling, the effort must come from the quarter whence we maintain it arose—from humanity itself. In the life of the individual, as in the life of nations, there are certain ideas, feelings, and reactions which are cultivated and retained although those who are subject to them know better. For the individual, as for the nation, they constitute not that which is denied them, but that which they deny themselves. Anti-Semitism is one of those feelings of aloofness, which mankind uses in order to set up a barrier between itself and the ultimate fulfilment of its human obligations.

CENTRALIZATION

THE end of the nineteenth century constituted for Judaism a period of decisions and separations, of disintegration and resolution. It is the last historical period in the life of the Jews that we can view as a whole, and during it we find centralization taking place. Both geographical and spiritual centres were sought; the aim was not limited to discovering a single centre; sometimes a centre would be established not among the Jews themselves, but outside in their environment or in the world about them. Even in those cases where the striving was not towards Judaism, but away from it, every repudiator of his own people, every renegade and every assimilated Jew, was still animated by the Jewish aspiration to be drawn within the sphere of some spiritual idea in the world; there was a passionate longing not to be an isolated individual contemptuously exploited by those about him, but a fellow-creature working with others to serve the world or some idea connected with it. For better for worse, the Jews are all filled with the idea of sharing something in common with others.

Although the Anti-Semitic movement we have just described has been shown to be a Gentile problem, it exercised a certain practical influence on Jewish ideology, inasmuch as it presented an obstacle to the line of thought and interests of the assimilated Jews, who endeavoured to overcome it. Their behaviour was entirely consistent. The various countries, when they granted emancipation to the Jews, demanded the renunciation of their national exclusiveness and attitude, and western Judaism responded to this demand by immediately separating the Jewish religion from its national elements. And on this plane it delivered itself up to assimilation. Whereupon, Anti-Semitism sprang into being and, on national grounds, again set up between the assimilated Jews and their environment a barrier which could be broken down only if the Jews resolutely and with fixed determination showed that their sole aim was to become attached to the particular country they happened to live in. But by so doing they tacitly admitted that the existence of a group of men, forming merely a religious community in an environment organized on national lines, was quite impossible. The tragedy of this consistency on the part of the Jews, however, lay in the fact that the national argument brought forward by those about them did not constitute an end in itself, but was only one of the pretexts for a fresh manifestation of hostility against the Jews, and that the motivation which had ceased to apply after the latter had become very largely assimilated to the various countries in which they lived, was forthwith replaced by another motivation. The Jew was now punished for his loss of historical perspective, and was forced to devote his energies to a hopeless struggle in which his strength was squandered. This happened in various ways; he was kept constantly on the defensive, offering excuses for himself and developing the idea of a Judaism without a nationality of its own, the direct and indirect consequence of which was to reduce its political and spiritual power.

The Jews, particularly in Germany, tried to meet the first fury of the Anti-Semitic movement by appealing to the governments of their respective countries, but as the latter, including the administration of Bismarck, found Anti-Semitism favourable to their policy, these efforts were naturally foredoomed to failure, while an energetic literary campaign, which in all good faith emphasized the fact that national Judaism was nonexistent, could not possibly have any effect on a movement, which, being based on no arguments from facts, was also inaccessible to such arguments. That Anti-Semitism set out with the objective truth that a Jewish nation did exist, was beside the point, for it abused the objective fact by making it merely the basis for a subjective valuation. But the effect of this polemical literature on the Jews themselves was much more important than its impotence in face of the hostility of the outside world; for the denial that the Jews constituted a nation, pronounced by men of such authority as Lazarus and Hermann Cohen, actually created among the western Jews an atmosphere in which an appeal to a living national body failed to meet with any response, and was bound to do so, since the consciousness of the thing was lacking. A change of consciousness had come about, though it was incomplete; for, if a Jew *qua* Jew was ill treated in any part of the world, there was still an immediate spontaneous reaction on the part of every member of his race which betrayed the fateful relationship.

It is only fair to add that both in Germany and in Austria (1890–1891) leading men lent their support to societies formed for combating Anti-Semitism, and that non-Jews played a prominent part in them. Their efforts deserve acknowledgment, though their inability to solve the problem is comprehensible enough. In due course the Jews resolved to organize a defensive movement of their own and formed the "Central Union of German Citizens of Jewish Faith," which did all that could be done to combat Anti-Semitism, meeting individual cases of illegal attack by legal means. In this connexion it did very good work, and its inability to cope effectively with the question was not its fault, since the problem was insoluble. But it was also largely responsible for the fact that one of the weapons of resistance possessed by the Jew—his consciousness of his relationship to all the other Jews of the world—was sensibly weakened. One of the cardinal principles that animated it was: "We are no more related to the Jews of other countries than the Catholics and Protestants of Germany are related to the Catholics and Protestants of other countries."

This maxim became something more than the device of a particular union. It developed into the standard governing the attitude of the majority of western Jews. It was the coping-stone of a century of development, and the national creed of a generation that had grown up in the national schools of the country of their adoption. It also, quite unwittingly, became the starting-point for the gradual disintegration of the Jewish population of western Europe. It was the formula which precipitated and made possible the transition from cultural assimilation to complete separation from Judaism. The idea of assimilation lost its unequivocality, and began to mean ever less and less the vital process of laying hold of the cultural treasures of the world, and became more and more a term denoting flight from Judaism, both racially and spiritually. Assimilation in this sense became a permanent phenomenon in western Jewry, and conversions to Christianity continued to take place regularly. Mixed marriages increased. As early as 1899 in Germany one Jew in five married a Gentile, and the loss in strength to the Jews as the result of mixed marriages during the last half century in Germany alone is enormous. Thus, to give an example, of 103,000 Jewish marriages celebrated between 1900 and 1927, 33,800, or about a third, were mixed marriages. The fact that, in spite of this, the total population of Jews throughout the world numbered about 15,000,000 in 1925, is certainly not to be placed to the credit of the western Jew. These figures merely help us to arrive at certain conclusions in connexion with the Jews of western Europe—their distribution, their numbers, their professional occupations, their legal and social position—but they tell us nothing whatever about the most important point of all, which is what their active or passive attitude was as Jews conscious of their connexion with Judaism. The problem of assimilation has burdened Jewry with an entirely new type, in the shape of the passive Jew, who does not go so far as to be baptized or to contract a mixed marriage, but whose relationship to Judaism is confined to his capacity for inertia. No country in the world, which has a Jewish population, is free from this class of Jews, particularly countries like Austria, Hungary, Germany, Switzerland, France, Holland, England, and Italy. The atomization of the Jews has been effectively accomplished. In the World War, an opportunity was afforded of proving this, and on all fronts Jew stood opposed to Jew. This was a tragedy for which, however, no one was responsible, and which will be repeated so long as wars continue to be fought and Jews are compelled to fulfil their duties as citizens of the lands of their adoption. But in the last war, the most appalling feature of all was that rabbis, "Jewish field padres," blessed the arms which were to consummate the doom of fellow-creatures who were Jews fighting on the opposite side. This was a crime for which we all have to answer. What advantage has been gained by the Jews who in this great conflict gave proof of their passionate will to assimilation cannot yet be historically determined. The sacrifices they made at home and abroad were very great, and yet the Jews are hated as much as ever. Thus these sacrifices for the various countries concerned must have a meaning which for the time being is still hidden from us.

We have been compelled to witness the atomization of the Jews as an accomplished fact. And we must now determine whether Jewry as a whole has accepted this fact without protest and without opposition. History has already given us a reply to this question in the shape of the Jewish national movement, which constitutes another aspect of the recent idea of centralization and makes the acquirement of a separate nationality of their own the deliberate and conscious cultural aim of the Jews. This movement includes all those Jews who could not and would not adopt the alternative of assimilation and mergence with their environment, because they recognized their common kindred as a people living according to its own laws, and had not yet lost faith in the creative power of their nation. We are here concerned, therefore, with one of those decisions taken by Judaism in the midst of one of its crises. There were various motives actuating the individual to come to this conclusion. It was not everywhere that the idea of a "nation" came spontaneously and forcibly into being, and the world about them played an important part in turning the Jews in this direction; for its method of reacting to their presence in every imaginable circumstance and with every possible means was bound to lead to the conclusion that there was no possibility of discovering a peaceful and objective solution of the Jewish question, and that consequently there was no solution, and certainly not one along the lines of assimilation. So long, therefore, as there was any life left in Judaism, the only path that remained open to the Jews was that which led back to themselves, with the full consciousness, however, that even this turning towards their own race and nationality would provoke the same hostile reactions as the turning away from themselves towards a strange nationality had done. If, as appears to be the case, the hostility of one species to another is a law of nature, then a nation's surrender of its particular type is a futile and foolish sacrifice.

This was first discovered in the East, particularly in Russia, by those who, in conjunction with the Russian liberals and radicals, were working at a liberal development of Russia and had accepted the principle of Russification in its widest sense. But events taught them that it was impossible to solve anything more than their own personal problem by means of Russification. The great mass of Jews, who did not and would not adopt this means, were left hopelessly at the mercy of oppression and annihilation. At the root of their deliberations was the consciousness of the appalling misery of the Jews, which must be relieved. Their object was to help, not to restore. But they would not have been Jews if, when they came to consider how help was to be given at the moment, they had not wondered how assistance of a more general and lasting kind could be rendered. This line of thought inevitably led to the conclusion that the laws governing both the Jew and his environment, and which determined their respective beings and their relation to each other, must be discovered. In his treatise, *Auto-Emancipation* (1882), Leon Pinsker was the first to establish a connexion between the fact of the Diaspora and the stunted and etiolated life of the Jewish people. And he proposed that the Jews should convert their shadowy existence into something tangible either in America or Palestine. The idea of forming a new and conscious centre became acute, and eyes were turned to the only two countries which could promise the Jews the opportunity of realizing their aim—America, the land where the realization would be practicable, and Palestine, where the realization would be in keeping with the highest ideals of the race.

Meanwhile, the hopes that were centred in America seemed nearer to realization than those centred in Palestine, for events had anticipated the movement. America had become a country to which Jews emigrated, for every fresh act of oppression in Europe had led them to seek refuge in the New World. It was a country which had not yet developed national haughtiness and it had no ecclesiastical tradition to enslave men's minds and turn their piety into hatred of the Jews. And it was not only the land of freedom, but also one in which there was a vast concentration of Jews. As early as 1880 there were about 250,000 Jews in America, 60,000 of whom had settled in New York. And this new colony exercised a suggestive power over the Jews, drawing them to itself. Millions of Jewish emigrants instinctively found their way thither, Jew drawing Jew, in response to the desire for close association and a communal existence which still survived. And thus began what was numerically the greatest Jewish migration that has ever been known. In fact it constituted a "migration of the people" in every sense of the term, for such migrations are undertaken only by peoples and never by religious communities. In Galicia all those Jews who could no longer survive under the Polish boycott fled to America; in Romania all who refused to live under the legal pogroms did likewise. After the Russian massacre of 1881, many thousands fled in frenzied haste to America. This also happened after the pogrom of 1882. Under the reactionary policy of Alexander III, an average of 30,000 emigrated annually, and in the two years, 1891 and 1892, over 100,000, and between 1903 and 1905 over 125,000. A people had started to move, and the great pendulum motion so characteristic of the Jewish Diaspora was set going and began to swing back.

Although economic causes constituted the deciding factor in this migratory movement, its essence and inner working made it a national migration, not merely from the standpoint of numbers but also from that of the ideas that animated it, the first being expressed by the formation of an enclosed settlement area in the downtown district of New York, and the second being the conviction that the Jews must return to agriculture. Though the exceptional difficulties of building up a new life, and the inexperience of the first colonists, led to the latter aim being only inadequately realized, we nevertheless find the Jews again endeavouring to contrive the most radical solution for a state of homelessness by becoming rooted to the soil. It is this feeling which inspired the grand scheme promoted by Baron Moritz Hirsch in 1891, by which he planned to reduce the Jewish population of Russia through an organized emigration of a third of their number, who were to be settled as farmers on the land. With this object in view he arranged to buy some land in the Argentine, whither Jews had already emigrated in 1889. In the autumn of 1891 he founded the Jewish Colonization Association, which was to organize a mass emigration of Russian Jews to various parts of America, particularly the Argentine. But for various reasons the organization never succeeded in effecting a mass emigration. Not only were means lacking for an undertaking which was far too ambitious, but serious mistakes were also made in the administration of the scheme. The most important fact, however, was that the mere prospect of leading a life free from outside hostility did not in itself prove a sufficient attraction to the Jews. Of two modes of life the Jew will always choose the worse, if other Jews happen to be close at hand to share it with him, thereby providing him with the possibility of forming a community. It was for this reason that the Jewish settlement in the Argentine numbered only 7000 in 1900.

But the call of the land, which now re-echoed for the first time for hundreds of years in the hearts of the Jews, could no longer be silenced. It meant a fundamental revolution in Judaism, for this people, which had risen from agriculture, had for centuries been excluded both voluntarily and involuntarily from the soil—involuntarily through legislation, and voluntarily because "soil" to them meant Palestine, and because they now once again saw a connexion between a land and their destiny. Land, after all, was the promise on which Judaism had been reared. The "Holy Land" is a Jewish concept and a Jewish idea. A return to this concept and this idea implied a return to the beginning of their evolution. Irrespective of all party prejudice, the resuscitated formative will of a community is to be recognized in this and commands our respect.

The call of the land developed into a movement as early as 1882, when in Kharkov a number of young people, most of them students, founded the Bilu, the object of which was to open up agricultural colonies in Palestine, and societies formed by the "Friends of Palestine," the *Choveve Zion,* spread all over the Russian settlement areas. In the summer of 1882, the first Bilu contingent landed in Palestine. If ever any people have deserved the right to be called self-sacrificing pioneers, it was these people, who by their superhuman labours prepared the arid soil. Slowly and with the utmost difficulty colonies began to form. Groups of Romanian Jews appeared and settled down, and at first all the colonists had to fight against the ravages of disease. In the hour of direst need, Edmond Rothschild, the Parisian financier, came to the rescue and arranged for an autonomous administration of the colonies, which paid the settlers and enabled the settlements to be carried on, in spite of many abuses. Gradually, after many setbacks and sacrifices, a network of Jewish colonies spread over the country, and, when the war broke out, they numbered forty-three. By this time they had already been drawn within the sphere of interest and influence of a movement, which the national ideology had shaped into an organized form, namely, Zionism.

The essentials of Zionism had already existed in the ideas of men like Hess, Kalischer, and Pinsker, and all those who were anxious to discover a practical solution of the Jewish question on the basis of its real historical principles. According to the laws of evolution, its development was just as necessary as that of the opposite movement, the tendency in Judaism to disintegrate, had been. It was indeed bound to develop, for being diametrically opposed to every aspect of the assimilative movement, it provoked the hostility of those who denied the first principle of Zionism, which was that the Jewish people constituted a nation. However opposed the orthodox and the liberals might be on the question of religion itself within that vestigial Judaism confined to religion alone, there was one point on which both parties were in entire agreement; they were unanimous in maintaining that the Zionist movement must be opposed on the score of its national implications. And thus the peculiar fate of the Jews once more emerged, inasmuch as they are the only people who, in the throes of a struggle to achieve their own reconstruction along creative lines, encountered their bitterest foes in their own camp. But apart from any question of resentment, it must be remembered that in this matter the Jews were concerned with two historic factors, which embody the extreme potentialities of a people, and which, therefore, must necessarily be hostile to each other.

The rise of the Zionist movement is inextricably associated with the name of Theodor Herzl. A member of a middle-class, liberal, and assimilated Budapest family, he differed but little from other intelligent Jews of his age and circle, until the details of the Dreyfus case, with which, as a journalist, he became acquainted, suddenly changed his outlook. He himself declared that his dislike of assimilated Judaism, and his interest in the national idea, dated from this moment. So violent was the change that occurred in him, that it soon led to the development of a concrete formula. At first he regarded the Jewish question and its solution as being a purely political matter. "It is a national question, and in order to solve it we must first of all make it a political question which will have to be settled in the councils of the civilized nations of the world," he declared. The object he had in view was "to establish a publicly and legally assured home for those who cannot and will not become assimilated." He wrote a treatise, *The Jewish State,* embodying this idea; it was published in 1896, and laid the problem open to public discussion. In this work he still shows himself undecided as to whether the Argentine or Palestine should be the site of this home of refuge; but the response his work received led him to the conclusion that it could be only Palestine. The problem—Palestine or some other country—again became topical, when the British government placed some land in Uganda (British East Africa) at the disposal of the Zionists for the purpose of a mass emigration of Jews. After passionate disputes within the party, the offer was declined. This was only logical. Even in the purely political form in which Herzl had at first conceived of Zionism, a number of imponderabilia, which constituted the heart and soul of the movement, were brought into play—attachment to the homeland for which the Jews had shed more blood than any other people had ever done for their country, and in which they had never ceased to live even after they had been dispersed. It is conceivable that, from the practical point of view, other countries might have been more suitable for a Jewish colony. But they lacked the spiritual appeal.

In 1897 the Zionist movement organized its propaganda and formed its representative body. The first congress met in Basel in August of that year and the programme was formulated which holds good to this day: "Zionism aims at establishing for the people a publicly and legally assured home in Palestine." And the executive was formed, the first embodiment of a real Jewish International. The congresses became a regular institution, and all the changes which were introduced into Zionism during its comparatively short existence were passionately discussed at these meetings. As early as the second congress held in Basel in 1898, it was shown that Zionism constituted a real *movement,* but that, whereas all were agreed as to its aim, views differed widely regarding methods and means. Some were in favour of concentrating upon practical constructive work in Palestine, while others hoped that everything would be accomplished by political means. And such political means were actually employed. Herzl worked indefatigably. He made repeated attempts to obtain a charter from the Turkish government, a sort of permit for the Jewish colony in Palestine. But he met with no success. In the opinion of the great powers, Zionism had not yet been universally accepted, and political efforts were therefore bound to fail. But it was not merely the idea behind the movement, but also the growing misery of the Jews in the East that made it necessary not to neglect practical work for these endeavours in the political sphere. The work of building up the Jewish colonies in Palestine was therefore begun. As early as the tenth congress, the new president, David Wolffsohn, declared: "We do not wish to create a Jewish state, but merely a homestead on the ancient soil of our remote ancestors." This declaration acquired exceptional importance, and has often been regarded as the official signal for retreat on the part of political Zionism. But to us its importance seems to lie in the fact that it puts into words the recognition of a particular truth—that a state, in the sense understood for ages by the national egoism of peoples, was unnecessary and indeed inadequate for the development of a Jewish centre. Nevertheless, even when the policy of obtaining a charter was abandoned, Zionism remained a political movement within the compass of Judaism. But as such, and as a movement serving only political ends, it could not possibly be representative of Judaism and of the formative will of the Jews. Politics are merely the technical means of realization. They may on a very high plane serve the idea. This was recognized very early in the history of the Jewish national movement. It was not enough merely to perceive that a meaning and a spiritual entity lay implicit in Judaism and its history, and it had become more than ever necessary once again consciously to give the spiritual significance of Judaism creative expression, so that every movement which undertook to solve the Jewish problem should not end in mere practical measures.

This idea of giving a spiritual basis to Zionism first found real expression in the figure of Achad Haam. He was not concerned with preparing a land for a people, but with preparing a people for a land. He was not interested in colonization but in returning home. "The national centre must be a home of refuge not for Jewry but for Judaism." This statement was inspired by the recognition of the fact that for practical reasons alone a country like Palestine could not possibly accommodate all the Jews of the world, a fact which has always provided one of the strongest arguments against Zionism. But people who use this argument are generally those who do not wish to hear anything about the idea of returning home. And they confound the idea with the mass of people who in practice might share in its realization. The same argument applies to the feeling for religion. When once it is in possession of the idea of God, it can lead men to pray to Him inside or outside the Temple. But it is necessary first of all to grasp the idea of God.

And it was with this grasping of the idea that a man like Achad Haam was chiefly concerned. He introduced the factor of evolution into Zionism. Thus he called attention to the eternity of the problem, and made clear the contrast between his spiritual view of the matter and the idea of making the centre of Judaism a colony based merely on the grant of political concessions. Thus, when the day came for this political concession to be granted, it was no longer capable of proving a menace to the idea, for the idea had already acquired an independent existence which made it impossible for political success to degrade it to the level of a mere colonizing venture. The coping-stone was put in the form of a letter addressed on November 2, 1917, by Lord Balfour, in the name of the British government, to Lord Rothschild in London. It read as follows:

Foreign Office,
November 2, 1917.

Dear Lord Rothschild,

I have much pleasure in conveying to you, on behalf of His Majesty's Government, the following declaration in sympathy with Jewish Zionist aspirations, which has been submitted to, and approved by, the Cabinet:

"His Majesty's Government view with favour the establishment in Palestine of a national home for the Jewish people, and will use their best endeavours to facilitate the achievement of this object, it being clearly understood that nothing shall be done which may prejudice the civil and religious rights of the existing non-Jewish communities in Palestine, or the rights and political status enjoyed by Jews in any other country."

I should be grateful if you would bring this declaration to the knowledge of the Zionist Federation.

Yours sincerely,
ARTHUR JAMES BALFOUR.

On the basis of this declaration and the newly created institution of the mandates, Palestine, after the World War, was placed under a British mandate. We cannot here concern ourselves with the outcome of this, which belongs to current history. It has yet to be proved whether and how it will become enshrined in history.

But what has already passed into history and is now less likely to be lost than the facts themselves, which tomorrow may be modified, is the spiritual situation which has resulted from the resuscitation of the national idea. This Jewish nationalism has nothing in common with chauvinism, because it does not erect a barrier of valuations between itself and other nations. Jewish nationalism will never lead to war, for it represents no empire. It is the continuation of a history, nothing more. It does not mean the abolition of the Diaspora in so far as its personnel is concerned, but it does not see in the Diaspora the real mission of Judaism, as do those Jews who are opposed to the national idea. The Diaspora is part of the destiny of Judaism, but it does not constitute its significance or its mission, its task or its fulfilment. The Diaspora has merely become the field in which the great division of spirits has taken place, the division between those who regard the people as a living unity, and those who regard it as made up of atoms, or, stated in political terms, the division between the national and the assimilated Jew. The latter reacted to the strange conditions of his environment, the former created conditions of his own; the latter assimilated himself to the foreign culture, the former assimilated the foreign culture to himself; the latter, despite all his efforts, never became united with the world about him, the former was able to create a unity of his own; the latter lived on the periphery of Judaism, the former in its very core; the latter now and again vouchsafed his Judaism a glance of recognition, a fleeting acknowledgment of its traditions and his duty towards it, the former endeavoured to restore the whole. The primeval antithesis which we have seen drawing its trail across all Jewish history, the antithesis between the Halakah and the Haggadah, between law and legend, reappeared once more in a different form. While some cried out for a formula for their Judaism, for a norm, belief in which was all that was necessary for salvation, others allowed themselves to be mastered by the secret of life, and stepped forward to continue to create their Judaism. It is really all a question of love and faith.

EPILOGUE

If a literature can be called rich which possesses a few classical tragedies, what place should be given to a real tragedy, which has lasted one thousand five hundred years, and has been written and acted by the heroes themselves?

—Zunz.

WE have endeavoured to lay bare the core of a people's three thousand years of history, as we seemed to see and divine it, and the essential characteristic of which appeared to us not as a state or condition, but always as a movement. Both in its political and spiritual aspects, the history of this people is wholly occupied with movements, which take place in the spiritual and the earthly sphere. Time, says Bergson, is movement in space. Looked at in this way, the history of Judaism consists of "time."

The primitive religious concepts of the Jews were the first in the history of mankind to be associated with a dawning notion of unity, and from these beginnings they proceeded to a sharply defined concept of a one and only God. On the basis of this idea they tried to mould their lives in the shape of a theocracy. In this they were not altogether successful, but substituted for the theocracy a mundane monarchy, an earthly king. It was through this that they drew nearer to worldly forms and to the standards of those about them, that the social forms of other nations were imitated, and religious syncretism, or the incorporation of foreign forms of worship in a strict monotheism, took place. It was a refusal to be consistent and a refusal to be exclusive. The bulk of the people, the ten tribes of the kingdom of Samaria, were sacrificed to it. Among the remainder, in the kingdom of Judah, a spiritual revolution took place under the blow of this calamity, which elevated the idea of God above that of a mere tribal or national deity and made Him a universal God. The impetus of this idea liberated a force, which we call prophecy, and which necessarily arose as soon as a certain idea of God aspired to dominion over the whole world. In order, however, to be able to grasp that the whole world, and not merely the little country of Judah, was God's habitat, it was necessary for the Jews to be removed from their circumscribed centre, into the periphery beyond; for the cumulative gaze from a point on the periphery to the centre is stronger than that from the centre to some given point on the periphery. And thus they were called upon to endure the Babylonian captivity. It was here that the Jewish idea of life under the theocracy developed into the *noblesse oblige* of being the Chosen People, and led to the idea of the dominion of one God over the whole world. When they were allowed to return home in possession of this new spiritual treasure, they entered upon a period in which they endeavoured to prove their worth. But all too soon the great powers of the world closed upon them, and made it their solemn aim by their influence to refute the Judaic idea. They did not succeed. All they could do was to destroy the communal state, to shatter the external form, which with its constant failures in the face of the demands of everyday life, had but seldom shown itself worthy of the idea. Then came the beginning of the Diaspora, and the Jews were scattered over the face of the earth with the twofold task before them of discovering ever fresh forms for their lives, and ever fresh ways of proving their personal worth, and their worth in relation to the idea. In their effort to accomplish this task, they fashioned a double-edged sword for themselves—the binding moral law of the Torah, the Direction, and its derivatives, which were welded into a brazen fence in the Talmud. From being supported by their law, they soon became subjugated by it, for in religious life the free consent and surrender of the heart is always more essential than the voluntary submission of the will, and voluntary obedience. Thus these two forces—obedience and faith, the law and mysticism—struggled together in the hearts of the Jews, and became a burden, for in course of time their freedom for natural development was restricted, and in the end it was impossible to replace this freedom by a fiction. Nevertheless, disintegration was already implicit in the tragedy of their situation; for their compulsory settlement in every quarter of the globe eventually imparted to the Jews a new world sense, and they were able, spiritually gifted as they were, to regard that part of the world which they wished heart and soul to penetrate, as their natural habitat, their home. They were able, in the spiritual sense, to convert every point in the world's periphery, into a centre, and then to work and strive as they thought right and best. The reality which they needed as their standard was conceived as being in the process of formation in the old homeland which they had never forgotten.

In addition to this spiritual mobility, Jewish history was also characterized by external mobility, the results of which also made themselves felt in the world at large and its activities. At the turning point of Jewish history, the western world, in the form of Greece and Rome, burst into the sphere of Judaism, which was a self-contained fragment of the East. This encounter between East and West led to a twofold movement in the world—the spread of Christianity and the spread of Judaism, the former as a triumphant conquest, the latter as a dispersion. The two together inaugurated a political movement—the struggle between Christianity and Judaism, the blend of East and West against the East. The great recoil stroke of the pendulum followed in the shape of the invasion of the West by the East, which constituted the triumph of Islam. The Jews also joined in this movement, but they held their ground when the West retaliated with its Crusades against the East and also drove the Moors out of Spain. Thus the Jews made the West their home and the scene of their various movements. But in so doing they placed themselves at its mercy. The West drove them eastwards by means of bloody persecutions; the East drove them all over the world by means of massacres unparalleled in history, until the great migration to America and the lesser migration to Palestine began; the former had for its object the salvation of their bodies, the latter the salvation of their souls, and the united aim of both was that the two should one day balance and complete each other.

As the result of these movements, the Jews while still in search of a centre, have at the same time become absorbed in the world. This is more than a bare fact, for it leads to consequences of a spiritual nature, both for the Jews and the Gentiles; they can no longer remain neutral to each other. The Gentile cannot be neutral, because in view of his own feelings of constraint, he confronts the Jew with a feeling of strangeness. But even less can the Jew be neutral. For centuries he has been called upon to make decisions both in the spiritual and the material sphere, about God and the world, about himself and the stranger, and they have always been decisions in which his very existence was at stake. It cannot be wondered at that, in such circumstances, he has become at once accommodating and apodeictic, humble and haughty, a freeman of the spirit and a bondman of society, a capitalist and a social revolutionary, the most pious of men and also the greatest nihilist of the spirit. He has been obliged to respond to every outcry on the part of the world, for whenever an outcry has been raised he has always been the object of it. Other peoples have been able to remain silent, or to make a negative response when an appeal has reached them which they either did not wish to hear, or were not allowed to hear. But the Jew was not permitted to turn a deaf ear, for there is no idea on earth which he, as a man who believed in universal salvation, was not bound to test for its saving quality. And there is no idea in the world for which he, as a man devoid of power and capacity for violence, has not been obliged to make every imaginable sacrifice. On his head all the woe of mankind has been vented, and that is why, willynilly, he is bound to accept all the good and evil that is born into the world.

His life has not been easy, and it is not easy even today, hampered as he is in all directions, to find a path which is his path, and which will also enable him to fulfil his destiny. So terrible has been his suffering, in small things as in great, that fear and danger have driven him into the neglected bypaths, the blind alleys of evolution. As in this work we have been concerned with depicting the past of a people, it has been impossible to shut our eyes to the cruel misery and mass martyrdom inflicted on the Jews by those about them, and with unremitting persistence through the medium of Christianity. We could not have kept silence about the slaughter and murder of millions of Jews, without being guilty of distorting history. But now that we are concerned with the prospects of the future, it is no more incumbent upon us to drag this load of memories along with us, than it is to perpetuate hatred in the world. It is not for us to make good these injustices. History is not a chain of facts linked together mechanically by cause and effect, action and reaction. It consists of the projection of a living idea, an ideated force liberated from the cosmos upon the living reality of communities. The life of the individual runs its course in relation to the cosmos, and the life of humanity as a whole does likewise. The transgression of the individual, and the transgression of the whole, have the same significance—the disturbance of the course of cosmic events. They also have the same effect—the recoil stroke of the disturbed course of events, or what we call retribution. Thus sins are requited not because they work havoc with our neighbour, but because they work havoc with ourselves. This the Jew has experienced times without number in his own fate, and he is still experiencing it. The fact that he now sees this law also operating against those who have for centuries martyrized him can mean nothing more to him than that he himself is a portion of the whole, and is included in the plan of cosmic processes. This may sound romantic, but it is based on reality.

Our Judaism is both a reality and an assumption, an imperfect existence aiming at perfection. In the face of our will to continue this existence, it is impossible to find any formula or formulation of what we are and what we wish to achieve; no definite course can be marked out. Life knows only movable goals. But knowledge of the starting-point, of the living ground, the root basis of the soul, has been revived in our own day. We call it, if we see things historically, a nation. Any other term could be used provided it does not deny the vital laws of this community, its biological and utopian, its sociological and religious quality, its historical objectivity and its Messianic creative power. These are world forces, which are certainly to be found everywhere, but in Judaism they have been concentrated into a determination to overcome every obstacle and be realized some day. There is a certain quality which may be called the fluid of the world's spirituality, and in this all conflicting elements will eventually have to be dissolved.

So there we stand; degenerate though we are, we are inspired by a great endeavour; we are weak and yet animated by an invincible will; surrounded by hostility, yet full of hope; an endless past behind us, a drab and sombre present with us, and beyond a future which can become a glorious reality only through the creative power of Jewish hearts. This history of a people is so full of wonder and horror, so much the sport of necessity and chance, so full of truth that never dies and elements that pass away, that it is impossible to approach it without becoming inspired by a religious faith which transcends all the dogmas of religion.

And so may God, our help in ages past, continue to guide us on our way!

INDEX

INDEX